Handbook of Rational-Emotive Therapy

Albert Ellis and Russell Grieger
with contributors

Springer Publishing Company/New York

Springer Publishing Company, Inc.
200 Park Avenue South
New York, N.Y. 10003

77 78 79 80 81 / 10 9 8 7 6 5 4 3 2 1

Designed by Patrick Vitacco

Library of Congress Cataloging in Publication Data

Main entry under title:

Handbook of rational-emotive therapy.

    Includes bibliographies.
    1. Rational-emotive psychotherapy. I. Ellis,
Albert, 1913–   II. Grieger, Russell.
[DNLM: 1. Psychotherapy—Handbooks. WM420 H2324]
RC489.R3H36   616.8′914   77–21410
ISBN 0–8261–2200–0
ISBN 0–8261–2201–9 pbk.

Printed in the United States of America

Handbook of Rational-Emotive Therapy

Albert Ellis, distinguished psychotherapist, marriage and family counselor, and exceptionally active writer and lecturer of international prominence, is the founder and executive director of the Institute for Advanced Study in Rational Psychotherapy in New York City. His widely read contributions in the areas of rational-emotive therapy and sexual fulfillment have established his reputation in and outside professional circles, here and abroad. Dr. Ellis, whose doctorate from Columbia University is in clinical psychology, is the recipient of the Humanist of the Year Award (1973), the Distinguished Professional Psychologist Award (1975, American Psychological Association, Division of Psychotherapy), and the Distinguished Sex Educator and Counselor Award (1976).

Russell Grieger teaches clinical and clinical-child psychology at the University of Virginia in Charlottesville, where he also conducts a private practice. Professor Grieger, who earned his doctorate from Ohio State University, is an associate fellow of the Institute for Advanced Study in Rational Psychotherapy and draws on a broad experience as a therapist and consultant on behalf of delinquent, emotionally disturbed, and learning-disabled youths, among others. He has published extensively on issues relevant to rational-emotive theory and therapy, and he frequently lectures and leads workshops on rational-emotive therapy.

Contents

58117

Part Three

Rational-Emotive Therapy: Primary Techniques and Basic Processes

Part Four

Rational-Emotive Therapy: Additional
Techniques and Related Approaches

Part Five

Rational-Emotive Therapy
with Children

Preface

By all accounts rational-emotive therapy has arrived. It is safe to say that it has become firmly established as a leading member of the psycho-therapeutic family in general and of the cognitive-emotive-behavioral therapy movement in particular. In its general or inelegant form, in fact, it is practically synonymous with what is usually called cognitive behavior therapy, since it employs a large variety of methods used in this form of therapy, and does so very consciously and determinedly, as part of its basic theory and practice. In its more specific or elegant form, RET particularly emphasizes the fact that emotional disturbance virtually always involves an absolutistic *should, ought,* or *must* that disturbed people are consciously or unconsciously demanding (or commanding) of themselves, of others, or of the universe; and that their *mus*turbatory thinking had better be scientifically disputed and surrendered—and so vigorously and persistently disputed that it will relatively rarely rise again to smite them in the future.

This is not to say that RET's acceptance has progressed in a particularly smooth manner or that the psychological community en masse has welcomed it with open arms. Acceptance has frequently been begrudgingly bestowed and is still not given in many quarters. But, alas, that is the way it should be (scientifically speaking), as rational-emotive therapy has distinctly flouted traditional psychological theory and rearranged psycho-therapeutic decor.

Despite all this, RET has seen an almost incredible growth in the twenty-two years since its birth in early 1955. During this period, literally hundreds of papers and scores of texts have been published that in part or in large measure focus on the theory and practice of RET. These include the many books listed at the beginning of Chapter 29 of this volume, as well as several basic texts by Ellis and his collaborators, such as, *Reason and Emotion in Psychotherapy, Growth Through Reason, Humanistic Psychotherapy: The Rational-Emotive Approach, Executive Leadership: A Rational Approach, A New Guide to Rational Living,* and *How to Live With—and Without—Anger.* Some indication of the wide-ranging scope of RET can also be found in the text by Wolfe and Brand, *Twenty Years of Rational Therapy.*

Precisely because so much has already been written about RET, we decided to assemble the present handbook—to collect in one source its major ideas and tools as they have developed during the last two decades and as they currently exist. Naturally, we have not been exhaustive; and, even as this book goes to press, we note that ideas and procedures are being articulated that we would have liked to have included in this volume. Perhaps we shall present these in Volume II of the *Handbook* in the not too distant future.

In spite of the constant revisions that are taking place in rational-emotive theory and practice, we think that a quote from *Reason and Emotion in Psychotherapy* is as appropriate today as it was in 1962 and that it accurately communicates some of the benefits that we hope will be derived from reading this *Handbook:*

> In any event, rational-emotive psychotherapy has, even in the few brief years of its existence, so far proven to be a highly intriguing and seemingly practical theory and method. It is hoped that the publication of this manual will bring it to the attention of many more individuals than those who are now conversant with its approach and that it will spur discussion and experimentation that will help develop its principles and its applications.

September, 1977

ALBERT ELLIS, PH.D.
Institute for Advanced Study
    in Rational Psychotherapy
New York, New York

RUSSELL GRIEGER, PH.D.
University of Virginia
Charlottesville, Virginia

Contributors

AARON T. BECK, M.D.
Department of Psychiatry
School of Medicine
University of Pennsylvania
Philadelphia, Pennsylvania

JOHN BOYD, PH.D.
Education Department
University of Virginia
Charlottesville, Virginia

ROY CAMERON, PH.D.
Department of Psychology
University of Saskatchewan
Saskatoon, Saskatchewan, Canada

CATHERINE DeVOGE, M.S.
Children's Unit
Larned State Hospital
Larned, Kansas

RAYMOND A. DiGIUSEPPE, PH.D.
Institute for Advanced Study
    in Rational Psychotherapy
and Long Island Jewish-Hillside
    Medical Center
New York, New York

ALBERT ELLIS, PH.D.
Institute for Advanced Study
    in Rational Psychotherapy
New York, New York

JOSEPH GOODMAN, PH.D.
Counseling Service
University of Waterloo
Waterloo, Ontario, Canada

RUSSELL GRIEGER, PH.D.
University of Virginia
and Clinical Psychologist in private practice
Charlottesville, Virginia

PAUL A. HAUCK, PH.D.
Clinical Psychologist in private practice
Rock Island, Illinois

WILLIAM J. KNAUS, ED.D.
Clinical Psychologist in private practice
New York, New York

ARTHUR J. LANGE, ED.D.
Center for Counseling and Special Services
University of California
Irvine, California

ARNOLD A. LAZARUS, PH.D.
Graduate School of Applied and Professional
    Psychology
Rutgers University
New Brunswick, New Jersey

MICHAEL J. MAHONEY, PH.D.
Department of Psychology
Pennsylvania State University
University Park, Pennsylvania

MAXIE C. MAULTSBY, JR., M.D.
College of Medicine
Albert B. Chandler Medical Center
University of Kentucky
Lexington, Kentucky

THOMAS A. McCLELLAN, M.S.W.
Outpatient Drug Treatment Program
Veterans Administration Outpatient Clinic
Fort Snelling
St. Paul, Minnesota

DONALD H. MEICHENBAUM, PH.D.
Department of Psychology
University of Waterloo
Waterloo, Ontario, Canada

NORMAN J. MILLER, PH.D.
Institute for Advanced Study
 in Rational Psychotherapy
and Southeast Nassau Guidance Center
New York, New York

BRIAN F. SHAW, PH.D.
Department of Psychology
University Hospital
London, Ontario, Canada

DONALD R. STIEPER, PH.D.
Psychology Service
Veterans Administration Outpatient Clinic
Fort Snelling
St. Paul, Minnesota

JOHN T. WATKINS, PH.D.
Department of Psychiatry and Behavioral
 Sciences
University of Oklahoma
Health Sciences Center
Oklahoma City, Oklahoma

Part One

Theoretical and Conceptual Foundations of Rational-Emotive Therapy

1

The Basic Clinical Theory of Rational-Emotive Therapy

Albert Ellis

Chapter 1 introduces the reader to the basic clinical theory of rational-emotive therapy. In this introduction, Albert Ellis, the founder and leading theorist/practitioner of RET, begins by stating the basic RET premise—that people largely control their own destinies by believing in and acting on the values or beliefs that they hold. He then outlines the now-famous A-B-C theory of emotional and behavioral reactions. Briefly stated, this theory holds that people do not directly react emotionally or behaviorally to the events they encounter in their lives; rather, people cause their own reactions by the way they interpret or evaluate the events they experience.

A second major component of Chapter 1 is an overview of the basic irrational beliefs that constitute most all instances of emotional disturbance. Ellis thoroughly explains these beliefs and shows through examples why each is patently absurd and self-defeating. Finally the reader is introduced to RET as a self-help tool. This process includes the detection of irrational beliefs, or the diagnostic process, and the heavy use of the logico-empirical methods of scientific inquiry: questioning, debating, challenging, and disputing of irrational beliefs. The purpose of this process is to induce the person to recognize the absurdity of his beliefs, to relinquish them, and to adopt new, more adaptive ones.

WHEN I FIRST STARTED using rational-emotive therapy (RET) in 1955 and gave my first paper on it at the American Psychological Association's annual meeting in Chicago on August 31, 1956, I viewed it as a quite simple theory of human personality and therapeutic practice. I mainly thought in terms of what I called the A-B-C theory of emotional disturbance, and I did damned well, by using this theory, at very quickly showing my clients some of their fundamental irrational premises, how these premises inevitably (well, *almost* inevitably) led to their "emotional" disturbances, and exactly what they could think and do to change their foolish ideas and their inappropriate feelings and thereby to overcome their "neurotic" symptoms.

How right—and how wrong—I proved! *Right,* in the sense that therapists (and a little later, the general public) soon began to acknowledge
me as one of the real pioneers in the fields of both cognitive and cognitive-behavior therapy. Although what I then called rational psychotherapy
actually had its roots in philosophic writings of the ancient Greek and
Roman stoics (especially, Epictetus and Marcus Aurelius [Hadas, 1963]),
and although several early twentieth-century writers had largely espoused
it (notably, Dubois [1907], Dejerine and Gaukler [1913], and Adler
[1927, 1929]), the analytic-emotive Freudian school (Freud, 1964)
had largely obliterated or driven it underground by the 1950s. As a result, what I began to vigorously say, from the public platform and in a
good many articles and books from 1955 onward, seemed highly original
and utterly heretical to most of those who heard me.

Actually, they attributed to me more originality than I merited. By the
late 1940s quite a few other therapists, most of them trained as I was in
the field of psychoanalysis, had begun to see the severe limitations and
myths of the analytic approach and had, whether they consciously
acknowledged it or not, moved much closer to Adler than to Freud. Some
of these included Karen Horney (1939), Franz Alexander and Thomas
French (1946), Eric Berne (1957), Alexander Herzberg (1945), George
Kelly (1955), Abraham Low (1952), Adolf Meyer (1948), E. Lakin
Phillips (1956), Julian Rotter (1954), Andrew Salter (1949), Frederick
Thorne (1950, 1961), and Harry Stack Sullivan (1947, 1953). I probably went beyond all these writers, in both my profoundly cognitive and
my strong behavioral emphasis; but even though I largely created RET
independently (since I read most of these writers after I had already published one book, *How to Live with a "Neurotic,"* and several papers on
rational-emotive methodology), many of them employed their own brands
of active-directive, cognitive-oriented therapy years before I did.

Largely on the basis of my clinical experimentation, I forged ahead in
the early 1950s to discover the gross ineffectuality of psychoanalysis and
to develop more rational and distinctly more efficient techniques with my
clients. And as I did so, I began to develop RET theory. For as I eliminated
one psychoanalytic technique after another—especially free association,
dream analysis, and the compulsive use of the transference relationship
between myself and my cleints—I realized more clearly that although
people have remarkable differences and uniquenesses in their tastes,
characteristics, goals, and enjoyments, they also have remarkable same-
ness in the ways in which they disturb themselves "emotionally." People
have, of course, thousands of specific irrational ideas and philosophies
(not to mention superstitions and religiosities) which they creatively invent, dogmatically carry on, and stupidly upset themselves about. But we

can easily put almost all these thousands of ideas into a few general categories. Once we do so, and then actively *look for* these categories, we can fairly quickly find them, show them to disturbed individuals, and also teach them how to give them up. This kind of categorizing, or theorizing (since we automatically tend to categorize on the basis of our own *assumptions* about what data seem important and what items suitably fit and do not fit under different headings and subheadings), helps us understand or explain disturbance, zero in on it with unusual dispatch, and do something about changing or eliminating it.

I can outline the main clinical theories of RET in several different ways, especially: (1) the A-B-C theory of how people create and can uncreate their own disturbances; (2) detecting irrational beliefs; (3) debating, discriminating, and disputing irrational beliefs; and (4) winding up with a new effect or philosophy. Let me, in this initial chapter, fill in the outlines of RET clinical theory under each of these main headings.

The A-B-C's of RET

Unlike most other systems of psychotherapy, including the psychoanalytic system, on the one hand, and the classical behaviorist system, on the other hand, RET does not start with the assumption that humans almost completely *get* conditioned or learn from others how to upset themselves. It assumes, naturally, that virtually everything people do includes very important learning elements. We have a strong innate or biological tendency, for example, to walk on the ground rather than (as monkeys have) to swing from trees. But we still learn, by the helpful teachings of others *and* by our own self-practice, how to walk better, faster, straighter, or longer. We innately tend to suckle at our mothers' breasts and later to eat nonliquid kinds of food. But we also learn bigger and better breast-sucking; and we learn to eat a tremendous variety of foods that we rarely would imbibe during our first few years of life. So biological inheritance *and* self- and social-learning tendencies combine to make us human and to provide us with our main goals and satisfactions, such as our basic values of staying alive and of making ourselves happy or satisfied in many ways while remaining alive.

Because of our innate and acquired tendencies, *we* largely (though not exclusively) control our own destinies, and particularly our emotional destinies. And we do so by our basic values or beliefs—by the way that we interpret or look at the events that occur in our lives and by the actions that we choose to take about these occurrences. We can put this in the A-B-C framework of RET, as follows:

At point A (an Activating Experience or Activating Event) something occurs. For example, you have a good job and get fired from it.

At point C, an emotional and/or behavioral Consequence, you react to the happenings at point A, and feel quite depressed about your job loss and tend to stay at home much of the time and avoid going out to look for another equivalent, or perhaps even better, job.

Noting, now, that the emotional and behavioral Consequence (C) almost immediately and directly follows after the occurrence of the Activating Experience (A), you (and others) falsely tend to assume that A *causes* C. And you (and they) erroneously make conclusions like: "I lost this good job and *that,* my loss, has depressed me and made me avoid looking for another one."

Actually, RET theory says, this conclusion doesn't follow, and represents what we call a non sequitur. For what really happened included A (the job loss) and C, the consequence of loss or deprivation or frustration (no longer getting what we wanted); and even at that, C didn't *automatically* follow from A but from B, your Belief about A. What Belief? Well, the fairly obvious Belief, "I *liked* the job I had; and because I liked it, I did not *want* to lose it; and because I did not want to lose it, I consider its loss bad, unfortunate, or disadvantageous."

In other words, if you have a job and feel completely neutral or indifferent about it, if you believe: "It doesn't really matter whether I keep it or lose it," and do not *evaluate* this job or your holding onto it one way or another, you would experience the Consequence, at C, of indifference or noninvolvement (meaning, virtually no feeling whatever) when you happened to lose the job. A, your Activating Experience, would consist of your loss of the job. B, your Belief or idea or evaluation about A, would consist of: "Who cares whether I keep this job or not?" And C, your emotional Consequence, would consist of indifference and inertia.

If you *merely* desire or wish or want the job, at point B, and tell yourself: "I definitely would like to have it, but if I don't, tough! I only find that unfortunate and undesirable, but hardly the end of the world," you then will tend only to feel disappointed, sorry, and regretful at C, after you experience the loss of the job, at A.

But if you *also* believe that you desperately *need* this job, by insisting to yourself, at point B, "I *must* have it! I can hardly exist without it and find it absolutely *awful* to lose it!" you will then experience something like a feeling of despair, depression, and complete inadequacy at point C, probably will feel unable to go out and look for another job, and will sit on your rear end or lie abed instead of forcing yourself out to try for other jobs.

RET theory strongly posits, then, that Activating Experiences at A, like the loss of a job, do *not* make you have emotional Consequences at C, such as feelings of depression, despair, and panic, and do *not* lead to behavioral Consequences such as inertia and avoidance. Rather, *you* mainly cause your own Consequences, at C, by strongly believing certain things at B—your innately predisposed *and* learned or acquired Belief System.

Do not the Activating Events (A) in your life definitely contribute in any way to your emotional or behavioral Consequences (C)? Indeed they do. For if you did not lose your job, you would hardly tend to feel sorry, regretful, and frustrated, nor certainly panicked, depressed, and inert about losing it. If *nothing* occurred in your life, at A, you would tend to have little or no behavioral Consequences at C. (Although, of course, you might have them. For even if you have virtually no chance of losing your job, you still might wrongly *think* you might lose it and also might have all kinds of awfulizing Beliefs [at B] about the very slight possibility of losing it; and, with these Beliefs, you could easily drive yourself to despair and depression. Thus, you could tell yourself, at B: *"Suppose* I lose my job. How absolutely awful! I just couldn't stand it at all! I'd have to take it with utter horror, and probably I'd have to go out and kill myself!" And with thoughts like these, even if you keep your job until you die in the saddle at the age of 95, you can thoroughly depress yourself with no trouble whatever!)

With somewhat greater difficulty, you could manage, at point A (Activating Experience) to lose an entire series of jobs, even lose them because of real job incompetence, and to keep concluding, at point B: "Well, there I go again. Another job down the drain. I guess I just have little ability to keep a good job. Hmm, well, too bad. Most unfortunate. But that just seems to remain the way I operate—not so hot at jobs. I guess I'll just have to keep sponging on my friends. Or go on Welfare. Or wait till my parents die and leave me enough money to live on. How sad! But I still have ways to enjoy myself. And I may yet find *some* kind of a job. So I think I'll keep trying, and keep myself busy until I do find one." If you maintained this kind of a philosophy at point B about losing many jobs at point A, you would certainly tend to feel sorry and regretful about your job experiences—but not utterly miserable; not depressed; not suicidal. Which tends to prove, again, that depression and inertia about the loss of one or more jobs do *not* stem from that loss itself but from what *you* tell yourself about the loss from B, your Belief System.

So says the central theory of RET (as Epictetus observed some 2000 years ago): The things that occur do not upset you—but your *view* of those things does. Or, in RET terms, A (Activating Event) does not directly cause C (emotional and behavioral Consequence); B (your Beliefs about A) does.

And further: Once you accept the fact that external events (including early conditioning) significantly contribute to but do not actually cause your feelings, and that you largely feel the way you think, you enormously increase your power over your own emotions. Although you can hardly change them at will, you can appreciably make them subject to your decision processes. You can, if you wish, decide to surrender to appropriate negative emotions, such as sorrow, regret, frustration, annoyance, and irritation, while refusing very often to give in to inappropriate and self-defeating feelings, such as anxiety, depression, hostility, and self-downing. How? By finishing the A-B-C's of RET with D and E. But that remains for later parts of this chapter. Next, I will talk about the skill of detection of irrational beliefs.

Detecting Irrational Beliefs

Now, how can you Detect irrational Beliefs so that you know, with good probability, that you have them and can go after them and surrender them? The main answer: *Cherchez le* "shoulds," *cherchez le* "musts." Or, in English: Look for your "shoulds," look for your "musts."

Not that *all* irrational Beliefs include a *should* or *must;* some of them merely consist of unempirical or unrealistic statements. Thus, if you get fired from a job and have a hard time getting an equivalent one, and if you then escalate that observation into the irrational Belief: "I'll never find a good job again! Life seems too hard to bear!" you make irrational or illogical conclusions from limited data. For if you look for a new job for a while and keep getting rejected by potential employers, your job-hunting data merely informs you that you cannot *quickly* find a suitable position and that you'll probably get many more rejections until you do find one. And it tells you that, consequently, your life has difficulties and frustrations, and probably will continue to have them.

You escalate this information, however, into the illegitimate conclusions that you'll *never* find a good job again and that life seems *too* hard to bear. These conclusions don't merely represent generalizations but *over*-generalizations from the data you observe. They go beyond and *distort* reality—make it worse than you actually find it.

These kinds of antiempirical conclusions, therefore, have *some* degree of validity—but not very much. And if you challenge them by asking yourself: "What evidence exists that I'll *never* find a job again? What makes my life *too* hard to bear?" you will quickly tend to interrupt and negate them.

For the most part, however, you tend, as a human, to make antiempirical overgeneralizations because you have a hidden *mus*turbatory agenda in your thinking. You sensibly want or desire to find a good job quickly, and you foolishly demand: "I therefore *must* immediately get what I desire." And, again, you sanely prefer a rather easy and enjoyable life and you insanely command that you *have to* get it right now, immediately, pronto! With such desires *and* demands, you will find it almost impossible *not* to make antiempirical conclusions about the world. For if you *must* get a good job *right now, this minute,* you will naturally conclude, when you do not immediately get it: "I'll never find a good job again. Life seems too hard to bear!" If you rigorously stayed with the rational Belief (rB): "I'd prefer to get a good job quickly, but if I don't, I don't," you would then tend to conclude: "Well, I haven't found a good job yet; but if I keep trying, I'll most probably find one in the not too distant future."

Almost always, therefore, irrational Beliefs (iB's) do not merely stem from your human tendency to see the world somewhat distortedly and to make antiempirical statements about what has happened and what probably will happen to you, but from your demanding, commanding statements about what *should* and *must* happen so that you can *absolutely* and *necessarily* get what you desire. If you really stayed with desires and preferences, and virtually never escalated them into needs and necessities, you would relatively rarely make antiempirical statements to yourself and others. But just as soon as you make your desires into dire needs, such unrealistic statements almost inevitably follow—and follow, frequently, in great numbers!

Back to the Detecting of irrational Beliefs. You first assume, on theoretical grounds, if you follow the RET approach, that when you feel anxious, depressed, self-downing, guilty, hostile, or otherwise emotionally upset, you have some kinds of *shoulds* or *musts* that you keep strongly telling yourself; and you *look for* these absolutes or magical demands. "What *should* or *must* do I keep telling myself to *create* my disturbance?" you ask yourself. "Do I have them in my social life? My sex life? My school life? My career? Where?"

Quite quickly, once you get adept at looking for these demands, you will start to find them. Then you can also do the same thing about your other irrational thinking, most notably your *awfulizing* and your *can't-stand-its* and your *damning* of yourself and/or others. For whenever you experience distinct emotional problems, you can assume that your irrational Beliefs take one or more of four basic forms, all of which appear related to each other: (1) you think that someone or something *should, ought,* or *must* be different from the way it actually does exist; (2) you find it *awful, terrible,* or *horrible* when it is this way; (3) you think that you *can't bear, stand,* or *tolerate* this person or thing that you concluded *should* not have been as it is; (4) you think that you or some other person (or people) have made or keep making horrible errors and that because you or they must not act the way they clearly do act, you or they deserve nothing good in life, merit *damnation,* and can legitimately receive the label of *louse, rotten person,* or *turd.*

To Detect your irrational Beliefs, then, when you have little conscious awareness of them, look at iC, your inappropriate behavioral or emotional Consequence, and look also at A, the Activating Experience or Event that tends to precede C immediately. By looking at this kind of evidence and scanning and analyzing your thought processes, you can almost always fairly quickly discover or figure out one or more of your iB's.

Suppose, for example, you feel very angry with your mother after she has falsely accused you of lying to her when you actually told her the truth. You know C (your feeling of anger) and you know A (the Activating Event). How about iB, your irrational Beliefs that instigated you to feel C? Suppose you really have little idea of what they consist. How do you find them? By the following process of self-questioning:

1. Look for your awfulizing. Ask yourself: "What do I think of as *awful* in connection with my anger at my mother?" Probable answer: "I think it *awful* that she dares to accuse me of lying when I *know* that I told her the truth—and, in fact, went out of my way, at some risk to myself, to tell it."

2. Look for something you think you can't stand. Ask yourself: "What about A, my mother's behavior, do I think I can't bear?" Probable answer: "I guess I think I can't *bear* her treating me in this shabby and falsely accusing way, especially when I've treated her so forthrightly and honestly."

3. Look for your musturbating. Ask yourself, "What *should* or *must* do I keep telling myself about this situation?" Probable answer: "I think I keep insisting that my mother *must* not falsely accuse me. Also, perhaps, that she *should* not make me angry. Also, that I *must* not take her so seriously."

4. Look for your damning of yourself or others. Ask yourself, "In what manner do I damn or down anyone in connection with my mother's falsely accusing me of lying?" Probable answer: "I obviously damn my mother and think of her as *a no-good bitch* for falsely accusing me. And I also seem to be downing myself for foolishly making myself angry, once again,

at my mother, when she probably can't even help acting in the negative way that she does."

By looking, in the above manner, for your awfulizing, for your can't-stand-it-itis, for your musturbating, and for your damning of yourself and others, you can easily come up with, and usually within a very few minutes, several related irrational Beliefs that you devoutly cling to and with which you keep making yourself angry. Similarly, whatever kind of emotional or behavioral disturbance you feel at point C, you can almost always zero in on your irrational Beliefs (iB's) that cause this disturbance if you look for these four basic kinds of demanding.

Can we say, then, that only these four kinds of irrationalities exist and that all disturbance, no matter what form it takes, stems from one or more of these demands? Probably not, since trying to put 100% of anything as pervasive and complex as emotional malfunctioning under only four headings may well not work. Various kinds of disturbance, such as dyslexia, mental retardation, hypoglycemic irritability, and neurological deficiencies that have physical, toxic, or other causes do seem to exist. So let us not overcategorize and insist that *all* behavioral disorders exclusively consist of demandingness et al. They most probably don't. But the vast majority of what we normally call emotional problems probably do. Look even a little closely at behavior that we tend to call "neurotic," "disturbed," or "disordered," and probably 90% or more of it involves a person's ab-solutistically demanding something, awfulizing about not getting what he or she demands, whining persistently about not getting it, and/or stupidly concluding that he or she, or someone else, is despicable for acting in a particular way. Certainly, we can, if we look hard enough, find other forms of "emotional disturbance." But not very often!

Another simple method of Detecting your irrational Beliefs when you want to work on them to undo them consists of assuming that they usually go under one of three major musturbatory ideologies: (1) "I *must* do well and *must* win approval for my performances, or else I rate as a rotten person;" (2) "You *must* act kindly and considerately and justly toward me, or else you amount to a louse;" (3) "The conditions under which I live *must* remain good and easy, so that I get practically everything I want without too much effort and discomfort, or else the world turns damnable, and life hardly seems worth living!" Although some kinds of "emotional disturbances" may exist without your strongly believing in one, two, or three of these absolutistic *musts,* I think you'll find it difficult to imagine them. Virtually every imaginable disturbed feeling, as far as I can see, seems closely linked with at least one, and often two or three, of these irrational Beliefs.

How about the various kinds of more specific irrational ideas which I have listed in my various articles and books under some ten or more major headings? How do they fit in with the three basic musturbatory notions? Well, I think we can list them as follows:

Musturbatory ideology 1: I must do well and win approval for my performances, or else I rate as a rotten person. Major sub-ideas:

a. I must have sincere love and approval almost all the time from all the people I find significant.

b. I must prove myself thoroughly competent, adequate, and achieving, or at least have real competence or talent at something important.

c. My emotional misery comes almost completely from external pressures that I have little ability to change or control; unless these pressures change, I cannot help making myself feel anxious, depressed, self-downing, or hostile.

d. If events occur that put me in real danger or that threaten my life, I have to make myself exceptionally preoccupied with and upset about them.

e. My past life influenced me immensely and remains all-important because if something once strongly affected me it has to keep determining my feelings and behavior today; my early childhood gullibility and conditionability still remains, and I cannot surmount it and think for myself.

f. I must have a high degree of order or certainty in the universe around me to enable me to feel comfortable and to perform adequately.

g. I desperately need others to rely and depend upon; because I shall always remain so weak, I also need some supernatural power on which to rely, especially in times of severe crisis.

h. I must understand the nature or secret of the universe in order to live happily in it.

i. I can and should give myself a global rating as a human, and I can only rate myself as good or worthy if I perform well, do worthwhile things, and have people generally approve of me.

j. If I make myself depressed, anxious, ashamed, or angry, or I weakly give in to the feelings of disturbance that people and events tend to make me feel, I perform most incompetently and shamefully. I must not do that, and I amount to a thoroughly weak, rotten person if I do.

k. Beliefs held by respected authorities or by my society must prove correct and I have no right to question them in theory or action; if I do, people have a perfect right to condemn and punish me, and I cannot bear their disapproval.

Musturbatory ideology 2: Others must treat me considerately and kindly, in precisely the way I want them to treat me; if they don't, society and the universe should severely blame, damn, and punish them for their inconsiderateness.

a. Others must treat everyone in a fair and just manner; and if they act unfairly or unethically they amount to rotten people, deserve damnation and severe punishment, and the universe will almost certainly see that they get this kind of retribution.

b. If others behave incompetently or stupidly, they turn into complete idiots and ought to feel thoroughly ashamed of themselves.

c. If people have the ability to do well but actually choose to shirk and avoid the responsibilities they should accept and carry out, they amount to rotters and should feel utterly ashamed of themselves. People must achieve their full potential for happy and worthwhile living, else they have little or no value as humans.

Musturbatory ideology 3: Conditions under which I live must get arranged so that I get practically everything I want comfortably, quickly, and easily, and get virtually nothing that I don't want.

a. Things must go the way I would like them to go, because I need what I want; and life proves awful, terrible, and horrible when I do not get what I prefer.

b. When dangers or fearsome people or things exist in my world, I must continually preoccupy myself with and upset myself about them; in that way I will have the power to control or change them.

c. I find it easier to avoid facing many of life's difficulties and self-responsibilities than to undertake more rewarding forms of self-discipline. I need immediate comfort and cannot go through present pain to achieve future gain.

d. People should act better than they usually do; and if they don't act well and do create needless hassles for me, I view it as awful and horrible and I can't stand the hassles that they then create.

e. Once handicaps exist in my life, either because of my hereditary tendencies or the influences of my past or present environment, I can do practically nothing to change them; I must continue to suffer endlessly because of these handicaps. Therefore life hardly seems worth continuing.

f. If changing some obnoxious or handicapping element in myself or my life proves hard, that difficulty ought not exist. I find it *too* hard to do anything about it; I might as well make no effort, or very little effort, to change it.

g. Things like justice, fairness, equality, and democracy clearly have to prevail; when they don't, I can't stand it and life seems too unbearable to continue.

h. I must find correct and practically perfect solutions to my problems and others' problems; if I don't, catastrophe and horror will result.

i. People and external events cause practically all my unhappiness and I have to remain a helpless victim of anxiety, depression, feelings of inadequacy, and hostility unless these conditions and people change and allow me to stop feeling disturbed.

j. Since I managed to get born and now remain alive, my life has to continue forever, or just about as long as I want it to continue. I find it completely unfair and horrible to think about the possibility of my dying and no longer having any existence.

k. As long as I remain alive, my life has to have some unusual or special meaning or purpose; if I cannot create this meaning or purpose for myself, the universe or some supernatural force in the universe must give it to me.

l. I can't stand the discomfort of feeling anxious, depressed, guilty, ashamed, or otherwise emotionally upset; if I really went crazy and wound up in a mental institution, I never could stand that horror and might well have to kill myself.

m. When things have really gone bad for me for a reasonably long period of time and no guarantee exists that they will change or that anyone will take over my life and make things better for me, I simply can't bear the thought of living any longer and have to seriously consider killing myself.

Do these constitute practically all the important irrational Beliefs that you and other humans will likely tell yourself to create your emotional disturbances during your lifetime? By no means! Probably hundreds, if not thousands, of irrational ideas exist, and some day I may go to the trouble of making a more comprehensive list of the some 259 major self-defeating ones that I have already collected. The ones listed above merely seem basic in the sense that virtually all the others you can think of (and unfortunately believe in and act upon!) fall into subcategories under these major headings.

Let me diverge somewhat at this point before going on to Disputing Irrational Beliefs and take the opportunity to point out an additional cornerstone of RET. That is, human irrational thinking, emoting, and behaving seems intrinsically to have a distinctively biological basis.[1] Before arguing this point, let me define what I mean by the terms *biological basis* and *irrationality*. By *biological basis* I mean that a characteristic or trait has distinctly innate (as well as distinctly acquired) origins—it partly arises from the organism's natural, easy predisposition to behave in certain stipulated ways. I do not mean that this characteristic or trait has a

[1] The following comments arguing for a biological basis of irrational human thought are excerpted from an article by Albert Ellis titled "The Biological Basis of Human Irrationality," which appeared in the *Journal of Individual Psychology*, 1976, *32*(2), 145–168.

purely instinctive basis, that it cannot undergo major change, nor that the organism would perish, or at least live in abject misery, without it. I simply mean that, because of its genetic and/or congenital nature, an individual easily develops this trait and has a difficult time modifying or eliminating it.

By *irrationality* I mean any thought, emotion, or behavior that leads to self-defeating or self-destructive consequences that significantly interfere with the survival and happiness of the organism. More specifically, irrational behavior usually has several aspects: (1) The individual believes, often devoutly, that the irrationality accords with the tenets of reality, although in some important respect it does not; (2) People who adhere to the irrationality significantly denigrate or refuse to accept themselves; (3) Irrationality interferes with their getting along satisfactorily with members of their primary social groups; (4) It seriously blocks their achieving the kind of interpersonal relations that they would like to achieve; (5) It hinders their working gainfully and joyfully at some kind of productive labor; (6) It interferes with their own best interests in other important respects (Ellis, 1974a, 1975; Maultsby, 1975).

Now, on what grounds do I maintain the thesis that, in all probability, the various irrationalities have biological roots and stem from the fundamental nature of humans? On several important grounds, which I shall briefly summarize here. (The amount of supporting evidence assumes overwhelming proportions and would literally take several volumes to summarize properly.)

1. All the major human irrationalities, including the major four and all the ones under these four (awfulizing, I can't stand-it-itis, musturbation, and self-damning) seem to exist, in one form or another, in virtually all humans. Not equally, of course! Some of us, on the whole, behave much less irrationally than others. But go find *any*—yes, I mean *any*—individuals who do not fairly frequently in their lives subscribe to all of these major irrationalities. For example, do any of you know of a single man or woman who has not often slavishly conformed to some asinine social custom, given himself or herself global, total ratings, held strong prejudices, resorted to several kinds of illogical thinking, fooled himself or herself into believing that his or her strong feelings represented something about objective reality, acquired and persisted in self-defeating habits, had any pernicious addictions; or do you know anyone who has remained perfectly free of all neurotic symptoms, never subscribed to religious dogmas, and never surrendered to any foolish health habits? I practically defy you to come up with a single case!

2. Just about all the major irrationalities that now exist have held rampant sway in virtually all social and cultural groups that we have investigated historically and anthropologically. Although rules, laws, mores,

and standards vary widely from group to group, gullibility, absolutism, dogmas, religiosity, and demandingness *about* these standards remain surprisingly similar. Thus, parents and culture advise or educate people in the Western civilized world to wear one kind of clothes and people in the South Sea Islands to wear another kind. But while they tend to inform you, "You had better dress in the right or proper way, so that people will accept your behavior and act advantageously toward you," you irrationally escalate this "proper" (and not too irrational) standard into, "I *must* dress properly, because I absolutely *need* other people's approval. I *can't stand* their disapproval and the disadvantages that may thereby accrue to me; and if they do not like my behavior that means they do not like *me* and that I rate as a completely *rotten person!*" Although your parents and your teachers may encourage you to think in this absolutistic, self-downing manner, you seem to have the innate human propensity: (a) to gullibly take them seriously; (b) to carry on their nonsense for the rest of your life; and (c) to invent it yourself if they happen to provide you with relatively little absolutism.

3. Many of the irrationalities that people profoundly follow go counter to almost all the teachings of their parents, peers, and mass media. Yet they refuse to give them up! Few parents encourage you to overgeneralize, make antiempirical statements, or uphold contradictory propositions; yet you tend to do this kind of thing continually. Your educational system strongly encourages you to learn, unlearn, and relearn; yet you have great difficulty doing so in many important respects. You encounter strong persuasive efforts of others to get you to forego nonproductive and self-defeating habits like overeating and smoking. But you largely tend to resist this constant teaching. You may go, at your own choosing, for years of psychotherapy to overcome your anxiety or tendencies toward depression. But look at the relatively little progress you often make!

You may have parents who raise you with extreme scepticism or anti-religious tendencies. Yet you easily can adopt some extreme religious orthodoxy in your adult years. You learn about the advisability of regularly visiting your physician and your dentist from grade school onward. But does this teaching make you go? Does widespread reading about the facts of life quiet your Pollyannaism or utopianism or rid you of undue pessimism? Thousands of well-documented books and films have clearly exposed the inequities of wars, riots, terrorism, and extreme nationalism. Have they really induced you and your fellow men and fellow women to unalterably oppose these forms of political irrationality? I could multiply the examples for hours.

4. As briefly mentioned before, practically all the irrationalities listed in this article hold true not only for ignorant, stupid, and severely disturbed

individuals but also for highly intelligent, educated, and relatively undisturbed persons. Ph.D.s in physics and psychology, for example, have strong racial and other prejudices; indulge in enormous amounts of wishful thinking; believe that if someone believes something strongly or intensely experiences it, it must have objective reality and truth; fall prey to all kinds of pernicious habits (including addictions like alcoholism); foolishly get themselves into debt; devoutly think that they must have others' approval; believe in the power of prayer; and invent rumors about others which they then strongly believe. Unusually bright and well-educated people probably hold fewer or less rigid irrationalities than average members of the populace, but they hardly have a monopoly on rational behavior!

5. When bright and generally competent people give up many of their irrationalities, they frequently tend to adopt other inanities or to go to opposite irrational extremes. Devout religionists often turn into devout atheists. Right-wing political extremists wind up as left-wing extremists. Individuals who procrastinate mightily may later emerge as compulsive workers. People who surrender one irrational phobia frequently turn up with another equally irrational but quite different phobia. Extremism tends to remain as a natural human trait that takes one foolish form or another.

6. Humans who seem least afflicted by irrational thoughts and behaviors still revert to them, and sometimes seriously so, at certain times. A man who rarely gets angry at others or has temper tantrums may on occasion incense himself so thoroughly that he almost or actually murders someone. A woman who fearlessly studies difficult subjects and takes complicated examinations may feel that she can't bear rejection by a job interviewer and may fail to look for a suitable position. A therapist who objectively and dispassionately teaches his or her clients how to behave more rationally may, if one of them stubbornly resists, act quite irrationally and agitatedly dismiss that person from therapy. In cases like these, unusual environmental conditions often bring out silly behavior by normally sane individuals. But these individuals obviously react to these conditions because they have some basic disposition to go out of their heads under unusual kinds of stress—and that basic disposition probably has innate elements.

7. People highly opposed to various kinds of irrationalities often fall prey to them. Agnostics give in to devout, absolutistic thoughts and feelings. Highly religious individuals act quite immorally. Psychologists who believe that guilt or self-downing has no legitimacy make themselves guilty and self-downing.

8. Knowledge or insight into one's irrational behavior only partially,

if at all, helps one change it. You may know full well about the harmful-
ness of smoking—and smoke more than ever! You may realize that you
hate sex because your parents puritanically taught you to do so; but you
may nonetheless keep hating it. You may have clearcut "intellectual" insight into your overweening egotism but have little "emotional" insight into
how to change it. This largely arises from the basic human tendency to have
two contradictory beliefs at the same time—an "intellectual" one which
you lightly and occasionally hold and an "emotional" one which you
vigorously and consistently hold and which you therefore usually tend to
act upon. This tendency to have simultaneous contradictory beliefs again
seems part of the human condition.

9. No matter how hard and how long people work to overcome their
irrational thoughts and behaviors, they usually find it exceptionally difficult
to overcome or eradicate them; to some degree they always remain exceptionally fallible in this respect (Ellis, 1962; Ellis and Harper, 1975;
Hauck, 1973; Maultsby, 1975). We could hypothesize that because they
overlearn their self-defeating behaviors at an early age, they therefore find
it most difficult to recondition themselves. But it seems simpler and more
logical to conclude that their fallibility has an inherent source and that
their early conditionability and proneness to accepting training in dysfunctional behavior *itself* represents a significant part of their innate fallibility! Certainly, they hardly acquired conditionability solely through having someone condition them!

10. It appears reasonably clear that certain irrational ideas stem from
personal, nonlearned (or even antilearned) experiences; that we inven-
tively, though crazily, *invent* them in a highly creative manner. Suppose,
for instance, you fall in love with someone and you intensely feel, know,
and state, "I know I'll love you forever!" You certainly didn't *learn* that
knowledge. You not only read about Romeo and Juliet (a fictional pair,
of course) but also read lots of other information, such as divorce statistics,
which shows that people rarely romantically adore each other forever. You
consequently *chose* your "knowledge" out of several other bits of data
you could have chosen to "know." And you most probably did so because
romantic love among humans frequently carries with it the intrinsic illusion: "Because my feeling for you has such authenticity and intensity, I
know it will last forever." You, at least for the most part, autistically
create the false and irrational "knowledge" that goes with your genuine
(and most probably temporary!) feelings.

Again, you may get reared as a Jew or a Moslem and may convert yourself to Christianity and conclude, "I feel Jesus as my Savior; and I feel certain that He exists as the Son of God." Did your experience or your environmental upbringing lead to this feeling and belief? Or did you, for

various reasons, invent it? The natural tendency of humans seems to consist of frequent dogmatic beliefs that their profound feelings prove something objectively exists in the universe; this largely appears an innately-based process of illusion.

11. If we look closely at some of the most popular irrational forms of thinking, it appears clear that humans figure them out. They start with a sensible or realistic observation, and they end up with a non sequitur type of conclusion. Thus, you start with, "It would feel enjoyable and I would have advantages if Jane loved me." You then falsely conclude, "Therefore she *has* to love me, and I find it *awful* if she doesn't." If you begin with an even stronger observation, "I would find it *exceptionally* and *uniquely* enjoyable if Jane loved me," you have even more of a tendency to conclude, "Therefore she must!" But no matter how true the first part of your proposition proves, the second part remains a non sequitur, making no sense whatever.

Similarly, you tend to irrationally conclude, "Because I find order desirable, I *need* certainty." "Because I find failure most undesirable: (1) I *must* not fail; (2) I did not cause myself to fail (he made me do it); and (3) Maybe I didn't really fail at all." Another example is: "Because it would prove very hard for me to give up smoking, I find it *too* hard; I *can't* do it." All these non sequiturs stem from autistic, grandiose thinking —you simply *command* that what you desire must exist and what you find obnoxious must not. This kind of autistic thinking largely appears innate.

12. Many types of irrational thinking largely consist of arrant over-generalizations; as Korzybski (1933) and his followers have shown, over-generalization seems a normal (though foolish) part of the human condition. Thus, you easily start with a sensible observation, "I failed at that test," and then you overgeneralize to "I will always fail; I have no ability to succeed at it." Or you start with, "They sometimes treat me unjustly," and you overgeneralize to, "They always treat me unjustly and I can't stand their continual unfair treatment!" This seems to be the way that normal humans naturally think. Children, as Piaget and his associates (Piaget and Inhelder, 1974) have shown, lack good judgment until the age of seven or eight. Adults frequently lack it forever!

13. Human thinking significantly varies in relation to people's intelligence levels; also, some forms of thinking stem largely from left-brain or right-brain functioning. Both intelligence and left-brain and right-brain functioning have a significant hereditary element and do not arise merely out of learned experiences (Austin, 1975; Sperry, 1975).

14. Some evidence exists that people often find it much easier to learn self-defeating than non-self-defeating behavior. Thus, they very easily overeat but have great trouble sticking to a sensible diet. They can learn,

usually from their foolish peers, to smoke cigarettes; but if other peers or elders try to teach them to give up smoking or to act more self-disciplinedly in other ways, they resist this teaching to a fare-thee-well! They fairly easily pick up prejudices against blacks, Jews, Catholics, and Orientals; but they rarely heed the teachings of thoroughly tolerant leaders. They quickly condition themselves to feel anxious, depressed, hating, and self-downing; but they take an enormous amount of time and effort getting rid of these disturbed feelings. They don't seem exactly doomed to a lifetime of stupid, foolish, asinine behavior, but pretty nearly!

To summarize, however we categorize or slice them, humans seem to have a fairly limited number of basic or *fundamental* irrational Beliefs (iB's), albeit at the same time having an almost unlimited number of variations and mutations of these basic irrationalities, which seem to have a large biological basis. Consequently, if you know what the main headings consist of (such as the three major forms of musturbation and the four major categories of irrationality), you can fairly easily ferret out the particular irrational Beliefs that you employ to create your own disturbed Consequences. Then you can get on to the Debating and Discriminating, which I will now do.

Disputing: Debating, Discriminating, and Defining

As you may or may not have discovered as yet, RET largely consists of the use of the logico-empirical method of scientific questioning, challenging, and debating. You take each of your irrational Beliefs that you arrived at during the Detecting process and you ask: "What evidence supports it? In which way does it have truth—or falseness? What makes it so?"

This kind of Debating, of course, really consists of rhetorical questions designed to dispute and to rip up the *false* Belief. For in RET we assume that if you have a dysfunctional behavior or emotional Consequence (C) following the occurrence of some Activating Experience or Event (A), you almost certainly have some kind of Belief (B) that directly sparks this Consequence, and that Belief has irrational elements in it and therefore constitutes an irrational Belief (iB). The scientific method takes any shaky hypothesis, particularly one that leads to poor results, and actively, vigorously disputes it, until it gets surrendered or sustained.

If you find evidence to back this hypothesis, fine: You keep it. If you find evidence against it, or if you don't find any to support it, you give it up and look for a better one. Your Debating, therefore, involves an internal Debate between you and you—between your rational and irrational

Beliefs. And the object of the Debating? To destroy, or at least minimize, your iB's.

And *Discriminating*? Of what does that consist? It consists of your clearly distinguishing between your wants and your needs, your desires and your demands (or musts), your rational and irrational ideas. The process consists of showing yourself the good as well as the bad points in your behavior; noting the difference between undesirable and "unbearable" results in your life; showing yourself that hassles do not amount to "horrors"; differentiating between logical conclusions about your life and non sequiturs; and discerning various other kinds of inconsistencies and contradictions in your thoughts and behaviors as you Debate with yourself the irrational Beliefs that you have Detected at point D in the RET process.

We might call another aspect of D the act of *Defining*. The scientific method usually starts off with some kind of definition of terms and ends up with even finer and more discriminative definitions. It tends to employ the principle of parsimony, sometimes called Ockham's razor. Like the practice of general semantics, originated by Alfred Korzybski (1933), it particularly avoids and undercuts overgeneralizations, since they contradict some of the basic principles of logic.

For example, if you feel depressed about acting foolishly on your job and thereby contributing to your losing it, and remain handicapped in getting another desirable position, you tend to use several semantic absolutes of overgeneralization. In the process of RET Defining, you can attack these and give them up. You probably tell yourself, when depressed, irrational Beliefs such as: (a) "I *always* act foolishly, as I did on my last job; therefore I'll *never* have the ability to keep a good one if I get one again"; (b) "Now that I feel severely depressed about my job loss, I *can't* stop feeling this way, and I'll continue feeling so *forever*"; (c) "Because I've shirked on several jobs before and have again shirked on the last one, I *am* an inveterate *shirker*."

In RET, we interrupt this kind of semantic looseness and induce you to Define your terms more precisely, so that you see: (a) You need not *always* act foolishly, even though you did so on your last job and perhaps on some other jobs. You *do* have the ability to keep a good position if you get one; (b) You *can* stop feeling the depressed way you now feel. You certainly need not feel that way *forever*; (c) Although you may have shirked on several jobs before, this doesn't mean you *are* an inveterate shirker or *are* anything else. You exist as a human who tends to *do* certain things, but who practically never has to do them all the time under all conditions. And you can therefore act nonshirkingly in the future.

RET Disputing, in sum, consists of several kinds of cognitive restructuring, including Detecting your irrationalities, Debating against them, Discriminating between logical and illogical thinking, and semantic Defining and reDefining that helps you to stop overgeneralizing and stick closer to reality.

Thus, in the example we have used earlier about losing your job, we can summarize the problem in the following A-B-C manner:

A (Activating Experience). Your boss fires you from a job you would prefer to keep, saying "I've had it! You keep coming in late after I've warned you about this many times. And, in addition, you pay little attention to what you do while on the job, constantly daydream about other things, and do poor work. Enough! You can stay till the end of the week. No longer!"

B (rational Belief). "I wish he hadn't done that! I don't like getting fired. How unfortunate that I kept coming in late and that I didn't pay enough attention to the job to do it better. I've really put myself in a lousy position, and I foolishly got myself on the Unemployment rolls. What crummy behavior!"

aC (appropriate Consequence). Feelings of disappointment; strong determination to change your behavior in the future; displeasure.

iB (irrational Belief). "How awful that I behaved so stupidly! I can't stand my behavior! I should not have acted so foolishly when I had such a good job. And because I did what I *should* and *must* not have done, I can only see myself as a rotten person who will always keep acting this stupid way and who deserves nothing good in life!"

iC (inappropriate Consequence). Feelings of depression, despair, shame, and severe inadequacy, inertia and little inclination to overcome it or to seek new employment.

Having summarized the problem you now can go on to D (Disputing) like this:

1. "Assuming that I really did behave stupidly and needlessly got myself fired from this job, how can I substantiate the *awfulness* of my stupid behavior?" Answer: "I can't. For although I well may have acted wrongly or foolishly about the job, *awful* doesn't merely mean that. It means much more than that. It means, first, that I behaved *totally* stupidly about having the job and that I would presumably behave that same way again if I got any kind of an equivalent position and that there is no behavior in the universe worse than the way I behaved. This seems most unlikely because:

(a) My behaving *quite* badly or *very* badly on the job—assuming that I actually did behave that way when I had it—hardly means that I behaved *totally* badly. Most probably, I also behaved well or at least moderately well in some respects. I most likely did *some* good things while

I held the job. And even the bad things that I did, I partly did in the process of learning how to do better. So if I got another equivalent job and I learned by my mistakes on this last one, I would presumably do decidedly or considerably better.

(b) My behaving *totally* badly when I held the job and my viewing it as *awful* that I behaved that way implies that I have no capacity whatever to do better on an equivalent job in the future. But my poor past performance hardly proves that I cannot make progress in the future; no way exists, actually, of showing that I *cannot* improve, even though up to the present time I may not have done so. So my concepts of *total* badness and the *awfulness* of the badness of my performance contain a predictive element that has a magical, unprovable quality about it.

(c) My behaving *totally* badly on the job from which I got fired implies that I could not possibly have behaved worse or that I acted as poorly on this job as anyone else could possibly have acted. But this again implies an impossibility. For no matter how badly I did the job, I could almost certainly have done it worse. And if I could not have performed worse on it, some other human definitely could. So the concept of 100% badness, or awfulness in that sense of the term, *theoretically* exists but *actually* does not. The very worst thing that could happen to me or any other person would presumably consist of our getting tortured to death very slowly. But even that would not be 100% badness—for we could always get tortured to death *even slower*! The 100% badness, therefore, of my behavior on the job or the 100% badness of my getting fired for doing badly at the job (and perhaps remaining unemployed for a long period of time or having to wind up with a considerably worse job) only exists in theory and not in practice. *No* human ever seems to actually create or receive this kind of a 100% penalty—although the term *awful* implies that he or she does.

In addition to implying that I behaved 100% badly on the job and that my penalties in losing it also equal or come close to 100% badness, when I tell myself, "How awful to fail!" I really imply that I view such a failure as *more than* bad—or at least 101% bad. For *awfulness,* again, has a truly magical connotation and does not merely mean totally bad. It really includes *surplus* badness—or badness that ranges from 101% to infinity.

Do I merely play with words when I say this, and invent a semantic quibble? Not at all. If I say to myself or to others, "I see it as very bad that I shirked while having this job and finally, because of my irresponsibility, lost it," I clearly remain on a continuum of badness, disadvantageousness, or inconvenience that ranges from .1 to 99.9. For I could view it as slightly bad (say, 5%), moderately bad (say, 25%), quite bad (say, 80%), or exceptionally bad (say, 99%). And, by the same token, I would therefore tend to feel, regarding my bad behavior, slightly disappointed in it, moderately disappointed, quite disappointed, or exceptionally disappointed.

My viewing my behavior as bad (or disadvantageous or self-defeating) clearly remains on a reality level. For I start, as practically all humans do, with the reasonably realistic values that I would like, wish, prefer, or desire to remain alive and to experience a decent degree of happiness while I live; as a subheading under this value, I start with the premise or goal that I would like, while remaining alive, to have a fairly good or advantageous job or career which will help me remain alive and decently happy. Consequently, if I do poorly on my job or in my career, I go against my values of survival and happiness and I can, with at least some degree of accuracy, *measure* how "well" I abet or how "badly" I sabotage these values. Once I decide or choose values like living and remaining happy, and, specifically, gaining satisfaction in the world of work, I can realistically and empirically measure how much or how little I achieve these goals and call the achievement of them "good" and their nonachievement "bad." So when I tell myself: "I view it as good when I work well and keep my job (or some equivalent job) and bad when I work poorly and get fired," I state a realistic proposition.

As soon as I jump to a statement like, "I find it *awful* when I work poorly and get fired," however, I make a magical leap to a nonexistent and absolutistic *second* continuum of evaluation whose "measurements," as stated earlier, really run from 101% badness to infinite badness. For if I look truthfully into my own heart, I will almost certainly find that by *awful* I mean *more than* bad or *infinitely* bad. And although such a degree of badness may easily exist in my thinking—just as demons, hobgoblins, and fairies may easily exist in my imagination—it really does not exist in the empirical world.

The proposition, "I find it *awful* when I work poorly and get fired," can get disputed (at D), as follows: "What makes it awful when I work poorly and get fired?" Specious answer: "Because I lose money; I get a poor recommendation for my next job; I remain bored when unemployed; I feel lonely when I stay at home and don't work; and I bring on myself various other kinds of disadvantages." Disputing, again: "No, those amount to reasons why you find unemployment inconvenient or disadvantageous. But you still haven't shown how those inconveniences and disadvantages merit the rating of *awful.*" Specious answer: "Well, I *feel* awful when I foolishly get myself fired and remain out of work because of my own foolishness. Doesn't *that* make it awful?" Disputing, again: "No, your feeling proves nothing except that you feel. It tells us nothing about what actually exists in the universe. If you say, 'Whenever I perform a foolish act, I feel like a donkey and I prance around and try to wag my tail,' that hardly proves that you truly turn into a donkey when you feel and act that way. You can *believe,* to whatever extent you like, that you metamorphize into a donkey when you act idiotically; but you can only prove, at most, the idiocy of your behavior and certainly not your donkeyhood!" Specious answer: "You seem to resort to semantic quibbling." Disputing: "Not at all. I merely keep forcing you to define your terms; and when you do so, you come up with unprovable statements. Really, you have two different views which you keep illegitimately coalescing, and if I force you to separate them, I think you'll easily find the illegitimacy of one of them. Your first view seems sane and empirical: 'I find it highly inconvenient and disadvantageous when I foolishly get myself fired and remain out of work because of my own foolishness.' But your second view, which you put together with this first one, makes little sense: namely, 'I find it awful *that* I bring on these inconveniences and disadvantages.' The *awfulness* that you invent *about* your disadvantaging yourself really doesn't exist, and represents something of a demon. You might just as well say: (a) 'I stupidly ate cattle manure instead of steak and got myself a stomach ache and a bad taste in my mouth,' and (b) 'How awful that I did this stupid act! The devil will get me and punish me further for having stupidly done it!' Although the first of these statements makes very good sense, the second amounts to nonsense. *All* awfulness or awfulizing, as far as I can see, makes similar nonsense—because it goes *beyond* empirical reality and invents a *surplus* badness or greater-than-badness to add to the obnoxious elements in human living that, because of our choice of basic values (again, surviving and remaining reasonably happy while surviving), actually exist."

Finally, you can Dispute (at point D) your awfulizing (at point iB) even when you remain relatively sane and don't claim 100% or 101% badness from your wrong acts, such as the act of foolishly shirking on a job and thereby losing it. For if you still, under these conditions, term your job loss and its consequences *awful,* you seem to mean: (a) "I did the wrong thing by shirking and losing my job, and I see that as only 60% or 65% bad," but (b) "I *shouldn't* have acted that badly but should have acted, say, only 59% badly and *no more* than that." If so, you can Dispute by asking yourself: "Why *shouldn't* I have acted 60% badly? What evidence exists that I must act *only* 59% badly and not a single degree more than that?"

Your answer: "No reason exists why I *shouldn't* act exactly as badly as I *did* act. If I did behave 60% badly, then I *should have* behaved that badly—because I *did*! I would have found it *preferable,* of course, to act less badly than I did. But *preferable* never means *necessary*. And no matter how badly I do behave, that remains that. Whatever I do, I do. Tough! Why *must* I not do what I indubitably do? Again, no reason exists why I mustn't. Whatever exists, exists!"

2. If you contend that you *can't stand* or *can't tolerate* your bad behavior, you can dispute this statement by asking yourself, at D again: "In what way *can't I stand it*? Prove that I can't. In what manner can't I?" And the fairly obvious answers come back, if you persist at asking these questions: "I obviously *can* stand my behavior, no matter how much I don't like it! In fact, I can stand *anything* that I do or that exists in the universe, as long as I still exist. Even if the most obnoxious thing possible happens to me—such as a steam roller rolling over me—I can clearly stand it until I die of it. For once I die of it, *I* no longer exist at all; and at *that* time, no question of my standing or bearing remains!"

In other words, whenever you claim that you *can't bear* or *can't stand* something, that statement makes no sense. For whatever exists, again, clearly exists; you can bear *anything* that happens to you, up to the time you expire. Even if a band of ruffians tortures you slowly to death, you can *still* stand their torture until you die of it; the declaration, "I can't stand those ruffians torturing me!" just doesn't hold true. You *always* can stand it, no matter *how* little you like it! Maybe you had better *not* stand some of the things you don't like, such as getting tortured; maybe you had better kill yourself rather than go on experiencing it. But until you do kill yourself, you obviously can bear whatever you deplore, hate the existence of, and *believe* that you can't abide. Or, as I keep assuring my clients, "You can always lump what you don't like. Though, of course, you rarely *have* to!"

3. You have made yourself disturbed, rather than merely sorry and displeased, about your boss firing you after you have shirked on your job by telling yourself, "I should not have acted so foolishly when I had such a good job." Here we come to the real core of your, and virtually everyone else's emotional problem: shoulding, oughting, and musting. I saw this quite clearly when I first originated RET—but not nearly as clearly as I see it now. Emotional disturbance rarely consists of desiring, preferring, wishing, or wanting. No matter what you desire, even the moon, you can always conclude in the end, "Well, I just don't seem to get what I want, and maybe I'll never get it. Too bad! I'll just have to live without it, for now and probably forever. Why do I *have* to get it?" As soon, however, as you make your wishes into demands, commands, or absolute insistences, you give up this leeway. If you don't get what you prefer—tough! But if you don't get what you absolutely *need* (or, more accurately, of course,

think you need), how can you help concluding "How awful! I can't stand it! I'll *never* find any real happiness in life!"

What we normally call "emotional disturbance," "neurosis," or "mental illness," then, largely consists of demandingness—or what I now refer to as *musturbation.* And when you devoutly tell yourself, "I should not have acted so foolishly when I had such a good job," the "should" you include in this Belief practically never means, as it theoretically could mean, "*It would have proved better* if I had acted differently." Oh, no! It may well mean that; but it also, and very pronouncedly means, "Because it would have proved better for me to have behaved differently and kept my job, and because I could have behaved that better way, I absolutely and with no exceptions about it *should have, must have* behaved as I definitely did not!" Without your dogmatically and damningly foisting upon yourself this kind of an unqualified, totalitarian, Jehovahistic (not to mention Paulistic and Mohammedanistic) *should, ought,* or *must,* and without your commanding that other humans and world conditions follow it as well, you would rarely (as I shall show in more detail below) make yourself emotionally upset.

Back to D—Disputing. You can determinedly, scientifically ask yourself, "What evidence exists that I *should* not have acted so foolishly when I had such a good job?" Or, if you want to Dispute even more clearly: "Prove that I *must* have behaved better in regard to my job, and thereby kept it and its advantages."

Answer: "No evidence whatever exists that I *should* not have acted so foolishly when I had such a good job. I have evidence for several other facts in connection with that job, namely: (a) 'I got distinct advantages from it and definitely desired to keep it'; (b) 'I did act badly while holding it and contributed significantly to getting myself fired'; (c) 'Because I found the job advantageous, I greatly dislike my present state of unemployment'; (d) 'I can now appropriately feel quite sorry and annoyed about my behaving badly on this desirable job and getting myself fired for behaving that way'; (e) 'I probably will have a pretty rough time getting an equally good job again, and I certainly feel displeased about that'; (f) 'I think I'll learn a lesson from what happened on this job and use it to encourage myself to act differently on my next position.' All these factual points, however, and the appropriate feelings I now experience as a result of facing them do not in any way constitute evidence for the proposition that I *should* and *must* have acted differently from the way I did act. I can now clearly see that acting differently would have proved preferable—very preferable. But that preference never equals an absolutistic *should* or *must!*

"Besides, the statement 'I *should* have done better on this job' implies that a law of the universe exists that unequivocally commands that I must have acted differently. But if such a law actually existed, I would have had no choice and would have *had* to act well on the job. Actually, of course, I didn't do what I *must* have done. Which means, obviously, that that *must* has only a fictional existence in my head, and certainly does not exist in reality!"

Again: "Once I have completed an act badly, I have little choice but to acknowledge that I *had* to do it badly—because I did! Whatever I did, I *should* have done—for the simple reason that I actually did it. When I think or talk about a *future* event, I can sensibly conclude: 'I should not do that, because I will bring about bad results if I do.' By the term *should* in this sentence I really mean, 'had better not,' or 'preferably should not,' do this act, because I wouldn't want to harm myself by doing it. But even about a future act I cannot legitimately conclude: 'I absolutely must never, under any conditions, do this, because I will bring about bad results if I do.' Because I then command, wrongly, that I have no right as a human to act badly—and even that I have no power to do so. But, of course, as a fallible person, I definitely do have the right to act wrongly; and I easily can!

"Granted that the statement 'I should not do that, because I will bring about bad results if I do' makes *some* sense if I stick to future events, it makes no sense whatever when I talk about what has *already* occurred. For the statement 'I should and must not have done that because I *now* see that I have brought about bad results by doing it' means: (a) 'I should have *then,* before I did this act, realized fully what kind of bad results it would bring about'; (b) 'Having known this, I had no right at all to do this disadvantageous act'; (c) 'I *had to* fully realize, then, what I obviously did not fully realize'; (d) 'Because I did not realize and stop myself from doing what I now realize I *must* have realized and stopped myself from doing, I clearly have little worth as a human and better denigrate and damn myself totally for the rest of my life!' "

All these propositions seem arrant nonsense. And by actively, vigorously Disputing them—at point D—you can get yourself to disbelieve them. Moreover, the theory of RET states if you persistently, steadily keep Disputing them, you will fairly easily and automatically, after a period of time, give them little credence and will give up your demandingness and your commandingness, join the human race, and generally live as a *non-musturbator.*

4. Your final highly irrational Belief (iB) about yourself when you foolishly lose your job and find it most difficult to replace it with an equivalent or better one and when you feel depressed after this sequence

of events has occurred, tends to run this way: "Because I did what I *should* and *must* not have done on this job, I can only see myself as a rotten person who will always keep acting this stupid way and who deserves nothing good in life!" This proposition arises as a somewhat logical deduction from an irrational premise. For if we could really prove that you *must* have behaved better about the job you lost and you willfully chose to ignore and go against this law of the universe, we might also justifiably conclude that the universe (or the presumed gods who run it) will almost certainly damn you forever for flouting such immutable laws and will make sure that nothing good will ever happen to you again—either in your present life or in any possible eternal existence that your "soul" will have.

Actually, however, your Belief about your essential rottenness and likely damnation for having acted so badly about losing your job seems most implausible on several fairly obvious counts. You can Dispute it, at D, as follows:

(a) "Assuming that I did a really rotten thing by shirking on the job and making myself thereby lose it, how does that make me an R.P.—a rotten person?" Answer: "It doesn't! For a rotten person would consist of an individual who had rottenness to the very core; and who consequently did, and would forever after always do, *everything* rottenly. Just as the term 'a rotten apple' doesn't mean an apple with a blemish or an apple with rotten parts, but one that we see as *totally* bad and *thoroughly* uneatable, so would we place 'a rotten person' in the same class: one who has *no* goodness or utility about him or her. Maybe I do a good many rotten things, but I don't think I can legitimately call myself *that* bad!"

(b) "If a 'rotten person' truly existed, that individual would have to inevitably, for all time and at all times, act rottenly. Can we ever, however, prove about *anyone* that he or she, because of present bad behavior, must always act the same way, under all possible conditions, in the future? Hardly! Then how can I accurately put myself in such a nonexistent category? I can't!"

(c) "If I rated as truly rotten to the core, because I could have acted better on my job and lost it when I refused to act well, I might possibly deserve nothing good in life. But this, too, remains an unprovable proposition. Since when does the universe spy on my performances, clearly note how badly I do, and decide to render me undeserving of any good things? According to the law of probability I *very likely* will get few rewards for bad behavior and more rewards for good behavior. But this never means that I *must*. A great many 'schlemiels' and 'undeserving' people reap unusually fine rewards during the course of their lifetime; a great many outstandingly competent and 'deserving' people reap little. Deservingness simply doesn't exist—except on a highly probabilistic basis. It has no absolute existence such as the absoluteness I invent when I insist that when I behave poorly I turn into an utterly rotten person who doesn't deserve any goodness and will undoubtedly suffer for the rest of my days."

(d) "In the very final analysis, by seing myself as a rotten and totally undeserving person, I posit immortality of the soul and devoutly believe that for doing good deeds during this earthly existence I will ultimately go to Heaven and lead a beatitudinous, angelic existence for eternity, and that for doing bad deeds while I reside on earth I will ultimately go to Hell and eternally lead a horrible, demon-ridden existence. For although I may well rate the goodness of my *acts,* in accordance with the values I choose to achieve by doing them, I cannot legitimately rate the total or global goodness of *me* who performs these acts; and when I do so I really opt for nobility, sacredness, and godliness. By the same token, when I ascend from empirically rating the badness of my acts (in terms of how they will likely sabotage my basic goals and purposes) to making a total or global rating of the badness of *me,* I opt for ignobility, unholiness, and demonization. But clearly no proof of sacredness, godliness, and demoniac qualities exists. Only my irrational and devout *beliefs* in these 'entities' will make them 'true.' So I'd better stop this nonsense and remain within the realm of empirical reality!"

By Disputing your irrational Beliefs (iB's) that make you and keep you emotionally disturbed at point D in the RET A-B-C-D-E's of human disturbance, you finally get to surrender these Beliefs and, ultimately, if you do so frequently enough, to rarely reinstate them. Disputing, or the logico-empirical method of science, is the main therapeutic approach of RET; it is a very powerful approach if you choose to make it so!

Winding Up with a New Effect or Philosophy

The end result of RET consists of your acquiring a new Effect (E) or philosophy that enables you semi-automatically to think about yourself, others, and the world in a more sensible way in the future. Thus, if you had the trouble about your job that we have used as an example, and if you Disputed (at point D) along the lines we have suggested, you would tend to wind up with this kind of new Effect, or philosophy, at E:

"I realize that I have shirked at my last job and perhaps at other jobs I have held, and that this kind of shirking remains quite undesirable and self-defeating. I also realize that, because of my human fallibility, I have little likelihood of never shirking again in my future jobs. For no one, including myself, works perfectly at all times at all the positions that he or she may hold.

"Nevertheless, on the basis of my past and present experience, I feel determined to change my ways in the future and to keep looking for another job until I finally find one and when I do, to work hard at coming on time, getting along with others, and trying to please my supervisors and bosses and avoid some of the worst mistakes that I have made in the past. If I do well at getting and keeping a job, fine. If I somehow do poorly, I will view that as highly unfortunate—but *not* as terrible or horrible. I can and will stand doing poorly on the job—just as I also can stand, though I clearly won't like, my present state of unemployment.

"Moreover, although I can find several excellent reasons for finding and keeping a good job, I can see no reason why I *have to* do so. Having the kind of job I enjoy will prove most *desirable,* but hardly *necessary.* I can live as a happy, though perhaps a distinctly less happy, individual if I remain unemployed. And whether I have a good job or not hardly makes me a *good person.* I, as a total individual, have too much complexity and ongoingness to merit a single rating or report card. Although I can rate my various acts or behaviors in terms of whether they help me survive and enjoy myself, I cannot legitimately assess or evaluate my *total self,* or my *humanity.* That merely exists and has no global value or rating. I intend to acknowledge myself and accept my identity (my separateness and uniqueness from all other individuals). But I shall not make my self-acknowledgment into a self-rating. Not if I can help it!"

With this kind of Effect (at E), you come to the end of the RET process. For, along with this cognitive Effect (cE), or new philosophy, you will, if you truly believe in it and follow what you believe, have a new emotive Effect (eE) and behavioral Effect (bE) as well. Thus, you will feel undepressed (though still sorry) and unanxious (though still concerned) about your not having a job right now. And, instead of avoiding looking for one, you will tend to get off your butt and actively and assertively do what you can to find the kind of employment you would feel good about it.

Is there anything else to RET than the use of the A-B-C's and the D-E's in the manner just described? Oh, yes: lots more! For, as shown in other parts of this book, RET strongly emphasizes emotive-evocative methods of therapy (such as rational-emotive imagery, shame-attacking exercises, and therapists giving their clients unconditional positive regard or full nondamning acceptance), and it emphasizes a large variety of behavioral homework assignments (particularly action-oriented, in vivo desensitization exercises). For its theory, while stressing the cognitive components in human disturbance and personality change, also states that people *strongly, forcefully,* and *dramatically* hold on to their ideas and behaviors and that to make real and lasting changes, they had better therefore strongly, forcefully, and emotively work at modifying their dysfunctional conduct.

RET theory also emphasizes the human tendency toward *habituation*. If you let yourself shirk at work, you tend to *habituate* yourself, by repetition and practice, to shirking. And if you tell yourself, many times and with great vigor, that you rate as a louse or a no-goodnik for your shirking and for causing yourself to lose jobs, you *habituate* yourself to easily believing and resistantly hanging on to this foolish, magical belief.

RET theory and practice forcefully says, therefore, that only by doing your A-B-C's and your D-E's many many times, and only by doing them in an emotive and action-oriented framework, will you likely undo your irrational Beliefs and *keep* them permanently undone. In fact, rational-emotive theory postulates that your tendency to think irrationally, emote inappropriately, and act dysfunctionally has a strong biological as well as a significant learned element to it; it therefore seems highly unlikely that you will *ever* behave as a completely rational, un-self-defeating creature. However, if you learn your A-B-C's of RET really well and back them up with vigorous and persistent emotive and behavioral action, you can go surprisingly far in this lovely direction!

References

Adler, A. *Understanding human nature*. New York: Greenberg, 1927. Paperback edition: Greenwich, Conn.: Fawcett World, 1968.

Adler, A. *The science of living*. New York: Greenberg, 1929. Paperback: New York: Doubleday, 1969.

Ainslie, G. Specious reward: A behavioral theory of impulsiveness and impulse control. *Psychological Bulletin,* 1975, *82,* 463–496.

Alexander, F., & French, T. M. *Psychoanalytic therapy.* New York: Ronald Press, 1946.

Austin, J. H. Eyes left! Eyes right! *Saturday Review,* August 9, 1975, 32.

Berne, E. Ego states in psychotherapy. *American Journal of Psychotherapy,* 1957, *11,* 293–309.

Bok, B. J. A critical look at astrology. *The Humanist,* 1975, *35*(5), 6–9.

Dejerine, J., & Gaukler, E. *Psychoneurosis and psychotherapy.* Philadelphia: Lippincott, 1913.

Dubois, P. *The psychic treatment of nervous disorders.* New York: Funk and Wagnalls, 1907.

Ellis, A. *Reason and emotion in psychotherapy.* New York: Lyle Stuart, 1962.

Ellis, A. *Executive leadership: a rational approach.* New York: Citadel, 1972 (a).

Ellis, A. *How to master your fear of flying.* New York: Pinnacle Books, 1972 (b).

Ellis, A. What does transpersonal psychology have to offer the art and science of psychotherapy? *Rational Living,* 1973, *8* (1), 20–28.

Ellis, A. *Humanistic psychotherapy: the rational-emotive approach.* New York: Julian Press, 1973. Paperback edition: New York: McGraw-Hill, 1974 (a).

Ellis, A. *Growth through reason.* Palo Alto: Science and Behavior Books, 1971. Hollywood: Wilshire Books, 1974 (b).

Ellis, A. *How to live with a "neurotic."* New York: Crown Publishers, 1957. Revised edition: New York: Crown Publishers, 1975.

Ellis, A. *Sex and the liberated man.* New York: Lyle Stuart, 1976.

Ellis, A. Why "scientific" professionals believe mystical nonsense. *Psychiatric Opinion,* 1977, *14* (2), 27–31.

Ellis, A. & Gullo, J. *Murder and assassination.* New York: Lyle Stuart, 1972.

Ellis, A. & Harper, R. A. *A guide to rational living.* Englewood Cliffs, N.J.: Prentice-Hall, and Hollywood: Wilshire Books, 1961.

Ellis, A. & Harper, R. A. *A new guide to rational living.* Englewood Cliffs, N.J.: Prentice-Hall, 1975, and Hollywood: Wilshire Books, 1975.

Ellis, A., & Harper, R. A. *Creative marriage.* New York: Lyle Stuart, 1961. Paperback edition: *A guide to successful marriage.* Hollywood: Wilshire Books, 1973.

Ellis, A., Wolfe, J. L., & Moseley, S. *How to prevent your child from becoming a neurotic adult.* New York: Crown Publishers, 1966. Paperback edition: *How to raise an emotionally healthy, happy child.* Hollywood: Wilshire Books, 1974.

Frankel, C. The nature and sources of irrationalism. *Science,* 1973, *180,* 927–931.

Frazer, J. G. *The new golden bough.* New York: Criterion, 1959.

Freud, S. *Collected papers.* New York: Collier Books, 1964.

Friedman, M. *Rational behavior.* Columbia, S.C.: University of South Carolina Press, 1975.

Hadas, M. (Ed.) *Essential works of stoicism.* New York: Bantam, 1963.

Hauck, P. A. *Overcoming depression.* Philadelphia: Westminster Press, 1973.

Herzberg, A. *Active psychotherapy.* New York: Grune and Stratton, 1945.

Hoffer, E. *The true believer.* New York: Harper, 1951.

Hook, S. The promise of humanism. *The Humanist,* 1975, *35*(5), 41–43.

Horney, K. *New ways in psychoanalysis.* New York: Norton, 1939.

Jerome, L. E. Astrology: magic or science? *The Humanist,* 1975, *35*(5), 10–16.

Jurjevich, R. M. *The hoax of Freudism.* Philadelphia: Dorrance & Company, 1974.

Kelly, G. *The psychology of personal constructs.* New York: Norton, 1955.

Korzybski, A. *Science and sanity.* Lancaster, Pa.: Lancaster Press, 1933. Paperback edition: San Francisco: Institute for General Semantics, 1973.

Kurtz, P. The original sins: Gullibility and nincompoopery. *Journal of Religious Humanism,* Winter 1975, 2–9.

Lazarus, A. A. *Behavior therapy and beyond.* New York: McGraw-Hill, 1971.

Leites, N. *The new ego.* New York: Science House, 1971.

Le Shan, L. The achievement ethic and the human potential movement. *Association for Humanistic Psychology Newsletter,* July 1975, 13–14.

Levi-Strauss, C. *Savage mind.* Chicago: University of Chicago Press, 1970.

Low, A. *Mental health through will-training.* Boston: Christopher Publishing Company, 1952.

Maultsby, M. C., Jr. *Help yourself to happiness.* New York: Institute for Rational Living, 1975.

Maslow, A. H. *Toward a psychology of being* (2nd ed.) New York: Van Nostrand Reinhold, 1974.

Meyer, A. *The commonsense psychiatry of Dr. Adolf Meyer.* New York: McGraw-Hill, 1948.

Parker, R. S. *Emotional common sense.* New York: Harper, 1973.

Phillips, E. L. *Psychotherapy.* Englewood Cliffs, N.J.: Prentice-Hall, 1956.

Piaget, J., & Inhelder, B. *Psychology of the child.* New York: Basic Books, 1974.

Pitkin, W. B. *A short introduction to the history of human stupidity.* New York: Simon and Schuster, 1932.

Rachleff, O. *The occult conceit: A new look at astrology, witchcraft and sorcery.* New York: Bell Publishing Company, 1973.

Rogers, C. R. *On becoming a person.* Boston: Houghton Mifflin, 1974.

Rotter, J. B. *Social learning and clinical psychology.* New York: Prentice-Hall, 1954.

Salter, A. *Conditioned reflex therapy.* New York: Creative Age, 1949. Paperback edition: New York: Putnam, 1961.

Shibles, W. *Emotion: The method of philosophical therapy.* Whitewater, Wisconsin: The Language Press, 1974.

Skinner, B. F. *Beyond freedom and dignity.* New York: Knopf, 1971. Paperback edition: New York: Bantam, 1972.

Sperry, R. W. Left-brain, right-brain. *Saturday Review,* August 9, 1975, 30–33.

Strupp, H. H. The therapist's personal therapy: the influx of irrationalism. *The Clinical Psychologist,* 1975, *28*(3), 1, 11. (a)

Strupp, H. H. Training the complete clinician. *The Clinical Psychologist,* 1975, *28*(4), 1–2. (b)

Sullivan, H. S. *Conceptions of modern psychiatry.* Washington: William Alanson White Foundation, 1947.

Sullivan, H. S. *The interpersonal theory of psychiatry.* New York: Norton, 1953.

Thorne, F. C. *Principles of personality counseling.* Brandon, Vermont: Journal of Clinical Psychology Press, 1950.

Thorne, F. C. *Personality: a clinical eclectic view.* Brandon, Vermont: Journal of Clinical Psychology Press, 1961.

Watzlawick, P., Weakland, J., & Fisch, R. *Change: Principles of problem formation and problem resolution.* New York: Norton, 1974.

2

Research Data Supporting the Clinical and Personality Hypotheses of RET and Other Cognitive-Behavior Therapies

Albert Ellis

No theory of psychotherapy stands up well without a good body of experimental evidence to support it. Fortunately, RET has this evidence, gathered from many studies, some of which were conducted by researchers who wanted to test RET theories, but most of which came from researchers who had no stake in validating or disputing RET at all.

This chapter explains 32 clinical and personality hypotheses of rational-emotive therapy and other modes of cognitive-behavior therapy. It cites specific studies testing each hypothesis and refers the reader to other reviews of the literature.

N O THEORY OF psychotherapy stands up well without a good body of experimental evidence to support it. Although rational-emotive therapy (RET), like many other theories of personality change, sounds fine, hangs together with a good deal of logical consistency, and seems (on the basis of clinical and anecdotal evidence) to get favorable results, it does not merit much faith as a "good" theory unless it has more rigorously-obtained research evidence behind it. Fortunately, it has. RET's main propositions are stated in such a clearcut, testable manner that an unusually large number of studies have appeared since I systematically formulated them in the late 1950s and early 1960s (Ellis, 1958, 1962). Well over 90% of the studies have offered statistically confirming evidence favoring RET hypotheses.

The bibliography for this chapter contains some 987 references and, because of its length, is not contained herein. The interested reader can refer to *The Counseling Psychologist* (1977), where the material in this chapter is also being published, or to *A comprehensive bibliography of materials on rational-emotive therapy and cognitive-behavior therapy* (New York: Institute for Rational Living, 1978).

The author wishes to thank Linda Eckstein for help in organizing and collating the material in this chapter.

Outcome studies of rational-emotive therapy appear elsewhere in this handbook (see DiGiuseppe and Miller, chapter 3). I shall therefore omit these data from the present chapter and merely note that they seem impressive. Researchers have tested RET procedures against other therapies and against control groups in about 75 instances and have found almost uniformly favorable results. Another 25 or so studies of rationality scales derived from RET have also appeared and virtually all of them have shown that the dozen basic irrational ideas that I first formulated in 1957 (Ellis, 1957, 1958) significantly differentiate various kinds of emotionally disturbed people from controls. So RET's clinical record, as measured by controlled experiments, appears unusually good. As Glass and Smith (1975) have shown in a review of hundreds of psychotherapy research experiments, RET proved second only to systematic desensitization in this respect, with eight other leading types of psychotherapy following behind these two. A notable record—especially considering that RET entered the field relatively late and that the populations in the RET studies had more complicated and more typical emotional disorders than the target symptoms of the systematic desensitization studies—which often included atypical "neurotic" reactions, such as fear of snakes.

The present chapter reviews a good many major clinical and personality hypotheses of RET and the research studies that appear to support these hypotheses. I found that well over 90% of the published studies supported the RET theory, while less than 10% gave equivocal or negative results. Some of these findings stemmed from faulty methodology; others pose questions for future research. Because I located so many confirmatory researches and have only limited space in this review, I shall largely omit the nonconfirmatory studies. And to keep the present chapter to a manageable length, I shall also concentrate on recent researches and cite older ones mainly when they included pioneering or classic research.

Most of the researches cited in this chapter included experimental and control groups and had a statistical analysis of obtained differences in the performances of these groups. A few papers were not experiments but, rather, reviewed many experiments; a few consisted of clinical studies of a number of individuals, with statistical differentiation of groups or subgroups but with no actual control group. Although many of the studies cited below originated with clinicians who specifically wanted to test RET or cognitive-behavior theories, most of the studies came from the psychological laboratories of literally hundreds of experimental, social, developmental, and other psychologists who have no particular stake in validating or disputing RET, who do not practice psychotherapy, who often seem completely unaware of rational-emotive theory, and who cite no references to it in their bibliographies. That so many non-RET-oriented researchers have published data supporting many of the most important RET theories impressively substantiates the RET hypotheses, I believe.

The A-B-C Theory of RET

Hypothesis 1: thinking creates emotion. Human thinking and emotion do not constitute two disparate or different processes, but significantly overlap. Cognition represents a mediating operation between stimuli and responses. What we call emotions and behaviors do not merely stem from people's reactions to their environment but also from their thoughts, beliefs, and attitudes about that environment. In terms of the RET theory of emotion and personality, A (an Activiting Event or Activating Experience) does not exclusively cause C (an emotional Consequence in the gut); B (people's Beliefs about A) more importantly and more directly contributes to or "causes" C (Ellis, 1957, 1958, 1962, 1975a).

This hypothesis is central to the whole field of RET and cognitive behavior therapy and has an enormous amount of research that solidly supports it. Pioneer researchers and theoreticians in the area include: Bandura (1969, 1974); Bannister (1971); Bannister and Mair (1968); Bannister and Fransella (1973); Bem (1967); Davitz (1969); Gray, Gray, and Gray (1975); Irwin (1971); Kagan (1972); Kelly (1955, 1969); Kendler (1971); Kilty (1969); Langner (1966); A. Lazarus (1971, 1974, 1976); R. Lazarus (1966); Lazarus and Averill (1975); Lazarus, Averill, and Opton (1970); London and Nisbett (1974); Luria (1961); Luria and Yudovich (1959); Mandler (1975); Meichenbaum (1974, 1975, 1977); Mischel (1968, 1976); Neisser (1966); Pavlov (1941); Rokeach (1960, 1968, 1973); Schacter (1965, 1966, 1971); Schacter and Singer (1962); and Zimbardo (1969). Almost innumerable studies and reviews of research have appeared that support the view that, in general, human emotion and behavior include cognitive mediation and for the most part have important cognitive origins. I list scores of these studies below under more specific headings. You may find additional general confirmation of this central RET theory in Bergin (1970); Bergin and Strupp (1970); Deci (1975); Guernette (1972); Jacobs and Sachs (1971); Kaplan (1972); Lewis, Wolman, and King (1971); Loveless and Brody (1974); Luce and Peper (1971); Norman (1975); Poetter (1970); Rollins (1975); Russell and Brandsma (1974); Si (1973); Spivack and Shure (1974); Theisen (1973); Wardell and Royce (1975); Weimer and Palermo (1974); and Weiner (1974).

Hypothesis 2: semantic processes and self-statements affect behavior. People invariably talk to themselves; the kinds of things they say to themselves, as well as the form in which they say these things, significantly affect their emotions and behavior and sometimes lead them to feel emotionally disturbed. Effective psychotherapy partly consists of helping them talk to themselves more precisely, empirically, rationally, and unabsolutistically.

Pioneers in the field of psychotherapy and allied disciplines who have espoused this hypothesis and worked to develop techniques of semantitherapy include Beier (1966); Blois (1963); Bois (1966, 1972); Bourland (1968, 1969); Chemodurow (1971); Ellis (1958, 1962, 1971a, 1973d, 1975a, 1977a); Ellis and Harper (1975); Kelly (1955); Korzybski (1933); Mahoney (1974); Meichenbaum (1974, 1975, 1977); Mosher (1966); Osgood (1971); Phillips (1956); and Velten (1968).

Studies that confirm the importance of semantic processes in human emotion and in psychotherapeutic change include those by Alperson (1975); Beilin, Lust, Sack, and Natt (1975); Boudewyns and Tanna (1975); Davitz (1969); Early (1968); Hays and Waddell (1976); Kaplan (1970); Levin, Davidson, Wolf, and Citron (1973); McGuigan (1970); O'Donnell and Brown (1973); Osgood (1971); Payne (1970); Perlman (1972); Rimm and Litvak (1969); Rychlak (1973); Schill, Evans, Munroe, and Ramanaiah (1976); Staats (1975); Staats, Gross, Guay and Carlson (1973); and Walton (1971).

Hypothesis 3: mood states depend on cognition. People's mood states significantly depend upon what they believe or tell themselves. When they tell themselves and believe in optimistic, hopeful, cheerful ideas they tend to feel happy, elated, joyous, or serene; when they tell themselves and believe in pessimistic, cynical, hopeless ideas and make predictions about an unenjoyable future, they tend to feel sad, morose, miserable, and depressed. Effective therapy often includes helping clients to have optimistic and cheerful ideas and to surrender their unduly pessimistic views of the present and future.

This hypothesis about mood states represents an important subheading under the general idea of cognitions significantly contributing to emotions; it also relates to the subjects of expectancy, positive thinking, and learned helplessness. As an hypothesis in its own right, it stems mainly from the theorizing of the cognitive-behavior therapists and philosophers listed in the previous sections of this article, and from my own particular theories of rational-emotive therapy (Ellis, 1958, 1962, 1971a, 1973c, 1973d, 1973e, 1975e, 1977a; Ellis and Harper, 1975).

The pioneering study confirming Hypothesis 3 was Velten's (1967, 1968) investigation. In Velten's study, one group of female college students concentrated on 60 self-referent statements intended to produce elation; a second group concentrated on 60 statements intended to produce depressing moods; and a third group concentrated on statements intended as neither self-referent nor pertaining to mood. Significant differences appeared in the moods of all three groups and Velten concluded: "Post-experimental questionnaire data strongly supported the conclusion that elation and depression treatments had indeed respectively induced elation and depression."

Velten's study has had several replications, just about all of which have confirmed his original findings, including studies by Aderman (1972), Blue (1975), Coleman (1975), and Hale and Strickland (1976).

Hypothesis 4: awareness, insight, and self-monitoring affect behavior. Humans not only have the ability to think (and generalize), but to think about their thinking and to think about thinking about their thinking. They almost invariably observe and cognize about their behavior; by such observation and cognition they significantly affect or change this behavior. Whenever they feel emotionally disturbed (e.g., anxious, depressed, or hostile), they tend to perceive and think about their disturbance and thereby either make themselves more disturbed (e.g., anxious about their anxiety or depressed about their feelings of depression) or make themselves less disturbed. Awareness, insight, understanding, and self-monitoring, therefore, comprise cognitive processes that significantly affect behavior and behavior change. Psychotherapists have as one of their main functions the helping of their clients to increase their awareness of precisely what they do to disturb themselves and to use this awareness to change their dysfunctional behavior.

In various ways, important elements of this hypothesis exist in virtually all the major systems of psychotherapy—including those advocated by Adler (1927, 1929); Berne (1961, 1964); Ellis (1957, 1958, 1962, 1973c); Freud (1965); Jung (1954); Kelly (1955); and Perls (1969). Even the presumably abreactive, nonverbal, or physically oriented systems of psychotherapy importantly use, whether consciously or unconsciously, highly cognitive, awareness-related elements (Ellis, 1970, 1973d, 1974a, 1974b, 1974c; Raimy, 1975).

Clinical presentations showing that awareness or insight helps humans change their dysfunctional behavior abound in the professional literature, including the references cited in the previous paragraph. With increased frequency in recent years, controlled experimental studies have appeared that indicate that when subjects get specifically aware of their cognitions (and other aspects of their behavior), they make greater changes or retain these changes in their emotions and behaviors better than when they have little or no specific awareness.

Other studies show that various kinds of performances and emotions lead to significantly improved results when coding, cognitive rehearsal, and various other kinds of mental practice occur. Researches demonstrating the efficacy of awareness and cognitive rehearsal include those by Bandura and Jeffrey (1973); Batson (1975); Cradler and Goodwin (1971); Friedman (1972); Geen, Rakosky, and Pigg (1972); Jones (1965); Muehlman (1972); O'Donnell and Brown (1973); Rokeach (1971); Schumsky (1972); Thorpe, Amatu, Blakey, and Burns (1975); Vargas and Adesso (1976); Vandell, Davis, and Clugston (1943); Wagner (1973); Wexler (1974a, 1974b); and Wortman (1974).

A related set of studies stems from the work on cognitive dissonance by Festinger (1957) and Heider (1946), whose theory holds that humans have great trouble holding two dissonant ideas and that they have an innate and pronounced tendency to make adjustments to "resolve" this dissonance in some semisatisfactory manner. Scores of researches have attested at least to the partial validity of this hypothesis and have found that cognitive processes that reduce dissonance serve as a highly important factor in personality integration and disorder. Festinger (1957, 1962) has summarized some of the main literature; other relevant studies include those of Innes (1972); Rosen and Wyer (1972); and Zanna and Cooper (1974).

Another large series of studies of the effects of self-monitoring on psychotherapeutic and other behavioral change has appeared in the behavior therapy literature during the last decade. The studies almost uniformly tend to show that when people monitor their own behavior (e.g., record the number of cigarettes they smoke or the amount of calories they use every day), they frequently change their dysfunctional habits without employing any other kinds of reinforcements or penalties. The self-monitoring process and the other cognitions that go with it seem to provide them with sufficient intrinsic reinforcements or penalties. Similarly, studies have shown that self-monitoring frequently brings better therapeutic results than monitoring by outside observers, and that self-monitoring methods, when added to other cognitive-behavioral techniques, increase the efficacy of these other techniques. Experimenters who have presented evidence in these connections include Johnson and White (1971); Kanfer (1970a, 1970b); Kazdin (1974); Mahoney, Moore, Wade, and Moura (1973); Mahoney, Moura, and Wade (1973); Pribram and McGuiness (1975); and Richards, McReynolds, Holt, and Sexton (1976).

Hypothesis 5: imaging and fantasy mediate emotions and behaviors. People not only think about what happens to them in words, phrases, and sentences but also do so in nonverbal ways, including images, fantasies, dreams, and other kinds of pictorial representations. Such images contain the same kind of cognitive mediating messages as do verbal self-statements, and these cognitions contribute significantly to emotions and behaviors, to emotional disturbances, and to helping people change their emotions, behaviors, and disturbances.

In particular, psychoanalytic writers have pioneered in proposing that images and fantasies have enormous influence over the emotions and behavior of most people (Freud, 1965). Many nonpsychoanalytic therapists, such as Assagioli (1965), have also emphasized fantasy in their work with clients. But as Singer (1974) points out in a most impressive review of the imagery literature, both the more orthodox behavior therapists—such as Cautela (1966) and Wolpe (1958)—and the cognitive-behavior therapists—such as Bandura (1969); Beck (1970); Brown (1967); A. Lazarus (1971, 1976); and Stampfl and Levis (1967)—also make extensive use of imaginative methods. Singer properly notes: "When the behaviorists flock over into so extensive a reliance on private 'internal' processes, we know the cognitive revolution is really on its way."

Specific studies that validate the important connection between subjects' imaging and emotive and behavioral changes include those by Barrett (1970); Barlow and Agras (1973); Berecz (1972); Chappell and Stevenson (1936); Grossberg and Wilson (1968); Haney and Euse (1976); Laws and Pawlowski (1974); Levinson, Davidson, Wolff, and Citron (1973); McConaghy (1967); Rychlak (1973); Spanos, Horton, and Chaves (1975); and Wenger, Averill, and Smith (1968). Singer (1974) includes scores of other interesting and relevant studies.

Although Joseph Wolpe (1958) has minimized cognitive factors in behavior therapy and has talked about deconditioning or desensitizing procedures as if they utilized almost pure instrumental or Pavlovian conditioning, and although B. F. Skinner (1953, 1971) has steadfastly refused to look in the "black box" of cognition that seems to lie behind operant conditioning, we can ironically observe that the most popular and one of the most effective of all the conventional behavior therapy techniques used in psychotherapy consists of Wolpe's systematic desensitization method. In this method, clients imagine disturbance-provoking stimuli (such as approaching a snake or delivering a public speech). Imagination, of course, constitutes a highly cognitive process. Clients then focus (another cognitive method!) on relaxing their muscles and feeling unanxious, until they gradually desensitize themselves to the images they fear. Finally, they seem to conclude—yes, *cognitively* conclude—that they need not fear snakes or public speaking.

A great many controlled studies of systematic desensitization have appeared showing the efficacy of this imaging method. Instead of listing them here, let me cite some comprehensive reviews of the literature which include them: Bandura (1969); Eysenck (1960, 1964); Franks (1969);

London (1969); Paul (1966); Rachman (1968); Ullman and Krasner (1965); Wolpe (1958, 1973); Wolpe and Lazarus (1966); Yates (1976).

Building on the work of Wolpe and of Homme (1965), Cautela (1966a, 1966b, 1967, 1971, 1973) created a form of behavior therapy called *covert desensitization,* in the course of which clients imagine the maladaptive behavior they want to control, such as smoking or overeating, and then imagine in vivid detail a noxious or aversive scene, such as feeling sick and vomiting. Similarly, in covert reinforcement, clients can strengthen their desirable behaviors by imagining reinforcing images and rewarding themselves in their heads rather than in vivo. Although, like all behavioral and imaginative methods, covert desensitization and reinforcement has its limitations, many studies show its effectiveness, including those by Ashem and Donner (1968); Barlow, Leitenberg, and Agras (1973); Bellack, Glanz, and Simon (1976); Binder (1975); Cautela, Walsh, and Wish (1971); Diament and Wilson (1975); Hekmat and Vanian (1971); Horan, Baker, Hoffman, and Shute (1975); Hurley (1976); Janda and Rimm (1972); Mahoney (1969); Marshall, Boutilier, and Minnes (1974); Mullen (1968); Segal and Sims (1972); Viernstein (1968); and Wisocki (1973).

Hypothesis 6: cognition, emotion, and behavior are interrelated. Human cognition, emotion, and behavior do not constitute separate entities but all significantly interrelate and importantly affect each other. Cognition significantly contributes to emotion and to action; emotion to cognition and to action; and action to cognition and to emotion. When people change one of these three modalities of behaving, they concomitantly tend to change the other two. Effective therapy consists of the therapist's consciously trying to help clients ameliorate their emotional disturbances and behavioral dysfunctioning by teaching them a variety of cognitive, emotive, and behavioral techniques of personality change. Although virtually all systems of psychotherapy seem to subscribe to this hypothesis implicitly or unconsciously, few of the well-known systems do so explicitly; RET represents a notable exception in this respect (Ellis, 1958, 1962, 1968, 1971a, 1973d, 1977a; Ellis and Harper, 1975). Some of the main therapists who have forcefully espoused an interactional, cognitive-affective-behavioral system of psychotherapy include Goldfried and Davison (1976); A. Lazarus (1971, 1976); Meyer (1948, 1958); and Pion (1976).

Some experimenters who have shown that when subjects experience distinct changes in their behavior they also experience significant changes in their cognitions and emotions include Becker, Horowitz, and Campbell, (1973); Bell (1972); Briggs and Weinberg (1973); Bull (1960); Byrne, Fisher, Lamberth, and Mitchell (1974); Caulfield and Martin (1976); Cooper and Goethals (1974); Detweiler and Zanna (1976); Diamond and Shapiro (1973); Dua (1970); Fisher and Winkler (1975); Grezsiak and Locke (1975); Jacobs, Jacobs, Cavior, and Burke (1974); Kopel and Arkowitz (1974); Krisher, Darley, and Darley (1973); Laird (1974); Leitenberg, Agras, Butz, and Wincze (1971); Levey and Martin (1975); Maranon (1924); Perez (1973); Ryan, Krall, and Hodges (1976); Schacter and Singer (1962); and Strong and Gray (1972).

Experimenters and reviewers who have confirmed the idea that changes in cognition tend to produce significant changes in emotion and behavior include Acock and deFleur (1972); Arnheim (1969); Arnold (1960); Bandura (1974); Batson (1975); Brown (1973); Dienstbier, Hillman, Lehnhoff, Hillman, and Valkenaar (1975); Hickey (1976); Kiesler (1971); Klix (1971); Longstreth (1971); Lott and Murray (1975); Marshall, Strawbridge, and Keltner (1972); McReynolds, Barnes, Brooks, and Rehagen (1973); Raimy (1975); Spielberger and Gorsuch (1966); Start (1960); Wexler (1974a, 1974b); and Yulis, Brahm, Charnes, Jacard, Picota, and Rutman (1975).

Studies that present evidence that changing human emotions significantly affects subjects' cognitions and behaviors include those by Cook, Pallak, and Sogin (1976); Coons and McEachern (1967); Dutta, Kanungo, and Friebergs (1972); Giesen and Hendrick (1974); Hale and Strickland (1976); Horowitz (1973); Horowitz and Becker (1971a, 1971b, 1971c); Horowitz, Becker, and Moskowitz (1971); Landfield (1971); Levey and Martin (1975); Strickland, Hale, and Anderson (1975); and Wine (1971).

Hypothesis 7: cognition can affect biofeedback and control of physiological processes. When people perceive their own thinking, emotive, and physiological processes, they think about (and often awfulize about) these processes; they thereby significantly affect their subsequent behavior, both in healthy (self-helping) and unhealthy (self-defeating) ways. By perceiving, focusing on, and cognizing about their physiological reactions, they can sometimes change these reactions dramatically, either consciously or unconsciously—e.g., they increase or decrease their pulse rates, their galvanic skin reactions, their experiences of pain, and many central or autonomic nervous system functions that they usually do not voluntarily control. Their ability to do so apparently depends to a large degree on their cognitions; this provides clearcut evidence of the significant influence of cognition on emotive and behavioral functions.

Pioneering studies and theoretical formulations in regard to biofeedback processes have emerged from the work of Green (1973); Kamiya (1968); N. Miller (1969); Olds (1960); and many other researchers. Their work has sparked other studies by a large number of investigators, just about all of which indicate that biofeedback, perceptual feedback, and other forms of cognitive-physical processes help subjects change their thinking, emoting, and behaving. Relevant studies and reviews in this area include those by Borkovec (1973); Friar and Beatty (1976); Herman and Prewett (1975); Jacobs, Jacobs, Feldman, and Cavior (1973); Laird (1974); Lang, Sproufe, and Hastings (1967); Melnick (1973); Mulholland (1973); Powers (1973); Riddick and Meyer (1973); Roberts and Kewman (1973); Rokeach (1975); Rutner (1973); Schwartz (1973); Sirota, Schwartz, and Shapiro (1974); Thomas (1973); and Trotter (1973).

A special series of studies indicates that people have much more ability than they generally recognize to control and regulate their feelings of physical pain. This includes studies by Bobey and Davison (1970); Chaves and Barber (1974); Crue (1975); Holmes and Frost (1976); Nisbett and Schacter (1966); and Spanos, Horton, and Chaves (1975).

A vast number of studies indicate that cognitive processes can significantly influence many different kinds of physiological reactions, including respiratory rate, electrodermal and vasomotor activity, cardiac activity, and sexual arousal. Research papers and reviews in this area include those by Adamson, Romano, Burdick, Corman, and Chebib (1972); Allison (1970); Altman (1973); Baer and Furher (1970); Black (1970); Burdick (1972); Carlson, Travers, and Schwab (1969); Cook and Harris (1937); Graham (1972); Grossberg (1968); Haney and Euse (1976); Henson and Rubin (1971); Jordan and Kempler (1970); Jordan and Simprelle (1972); R. Lazarus (1966, 1975); Loftis and Ross (1974); Mathews (1971); McCarron and Appel (1971); May (1974); Mowrer (1938); Post (1973); Proctor and Malloy (1971); Rakover and Levita (1973); Ray and Walker (1973); Rule and Hewitt (1971); Russell and Brandsma (1974); Shean, Faia, and Schmaltz (1974); Vantress and Williams (1972); Warson and Huey (1973); Wenger, Averill, and Smith (1968); and Wooley (1972).

Hypothesis 8: there are innate influences on emotions and behavior. Humans appear to have very strong innate as well as acquired tendencies to think, emote, and behave in certain ways, although virtually none of their behavior stems solely from instinct and just about all of it has powerful environmental and learning factors that contribute to its causation. Particularly in the field of disturbed emotions, both innate biological tendencies and acquired learning help create and sustain what we call emotional disturbance. Therapists would do better, therefore, to face these facts and sometimes communicate them to clients, in order to help these clients see: (1) the complex reasons for their disturbance; (2) how hard they will probably have to work to make themselves less disturbed; and (3) how easily they can fall back to dysfunctional behavior that they have previously ameliorated.

Almost all leading psychotherapists tend to emphasize, and probably to overemphasize, the importance of early childhood training or conditioning in the creation of human disturbance; very few of them importantly stress genetic or constitutional factors, even though their basic theories implicitly and often very strongly subsume such factors. Although Freud (1965) and Adler (1927, 1929) had some strong biological leanings, most of their followers have ignored these leanings and almost exclusively stressed the role of environmental forces in disturbance. Body-oriented therapies, such as those stemming from the theories of Reich (1949), clearly involve biological underpinnings. But virtually all the practitioners of these theories, including Reich himself, so intensively stress the importance of environmental teaching and training in overcoming tendencies to disturbance that they imply or unequivocally state that such tendencies also derive from almost purely environmental influences. They tend to neglect almost entirely the fairly obvious point that even when a physical or emotional disorder, such as a muscular weakness, dyslexia, or childhood autism, has distinct biological determinants, we can often help those afflicted with such a disorder by specific education, conditioning, and retraining.

RET seems to be one of the few major psychotherapies that frankly and unapologetically stresses the powerful organic and biological factors that exist in human disturbance (Ellis, 1962, 1971a, 1973d, 1974a, 1974b, 1977b; Maultsby, 1975). I have for many years collected data on the biological basis of human disturbance that support RET hypotheses in this connection; if published, this material would doubtless require several thick volumes. Let me cite here just a few of the important studies and reviews that tend to prove, though not of course with absolute certainty, that emotional disturbance springs from profound and complex biological as well as sociological influences; that early childhood learning definitely contributes to psychological disorder but has a significantly greater effect on innately vulnerable than nonvulnerable children; that certain serious psychological ailments, such as manic-depressive psychosis and schizophrenia, almost surely have a powerful biological (as well as environmental) basis; and that social and therapeutic conditioning can greatly help disturbed individuals even when they clearly appear to have innately predisposed handicaps.

A small sample of relevant research studies and reviews in this area includes those by Ainsworth (1969); Altman (1972); Bender (1953, 1963, 1968); Bowers (1971); Browning (1971); Brainerd (1970);

Cameron, Gnadinger, Kostin, and Kostin (1973); Casler (1974); Chess, Thomas, and Birch (1965); Churchill (1969); Confino (1973); Etzioni (1968); Freedman (1974); Freedman and Keller (1963); Garmezy (1972); Jellinek (1973); Kalish (1970); Kallman (1960); Kety (1967); Kraines (1966); Lovass and Schriebman (1971); Mahler (1968); Mandell, Segal, Kuszenski and Knapp (1972); Marks (1970); McWhinnie (1967); Meehl (1962); Novak and Van der Veen (1968); Oltman and Friedman (1965, 1966); Osborn (1968); Rimland (1964); Rosenthal (1962, 1970, 1973); Rosenthal and Kety (1968); Russell and Russell (1957); Schmeck (1972); Schopler and Loftin (1969); Seligman (1971); Slater and Cowie (1971); Thomas, Chess, and Birch (1968, 1970); Van den Berg (1972); Wender (1969); Willner and Struve (1970); and Wolpe (1970).

Hypothesis 9: expectancy influences behavior. When people expect that something will happen or expect that others will act or respond in a certain way, they act significantly differently than when they have other kinds of expectancies. Their cognitive expectancy importantly influences both their degree of emotional disturbance and the ways in which they react to therapy and to their therapists. In RET and related cognitive behavior procedures, therapists can use clients' expectancies to help them overcome their disturbances.

This expectancy hypothesis has received pioneering confirmation by therapists like Jerome Frank (1961, 1968); Meichenbaum and Smart (1971); Mowrer (1938); Rosenthal and Frank (1956); R. Rosenthal (1966, 1973); and many others. They have shown that clients' and therapists' expectations significantly affect the outcome of psychotherapy; that students who receive direct expectancy statements improve significantly relative to control groups; that subjects' expectations seem more powerful than their experiences in establishing conditioned galvanic skin responses; that a very powerful placebo effect exists in psychotherapy; that all kinds of psychological experimenter expectancies seriously affect the outcomes of behavioral researches; and that demand or conformism expectancies induce clients and others to emote and behave in special ways.

Literally scores of researchers have done controlled experiments showing that different kinds of expectancy influence people to make emotional and behavioral changes. Confirmatory studies in this area include those by Austin and Walster (1974); Babad (1973); Borkovec (1972, 1973); Breznitz (1967); Brickman and Hendricks (1975); Brickman and McCareins (1976); Cook and Harris (1937); Davison, Tsujimoto, and Glaros (1973); Deane (1966); Ducette and Wolk (1973); Dweck (1975); Eagly and Acksen (1971); Garfield, Gershon, Sletten, Sundland, and Ballon (1967); Grings (1973); Johnson (1973); Lang, Goeckner,

Adesso, and Marlett (1975); Legant and Mettee (1973); Lick and Bootzin (1975); Loeb, Beck, Diggory, and Tuthill (1967); Lott and Murray (1975); Marcia, Rubin, and Efran (1969); McMahan (1973); Meichenbaum, Bowers, and Ross (1969); Nowicki and Walker (1974); Persely and Leventhal (1972); Pope, Siegman, Cheek, and Blass (1972); Rappaport (1972); Rosen (1975, 1976); Rubovits and Maehr (1973); Schaefer, Tregerthan, and Colgan (1976); Snyder, Schulz, and Jones (1974); Tori and Worell (1973); Wilson and Rappaport (1974); Wilson and Thomas (1973); Wyer (1973); and Ziemelis (1974).

In addition to these studies, another group of studies exists that specifically shows that when experimenters give placebos to psychotherapy clients or other subjects and deliberately lead them to believe that these placebos have a therapeutic effect, the clients or subjects actually experience pronounced emotional and behavioral changes. Validations of the efficacy of placebos include experiments by Jellinek (1946); Paul (1966); Rosenthal and Frank (1956); Steinmark and Borkovec (1974); Wolf (1950); and Wolf and Pinsky (1954).

Another related area of cognitive expectation consists of the field of conformism or demand expectancy. Asch (1952) and his associates discovered that humans, including intelligent college students, when asked to make antiempirical choices (e.g., declare that they see a 2½″ stick as shorter than a 2″ stick) will very frequently make such a choice if they think that people around them have also made this antiempirical decision. They have such a dire love need or conformism need—in RET terms—that they actually make themselves falsely view reality, or at least falsely report on their views of it, in order to please others.

Following up on Asch's work, many investigators have reported that subjects significantly change their thoughts, feelings, and behaviors when they expect that others want them to do so. They give in to what they conceive of as the "demands" of these others and go out of their way, often against their own best interests, to fill these demands. In the field of psychotherapy, in particular, clients frequently give responses to therapists and actually change their behaviors as much or more in accordance with what they think their therapists want them to do as in accordance with their own basic wishes. Many experiments have provided evidence of this expectancy demand characteristic of subjects and of clients, including those by Berquist and Klemm (1973); Borkovec and Glasgow (1973); McReynolds and Tori (1972); Milgrim (1974); Page (1972); and Pliner and Cappell (1974).

Hypothesis 10: perceived locus of control influences behavior. When people view situations, others' reactions, and their own behavior as within their control, they act differently than when they view these situations and behaviors as stemming from external sources or as outside their control. They can therefore improve their dysfunctional emoting and behaving if a therapist helps them see how they *use* external sources to form reactions and how they can take control of their own thoughts, feelings, and actions to a large degree, thereby minimizing their disturbances.

In the field of psychology, this hypothesis stems from the pioneering work of many experimentalists, particularly Witkin (1954), who developed tests showing how some people have field dependency, and let themselves feel influenced by environmental conditions around them, while others seem "field-independent," and let themselves feel less influenced in a passive-dependent manner by their environment. Going beyond Witkin's work, Rotter (1954, 1964, 1966, 1971, 1975) and his associates have done an immense amount of work on the problem of locus of control for more than twenty years. As Lefcourt (1976) indicates in a comprehensive review of the literature inspired by Witkin, Rotter, and other researchers on locus of control: "Whether people, or other species for that matter, believe that they are actors and can determine their own fates within limits will be seen to be of critical importance to the way in which they cope with stress and engage in challenges."

Lefcourt (1966, 1976) lists over 200 studies concerned with locus of control, virtually all of which show that people do think, emote, and act differently when they believe that they control important aspects of their lives than when they see these aspects as beyond their own control. Typical studies of locus of control, including some from Lefcourt's list, are those by Brisset and Nowicki (1973); Calhoun, Cheney, and Dawes (1974); Chaikin and Karley (1973); Ehri and Muzio (1974); Felton and Biggs (1972); Gilbert (1976); Harris (1976); Houston (1972); Levenson (1973); Nowicki, Bonner, and Feather (1972); Nowicki and Walker (1974); Phares (1971); Pines (1973); Riemer (1975); Roth and Bootzin (1974); Snyder, Schulz, and Jones (1974); Sogin and Pallak (1976); Williams and Stack (1973); Wolman, Lewis, and King (1971); and Worchel and Andreolo (1974).

Hypothesis 11: attribution errors influence emotions and behavior. Humans attribute motives, reasons, and causes to other people and to external events and internal physical states; they significantly influence their own emotions and behavior by these attributes, even when they base them on quite false or misleading perceptions and conceptions. A good deal of their emotional disturbance stems from misattributions. We may often help them overcome such disturbance by helping them to understand and change their cognitive misattributions.

Many social and experimental psychologists, such as Bem (1965, 1966, 1967), Kelley (1968), and Schacter and Singer (1962), have pioneered in formulating attribution theory. Their formulations have led to a vast number of studies, almost all of which confirm this theory. Classic experiments by Davison, Tsujimoto, and Glaros (1973), and by Davison and Valins (1969), showed how subjects who attributed their physiological changes to themselves rather than to a drug made significantly greater therapeutic gains than those who falsely made drug attributions. A study by Geer, Davison, and Gatchel (1971) indicated that subjects who believed they had control over their reaction time had fewer spontaneous skin conductance responses (SCR's) and smaller SCR's to shock than subjects who did not feel they had control. Nisbett and Schacter (1966) showed that subjects will behave more emotionally if they identify an emotional stimulus as the source of their arousal or pain than if they do not identify the stimulus as the source. Schacter and Singer (1962) found that: "Given a state of physiological arousal for which an individual has no immediate explanation, he will label this state and describe his feelings in terms of the cognitions available to him." Valins (1966, 1967) found that when a subject thinks his heart rate has changed in response to a photo of a nude female, he will consider her more attractive and desire a copy of her photo more than another photo to which he falsely thinks his heart rate has not changed. Valins and Ray (1967) led subjects to believe that snake stimuli did not affect them internally and found that these subjects, in comparison to suitable controls, later manifested more approach behavior when confronted with a live snake.

Similar experiments, showing that subjects significantly emoted or acted differently from controls when they falsely believed certain "facts" about external conditions or about their own reactions, almost uniformly support the attribution hypothesis. These include studies by Batson (1975); Blechman and Dannemiller (1976); Borkovec (1973); Cantor, Zillmann, and Bryant (1975); Colson (1974); Cook, Pallak, and Sogin (1976); Detweiler and Zanna (1976); Elliott and Denney (1975); Geen, Rakosky, and Pigg (1972); Giesen and Hendrick (1974); Harris and Katkin (1975); Hitschman (1975); Holmes and Frost (1976); Kleinke (1975); Koenig (1973); Kravetz (1974); Krebs (1975); Krisher, Darley, and Darley (1973); Lick (1975); Loftis and Ross (1974a, 1974b); Riddick and Meyer (1973); Rodin (1976); Ross, Lepper, and Hubbard (1975); Sullivan (1969); Whalen and Henker (1976); and Wooley (1972).

A large series of attribution studies examines the results of people attributing certain phenomena either to their own behavior, control, or self-rating or to other sources. These studies overlap with the locus of control studies and, to some extent, also overlap with self-rating studies considered below. Almost all the studies indicate that there are significant behavioral and emotional changes when people see themselves in certain ways and attribute events and feelings to themselves, compared with the changes they show when they attribute the same events and feelings to external conditions or to nonself causes. Reported studies in this area which tend to confirm RET hypotheses include those by Bandler, Madaras, and Bem (1968); Bem (1970); Bugenthal, Whalen, and Henker (1975); Corah and Boffa (1970); Dienstbier and others (1975); Jones, Kanouse, Kelley, Nisbett, Valins, and Wiener (1972); Kopel and Arkowitz (1975); Miller, Brickman, and Bolen (1975); and Pennebaker and Sanders (1976).

Increasing attention gets paid these days to techniques of helping people change their false and misleading attributions when these lead to dysfunctional results, but few studies showing empirical validation of such techniques exist at present. Confirmatory evidence in this area appears in studies and reviews by Dweck (1975); Rimm and Masters (1974); and Wein and Odom (1975).

Cognitive Mediation of Emotional Disturbance

Hypothesis 12: humans have an innate and acquired tendency to think irrationally. Humans have strong innate and acquired tendencies to set up basic values (especially the values of survival and happiness) and to think and act both rationally (abetting the achievement of their basic values) and irrationally (sabotaging the achievement of such values). Virtually all humans frequently have several important irrational ideas or absolutistic and antiempirical modes of thinking that interfere with their healthy thoughts, emotions, and behaviors. When they change these ideas, their dysfunctional behavior also tends to change significantly. In efficient therapy, the therapist attempts to show clients their irrational thinking and behaving. Many pioneering psychotherapists have promulgated or endorsed this hypothesis—including Adler (1927, 1929); Dubois (1907); Ellis (1962); Kelly (1955); Low (1952); Phillips (1956); and Wolberg (1967). Freud specifically endorsed it in his original formulations (Breuer and Freud, 1895/1957) by calling emotional disturbance ideogenic; although he and most psychoanalysts later focused more on transference methods and other emotive aspects of therapy, they have often implicitly tried to show clients their unrealistic and irrational thinking and to help them give it up.

An impressive amount of data now demonstrates that the specific kinds of irrational thoughts posited by RET (Ellis, 1957, 1958, 1962, 1971a, 1973d, 1975a; Ellis and Harper, 1975) exist in different populations and have significant correlations with emotional disturbance. These data have been summarized in DiGiuseppe, Miller, and Trexler (1977) and Murphy and Ellis (1978), so I shall not repeat them here.

Scores of related studies experimentally show that various kinds of disturbed or malfunctioning populations employ significantly more disordered or irrational thinking than do less severely disturbed groups. Let me list a few of these studies, most of them recent and a few of them pioneering or classic. Disturbed or peculiar individuals tend to have various kinds of cognitive difficulties and to think irrationally or disorderedly in many different ways, including: abstraction difficulties (Braff and Beck, 1974; Wright, 1973); analytic thinking problems (Ehri and Muzio, 1974); closedness (Heibrun, 1973); conceptual organization difficulty (Depue and Fowles, 1974); decentering (Suchotliff, 1970); disattending to strong aspects of meaning (Chapman, Chapman, and Daut, 1976); gullibility (Dmitruk, Collins, and Clinger, 1973); idiosyncratic construct systems (Widom, 1976); hopelessness (Cassidy, Flanagan, and Spellman, 1957; Seligman, 1975); incapacity for formal operations (Kilburg and Siegel, 1973); injustice-collecting (Collins, 1974); intrusive thoughts (Horowitz, Becker, and Malone, 1973); logical deviation (DeWolfe and McDonald, 1972); magical thinking (Collins, 1974); mnemonic disorganization (Larsen and Fromholt, 1976); overgeneralization (Mourer, 1973); overinclusive thinking (Harrow, Himmelhoch, Tucker, Hersh, and Quinlan, 1972; Craig, 1973; Davis and Blaney, 1976); and role-taking deficiencies (Davis and Blaney, 1976).

In a review of the nature and ubiquity of human irrationality in the first chapter of this book, I list literally scores of basic and important irrational beliefs and behaviors of humans and show how they commonly exist in virtually all people at all times in all climes (Ellis, 1977b). I cite some of the researchers who have presented large amounts of evidence for the hypothesis that all humans often tend to act irrationally and that they probably have a pronounced biological, as well as cultural, tendency to do so—including Frankel (1973), Frazer (1959), Hoffer (1951), Korzybski (1933), Kurtz (1973), Levi-Strauss (1970), Pitkin (1932), Rachleff (1973), and Sperry (1975).

Psychologists have presented evidence showing the ubiquity of many forms of irrational thinking, particularly authoritarianism, bigotry, and prejudice. They have shown how prejudiced cognitions significantly affect many different kinds of emotional and behavioral reactions; how such irrational prejudices often correlate with emotional disturbances; and how the diminishing or extirpation of these prejudices may have important therapeutic results. These include studies by Alexander and Sagatun (1973); Becker (1960); Becker, Spielberger, and Parker (1963); Davies

(1970); Dunlap, Gaertner, and Mangelsdorff (1973); Dutton and Lake (1973); Fox (1969); Geller and Berzins (1976); Genther, Shuntich, and Bunting (1975); Kemp (1961); Landy and Sigall (1974); Langer and Abelson (1974); Lincoln and Levinger (1972); Long (1976a, 1976b, 1976c); Marquis (1973); McCrame and Kimberly (1973); Ray and Walker (1973); Rosen, Johnson, Johnson, and Tesser (1973); Ross, Lepper, and Hubbard (1975); Rubovits and Maehr (1973); Silverman and Cochran (1972); S. Schwartz (1973); Stephan, Lucker, and Aronson (1976); Tesser and Conlee (1975); West and Schultz (1976); Wyer (1976); and Ziemelis (1974).

Hypothesis 13: humans tend to self-rate. People have very strong innate and acquired tendencies not only to rate their acts, behaviors, performances, and traits as "good" or "bad" but to rate their *selves,* their *essences,* their *totalities* in the same manner. Their self-ratings profoundly influence their emotions and behaviors and constitute one of the main sources of their emotional disturbances. Effective psychotherapy importantly consists of helping individuals who denigrate themselves to have high self-esteem and to rate themselves unconditionally as good; or, preferably, to continue to rate their acts and traits, in accordance with the enjoyable or unenjoyable results they produce, but to refuse to rate their *selves* or *essences* at all.

The first part of this hypothesis—that people do rate themselves, usually or frequently end up with low self-esteem, and would better learn to rate themselves unconditionally as good—seems implicit in the work of Freud (1965) and his followers, but has more explicit formulations in the writings of Adler (1927, 1929), Berne (1964), Branden (1969), Fromm (1941, 1947), Horney (1965), Jung (1954), Lecky (1945), and Rogers (1961, 1971). The second part of this hypothesis—that people had better learn to refuse to rate their selves or essences at all, while still continuing to rate their traits—gets vaguely hinted at in some writings, particularly Zen Buddhist literature (Suzuki, 1956; Suzuki, Fromm, and DeMartino, 1963), but only rational-emotive writings appear to state it with great clarity and precision (Ellis, 1971a, 1973d, 1975a, 1977a; Ellis and Harper, 1975; Ellis and Knaus, 1977; Lembo, 1976; Morris and Kanitz, 1975; and Young, 1974).

Considerable experimental evidence exists showing that humans do rate themselves and that they affect their emotions and behaviors enormously by the kind of self-ratings they choose. Verifying studies include those by Beck (1967); Beck and Hurvich (1959); Beck and Stein (1967); D. V. Bem (1967); Brainerd (1969); Cunningham and Berberian (1976); Forrest and Hokanson (1975); Glasgow and Arkowitz (1975); Grossack, Martin and Lussiev (1966); Kaczkowski and Owen

(1972); Kaplan and Pokorny (1969); Kingsbury, Stevens, and Murray (1975); Lapuc and Harmatz (1970); Maracek and Mettee (1972); Meichenbaum and Smart (1971); Mischel, Ebbesen, and Zeiss (1976); Nosanchuk and Lightstone (1974); Regan, Gosselink, Hubsch, and Ulsh (1975); Rychlak, Carlsen, and Dunning (1974); Sheehan and Marsh (1974); Shortell and Biller (1970); Shrauger and Terbovic (1976); Steber (1974); Vidman (1972); Walster, Walster, Piliavin, and Schmidt (1973); and Wine (1971).

Few studies exist investigating the validity of the RET hypothesis that unconditional self-acceptance or self-regard would better consist of no rating of oneself or essence, although there is a partially confirming study by T. Miller (1976). More studies of this specific RET hypothesis would seem advisable.

Hypothesis 14: cognitive defensiveness depends on self-damning. When people perceive their behavior as "bad," "wrong," "incompetent," or "shameful," they frequently refuse to acknowledge to themselves and/or to others that they have thought or acted "badly" and they use various kinds of cognitive defenses to obscure or deny their "wrong" acts. To this end, they rationalize, project, repress, compensate, use reaction formation, and employ other modes of defense mechanisms. Their main motive for utilizing such cognitive defenses stems from their self-rating and self-damning. A highly effective technique for undoing these defenses, and for helping people change the dysfunctional behavior that they defend themselves from perceiving, consists of enabling them to give up their self-condemnation and to stop their awfulizing about frustrations and inconveniences they encounter.

Freud (1965) and his followers (A. Freud, 1948/1975; Fenichel, 1945) formulated the theory of cognitive defensiveness and, to my way of thinking, thereby made perhaps the most useful contribution of psychoanalysis to effective psychotherapy. Many experimental studies presenting evidence for defense mechanisms and their significant effects on human emotion and behavior have appeared. Rather than list them here, I shall refer the reader to summary reviews of the literature by Blum (1966); Ellenberger (1970); Ellis (1950); Jurjevich (1974); and Sears (1943). A few recent studies showing evidence for defensiveness include those by Love, Sloan, and Schmidt (1976); Muehleman (1973); Pagano (1973); and Regan, Gosselink, Hubsch, and Ulsh (1975).

I have as yet found no studies that specifically test the RET hypothesis that cognitive defensiveness will get minimized or disappear when people change their irrational ideas abolt self-rating and self-damning. This seems a fruitful field for future study.

Hypothesis 15: humans have a tendency to low frustration tolerance.

54   *Theoretical and Conceptual Foundations*

People have an innate and acquired tendency to have low frustration tolerance (LFT)—to do things that seem easier in the short run even though they often bring poor results in the future; to go for immediate gratification and stimulation-seeking that offer highly specious rewards; and to procrastinate and avoid behaviors and disciplines that would bring them greater ultimate rewards. While their hedonistic views and ways help them survive and achieve greater happiness in some respects, their powerful tendencies to short-range rather than long-range hedonism frequently prove self-defeating.

Emotional disturbance largely consists of or involves distinct low frustration tolerance. Whenever people make themselves anxious, depressed, hating, or undisciplined, even when they note their symptoms and determine to work to ameliorate them, they usually sabotage their therapeutic efforts to some extent, or they make temporary gains and fall back to previously disturbed ways, partly or largely as a result of their seeking immediate ease or comfort and giving in to their LFT. Effective therapy often consists of enabling clients to achieve higher frustration tolerance or a philosophic outlook that acknowledges that gain rarely exists without pain, that they would better work at changing themselves, and that the human condition ordinarily requires, for maximum happiness and freedom, a considerable amount of lifelong discipline, including an active determination to change obnoxious stimuli when possible but also to accept them when they prove unchangeable.

Although many therapists—including Adler (1927, 1929) and Freud (1965)—have pointed out that humans had better resort to delayed gratification in order to act sanely, few psychotherapies have stressed this point to any considerable degree. RET (Ellis, 1962, 1971a, 1974c, 1975a; Ellis and Harper, 1975; Ellis and Knaus, 1977) and reality therapy (Glasser, 1965) have perhaps pioneered in this respect.

Many psychological studies, especially in recent years, have presented evidence that low frustration tolerance looms importantly in human disturbance. Ainslie (1975) and Mischel (1975) have presented comprehensive reviews of the large amount of data that has accumulated to support the hypotheses that LFT mightily contributes to emotional disturbance and behavioral malfunctioning and that this disturbance ameliorates when experimenters or therapists help people to gain higher frustration tolerance. Some relevant studies in this area include: Hildebrandt, Feldman, and Ditrichs (1973); Leon and Chamberlain (1973); Miller and Karniol (1976); Mischel and Baker (1975); Mischel and Ebbesen (1970); Mischel, Ebbesen, Zeiss, and Raskoff (1972); Mischel and Gilligan (1964); Mischel and Moore (1973); Mowrer and Ulmann (1945);

Patterson and Mischel (1976); Shaffer and Hendrick (1974); and White-hill, DeMeyer-Gapin, and Scott (1976).

Hypothesis 16: anticipation of threat often mediates emotional disturbance. People not only react to real threat and display fear or anxiety when such danger exists, but they also anticipate or imagine conditions of threat and often react with as much disturbance to such anticipation or imagination as they do to actual conditions of threat. Anticipation of threat therefore constitutes an important cognitive mediating process in emotional disturbance; and in effective psychotherapy, therapists had better deal with it or head it off.

A good many researchers have investigated the idea that various kinds of anticipation of threat or stress lead to emotional disturbance and that certain other kinds of anticipation minimize or alleviate disturbance. Fritz and Marks (1954) found that a one-minute tornado warning proved more disruptive of effective behavior than none at all or than a much longer warning period and that people who have a long time to make anticipatory preparation may feel significantly more disturbance than those who have a shorter waiting period. Additional confirmation of this and related hypotheses appears in studies by Folkins (1970); Grings (1973); Krupat (1974); Jordan and Kempler (1970); Jordan and Simprelle (1972); R. Lazarus (1966); Nomikos, Opton, Averill, and Lazarus (1968); Rakover and Levita (1973); Szpiler and Epstein (1976); and Suls and Miller (1976).

Rational-Emotive Therapy Techniques

Hypothesis 17: active-directive therapy is more helpful than passive therapy. Because people have very powerful innate and acquired tendencies to disturb themselves emotionally and to act dysfunctionally; because they think, feel, and behave in self-defeating ways from early childhood onward; because they adhere strongly to their self-sabotaging thoughts and feelings; and because they easily fall back into them once they have temporarily changed, they will tend to receive more effective help from a highly active-directive therapy than from a more passive and unintrusive psychotherapeutic approach.

Outstanding theoreticians and researchers endorsing the active-directive position in psychotherapy have included Adler (1927, 1929); Alexander and French (1946); Ellis (1957, 1958, 1962, 1972a, 1972b, 1974b); Ferenczi (1952); Garner (1970); Goldfried and Davison (1976); Goldfried and Merbaum (1973); Greenwald (1967); Haley (1961, 1963); Herzberg (1945); Hill (1955); Homme (1969); Janov

(1970); Jurjevich (1973); Kelly (1955); Lange and Jakubowski (1976); Matarazzo (1962); O'Connell (1966); Perls (1969); Piaget (1970); Regardie (1952); Reich (1949); Rosen (1953); Salter (1949); Salzman (1963); Thorne (1950); Wolberg (1967); Wolpe (1956); and Wolpe and Lazarus (1966).

More concrete studies and reviews presenting evidence favoring the effectiveness of active-directive forms of therapy over more passive forms have recently appeared in many books and journals, including writings by Blumberg (1972); Coons (1972); Curren, Gilbert, and Little (1976); Doster (1972); Harari (1971); Kanfer and Karas (1959); Mendel (1970); Mitchell and Namenkek (1972); O'Connell, Baker, Hanson, and Ermalinski (1973); Pachwood (1974); Padfield (1976); Schiavo, Alexander, Barton, and Parsons (1976); Vernallis, Holson, Shipper, and Butler (1972); Warren and Rice (1972); and Winship and Kelley (1976).

Hypothesis 18: therapist's disputing and persuasion are desirable. People frequently hold irrational, logically inconsistent, antiempirical, and absolutistic ideas. These ideas tend to bring them needless self-defeating results. Because these ideas do not accord with reality, a therapist or other helper or teacher can show people how their irrational beliefs do not hold up as true and can demonstrate that continuing to believe irrationalities will almost inevitably bring them gratuitous pain. Such a therapist or helper can often persuade people to change or surrender their irrational beliefs and the dysfunctional behaviors to which they contribute. Effective psychotherapy importantly includes the therapist's actively and directively disputing, challenging, and questioning clients' irrational philosophies and persuading them to adopt less self-defeating beliefs.

Although many therapists, as indicated previously in this chapter, have acknowledged the profound influence of irrational thinking on the creation and maintenance of emotional disturbance, surprisingly few have unequivocally advocated active-directive methods of disputing these beliefs. To some extent, however, Adler (1927, 1929); Dreikurs (1964); Dubois (1907); Ellis (1958, 1962, 1971a, 1973d, 1973e, 1974b, 1974c, 1975a, 1975c, 1975d, 1976c); Ellis and Gullo (1972); Ellis and Knaus (1977); Frankl (1966); Jurjevich (1973, 1974); Phillips (1956); and Raimy (1975) have taken a distinctly persuasive therapeutic stance.

Many studies showing the importance and effectiveness of persuasion appear in the experimental and social psychology literature. I refer the reader to the reviews of the literature by Abelson (1975), Hovland and Janis (1959), and Rosnow and Robinson (1967). Some of the more recent relevant studies, showing the effect of persuasion on personality change, include those by Bem (1965, 1966); Beutler, Jobe, and Elkins (1974);

Miller, Brickman, and Bolen (1975); Packwood and Parker (1973); Reed and Janis (1974); Steele and Ostrom (1974); and Truax, Fine, Moravec, and Millis (1968).

A special RET hypothesis that I formulated a number of years ago states that when therapists or others try to persuade people to give up their irrational ideas and to adopt less self-defeating notions, not only do these people get helped but, consciously or unconsciously, the therapists tend to help themselves give up their own irrationalities and improve their own functioning. This hypothesis receives some confirmation in studies by Bard (1973) and Perlman (1972).

Hypothesis 19: homework is desirable. People habituate themselves to thinking, emoting, and acting in certain dysfunctional ways and consciously or unconsciously overpractice these behaviors for many years until they turn into their "second nature." For this reason, people resist change with great difficulty and almost always require considerable active practice to undo their self-defeating habits and to keep them from recurring. Effective psychotherapy therefore includes assigning a considerable amount of active-directive homework, especially in the form of in vivo practice that interrupts or contradicts dysfunctional behavior. It often includes forced, repetitive, and massed cognitive, emotive, and behavioral in vivo and imaginative practice.

Therapists probably have unofficially used active-directive homework assignments since the beginning of man and woman. Modern therapists who have particularly pioneered in advocating such assignments include Ellis (1954, 1962, 1971a, 1973a, 1973e, 1974c, 1975a, 1976c, 1976d); Ellis and Harper (1975); Ellis and Knaus (1977); Herzberg (1945); Masters and Johnson (1970); Maultsby (1971, 1975); Maultsby and Ellis (1974); Salter (1949); Shelton and Ackerman (1974); and Wolpe (1958).

Many researchers have confirmed the value of active-directive homework procedures in psychotherapy, including: Azrin and Powers (1975); Bandura, Jeffrey, and Gajdos (1975); Barlow, Leitenberg, Agras, and Wincze (1969); Boulougouric and Bassiakos (1973); Christensen and Arkowitz (1974); Christensen, Arkowitz, and Anderson (1975); Clore and Jeffrey (1972); Crowe, Marks, Agras, and Leitenberg (1972); Dua (1972); Eberle, Rehm, and McBurney (1975); Everaerd, Rijken, and Emmelkamp (1973); Gelder, Bancroft, Gath, Johnston, Mathews, and Shaw (1973); Hoehn-Saric, Frank, and Gurland (1968); Leitenberg, Agras, Butz, and Wincze (1971); Leitenberg and Wincze (1970); Mitchell and Mitchell (1971); M. Rosenberg (1960); and Sherman, Mulac, and McCann (1974).

A more specific RET hypothesis, which I have held ever since I created this system of psychotherapy early in 1955, states that in vivo homework assignments will usually tend to help emotionally disturbed people more than will various other kinds of active-directive therapy methods (such as systematic desensitization) which tend to remain more imaginative and theoretical than does contact desensitization. For example, this hypothesis proposes that if clients who have a fear of approaching members of the other sex actually go out and force themselves to encounter a number of members of the other sex, they will tend to experience greater reduction of their fears than if they practiced systematic desensitization during therapy sessions or by themselves. Similarly, RET hypothesizes that clients who practice only rational-emotive imagery (Maultsby, 1971; Maultsby and Ellis, 1974) will overcome their disturbances to a lesser degree than those who also do in vivo homework in connection with these disturbances.

Evidence that in vivo or contact homework assignments are more effective than other kinds of assignments or other therapeutic procedures appears in research studies by Cooke (1966); Davison (1965); Dua (1970); D'Zurilla, Wilson, and Nelson (1973); Emmelkamp and Wessels (1975); Garfield, Darwin, Singer, and McBrearty (1967); Gentry (1970); Hodgson, Rachman, and Marks (1972); Kirsch, Wolpin, and Knutson (1975); Leitenberg, Agras, Edwards, Thompson, and Wincze (1970); Leitenberg and Callahan (1973); Litvak (1969a, 1969b); Marks (1971); Marks, Viswanathan, Lipsedge, and Gardner (1972); Murphy and Bootzin (1973); Rimm and Medeiros (1970); Ritter (1968); Schopler and Compere (1971); Schroeder and Rich (1976); Sherman (1972); Stradter (1973); Watson, Gaind, and Marks (1972); Wilson and Davison (1971); and Zajonc (1968).

Hypothesis 20: perceived insult and intent causes behavior change. People tend to feel more disturbed and change their behavior more drastically when they think that others have tried to denigate or insult them than they do when they see these others as acting badly but not insultingly. Their perceptions of others' intentions to harm or down them often tend to affect them more than their perceptions of the actual harm these others cause them. Efficient therapy therefore often consists of helping clients not to take others' insults too seriously and of helping them noncondemningly to accept others who act against them even when these others do so intentionally.

Few of the major schools of therapy emphasize this point very clearly or specifically, although it is a cornerstone of RET (Ellis, 1962, 1971a, 1974c, 1975a, 1977a; Ellis and Harper, 1975). Other RET practitioners and I continually show our clients that insults really do not hurt them unless they take such insults too seriously; and that even when others do intentionally harm or down them, these others have a right to act wrongly (because of their human fallibility), and that refusing to give them this right will cause more disturbance than the harm they try to cause.

Evidence that people distinctly upset themselves or make significant changes in their behavior when they feel insulted appears in scores of studies of attribution, expectancy, rating, and the instigation of anger, many of which I list in other sections of this chapter. Other studies of a confirming nature include those by Lang, Goeckner, Adesso, and Marlett (1975); Rule and Hewitt (1971); and Steele (1975).

Studies showing that subjects' perception of the "good" or "bad" intentions of others (even when these perceptions had no empirical foundation) significantly affected their attitudes and behavior toward themselves and toward these others include experiments by Ellsworth and Langer (1976); Greenwell and Dengerink (1973); Harris and Huang (1974); Heller, Pallak, and Picek (1973); Legant and Mettee (1973); Lincoln and Levinger (1972); and Salili, Mach, and Billmore (1976).

Hypothesis 21: abreaction of dysfunctional emotions is not therapeutic. Abreaction or catharsis of dysfunctional emotion, and particularly of various forms of anger (including hostility, resentment, rage, and physical aggression), may have palliative effects on relieving these emotions but often proves iatrogenic in that it tends to reinforce the philosophies or beliefs that people employ to create these feelings. Thus, the philosophy behind anger almost invariably includes the rational belief, "I don't like your behavior and I wish you would stop it!" and the irrational belief, or absolutistic command, "Because I don't like your behavior, you must stop it! And you rate as a rotten person if you don't!" Expression or abreaction of anger reinforces people's irrational belief and thereby helps them *feel* better instead of *get* better. By giving up the irrational command that others treat them fairly or that the world must provide what they want, humans lose rather than suppress or repress anger; they thereby improve their emotional health and render themselves less prone to future anger.

The RET view that people create their own angry reactions and have a great deal of ability to expunge their anger and minimize their feeling it, even when unjustly provoked, originated largely with philosophers rather than psychologists—including such thinkers as Epictetus (1899); Marcus Aurelius (1900); Melden (1969); Shibles (1974); Spinoza (1901); and Wittgenstein (1958). Some psychologists, however, have at least partly espoused it—including Charny (1968); deRivera (1970); Ellis (1962, 1971a, 1973d, 1975a, 1975b, 1976a, 1977a); Ellis and Gullo (1972); Ellis and Harper (1975); Hauck (1974); Knaus (1974); Lange and Jakubowski (1976); Lembo (1976); Low (1952); Maultsby (1975); Novaco (1975); Peters (1970); and Tosi (1974).

Various experimenters have investigated the theory that anger partly or largely originates in human cognitions and have come up with data supporting this theory—including Bandura and Walters (1963); Berkowitz and Alioto (1973); Berkowitz, Lepinski and Angulo (1969); Block (1975); Frodi (1974); Geen and Stonner (1973); Konecni (1975); Lang, Goeckner, Adesso, and Marlett (1975); Legant and Mettee (1973); Lehman (1972); Novaco (1975); Pastore (1950, 1952); and Pisano and Taylor (1971). Incidentally, I may note that just as anger seems to have its cognitive origins, so also does love. Various modern investigators—including Bleda (1974); Duck and Spencer (1972); Landy and Sigall (1974); and Walster, Walster, Piliavin, and Schmidt (1973)—have come up with experimental evidence backing this hypothesis.

More to the point, the RET theory that abreaction has only limited therapeutic effects and that it often leads to an increase in hostility and punitiveness has received confirmation in literally scores of recent experiments, as Berkowitz (1970) has shown in a brilliant review of the literature. Some of the many important studies in this respect are by Averswald (1974); Bandura (1973); Bandura and Walters (1963); Bandura and Wittenberg (1971); Baron (1974); Berkowitz (1964, 1966, 1970); Berkowitz and Alioto (1973); Berkowitz, Green, and Macaulay (1962); Berkowitz, Lepinski, and Angulo (1969); Berkowitz and Rawlings (1963); Drabman and Thomas (1974); Feshbach (1971); Frodi (1974); Geen and Stonner (1973); Geen, Stonner, and Hope (1975); Hokason (1970); Konecni (1975); Leyens, Camino, Parke, and Berkowitz (1975); Liebert and Baron (1972); Nelson, Gelfand, and Harmann (1969); Strauss (1974); and Wagner (1968).

Not too much attention has yet been given to the experimental study of relieving or removing feelings of anger by cognitive methods. But some confirmation of the basic RET hypotheses in this connection appears in studies by Barton (1972), Block (1975), Kaufmann and Feshbach (1963), Novaco (1975), and Pisano and Taylor (1971).

Hypothesis 22: people have the choice of behavioral change. Although pure free will does not seem to exist, and although human behavior gets determined at least in part by biological and environmental factors or "causes" over which an individual has relatively little control, so that a high degree of probability exists that people will do one thing and will not do another, people do still have a large degree of choice or will, and they can (with considerable amounts of work) partly determine how they feel and act. Because of their ability in this respect, clients can come to therapy and choose to work (or not to work) at helping themselves; they can thereby choose significantly to change some of their most "natural" and long-practiced disturbances. As people remove their emotional blocks, they can also choose to actualize their potential for greater enjoyment and personality growth.

This hypothesis, or aspects of it, underlies virtually all forms of psychotherapy; but various therapists and educators have particularly emphasized it—including Adler (1927, 1929); Assagioli (1965); Dewey (1930); Ellis (1962, 1973d); Ellis and Harper (1975); Friedman (1975); Perls (1969); and Rogers (1961, 1971). Although some degree of free choice remains central to the entire field of psychotherapy (and of liberal education), few experiments have specifically tested this theory. A review of the research literature on attitudes led Ajzen and Fishbein (1973) to conclude: "The most immediately relevant predictor of a specific action is the person's behavioral intention. Although problems can arise with regard to the intention-behavior relationship, empirical research has shown that high correlations between these two variables can be obtained." Some experiments which have validated the hypothesis that humans can to some degree choose how they think, emote, and behave are discussed below.

Cappell and Pliner (1973) found that subjects do have volitional control over marijuana intoxication and can make themselves come down from such intoxication if they wish to do so. Ellsworth and Langer (1976) showed that a stare does not have to get perceived as a threatening signal; nor does it automatically elicit flight. Subjects have the ability to interpret it in such a manner as to approach strangers in a friendly, helpful way. Davison and Steiner (1971) found that subjects can interpret reinforcements and penalties in different ways and that therefore: "Behavior therapy may be assumed to evoke complex cognitive and evaluative processes which are not comfortably handled by the Skinnerian model. To a greater degree than rats or even chimpanzees, humans appear to impose meaning upon social situations." Zimbardo (1973) discovered that when people agree to play the role of prisoner to another they frequently choose to restrict themselves unduly; he concluded that in self-chosen situations, such as marriage, many of us "choose to remain prisoners because being passive and dependent frees us from the need to act and be responsible for our actions. The prison of fear constructed in the delusions of the paranoid is no less confining or less real than the cell that every shy person erects to limit his own freedom in serious anticipation of being ridiculed and rejected by his guards—often guards of his own making."

These studies tend to show, in other words, that people to a large extent choose their emotional disturbances—and therefore can distinctly choose to surrender them, which tends to confirm one of the main RET hypotheses!

Hypothesis 23: cognitive-behavior methods of self-control are effective. When people perceive their behavior as less than desirable, or when they feel emotionally disturbed, they have considerable ability to decide to change and to follow various kinds of self-control or self-management procedures to bring about such change. They often modify their emotions and behavior more by using self-control principles than they change when controlled or directed by others. Self-control has very strong cognitive (as well as behavioral) elements and effective therapy often consists of helping clients to use a considerable amount of cognitive-related self-management.

I have cited some amount of research studies favoring this hypothesis earlier in this chapter—especially under the headings of self-perception, biofeedback, imaging, homework, and self-monitoring. In spite of this evidence, most major psychotherapies have neglected self-management principles in the past; only a few—for example, behavior therapy (Wolpe, 1958, 1975; Wolpe and Lazarus, 1966), rational-emotive therapy (Ellis, 1962, 1969, 1971a, 1973a, 1973d, 1974a; Ellis and Harper, 1975), and reality therapy (Glasser, 1965)—have very clearly espoused encouraging clients to use systematic self-control.

Pioneers in the theory and practice of self-control have included many cognitive-behavior therapists, including Cautela (1969), Goldfried and Davison (1976), Goldfried and Merbaum (1973), Kanfer (1970a, 1970b), Meichenbaum (1975); Meichenbaum and Cameron (1973), Mischel and Mischel (1975), Stuart (1969), and Watson and Tharp (1972).

Many studies have appeared demonstrating that cognitive-behavioral self-control methods work; that they frequently have advantages over externally directed behavior change; and that self-control procedures, even when highly "behavioral," have clearcut and important cognitive elements. These include studies by Baker, Cohen, and Saunders (1973); Batterson and Mischel (1976); Blackwood (1970); Davison (1968); Drummond (1974); Felixbond and O'Leary (1973); Goldfried (1971); Gottman and McFall (1972); Harris (1969); Harris and Bruner (1971); Harris and Rothberg (1972); Knapp (1976); Levinson, Shapiro, Schwartz, and Tursky (1971); Mann (1972); Marston (1972); McReynolds and Church (1973); Rose, Glasgow, and Barrera (1976); Sherman and Plummer (1973); Sobell and Sobell (1973); and Spiegler, Cooley, Marshall, Prince, Puckett, and Slenzy (1976).

Hypothesis 24: coping with distress and threat relates to self-perception. People's ability to cope with distress and threat seems significantly affected by their conceptions of how well they think they can cope. Teaching them skills or strategies of coping may help them cope—not so much because they can thus deal with people and things better, but because they *conclude* that they can and thereby increase their *confidence* in their ability to do so. Having greater confidence, they usually cope better—or cope worse but think they do better. Even when they learn poor strategies, such as whining and screaming about the hassles that beset them, or dealing with others aggressively instead of assertively, they may feel much better because they view such "coping" behavior as "good" and "effective." Both the teaching of coping skills and helping clients to strongly believe that they can cope with conditions of distress and threat constitute effective methods of psychotherapy or behavior change.

Studies of and theorizing about coping behavior and people's attitudes toward their ability to cope stem from the work of Richard S. Lazarus and his associates (Lazarus, 1966; Lazarus and Alpert, 1964). Following up on Lazarus' work, and especially investigating the attitude of learned helplessness and its relationship to feelings of depression, Martin Seligman and his associates (Seligman, 1975) have provided a large body of significant research and have sparked many other relevant studies.

Researches that tend to confirm the importance of an individual's perceptions and attitudes about his or her coping ability appear in a comprehensive review of the literature by Averill (1973). Some specific confirmatory findings relating to the RET hypothesis about coping appear in publications by Averill, Opton, and Lazarus (1969); Davison (1967); Glass and Singer (1972); Glass, Singer, and Friedman (1969); Goldfried and Trier (1974); Houston (1975); Kazdin (1973); Neufeld (1976); Sanchez-Craig (1976); and Speisman, Lazarus, Mordkoff, and Davison (1964).

Learned helplessness studies, according to Seligman's (1975) conclusions and interpretations, generally show that when children, adolescents, and adults feel consistently thwarted in the fulfillment of some important desire, they frequently conclude (rightly or wrongly) that they have no hope of ever achieving such fulfillment and they tend to severely depress themselves because of their cognitions about their frustrated and "impossible" state. Specific confirmation of this hypothesis appears in studies by Dweck and Reppucci (1973); Gatchel, Paulus, and Maples (1975); Gatchel and Proctor (1976); Glass, Singer, and Friedman (1969); Hiroto and Seligman (1975); Klein, Fencil, and Seligman (1976); and Seligman (1973). Studies which show that learned helplessness can also get reversed, so that cognitions of hopelessness change along with feelings of depression, include those published by Klein and Seligman (1976), Schmickley (1976), and Seligman (1975).

Hypothesis 25: diversion or distraction has therapeutic value. People tend to focus mainly on one thing at a time. If they want to stop concentrating on one set of disturbing thoughts (such as awfulizing about failure, rejection, or frustration), they can significantly change their emotions and behaviors, at least temporarily, by concentrating on other nondisturbing cognitions or occurrences (e.g., on pleasure, meditation, fantasies, relaxation, or physical sensations). A great deal of psychotherapy consequently consists of cognitive diversion or distraction. This form of treatment can often lead to good therapeutic results.

Although virtually all forms of psychotherapy in one way or another utilize important elements of cognitive diversion, not many authorities seem to have specifically acknowledged this point. The few formulators in this area include Benson (1975); Ellis (1962, 1971a, 1973d, 1977a); and Ellis and Harper (1975). By consciously advocating the techniques of noncoital concentration, the sensate focus, and the use of concrete imaging, many leading sex therapists seem to acknowledge the importance of diverting or distracting cognitions. Pioneers in this regard include Ellis (1954, 1975c, 1976d), Hartman and Fithian (1972), H. Kaplan (1974), Masters and Johnson (1970), and Semans (1956).

Evidence that people significantly change their behaviors when they distract themselves in various ways from disturbed thoughts, feelings, and actions is found in studies of Geer and Fuhr (1976); Lewinsohn and Graf (1973); Linden (1973); Little and Jackson (1974); Miller, Baron, and Baron (1973); Mischel, Ebbesen, Zeiss, and Raskoff (1972); Patterson and Mischel (1976); Sergio, Brahm, Charnes, Jacard, Luz, Picota, and Rutman (1975); Trotter (1973); and Wallace (1970).

Wolpe (1958; Wolpe and Lazarus, 1966) has recommended thought-stopping procedures as a therapeutic technique for allaying anxiety; a study by Rimm, Saunders, and Westel (1975) has confirmed the efficacy of this diversionary method. Mischel and Walther (1973) investigated the hypothesis that children's ability to wait for a delayed reward significantly depends on whether they focus on rewards abstractly, and thereby remind themselves of the advantages of delay, or whether they focus concretely on the arousing quality of the rewards and thereby make themselves feel more frustrated and undermine their self-control. Mischel and Walther found that the different kinds of focusing or concentrating did indeed significantly affect the children's frustration tolerance. These and similar studies support the RET hypothesis that focusing on one kind of thinking or diverting oneself with another kind of thinking importantly influences human behavior.

Hypothesis 26: education and information play an important role in therapy. People largely teach or condition themselves to emote and behave in various ways, in addition to accepting the teachings of others. Their self-conditioning and acceptance of the teachings of others significantly contribute to their emotional disturbances. An important function of effective psychotherapy is education and reeducation: providing salient information and instruction to clients in a variety of ways to help them understand what they have done to disturb themselves and what they can do to make themselves less disturbed.

Almost all psychotherapies appear educational and information-giving; however, perhaps the majority of leading theorists and practitioners minimize or ignore this aspect and emphasize or overemphasize various other therapeutic aspects. For example, they emphasize the relationship between client and therapist; the ventilation of feelings by the client; and the uncovering of unconscious motivations and blockings—ignoring the fact that even these aspects of therapy include highly educative and informational elements! Some therapeutically oriented writers, however, have frankly and unashamedly endorsed the role of education in personality change. These include Adler (1927, 1929), G. Brown (1971), Dinkmeyer (1973), Dreikurs (1974), Educational Research Council (1971a, 1971b), Ellis (1962, 1973a, 1973b, 1977a), Knaus (1974), and Raimy (1975).

Although rational-emotive education has arrived lately on the scene of emotional education, and although the first publications in the area have recent origins (D. A. Brown, 1974a, 1974b; Ellis, 1971b, 1972a, 1973b; Knaus, 1974), quite a few research studies have already appeared confirming the RET view that rational-emotive methods, taught to children or adults in classroom settings, usually by regular teachers, can help people significantly to overcome their tendencies to emotional disturbance. Such studies include presentations by Bokor (1971), Brody (1974), Cooke (1974), deVoge (1974), DiGiuseppe (1975), Gustav (1968), Katz (1974), Knaus and Bokor (1975), Kujoth (1976), Lafferty (1962), Sharma (1970), Sydel (1972), Taylor (1975), and Zingle (1965).

Related studies showing that other forms of education or instruction can help individuals significantly to change their emotions and behavior include those by Dell (1973); Doster (1972); Dua (1971); Eisler, Hersen, and Agras (1973); Green and Marlatt (1972); Heitler (1973); Hoxter (1967); Meichenbaum, Turk, and Rogers (1972); Palkes, Stewart, and Kahana (1968); Rogers and Deckner (1975); Sarason and Ganzer (1973); Schleifer and Douglas (1973); Schumsky (1972); and Taffel, O'Leary, and Armel (1974).

Another series of controlled studies tests the hypothesis that the giving of specific information will help various kinds of subjects significantly change their feelings and behaviors. Confirmatory evidence in this connection appears in published papers by Crawford and Haaland (1972); Davison and Denney (1976); Diamond (1972); Kaplan and Anderson (1973); Nisbett and Borgida (1975); Shapiro, Litman, and Hendry (1973); Singerman, Borkovec, and Baron (1976); and Wyler (1973).

Other studies present evidence that certain kinds of self-instruction will help change the dysfunctional behavior of groups of subjects. This includes studies by Bornstein and Quevillon (1976); Hartig and Kanfer (1973); Robin, Armel, and O'Leary (1975); Smith (1975); and Thorpe (1975).

A number of researchers have investigated the effects of using special kinds of information-giving, including the use of bibliotherapy, programmed texts, and audiovisual materials, to help promote personality change. Studies in this area which show positive results include those by Allen (1973); Atkinson (1974); Bastien and Jacobs (1974); Fielding, Errickson, and Bettin (1971); Hagen (1974); Hagen, Foreyt, and Durham (1976); Hunt and Azrin (1973); LaFleur and Johnson (1972); McClellan and Stieper (1973); Parrino (1971); and Saltmarsh (1973).

Hypothesis 27: suggestion, autosuggestion, and hypnotic suggestion strongly influence behavior. Humans have a strong tendency to think, emote, and behave in accordance with the suggestions of others, even when these suggestions lead to poor individual or social results. They take such suggestions and make them into powerful autosuggestions, on the basis of which they significantly affect their own behavior. Their strong tendencies to act gullibly contribute to much of their emotional disturbance. By the same token, they can frequently ameliorate disturbance by acting on autosuggestion, on the suggestion of others, or on hypnotic suggestion. Almost all psychotherapy contains mighty elements of suggestion; an effective form of therapy consciously uses it to some extent. However, efficient or elegant therapy at the same time tries to help clients to achieve less suggestibility, and to make themselves more influenceable by their own empirically and experimentally based thinking and less influenceable by the absolutistic suggestion of others.

Bernheim (1947, orig. 1886) may have been the first clearly to state the hypothesis that suggestion and autosuggestion, rather than mesmerism, animal magnetism, or some other mysterious force, make hypnosis a powerful therapeutic tool. Freud (1965), who used a good deal of hypnosis in his early experiments with clients, also finally realized that it had few special qualities in its own right and that it largely consisted of suggestion. Modern therapists and researchers have clearly seen that suggestion has powerful effects on both disturbance and the amelioration of disturbance, and that much of the behavioral and therapeutic effects achieved by hypnosis stem from the suggestive elements that almost always constitute a large part of the hypnotic state. They include Barber (1961; 1966, 1969); Blum and his associates (Blum, Geiwitz and Steward, 1967; Blum and Porter, 1974; Blum and Whol, 1971); Coué (1923); Ellis (1962, 1974c, 1977a); Hart (1956); Levitt and his associates (Levitt, Den

Breeijen, and Persky, 1960; Levitt, Persky, and Brady, 1964); and Peale (1948, 1962).

A great many experimental studies and reviews have appeared showing that different kinds of suggestion contribute to people's experiencing profound behavioral changes. I have already listed some in this chapter under the headings of attribution and expectancy. Various other confirmatory studies have appeared, including those by Berzins and Ross (1972); Borkovec (1973); Foreyt and Hagen (1973); Gliedman, Nash, Imber, Stone, and Frank (1958); Hampson, Rosenthal, and Frank (1954); Morrison and Walters (1972); Meath, Feldberg, Rosenthal, and Frank (1954); Nowlis and Nowlis (1956); Shaw and Margulis (1974); Sloane, Cristol, Pepernik, and Stapels (1970); Snyder and Larson (1972); Sparks (1962); and Wolf (1950).

A large number of studies have also appeared that clearly demonstrate the effectiveness of hypnotic suggestion on behavior change, including those by Barber and Calverley (1965, 1966); Barber, Walker, and Hahn (1973); Baunitz, Unesthal, and Berglund (1975); Bowers (1973); Dalal and Barber (1969); Diamond, Gregory, Lenney, Steadman, and Talone (1974); Gibbons, Kilbourne, Saunders, and Castles (1970); Gordon (1967); Greene and Reyher (1972); Hilgard, MacDonald, Marshall, and Morgan (1974); Lauer (1968); Roberts, Kewman, and MacDonald (1973); Roper (1967); Sheehan and Bowman (1973); Sparks (1962); Weinstein, Abrams, and Gibbons (1970); and Zimbardo, Marshall, and Marlash (1971).

The specific hypothesis of Coué (1923), Peale (1948, 1962), and others was that positive thinking, or autosuggestively convincing oneself that one can do certain tasks well, often produces good results. It has occasionally been tested and confirmed—as in studies by Kanfer, Karoly, and Newman (1975) and Suinn and Richardson (1971). The specific hypothesis of RET that positive thinking works, but that it remains a less elegant and less effective form of therapy than helping people to scientifically attack and invalidate their negative thinking (Ellis, 1962; Ellis and Harper, 1975), does not seem to have led to any validating studies yet.

Hypothesis 28: modeling and imitation produce behavior change. People have innate and acquired tendencies to imitate or model themselves after others and to significantly change their thoughts, emotions, and actions in accordance with those they perceive in their models. They frequently acquire or ameliorate their emotional disturbances by conscious or unconscious modeling. Imitating and modeling almost always involve powerful cognitive mediating processes. When people explicitly perceive how they can use modeling to help themselves, they can more easily and intensively help themselves than when they have little or no awareness of using imitation. Effective therapy often includes the therapist's consciously using modeling procedures and sometimes helping clients gain specific awareness of how they can employ imitation to help themselves overcome their disturbances.

Bandura (1968, 1969) and his associates have pioneered in the theory and practice of modeling for behavior change. Other psychotherapists—for example, Ellis (1962, 1971a, 1974c, 1977a) and Rogers (1961, 1971)—have also indicated that what often seems "relationship" or "reinforcement" in therapy to a large degree really consists of modeling.

Thus, the existentialist, client-centered, or RET therapist reveals himself or herself to clients, shows a minimum of upsetness and a maximum amount of openness, and thereby models "good" or "healthy" behavior—which clients can then consciously or unconsciously adopt in part, and thereby help themselves to change.

Many experimenters have presented evidence that modeling helps instigate significant behavior change, that it involves distinct cognitive mediating processes, and that modeling with specific informational and awareness elements often proves more helpful than modeling without such elements. Some of the main studies in this connection include those by Braun (1972); Denney (1975); Denney and Sullivan (1976); Fiedler and Windheuser (1974); Goodwin and Mahoney (1976); Hall and Hinkle (1972); Harris (1970); Jabichuk and Smeriglio (1975); Kauffman, Lafleur, Hallahan, and Chanes (1975); LaFleur and Johnson (1972); Leitenberg and Wincze (1970); Marburg, Mouston, and Holmes (1976); Meichenbaum, Turk, and Rogers (1972); Moore and Sipprelle (1971); O'Connor (1972); Olson (1971); Pathus (1973); Prentice (1972); Rachman (1972); Rachman, Hodgson, and Marks (1971); and Sarason 1973).

Hypothesis 29: increasing problem-solving skills is therapeutic. People tend to use problem solving and related cognitive methods in dealing with and overcoming their emotional disturbances and their behavioral dysfunctioning. Those deficient in problem-solving abilities and skills tend to wind up more disturbed and malfunctioning than those with greater skills in this area. Showing clients how to increase their problem-solving skills constitutes one effective cognitive form of psychotherapy.

Problem-solving methods of therapy have had pioneering applications in the theories and practices of Ellis (1962, 1971a, 1974c, 1977a; Ellis and Harper, 1975) and Goldfried (D'Zurilla and Goldfried, 1971; Goldfried and Davison, 1976; Goldfried and Goldfried, 1975); Goldfried and Merbaum, 1973). Gagne (1959), although not a therapist, has also pioneered in theorizing about the efficacy of problem-solving methods.

Confirmatory studies have shown that people with problem-solving deficiencies do tend to behave in a more disturbed fashion than those without such deficiencies and that the teaching of problem-solving methods to clients can serve as a highly effective therapeutic technique. Relevant studies include those by D'Zurilla and Goldfried (1971); Levenson and Neuringer (1971); Mendonca and Siess (1976); Platt, Spivack, Altman, and Altman (1974); and Vincent, Wiess, and Birchler (1975).

Hypothesis 30: role playing and behavioral rehearsal have cognitive components and may be therapeutic. When people adopt a role and role play an important event or hypothetical event, they frequently influence themselves to experience thoughts, feelings, and behaviors that significantly differ from those they would otherwise experience. They can often disturb themselves and also help ameliorate their disturbances by role-playing experiences. Like modeling and imitation, role playing includes distinct cognitive elements and these elements help people change their dysfunctional feelings and action. Role playing that includes a clearcut cognitive analysis of the feelings invoked during role-enactment and that includes cognitive restructuring of the attitudes revealed by the role-playing experiences will prove more therapeutically effective than role playing without this kind of cognitive analysis or cognitive restructuring.

J. L. Moreno (1934, 1947) has done outstanding role playing theory and research, as have some of his followers, including Corsini (1966); Corsini, Shaw, and Blake (1961); Greenberg (1974); and Yablonski (1965). In the field of psychotherapy, Kelly (1955) has enthusiastically favored role playing as a therapeutic technique; many behavior therapists have used it under the name of behavior rehearsal (Lazarus, 1971, 1976).

Research backing the thesis that role playing has specific cognitive-behavioral components, and that when it goes with rational or cognitive restructuring it has distinct therapeutic benefits, appears in studies by O'Connell (1972); O'Connell, Baker, Hanson, and Emalinski (1973, 1974); O'Connell and Hanson (1971); Schopler and Compere (1971); and Zimbardo and Ebbesen (1970).

Hypothesis 31: skill training may have therapeutic effectiveness. When people receive effective training in certain skills—e.g., in assertion, in socializing, in sex technique, or in values clarification—they frequently significantly change their thinking, emoting, and behaving and sometimes make themselves considerably less emotionally disturbed. These changes do not merely arise from their increased skills but also from their perceptions of their abilities and their self-ratings about their newly acquired competencies. Effective therapy often includes some amount of skill training and the helping of clients to perceive their abilities and capacities differently as they acquire new skills. It also includes helping them to accept themselves unconditionally in spite of their remaining lack of skills. Just as skill training enables clients to change their perceptions of their abilities, so does helping them to perceive themselves differently enable them to acquire better skills.

The older and more conventional psychotherapies usually tend to neglect skill training, although they may unacknowledgedly do some amount of it. RET, however, has emphasized skill training from its earliest days (Ellis, 1962, 1969, 1971a, 1972a, 1973d; Ellis and Harper, 1975). Behavior therapy has particularly pioneered in skill training (Goldfried and Davison, 1976; Lange and Jakubowski, 1976; A. Lazarus, 1971, 1976; LoPiccolo, 1971; LoPiccolo and Miller, 1975; Masters and Johson, 1970; Rimm and Masters, 1974; Salter, 1949; Wolpe, 1958; Wolpe and Lazarus, 1966).

Many studies have appeared that demonstrate the therapeutic effectiveness of skill training and the existence of an important cognitive element in skill training. Let me list a few: Argyle, Bryant, and Trower (1974); Byrne (1973); Christensen (1974); Curran and Gilbert (1975); Glasgow and Arkowitz (1975); Glass, Gottman, and Shmurak (1976); Hodgson and Urban (1975); Rehm, Fuchs, Roth, Kornblith, and Roman (1975); Schwartz and Gottman (1974); Usher (1974); and Yulis (1976).

Hypothesis 32: there are significant differences between RET and other types of therapy. Although RET uses many techniques that partially overlap with those used in other systems of therapy, significant differences exist between the practice of RET and that of several other major therapies.

I conceive of RET as particularly overlapping with cognitive-behavior therapy and as one of the major cognitive-behavior techniques (Ellis, 1969). Several other authorities also see it as an integral part of the cognitive-behavior therapy movement (Beck, 1976; Goldfried and Davison, 1976; Lazarus, 1971, 1976; Mahoney, 1974, Meichenbaum, 1974, 1977; Rimm and Masters, 1974). At the same time, RET differs in many respects from most other major systems of psychotherapy, including Gestalt therapy, experiential therapy (Ellis, 1976b, 1976c, 1977a), client-centered therapy, and psychoanalysis.

Research data showing some significant differences between the practice of RET and the practice of other forms of therapy have appeared in studies by Raskin (1965, 1966); Woodard, Burck, and Sweeney (1975); Zimmer and Cowles (1972a, 1972b); Zimmer and Pepyne (1971); and Zimmer,

Wightman, and McArthur (1970). Significant differences in the practice as well as the outcome of RET, when compared to other types of therapy, also exist in many of the clinical outcome studies reported by DiGiuseppe and Miller (1977).

Discussion

This chapter states many of the important clinical and theoretical hypotheses of rational-emotive therapy (RET) in particular, and of cognitive-behavior therapy in general, and lists a great number of research studies that provide empirical confirmation of these hypotheses. It concentrates mainly on recent researches; and it largely omits a good deal of additional evidence that one can find in studies of the clinical outcome of RET procedures when used in controlled experiments and in studies of irrational ideas, since DiGiuseppe and Miller (1977) cover some of this evidence in the next chapter of the present handbook. It also omits a huge amount of corroborative clinical and anecdotal data included in literally hundreds of articles and books that Murphy and Ellis (1978) will soon publish in a comprehensive bibliography of rational-emotive therapy and cognitive-behavior therapy, and it further omits some corroborative material included in the bibliographies of Mahoney (1974), Meichenbaum (1974, 1976), and Zingle and Mallett (1976).

I think I can safely conclude, on the basis of the studies cited in this article, that: (1) a vast amount of research data exists that tends to confirm the major clinical and theoretical hypotheses of RET; (2) the amount of data keeps increasing by leaps and bounds; (3) RET hypotheses nicely lend themselves to experimental investigation and have therefore encouraged an enormous amount of research, especially considering that RET formulations have arrived so recently on the scene; (4) researchers have not yet tested some of the important RET formulations and could do so with much profit to the field of psychotherapy and personality theory.

RET, like classical behavior therapy, stems from empirical clinical observations and tries to rigorously confirm its theories by using the scientific method. Moreover, it employs criteria of rationality and effective living that stress scientific investigation, scepticism, empiricism, and antiabsolutism (Bartley, 1962, 1968; Ellis, 1971a, 1973d, 1973e, 1977a, 1978; Mahoney, 1976). It seems amazing that some critics, such as Arbuckle (1975), would see it as authoritarian and that other critics, such as Wolpe (Ellis and Wolpe, 1974), would see it as lacking empirical confirmation. I hope that the present review helps to dispel such misperceptions and doubts.

See note on page 35 for information about the references for this chapter.

3

A Review of Outcome Studies on Rational-Emotive Therapy

Raymond A. DiGiuseppe and Norman J. Miller

Chapter 3 is a companion to the preceding chapter by Ellis. It reviews studies of RET vs. nontreatment groups in reducing anxiety; it also reviews comparative studies of the efficacy of RET, systematic desensitization, client-centered therapy, and assertive training. DiGiuseppe and Miller conclude that recent research provides support for the efficacy of RET. Specifically, they conclude that: (1) RET is more effective than client-centered therapy with introverted persons; (2) it is more effective than systematic desensitization in reducing general anxiety; and (3) cognitive therapy plus behavior therapy seems to be the most efficacious treatment for depression. However, they conclude that the effectiveness of RET compared to assertive training has not yet been clearly demonstrated.

The chapter also assesses studies of the use of RET to prevent psychopathology in student populations.

The authors discuss methodological limitations of the studies reviewed and make suggestions for the design of future experiments.

WHEN ELLIS FIRST introduced the theory and practice of rational-emotive psychotherapy in 1957, there were few therapists sympathetic to such a view. Psychoanalysis was still in its prime and behaviorism was just beginning to become popular in clinical circles. Everyone was yelling, "Where is the evidence?"

Since then there have been scores of studies that relate to the basic theoretical and therapeutic hypotheses on which RET is based. Ellis has reviewed this literature in the previous chapter and has found the evidence overwhelmingly supportive of RET. Chapter 3 focuses on research that investigates the effectiveness of RET. The number of such studies has dramatically mushroomed in the past five years and hopefully will continue to do so.

Some of the papers included in this review are not, strictly speaking, rational-emotive psychotherapy outcome studies. They fall under a variety of rubrics, such as "cognitive therapy," "self-instructional training,"

Chapter 3 is scheduled for 1977 publication in *The Counseling Psychologist* and appears here courtesy of that journal.

"cognitive-behavior therapy," and "cognitive restructuring." Their overall similarity to RET, or emphasis upon key elements thereof, makes it necessary to include them as relevant to the test of rational-emotive psychotherapy principles. We have tried to choose studies in which the core ingredient is some form of cognitive modification or cognitive restructuring, to the end that what clients think and believe becomes more rational in order to effect desired emotive and behavioral changes.

Our inclusion of such non-RET outcome studies does not mean we have ignored Meichenbaum's (1975) warning that the "uniformity myth" not be applied to the semantic or cognitive therapies. We also note his encouragement of therapy process and outcome studies directly comparing different cognitive approaches. We simply believe it would be amiss to leave out studies that include treatment conditions which are in important respects close to rational-emotive therapy and therefore contribute to our examination of its therapeutic effectiveness.

Noncomparative Studies

In this section, we review outcome studies that do not compare RET with other types of psychotherapy. These studies by and large measure the benefits of RET on a pretreatment-posttreatment basis, or compare the effectiveness of RET with various placebo or no-treatment groups. In general, the reported studies support the efficacy of RET, even though many have methodological problems that limit their uncritical acceptance.

The first study documenting the effectiveness of rational-emotive psychotherapy was published by Ellis in 1957. In this effort, admittedly weak in sufficient experimental control, Ellis studies his own effectiveness as a therapist during three periods of his professional practice: (1) orthodox psychoanalysis; (2) more directive, psychoanalytically oriented psychotherapy; and (3) rational-emotive psychotherapy. To compare the three approaches, he compiled 78 cases which he treated while using an analytically oriented approach, 16 cases treated by orthodox analysis, and 78 cases treated by rational-emotive therapy. The minimum duration of treatment was ten sessions and patients were matched on severity of diagnosis, sex, age, and socioeconomic status. The mean number of sessions for orthodox analysis was 93; for the analytically oriented therapy, 35; and for rational-emotive therapy, 26. The criterion for improvement was therapist ratings at the time of termination. Ellis used the following categories: (1) little or no progress, (2) some distinct improvement, (3) considerable improvement. He determined that with those receiving orthodox psychoanalysis, 50% showed little or no improvement, 37% showed some distinct improvement, and only 13% were deemed as considerably improved. With the analytically oriented therapy, 37% were rated in category 1, 45% were in category 2, and 18% were in category 3. Only those treated with rational-emotive therapy showed a trend toward success: 10% were rated as having improved very little, 46% showed distinct improvement, and 44% had improved considerably. An additional discovery was that 22 patients treated by rational-emotive therapy showed considerable improvement in one to five sessions, as compared to only seven analytically oriented cases and no orthodox analysis cases which showed as much improvement within the same number of sessions.

Most of the subsequent noncomparative evaluations of RET concerned themselves with the reduction of anxiety. Jacobs (1971) studied the effectiveness of rational-emotive psychotherapy in reducing anxiety in college students. Treatment consisted of five one-hour sessions. Two control groups and a no-contact control, as well as a placebo group, were utilized. After treatment, the rational-emotive group differed significantly from the two control groups in showing less anxiety on the Adult Irrational Idea Inventory (Jones, 1968) and the trait scale of the State-Trait Anxiety Inventory, and presented fewer problems on the Mooney Problem Check List.

Working with a test-anxious college student population, Wine (1971) attempted to ascertain the effects of various components of rational therapy. A first group received six hours of rational therapy that included both insight into students' irrational ideas and also modeling and behavioral rehearsal of rational self-statements. The students in the second group were given insight into their irrational ideas without having an opportunity to model and rehearse rational alternatives. Results favored the insight-plus-rehearsal condition; the behavioral-rehearsal-plus-modeling group improved significantly more than the insight group. Wine (1971) hypothesized that a rational-emotive therapeutic approach that focuses only on the exploration of the irrational beliefs, without also emphasizing the rehearsing of more appropriate rational self-statements, would not achieve the goal of reducing self-defeating emotions and behaviors.

Karst and Trexler (1970) investigated the effectiveness of rational-emotive and fixed role therapy (Kelly, 1955) in the reduction of speech anxiety in college students. Results indicated no difference between the two therapies, although both were significantly more effective than no treatment. In a replication and expansion of their study, Trexler and Karst (1972) compared the efficacy of rational-emotive therapy to an attention placebo group and to a no-contact control group in the treatment of public speaking anxiety. The groups were equated on initial intensity of their anxiety and randomly assigned to the respective treatments. The rational-emotive treatment consisted of teaching about 11 irrational beliefs and teaching techniques for disputing them and for generating rational self-statements. The attention placebo procedure consisted of relaxation training without the standard hierarchies used in desensitization. Duration of treatment was four sessions. The results demonstrated that rational-emotive therapy was more effective than the placebo or no-treatment conditions. A subsequent follow-up six months after completion revealed that improvement had been maintained.

In a study patterned after the Trexler and Karst (1972) experiment, Straatmeyer and Watkins (1974) also investigated the effects of rational-emotive psychotherapy on public-speaking anxiety. They worked with 57 college students who were assigned to one of four treatment conditions: (1) traditional rational-emotive therapy; (2) rational-emotive therapy without the disputing components—subjects were given "insight" into the irrational beliefs, but were given no techniques in disputing or attacking them; (3) attention-placebo group in which discussions on anxiety were conducted; and (4) a no-treatment group. Two self-report and two behavioral ratings were used as dependent measures. As a way of measuring generalization outside treatment, DiLoreto's (1971) Interpersonal Activity Anxiety Scale was also used. Analysis of covariance indicated no statistical significance between the four groups on any of the measures related to speech anxiety. However, when mean change scores were analyzed between the pre- and post-measures, the traditional rational therapy group showed a significant decrease in anxiety on all measures. On the generalization measure, both rational-emotive therapy groups showed transfer-of-training effects. The authors attribute the lack of support for all their hypotheses to the "gross within-cell variance" which resulted in extremely large error terms. They suggest a replication of the study with subjects placed in equivalent groups that are matched on their initial level of speech anxiety. In addition, they suggest that the rational-emotive therapy group receive treatment for more than five weeks so as to enhance the effects of the approach.

In a similar vein, Keller, Croake and Brookings (1975) investigated the use of rational-emotive therapy in reducing irrational thinking and self-reported anxiety in a geriatric population. Treatment consisted of an intensive 4-week program which met once a week for two hours and included readings and homework. A control group was seen for only the pretesting and posttesting. The members of the experimental group showed significant reductions in the dependent measures at the posttest, while the control group showed no change. This study, along with the Ellis (1957) and the Jacobs (1971) studies mentioned before, suggest that RET can have significant positive benefits in a rather short period of time. The positive results in so few sessions are impressive for psychotherapy research.

Finally, several studies have investigated the therapeutic benefits of certain aspects of RET. Bard (1973b) compared two groups of college students on their acquisition of rational beliefs. Both groups were enrolled in a psychology course emphasizing rational-emotive principles. He gave the assignment to one group of students to "teach rational-emotive therapy principles to a friend" (rational proselytizing). The second group was not given the assignment. On measures of irrational beliefs, the rational proselytizers endorsed fewer irrational beliefs than their counterparts. In addition, their knowledge of the rational-emotive therapy principles, as shown on tests of content acquisition, was significantly greater than the passive learners. He concluded that actively participating in a rational thinking process has greater benefits than passive participation.

The use of the bibliotherapy as a therapeutic adjunct is a common practice among rational-emotive therapists. Ellis and his colleagues frequently assign clients *A New Guide to Rational Living* (Ellis and Harper, 1975), as well as other material to be read after the first session. Jarmon (1972) attempted to isolate and evaluate the effectiveness of bibliotherapy as an adjunct to rational-emotive psychotherapy in the reduction of speech anxiety. He randomly assigned 54 college students into one of four groups. The first group received the standard rational-emotive therapy treatment and in addition read related materials. The second condition consisted of group rational-emotive psychotherapy. The third group was the attention placebo condition. The fourth group was a no-contact control. The dependent measures included behavioral, self-report, and physiological scales. The results showed that on all of the dependent measures, the bibliotherapy, rational-emotive therapy group demonstrated a significant decrease in anxiety relative to the other three groups. Despite these positive findings, the differences were not maintained at follow-up. Jarmon believed that this was due to the low level of initial anxiety among students as well as the short duration of treatment. It is also possible that therapeutic readings carries a placebo effect.

In addition to adjunct bibliotherapy, rational-emotive therapists frequently assign written homework to clients between sessions to help them dispute their irrational ideas. Maultsby (1971) investigated the usefulness of utilizing written homework as therapy. He assigned 87 psychiatric outpatients to a homework therapy condition for ten weeks. The patients rated their consistency at the task, their degree of improvement, and the degree to which they believed the homework sheets helped them. After treatment the patients were divided into three groups based on degree of improvement: (1) no improvement; (2) moderate improvement; and (3) much improvement. Criterion for the above was based on self-evaluation forms that were rated by Maultsby and three independent judges. Concomitant with the therapist's ratings, each patient subjectively rated the effectiveness of the written homework assignments. Results demonstrated that 85% of the patients who were judged most improved rated the assignments as an effective adjunct to their therapy.

Comparative Studies

The preponderance of outcome studies have compared the effects of rational-emotive psychotherapy with some form of behavior therapy, either systematic desensitization or behavioral rehearsal. There have been a few comparing RET with client-centered therapy, but none has appeared in the literature comparing the efficacy of RET with other major schools, such as Gestalt therapy, psychoanalytic therapy, or reality therapy.

RET and Systematic Desensitization

Maes and Heiman (1972) compared the effectiveness of rational-emotive therapy to client-centered therapy, to systematic desensitization, and to a no-contact control group in the treatment of test-anxious high school students. Thirty-three male and female college students who obtained either high or low anxiety scores on the Spielberger, Edwards, Montouri and Lushene (1975) State-Trait Anxiety Inventory participated in the study. Each subject in the treatment groups was seen individually between 7 and 11 times over a 5-week period. To measure the effects of the therapeutic interventions, the students were placed in a simulated classroom IQ test. Dependent measures were scores on the anxiety inventory and changes in galvanic skin response (GSR) and heart rate. The results showed no significant differences between the four groups on the State-Trait Anxiety measure. However, significant differences were found on the GSR and heart rate measures in favor of rational-emotive psychotherapy and systematic desensitization over the client-centered and no-contact control groups. Through a post hoc reanalysis of the data using a more conservative test of significance (the Mann-Whitney U Test), the authors found that only the rational-emotive therapy group differed from the controls on all three measures. While this study is important, it has several methodological limitations: the failure to match subjects on initial level of anxiety makes it difficult to assume that there were no initial differences between groups; the small N prevented use of more powerful statistical tests; the study lacked a placebo control group; and a significance level of .10 was chosen.

DiLoreto (1971) investigated the effectiveness of systematic desensitization compared to rational-emotive psychotherapy and client-centered therapy in the treatment of subjects with interpersonal anxiety who were classified as either introverted or extroverted. He assigned 100 college students to 1 of 10 introvert and 10 extrovert groups. Each of the 20 groups consisted of 5 subjects. He then randomly assigned each group to 1 of the 3 treatment conditions or to the 2 control conditions (attention-placebo and no-contact). All subjects in the treatment groups received 11 hours of group counseling by graduate students. The dependent measures included a behavioral checklist of interpersonal anxiety scored by trained observers, self-report scales of interpersonal anxiety, and a variety of personality assessment scales including the Trait Anxiety Inventory, State Anxiety Inventory, and the Edwards Social Desirability Scale.

DiLoreto hypothesized that all three treatment approaches would produce significantly more anxiety reduction than either control procedure. Based on other research, he hypothesized that the order of effectiveness of the treatment approaches would be client-centered, rational-emotive therapy, and systematic desensitization with extroverts; with introverts, the order of effectiveness of the treatment approaches would be systematic desensitization, rational-emotive therapy and client-centered therapy, he hypothesized.

The results indicated that all the treatment conditions significantly differed from both control conditions on all the dependent measures, with the exception of the client-centered group, which did not achieve significance on the self-report scale of interpersonal anxiety. However, a further analysis of the results did reveal some differences among treatments. Systematic desensitization achieved the greatest amount of anxiety reduction with both personality types; rational-emotive therapy produced more significant decreases in anxiety with introverts than did client-centered therapy; and client-centered therapy was more effective than rational-emotive therapy with extroverts. However, a follow-up measure showed that, three months after termination, students who received rational-emotive therapy indicated more interpersonal interactions and assertive behavior than students who had received either desensitization or client-centered therapy.

The DiLoreto study is one of the most advanced comparative studies to date in psychotherapy. Bergin and Strupp (1972) commented that "the phenomena and processes involved were somewhat closer to the real thing" (p. 511), but the significance of the results was limited due to the nature of the subjects and therapists. The interpersonally anxious college students are not exactly equivalent to actual psychotherapy clients, and graduate students, regardless of training, are not the equivalent of experienced therapists. Another major criticism appears to be the nature of the placebo treatment. This group met for discussions of university life, academic problems, and study skills for only three sessions. Thus, they could have been cued that this was not a treatment situation and that they were not expected to change.

Ellis (DiLoreto, 1971), in his review of this study, also noted that the RET therapists used a "watered-down" approach. According to Ellis, the therapists did not demonstrate why the students' beliefs were irrational, did not give enough stress to the necessity for work and practice, and tended to be too generally didactic and lecturing. Ellis' comments re-emphasize the difficulty in assessing studies using graduate students as opposed to experienced therapists.

Meichenbaum, Gilmore, and Fedoravicius (1971) investigated the effectiveness of group rational-emotive psychotherapy and group systematic desensitization on the treatment of speech anxiety in college students. In addition, they included a third group which received both systematic desensitization and RET. An attention-placebo group and a no-contact control group were also included. Treatment was carried out over eight sessions lasting one hour each. The dependent measures included a behavioral checklist, recorded speech behavior, self-reports, and a cognitive measure of anxiety. Measures were taken in connection with test speeches occurring prior to and following treatment. The major finding was that subjects receiving systematic desensitization only, or rational-emotive therapy only, showed the greatest improvement in reducing speech anxiety. Their level of speech performance following treatment matched that of an additional group of low speech-anxious subjects, included to provide a standard for adaptive responding in group speech situations. Self-report follow-up measures taken three months after the conclusion of treatment indicated that improvement had been maintained. In addition, a post hoc analysis found that desensitization and rational-emotive therapy had differential effects depending upon the type of speech anxiety the students displayed. Desensitization appeared to be more effective than rational-emotive therapy with students for whom speech anxiety was confined to situationally specific stimuli; conversely, rational-emotive therapy was more effective with students who suffered anxiety in a variety of social situations. This finding is consistent with previous research (Lazarus, 1974; Meichenbaum, 1973) which suggests that systematic desensitization is a more effective treatment with persons with monosymptomatic phobias, while a cognitive approach such as rational-emotive therapy works better with those who demonstrate free-floating anxiety states or the "social phobias" (Lazarus, 1974).

Meichenbaum (1972) compared the relative efficacy of "cognitive modification," systematic desensitization, and a waiting-list control group with test-anxious college students. The "cognitive modification" group was given a combination of rational-emotive therapy with a modified desensitization procedure. In this group, subjects were taught to become aware of the self-defeating irrational self-statements they were emitting when they became anxious. They were also trained to emit task-relevant rational self-statements while performing anxiety-inhibiting behaviors such as relaxation. To achieve this, the subjects were asked to visualize themselves becoming anxious and then to visualize themselves coping with the anxiety by relaxing and verbalizing rational self-statements, either overtly or covertly, which could serve to inhibit task-irrelevant irrational self-statements. The results of the study indicated that the "cognitive modification" procedure, as compared with standard systematic desensitization and the control conditions on self-report measures, was significantly more effective in reducing test anxiety in an analog test situation and in improving grade point average. This improvement was maintained in a one-month follow-up.

In an attempt to isolate and assess the relative contributions of the components in Meichenbaum's cognitive modification treatment package, Thompson (1974) conducted a study using standard systematic desensitization, desensitization using coping imagery, cognitive modification, and rational-emotive therapy. He also utilized test-anxious college students. The cognitive modification group procedures were identical to Meichenbaum's. The rational-emotive therapy group focused on the specific irrational beliefs which led to test anxiety and did not use coping imagery or relaxation. The procedure is similar to the rational-emotive imagery technique of Maultsby (1974). The results indicated that the rational-emotive therapy group showed the most significant improvement on self-report and test-anxiety inventories. Thompson (1974) concluded that the results found in Meichenbaum's (1972) study were due to cognitive components of his treatment plan, rather than to relaxation or coping imagery.

Kanter's (1975) investigation is closer to the "real thing" than most outcome studies in the field, equaled only by DiLoreto's (1971) in complexity and thoroughness. Kanter attempted to compare the relative effectiveness of systematic desensitization and systematic rational restructuring. Systematic rational restructuring is a method very similar to rational-emotive therapy devised by Goldfried, Decenteceo, and Weinberg (1974). These two procedures were also compared to a combined treatment of desensitization and systematic rational restructuring and to a waiting-list control group. The subjects were divided according to pretest difference in anxiety into high, medium, and low anxiety groups. Kanter obtained subjects for the study by advertising in two local newspapers. The advertisements asked for persons with social anxiety and specified that the treatment would be experimental in nature. The mean age of this population was 35.6. The subjects were screened to eliminate any who manifested signs of psychosis or were presently receiving psychotherapy. Two phases of the experiment were run, each serving as a replication of the other. Pretest and posttest measures were taken on several self-report scales of social anxiety, Jones' (1968) Irrational Beliefs Test, behavioral ratings, and pulse rate during an analog test situation. Only the self-report measures were taken at a ninth week of follow-up. All treatments consisted of seven weekly meetings of 1½ hour duration with groups of eight to ten clients.

Kanter predicted that the combined treatment condition would be the most effective and that the desensitization and restructuring treatments would be equally effective. While all treatments showed significant reductions in anxiety from pretests to posttests and all were significantly more effective than the control condition, the rational restructuring approach was the most effective, followed in order by the combined approach and then the desensitization alone. These results were maintained at the follow-up. Kanter also predicted that the treatments would have differential effectiveness at various levels of anxiety. Specifically, he predicted that the cognitive therapy would be least effective with subjects with high degrees of anxiety. This prediction was not supported since none of the main effects or interactions of the anxiety level variables was significant.

Kanter's study had a number of shortcomings. The faults involved the failure to control for experimenter bias and the lack of behavioral measures in the follow-up data. Since the experimenter led all of the therapy groups for all the treatments, the possibility of experimenter bias remains. Further, a longer follow-up period and the inclusion of behavioral and other assessments with more reliable measures than self-report scales would have strengthened the results. Despite these shortcomings, this attempt comes closest to an actual test of psychotherapy, since the subjects were persons seeking therapy for anxiety problems and, even though they may have been drawn from a select group, they are close to approximating an actual outpatient population. These results add support for the efficacy of rational-emotive and related therapies.

The first study to include an actual patient population was that of Moleski and Tosi (1976). The authors hypothesized that rational-emotive therapy would be more efficient than systematic desensitization in the treatment of adult stutterers. This was based on the observation that stutterers hold irrational beliefs about speaking and that these ideas serve as cues which elicit the anxiety that disrupts their speech. In addition, the contribution of in vivo practice to both forms of therapy was assessed. In all, there were four treatment groups plus a no-contact control group. Dependent measures included self-report scales of anxiety and attitudes towards stuttering, as well as two behavioral measures of speech disfluency taken during speaking tasks. Each client received eight 45-minute individual therapy sessions. The dependent measures were administered immediately before and after the therapy as well as one month after termination.

To guard against experimenter biases, two therapists were employed; two experienced raters, trained in behavior therapy, evaluated random segments of the tape-recorded sessions. Both raters agreed that the therapists were, in fact, adhering to the techniques of both psychotherapy systems. Also there were no statistically significant differences between the therapists on any of the outcome measures. This represents the most rigorous effort to date to avoid experimenter bias in rational therapy research. The results of this study strongly support the relative effectiveness of rational-emotive therapy over systematic desensitization in reducing stuttering behavior as well as the accompanying anxiety and irrational attitudes concerning the behavior. These results were sustained at one-month follow-up.

Moleski and Tosi's (1976) study is among those which offer strong support for rational-emotive therapy. The inclusion of multiple therapists and raters who can guard against bias is strongly recommended for all future studies. Follow-up data is important for evaluating the permanence of therapeutic outcomes. However, it is suggested that follow-up tests be administered at progressively longer intervals after the conclusion of treatment.

In a well-controlled study, Wein, Nelson and Odom (1975) attempted to ascertain if the gains made by cognitive restructuring therapies in treating phobias were due to a cognitive "relabeling" of fear-provoking stimuli or due to verbal extinction. They argued that the effectiveness of cognitive restructuring could be explained by either a reattribution of the feared behaviors from the phobic stimuli to the client's irrational beliefs about the stimuli, or an extinction process consisting of prolonged verbal exposure to threatening stimuli via talking about their fears. This second explanation is based on the assumption that overt and covert behaviors obey the same psychological laws (Bandura, 1969). The cognitive restructuring therapy used in this study was that of D'Zurilla, Wilson, and Nelson (1973), which is considered similar to rational-emotive therapy.

The subjects were female college students with snake phobias. The experimental design consisted of five treatments: cognitive restructuring, a verbal extinction therapy, systematic desensitization, an attention placebo group, and a no-contact control group. Two therapists were used to reduce the possibility of experimenter bias. All treatments consisted of six sessions. In the verbal extinction condition, the clients were encouraged to express their images and past memories of snakes. The therapist directed the discussion away from any tendency toward relabeling or emitting rational self-statements about snakes. The four dependent measures were: the behavioral avoidance test (Bandura, Blanchard, and Ritter, 1969); two self-report measures of anxiety—the Fear Thermometer (Walk, 1956) and the Personal Reactions Questionnaire of the Systematic Restructuring Inventory of Anxiousness (Endler, Hunt, and Rosenstein, 1962); and a measure of heart rate. Subjects were matched on all dependent measures. An analysis of variance of the pretreatment scores of the students failed to show any significant differences. Change scores from pretreatment and posttreatment measures were used in all statistical analyses. The results for the behavioral measure indicated that cognitive restructuring was as effective as systematic desensitization in increasing approach behavior; both were more effective than the verbal extinction treatment and the two control conditions. The cognitive restructuring condition was the only effective treatment as measured by self-report measures. On only one self-report measure did the verbal extinction condition differ significantly from the placebo. There were no significant differences on the heart rate measure.

These results support the effectiveness of cognitive therapy and indicate that it is equally efficacious, if not more efficacious, than desensitization. The comparison between the restructuring and extinction groups confirm that it is the cognitive reappraisal that accounts for the therapeutic gains of rational-emotive therapy and similar cognitive therapies, not extinction. These results are similar to those of Wine (1971), who demonstrated that providing the client with alternate cognitions while viewing a situation is a critical component of therapy. The lack of follow-up leaves unclear the long-term effectiveness of the intervention.

Holroyd (1976) reported the results of a comparative assessment of the effects of rational-emotive psychotherapy, systematic desensitization, a treatment approach that combined RET and systematic desensitization, a pseudotherapy/meditation control group, and a waiting-list control group on test anxiety. Dependent measures included the Debilitating Anxiety Scale of the Achievement Anxiety Test (Albert and Haber, 1960), performance in an analog testing situation, academic achievement, and two additional measures of frustration: The Frustration Tolerance Test and The Frustration Thermometer (McReynolds and Tori, 1972). Subjects were 60 test-anxious volunteers who fell approximately in the upper 13% of the distribution on the Debilitating Anxiety Scale of the Achievement Anxiety Test. Six were assigned to each treatment group and the pseudotherapy control group and 12 to the waiting-list control group. Two advanced graduate students who had completed a one-year sequence in behavior modification, a year of supervised practicum in psychotherapy, and a one year APA-approved internship in clinical psychology served as therapists. Each therapist conducted one group of each type to control for therapist skill or bias. All groups met one hour a week for seven weeks.

The major finding of this study was that the RET condition was significantly effective in reducing test anxiety as assessed by all dependent measures on both an immediate posttreatment and one month follow-up basis. Moreover, the RET condition fared quite well in comparison with the other treatment and control conditions. Specifically, on the analog measures and on academic performance, RET obtained significantly more positive measures than the remaining treatment groups and pseudotherapy groups, which in turn obtained significantly more positive measures than the waiting-list control group. On the Debilitating Anxiety Scale and The Frustration Thermometer, all treatment groups and the pseudotherapy group differed significantly from the waiting-list control group but did not differ from each other.

To summarize the comparative studies of RET and systematic desensitization, while it appears that the present data support the hypothesis that rational-emotive therapy is more effective in eliminating anxiety than systematic desensitization, more research is needed to assess the relative contributions of the various components in cognitive therapy with actual clinical populations.

Of particular interest would be an experimental test of Meichenbaum, Gilmore, and Fedoravicius' (1971) post hoc findings that desensitization was most effective with subjects with more situationally specific anxiety, while cognitive therapy was more efficacious with subjects with more generalized social anxiety. In addition, research is needed to explore the relationship between other patient characteristics and the relative effectiveness of these approaches. DiLoreto's (1971) findings concerning introversion and extroversion need to be replicated.

RET and Assertive Training

There have recently been a large number of studies in the treatment of interpersonal anxiety vis-à-vis assertive training. Results have shown that assertive training is a useful technique in promoting assertive behavior and reducing interpersonal anxiety (Lazarus, 1966; McFall and Lillesand, 1971; McFall and Marston, 1970; Young, Rimm, and Kennedy, 1973).

Most behavior therapists conceptualize assertion through a reciprocal inhibition model. Assertion and anxiety are to a considerable degree incompatible responses; through behavior rehearsal, modeling, and in vivo graduated life situations, the individual can "learn" to emit assertive responses in lieu of the previously learned, nonassertive, anxiety-ridden responses. Such a conceptualization, however, minimizes the importance of an individual's cognitions and basic belief system in the acquisition of assertive responses. Research has demonstrated that an individual's irrational beliefs about an interpersonal situation can lead to unassertive behavior (Wolfe, 1975). Most practitioners of assertive training now recognize the importance of providing both a cognitive and a behavioral component in promoting assertive behavior (Wolfe and Fodor, 1975). The subsequent section reviews the comparative effectiveness of assertive training, with and without rational-emotive therapy, in the reduction of interpersonal anxiety.

Wolfe (1975) investigated the efficacy of modeling and behavioral rehearsal as an adjunct to rational-emotive therapy in increasing assertive responses in women. She randomly assigned 64 women recruited from a waiting list for assertive training groups at an outpatient psychotherapy clinic into one of four conditions. In the first condition the women observed the experimenter model the appropriate assertive response, which they then rehearsed. The second condition consisted of rational-emotive therapy, which focused on identifying and challenging the irrational beliefs that blocked assertion. In addition, they observed the therapist model an assertive response and later role-played this response. A third group, serving as an attention-placebo group, discussed "early socialization" experiences behind nonassertiveness. The fourth group was a waiting-list control group. Each group ran for two 2-hour sessions. Wolfe hypothesized that the combination of rational-emotive therapy and behavioral rehearsal/ modeling would be more effective than behavioral rehearsal/modeling alone. In addition, she hypothesized that the combined approach would show greater generalization of treatment effects. Dependent measures included self-report measures of assertiveness and situational and general measures of anxiety. The results indicated that both the modeling/behavioral rehearsal group and the combined treatment of modeling/behavioral rehearsal and RET group showed significantly more improvement on measures of assertiveness than the control groups. On the measure of situational anxiety, the combined group was significantly better than the other three groups. However, the hypothesis that the combined approach would show greater generalization was not borne out. A possible explanation for this last finding can be attributed to the rather short duration of treatment. Since treatment consisted of four hours, and within that time rational-emotive principles had to be taught in addition to behavioral rehearsal, it is not surprising that the combined approach did not elicit greater reduction in social anxiety. Additionally, experimenter bias was not controlled for, since the same therapist was used for all treatments.

Tiegerman (1975) tested the success in reducing interpersonal anxiety in college students of rational-emotive therapy, assertive training, and a combined treatment of both. As controls there were an attention-placebo group and a no-contact group. The treatment was given in ten 1-hour sessions. Although Tiegerman did not specifically isolate behavioral rehearsal as a variable, his assertive training treatment primarily entailed the use of behavioral rehearsal and modeling. Tiegerman hypothesized that both assertive training and rational-emotive therapy would increase assertiveness and that the combined approach would be superior to either component in isolation. Dependent measures included self-report scales of assertiveness and interpersonal anxiety. Two therapists were used for each treatment, thus reducing the possibility of experimenter bias. There was no significant main effect or interaction for the effect of therapists.

Results provided partial support for the relative efficacy over the control groups of all three treatment approaches in promoting assertion. The assertive training group showed the most consistent gains, followed by the combined approach and the rational-emotive therapy group. The lack of superiority of the combined treatment was considered a function of the limited number of sessions. Although both behavioral and cognitive components were introduced at the beginning of treatment, postexperimental interviews revealed that the students in the combined treatment reported: "Too much material was presented in a small amount of time." The failure of the rational-emotive therapy condition to be as effective as assertive training or the combined treatment was considered a function of the missing behavioral component. The subjects within the rational-emotive therapy group only received the cognitive components of the rational-emotive therapy approach; this treatment approach is in direct contrast to the usual rational-emotive therapy procedure which relies heavily on behavioral components such as behavioral rehearsal and outside assignments.

Thorpe (1975) designed a study comparing the merits of rational-emotive therapy (self-instructional training), systematic desensitization, behavior rehearsal, and a placebo control group, in increasing assertiveness in college students. Students in the rational-emotive therapy group were made aware of their irrational self-statements and rehearsed more appropriate rational statements. In the systematic desensitization condition, students were desensitized to making assertive responses via relaxation. Students in the behavior rehearsal group observed the therapist model the appropriate response, which they then rehearsed. In the placebo control group, students discussed the etiology of nonassertiveness. The length of treatment was six sessions. Dependent measures included self-report, behavioral, and physiological ratings for a situational test in which the students had to respond assertively. Results indicated the general superiority of the rational-emotive therapy group, followed by the behavior rehearsal group. However, one cannot singularly attribute the success of the self-instructional group to the cognitive components of rational-emotive therapy, since Thorpe did not isolate the behavioral and cognitive components of rational-emotive therapy.

In sum, the research in the area of assertive training as an adjunct to rational-emotive therapy has been minimal and at best equivocal. Additionally, a closer review of the cognitive-behavioral literature (Meichenbaum, 1972; Tiegerman, 1975; Thorpe, 1975; Wolfe, 1975) reveals three essential unresolved problems: (1) inadequate isolation of the behavioral and cognitive components of the rational-emotive therapy procedure; (2) limited duration of the treatment period; and (3) no adequate follow-up data. It is only when the above requisite conditions are met that the beneficial effects of a combined cognitive-behavioral approach to assertive training will be demonstrated.

RET as Primary Prevention

It has been claimed that in addition to reducing inappropriate, excessive negative emotions, rational-emotive therapy can also be applied to the prevention of psychopathology. Maultsby (1974) has developed a program with rational-emotive therapy that is essentially designed for use in high schools and college classrooms. His goal is to teach students to utilize rational-emotive therapy in analyzing their emotional upsets and to give them an effective method for solving their personal conflicts.

Maultsby, Knipping, and Carpenter (1974) investigated the efficacy of rational-emotive therapy as a preventive measure. In a pilot study, two groups of emotionally disturbed high school students were used as the sample population. One group received the rational-emotive therapy course and the other group served as a control group. Dependent measures included several personality assessment scales—the Rotter Scale (Rotter, 1966); the Personal Orientation Inventory (Shostram, 1976); and the Maultsby Common Trait Inventory (Maultsby, 1974). Results indicated significant differences in the positive direction on all three measures in the group receiving the rational-emotive course. A second study using college students again demonstrated that the group receiving the rational-emotive course showed more pretest-posttest improvement on scales that were highly correlated with emotional adjustment.

Maultsby, Costello, and Carpenter (1974) attempted to validate the efficacy of rational-emotive therapy as a preventive mental health program with college students. The sessions lasted for 75 minutes and met twice a week for 15 weeks. The instructor of the course was unaware of the nature of the hypotheses. A control group consisted of 30 students who were enrolled in an introductory psychology course taught by the same instructor. The dependent measure was a mental health adjustment scale. The results, as measured by the scores on the mental health adjustment scale, showed that the rational-emotive therapy group yielded more positive results than the control group.

The above studies demonstrate that rational-emotive therapy principles applied through a didactic experience can be used effectively as a preventive mental health educational model with "normal" populations and that RET's effectiveness is not limited to clinical problems. Despite these claims, the above studies must be taken as tentative until further and more controlled studies are conducted.

Since the elementary school environment may be an important setting for instituting preventive efforts, there has been increasing interest in developing mental health programs that would promote emotional and behavioral adjustment (Ivery and Alchuler, 1973; Spivack and Shure, 1974). In concordance with these views, Ellis has recommended that the principles of rational-emotive therapy be taught to elementary school children.

Rational-emotive education (Knaus, 1974) is a direct extension of rational-emotive therapy. Children are taught many of the same principles of RET, including the 11 common irrational beliefs that Ellis (1962) articulated, as well as the concepts of self-acceptance and mistake-making. In addition, specific lessons are designed to help children cope with disappointments and frustrations by teaching them to limit their "musts," "shoulds," and "demands." Materials used in rational-emotive education are simplified for easier understanding by children.

The research in this area is summarized in Chapter 27 so there is no need to review it again at this point. Suffice it to say that the research supports the hypothesis that elementary school children are capable of acquiring knowledge of rational-emotive principles and that the modification of a child's self-verbalizations or irrational self-statements can have a positive effect on personal adjustment (Albert, 1972; Brody, 1974; DiGiuseppe and Kassinove, 1976; Knaus and Bokor, 1975); and on behavior (Katz, 1974).

Discussion

Since the last review of the outcome literature on rational-emotive therapy (Mahoney, 1969), there has been considerable research activity. The results of this research, as well as a growing body of literature in many related areas, such as Beck's cognitive therapy (see Chapter 21), does provide support for the efficacy of the rational-emotive psychotherapy approach. Specifically, the research does suggest that: (1) rational-emotive therapy is more effective than client-centered therapy with introverted persons; (2) it is more effective than systematic desensitization in the reduction of general or pervasive anxiety; (3) a combination of cognitive therapy and behavior therapy appears to be the most efficacious treatment for depression; (4) the relative effectiveness of rational-emotive therapy versus assertive training is inconclusive due to limited and confounded research.

The present review of the literature in rational-emotive therapy contains studies with the same methodological limitations that are generally found in psychotherapy outcome research. For example, several of the reviewed studies used inadequate control groups and failed to make comparisons with other forms of psychotherapy.

Another major criticism of the above studies is the extensive use of nonrepresentative subject pools. Generally they included college or high school students with varying degrees of test-taking, public speaking, or interpersonal anxiety. While it is advantageous to use such populations because it insures more scientific rigor, they can be considered analog studies at best, since the results can not be generalized to clinical populations. One of the reasons for this is that nonclinical populations may not exhibit a high enough level of anxiety or pathological behavior for the effectiveness of therapy to be adequately measured. Some notable exceptions in this area have been the studies by Kanter (1975) and Moleski and Tosi (1976), which utilized clinical populations. The efficacy of rational-emotive therapy or any other therapeutic system can only be demonstrated when actual clinical populations are used. The goal of any psychotherapy outcome research is to answer the question: "Which therapy works for what clients under what conditions?" Insufficient attention has been paid to the influence of specific client variables in this research.

The outcome literature in psychotherapy suggests that any therapy is most efficacious with high socioeconomic status (SES) intelligent clients. Except for the study of DiLoreto (1971), comparing introverted and extroverted subjects, no research has been done which investigated the effects of client variables. While practitioners of rational-emotive therapy agree that it is more effective with high SES clients (Ellis, personal communications, April, 1976), it is possible that it may be more effective with low SES clients than other forms of therapy. Research has shown that low SES clients often become dissatisfied and drop out of therapy because of the nondirective, non-goal-oriented behaviors of therapists (Heitler, 1976). Furthermore, low SES clients expect therapists to be active and directive. Given these results and the fact that rational-emotive therapy is active and directive, it can be hypothesized that low SES clients may do better, or at least drop out less frequently, with rational therapy. Such speculations are waiting systematic research.

The lack of adequate dependent variables and the limited number of follow-up measures also limit the generalizability of the findings in this area. Many of the studies utilized scales assessing the endorsement of irrational belief systems. While it is important to demonstrate that rational-emotive therapy produces a decrease in irrational beliefs, as well as psychopathology, there are substantial difficulties in assessing such beliefs. Lane, Bessia, and Bard (1975) and Wessler (1976) have concluded that the existing scales are psychometrically poor and lacking in reliability and validity. Unfortunately, many studies have included such measures as dependent variables. It is suggested that future studies avoid self-report measures of this type and use more psychometrically valid instruments and, if possible, behavioral measures. In addition, follow-up data is essential in determining the permanence of any behavior change. The absence of such in many studies seriously weakens the support for the effectiveness of rational-emotive therapy. It is suggested that all future studies include follow-up data of at least six months' duration.

Two methodological limitations that minimized a positive outcome in studies of rational-emotive therapy have been the short duration of treatment and the level of training of the therapists. Since most of the studies utilized treatment of ten weeks or less, the number of significant findings is quite impressive. However, this finding may be due to the use of non-clinical populations. Longer durations of treatment may be necessary with more disturbed subjects. The other limitation is that most of the studies utilized graduate students as therapists. Again, more positive results could have been expected if experienced therapists were employed. While most of the investigators listed here claimed to use rational-emotive therapy, there were no assurances that they actually did so. It is conceivable that many of the studies used "watered-down" versions of the rational approach. This, in fact, was one of the major criticisms by Ellis of the DiLoreto (1971) study. To guard against this, it is strongly suggested that researchers publish therapist manuals of the technique actually used in their studies. This would assume that they practiced what they claim and would make replication much easier. DiGiuseppe and Kassinove (1976), Katz (1974), Kanter (1975), and Meichenbaum and Cameron (1973) have included such step-by-step manuals.

Perhaps the most dangerous of all experimental shortcomings is the use of a single therapist in most of the studies. This, of course, increases the likelihood of experimenter bias. A major reason for the inclusion of only one therapist in the present literature is that most of the studies were dissertations, in which manpower is limited by financing. It is strongly suggested that more complicated experimental designs be employed which include multiple therapists. Another possible way of avoiding experimenter bias is to utilize blind raters to assess the dependent measures. This was used too rarely in the present group of studies.

Finally, research isolating the critical components of rational-emotive therapy is absent; we believe that there are at least five major cognitive components and one behavioral component. In actual practice, rational-emotive therapy consists of the following: (1) identifying the client's irrational beliefs; (2) disputing these beliefs; (3) changing the client's illogical thinking patterns and tendencies to distort reality; (4) teaching social-problem-solving skills, à la D'Zurilla & Goldfried (1971); (5) teaching appropriate rational self-statements; and (6) in vivo behavioral rehearsal and practice. Steps three and four are altogether absent from Ellis' (1962) writings but are definitely present in his and other rational therapists' practice today. While some of the research has attempted to assess the relative contributions of teaching rational self-statements and the behavioral assignments, there has been insufficient research to enable the critical components to be identified.

To summarize, there has been a substantial amount of research since Mahoney (1974) last reviewed the literature on rational-emotive therapy. While the results are positive and hopeful, they are far from conclusive. It is hoped that future research will address itself to some of the issues raised here.

References

Albert, R., & Haber, R. N. Anxiety in academic achievement situations. *Journal of Abnormal and Social Psychology,* 1960, *61,* 207–215.

Albert, S. A study to determine the effectiveness of affective education with fifth grade students. Unpublished master's thesis, Queens College, 1972.

Argabute, A. H., & Nidorf, L. J. Fifteen questions for rating reason. *Rational Living.* 1968, *3,* 9–11.

Bandura, A. *Principles of behavior modification.* New York: Holt, Rinehart, & Winston, 1969.

Bandura, A., Blanchard, E. B., & Ritter, V. The relative efficacy of desensitization and modeling approaches for inducing behavioral, affective, and attitudinal changes. Unpublished manuscript, Stanford University, 1969.

Bard, J. A self-rating scale for rationality. *Rational Living,* 1973(a), *8,* 19.

Bard, J. Rational proselytizing. *Rational Living,* 1973(b), *8,* 24–26.

Beck, A. T. *Cognitive therapy and the emotional disorders.* New York: International Universities Press, 1976.

Beck, A. T. Cognitive therapy: Nature and relation to behavior therapy. *Behavior Therapy*, 1970, *1*, 184–200.

Beck, A. T. *Depression: Clinical, experimental and therapeutic aspects.* New York: Harper and Row, 1967.

Bergin, A. E., & Strupp, H. H. *Changing frontiers in the science of psychotherapy.* Chicago: Aldine, 1972.

Brody, M. The effect of the rational-emotive affective education approach on anxiety, frustration tolerance and self-esteem with fifth grade students. Unpublished doctoral dissertation, Temple University, 1974.

Coopersmith, S. *The antecedents of self-esteem.* San Francisco: Freeman, 1967.

DiGiuseppe, R., & Kassinove, H. Effects of a rational-emotive school mental health program on children's emotional adjustment. *Journal of Community Psychology*, 1976, *4*(4), 382–387.

DiLoreto, A. *Comparative psychotherapy.* Chicago: Aldine, 1971.

Dollard, J., & Miller, N. *Personality and psychotherapy.* New York: McGraw-Hill, 1950.

D'Zurilla, T. J., & Goldfried, M. R. Problem solving and behavior modification. *Journal of Abnormal Psychology*, 1971, *78*, 107–126.

D'Zurilla, T. J., Wilson, T., & Nelson, R. A preliminary study of the effectiveness of graduated prolonged exposure in the treatment of irrational fear. *Behavior Therapy*, 1973, *4*, 672–685.

Ellis, A. Are cognitive behavior therapy and rational therapy synonymous. *Rational Living*, 1973, *8*, (2), 8–11.

Ellis, A. Emotional education in the classroom. *Journal of Clinical Child Psychology*, 1972, *1*, 19–22.

Ellis, A. *Growth through reason.* Palo Alto: Science and Behavior Books, 1971.

Ellis, A. Outcome of employing three techniques of psychotherapy. *Journal of Clinical Psychology*, 1957, *13*, 344–350.

Ellis, A. *Reason and emotion in psychotherapy.* New York: Lyle Stuart, 1962.

Ellis, A. Teaching emotional education in the classroom. *School Health Review*, 1969, November, 10–13.

Ellis, A., & Harper, R. *A new guide to rational living.* North Hollywood, Calif.: Wilshire, 1975.

Ellis, A., Wolfe, J. L., & Mosley, S. *How to prevent your child from becoming a neurotic adult.* New York: Crown Publishers, 1966.

Endler, N. S., Hunt, J., & Rosenstein, A. An S-R inventory of anxiousness. *Psychological Monographs*, 1962, *76* (Whole Number 536).

Eysenck, H. J. The effects of psychotherapy. In H. J. Eysenck (Ed.), *Handbook of abnormal psychology.* New York: Basic Books, 1961.

Eysenck, S. *Manual for the junior Eysenck personality inventory.* London: University of London Press, 1965.

Fox, E., & Davies, R. Test your rationality. *Rational Living*, 1971, *5*, 23–25.

Glass, D. C., & Singer, J. E. *Stress and adaption: Experimental studies of behavioral effects of exposure to aversive events.* New York: Academic Press, 1972.

Glicken, M. Rational counseling: A new approach to children. *Journal of Elementary School Guidance and Counseling*, 1968, *2*, 261–267.

Goldfried, M. R. Postdoctoral training in clinical behavior therapy. In I. B. Wiener (Ed.), *Postdoctoral education in clinical psychology.* Topeka, Kansas: Menninger Foundation, 1973.

Goldfried, M. R., Decenteceo, E. T., & Weinberg, L. Systematic rational restructuring as a self-control technique. *Behavior Therapy*, 1974, *5*, 247–254.

Goldfried, M. R., & Sobocinski, D. The effect of irrational beliefs on emotional arousal. *Journal of Consulting and Clinical Psychology*, 1975, *43*, 504–510.

Hauck, P. A. *The rational management of children.* New York: Libra Publishing, 1967.

Heitler, J. B. Preparatory techniques in initiating expressive psychotherapy with lower class unsophisticated patients. *Psychological Bulletin,* 1976, *83,* 339–352.

Holroyd, K. A. Cognition and desensitization in the group treatment of test anxiety. *Journal of Consulting and Clinical Psychology,* 1976, *44,* 991–1001.

Ivery, A., & Alchuler, A. Getting into psychological education. *Personnel and Guidance Journal,* 1973, *51,* 682–691.

Jacobs, E. E. The effects of a systematic learning program for college undergraduates based on rational-emotive concepts and techniques. Unpublished master's thesis, Florida State University, 1971.

Jarmon, D. S. Differential effectiveness of rational emotive therapy bibliotherapy and attention placebo in the treatment of speech anxiety. Unpublished doctoral dissertation, Southern Illinois University, 1972.

Jones, R. A factored measure of Ellis' irrational belief systems with personality and maladjustment correlates. Unpublished doctoral dissertation, Texas Tech College, 1968.

Kanter, N. J. A comparison of self-control desensitization and systematic rational restructuring for the reduction of interpersonal anxiety. Unpublished doctoral dissertation, SUNY at Stony Brook, 1975.

Karst, S., & Trexler, L. An initial study using fixed role and rational-emotive therapies in treating public speaking anxiety. *Journal of Consulting and Clinical Psychology,* 1970, *34,* 360–366.

Katz, S. The effects of emotional education on locus of control and self concept. Unpublished doctoral dissertation, Hofstra University, 1974.

Keller, J., Crooke, J., & Brookings, J. Effects of a program in rational thinking on anxiety in older persons. *Journal of Counseling Psychology,* 1975, *22,* 54–57.

Kelly, G. *The psychology of personal constructs.* New York: Norton, 1955.

Knaus, W. *Rational-emotive education: A manual for elementary school teachers.* New York: Institute for Rational Living, 1974.

Knaus, W., & Bokor, S. The effect of rational-emotive education lessons on anxiety and self-concept in sixth grade students. *Rational Living,* 1975, *11,* 7–10.

Lane, S. H., Bessia, J. L., & Bard, J. A. Irrational beliefs assessment: perspectives. First National Conference on Rational Psychotherapy. Chicago: June, 1975.

Laughridge, S. Differential diagnosis with a test of irrational ideation. *Rational Living,* 1975, *10* (2), 21–23.

Lazarus, A. A. Behavioral rehearsal vs non-directive therapy vs advice in effecting behavior change. *Behavior Research and Therapy,* 1966, *4,* 209–212.

Lazarus, A. A. *Behavior therapy and beyond.* New York: McGraw-Hill, 1971.

Lazarus, A. A. Desensitization and cognitive restructuring. *Psychotherapy: Therapy, Research, and Practice,* 1974, *11,* 98–102.

Lewinsohn, P. M. A behavioral approach to depression. In R. J. Friedman, & M. M. Katz (Eds.), *The psychology of depression: Contemporary theory and research.* New York: John Wiley, 1974.

MacDonald, A., & Games, R. Ellis' irrational ideas: A validation study. *Rational Living,* 1972, *7* (2), 25–29.

Maes, W., & Heiman, R. The comparison of three approaches to the reduction of test anxiety in high school students. Final report project 9-1-040. Washington Office of Education, United States Department of Health, Education and Welfare, October, 1972.

Mahoney, M. *Cognition and behavior modification.* Cambridge, Mass.: Ballinger Press, 1974.

Maultsby, M. The classroom as an emotional health center. *The Educational Magazine,* 1974, *31* (5), 8–11.

Maultsby, M. Systematic written homework in psychotherapy. *Psychotherapy: Theory, Research, and Practice,* 1971, *8,* 195–198.

Maultsby, M., Costello, P. T., & Carpenter, L. Classroom rational self-counseling.

Mimeographed paper, University of Kentucky Medical Center, 1974.

Maultsby, M., Knipping, P., & Carpenter, L. Teaching self-help in the classroom with rational self-counseling. *Journal of School Health,* 1974, *44,* 445–448.

McFall, R. M., & Lillesand, D. B. Behavioral rehearsal with modeling and coaching in assertive training. *Journal of Abnormal Psychology,* 1971, *77,* 313–323.

McFall, R. M., & Marston, A. R. An experimental investigation of assertive training. *Journal of Abnormal Psychology,* 1970, *76,* 295–303.

McReynolds, W. T., & Tori, C. A further assessment of attention-placebo effects and demand characteristics in studies of systematic desensitization. *Journal of Consulting and Clinical Psychology,* 1972, *38,* 261–264.

Meichenbaum, D. Cognitive factors in behavior modification: Modifying what clients say to themselves. In A. A. Lazarus (Ed.), *Advances in behavior modification.* Vol. 4. New York: Academic Press, 1973.

Meichenbaum, D. Cognitive modification of test-anxious college students. *Journal of Consulting and Clinical Psychology,* 1972, *39,* 370–380.

Meichenbaum, D. Towards a cognitive theory of self-control. In G. Schwartz & D. Skopiro (Eds.), *Consciousness and self-regulation: Advances in research.* New York: Plenum, 1975.

Meichenbaum, D., & Cameron, R. Stress innoculation: a skills training approach to anxiety management. Unpublished manuscript, University of Waterloo, 1973.

Meichenbaum, D., & Cameron, R. The clinical potential of modifying what clients say to themselves. *Psychotherapy: Theory, Research and Practice,* 1974, *11,* 103–117.

Meichenbaum, D., Gilmore, J., & Fedoravicius, D. Group insight versus group desensitization in treating speech anxiety. *Journal of Consulting and Clinical Psychology,* 1971, *36,* 410–421.

Meichenbaum, D., & Goodman, J. Training impulsive children to talk to themselves. *Journal of Abnormal Psychology,* 1971, *77,* 115–126.

Meltzoff, J., & Kornreich, M. *Research in psychotherapy.* New York: Atherton, 1971.

Moleski, R., & Tosi, D. Comparative psychotherapy: Rational-emotive therapy versus systematic desensitization in the treatment of stuttering. *Journal of Consulting and Clinical Psychology,* 1976, *44,* 309–311.

Newmark, C. Professional opinions with regard to Ellis' irrational ideas. *Journal of Clinical Psychology,* 1972, *25,* 452–456.

Newmark, C., Frerking, R., Cook, L., & Newmark, L. Endorsement of Ellis' irrational beliefs as a function of psychopathology. *Journal of Clinical Psychology,* 1973, *29,* 300–302.

Nisbett, R. E., & Schachter, S. Cognitive modification of pain. *Journal of Experimental and Social Psychology,* 1966, *2,* 227–236.

Palkes, H., Stewart, W., & Kahana, B. Porteus maze performance of hyperactive boys after training in self-directed verbal commands. *Child Development,* 1968, *39,* 817–826.

Rimm, D. C., & Litvak, S. B. Self-verbalization and emotional arousal. *Journal of Abnormal Psychology,* 1969, *74,* 181–187.

Rimm, D. C., & Masters, J. C. *Behavior therapy: Techniques and empirical findings.* New York: Academic Press, 1974.

Rotter, J. Generalized expectancy for internal versus external control of reinforcement. *Psychological Monographs,* 1966, *80,* No. 1 (Whole No. 609).

Sarason, S. B. *Anxiety in the elementary school.* New York: John Wiley, 1960.

Shostram, E. L. *Handbook of the Personal Orientation Scale.* San Diego, Calif.: Educational and Industrial Testing Service, 1976.

Spielberger, C., Edwards, C., Montouri, J., & Lushene, R. *Children's state-trait anxiety inventory: Preliminary manual.* Palo Alto: Consulting Psychology Press, 1973.

Spielberger, C., Gorsuch, R., & Lushene, R. *State-Trait Anxiety Inventory.* Palo Alto: Consulting Psychology Press, 1975.

Spivack, G., & Shure, M. *Social adjustment of young children*. San Francisco: Jossey-Bass, 1974.

Spivack, G., & Swift, M. *Devereux elementary school behavior rating scale manual*. Devon, Pa.: Devereux Foundation Press, 1967.

Straatmeyer, A. J., & Watkins, J. T. Rational-emotive therapy and the reduction of speech anxiety. *Rational Living*, 1974, 9 (1), 33–37.

Thompson, S. The relative efficacy of desensitization, desensitization with coping imagery, cognitive modification, and rational-emotive therapy with test-anxious college students. Unpublished doctoral dissertation, University of Arkansas, 1974.

Thorpe, G. L. Desensitization, behavioral rehearsal, self-instruction training and placebo effects on assertive-refusal behavior. *European Journal of Behavior Analysis and Modification*, 1975, 1, 30–44.

Tiegerman, S. Effects of assertive training, and cognitive components of rational therapy on the promotion of assertive behavior and the reduction of interpersonal anxiety. Unpublished doctoral dissertation, Hofstra University, 1975.

Trexler, L., & Karst, J. Further validation for a new measure of irrational cognitions. *Journal of Personality Assessment*, 1973, 37, 150–155.

Trexler, L., & Karst, J. Rational-emotive therapy, placebo and no-treatment effects on public speaking anxiety. *Journal of Abnormal Psychology*, 1972, 79, 60–67.

Valins, S. Cognitive effects of false heart-rate feedback. *Journal of Personality and Social Psychology*, 1966, 7, 400–408.

Valins, S., & Ray, A. Effects of cognitive desensitization on avoidance behavior. *Journal of Personality and Social Psychology*, 1967, 7, 345–350.

Velton, E. A. A laboratory task for induction of mood states. *Behavior Research and Therapy*, 1968, 6, 473–482.

Walk, R. D. Self-ratings of fear in a fear-provoking situation. *Journal of Abnormal and Social Psychology*, 1956, 52, 171–178.

Waugh, N. M. Rationality and emotional adjustment: A test of Ellis' theory of rational-emotive therapy. Unpublished doctoral dissertation, Case Western Reserve University, 1975.

Wein, K. S., Nelson, R. O., & Odom, J. V. The relative contribution of reattribution and verbal extinction to the effectiveness of cognitive restructuring. *Behavior Therapy*, 1975, 6, 459–474.

Wessler, R. L. On measuring rationality. *Rational Living*, 1976, 11 (1), 25.

Wine, J. Investigations of attentional interpretations of test anxiety. Unpublished doctoral dissertation, University of Waterloo, 1971.

Wolfe, J. L. Short-term effects of modeling/behavior rehearsal, modeling/behavior rehearsal plus rational therapy, placebo, and no-treatment on assertive behavior. Unpublished doctoral dissertation, New York University, 1975.

Wolfe, J. L., & Fodor, I. G. A cognitive/behavioral approach to modifying assertive behavior in women. *The Counseling Psychologist*, 1975, 5 (4), 45–52.

Wolpe, J. *Psychotherapy by reciprocal inhibition*. Stanford: Stanford University Press, 1958.

Wolpe, J., & Lazarus, A. A. *Behavior therapy techniques*. New York: Pergamon Press, 1966.

Wolpin, M., & Raines, J. Visual imagery, expected roles and extinction as possible roles in reducing fear and avoidance behavior. *Behavior Research and Therapy*, 1966, 9, 3–7.

Young, E. R., Rimm, D. C., & Kennedy, T. D. An experimental investigation of modeling and verbal reinforcement in the modification of assertive behavior. *Behavior Research and Therapy*, 1973, 11, 317–319.

Part Two

The Dynamics
of Emotional Disturbance

4

Psychotherapy and the Value of a Human Being

Albert Ellis

Rational-emotive psychotherapists share with most other theoreticians and practitioners the belief that one's estimation of his or her own value or worth is exceptionally important. Rational-emotive psychotherapists go further than most psychotherapists in viewing the control dynamics of a good many forms of emotional disturbances, no matter what other problems coincide or overlap, as foolishly, unrealistically, and unempirically rating or judging oneself as globally "good" or "bad" as a human being. At the core, many emotionally disturbed people demand that they succeed in being loved or in being successful in their undertakings, lest they rate or condemn themselves as bad, lousy, or unworthy, and feel guilty and depressed. Alternatively, they fear failing in being loved or successful, and end up feeling anxious as well.

In Chapter 4, Albert Ellis elaborates on the dynamics of self-acceptance problems. After making the important distinction between self-acceptance and self-esteem, he shows why self-rating is absurd, theoretically untenable, and virtually always self-defeating. He then enumerates the many negative results of engaging in such a philosophic-cognitive process.

ALMOST ALL MODERN authorities in psychotherapy believe that the individual's estimation of his own value or worth is exceptionally important and that if he seriously denigrates himself or has a poor self-image, he will impair his normal functioning and make himself miserable in many significant ways. The proponents of rational-emotive psychotherapy are no different than most and, in fact, go even further in stressing that a disproportionately high percentage of disturbed people become so because they estimate themselves negatively. Consequently, one of the main functions of psychotherapy is to enhance the individual's self-respect (or "ego strength," "self-confidence," "self-esteem," "feelings of personal worth," or "sense of identity") so that he may thereby solve the

A longer version of Chapter 4 first appeared in *Value and Valuation: Aetiological Studies in Honor of Robert A. Hartman,* ed. William Davis (Knoxville: University of Tennessee Press, 1972).

problem of self-evaluation (see Adler, 1927, 1931; Ellis, 1962, 1966; Ellis and Harper, 1967b; Kelly, 1955; Lecky, 1945; Rogers, 1961).

Moreover, when an individual does not value himself very highly, innumerable other problems result. He frequently will focus so intensely on what a rotten person he is that he will distract himself from problem-solving and will become increasingly inefficient. He may falsely conclude that a rotter such as he can do virtually nothing right, and he may stop trying to succeed at the things he wants to accomplish. He may look at his proven advantages with a jaundiced eye and tend to conclude that he is a "phony" and that people just haven't as yet seen through him. Or he may become so intent on "proving" his value that he will be inclined to grovel for others' favors and approval and will conformingly give up his own desires for what he thinks (rightly or wrongly) they want him to do (Ellis, 1967; Hoffer, 1955; Lecky, 1945; Nietzsche, 1965). He may tend to annihilate himself, either literally or figuratively, as he desperately tries to achieve or to please (Becker, 1964; Hess, 1966; Watzlawick, 1967). He may favor non-commitment and avoidance, and become essentially "nonalive," and he may sabotage many or most of his potentialities for creative living (May, 1969). He may become obsessed with comparing himself to others and their achievements and tend to be status-seeking rather than joy-exploring (Farson, 1966; Harris, 1963). He may frequently be anxious, panicked, terrified (Branden, 1964; Ellis, 1962; Coopersmith, 1968; Rosenberg, 1962). He may tend to be a short-range hedonist and to lack self-discipline (Hoffer, 1955). Often he may become defensive and thus act in a "superior," grandiose way (Adler, 1964; Anderson, 1962, 1964; Low, 1967). He may compensatingly assume an unusually rough or "masculine" manner (Adler, 1931; Maslow, 1966). He may become quite hostile toward others (Anderson, 1964; Low, 1967). He may become exceptionally depressed (Anderson, 1964). He may withdraw from reality and retreat into fantasy (Coopersmith, 1968; Rosenberg, 1962). He may become exceptionally guilty (Ellis, 1967; Geis, 1965). He may present a great false front to the world (Rosenberg, 1962). He may sabotage a number of special talents which he possesses (Coopersmith, 1968). He may easily become conscious of his lack of self-approval, may berate himself for having little or no confidence in himself, and may thereby reduce his self-image even more than he has done previously (Ellis, 1962; Ellis and Harper, 1967). He may become afflicted with numerous psychosomatic reactions, which then encourage him to defame himself still more (Coopersmith, 1968; Rosenberg, 1962).

An obvious question therefore presents itself: If the individual's perception of his own value or worth so importantly affects his thoughts, emotions, and actions, how and why does a person foolishly denigrate him-

self and how is it possible to help him consistently to appraise himself so
that, no matter what kind of performances he achieves and no matter how
popular or unpopular he is in his relations with others, he almost invariably accepts or respects himself? Oddly enough, modern psychotherapy
has not often posed this question—at least not in the form just stated. Instead, it has fairly consistently asked another, and actually almost antitheti-
cal, question: Since the individual's self-acceptance seems to depend on
(1) his succeeding or achieving reasonably well in his society and on (2)
his having good relations with others, how can he be helped to accomplish
these two goals and thereby to achieve self-esteem?

The answer, I think, lies in the distinction between self-acceptance and
self-esteem. At first blush they appear to be very similar; but actually,
when they are clearly defined, they are quite different. Self-esteem—as it
is fairly consistently used by Branden (1964), Rand (1961, 1964), and
other devotees of Ayn Rand's objectivist philosophy—means that the individual values himself because he has behaved intelligently, correctly, or
competently. When taken to its logical extremes, it "is the consequence,
expression and reward of a mind *fully* committed to reason" (Branden,
1965; italics mine); and "an *unbreached rationality*—that is, an unbreached determination to use one's mind to the fullest extent of one's
ability, and a refusal *ever* to evade one's knowledge or act against it—
is the *only* valid criterion of virtue and the *only* possible basis of authentic
self-esteem" (Branden, 1967; italics mine).

While this is a highly interesting position, there is a great deal of trouble
with the inelegance of its philosophic premise. Granted that man's thinking of himself as bad or worthless is usually pernicious and that his thinking of himself as good or worthwhile is more beneficial, I see no reason
why these two hypotheses exhaust the possibilities of useful choices. I believe, instead, that there is a third choice that is much more philosophically
elegant, less definitional, and more likely to conform to empirical reality.
And that is the seldom-posited assumption that value is a meaningless term
when applied to man's being, that it is invalid to call him either "good" or
"bad," and that if educators and psychotherapists can teach people to
give up all "ego" concepts and to have no "self-images" whatever, they
may considerably help the human dilemma and enable men and women
to be much less emotionally disturbed than they now tend to be.

This is the essence of self-acceptance. Self-acceptance means that the
individual fully and unconditionally accepts himself whether or not he
behaves intelligently, correctly, or competently and whether or not other
people approve, respect, or love him (Bone, 1968; Ellis, 1962, 1966;
Rogers, 1961). Whereas, therefore, only well-behaving (not to mention
perfectly behaving) individuals can merit and feel self-esteem, virtually

all humans are capable of feeling self-acceptance. And since the number of consistently well-behaving individuals in this world appears usually to be exceptionally small and the number of exceptionally fallible and often ill-behaving persons appears to be legion, the consistent achievement of self-esteem by most of us would seem to be remote while the steady feeling of self-acceptance would seem to be quite attainable.

Must man actually be a self-evaluator? Yes and no. On the yes side, he clearly seems to be the kind of animal who is not merely reared but is also born with strong self-evaluating tendencies, as I stated in the first chapter of this handbook. For nowhere in the world, to my knowledge, does civilized man simply accept that he is alive, go about the business of discovering how he can enjoy himself more and discomfort himself less, and live his century or so of existence in a reasonably unselfconscious, nondamning, and nondeifying manner. Instead he invariably seems to identify and rate his *self* as well as his *performances,* to be highly ego-involved about accomplishing this and avoiding that deed, and to believe and feel strongly that he will end up in some kind of heaven or hell if he does the "right" and eschews the "wrong" thing.

But, is it really worth it? Does man absolutely have to rate himself as a person and evaluate others as people? My tentative answer to both these questions, after spending a quarter of a century busily engaged as a psychotherapist, writer, teacher, and lecturer, is: "No." By very hardheaded thinking, along with active work and practice, he can persistently fight against and minimize this tendency; if he does, he will, in all probability, be considerably healthier and happier than he usually is. Instead of strongly evaluating his and other people's selves, he can pretty rigorously stick to rating only performances; instead of damning or deifying anyone or anything, he can adhere to reality and be truly demonless and godless; and instead of inventing demands and needs, he can remain with desires and preferences. If he does so, I hypothesize, he will not achieve utopia (which itself is changeless, absolutistic, and unrealistic), but he most probably will achieve more spontaneity, creativity, and satisfaction than he has ever previously achieved or presently tends to attain.

I have illustrated this human tendency with a typical case of rational-emotive psychotherapy in the first chapter of this handbook. Arnold Lazarus does so in "Toward an Egoless State of Being," Chapter 5 of this book. Rather than spending additional time on another clinical example, I will detail some of the main reasons for my espousing man's taking a nonevaluative attitude toward himself (while still evaluating many of his traits and performances):

1. Both positive and negative self-evaluation are inefficient and often seriously interfere with problem-solving. If one elevates or defames him-

self because of his performances, he will tend to be self-centered rather than problem-centered, and these performances will, consequently, tend to suffer. Self-evaluation, moreover, is usually ruminative and absorbs enormous amounts of time and energy. By it one may possibly cultivate his "soul" but hardly his garden!

2. Self-rating only works well when one has many talents and few flaws; but, statistically speaking, few are in that class. It also tends to demand universal competence. But, again, few can measure up to such a demand.

3. Self-appraisal almost inevitably leads to one-upmanship and one-downmanship. If one rates himself as being "good," he will usually rate others as being "bad" or "less good." If he rates himself as being "bad," others will be seen as "less bad" or "good." Thereby he practically forces himself to compete with others in "goodness" or "badness" and constantly feels envious, jealous, or superior. Persistent individual, group, and international conflicts easily stem from this kind of thinking and feeling; love, cooperation, and other forms of fellow-feeling are minimized. To see oneself as having a better or worse *trait* than another person may be unimportant or even beneficial (since one may use his knowledge of another's superior trait to help achieve that trait himself). But to see oneself as being a better or worse *person* than another is likely to cause trouble for both.

4. Self-evaluation enhances self-consciousness and therefore tends to shut one up within himself, to narrow his range of interests and enjoyments. "It should be our endeavor," said Bertrand Russell, "to aim at avoiding self-centered passions and at acquiring those affections and those interests which will prevent our thoughts from dwelling perpetually upon ourselves. It is not the nature of most men to be happy in a prison, and the passions which shut us up in ourselves constitute one of the worst kinds of prisons. Among such passions some of the commonest are fear, envy, the sense of sin, self-pity, and self-admiration" (Russell, 1952).

5. Blaming or praising the whole individual for a few of his acts is an unscientific overgeneralization. "I have called the process of converting a child mentally into something else, whether it be a monster or a mere nonentity, *pathogenic metamorphosis*," Jules Henry declared. "Mrs. Portman called [her son] Pete 'a human garbage pail'; she said to him, 'you smell, you stink'; she kept the garbage bag and refuse newspapers on his high chair when he was not in it; she called him Mr. Magoo, and never used his right name. Thus he was a stinking monster, a nonentity, a buffoon" (Henry, 1963). But Henry failed to point out that had Mrs. Portman called her son, Pete, "an angel" and said to him, "you smell heavenly," she would have equally converted him, by the process of

pathogenic metamorphosis, into something he was not; namely, a godlike being. Peter is a human person who sometimes smells bad (or heavenly); he is not a *bad-smelling* (or heavenly-smelling) *person*.

6. When human selves are lauded or condemned there is a strong implication that people should be rewarded or punished for being "good" or "bad." But, as noted above, if there were "bad" people, they would already be so handicapped by their "rottenness" that it would be thoroughly unfair to punish them further for being "rotten." And if there were "good" people, they would already be so favored by their "goodness" that it would be superfluous or unjust to reward them for it. Human justice, therefore, is very badly served by self-evaluations.

7. To rate a person high because of his good traits is often tantamount to deifying him; conversely, to rate him low because of his bad traits is tantamount to demonizing him. But since there seems to be no way of validating the existence of gods and devils and since man can well live without this redundant hypothesis, it merely clutters human thinking and acting and probably does much more harm than good. Concepts of god and the devil, moreover, obviously vary enormously from person to person and from group to group; they add nothing to human knowledge; and they usually serve as obstructions to precise intrapersonal and interpersonal communication. Although it is possible that people who behave stupidly and weakly may derive benefits from inventing supernatural beings, there is no evidence that those who act intelligently and strongly have any need of them.

8. Bigotry and lack of respect for individuals in their own right are consequences of self- and other-evaluation. For if you accept A because he is white, Episcopalian, and well-educated and reject B because he is black, Baptist, and a high school dropout, you are clearly not respecting B as a human—and, of course, are intolerantly disrespecting millions of people like him. Bigotry is arbitrary, unjust, and conflict-creating; it is ineffective for social living. As George Axtelle has noted, "Men are profoundly social creatures. They can realize their own ends more fully only as they respect one another as ends in themselves. Mutual respect is an essential condition of effectiveness both individually and socially. Its opposites, hatred, contempt, segregation, exploitation, frustrate the realization of values for all concerned and hence they are profoundly destructive of all effectiveness" (Axtelle, 1956). Once you damn an individual, including yourself, for having or lacking any trait whatever, you become authoritarian or fascistic; for fascism is the very essence of people-evaluation (Ellis, 1965a, 1965b).

9. By evaluating an individual, even if only in a complimentary way, one is often trying to change him or trying to control or manipulate him;

and the kind of change envisioned may or may not be good for him. "Often," Richard Farson notes, "the change which praise asks one to make is not necessarily beneficial to the person being praised but will redound to the convenience, pleasure or profit of the praiser" (Farson, 1966). Evaluation may induce the individual to feel obligated to his evaluator; to the degree that he lets himself feel compelled or obligated to change himself, he may be much less of the self that he would really like to be. Positive or negative evaluation of a person, therefore, may well encourage him to be less of a self or of a self-directed individual than he would enjoy being.

10. Evaluation of the individual tends to bolster the Establishment and to block social change. For when one gives himself a report card he not only becomes accustomed to telling himself, "My deeds are wrong, and I think I'd better work at improving them in the future," but also, "I am wrong, I am a 'no-goodnik' for performing these poor deeds." Since "wrong" acts are largely measured by societal standards, and since most societies are run by a limited number of "upper level" people who have a strong, vested interest in keeping them the way they are, self-evaluation usually encourages the individual to go along with social rules, no matter how arbitrary or foolish they are, and especially to woo the approval of the powers that be. Conformism, which is one of the worst products of self-rating, generally means conformity to the time-honored and justice-dishonoring rules of the "Establishment."

11. Self-appraisal and the measuring of others tends to sabotage empathic listening. Close and authentic relationships between two people, as Richard Farson points out, are often achieved through intensive listening: "This does not merely mean to wait for a person to finish talking, but to try to see how the world looks to this person and to communicate this understanding to him. This empathic, non-evaluative listening responds to the person's feelings as well as to his words; that is, to the total meaning of what he is trying to say. It implies no evaluation, no judgment, no agreement (or disagreement). It simply conveys an understanding of what the person is feeling and attempting to communicate; and his feelings and ideas are accepted as being valid for him, if not for the listener" (Farson, 1966). When, however, one evaluates a person (and oneself) as one listens to the other person, one is usually prejudicedly blocked from fully understanding him, seeing him as he is, and uncompetitively understanding and getting close to him.

12. Person-rating tends to denigrate human wants, desires, and preferences and to replace them with demands, compulsions, or needs. If you do not measure your selfness, you tend to spend your days asking yourself, "Now what would I really like to do, in my relatively brief span of existence, to gain maximum satisfaction and minimum pain?" If you do

measure your selfhood, you tend to keep asking, "What do I have to do to prove that I am a worthwhile person?" As Richard Robertiello has observed, "People are constantly negating their right to take something just purely because they want it, to enjoy something simply because they enjoy it. They can hardly ever let themselves take anything for pure pleasure without justifying it on the basis of having earned it or suffered enough to be entitled to it or rationalizing that, though they enjoy it, it is really an altruistic act that they are doing for someone else's good. . . . It seems as if the greatest crime is to do something simply because we enjoy it and without any thought of doing good for anyone else or of serving an absolute need in us that is essential for our continued survival" (Robertiello, 1964). Such is the folly born of self-deservingness!

13. Placing a value on a human being tends to sabotage his free will. One has little enough self-direction in the normal course of events! Even his most "voluntary" activities are significantly influenced by his heredity and environment; when he thinks that one of his thoughts, feelings, or actions is really "his," he is ignoring some of its most important biosocial causes. As soon as one labels himself as "good" or "bad," as a "genius" or as an "idiot," he so seriously stereotypes himself that he will almost certainly bias and influence much of his subsequent behavior. For how can a "bad person" or an "idiot" determine, even to a small degree, what his future actions will be, and how can he work hard at achieving his goals? Moreover, how can a "good person" do non-good acts, or a "genius" turn out mediocre works along with his outstanding ones? What asinine, creativity-downing restrictions one almost automatically places on himself when he thinks in terms of these general designations of his selfness!

14. To give a human an accurate global rating is probably impossible for several reasons:

a. The traits by which he is to be rated are very likely to change from year to year, even from moment to moment. Man is not a thing or an object, but a process. How can an ever-changing process be precisely measured and rated?

b. The characteristics by which a person is to be evaluated have no absolute scale by which they can be judged. Traits which are highly honored in one social group are roundly condemned in another. A murderer may be seen as a horrible criminal by a judge but as a marvelous soldier by a general. A man's qualities (such as his ability to compose music) may be deemed fine in one century and mediocre in a later age.

c. To rate a human globally, special weights would have to be given to each kind of positive and negative action that he performed. Thus, if a man did a friend a small favor and also worked very hard to save a hundred people from drowning, his latter act would normally be given a much higher rating than his former act; if he told a lie to his wife and also battered a child, his second deed would be considered much more heinous than his first. But who is to give an exact weight to his various deeds, so that it could finally be determined how globally "good" or "bad" he is? It might be convenient if there existed on earth some kind of St. Peter, who would have a record of every single one of his deeds (and, for that matter, his thoughts) and who could quickly assess him as a potential angel or as hell-bound. But what is the likelihood of such a St. Peter's ever existing (even in the form of an infallible computer)?

d. What kind of mathematics could we employ to arrive at a single, total rating of a human being's worth? Suppose an individual does a thousand good acts, and then he fiendishly tortures someone to death. Shall we, to arrive at a general evaluation of his being, add up all his good acts arithmetically and compare this sum to the weighted sum of his bad act? Shall we, instead, use some geometric means of assessing his "goodness" and "badness"? What system shall we employ to "accurately" measure his "value"? Is there, really, any valid kind of mathematical evaluation by which he can be rated?

e. No matter how many traits of an individual are known and employed for his global rating, since it is quite impossible for him or anyone else to discover all his characteristics and to use them in arriving at a single universal rating, in the final analysis the whole of him is being evaluated by some of his parts. But is it ever really legitimate to rate a whole individual by some (or even many) of his parts? Even one unknown, and hence unevaluated, part might significantly change and, hence invalidate the final rating. Suppose, for example, the individual is given (by himself or others) a 91% general rating (that is, is considered to have 91% of "goodness"). If he unconsciously hated his brother most of his life and actually brought about the early demise of this brother, but if he consciously only remembers loving his brother and presumably helping him to live happily, he will rate himself (and anyone but an all-knowing St. Peter will rate him) considerably higher than if he consciously admitted his hatred for his brother and causing this brother needless harm. His "real" rating, therefore, will be considerably lower than 91%; but how will this "real" rating ever be known?

f. If an individual is given a very low global rating by himself and others—say, he winds up with a 13% general report card on himself—it presumably means that: (1) he was born a worthless individual; (2) he never possibly could become worthwhile; and (3) he deserves to be punished (and ultimately roasted in some kind of hell) for being hope-

lessly worthless. All of these are empirically unverifiable hypotheses which
can hardly be proved or disproved and which tend (as stated above) to
bring about much more harm than good.

g. Measuring a human being is really a form of circular thinking. If a
man is "good" because he has "good" traits, his "goodness," in both
instances, is based on some kind of value system that is definitional; for
who, again, except some kind of deity is to say what "good" traits truly
are? Once his traits are defined as being "good," and his global "goodness" is deduced from his specific "goodnesses," the concept of his being
globally "good" will almost inevitably prejudice one's view of his specific
traits—which will then seem "more good" than they really may be. And
once his traits are defined as being "bad," the concept of his being
globally "bad" will almost inevitably prejudice one's view of his specific
traits—which will then seem "more bad" than they really may be. If the
"good" traits of a person who is rated as being globally "good" are
prejudicedly seen as being "more good" than they really are, one will
keep seeing him, by prejudice, as being "good," when he may not actually
be. Globally rating him, in other words, includes making a prophecy
about his specific "good" traits; rating his specific traits as "good" includes
making a prophecy about his global "goodness." Both these prophecies,
in all probability, will turn out to be "true," whatever the facts of his
specific and general "goodness" actually are; for "goodness" itself can
never accurately be determined, since the entire edifice of "goodness" is
based, as I have said, on concepts which are largely definitional.

h. Perhaps the only sensible way of making a global rating of an individual is on the basis of his aliveness: that is, assuming that he is intrinsically good just because he is human and alive (and that he will be
nongood or nonexistent when he is dead). Similarly, we can hypothesize, if we want to accept redundant and unnecessary religious assumptions, that an individual is good because he is human and because Jehovah,
Jesus, or some other deity in whom he believes, accepts, loves, or gives
grace to all humans. This is a rather silly assumption, since we know (as
well as we know anything) that the individual who believes in this assumed deity exists, while we have no way of proving the existence (or
nonexistence) of the deity in which he believes. Nonetheless, such an
assumption will work, in that it will refer back to the more basic assumption that a human is globally "good" just because he is human and alive.
The trouble with this basic concept of general human "goodness" is that it
obviously puts *all* humans in the same boat—makes them all equally
"good" and leaves no room whatever for any of them to be "bad." Consequently, it is a global rating that is not really a rating, and it is entirely
definitional and is rather meaningless.

i. The concept of giving any human a general or global evaluation may be an artifact of the inaccurate way in which almost all humans think and communicate with themselves and each other. Korzybski (1933, 1951) and some of his main followers, such as Hayakawa (1965) and Bourland (*Time* magazine, 1969), have pointed out for a good many years that just as pencil$_1$ is not the same thing as pencil$_2$, so individual$_1$ is hardly the same as individual$_2$. Consequently, generalizing about pencils and about individuals is never entirely accurate. Bourland has especially campaigned, for the last decade, against our using any form of the verb *to be* when we speak about or categorize the behavior of a person. Thus, it is one thing for us to note that "Jones has (or possesses) some outstanding mathematical qualities" and another to say that "Jones is an outstanding mathematician." The former sentence is much more precise and probably "truer" than the latter. The latter sentence, moreover, implies a global rating of Jones that is hardly warranted by the facts, if these can be substantiated, of Jones's possessing some mathematical qualities. If Korzybski and his followers are correct, as they in all probability are (at least to some degree), than global terms and ratings of humans are easily made (indeed, it is most difficult for us not to make them) but would better be fought against and transformed into more specific evaluations of their performances, talents, and traits. Such generalized (or overgeneralized) grades exist (since we obviously keep employing them), but it would be much better if we minimized or eliminated them.

j. All of man's traits are different—as apples and pears are different. Just as one cannot legitimately add and divide apples and pears and thereby get a single, accurate, global rating of an entire basket of fruit, so one cannot truly add and divide different human traits and thereby obtain a single, meaningful, global rating of a human individual.

What conclusions can be drawn from the foregoing observations and deductions about psychotherapy and human value? First, that self-reference and self-evaluation are a normal and natural part of man. It seems to be much easier for him to rate his self, his being, as well as his performances, than it is for him only to assess the latter and not the former.

When man does appraise himself *globally,* he almost invariably gets into trouble. When he terms himself "bad," "inferior," or "inadequate," he tends to feel anxious, guilty, and depressed, and to falsely confirm his low estimation of himself. When he terms himself "good," "superior," or "adequate," he tends to feel forever unsure of maintaining his "goodness," to spend considerable time and energy "proving" how worthwhile he is, but still to sabotage his relations with himself and others.

Ideally, it would seem wise for man to train himself, through rigorous thinking about and working against some of his strongest inborn and environmentally bolstered tendencies, to refuse to evaluate himself at all. He had better continue, as objectively as he can, to assess his traits, talents, and performances, so that he can thereby lead a longer, pain-avoiding, and satisfaction-filled life. But, for many reasons which are considered in detail in this chapter, he would better also accept rather than rate his so-called self and strive for the enjoyment rather than the justification of his existence. According to Freud (1963), the individual attains mental health when he follows the rule. "Where id was, there shall ego be." Freud, however, did not mean by *ego* man's self-evaluating but his self-directing tendencies. According to my own views (Ellis, 1962, 1966, 1968, 1971) and the principles of rational-emotive therapy, man attains maximum understanding of himself and others and minimum anxiety and hostility when he follows the rule "Where ego was, there shall the person be." By *ego,* of course, I mean man's self-rating and self-justifying tendencies.

For man, as an individual living with other individuals in a world with which he interacts, is too complex to be measured or given a report card. He may be legitimately "valued," in the sense of accepting and abiding by the empirically determinable facts that (1) he exists, (2) he can suffer satisfaction and pain while he exists, (3) it is usually within his power to continue to exist and to experience more satisfaction than pain, and (4) it is therefore highly probable that he "deserves" to (that is, would better) go on existing and enjoying. Or, more succinctly stated, man has value because he decides to remain alive and to value his existence. Observations and conclusions other than those based on these minimal assumptions may well be foolishly egocentric and fictional, and in the final analysis human—all too human, but still essentially inhumane.

References

Adler, Alfred. *Understanding Human Nature*. New York: Greenberg, 1927.
———. *What Life Should Mean to You*. New York: Greenberg, 1931.
———. *Social Interest: A Challenge to Mankind*. New York: Capricorn, 1964.
Anderson, Camilla. *Saints, Sinners and Psychiatry*. Portland, Ore.: Commonwealth Fund, 1962.
———. "Depression and Suicide Reassessed." Reprint from *Journal of the American Medical Women's Association* (June, 1964).
Axtelle, George E. "Effectiveness as a Value Concept." *Journal of Educational Sociology,* 29 (1956): 240–46.
Becker, Ernest. *The Revolution in Psychiatry*. New York: Free Press, 1964.
Bone, Harry. "Two proposed alternatives to psychoanalytic interpreting." In Emmanuel F. Hammer, ed. *Use of Interpretation in Treatment*. New York and London: Grune & Stratton, 1968, pp. 160–96.
Bourland, D. David. "Language." *Time* (May 23, 1969): p. 69.

Branden, Nathaniel. "Pseudo-Self-Esteem." *Objective Newsletter,* 3, No. 6 (June, 1964): pp. 22–23.

———. *Who Is Ayn Rand?* New York: New American Library, 1965.

———. "Self-esteem." *Objectivist,* 6 (March, 1967): pp. 1–17; (April, 1967): pp. 5–10; (May, 1967): pp. 8–10; (June, 1967): pp. 5–8.

Coopersmith, Stanley. "Studies in Self-esteem." *Scientific Monthly,* 218, No. 2 (February, 1968): pp. 96–106.

Danielsson, Bengt. *Love in the South Seas.* New York: Reynal, 1956.

———. "Sex Life in Polynesia." In Albert Ellis and Albert Abarbanel, eds. *The Encyclopedia of Sexual Behavior.* New York: Hawthorn, 1967, pp. 832–40.

Ellis, Albert. *Reason and Emotion in Psychotherapy.* New York: Lyle Stuart, 1962.

———. *Sex Without Guilt.* New York: Lyle Stuart, 1965a.

———. *Suppressed: Seven Key Essays Publishers Dared Not Print.* Chicago: New-classics House, 1965b.

———, with Janet L. Wolfe and Sandra Moseley. *How to Prevent Your Child From Becoming a Neurotic Adult.* New York: Crown, 1966.

———. "Psychotherapy and Moral Laxity." *Psychiatric Opinion,* 4, No. 5 (1967a): pp. 18–21.

——— and Robert A. Harper. *A Guide to Rational Living.* Englewood Cliffs, N.J.: Prentice-Hall, 1967b.

———. *Is Objectivism a Religion?* New York: Lyle Stuart, 1968.

——— and John M. Gullo. *Murder and Assassination.* New York: Lyle Stuart, 1970.

———. *Growth Through Reason.* Palo Alto: Science & Behavior Books, 1971.

Farson, Richard A. "A Praise Reappraised." *Encounter,* No. 1 (1966): pp. 13–21. Reprinted from *Harvard Business Review* (September-October, 1963).

Freud, Sigmund. *Collected Papers.* New York: Doubleday-Anchor, 1963.

Geis, H. Jon. "Guilt Feelings and Inferiority Feelings: An Experimental Comparison." Ph.D dissertation, Columbia University, 1965.

Harris, Sydney J. "A Man's Worth Is Not Relative." *Detroit Free Press* (December 12, 1963).

Hartman, Robert S. *The Measurement of Value.* Crotonville, N.Y.: General Electric, 1959.

———. "Sputnick's Moral Challenge." *Texas Quarterly,* 3, No 3. (Autumn, 1960): pp. 9–22.

———. *The Individual in Management.* Chicago: Nationwide Insurance, 1962.

———. *The Structure of Value.* Carbondale, Ill.: Southern Illinois University Press, 1967a.

———. Letter to Albert Ellis, June 27, 1967b.

Hayakawa, S. I. *Language in Action.* New York: Harcourt, Brace, 1965.

Henry, Jules. *Culture Against Man.* New York: Random House, 1963.

Hess, John L. "Michelin's Two Stars Lost, Paris Chef Shoots Himself." *New York Times* (October 14, 1966).

Hoffer, Eric. *The Passionate State of Mind.* New York: Harper, 1955.

Kelly, George. *The Psychology of Personal Constructs.* New York: Norton, 1955.

Korzybski, Alfred. *Science and Sanity.* Lancaster Pa.: Lancaster Press, 1933.

———. "The Role of Language in the Perceptual Process." In R. R. Blake and G. V. Ramsey, eds. *Perception.* New York: Ronald Press, 1951, pp. 170–202.

Lecky, Prescott. *Self-consistency.* New York: Island Press, 1945.

Low, Abraham. *Lectures to Relatives of Former Patients.* Boston: Christopher, 1967.

Marston, Albert R. "Self Reinforcement: The Relevance of a Concept in Analogue Research to Psychotherapy." *Psychotherapy* (Winter, 1965): p. 2.

Maslow, Abraham H. *The Psychology of Science.* New York: Macmillan, 1966.

May, Rollo. *Psychology and the Human Dilemma.* Princeton: Van Nostrand, 1967.

———. *Love and Will.* New York: Norton, 1969.

Nietzsche, F. W. In H. J. Blackman, ed. *Reality, Man and Existence: Essential Works of Existentialism.* New York: Bantam, 1961.

Rand, Ayn. *For the New Intellectual.* New York: New American Library, 1961.
————. *The Virtue of Selfishness.* New York: New American Library, 1964.
Robertiello, Richard. *Sexual Fulfillment and Self-Affirmation.* Larchmont: Argonaut, 1964.
Rogers, C. C. *On Becoming a Person.* Boston: Houghton Mifflin, 1961.
Rosenberg, Morris. "The Association Between Self-Esteem and Anxiety." *Psychiatric Research* 1 (1962): pp. 135–52.
Russell, Bertrand. *The Conquest of Happiness.* New York: Bantam, 1952.
Watzlawick, P., and others. *Pragmatics of Human Communication.* New York: Norton, 1967.

5

Toward an Egoless
State of Being

Arnold A. Lazarus

*In Chapter 5, Arnold Lazarus gives some excerpts from a therapy session
in which the client and therapist confront the patient's global self-rating
and discuss its detrimental effects. As does Ellis, Lazarus recognizes that
self-condemnation problems are at the core of most human suffering.
Lazarus discusses some of the exercises in his multimodal therapy which
enabled the client to overcome his severe public-speaking anxiety.*

AMONG THE MOST perniciously self-destructive habits of thought
and action is the widespread tendency to place one's "ego" on the
line. This unfortunate proclivity is probably at the core of most
fallacious thinking. The "overgeneralized self" is involved in errors of
absolutistic thinking, poor "self-worth," blaming and damning, categorical
imperatives, and a host of other crazy-making propensities that RET so
aptly underscores. Inappropriate and overextended ego-involvement is
probably responsible for the bulk of anxiety, guilt, and depression-related
reactions from which so many people suffer. Effective therapy succeeds
in showing clients how to dissociate a unitary "self" from the numerous
situations that pervade their lives. Instead, emphasis is placed upon clients
learning to see a plurality of "selves" across innumerable situations.

The rational therapist endeavors to impart the knowledge that the concept of "ego" or "self" amounts to one's *total being*. It comprises every
conceivable role, action, value, belief, attitude, etc. that occurs throughout one's life. When our clients make statements such as, "I am useless!"
we point out that this implies a self-statement that they are of zero value
in all areas of life—useless as a son, brother, husband, father, friend,
acquaintance, colleague, movie-goer, theater-lover, tennis player, oyster-
eater, plus innumerable other roles and activities that constitute the
"self." We teach our clients about the profound differences between
statements such as "I am a failure," versus "I failed in that particular
situation." And even more elegantly and thoroughly, we school them in
the virtues of adopting E-prime (Ellis, 1975), so that the " 'is' of identity"
no longer contaminates and confuses their sense of being. The following
excerpts from a therapy session illustrate the dynamics of "self-esteem"

113

or "ego" problems. They also describe some techniques that have been helpful in achieving the aforementioned ends. A specific case study is helpful in conveying precisely how placing one's "ego" on the line leads to anxiety and also shows ways in which egolessness as an antidote to anxiety was successfully administered as part of a multimodal treatment program (Lazarus, 1976).

A Case of Public-Speaking Anxiety

A young professional man whose occupation called for a considerable amount of public speaking found himself acutely anxious whenever addressing audiences in excess of five or six people. He had been forcing himself over a period of three years not to avoid these speech-making situations, but his anxiety had only become more intense over time. A behavior therapist had attempted to desensitize him, but the client found himself temperamentally unsuited to relaxation training. He commented: "It made me feel even more tense, bored and restless!" He was unable to picture images with sufficient clarity to engender anxiety.

By the time he consulted me, he felt that his job was in jeopardy and this heightened his specific fears. Below is the dialogue which ensued.

THERAPIST   What would happen if your employer called you in and told you to start looking for another job?

CLIENT   I know what you're getting at. So it wouldn't be the end of the world, and it wouldn't be awful or terrible. But it would be a damn sight more than merely inconvenient. First off, I get a salary that would be very tough to duplicate in this day of economic uncertainty and besides, there are chances for advancement and promotion that far exceed just about anything I am likely to get elsewhere. I've read Ellis and I am not demanding or insisting that I must or should hold onto this job, but it does go a bit deeper than merely preferring to live in the style to which I am accustomed. I want to very much, and that strikes me as perfectly sane. But long before the job was at stake I got uptight when giving talks. Now we just have another real threat added to it.

THERAPIST   Despite your words to the contrary, I think that you are insisting and demanding that you *should* not have to compromise your standard of living.

CLIENT   Well, let me ask you the same thing. Suppose you were banned from practicing psychotherapy and from teaching psychology. I mean how would you feel?

THERAPIST   Are you implying that the loss of your job would be identical to my being expelled from the fields of psychology and psychotherapy?

CLIENT   No, I realize that you have invested far more time and effort and all that into your career, but what I'm driving at is that you would be more than "inconvenienced" if you had to find a new way of earning a living.

THERAPIST   Sure, it would be extremely inconvenient and very disruptive, but hardly catastrophic.

CLIENT   Oh, come now!

THERAPIST   Here's the crucial factor. Are you listening? I want you to hear this very clearly. *I am not a psychotherapist. I am a person who practices psychotherapy.* Suppose I'm kicked out of psychology and I'm looking around for another career and a new source of income. I study, take some exams and end up teaching high school English.

CLIENT   And now you have less income and less status and less prestige. You would probably sell your house and move into a less expensive neighborhood. . . .

THERAPIST   But I can envision myself still being reasonably happy and fulfilled despite adopting a different modus vivendi. I am still the same person, the same husband, father, friend, brother. . . .

CLIENT   You might lose some so-called friends.

THERAPIST   And I might gain others.

CLIENT   But I wonder how many people really like us for ourselves?

THERAPIST   Is there such an entity as a "self"? What does it mean to be "liked for one's self?" I suppose that there are certain continuities in behavior that let us make predictions about our responses and other people's reactions in different situations, but we are still talking about *behavior*. If people like me for "myself" it means that they value or respect the way I behave at various times and across different situations.

CLIENT   That's my point! No matter what situation you are in you are always responded to by others as Dr. Lazarus. But if you had to eke out a living in trying to teach kids how to punctuate sentences, a lot of people might decide that you are no longer worth having over for dinner—if you see what I mean.

THERAPIST   So what you seem to be saying is that in your own life situation, you cannot really see yourself adjusting to an entirely different lifestyle.

CLIENT   Wait a minute. Please answer my question first. How would you feel about being dropped by many people who are presently in your social circle?

THERAPIST   My *friends* get a lot more from me than my professional expertise. Some of my acquaintances might drop me, but they would be replaced by other casual contacts. And this is not true across the board. The people who play tennis with me are not interested in my occupation. The people with whom I play cards, enjoy music, go bowling, or boating would not reject me. My wife and children would not desert me. . . .

CLIENT   How can you be so sure? Perhaps your wife might stick it out, but she would doubtless let you know about her basic resentment in other ways.

THERAPIST So I have to actively practice psychotherapy in order to maintain the love of my wife, the caring of my children, the respect of my friends. According to you, my occupation is at the core of my very existence. No wonder you become so anxious when speaking in public. Your whole being is under the gun. If you give a poor performance, everything can be threatened. It's not merely your job that is on trial, but as you stand before the audience, you are on trial as an employee, a husband, a friend, as a total person. If someone warned me that the next time I gave a public talk, I would lose everything—job, home, friends, family, self-respect— unless I gave a sterling performance, I too would be anxious.

CLIENT   (*long pause*) Do you think that's it?

THERAPIST I'm pretty sure that is a large part of the problem.

CLIENT   You could be right. So where can I start?

THERAPIST Well, how about developing an *image* in which you see yourself losing your job and ending up with less lucrative and less prestigious work but nonetheless retaining the full love and respect of your wife, family, and friends? Do you think that you can really develop that scenario? Would you practice that image at least twice a day?

CLIENT   Yes, I'll work at that if you think it would help.

THERAPIST Do you understand exactly what I would like you to accomplish in the image?

CLIENT   Yes. I will picture myself in a less gainful life circumstance but without the loss of my wife and friends.

THERAPIST Can you picture something like that right now?

CLIENT   (*closes his eyes*) I'll need some time to make it feel for real. Yes, I'll practice it. But I have an immediate problem. Tomorrow I am scheduled to give a presentation at work and, if I am to judge from past experience, I'll go through hell.

THERAPIST Tomorrow while giving your presentation I want you to focus on something you have never done before. Instead of trying to minimize your feelings of anxiety and seeking to escape from them, I want you to study them with extreme attention. Examine precisely how every part of your body reacts while you are anxious. I want you to study all of your *senses*. How every part reacts from the top of your head to the soles of your feet. Afterwards I want you to write down as much as you can remember in meticulous detail. I'm asking you to note if there are different sensations in each finger, whether your toes, ankles, calves, knees, thighs, hips, back, stomach, chest, arms, shoulders, neck, throat, face, lips, tongue, eyes, nose, forehead, scalp are affected in any way. Examine your sense of smell, taste, sight, hearing. Do you tremble? If so where and how? Do you get hot and cold, neither, just one or the other? In other words, study every minute sensation in tremendous detail.

CLIENT   But what will that achieve? Won't it make me even more anxious?

THERAPIST   Most people find that by focusing on all the sensory concomitants of anxiety, the negative feelings not only diminish but also often disappear. Are you willing to test it out?

CLIENT   But what if it makes me feel worse?

THERAPIST   "What if." That's the prime anxiety thought. Try putting a "so" in front of it. "So what if it makes me worse? Then I'll know not to do it in future." But my hypothesis is that sensory focusing will lessen the unpleasant feelings—if you really get into them.

CLIENT   I'd hate to make a fool of myself.

THERAPIST   There you go again putting your entire being on the line. Here's a simple technique that might help you. Tomorrow, instead of saying "I am giving a speech," think of your "self" not as one big *"I"* but as a whole complex of iiiiiiiiii's. Each little *"i"* corresponds to some facet of your being. So tomorrow, instead of saying "*I* am giving a speech," consider the fact that *you* are not on trial. It's not the total you. Think instead: "*i* am giving a speech."

CLIENT   So if it goes poorly, instead of saying, "I gave a bad speech," it would be "i gave a bad speech." It's not *me* but merely a small part of me.

THERAPIST   Correct! But if you want to go one better, try leaving the big "I" and the little "i" out completely. You can say: "A bad speech was given." Or: "The speech was not very good." Make it task-oriented. Keep your "self" out of it completely. The goal of life is to have as many positively reinforcing little i's as possible.

Discussion

The foregoing dialogue illustrates the ways that total self-ratings, that is, placing oneself on the line because of a certain behavioral performance, cause people to suffer and to perform poorly in a myriad of endeavors. The sensitive and knowledgeable therapist, knowing that this habit is at the base of most problems, looks for clues as to its nature and goes after it. Once the client saw that he was staking *everything* on how well he gave a public talk—his job, the esteem of his acquaintances, his own self-esteem—we were able to get somewhere.

This dialogue, together with the various suggestions, homework assignments and prescriptions, enabled the client to reduce his anxiety, but he required an additional two in vivo role-playing sessions before his public-speaking anxiety was completely eliminated. A group of students and secretaries made up the audience; while the client was speaking, each person had been primed to hurl insults and verbal abuse while the client, undaunted, was to continue his speech. This "bull-baiting" technique continued for at least five minutes and tended to arouse considerable anxiety despite the contrived nature of the exercise. When anxiety was at a fairly high intensity, the audience stopped their verbal expletives and simply listened attentively while the client continued his speech. At this stage, he was instructed to engage in sensory focusing so that he could describe a precise range of concomitant sensations to the group. He was also instructed to employ the "little i strategy."

This case is another example of multimodal therapy (Lazarus, 1976) in which each dimension of "personality"—behavior, affect, sensation, imagery, cognition, and interpersonal relations—was specifically and deliberately included in the treatment program. It is significant that only three sessions, over a span of four weeks, were required to overcome a severe anxiety reaction that had not abated after a period of years.

References

Ellis, A. *How to live with a neurotic.* New York: Crown, 1975.
Lazarus, A. A. *Multimodal behavior therapy.* New York: Springer Publishing, 1976.

6

Cognitive Approaches to Depression

Aaron T. Beck and Brian F. Shaw

Although not a member of the RET camp by strict definition, Aaron Beck has been a pioneer in developing cognitive theories of psychopathology and cognitive approaches to personality change for several decades. In this chapter, he and Dr. Brian Shaw summarize their work on the cognitive basis of depression. First they discuss the core cognitive triad in depression —a negative, condemning view of the self; an awful picture of the outside world; and a negative view of the future—and cite research that supports its validity. In the second section, "Cognitive Schemas and Depression," they describe the pathogenesis of depression and highlight the role that primitive cognitive organization plays in the development and maintenance of depression. They show how resulting errors in information processing such as overgeneralizing and dichotomous thinking perpetuate both the cognitive triad and the depressive emotions. Finally, Beck and Shaw explain how the cognitive distortions precipitate the other phenomena of depression, including sadness and loneliness, loss of motivation, and motor retardation and fatigue. All in all, they present an extremely important and cogent position regarding the cognitive dynamics of depressive phenomena.

MANY THEORIES HAVE BEEN proposed to explain the etiology of depression. The explanatory model which is presented here focuses on the importance of cognitive factors in the development and maintenance of depression. While cognitive theories have been postulated (Ellis, 1962; Lazarus, Averill, and Opton, 1970), these theories attempted to account for the development of emotional responses and affective disturbance *in general*. In contrast, this chapter outlines a cognitive model that is specific to the clinical state of depression.

The cognitive model of depression differs from traditional views which hold that all other symptoms are secondary to the basic affective disturbance. The central tenet of the cognitive model is that the idiosyncratic, distorted conceptions of depressed patients are central in the development and maintenance of depressive symptomatology. Of particular importance is the "cognitive triad" (Beck, 1967) which consists of a

119

negative view of the self, of the outside world, and of the future. Depressed patients see themselves as deprived, frustrated, humiliated, rejected, or punished ("losers," in the vernacular). They construe their experience in terms of failure and regard the future as hopeless. The critical importance of these negative conceptions to the understanding of depression will become evident later in the chapter. At this point, it is most relevant to review the correlation and experimental studies that outline this cognitive triad and the related behavioral manifestations of depressed patients.

The Cognitive Triad in Depression

One of the most widely accepted and intriguing notions regarding depression is that the condition is characterized by a core of inverted hostility. This "retroflected-hostility" or "need-to-suffer" concept was the initial focus of Beck's research with depressed patients and eventually led to the cognitive model. In a study of depressed patients in psychotherapy, Beck and Hurvich (1959) found that depressed patients showed a higher proportion of "masochistic dreams" than a matched group of nondepressed patients. The ideational material consisted of a specific thematic content: The depressed dreamer portrayed himself as a "loser" in some respect; that is, he suffered deprivation of some tangible object, experienced a loss of self-esteem in an interpersonal relationship, or experienced a loss of a person to whom he was attached. Other common themes included the depressed patient as thwarted in attempting to reach a goal or portrayed as inept, repulsive, or defective.

The findings of the Beck and Hurvich (1959) study were supported by a second, more refined study of the most recent dreams of 218 depressed and nondepressed psychiatric patients (Beck and Ward, 1961). Hauri (1976) further substantiated these findings in a study of individuals remitted from a serious reactive depression. Finally, Beck (1961) constructed a focused fantasy test consisting of a set of cards, each card containing four frames that portrayed a continuous sequence of events involving a set of identical twins. One of the twins was subjected to an unpleasant experience while the other twin either avoided the unpleasant experience or had a pleasant experience. The themes were similar to those found in dreams of depressed patients in that the hero loses something of value, is rejected, or punished. It was found that the depressed patients identified with the loser significantly more frequently than did the nondepressed patients. From all this evidence, Beck concluded that the data did not warrant the interpretation that depressed patients "need to suffer" because of inverted hostility, but, more parsimoniously, that the depressed person actually perceived himself as a "loser."

This latter hypothesis was pursued in a clinical study by Beck (1963, 1964). He analyzed verbatim recorded interview material of depressed and nondepressed patients in psychotherapy. The content of the reports of the depressed patients showed a continuity with the thematic content of their dreams in that the depressed person saw himself as a "loser." Furthermore, the depressed patients' reports showed other idiosyncratic negative thematic *content* not observed in those of nondepressed patients, to wit:

A negative view of self. The depressed individual shows a marked tendency to view himself as deficient, inadequate, or unworthy, and to attribute his unpleasant experiences to a physical, mental, or moral defect in himself. Furthermore, he regards himself as undesirable and worthless because of his presumed defect and tends to reject himself (and to believe others will reject him) because of it.

A negative view of the world. His interactions with the environment are interpreted as representing defeat, deprivation, or disparagement. He views the world as making exorbitant demands on him and presenting obstacles which interfere with the achievement of his life goals.

A negative view of the future. The future is seen from a negative perspective and revolves around a series of negative expectations. The depressed patient anticipates that his current problems and experiences will continue indefinitely and that he will increasingly burden significant others in his life.

Beck (1963, 1964) further noted the *way* depressed patients interpreted their current life experiences. The depressed patients tended to distort their experiences: they misinterpreted specific, irrelevant events in terms of personal failure, deprivation, or rejection; they tended to greatly exaggerate or overgeneralize any event that bore any semblance of negative information about themselves; they also tended to perseverate in making indiscriminate, negative predictions of the future. It is important to note that the depressed person's cognitions reflect a *systematic bias* against himself. Because of this overemphasis of negative data to the relative exclusion of positive data, the label "cognitive distortion" is most appropriate when describing the thinking of depressed patients.

In the past 15 years, Beck and his associates, as well as other investigators, have conducted studies designed to test these initial observations and the results are by and large supportive. Significant correlations were found between a measure of the severity of depression (the Beck Depression Inventory) and measures of pessimism ($r = 0.56$) and negative self-concept ($r = 0.70$) in hospitalized patients (Vatz, Winig, and Beck,

1969). After recovery from depression, all scores showed substantial decrements, and change scores (between the time of admission and discharge) on the measures of pessimism and negative self-concept correlated 0.49 and 0.53, respectively, with the change scores on the Depression Inventory. These findings supported the notion that the state of depression is associated with a negative view of the self and the future.

A further line of inquiry involved the experimental manipulation of certain cognitive variables and the assessment of the effects upon other variables relevant to depression. According to our formulation, the depressed patient is characterized by unrealistically low concepts of his capabilities. If this negative orientation can be ameliorated, then the secondary symptoms of depression, such as the dysphoria and the reduction of goal-directed behavior, can be expected to improve.

A study by Loeb, Feshbach, Beck, and Wolf (1964) revealed that outpatients in a superior performance group on a card-sorting task were more self-confident, rated themselves as happier, and perceived others as happier than did outpatients in an inferior performance group. Depressed patients were more affected than nondepressed patients in task performance by estimating how they would do in a future task. They also showed greater changes in their self-ratings on the happiness-sadness continuum; however, the increment (or decrement) in their mood failed to reach a statistically significant level ($p = .10$).

A later experiment (Loeb, Beck, and Diggory, 1971) showed that depressed outpatients were significantly more pessimistic about their likelihood of succeeding on a task and made significantly lower ratings of their performance, even though they performed as well as or better than a matched control group of nondepressed outpatients. On a second task, the previous experience of success or failure had different effects on the actual performance of the two groups: Success *improved the performance of the depressed group,* whereas failure improved the performance of the nondepressed group. The depressed patients in the success group, though positively affected by success, still showed lower probability-of-success estimates and lower self-evaluations than did the successful nondepressed group.

The two studies of depressed outpatients by Loeb et al. (1964, 1971) were replicated in a study of depressed inpatients (Beck, 1974). In addition to specific measures of self-confidence and expectancies regarding test performance, the Hopelessness Scale (Beck, Weissman, Lester, and Trexler, 1974) and the Stuart Self-Evaluation Test (Stuart, 1962) were included. Following a successful experience there was not only an improvement in ratings relevant to test performance, but also a generalized increase in self-esteem and optimism. Thus, the patients made more positive ratings about their personal attractiveness, ability to communicate, and social interest. They also saw the future as brighter and had higher expectations of achieving their major objectives in life.

Another study of depressed inpatients presented a hierarchy of tasks in a verbal dimension. The patients progressed from a simple task (reading a paragraph aloud) up to the most difficult items in the hierarchy (improvising a short talk on a selected subject and trying to convince the experimenter of their point of view). Again, significant improvements in global ratings of self-concept and optimism were found (Beck, 1974).

Since Beck's early studies, other investigators have continued a similar line of investigation. Hammen and Krantz (1976) reported the results of a study which compared the changes in self-ratings of depressed and nondepressed female subjects as a function of feedback on a performance task. The depressed subjects were found to evaluate their personal qualities significantly more negatively than nondepressed subjects. In response to an experimental manipulation (positive feedback about their performance, negative feedback, or no feedback), the depressed subjects typically demonstrated strongly negative reactions to failure, compared with the neutral condition. Specifically, the depressed subjects became more pessimistic in the prediction of their future performance following the negative feedback.

In addition, Hammen and Krantz (1976) evaluated the hypothesis that depressed and nondepressed patients would differ in their cognitive responses to a number of standardized stories which involved problematic situations. The potential response choices available to subjects were designed to include each of the following: depressed-distorted, depressed-nondistorted, nondepressed-distorted and nondepressed-nondistorted. Consistent with their hypotheses, depressed subjects selected significantly more depressed-distorted responses and less nondepressed-nondistorted responses. These findings again suggest that depressed persons systematically select dysfunctional cognitions which maintain if not enhance depression and hopelessness.

The work of Hammen and Krantz (1976) provides further support of the importance of the cognitive triad in clinical depression. In addition, two other studies have investigated the importance of cognitions in depression with "normal" individuals. To date, preliminary studies have supported the significance of the association between negative cognitions and negative affect. Velten (1968) used a group of statements designed to be "depressing" and controlled for the subjects' pretreatment mood level and suggestibility. He found that depressed mood was induced by the depressing statements. Coleman (1975) adapted Velten's (1968) methodology and also concluded that the induction of positive versus negative cognitions produced significant differences in elation-depression on multiple measure. Subjects who were defined as either "elated" or "depressed" were able to experience opposite mood states as a result of the cognitive intervention.

Weintraub, Segal, and Beck (1974) examined the relationship between cognition and affect in a longitudinal study of male college students. Using a measure of self-reported depressed mood and a scale of cognitive process, a time-specific relationship between cognition and depressed mood was observed. A negative cognitive set emerged as a more stable characteristic of the subjects than the depressed affect. Further studies in this area are obviously needed, but based on these and the previously mentioned investigations, there is a significant body of evidence for the primacy of cognition in the development of depression.

To summarize, cognitive factors are proposed as having central etiological significance in the development and maintenance of the symptoms of depression. The depression-prone individual has acquired specific negative attitudes about himself, his environment, and his future. These cognitive constellations have been labeled the "cognitive triad of depression."

Cognitive Schemas and Depression

The clinical observations and the results of the experimental and correlational studies provide the basis for a description of the pathogenesis of depression.

An individual's concepts—realistic as well as unrealistic—are drawn from his experiences, from the attitudes and opinions communicated to him by others, and from his identification (or his social role-models).

Once a specific concept (attitude or assumption) has been formed, it can influence subsequent judgments and, therefore, becomes more firmly set. For instance, the child who gets the notion that he is inept, as a result of either failure experiences or the attributions of others, may interpret subsequent experiences according to this notion. Each time that he encounters difficulties in manual tasks, he may have a tendency to judge himself inept. Each negative judgment, irrespective of actual performance or objective criteria, tends to reinforce the negative concept. Thus, a cycle is established: Each negative judgment reinforces the negative self-concept which in turn facilitates a negative interpretation of subsequent experiences. Unless this negative self-concept is altered, it becomes structuralized, i.e., it becomes a permanent formation of the cognitive organization. Once a concept is structuralized, it remains permanently even though it may be dormant; it becomes a cognitive structure, or schema.

Among the concepts that are prominent in the pathogenesis of depression are the individual's concepts toward himself, his environmental consequences, and his future. Included in positive self-concepts are such schemas as "I am capable," "I can control my immediate environment," "I can understand problems and solve them." Examples of negative self-concepts are "I am weak," "I am inferior," "I can't do anything right." These negative self-concepts emerge with great force in depression.

While this is a highly simplified framework of cognitive processes, it is both theoretically and clinically useful to view psychological processes as belonging to one of two systems. These may be assumed to be a mature and a primitive system. The more mature system is involved in realistic information processing. This notion of a primitive organization is similar in many ways to Freud's description of the primary process and Piaget's formulation of early developmental levels of thinking. This primitive organization is composed of relatively crude concepts and ways of thinking. In contrast to the more mature levels of organization (for example, the secondary process), these concepts are framed in absolute rather than relative terms, are dichotomous rather than graduated, and are global rather than discriminative. Under normal conditions, the mature psychological processes (i.e., information processing) are generally dominant, although more primitive levels of thinking may be detected in sporadic illogical ideas, in disproportionate or inappropriate reactions to specific life events, and in dreams and waking fantasies.

The principle postulate of this formulation is that in depression (as in other psychopathological conditions) the primitive cognitive organization becomes dominant. Depression is likely to be precipitated when a depression-prone individual (i.e., an individual who has incorporated a constellation of negative schemas) is either subjected to specific stresses which activate his negative schema or to a series of specific events which are not highly structured individually but have an additive effect. The most notable feature of the individual's interpretation of these stressful situations is that they represent a personal loss and thus have substantial significance. Typically, the outcome of the precipitant situation is associated with a negative value judgment and is attributed to a defect or deficiency in the individual.

As depression develops, the primitive organization preempts the more mature system in areas of experience relevant to self-evaluation and expectancy so that the depressed patient's negative ideation about himself, his environmental interactions, and his future are subject to distortions of reality that perpetuate the cognitive triad. The operations of the primitive organization are evident in both the content and the form of the depressed patient's ideation. To a large extent, the cognitive schemas dictate the meanings and even the "facts" of observation. The external stimulus configurations are screened and molded to conform to the content of these ideas. Therefore, the patient's interpretations of experiences, his expectancies, his reminiscences are congruent with the idiosyncratic schemas. The prevailing content of his ideation is consistent with the themes of the schemas: "I am inferior," "I will never feel better," "I cannot cope."

An observation of the thinking style of depressed patients reveals that those patients typically exhibit a thinking disorder. The kinds of fallacious thinking include the following:

Arbitrary inference, the process of drawing a conclusion when evidence is lacking or is actually contrary to the conclusion. This type of dysfunctional thinking usually takes the form of personalization (or self-reference). For instance, a depressed patient who saw a frown on the face of a passerby thought, "He has deliberately left in order to avoid seeing me."

Overgeneralization, the process of making an unjustified generalization on the basis of a single incident. An example is a patient who thinks, "I never succeed at anything" when he has a single isolated failure.

Magnification, the propensity to exaggerate the meaning or significance of a particular event. A person with a fear of dying, for instance, interpreted every unpleasant sensation or pain in his body as a sign of some fatal disease such as cancer, heart attack, or cerebral hemorrhage. Ellis (1962) applied the label "catastrophizing" to this kind of reaction.

To sum, the formal disturbances of thinking in depression can be attributed to the dominance of the idiosyncratic schemas, which override the demand characteristics of the external stimulus situation. The crude, undifferentiated nature of the schemas may account for the overgeneralizations and blurring of discriminations. Extreme judgments and overgeneralizations may be explained by the properties of the primitive schemas, namely, their breadth, rigidity, and dichotomous structure. Selective abstraction and selective recall may be attributed to the extraction of data isomorphic to the primitive schemas which are dominant in depression.

The manner in which a precipitating event involving loss leads to the constellation of depressive symptoms may be outlined by an illustrative case: a man whose wife has unexpectedly deserted him.

The effect on the deserted mate cannot necessarily be predicted in advance. Obviously, not every person deserted by a spouse becomes depressed. He may have other sources or areas in his life which provide adequate satisfactions to maintain his "psychological equilibrium." He may not believe that he was one of the causal factors which determined her behavior. Alternately, the deserted husband may not consider his wife to be a crucial source of happiness in his life. If the problem were simply a new hiatus in his life, it would seem plausible that in the course of time he would be able to adapt, at least in part, to the loss without becoming clinically depressed. Nonetheless, we know that certain vulnerable individuals respond to such a loss with the profound disturbance called depression.

The impact of the loss depends in part on the kind and intensity of the meanings attached to the key person. The deserting wife may have been the hub of shared experiences, fantasies, and expectations. The deserted husband (in this example) has built a network of associations around his wife, such as "She is part of me," "She is everything to me," "I enjoy life because of her," "She is my mainstay," or "She comforts me when I am down." These positive associations range from the realistic to the extremely unrealistic or imaginary. The more absolute these positive concepts, the greater the damage.

If the damage to his psychological domain is great enough, it sets off a chain reaction. The positive values he attributes to his wife appear to be totally and irrevocably lost. Therefore, the greater and more absolute these positive associations, the greater the sense of loss. The extinction of "assets" such as "the only person who can make me happy" or "the essence of my existence" magnifies the impact of the loss and generates further sadness. Consequently, our deserted husband begins to make extreme, *negative* conclusions which parallel the extreme *positive* associations to his wife. He interprets the consequences of the loss as "I am nothing without her," "I can never be happy again," and "I can't go on without her."

The further reverberations of the desertion lead the husband to question his own validity and worth: "If I had been a better person, she wouldn't have left me." Further, he predicts other negative consequences of the breakup of the marriage: "All of our friends will go over to her side," "The children will want to live with her, not with me," and "I will go broke trying to maintain two households."

As the chain reaction progresses to a full-blown depression, the husband's self-doubts and gloomy predictions expand into negative generalizations about himself, his world, and his future. He starts to see himself as permanently impoverished both financially and in terms of emotional satisfactions. In addition, he exacerbates his suffering by overemphasizing the event: "It is too much for a person to bear" or "This is a terrible disaster." Such ideas undermine his ability and motivation to absorb the shock.

Since the chain reaction feeds upon itself, the depression goes into a downward spiral. The various symptoms—sadness, decreased physical activity, sleep disturbances—feed back into the psychological system. Hence, as the patient experiences sadness his generalized pessimism leads him to conclude, "I will *always* be sad." This conclusion leads to more sadness, which is further interpreted in a negative way. Similarly he thinks, "I will never be able to eat or to sleep well again" and concludes that he is rotting or deteriorating physically. As the patient observes the various manifestations of his disorder (decreased productivity, avoidance of responsibility, withdrawal from other people), he becomes increasingly critical of himself. His self-criticisms lead to deeper sadness and we thus see a continuing vicious cycle.

Cognition and Concomitant Depressive Symptomatology

In previous sections, the cognitive manifestations have been described and evidence for their primary etiological position presented. As with any model, it is critical to provide a satisfactory explanation of the associated phenomena of depression.

Sadness and Loneliness

Although the onset of depression may be sudden, its full development spreads over a period of days or weeks. The patient experiences a gradual increase in intensity of sadness and of other symptoms until he "hits bottom." Each repetition of the *idea* of loss constitutes a fresh experience of loss which is added to the previous reservoir of perceived losses. With each successive "loss" further sadness is generated.

One of the most notable cognitive aspects of depression directly related to dysphoric mood is the selective recall of experiences. A depressed individual is facile in recalling past unpleasant experiences while "drawing a blank" when questioned about positive experiences. A similar selectivity can be observed in his perception of current events; he is hypersensitive to the stimuli suggestive of loss and insensitive to stimuli representing gain.

As a result of this "tunnel vision," the patient becomes relatively impermeable to stimuli that can arouse pleasant emotions. Although he may be able to acknowledge that certain events are favorable, his attitudes block any happy feelings: "I don't deserve to be happy," "I'm different from other people," "I can't feel happy over the things that make them happy," "How can I be happy when everything else is bad?" Similarly, comical situations do not strike him as funny because of his negative set and his tendency toward self-reference: "There is nothing funny about my life." He has difficulty in experiencing anger and making assertive responses, since he views himself as responsible for and deserving of any rude or insulting actions of other people.

Freud and more recent writers have held that the sadness is a transformation of anger turned inward. By a kind of "alchemy," the anger is supposedly converted into depressive feelings. A more plausible explanation is that the sadness is the result of the self-instigated lowering of the self-esteem. Suppose a student is informed that his performance is inferior and he accepts the assessment as fair. Even though the evaluation is communicated without anger and may, in fact, be expressed with regret or empathy, he is likely to feel sad. The lowering of his self-esteem by an objective evaluation is sufficient to make him sad—even without an expression of anger. Similarly, if the student makes a negative evaluation of himself, he feels sad. The depressed patient is like the self-devaluating student; he feels sad because he lowers his sense of worth by his negative evaluations. There is no reason to postulate that he is unconsciously angry at someone else and that his anger is transformed into sadness.

When a depressed patient makes a negative evaluation of himself, he generally does not feel anger at himself; he is, in his frame of reference, simply making an objective judgment. Similarly he reacts with sadness when he believes that somebody else is devaluating him, even though this external devaluation may be devoid of any anger. Closely associated with his negative self-evaluation is the tendency to think in absolute terms which contributes to the cumulative arousal of sadness. The patient tends to dwell increasingly on extreme ideas such as "Life is meaningless," "Nobody loves me," "I'm totally inadequate," or "I have nothing left."

By downgrading qualities that are closely linked with gratification, the patient is in effect taking gratification away from himself. In calling herself unattractive, a woman is in effect saying, "I no longer can enjoy my physical appearance, or compliments I receive for it, or friendships that it helped me to form and maintain."

The loss of gratification leads to sadness; the prevailing pessimism maintains a continual state of sadness. If the usual consequence of loss is sadness, then giving up is followed by apathy. When the depressed patient regards himself as defeated or at least thwarted in his life's major goals, he is apt to experience a state of indifference or apathy.

Motivational Changes

The reversals in major goals and objectives are among the most puzzling characteristics of the seriously depressed patient. He not only desires to avoid experiences that formerly gratified him or represented the mainstream of his life, but he is drawn toward a state of inactivity. He even seeks to withdraw from life completely through suicide.

To understand the link between the changes in motivation and cognitions, it is valuable to consider the ways in which the patient has "given up." He no longer feels attracted to the kinds of enterprises that ordinarily he would engage in spontaneously. In fact, he finds that he has to force himself into any undertaking. He goes through the motions of attending to his routine affairs because he believes he should, or because he knows it is "the right thing to do," or because others urge him to do it, but not because he wants to. He finds that he has to work against a powerful inner resistance as though he were trying to drive an automobile with the brakes on or to swim upstream.

In the most extreme cases, the patient experiences "paralysis of the will." He is completely devoid of any spontaneous desire to do anything except remain in a state of passive inertia. Nor can he mobilize "will power" to force himself to do what he believes he "ought to do." His inertia, however, is deceptive in that it derives not only from a desire to be passive, but also from a less obvious desire to shrink from any situation that he regards as unpleasant. He feels repelled by the thought of performing even elementary functions such as getting out of bed, dressing himself, and attending to personal needs. A retarded, depressed woman would rapidly dive under the covers of her bed whenever her therapist entered the room. She would become exceptionally aroused and even energetic in attempting to escape from an activity in which she was pressed to engage.

The depressed patient's desires to avoid activity and escape from his present environment are the consequences of his peculiar constructions— a negative view of his future, of his environment, and of himself (the cognitive triad).

Everyday experience, as well as a number of well-designed experiments, demonstrates that when a person believes he cannot succeed at a task, he is likely to give up or not even attempt to work at it. He adopts the attitude that "there's no use in trying" and does not feel much spontaneous drive. Moreover, the belief that the task is pointless and that even successful completion is meaningless minimizes his motivation.

An analogous situation is typical of depression. The depressed patient expects negative outcomes, so he does not experience ordinary mobilization of the drive to make an effort. Furthermore, he does not see any point in trying because he believes the goals are meaningless. There is a general tendency for people to avoid situations they expect to be painful. The depressed patient perceives most situations as onerous, boring, or painful; hence, he desires to avoid even the usual amenities of living.

These avoidance desires are powerful enough to override any tendencies toward constructive, goal-directed activity.

The background setting for the patient's powerful desire to seek a passive state is illustrated by this sequence of thoughts: "I'm too fatigued and sad to do anything. If I am active I will only feel worse. But if I lie down, I can conserve my strength and my bad feeling will go away." Unfortunately, his attempt to escape from the unpleasant feeling by being passive does not work; if anything, it enhances the dysphoria. The patient finds that, far from getting respite from his unpleasant thoughts and feelings, he becomes more preoccupied by them.

Suicidal Behavior

Suicidal wishes and suicidal attempts may be regarded as an extreme expression of the desire to escape. The depressed patient sees his future as filled with suffering. He cannot visualize any way of improving his lot. He does not believe that he will get better. Under these conditions, suicide seems to be a rational solution. It not only promises an end to his own misery but also presumably will relieve his family of a burden. Once the patient regards suicide as a more desirable alternative than living, he feels attracted to this kind of solution. The more hopeless and painful his life seems, the stronger his desire to end that life.

The wish to find surcease through suicide is illustrated in the following quotation from a depressed woman rejected by her lover: "There's no sense in living. There's nothing here for me. I need love and I don't have it any more. I can't be happy without love—only miserable. It will just be the same misery, day in and day out. It's senseless to go on."

The desire to escape from the apparent futility of his existence is illustrated by the statement of another patient: "Life means just going through another day. It doesn't make any sense. There's nothing that can give me any satisfaction. The future isn't there. I just don't want life any more. I want to get out of here. It's stupid just to go on living."

Another premise underlying the suicidal wishes is the patient's belief that everybody would be better off if he were dead. Since he regards himself as worthless and a burden, he considers as hollow the arguments that his family would be hurt if he died. How can they be injured by losing a burden? One patient envisioned suicide as doing her parents a favor. She would not only end her own pain, but would relieve them of psychological and financial burdens. "I'm just taking money from my parents," she said. "They could use it to better advantage. They wouldn't have to support me. My father wouldn't have to work so hard and they could travel. I'm unhappy taking their money and they could be happy with it."

Physical and Vegetative Symptoms

The explanation of the physical and vegetative symptoms of depression in the framework of a psychological model presents certain difficulties. Mixing different conceptual levels entails the risk of confounding rather than clarifying the problem. Furthermore, whereas patients' verbal material is a rich source of information for establishing meaningful connections between the psychological variables, it provides scanty data for determining psychophysiological relationships.

With these reservations in mind, an attempt can be made to relate the cognitive patterns to one of the physical correlates of depression, namely, the motor retardation and fatigue. Depressed patients have generally expressed attitudes of passive resignation to their supposedly terrible fate. Their attitude is expressed in such statements as "There's nothing I can do to save myself." In the most severe cases, such as the benign stupors, the patient may believe that he is already dead. In any event, the profound motor inhibition appears to be congruent with the patient's negative view of himself and loss of spontaneous motivation. When the patient's desire to do something is stimulated, retardation becomes temporarily reduced or disappears. Moreover, when the patient can entertain the idea of getting some gratification from what he is doing, there is a reduction in the subjective sense of fatigue.

The influence of psychological factors on the inertia, retardation, and fatigability of depression has been borne out by several systematic studies. It has been noted that when depressed patients are given a concrete task, such as the digit-symbol substitution test, they mobilize sufficient motivation to perform as well as other nondepressed patients of similar severity of illness (Beck, Feshbach, and Legg, 1962). Since this test is essentially a speed test, it should be particularly sensitive to psychomotor retardation. Similarly, Friedman (1964) found that depressed patients showed either no impairment or only minimal impairment when engaged in a variety of psychological tests.

The vegetative signs of depression, such as loss of appetite, loss of libido, and sleep disturbance, may be defined as the physiological concomitants of the particular psychological disturbance in a fashion analogous to the conceptualization of the automatic symptoms as correlates of anxiety. To complete the description, it may be speculated that the patient's perception of his vegetative and other somatic disturbances is processed by the typical idiosyncratic cognitive schemas. Hence, the meaning attached to sleep disturbance ranges from "I am going to pieces" to "I haven't slept at all for several weeks." The perception of loss of appetite and possibly reduction of other proprioceptive sensations from the gastrointestinal system may be woven into notions such as "I am an empty shell. I have lost my internal organs," in a severely depressed individual to "I'm too sick to eat" in a person who is less depressed.

Based on the clinical and experimental evidence presented, it is concluded that, in depression, distorted thinking constitutes the "eye of the storm." It is notable that cognitive factors have also been implicated in many other psychopathological conditions (see Beck, 1976). Although not always apparent to an untrained observer, the depressed patient's negative interpretation of reality contributes to the more obvious turbulence (sadness, agitation, insomnia, loss of appetite). As is noted in Chapter 22, this conceptualization provides a clue to success intervention with depressed patients. By aiming the therapeutic techniques at the center of the disturbance, the therapist can precipitate a "calming of the storm."

References

Beck, A. T. A systematic investigation of depression, *Comparative Psychiatry*, 1961, *2*, 162–170.

Beck, A. T. Thinking and depression: 1. Idiosyncratic content and cognitive distortions. *Archives of General Psychiatry*, 1963, *9*, 324–335.

Beck, A. T. Thinking and depression: 2. Theory and therapy. *Archives of General Psychiatry*, 1964, *10*, 561–571.

Beck, A. T. *Depression: Clinical, experimental, and theoretical aspects*. New York: Harper and Row, 1967. Republished as *Depression: Causes and treatment*. Philadelphia: University of Pennsylvania Press, 1972.

Beck, A. T. The Development of depression: A cognitive model. In R. Friedman, and M. Katz (Eds.), *Psychology of depression: Contemporary theory and research*. Washington, D.C.: Winston-Wiley, 1974.

Beck, A. T. *Cognitive therapy and the emotional disorders*. New York: International Universities Press, 1976.

Beck, A. T., Feshbach, S., and Legg, D. The clinical utility of the digit symbol test. *Journal of Consulting Psychology*, 1962, *26*, 263–268.

Beck, A. T., and Hurvich, M. S. Psychological correlates of depression: 1. Frequency of "masochistic" dream content in a private practice sample. *Psychosomatic Medicine*, 1959, *21*, 50–55.

Beck, A. T., and War, C. H. Dreams of depressed patients: Characteristic themes in manifest content. *Archives of General Psychiatry*, 1961, *5*, 462–467.

Beck, A. T., Weissman, A., Lester, D., and Trexler, L. The measurement of pessimism: The Hopelessness Scale. *Journal of Consulting and Clinical Psychology*, 1974, *42*, 861–865.

Coleman, R. Manipulation of self-esteem as a determinant of mood of elated and depressed women. *Journal of Abnormal Psychology*, 1975, *84*, 693–700.

Ellis, A. *Reason and emotion in psychotherapy*. New York: Lyle Stuart, 1962.

Friedman, A. S. Minimal effects of severe depression on cognitive functioning. *Journal of Abnormal Social Psychology,* 1964, *69,* 237–243.

Grinker, R. R., Sr., Miller, J., Sabshin, M., Nunn, R., and Nunnally, J. *The phenomena of depressions.* New York: Hoeber, 1961.

Hammen, C. L., and Krantz, S. Effects of success and failure on depressive cognitions. Unpublished manuscript, 1976.

Hauri, P. Dreams in patients remitted from reactive repression. *Journal of Abnormal Psychology,* 1976, *85,* 1–10.

Lazarus, R. S., Averill, J. R., and Opton, E. M., Jr. Towards a cognitive theory of emotion. In M. B. Arnold (Ed.), *Feelings and emotion.* New York: Academic Press, 1970.

Loeb, A., Beck, A. T., and Diggory, J. Differential effects of success and failure on depressed and nondepressed patients. *Journal of Nervous and Mental Disease,* 1971, *152,* 106–114.

Loeb, A., Feshbach, S., Beck, A. T., and Wolf, A. Some effects of reward upon the social perception and motivation of psychiatric patients varying in depression. *Journal of Abnormal Social Psychology,* 1964, *68,* 609–616.

Stuart, J. L. Intercorrelations of depressive tendencies, time perspective, and cognitive style variable. Doctoral dissertation, Vanderbilt University, 1962.

Vatz, K. A., Winig, H. R., and Beck, A. T. Pessimism and a sense of future time constriction as cognitive distortions in depression. Mimeographed. University of Pennsylvania, 1969.

Velten, E. A laboratory task for induction of mood states. *Behavior Research and Therapy,* 1968, *6,* 473–482.

Weintraub, M., Segal, R., and Beck, A. T. An investigation of cognition and affect in the depressive experiences of normal men. *Journal of Consulting and Clinical Psychology,* 1974, *42,* 911.

7

The Rational-Emotive Dynamics of Impulsive Disorders

John T. Watkins

A theoretically interesting and socially significant area for professional attention is the psychodynamics of impulse acting-out disorders. The literature on this area is extensive with regard to children, but it is relatively sparse regarding adults, except when acting out is considered to be the result of a sociopathic adjustment. In this highly interesting and informative chapter, John Watkins considers the relationship between cognition and impulse control. His major premise is that impulsive, acting-out behavior represents more than just deficiencies in "ego" functioning or a lack of reflection; rather it represents the presence of certain philosophic distortions or irrational beliefs.

Through client illustrations, Watkins proposes that three cognitive patterns underlie most impulse control problems: (1) infantilely believing that one has to have what one wants, or infantilely demanding, dictating, or insisting that desires be satisfied at all costs; (2) egocentrically believing that circumstances must not be difficult and that life should be easy; and (3) believing that any difficulty, delay, or inhibition is too awful to stand. It is interesting to note that Watkins has operationally defined low frustration tolerance in RET terms; that is, the tendency to be intolerant of deprivation, frustration, or emotional upset by holding the aforementioned beliefs or philosophies. Watkins supports his thesis by reviewing the literature on the cognitive control of impulsive behavior in children.

E XACTLY WHAT IS MEANT when we refer to a person as impulsive? Usually this refers to a person who acts without forethought, who acts on the spur of the moment, who expresses his urges upon experiencing them without reflection or prior deliberation. In the case of an adult whose behaviors are impulsive and lead him into social and legal difficulties, there is usually more behind his behavior than just an inadequacy of reflection. It is not that there is an absence of cognitions, but rather that he first holds irrational cognitions and furthermore fails to engage in any type of cognitive "checking" of what he is thinking.

135

The purposes of this chapter are to consider the dynamics of impulsive behaviors, to present corroborating research on the dynamics of impulse control problems, and to illustrate the cognitive dynamics through cases of several persons whose presenting problems were a lack of impulse control.

The Impulsive Person

Ray and Tom grow up experiencing many desires. As infants they both demand immediate gratification and the complete absence of discomfort. As we observe these two persons developing, we notice that Ray becomes more aware of the limitations of the environment in regard to meeting his every wish. He begins to develop a tolerance for some discomfort and delay in gratification and also begins to learn to manipulate the environment in ways instrumental in maximizing his chances for gratification. Later we notice that Ray's developing ability to operate on the environment has prepared him for beginning to handle the external values and sanctions imposed by other persons. He is able to respond to these contingencies by curbing his behavior via initially adopting the values of others and eventually developing and imposing his own internal values. Ray seems to be processing accurately the realities of his physical and interpersonal world and has the promise of functioning in a rational manner capable of minimizing the degree to which he emotionally disturbs himself.

Tom's course of development seems to have gone in a different direction. He too begins by experiencing many desires and demands for immediate gratification. However, Tom continues to function at the infantile level in that he operates *as if* his wants were organismic needs demanding to be met. He develops little tolerance for delay in gratification or for substitute satisfactions. Tom's desires take on the urgency of a screaming 3-month-old, lying rigidly on his back, beet-red, thrashing the air with his arms. He thinks he *has to* have what he wants *when he wants it* and, furthermore, that it is *too awful to stand* when he does not get what he wants. Tom has *low frustration tolerance* in that his impulses and desires are experienced as urgent and compelling. He goes through life insisting that the environment and others gratify his urges. His low frustration tolerance is further related to his acting as if the world *ought* to be there for his satisfaction, that life *should* be easy and pain-free for him, and that others *must* not deny or delay him. Either Tom is out of touch with reality in the sense of being unaware of or distorting the constraints of the environment, or else he is characteristically making irrational demands upon others and his environment. Having placed these demands upon himself, others, and the world, Tom has assured himself chronic frustration. He cannot tolerate not having his way and engages in *"awfulizing,"* stating that he "can't stand" not being gratified.

Given the above conditions, Tom assuredly will act upon his impulses. How could he do otherwise? After all, he *has* to do it. *It* (his urge) makes him do it, so he says. His wants have become needs and he is no longer personally responsible for his behavior, so he claims. Urges toward pleasure, which came to be viewed by Ray as mere preferences which he could choose to act upon or not, are experienced by Tom as demands insisting upon fulfillment. Tom is out of control, experiences low frustration tolerance, and feels angry toward the world and others for trying to interfere, believing that he should get what he wants and that it is all very unfair.

Ellis (1973) has described the state of mind of people like Tom. "The major forms of human disturbance can be summarized under the heading of childish demandingness. *Demandingness* or *dictating* seems to be, in fact, the essence of virtually all of what we normally call emotional upsetness. While the less disturbed individual strongly *desires* what he wants and makes himself appropriately sorry or annoyed if his desires are unfulfilled, the more disturbed person dogmatically *demands, insists, commands,* or *dictates* that his desires be granted and makes himself inappropriately anxious, depressed, or hostile when they are not," says Ellis (1973).

The above hypothetical cases of Ray and Tom are presented to highlight the cognitive dynamics involved in impulsive disorders. The case of Tom is quite descriptive of the developing dynamics of the impulsive individual. We now have offered a better understanding of how Tom and other impulsive individuals contribute to and perpetuate their being out of control. Our cognitive-behavioral model is meant to be descriptive, not necessarily explanatory in a final sense. We do not know, for instance, why Ray developed rational control over his impulses while Tom failed to do so. What factors predisposed Tom to turn out the way he did? Was nature or nurture more important? Was early conditioning all-determining, or is Tom culpable because he continues to indoctrinate himself with his distorted views? There is compelling logic in rational-emotive theory and impressive empirical findings support the contention that behaviors and emotions are caused by cognitions; however, answers to the ultimate *whys* are not required for our developing a meaningful understanding of dynamics. Rational-emotive theory is a cognitive-emotional-behavioral model for understanding human behavior; as a model it need not be isomorphic with physical reality to prove highly useful in describing human functioning and to provide a theoretical basis upon which behavioral and emotional change can be predicated.

At this stage of our theory development, "demandingness" could easily become reified as occurred with the concept "ego." For example, how might we *explain* Ray's behavior? We could attribute it to his "ego strength." More descriptive, and probably more useful, would be the observation that Ray effectively mediates between his impulses on one hand and the limitations of reality, external mores and taboos, and introjected values on the other hand. It would be easy to slip into saying that Tom continues to function at the infantile level because of his "demandingness," as if this were some sort of internal trait causing his behavior. The author prefers to think of Tom as operating *"as if* his wants are organismic needs demanding to be met . . . *as if* the world ought to be there for his satisfaction. . . ."

To summarize the dynamics of the impulsive individual: First, the impulsive person confuses wants with needs. He translates his preferences into demands and insists that his desires be met. The absolutist and dogmatic demanding, insisting, commanding, or dictating in which he engages are the result of his asserting, or acting *as if* he were asserting, that life should be easy for him, that the world ought to satisfy his every whim. Second, the impulsive person awfulizes. He not only believes rationally that it is unfortunate that he be denied or delayed in his wants, but that it is ungodly awful to be thwarted. Believing this, he tolerates frustration even less. Third, the impulsive person thinks that he cannot stand not having wishes gratified and cannot stand the attendant discomfort. The facts, of course, are that all people can always stand it.

Case Illustrations of Impulsive Disorders

The cases presented in this section illustrate the cognitive dynamics of persons with problems in impulse control. Some of the facts have been changed to protect the identity of the individuals concerned. However, the cases reported reflect accurately the ways in which impulsive individuals present themselves in therapy, the central dynamics of low frustration tolerance, and the treatment difficulties posed.

Most of the examples have come from a rational-emotive therapy group which was designed for impulsive individuals. The goal in this approach has been to help clients internalize cognitions which will permit them to gain control over their impulsive behavior. The types of problems treated have included the following: alcohol abuse, armed robbery, arson, burglary, car theft, exhibitionism, homosexuality, impulsive spending, obscene telephone calls, pedophilia, and voyeurism. The author has had a succession of interns and residents functioning as co-therapists in the group treatment program over a period of two years. The rational-emotive dynamics of the various disordered behaviors have appeared rather similar to the co-therapists. Several cases have been selected which best illustrate these dynamics.

The Impulsive Buyer

Wally was a big-time spender with a small-time pocketbook. Inside he felt rather small, but on the outside he was all show. He talked big, had been the high school clown, was the RET group therapy jester, and occasionally wore a big floppy leather Mexican hat to the group sessions. Wally was determined that people see him as "a big success." He had had a number of brushes with the law as a teenager, mainly as a result of pranks he played on the police department to gain the laughs and admiration of his friends. His most recent legal difficulty prior to coming to the group was his propositioning a female acquaintance over the telephone, for which he was arrested and charged with making an obscene phone call. According to him, it was all due to a mix up; she had led him on earlier, and he thought she'd be receptive to his pitch.

The outstanding problem Wally presented upon coming to therapy was the enormous debts he had run up. A family man in his early twenties, Wally had, through the use of charge cards, amassed a total of nearly $10,000 in bills. He claimed that he could not resist buying things. Wally wanted very much to convince his wife and relatives that he was "a big success." He bought all new furniture and a big car, and could not resist buying any material object that caught his eye. Wally had just declared bankruptcy upon entering treatment. One of his earliest statements was, "I didn't know how impulsive a buyer I was until I'd talked myself out of such buying, then got this new BankAmericard in the mail, and had the feeling to buy all over again." Having just gone through bankruptcy, he was in touch with how much he still was out of control and how he was in danger of repeating the whole pattern.

The formulation of his dynamics was that he had not learned to separate his impulses to buy from his assumptions that he had to do so. In the fourth session Wally revealed that he had gone into a large department store where before he had never left without buying at least some item. He reminded himself continuously throughout his browsing that he did not need to buy anything. After handling many items he finally left the store with no purchases and praised himself for his new behavior. The RET approach of learning to discriminate between wants and needs was successful in helping Wally solve his compulsive spending. As an additional test of his ability to challenge his "needs" for material objects, he carried his new BankAmericard with him. He made a contract with himself that he would only use the card if there were to be an emergency. The co-therapists were concerned about his ability to identify a real emergency and whether he would in a moment of poor judgment go on a spree. Only once did he use his credit card; this was to have his automobile tire repaired late at night when he did not have sufficient cash.

On his own, Wally began to generalize his learning of RET to other potentially disturbing areas. For example, while saving toward a large tuition payment for trade school, he used his new insights by acknowledging that *it would be a ball* "to blow the whole wad" but that he *did not have to*. In another situation he could have easily taken advantage of the sexual availability of a female but at considerable risk to his marriage. He identified that he initially said to himself "I should get a piece," but next found himself asking: "Why? Why should I, just because she's available?"

While Wally made exciting gains through discriminating between his wants and needs, he was quite fallible. Several weeks later he impulsively moved in with another female and did not let his family know where he was. After a few days he changed his mind and returned home to his very upset wife. The group pointed out to Wally that this behavior was similar to his use of credit cards, i.e., "Get what you want now, pay later." Wally assimilated this rather well, and continued to use RET both in therapy and between sessions.

The group also worked with Wally on his need to be approved by helping him see that while approval is nice to have, he did not need it. After three months the frequency of playing the group jester dropped, he became more serious, and he talked about how his behavior had changed, stating that he no longer was ashamed to tell others that he could not afford to spend money. About a month later his probationary period was up and he dropped out of therapy. To his and the group's satisfaction he had gained control over his impulsive spending. He also felt somewhat better about himself as a person; but he had begun to eat excessively because he "needed something to feel good." This was revealed to the group in his last session. Working toward clarifying the difference between his wants and needs had been instrumental in helping him to internalize controls over his spending and over some other areas of his behavior as well. However, we failed to help Wally as completely as we might have in regard to his stated "need to feel good," as attempts to persuade him to remain in therapy failed.

The Pedophile

Jerry was arrested for "taking indecent liberties with a female child." He had molested a girl of about 8 or 9 years of age and faced a stiff sentence of as much as twenty years if convicted. His attorney arranged for a 2-year deferred sentence contingent upon continued psychiatric care. He had been accepted for treatment in the RET behavior control group prior to his court hearing.

Jerry was nowhere near ready for treatment when first seen. He used many euphemisms for his molesting, such as touching, caressing, and being fatherly. "I just love children," he said, claiming that there had been nothing improper in his contacts and adamantly rejecting the suggestion that he might have experienced sexual arousal or satisfaction. The co-therapists suspected that in situations with young girls Jerry was telling himself two different things: (1) "I want to touch her"; (2) "I have to have sexual satisfaction; I need to touch her." However, Jerry could not begin to examine his cognitions since he had not yet acknowledged that he had any disturbed feelings or maladaptive behavior. It was not until the fourth session that he even used the word "molest," at which point he seemed stunned by his own admission. "I guess that's what I have been doing," he said. Describing his problem in the next session, he blocked on the word "molest" and could not recall the word. Jerry was ambivalent toward therapy, wanting to change but finding it painful to acknowledge that he had molested several girls in the past few years. He experienced guilt and shame and did not want to look at what he was doing.

In terms of Ellis' A-B-C's, the therapists first had to establish with the client that there was a C, that is, a behavioral and emotional consequence. After the behavior of molesting and the emotions of guilt and shame were established at point C, Jerry then denied having any cognitions: "I don't say anything to myself, and I certainly don't say 'I want to caress her,'" he exclaimed. It was hard for him to admit that he wanted to touch, molest, and be gratified by children. It was slow going at first, but finally Jerry admitted that he had had an erection "a couple of times" when caressing the girls. Later he admitted to moving his fingers over their vaginas, although he always claimed never to have attempted penetration with his penis. As his denial of sexual satisfaction gave way, he acknowledged his desires and self-talk of "I want to touch and fondle her."

Jerry's next level of resistance was in regard to the role of his cognition of "I need to" in his behavior. He could not see that he was saying this to himself. By chance, two young girls had been in the waiting room with him just prior to his sixth appointment. The therapists used this occurrence to advantage by putting two A-B-C paradigms on the chalkboard. The first paradigm was something like the following: A—Two girls in the waiting room. B—It would feel good to fondle them. C—No molesting, no guilt, no shame. The second paradigm was the following: A—Girl in my bedroom. B—It would feel good to fondle her. C—Molest her, with feelings of guilt and shame later. Jerry was then asked, "Given essentially the same situation of there being a girl, your being aroused and desiring to touch her, and your telling yourself 'I want to,' how is it that you are coming out with two different behavioral consequences?" Jerry dropped his defensiveness, admitting that there was something different going on in the two situations. He was given a homework assignment of comparing the two paradigms and figuring out what he was saying differently to himself in the second one.

Jerry returned to the seventh session and reported, "I've been conning myself. I must have been telling myself all along that I *should* get sexual satisfaction with those children, that I *needed* to touch them." This was the big breakthrough in treatment for Jerry. He rapidly progressed, using his new skills in RET to work on his impulsiveness in other situations, such as handling his anger as a business failure, controlling his temper with other drivers on the highway, and refraining from impulsively telling off his boss. He not only generalized from his RET work with his sexual desires to other areas, but generalized back from other areas to his sexual urges, illustrating time and again that controlling and directing his sexual urges were no different in principle from being in control of the rest of his life.

Jerry went on to become a most vigorous proselytizer, inducting new members coming into the group into the rational-emotive analysis of how they were out of control and were perpetuating their impetuousness. He was open and candid about his own sexual problem when illustrating to new members how they too could challenge their automatic thoughts. In the third month of treatment Jerry mentioned that children were not on his mind as much recently. In a later session he reported that his impulses toward children had diminished and he no longer felt attracted to them.

In the fourth month of treatment, the client reported that friends had left their children with him over the weekend while they went out of town. This had not been a homework assignment in that the therapists found it ethically unacceptable to imperil young children by having him test his control with them. When the group confronted Jerry as to why he put himself into a situation which could have had serious legal consequences for him, he replied, "Maybe to prove that I've beaten my problem." Once resistant, now he does not want to leave the group. He has developed a new philosophy of life which he is enjoying applying to other areas of his functioning. He is utilizing the group fruitfully to exorcise his "shoulds." If he does not terminate therapy himself, he soon will be faced by the group with his implied "need" to stay.

The Auto Thief

Although Tony was not old enough for a driver's license, he had stolen three automobiles. He got a thrill from driving cars and had taken several on the spur of the moment. The goal in therapy was to assist him in developing greater internal controls over his behavior. His cognitive dynamics seemed to be that he understandably enough enjoyed driving automobiles, but that he probably also was saying to himself something like: "I must have what I want when I want it. I can't stand waiting until I am of age. I've got to drive that car."

In the first few sessions, Tony worked on learning the distinction between his wants and needs. He learned to identify the statements he was making to himself between point A of seeing an automobile and point C of taking the car. He learned that he was telling himself both rational and irrational statements at point B: "I want to drive that car. I need to drive that car." After learning that there was no convincing evidence which could be given in support of his irrational claims, he came to the conclusion that while it would be a thrill to drive the car, he did not have to get into it or drive it. His homework assignment for the first few weeks was not to avoid situations in which there was an attractive automobile but, rather, to approach the car, look it over carefully, and fully acknowledge how tempting the car was. He was then to discriminate between his wants and needs and to challenge the irrational claim that he needed to drive that car. After carrying out the homework assignment, we would discuss the results in his next session:

THERAPIST Any temptations this week?
CLIENT Well, I saw this new blue Malibu, a real slick car.
THERAPIST What did you do?
CLIENT I said to myself, "I sure would like to burn rubber with that. I've got to drive that."
THERAPIST And then what?
CLIENT I said, "Wait a minute. I don't have to drive that car."
THERAPIST Why not?
CLIENT It's not an absolute necessity. I am not going to drop dead if I don't get into that car.
THERAPIST So, while you really would like to drive that car, you don't have to; the world isn't going to come to an end if you don't.

Tony was seen for a total of ten individual sessions. In the later sessions the therapist engaged in a technique called "counter-challenge" (Watkins, 1973), which involves testing the strength of the cognitive and behavioral effects produced by therapy. As Tony was relating how he had applied RET to himself in the face of his most recent temptation, the therapist would counter-challenge his rejection of his irrational demands by saying something like the following:

THERAPIST   What do you mean you don't have to burn rubber in that Charger with the overhead cam, 387 engine, and wide tires? Your eyes are the size of golf balls, bulging out of your head! Your tongue is hanging out all the way to the pavement; you're drooling all over yourself! Tell me you don't have to drive that car!

CLIENT   No, no I don't *have* to drive that car! I want to drive it, but I don't *need* to. It's not necessary that I drive it. I won't drop dead if I don't get into it!

There were no recurrences of auto theft during the four months Tony was in treatment. Follow-ups two, three, and five months later found him to be free of any further difficulties in controlling his impulses.

The Obscene Phone Caller

Rod was referred to therapy after appearing before the court for making obscene telephone calls. He had a history of impulse control problems including the loss of several jobs for failure to get out of bed and to work on time, numerous traffic citations for "hot rodding," and one previous arrest for nude "streaking." The intake evaluation described him as a rather immature, passive-aggressive personality. In his mid-twenties, Rod still lived at home with his parents, relied upon them in many ways, and was often treated like a little boy. When first seen in therapy, he displayed considerable feelings of inadequacy resembling closely the classic description of inadequacy to be found in voyeurs, exhibitionists, and pedophils.

At first it was difficult to discern what there was about the telephone calls that turned Rod on. He disavowed any sexual arousal or release. Eventually it was discovered that he enjoyed getting irate responses from his victims and, as a consequence, these persons received further calls from him. More often than not he simply made a general nuisance of himself. To call someone and get a rise out of them put him in a position of "one-upmanship." He had power over them and enjoyed this rare sense of adequacy.

The goals of therapy were to attack the low frustration tolerance beneath the obscene phone calls and also to assist him in beginning to experience himself as a more adequate human being. By the second therapy session, Rod had read Young's (1974) *Rational Counseling Primer* and was quickly able to get in touch with what he was saying to himself, i.e., "I am compelled to call." The co-therapists and other members of his RET group challenged his assertion that he was compelled to make these calls. By the third session, Rod was admitting that he often felt bored and particularly made telephone calls at these times because he thought he *"needed"* some excitement. "A guy ought to be able to have some excitement!" he claimed. With confrontation by the group, Rod was able to come to identify his own irrational demands and to dispute and reject them as "needs." To this point Rod had progressed quite well, but his progress than took a turn backwards. He went to the extreme of denying his desires or shielding himself from realizing them. He assigned himself numerous odd jobs which kept him away from telephones so as not to be tempted. The important dynamics here are that while he may *want* to have excitement, he *need* not make the phone calls. Although the impulses themselves may wane as they are not acted upon and as cognitive changes are taking place, it seems important to recognize, rather than deny, the presence of the strong desires while doing battle with the alleged necessity of acting upon them.

To combat his avoidance, Rod was given homework assignments of intentionally approaching telephones, looking at them, and saying to himself that he would like to make nuisance calls. This assignment was not immediately effective in that Rod came back to tell the group that in fact he did not experience any desire to make such calls. It was not until sometime later when he was rejected by a girlfriend and became quite angry that he wanted to vent his anger by making an annoying phone call. At this time he was able to carry out the assigned exercise of approaching a phone and successfully refuting his "need." Additional work was also done on his demand for acceptance and intolerance of rejection.

The above description demonstrates how, in working with an obscene phone caller, the discrimination between wants and needs operates and can be effectively dealt with. Another focus in RET could have been on his irrational beliefs that he must be a totally adequate person. However, the therapists chose to work next with other cognitions which seemed to be keeping him from developing greater confidence of which he was capable. Rod was unemployed and inactive much of the time. His self-defeating view was that a job opportunity should approach him. He was guided by the action that life *should* be easy and that some of the changes he wanted for himself *should* happen to him without any effort on his part. By working through these silly cognitions, he eventually became more active in pursuing regular employment and obtained a steady job. After several months of (1) making no further obscene phone calls; (2) a marked diminution, if not elimination, of desires to make such phone calls; (3) regular employment; and (4) a noticeable increase in self-esteem, Rod was discharged from the group as significantly benefited.

The Voyeur

Ralph became excited by looking in windows. The onset or original causative factor in his case was far clearer than is typically found by the clinician. His peeking started when he was a teenager and was dating a girl without her parents' knowledge or permission. She invited him to visit her one night at her bedroom window, which he found highly stimulating. Several days later he went back, saw her undressing, and stood there and masturbated.

Ralph came to therapy when his wife threw him out. She had caught him peeking in on her adolescent daughters several times. Each time he had promised never to do it again, but the last time he did it, his wife made him move out and told him to get help or stay away. In an initial interview he readily admitted that he found his stepdaughters arousing. He also disclosed that he peeked into windows of various other houses as well. He explained his peeking by saying that he experienced sexual arousal and found that peeking and masturbating provided an exciting sexual release to him. Ralph found sexual relations with his wife to be satisfactory, but due to their different work schedules she often was not available when he became aroused. Even when their schedules made sex convenient, he at times would impulsively look in a window while on his way to shop or while doing other errands.

By the third rational-emotive group session, Ralph was in harness. He acknowledged that he had recently wanted to look into a window, but "had better not—tough!" He had read the *Rational Counseling Primer* (Young, 1974) several times and was beginning to assimilate the ideas. The next week he told of driving by a house which he had previously found attractive, yet he drove on. The group examined how he checked himself. He indeed was using cognitive means, such as saying to himself to stop and think before acting and reminding himself of the dire consequences. It is interesting to note that Ralph's approach was a very familiar one in groups of acting-out individuals. Frequently they begin therapy by giving themselves injunctions that they should not act in the way they have and reminding themselves of the aversive consequences. For most impulsive persons, however, this merely provides a temporary deterrent for they eventually find themselves repeating. Clients also frequently use one of the three palliative A's in the initial stages of treatment: avoidance, activity, aversiveness. That is, they avoid the situation in which they have previously acted out, as was described in the case of the obscene phone caller. Others throw themselves into a high pitch of activity so as to crowd out time during which they might slip. And others like Ralph remind themselves of the aversiveness in the attempt to curb themselves.

In an attempt to help Ralph arrive at an in-depth solution, the co-therapists urged Ralph to challenge his irrational belief that he *had to* act on his urges. He was told, "Your wife's anger and the possibility of getting shot while looking in someone's window have never stopped you from repeating this before. Let's look at what you are saying to yourself that sets you up for doing this over and over." Ralph recognized and began challenging his beliefs that he needed to look in windows and that he had to have sexual release whenever or wherever he felt aroused. The sixth session he was given a homework assignment of viewing from a distance a favorite window where he had been visually delighted numerous times before. Before doing this, he practiced picturing himself sitting in his car looking at the window in the group session; acknowledging his strong desires to approach that window and look in; and challenging his "need" for sexual gratification at that moment. He also practiced substituting alternative statements to himself such as, "I can have intercourse with my wife (Ralph was now living at home). Even if my wife is not available, I can beat off in the bathroom. I may want to feast my eyes on that woman lying nude in bed, but I don't *need* to. It's only when I tell myself that I need to and ignore my other possibilities that I find myself having to peek."

The next week Ralph told the group that he had carried out his in vivo assignment only to find himself walking up to the window. He got within four feet of the window before he was able to use his practiced cognitions to control his urge. Ralph stopped by telling himself that he did not need to peek in. He turned, returned to his car, and left. He was anxious and shaken by his near loss of control. The therapists focused on his success in eventually stopping himself rather than his perfectly carrying out the homework assignment from his automobile. He was praised highly for his demonstrated ability to use his newly acquired cognitive approach. With tongue-in-cheek, the therapists told him they had confidence he would not get so close in the future. The therapists actually thought that there was a definite risk of his peeking. The next week he went to the same place as before, but this time stayed in his car. He was aroused and strongly attracted by the sight of the window. Ralph went back and forth telling himself that he wanted to but did not have to, yet having the urge emerge again, drawing him toward that window. Thus he had the opportunity several times in succession to challenge his irrational demand that he needed sexual satisfaction right then. Although he admitted to peeking on one occasion in the first two weeks after starting therapy, there were no further voyeuristic occurrences. In the next two months, he gave many examples of how he had used the distinction between wants and needs to maintain control. His relationship with his wife improved and he reported a reduction in the intensity of urges experienced upon seeing windows into which he had previously peeked. Shortly before discharge from the group he summed up where he was cognitively in his own shorthand version: while working at the chalkboard in front of the group: "Window, be nice, feel good, tuff, don't have to."

Role of Cognitions in Impulse Control

Direct empirical support that rational-emotive theory is an accurate conceptualization of the dynamics of impulsive disorders in adults is lacking. However, there are a number of experimental analog studies with children in which impulsivity has been altered via cognitive training.

Bem (1967) demonstrated that verbal self-control can be produced experimentally in 3-year-old children. Ridberg, Parke, and Hetherington (1971) reported that an impulsive cognitive tempo can be altered by modeling techniques. Following exposure to a reflective model, impulsive children showed a significant increase in response time and made significantly fewer errors. Hartig and Kanfer (1973) measured children's resistance to temptation. They found that self-instruction not to transgress, regardless of whether positive or negative consequences were included or not, were considerably more effective than neutral recitation or no self-instructions. Hartig and Kanfer further discovered that of their 220 subjects, the half who verbalized the self-instructions out loud had significantly longer latencies than nonverbalizers, confirming that overt recitation of self-instructions significantly affects the waiting interval in resisting a temptation. These findings are reminiscent of Luria's (1961) work, in which he suggested three developmental stages in the internalized control of behavior. The child's performance is first controlled by the verbal instructions from parents, he then begins to regulate some of his own actions through audible self-talk, and finally, the self-statements become covert and expand their extensive regulatory influences.

The most extensive research in the role of cognitions in impulse control has consisted of utilizing cognitive self-instructional training to alter the behavior of impulsive children. Meichenbaum and Goodman (1971) required children to talk to themselves, initially overtly and then covertly, to increase self-control (see Chapter 26 of this book). "Impulsivity" was characterized by extremely brief response latencies and a high frequency of errors. The Meichenbaum training procedures consisted of five steps. The child (1) observed an adult who modeled the task while talking to himself out loud, (2) performed the same task under the overt guidance by the model, (3) performed the task while instructing himself out loud, (4) whispered the instructions to himself as he performed the task, and (5) performed the task while guiding his performance via private speech. The children improved significantly on measures of cognitive impulsivity; improvement was still present one month later. Meichenbaum and Goodman further demonstrated that while cognitive modeling alone slowed down Ss' response time, only with the addition to self-instructional training was there a significant decrease in errors.

Camp (1976) has found that "aggressive" boys, in contrast to "normals," are characterized by immature and irrelevant private speech and fail to employ verbal mediational activity in many situations where it would be appropriate. Finch and Montgomery (1973) and Stein, Finch, Hooke, Montgomery, and Nelson (1975) have reported that children with an impulsive cognitive style think in pictures, while reflectives think with words. Finch, Wilkinson, Nelson, and Montgomery (1975) suggested that training in verbal self-instruction should maximize the likelihood of helping children respond more reflectively. Finch and his colleagues found that a cognitive training procedure which emphasized verbal self-instructions similar to those employed by Meichenbaum and Goodman (1971) resulted in significant modification in cognitive style with both an increase in latencies and decrease in errors.

Case studies by Kendall and Finch (1976) and Bornstein and Quevillon (1976) extend the work of Meichenbaum and Goodman (1971). Kendall and Finch treated a 9-year-old with a combination of verbal self-instructions and response cost. Treatment was sequentially applied to inappropriate "switches" (i.e., changing the focus of attention) in each of three target behaviors according to a multiple baseline design, i.e., a separate baseline was established for each respective behavior. Positive change in all target behaviors and in response latencies and errors were evident at post-treatment and six months later. Bornstein and Quevillon studied the effects of self-instruction using a multiple baseline design across subjects, i.e., a separate baseline was established for each child. Self-instructional training was initiated at different points in time for each of the three children in a classroom setting. On-task behaviors increased dramatically concomitant with the introduction of the self-instructional package for each respective child. Transfer of training effects from the experimental task to the actual classroom situation occurred and treatment gains were present five months later.

The impressive research in self-instructional training provides considerable support for the direct role of cognitions in changing behavior. Rational-emotive therapy can claim tentative and indirect support from these studies in that the treatment approaches were generically cognitive-behavior, although not specifically rational-emotive. Generalization is limited because the subjects investigated were children and because many of the studies were analog studies focusing upon target behaviors which were not clinical problems. The results, however, are most encouraging to rational-emotive therapists wishing to make an impact upon persons with impulsive disorders. There are notable similarities between self-instructional training procedures and rational-emotive therapy. Both approaches emphasize the role of covert self-talk in emotional distress and behavioral excesses and advocate either the installation of new thought patterns or the disputation of dysfunctional cognitions and affirmation of reality-based beliefs. Outcome studies are now needed in which rational-emotive therapy, as well as other cognitive training procedures, are applied to adults presenting genuine clinical problems of poor impulse control.

Summary and Notes on Treatment

In the case reports given in Chapter 7, the rational-emotive dynamics of impulsive behaviors have been discussed and illustrated. The impulsive individual is described as a person who misidentifies his wants as needs, *demanding* that his urges be satisfied. He is depicted as having "low frustration tolerance" in that he believes it *awful* not to have his wishes met and furthermore believes that he *can not stand* even temporary discomfort or forego the pleasures of the moment. He *dictates* that the world satisfy his wishes, *insists* that life be easy for him, and *commands* that others gratify him. Asserting that he *should* be gratified, the impulsive individual will predictably act out. In the face of social sanctions he may respond with anger and he may become further frustrated over what he perceives to be unjust interference.

To the author, the cognitive dynamics of impulsive disorders are far clearer than exactly how change is most effectively brought about in the impulsive person. From the clinical standpoint, it would seem to be the therapist's task to show his clients exactly how they display their low frustration tolerance, how they can give up childishly dictating that the world be completely and instantaneously gratifying to them, and how through a reality-centered existence they can be in control of their lives. These goals may best be achieved by taking the client through the logical disputation of his beliefs and the substitution of more rational assertions for them. Although less elegant, it may be sufficient for some clients simply to adopt the belief that "I do not *need* such and such, it is *only frustrating* not to get it, and *I can stand* to live without it." This could conceivably be accomplished through direct self-instructional training (Meichenbaum and Goodman, 1971) or via the experiencing of discomfort upon perceiving the relationship between cognitions and behavior. Thus self-instructional training with the statement, "I do not need . . ." may itself be effective. Or, dissonance and motivation for change may be created by demonstrating to the client that his "need and should" statements *cause* him pain and problems. From several sources in this chapter, we have evidence that initially verbalizing new cognitions aloud may accelerate the process of change. Eventually, silent self-instructions practiced in in vivo situations are likely to consolidate further the cognitive changes into behavioral effects. Process studies, as well as outcome research, will be useful in understanding and improving the therapy process with impulsive persons.

While the primary focus of this chapter has been on the dynamics of impulsive disorders, some consideration of treatment issues seems warranted. In treating acting-out adult clients, some degree of motivation for therapy by the client seems a prerequisite to change. Many persons involved in antisocial behavior are resistant, hostile, and/or obviously not interested in changing. If they are to be seen in therapy, the initial RET procedure should involve demonstrating to them how translating their *preferences* for gratifying their desires into an *insistence* on gratification is irrational and leads to their inefficient, self-destructive, punishment-eliciting behavior. In other words, such individuals first have to be sold on the concept that it is they who are responsible for their behavior and that it is the illogical equating of wants with needs which has led to their acting *as if* they ought to gratify themselves.

As conceptually sound as the above plan may be, good luck! Dealing with the resistances posed by clients can be a very slow process, as in the case of Jerry, the pedophil. Dealing successfully with the defiance and hostility of persons like Brad, an armed robber, is often futile; these individuals adamantly deny any responsibility for their present predicament, attribute the blame entirely to their employers, society, or the "pigs," and come to view the therapist as part of the system that frustrates them. At times the defenses presented are not unlike those found in the paranoid individual—denial, external attribution, projection. The author is convinced, however, that the effort with the resistive person is worth making, that even the most impulsively disturbed clients can be impacted by challenging their asserted "needs," and that predicting which resistant clients will be refractive is not possible until the clinical work is attempted with them for at least a few sessions.

References

Bem, S. L. Verbal self-control: the establishment of effective self-instruction. *Journal of Experimental Psychology,* 1967, *74,* 485–491.

Bornstein, P. H., and Quevillon, R. P. The effects of a self-instructional package with overactive pre-school boys. *Journal of Applied Behavioral Analysis,* 1976, *9,* 179–188.

Camp, B. W. Verbal mediation in young aggressive boys. Unpublished manuscript, 1976.

Ellis, A. *Humanistic psychotherapy: The rational-emotive approach.* New York: Julian Press, 1973.

Finch, A. J., Jr., and Montgomery, L. E. Reflection-impulsivity and information seeking in emotionally disturbed children. *Journal of Abnormal Child Psychology,* 1973, *1,* 358–362.

Finch, A. J., Jr., Wilkinson, M. D., Nelson, W. M., III, and Montgomery, L. E. Modification of an impulsive cognitive tempo in emotionally disturbed boys. *Journal of Abnormal Child Psychology,* 1975, *3,* 49–52.

Hartig, M., and Kanfer, F. H. The role of verbal self-instructions in children's resistance to temptation. *Journal of Personality and Social Psychology,* 1973, *25,* 259–267.

Kendall, P. C., and Finch, A. J., Jr. A cognitive behavioral treatment for impulse control: A case study. *Journal of Consulting and Clinical Psychology,* 1976, *44,* 852–857.

Luria, A. *The role of speech in the regulation of normal and abnormal behavior.* New York: Liveright, 1961.

Meichenbaum, D. H., and Goodman, J. Training impulsive children to talk to themselves: A means of developing self-control. *Journal of Abnormal Psychology,* 1971, *77,* 115–126.

Ridberg, E. H., Parke, R. D., and Hetherington, E. M. Modification of impulse and reflective cognitive styles through observation of film-mediated models. *Developmental Psychology,* 1971, *5,* 369–377.

Stein, A. B., Finch, A. J., Jr., Hooke, J. F., Montgomery, L. E., and Nelson, W. M., III. Cognitive tempo and the mode of representation in emotionally disturbed and normal children. *Journal of Psychology,* 1975, *90,* 197–201.

Watkins, J. T. Rational-emotive therapy and the treatment of behavioral excesses. *Rational Living,* 1973, *8,* No. 1, 29–31.

Young, H. S. *A rational counseling primer.* New York: Institute for Rational Living, 1974.

8

Sex and Love Problems in Women

Albert Ellis

In Chapter 8, Albert Ellis presents a very clear picture of the RET position regarding the nature of sexual dysfunctioning in women. Noting that the vast majority of women (as well as men) today "suffer from one or more fairly serious love and sex difficulties," he hypothesizes that women are prone to view themselves as inadequate without the love of a man, to repress and suppress their sexual arousability, and to allow themselves to be sexually and personally exploited. Starting from the above premises, Ellis presents the dynamics behind some of the main sex-love disturbances of females in Western civilization: love slobbism, sex-love hostility, sexual inadequacy, and general unassertiveness. Throughout this discussion, he broadens the notion of sexual dysfunction to include sex role problems (e.g., general unassertiveness) as well as problems in physical sexual performance (e.g., frigidity).

WHETHER WOMEN, just because they are female, have any different or greater sex and love problems than men is a highly debatable question. On the one hand, we have outstanding female writers and researchers, such as Mead (1955) and Thompson (1973), insisting that women are distinctly different from (though hardly inferior to) men and that therefore they have special kinds of sex-love difficulties. On the other hand, we have equally prominent and authoritative feminists, such as Chesler (1972), de Beauvoir (1953), and Millet (1971), claiming that practically all the "unique" psychological and sexual "disturbances" of women are culturally incited and that if male chauvinism stopped rearing its ugly head these "unique" problems would become practically nonexistent.

No one presently seems to know the indubitable answer to this important question, since all the published evidence is, to say the very least, inconclusive. What does seem reasonably clear is that whatever are women's "intrinsic" or "natural" sex and love problems, these difficulties

A somewhat longer version of Chapter 8, entitled "The Treatment of Sex and Love Problems in Women," appeared in *Women in Therapy*, ed. by Violet Franks and Vasanti Burtle (New York: Brunner/Mazel, 1974).

153

tend to become enormously exacerbated in any male-dominated culture. If women are easily prone, as they may possibly be, to viewing themselves as inadequate and undeserving, to being overly dependent and in dire need of others' love and approval, to letting themselves be sexually exploitable, and to unconsciously repressing or consciously suppressing their sexual arousability and orgasmic capacities, their "proneness" in these respects is certainly abetted by the tendency of a vast majority of human cultures—which generally tend to be male supremacist—to espouse a double standard of morality, to exploit women's weaknesses, and in one way or another (and usually quite significantly) to give females only second-class citizenship.

The sex-love problems to which women are so frequently heir are therefore in large part social and are inextricably meshed with the existing social order (Seward, 1973). If full, or even notable, solutions to some of these problems are ever to be achieved, this order will probably have to be significantly modified. For example, if females are to stop putting themselves down for having "unfeminine" bodies, the extremely unrealistic views of Hollywood, the TV industry, and the bathing beauty concepts of what the ideal female form absolutely *should* be would better undergo drastic revision (Ellis, 1961, Frumkin, 1973). For even the teachings of an efficient system of psychotherapy—like rational-emotive therapy—are going to be impeded if a woman's therapist shows her that she doesn't *have to* conform to societal standards of physical beauty while practically every movie and TV presentation that she sees tells her that she *does*.

Granting that women's sex-love difficulties are importantly intertwined with the social fabric in which they are reared and reside and that the elegant solution to these problems includes significant social change, the question still arises: What are some of the most common problems in this area with which, for one reason or another, women are afflicted? It is to this question that the present chapter will largely be devoted.

The vast majority of women today seem to suffer from one or more fairly serious love and sex difficulties. This may be seen as an exaggerated and alarmist statement, but let me hasten to add that I would make exactly the same assertion about the vast majority of men. Even if I forget about the literally thousands of clients whom I have worked with over the last 30 years, and even if I stick to the evidence I have gained from detailed conversations with hundreds of non-clients whom I have met during the same period in many different parts of the United States and Canada (and more occasionally in various other parts of the world), I would still stand by this declaration. From 80% to 90% of the males I have talked to are afflicted with some significant degree of inability to love, and of insensate jealousy, engaging in sex more for ego-raising games than for intrinsic enjoyment, varying degrees of impotence, compulsive homosexuality or virulent antihomosexuality, sexual anxieties and phobias, or other kinds of love-sex hangups. Come to think of it, I think I could easily (and safely) say 90% to 95%!

So women, even in our male-dominated culture, are hardly unique in their sexual and amative problems. But since this chapter, by arbitrary delimitation, is designed to be about women and sex, let me stick to that aspect of human affairs. And let me now list some of the main sex-love disturbances to which, on the basis of my many clinical and nonclinical intimate contacts with females, I think women in our culture (that is, Western civilization) are prone.

Love Slobbism

Women, as Lord Byron poetically and perspicaciously noted over a century ago, tend to make love not merely *an* important part of their lives but their whole existence. Although the women's liberation movement may eventually change this, it has not yet done so to any considerable extent. The average female, married or unmarried, believes that she *has* to be part of an intimate twosome; that she *must* be securely companioned by someone who dearly cares for her until the very end of her days; and that, if she has children, they've *got to* be interested in and want to regularly relate to her. When there is any good possibility—as there assuredly is, in the course of her everyday existence—that her dire need to love and be loved may not be successfully fulfilled, she often turns herself into a love slob and literally or figuratively licks the ass (or penis) of any man, woman, or child whose approval she thinks she absolutely must, must, must have. When her attempts to nail down love guarantees appear to be failing, she commonly makes herself feel desperately lonely, alienated, depressed, worthless, hopeless, or suicidal.

Love slobbism is a severe symptom of disturbance—or what I call point C (emotional Consequence) in the A-B-C's of rational-emotive psychology. It usually follows after, at point A (an Activating Event), a woman has been unable to find a suitable love partner or has found a potential mate and been rejected by him. Since most women (like most men) do not fully understand how emotional Consequences really occur, they falsely believe that Activating Events (A) cause these Consequences (C), and tell themselves (and others): "My lover rejected me and that made me depressed. His leaving me hurt me very much."

Hogwash! Activating Events (A) virtually never cause emotional Consequences (C). The real issue is B—the individual's Belief System, which *interprets* and *evaluates* the events at A. What happens, therefore, when a woman gets rejected, at A, and feels and acts like a love slob (that is, utterly dependent, depressed, and self-downing) at C, is that she believes, at B, a set of irrational ideas. And it is almost entirely these ideas (or attitudes, values, philosophies, or Beliefs) which determine whether or not she will take on the self-defeating behavior of love slobbism.

Such as? Such as: (1) "It's *awful* that my mate (or potential mate) rejected me!" (2) "I *can't stand* being rejected!" (3) "I *should have* been more beautiful, intelligent, and loving so that he then would not have rejected me." (4) "Because I didn't do what I *should have* done with him, I am a rotten person, a worm!" (5) "Since I'm so worthless, every partner I go with will recognize this, and I will *never* maintain a successful, ongoing relationship with a desirable person." (6) "If so, life won't be worth living at all, and I might as well kill myself as face such a horrible, hopeless existence!"

It is these irrational Beliefs (iB's), rather than the woman's being rejected (at point A), that cause her anguish, despair, and acute love slobbism (at point C). Even if she *continually* got rejected at A, and thereby failed to get what she wanted in the way of a deep, satisfying love relationship, this kind of steady rejection would merely be frustrating, depriving, and thwarting. Only by her irrational *evaluations* would she make it demeaning and depressing.

The solution? Pretty obvious, if I, as a therapist, can help this woman use rational-emotive psychology. For I then merely try to induce her to go on to D—to Dispute her irrational Beliefs. Thus, I persuade her, by teaching her the logico-empirical method of challenging and questioning her irrational hypotheses about herself and the universe, to Dispute as follows:

1. "Why is it *awful* if your mate (or potential mate) rejects you?" Answer: "It isn't! For *awful* means, first, *more than* obnoxious and unpleasant; and how could anything be *more than* very frustrating and unpleasant—even rejection by a person whom I deeply love? Second, if I say a thing is *awful* I really mean that because it is highly undesirable, it shouldn't, mustn't exist. But *why* shouldn't things I don't desire, like rejection, exist? No reason whatsoever! Whatever exists exists! Only God can mandate away unpleasantness; and, obviously, I'm no God!"

2. "Where is the evidence that *I can't stand* being rejected?" Answer: "Clearly, there isn't any. Of course, I'll never *like* rejection; but I can damned well stand what I don't like! No matter how many times I am

rejected by someone for whom I care, I'll still survive. What's more, I can even—at least, if I stop my whining—be happy surviving without him: though not, perhaps, *as* happy as I would be if I survived with his love."

3. "Why *should* I have been more beautiful, intelligent, and loving so that he then would not have rejected me?" Answer: "Only because I stupidly *think* I should! It would have been fine had I possessed exactly the kind of traits that he adores and if he consequently loved me. But just because *it would be desirable* if I had *x* or *y* or *z* hardly means that I *should* or *must* have it. There is no reason, in fact, why I must be *anything;* and I'd better accept that reality!"

4. "Even if I didn't do what I could have done to get him to accept me, how does it make me a rotten person or a worm for my acting so badly?" Answer: "It doesn't. Although my *traits* and *performances* can legitimately be rated, there is no accurate way of rating *me,* my totality, my essence, or my being. *I* consist of thousands of traits, some good, some bad; some of them one way today, much different tomorrow. I may, for example, be good at writing, but that hardly makes me a *good person.* And I may be bad at sex, but that doesn't make me a *bad individual.* All people, including me, are much too complex to be given a global, total rating. There are no human worms and there are no human angels. All humans are simply human—never subhuman or superhuman. I'd better, therefore, acknowledge the bad or inefficient *things* I did that may have kept me from winning him, but I'd better not say that the rating of those things (which I can helpfully use to change them) is the same thing as the rating of me. I, as a person, am not really ratable, even though most of my individual acts and performances may be."

5. "Is it likely, if the person who rejected me finds me (or, more accurately, my traits) of so little worth to him, that all other men whom I find attractive will recognize my total worthlessness and that I will therefore never be able to maintain a successful, ongoing relationship?" Answer: "Hardly! Individual tastes widely differ, and some males will accept me for the very reasons he rejected me. If he and many others reject me, that will tend to prove that *it will be difficult* for me to find the kind of partner I want. But difficult only means difficult—and not impossible. If I really am handicapped in finding the kind of person I want because some of my traits are not too attractive, then maybe I'd better look harder and work more energetically to discover and win this kind of partner."

6. "Is it true that if I never find the kind of sex-love partner I desire, life won't be worth living at all and that I might as well kill myself than face such a horrible, hopeless existence?" Answer: "Of course not! My

life will, of course, be *less* enjoyable without a good sex-love relationship than it would be with one. But there are many other things I can enjoy besides sex, love, and mating, and if these things are entirely unavailable to me for the rest of my days (which is highly unlikely, if I get off my butt and keep seeking them!) that's really going to be sad. But not awful or terrible—for I can still find *something* to make my life meaningful and happy!"

If, therapeutically, this rejected and despairing woman will Dispute, at D, her irrational Beliefs (iB's), and if she will continue to vigorously Dispute them until she no longer devoutly holds them, or until she at most subscribes to them lightly and occasionally, she will almost invariably be able to change her disturbed feelings, at C, from hurt, depression, horror, and withdrawal to sorrow, regret, frustration, and annoyance—or from highly inappropriate and self-defeating to distinctly appropriate and self-motivating feelings. She won't feel deliriously happy or even indifferent about being rejected—for those emotions, too, would be inappropriate and self-sabotaging—but she will feel suitably sad and concerned; and will be able to use these feelings to help herself in her future quest for sex-love acceptance.

Love slobbism, in other words, doesn't stem from a woman's strong *desire* or *preference* for relating intimately to others but from her grandiose *demand, command,* or *need* that she so relate. She makes herself into a love slob by sanely wanting intimacy and then by insanely escalating her wanting into a whining dictate. When she logically and empirically—that is, rationally—Disputes (at D) her own puerile demandingness and de-escalates it into a strong (though not necessitous) desiringness, she solves her emotional problems, learns to live with (though not necessarily like) harsh reality, and increases her chances of getting what she wants in the future. Her love slobbism then tends to evaporate.

Sex-Love Hostility

While most women (like most men) put themselves down when they act inadequately or get rejected by someone for whom they care, some heavily create feelings of hostility and rage rather than (or in addition to) feelings of shame and worthlessness when they are sexually or amatively thwarted. A typical example, in this connection, is the woman who is in an emotional relationship where the man, her lover or husband, says that he cares for her but keeps acting in a manner that she thinks is not too loving and seems to be interested in other women, too. At point A (the Activating Event) she observes his seeming lack of interest and at point C (the emotional Consequence), she becomes intensely jealous and hostile. Because of her jealousy and hostility, she frequently becomes so obnoxious in her behavior toward her partner that she appreciably helps to ruin their relationship.

In this kind of sex-love problem, B, her Belief System, is again the key issue. For no matter how much she tends to think that A causes C—"He lied to me about that other women he is interested in, and he thus upset me and made me angry!"—she really causes it by her own rational and irrational Beliefs. Her rational Beliefs (rB's) probably are: "He is neglecting me and I don't like that! I wish he were only enamored of me and it is most unfortunate that he isn't!" As in the illustration used under love slobbism, if she stayed with these Beliefs, and these alone, she would feel appropriately sorry, disappointed, and annoyed—but hardly insanely jealous and angry.

Her hostility comes from her concomitant irrational Beliefs (iB's); namely: "How horrible it is that he is treating me like this! How can he act so unfairly! He shouldn't be acting that way at all; what a louse he is for behaving the way he shouldn't!" These Beliefs are almost completely magical, unrealistic, and unprovable because: (1) It isn't *horrible* (that is, more than 100% unpleasant) that he is treating her this way—only highly inconvenient. (2) Even if he is acting unfairly (which, of course, he may not be), he can easily act in that manner, and has every right, as a fallible human, to make mistakes and commit injustices. (3) It would be lovely for her, no doubt, if he acted more lovingly. But that is hardly a reason why he *should, ought,* or *must* act that way. (4) He may indeed be behaving lousily but that hardly makes him, as a total human, a louse. In many other respects, toward her and others, he probably behaves quite unlousily, even remarkably well. She is therefore foolishly damning *him,* instead of some of his *behavior.*

The solution to this woman's problem of jealousy and hatred, therefore, is to work hard at changing her B's—her Beliefs—instead of inappropriately overfocusing on A (someone else's attitudes, emotions, and behavior) and C (her own feelings which stem from her irrational Beliefs). In looking at her irrational Beliefs (her demandingness about her husband or lover) she might also well look at some of her own irrational B's about herself (her underlying assumptions that she *must* have some man's complete and utterly guaranteed love if she is to accept herself and live a reasonably happy existence). It might, indeed, be *preferable* if her chosen partner deeply cared for her forever. But why *must* she depend on the attainment of a *preferable* state of affairs? Clearly—if she thinks about it and gives up her grandiose demands—she mustn't.

Sexual Inadequacy

If we go by ideal standards of sexual arousal and orgasmic achievement, most civilized females are frequently or usually inadequate. For it is only the rare woman who easily becomes aroused, who doesn't require some special condition (such as an intense romantic attachment to her partner) to let herself go sexually, who never is guilty about masturbation, who quickly comes to orgasm, who can almost always climax during intercourse, and who can achieve a minimum of several orgasms a week. Every study of female sexuality that has ever been done tends to show that even among selected women who are partly picked for their "normal" sexuality, high incidences of various kinds of sexual disability tend to exist (de Martino, 1969, 1973; Fisher, 1973; Kinsey, Pomeroy, Martin, and Gebhard, 1969; Masters and Johnson, 1966, 1971; Singer, 1973; Sorenson, 1973).

Even if we go by much less ideal standards and consider as sexually inadequate only those women who have great difficulty in becoming sexually aroused and who never or rarely achieve any kind of orgasm, we still are left with a quite sizable number, and a great many of these females tend to have some kind of psychological problem, particularly that of anxiety (Ellis, 1961, 1965a, 1965b, Masters and Johnson, 1971). Their irrational Beliefs (iB's), in these instances, overlap with the same kind of Beliefs that they are telling themselves about love and rejection, except that they are more specifically about sex failure.

By way of illustration, let us consider Sally G., who came to see me because she only occasionally came to a climax even when her lovers massaged her clitoral region for fifteen or twenty minutes and who recently had been becoming completely turned off to sex, so that virtually nothing aroused her. "The man I am going with now," she said, "is great. There's not a thing he wouldn't do to satisfy me. He really cares and *wants* me to be satisfied. And I love him for that—as well as for many other things. But nothing seems to work any more, and if it continues like this, I'm sure I'll ruin the best relationship I've ever had."

"And how do you feel about all this?" I asked.

"Feel! How would anyone feel in my position? Depressed, of course. Depressed like I've never been depressed before!"

Already, after knowing Sally for only a few minutes, I thought I knew the basic answer—and the solution—to her problem. For that is the advantage of an efficient theory of psychotherapy, such as RET. Give me A and C—which most clients are fully aware of and can exposit in from five to fifteen minutes—and I almost always know what B and D are. And also what can be done with and about them, to help solve the client's emotional difficulties.

Just to make no mistake about this, however (since even the best psychotherapists are hardly infallible!), I asked, "While you're having sex with your lover, what exactly are you saying to yourself? What are you thinking, at what I call B (your Belief System), about yourself, your partner, and the sex act itself?"

"Oh, that's easy. I'm saying many things to myself—all bad. I'm saying, first, that it's taking too long for me to get aroused. That I'll probably never come to orgasm. That he must be getting bored. That this will ruin our relationship. That there's something really wrong with me. That I might as well kill myself, if this keeps up!"

"Very sexy thoughts, I must say!"

"You're right. They're as sexy as the kitchen sink. But I *know* what's going to happen—or *not* happen. I really *know,* after all the experience I've had, the very dreadful experience I've had, recently. So what do you expect me to be saying to myself—that everything is glorious and I'm going to get sixteen orgasms before he can say Ms. Robinson?"

"No, I don't expect anything. But the point is: *You* do."

"I do?"

"Yes, you expect—or demand—that it *shouldn't* take so long for you to get aroused. That you've *got to* come to orgasm. That he *must not* get bored. That you *have to* maintain a good relationship with him. That there *ought not* be something wrong with you. That you *need* a good sex life to be a happy human being."

"Well, what's wrong with *those* expectations? *Shouldn't* I get aroused more easily, have orgasms, and maintain a good relationship with my lover? Why *shouldn't* I?"

"Because—if you stop to think about it (which few humans, alas, do) —there pretty obviously aren't any absolutistic shoulds, oughts, musts, necessities, got to's, or have to's in the universe. Not, at least, as far as anyone has ever scientifically proven."

"Nonsense! Don't I *have to* respond better sexually if I am to keep him or any other reasonably sexy man satisfied?"

"No, of course not. It would, in all probability, *be better* if you were sexually more arousable and orgasmic; but ten thousand *it would be betters* never equal a single *should.* For 'it would be better if I were sexier' means that *the chances are* that if you were, you would please your lover and *probably* have a more satisfying relationship with him. But some lovers, actually, might find your sexiness *dis*pleasing; and some would love you more without it."

"Damned few!" retorted Sally.

"Yes, probably. But the mere fact that most of your lovers most of the time would love you more if you were more arousable and orgasmic still doesn't equal (1) I *must* be loved and am a thoroughly worthless skunk if I am not, nor (2) There is an inalterable law of the universe which states that I *have to* be sexy to be loved."

"Are you trying to tell me that I must think in terms of 'it would be betters' rather than of 'musts' if I am to overcome my feelings of sexual anesthesia?"

"No—not you *must think that way,* but *it would be better if you did!*"

Whereupon I proceeded to show Sally that she had at least two serious emotional problems—or inordinate demands on herself—which seriously interfered with her functioning. First, she demanded and commanded that she be easily and fully sexually arousable, and because she was focusing so intently, during the sex act, on "I must succeed at sex; it's terrible to fail," she was not focusing on sexually exciting stimuli (such as her lover's body or his feelings for her) and was foredooming herself to failure.

Once Sally had sex (at A), told herself that she absolutely *had to* succeed (at B), and thereby brought on anxiety and frigidity (at C), she then perceived what was happening at C and turned this into another A and B. Thus, at the new A (Activating Experience), she experienced panic and sexlessness. At the new B (Belief System), she told herself, "It's horrible to be sexually inadequate! What a thorough, unlovable slob I am for being so inadequate!" At the new C (emotional Consequence), she then felt even more inadequate and hopelessly depressed.

Sally, in other words, had *two* intense fears of failure: first, her fear of failing sexually, which deflected her from thinking of arousing stimuli and which caused her to be frigid; and second, her fear of being worthless for *being* sexually inadequate. This same kind of doubleheaded fear is common in nonsexual disturbances as well. An individual is extremely anxious *lest* he or she fail at school, work, or social affairs; then, when anxiety actually brings on failure, he or she is exceptionally anxious *about* this anxiety and about the actual failure. Consequently, people circularly put themselves down, become panicked about being panicked, depressed about being depressed, and feel worthless about feeling worthless.

Sexual and General Unassertiveness

Until recently, perhaps the great majority of women, particularly in Western "civilization," have been much less assertive than it would have been preferable for them to be. Although women's lack of assertiveness tends to be something of a general trait, prevalent in many aspects of their lives, its sex-love aspects are notably pernicious. Thus, in our society, females tend to avoid actively pursuing relationships with males they care for. They often avoid taking the sex initiative, even when they are highly desirous, both before and after marriage. They go along with hypocritical double standards of sexual morality, even when actively discriminated against by these standards. They pretend that they are sexually satisfied when they really are not. They often accede to male demands, even when they feel sexually indifferent or revolted. They refrain from instituting separation or divorce proceedings, in spite of the unsatisfactory state of their marriages. They easily go along with conventional child-rearing traditions that make them virtually slaves to their children. They meekly accept work and household duties without asking sufficient support or cooperation from their husbands. Et cetera!

RET has always been in the forefront of those therapies that promulgate assertion training. It especially does so by activity homework assignments. Thus, females in individual or group rational-emotive therapy are frequently given graduated series of assignments that finally enable them to pick up attractive males in public places (such as dances, singles gatherings, or bars); to phone their men friends instead of passively waiting for the men to call; to make sexual overtures when they wish to do so; to ask their partners to engage in sex-love practices that they particularly enjoy; to stop taking too much responsibility for their children; and to do many other "unfeminine" things that they truly would like to do (Wolfe, 1973).

If they have great difficulty in asserting themselves in these ways, they are frequently put through role-playing forms of behavior rehearsal in the course of their individual or group therapy sessions. Thus, a shy and meek woman may be rehearsed, in the course of a group session, to ask a man to dinner, to go to a party alone and break in on the conversation of three people who are talking together, or to ask her lover to bring her to orgasm through oral-genital relations.

As usual, these behavior therapy aspects of RET are invariably accomplished by teaching women clients the philosophic A-B-C's of assertiveness and nonassertiveness. Susan G., for example, had the problem of never going after the male she really wanted when she and her womanfriend, Josephine, went to a social affair together and were approached by a couple of men. She almost always stood quietly by while Josephine picked the man she clearly wanted—who normally was easily the more attractive of the two—and maneuvered him into taking her home while Susan was left with the less desirable male.

Although Susan benefited during her RET sessions with activity homework assignments, assertion training, and operant conditioning in connection with forcing herself to be almost as determined as Josephine was in getting the man she wanted, a real breakthrough in this connection was not achieved until she finally, during her fifth session, saw what the A-B-C's of her unassertiveness were all about. Part of our dialogue during this session went as follows:

SUSAN   I'm afraid I blew it again! In spite of the great rehearsal we did last week, I went to a dance with Josephine last Saturday and let her do exactly what she's done twenty times before with me. And this time the guy I wanted obviously was much more interested in me than in her, and he and his friend, in fact, got talking to me first when Josephine was off in the ladies' room. Nonetheless, she just maneuvered herself into the front seat of the car with him, when they were taking us home, pushed me into the back seat with the other guy, and then got the good one to drive me and the other guy to my place first and to drive off with her to her place. And I just let her do it! I could have killed myself for not speaking up and insisting that the good guy was really with me. But I didn't speak up!

THERAPIST   Because?

SUSAN   Oh, I don't know. I just didn't.

THERAPIST   *Just?* You mean, don't you, that you told yourself something very specific and *then* you "just" didn't speak up to her. Or, in other words, at point C, the Consequence, you unassertively kept your mouth shut after, at point A, the Activating Experience, she arranged to let the "good guy" sit in the front seat with her and drive her home. Now the point is: What is point B, your Belief System, that led you to act so unassertively at C?

SUSAN   Well, I certainly know what my rational Belief was at B!

THERAPIST   What? What was it?

SUSAN   "There she goes again, that bitch! Going after what she wants, no matter what I want—and no matter what the guy wants. What a vile way to act!"

THERAPIST   You mean, that was your *almost* rational Belief. The first part, "There she goes again!" is an observation, and probably correct. The last part, "What a vile way to act!" is your rational evaluation, or Belief. For, according to your wishes and the way you would like things to turn out, it would have been better had she acted otherwise. Consequently, your evaluative conclusion, "In view of what I would want to have happened, and in view of the fact that I've told her about how displeased I am about the way she's behaved in the past and agreed with her that she was not to do this again, her action or behavior is indeed vile," is a reasonable or rational conclusion. But you are making an irrational judgment, too. What is that?

SUSAN   Oh, you mean about my designating her as a bitch?

THERAPIST   Yes, why is that an irrational—rather than a rational—Belief?

SUSAN   Because she *acts* bitchily but is not necessarily *always* going to do so.

THERAPIST   Yes. Accurately stated, she is a woman with highly bitchy behavior, and she might well behave that way again. But she *could,* at least theoretically, act better in the future, while *a* bitch, or someone who is a bitch to the core, could not. What, moreover, about your *condemning her* for acting bitchily?

SUSAN   Oh, yes. We've been through that before, too. And I guess you're right. I didn't get what you were saying about this, at first, because I really believed that people who act consistently bitchily *should be* condemned. Now I'm beginning to see that maybe it is better to avoid them, but that to condemn them means putting them down as being *totally* lousy. I'm beginning to agree with you about this, although I couldn't see it at first.

THERAPIST   All right: so it's irrational for you to call her *a* bitch, however bitchy her behavior may be (and even continue to be). What else are you saying, at point B, to make yourself give in to her when she goes after the fellow you want, and who you think wants you?

SUSAN   I guess, "If I interrupt and contradict her nerviness, she'll hate me and maybe never go out with me again."

THERAPIST   Right. But that, too, is merely an observation—and perhaps a true one. If you hold your ground and deflect her from waltzing off with the fellow you want, she may well hate you and refuse to go out with you again. But what's your evaluation, your irrational evaluation, of that possibility?

SUSAN   Mmm. I'm not sure. I don't know.

THERAPIST   You *do* know. Look for it!

SUSAN   No. My mind's blank.

THERAPIST   Well, unblank it! What would virtually any woman tell herself if her friend agreed not to go off with a male who was interested in her and then actually did so?

SUSAN   That that's a dirty deed!

THERAPIST   Yes, but that's a rational Belief again. For it probably *is,* empirically speaking, a dirty deed. Now, what's the irrational Belief?

SUSAN   (*Looks puzzled. Silence.*)

THERAPIST   And that dirty deed is—? What?

SUSAN   —Awful!

THERAPIST   Right! "It's *awful* that Josephine did that to me again! How *could* she do it? She *shouldn't* have done that dirty deed."

SUSAN   Right! she *shouldn't* have done it.

THERAPIST   Why the hell *shouldn't* she?

SUSAN   Well, I wouldn't do it to her, for one thing.

THERAPIST   And *therefore* she shouldn't do it to me? Does that really follow?

SUSAN   No. I see what you mean. No matter how I would behave, she has a perfect right to behave as she does.

THERAPIST   Even though you don't *like* her behavior?

SUSAN   Yes, even though I don't like it.

THERAPIST   And how about your statement, which you probably keep making to yourself, "How *could* she do it?"

SUSAN   She damned well could! In fact, she did!

THERAPIST   Yes, she easily can do whatever she does. The answer to the question, "How can she do this to me?" is almost invariably, "Easily!" In fact, it would be very hard for her *not* to do it—wouldn't it?

SUSAN   Yes, in Josephine's case, it certainly would be!

THERAPIST   And how about your irrational Belief, "She shouldn't have done that dirty deed!" Well?

SUSAN   Well, of course, that's nonsense. I can't command that she not do what she does.

THERAPIST   You can—but it won't get you very far! You don't control her behavior and your command says that you should control it—that "Because I don't like it, she shouldn't do it!" Drivel!

SUSAN   Yes, I see now. I am not God. I can only control myself—and *hope* or *wish*, not *command*, that people like Josephine will control themselves.

THERAPIST   Right. Now, let's review. Spell out the A-B-C's that you are making up about Josephine; and how you could Dispute, at D, your irrational Beliefs, at B.

SUSAN   All right. At A, she agrees not to be too pushy about walking off with all the attractive men we meet together, especially when one seems to be interested in me. And she then actually does me in and maneuvers the better of two guys to take her, instead of me, home. At C, I feel angry at her, but do nothing to stop her.

THERAPIST   Right. Because at B—what?

SUSAN   At B, I'm first telling myself, rationally, that she's doing a dirty deed to me, and I don't like it. Then I'm telling myself, irrationally, that she *shouldn't* be doing that bitchy deed and is *a* bitch for doing it.

THERAPIST   Correct. Now, what can you do, at D, to Dispute your irrational Belief?

SUSAN   Ask myself, *"Why* shouldn't she be doing that deed?" and "How does it make her *a* total bitch for doing it?"

THERAPIST   Exactly. And your answer, or the new philosophic Effect, at E?

SUSAN   That people behave the way they behave, including Josephine. That *it would be nice* if she didn't behave that way, but that's no reason why she *shouldn't*. And that she isn't *a* bitch, but merely a fucked up human who often acts bitchily.

THERAPIST   Good! I think you hit it right on the head. Except that we both made a mistake, you and I, and got so hung up on your anger at

	Josephine that we forgot the other very important C or Consequence: Your not assertively speaking up for yourself and trying to stop her from waltzing off with this "good guy." How about that A-B-C's of your inertia and unassertiveness?
SUSAN	Yes, we forgot that. But I can see that even without our discussing it, I have been getting myself all set to change it.
THERAPIST	How?
SUSAN	By—uh—. Well, let me do it A-B-C-wise again, just to get it utterly clear in my head and to aid my dealing with it next time.
THERAPIST	Fine.
SUSAN	Let me start with C, the way it tells you to do on your Homework Report. At C, I act unassertively and feel anxious. At A, Josephine is, as usual, trying to get her way and make off with the more attractive guy. Because at B, I am first telling myself, rationally, "I don't like her behavior, and I'd better stop her before she gets away with it!" But at B, I am also telling myself, irrationally, and much more strongly, "If I stop her, she won't like me—and that would be terrible! I *must* have Josephine's approval, even if I keep losing the guys I want because I let her go after them first." And my irrational idea, at B, is the real thing that makes me act so unassertively and weakly at C.
THERAPIST	Exactly! And what could D and E be?
SUSAN	Uh, let me see. D—"Why would it be terrible if Josephine doesn't like me?" And: "Where is the evidence that I *must* have her approval?" E— "It's not terrible if Josephine doesn't like me, only inconvenient. And it even has its conveniences! And there is no reason why I *must* have her approval, though it would be nice if I did have it."
THERAPIST	Right. And what behavioral Effect do you think you'd get, at E again, if you kept Disputing your irrational Beliefs persistently and strongly?
SUSAN	I think I'd begin to speak up, to assert myself in going off with the good guy, and probably much more often get what I really wanted.
THERAPIST	I think so, too. Why not try it and see? Force yourself to see the bullshit you are telling yourself, at B, and to Dispute it vigorously, at D. Also: let's give you the actual homework assignments of: (1) speaking to Josephine again about this general problem that you have with her, and (2) definitely speaking up and challenging her the very next time she attempts to walk off with a male in whom you are interested.
SUSAN	I'll definitely work on that.

And Susan did work on it and over the next few months became so assertive that she usually ended up with the "good guy" whenever she and

Josephine went to a social affair and met two males. Moreover, she began to be more assertive, at the same time, on her teaching job, with her family members, and with the males she dated. So her general as well as her sex-love assertiveness significantly increased.

Summary

Rational-emotive therapy deals with various sex-love problems of women (and, of course, of men) in a comprehensive, cognitive-emotive-behavioral way. It often employs a wide variety of therapeutic methods. But it does not do so merely in an eclectic, pragmatic way because one or more of these methods may work. It is primarily interested in helping women make a profound philosophic change, so that they will not only be able to overcome their existing emotional problems but also tackle any other difficulties that are likely to arise in the future. It is preventive as well as therapeutic and it follows the educational rather than the medical, psycho-dynamic, or encounter model (Ellis, 1972b). It essentially teaches troubled individuals to understand and employ the logico-empirical method in regard to their own thinking, feeling, and behavior rather than merely in regard to external problems (Ellis, 1971, 1972a).

RET accepts women in their own right and not merely as part of a man-woman relationship. It assumes that they are all individuals, with significant differences from all other individuals. It assumes that simply because they exist and are human they have a right (though not a necessity) to survive, to be as happy as they can teach themselves to be, to live in and get along satisfactorily with members of their social group, and to relate intimately (and sometimes sexually) to personally selected members of this group. It teaches women, in the pursuit of these individual and social goals, to accept themselves fully and unconditionally—that is, to rate their traits, deeds, acts, and performances (in order to know what they like and help themselves to get what they like) but *not* to rate their selves, beings, essences, or images (in order to become holier-than-thou and get into some kind of mythical heaven). While attempting to be ruthlessly scientific and empirical, RET is at the same time humanistic, egalitarian, and devoted to maximum utilization of self-choosing. Patricia Jakubowski-Spector (1973) and many other counselors who especially try to help women with problems of assertiveness frequently note that RET is the main cognitive-behavior therapy of choice. It is hardly surprising that I enthusiastically agree.

References

Chesler, Phyllis. *Women and Madness.* New York: Doubleday, 1972.

De Beauvoir, Simone. *The Second Sex.* New York: Knopf, 1953.

De Martino, M. *The New Female Sexuality.* New York: Julian Press, 1969.

De Martino, M. *Sex and the Intelligent Woman.* New York: Springer Publishing, 1973.

Ellis, A. *The American Sexual Tragedy.* New York: Lyle Stuart and Grove Press, 1961.

Ellis, A. *The Intelligent Woman's Guide to Manhunting.* New York: Lyle Stuart and Dell Books, 1965a.

Ellis, A. *The Art and Science of Love.* New York: Lyle Stuart and Dell Books, 1960, 1965b.

Ellis, A. *Growth through Reason.* Palo Alto, Calif.: Science and Behavior Books, 1971.

Ellis, A. *The Sensuous Person: Critique and Corrections.* New York: Lyle Stuart, 1972a.

Ellis, A. Emotional education in the classroom: The Living School. *Journal of Clinical Child Psychology, 1*(13), 19–22, 1972b.

Fisher, S. *The Female Orgasm.* New York: Basic Books, 1973.

Frumkin, R. M. Beauty. In A. Ellis and A. Abarbanel (Eds.), *Encyclopedia of Sexual Behavior,* New York: Jason Aronson, 1973.

Jakubowski-Spector, Patricia. Facilitating the growth of women through assertive training. *Counseling Psychologist, 4,* 75–86, 1973.

Kinsey, A. C., Pomeroy, W. B., Martin, C. E., & Gebhard, P. H. *Sexual Behavior in the Human Female.* New York: Pocket Books, 1969.

Masters, W. H., & Johnson, V. E. *Human Sexual Response.* Boston: Little, Brown, 1966.

Masters, W. H., & Johnson, V. E. *Human Sexual Inadequacy.* Boston: Little, Brown, 1971.

Mead, Margaret. *Male and Female.* New York: New American Library, 1955.

Millet, Kate. *Sexual Politics.* New York: Doubleday, 1971.

Seward, Georgene. Sex and the Social Order. In A. Ellis and A. Abarbanel (Eds.), *Encyclopedia of Sexual Behavior.* New York: Jason Aronson, 1973.

Singer, I. *The Goals of Human Sexuality.* New York: Norton, 1973.

Sorenson, R. C. *Adolescent Sexuality in Contemporary America.* New York: World Publishing, 1973.

Thompson, Clara. Femininity. In A. Ellis and A. Abarbanel (Eds.), *Encyclopedia of Sexual Behavior.* New York: Jason Aronson, 1973.

Wolfe, J. L. What to do until the revolution comes: An argument for women's rational therapy groups. Talk presented at the University of Wisconsin, November, 1973.

9

The Nature of Disturbed
Marital Interactions

Albert Ellis

In Chapter 9, Albert Ellis discusses what causes marriages to become dysfunctional. Contrary to most theories, which posit either dysfunctional communication or faulty childhood experiences on one or the other partner's part as the core of the problem, Ellis asserts that disturbed marital interaction results when each partner holds and acts upon irrational philosophies about the other partner and/or about marriage itself. Each partner irrationally demands that the other behave as he or she thinks the partner should and condemns the other for behaving the way he or she does. Another significant notion that Ellis introduces and explores in this chapter is the role of "human drifting" in causing and maintaining emotional and interpersonal disturbance. Human drifting refers to the tendency of most people to "pigheadedly cling to, and utterly refuse to work at eliminating, [their] self-defeating value systems." That is, not only do humans reindoctrinate themselves over and over with their irrational beliefs, but they also lazily refuse to think about and evaluate them so that these beliefs become daily more powerful. This important concept is more fully developed in Chapter 11.

Ellis also defines the irrational beliefs or philosophies behind anger and anger problems, although he does not directly address or elaborate upon them. In contrast to annoyance, irritation, and displeasure, anger is invariably a form of demandingness. Irritation starts with the rational premise or belief: "I don't like what you are doing, I want you to change it, and I intend to do something to change it." Anger, however, consists of the additional and highly irrational premises: "Because I don't like what you are doing, I can't stand what you are doing, you absolutely must not do it, and you are a total louse for doing that thing to me, and I'm going to get back at you for doing that if it is the last thing I do." These latter statements are rationally unfounded (see Chapter 1), display childish grandiosity, and either promote or exacerbate poor interpersonal relationships. The reader interested in a lengthier discussion of the psychodynamics of anger is referred to Ellis' debate with Daniel Casriel in Rational Living, *1971, 6, pages 2–21 and to his book,* How to Live With and Without Anger *(New York: Reader's Digest Press, 1977).*

L ET ME BEGIN THIS CHAPTER with a typical example of disturbed
marital interaction; then I shall try to show what the essential nature of this kind of neurotic interaction is; and, finally, I shall try
to indicate some of the remedies that can be taken to interrupt and
minimize it.

The husband of the couple I saw for marriage counseling was 32, very
bright and artistically talented, and desirous of having a mate who would
(a) be stimulating to live with and (b) give him sufficient time to be by
himself when he was home to pursue his writing. The wife was 30, warm
and beautiful, but interested far more in close ties with her husband and
two children than in intellectual pursuits. She also wanted sex relations
three or four times a week, while her husband was perfectly satisfied to
have intercourse about once every two or three weeks.

The husband was so unhappy over his wife's persistent demands for
companionship that he constantly criticized her, belittled her in front of
others, neglected his relations with his children, and became so depressed
on many occasions that he worked only sporadically at his writing. The
wife, in her turn, carried on side affairs with men for whom she had little
love or liking, constantly told the children what a poor father they had,
and found excuses to keep interrupting her husband on those days when
he finally did come out of his depressed moods and begin to do some work
on the novel he was desperately trying to finish. The mates fought viciously
over sex, and had highly unsatisfactory coitus on those relatively rare times
when they did agree to copulate.

Both these individuals were obviously disturbed in their own right. The
husband was needlessly condemning himself for not consistently buckling
down to his writing and was consequently becoming more and more depressed and doing less consistent writing. The wife was so direly in need
of being loved in order to sustain her own worth as a human being that
she was having side affairs with men whom she did not care for and who
had no great feeling for her. Both mates, therefore, were foolishly sabotaging their own main life goals and were needlessly creating self-hatred and
hostility to others.

Maritally, they were neurotically interacting because, after seeing that
they were frustrated in some of their main marriage goals, instead of
stoically facing and intelligently trying to minimize their disappointments,
they were insanely raging against these thwartings and thereby only balk-
ing themselves all the more. Thus, by denigrating his wife for not being
more self-sufficient and for demanding more of his time, the husband was
encouraging her to be still less able to be by herself and to be more upset

Chapter 9 previously appeared in *Marital Counseling,* ed. H. L. Silverman (Springfield,
Ill.: Charles C Thomas, 1967).

about his wanting more time to himself. And by angrily interrupting her husband's writing, the wife was helping to aggravate his desire for solitude; by excoriating him for being a poor father and bedmate, she made fatherhood and sexual copulation even less desirable to him.

Disturbed marital interaction, in other words, arises when one mate reacts badly to the normal frustrations and the abnormal and unrealistic demands of the other mate and in this process helps accentuate the frustrations and demands. Then the other mate, in his or her turn, also reacts poorly to the sensible requests and the unreasonable demands of the first mate; increasing low frustration tolerance and outbursts of temper on the part of both spouses ensue. Disturbed individuals tend to respond anxiously or angrily even to relatively good life-situations, since they have basically irrational or illogical attitudes or philosophic assumptions (2, 3, 4, 5, 6, 7). When external pressures are difficult, then they react even more neurotically or psychotically (8, 10, 13).

Disturbed people particularly often respond badly to marriage because, at best, monogamic mating is an unusually difficult business and because our expectations in regard to it are exceptionally unrealistic. It should be obvious to almost any sound-thinking person that while friends, lovers, and business associates are often on their best behavior, and consequently will treat one politely and hypocritically, spouses and children are *not* likely to be able to maintain the same kind of urbane pretense for any length of time. Consequently, domestic partners are almost certain to be frequently irritable, short-tempered, unresponsive, and difficult. Yet the average husband thinks that just *because* he is married, his wife should be consistently kind and mannerly, and the average wife thinks that just *because* her husband is married to her, he should be invariable sweet and responsive. Thus, two people who, if they were in the least realistic, would frequently expect the very *worst* kind of behavior from their mates, are quite irrationally asking—nay, demanding—the very best conduct from the other. The result of these highly untenable assumptions about what the married state *should* be can only lead to clearcut disappointment and disillusionment on the part of those who hold these assumptions; this especially is true for basically disturbed individuals, who tend to invent and cling to unsound premises in the first place and then roundly to give themselves a pain in the gut when reality proves these to be unwarranted.

The first and foremost cause of disturbed marital interaction, then, is the utterly unrealistic expectations which husband and wives tend to have, not merely about themselves and about others (as is the case with non-maritally upset individuals), but also about the marriage relation itself. They senselessly cling to the supposition that a spouse absolutely *should be* continually loving and forgiving—when, if they were wiser, they would believe that *it would be lovely* if a spouse were that way, but the chances very much are that he or she simply won't be. Then, after somehow imbibing this nonsensical belief, married individuals usually do one more thing that insures their neurotically interacting forever: Namely, they pigheadedly cling to, and utterly refuse to work at eliminating, this self-defeating value system.

This is the real tragedy, and in a profound sense the main cause of all emotional disturbance: human drifting or goofing. Granting that human beings acquire, usually early in their lives, major self-defeating philosophies and pernicious conditioned patterns of response, the fact remains that they theoretically are capable of changing these philosophies and of reconditioning themselves—and they usually don't. This, in fact, is why we usually refer to an irrational person as neurotic or disturbed rather than as stupid or incompetent: because he presumably *can* behave better than he currently is behaving. Neurosis, as I pointed out in my book, *How to Live with a Neurotic,* is essentially stupid behavior by a *non*-stupid person. The neurotic can do better, but he doesn't. Because, in regard to his self-defeating conduct, he drifts or goofs.

Take, for example, the husband of the couple I mentioned in the beginning of this paper. He was an unusually bright, well-educated and artistically talented individual. Nevertheless, he easily surrendered to several forms of idling in his disturbed relations with himself and his wife. First, he uncritically accepted the hypothesis that he *had* to succeed as a writer and that he was a worthless slob if he didn't. Second, when he became depressed about his sporadic attempts at writing, he lazily allowed himself to wallow in his depression for days or weeks at a time, without making any real effort to see what nonsense he was telling himself to cause this depression and to vigorously challenge and question this nonsense. Third, he made little effort, even though he expected to remain married indefinitely, to strive for true *marital* interaction with his wife and children, but instead largely tried to do exactly what he wanted to do, just as if he had no marital responsibilities. Fourth, he refused to make any allowances, along the lines we mentioned above, for the reality that marriage *is* the kind of a relationship where one is not overpolitely responded to by one's wife and children, who are generally preoccupied with normal and abnormal problems of their own. Fifth, when this husband's wife acted badly, he failed to let any of her mistakes go by, but felt constrained to open his big mouth and point all of them out to her in considerable detail. Sixth, when he observed that his wife was using his negative barbs against her to shatter herself with, he stubbornly stuck with the belief that his defamation of her would somehow magically do good rather than harm. Seventh, when he could have pacified his wife to some extent by having more frequent sex relations with her, he vindictively chose to have them even less than he personally desired.

In many ways, then, this husband not only acted ineffectually in his relationships with himself and his wife, but when his main premise (namely, that he *should* be happy in marriage, no matter how different from his wife and no matter what her and his emotional hangups were) obviously bore ill fruit, he did nothing to see, examine, or change this premise. On the contrary, he rigidly held on to it and preferred to believe that it was his wife's fault that his philosophy of life and marriage was not working out too well.

This tendency toward human drifting is so pronounced among disturbed people and their marriages that even the followers of Carl Rogers (12), who tend to believe that humans have an almost infinite capacity for self-actualization, have had to recently take cognizance of it. Thus, in the Rogerian-oriented course of programmed instruction in improving communication in marriage, the Human Development Institute of Atlanta (11) notes that both mates are responsible for poor communication: "Either one of them could do something to change things, but instead of doing so, they concentrate on blaming the other person and hoping that he will change. Naturally, nothing happens—and nothing *will* happen until one of the two stops trying to blame the other and asks himself, 'How can *I* be different? What can *I* do about this?' " Obviously, even the Rogerians have, albeit reluctantly, come around to the view that human drifting and blaming will indefinitely perpetuate marital discord and that therefore husbands and wives who are interacting in a disturbed fashion must somehow be persuaded not merely honestly to express their true feelings to each other but, much more importantly, to work their heads off at *changing* the blaming assumptions that create and perpetuate these feelings.

The more disturbed people and their negative interactions with each other that I see in my psychotherapy and marriage counseling practice, the more I am convinced that *all* forms of psychopathology are largely perpetuated by various kinds of drifting or goofing. Neurosis and psychosis, as I began to point out a decade ago, are so-called emotional disorders which are largely caused by crooked thinking (1, 3). The origin of this irrational cognizing is interesting but not too important in its treatment. Many patients, even before they come for psychotherapy, know full well just how they originally started having crazy thoughts and what they must do to give them up—just as most cigarette smokers know how they started smoking and what they must do to discontinue it. But, in spite of their insight, they continue their cognitive goofing and they refuse to work very hard at giving it up.

This is particularly true in marriage, where husbands, such as the one mentioned above, see clearly that their treatment of their wives is short-sighted and foolish, but nonetheless stubbornly continue this marital-defeating treatment. In the case in question I was able to show the husband that his expectations about marriage in general and his wife in particular were highly unrealistic and that he had no chance for a happy home life if he kept maintaining them. Somewhat to my surprise, he quickly went to work to challenge and question his own assumptions, began to hold his tongue when his wife and children behaved badly, concentrated more on solving his own writing problems than demanding that his wife change to suit him, and deliberately started to satisfy his wife sexually two or three times a week, whether or not he himself wanted coitus. His concerted work in this connection soon began to pay off. His wife stopped her outside affairs, encouraged the children to be more affectionate toward him, and voluntarily got herself absorbed in painting so that she easily was able to let him have more time for his writing. Although she did not significantly change her own basic assumptions that she direly needed his love to consider herself a worthwhile person in her own right, and hence remained fundamentally neurotic, she at least was able to live more successfully with her disturbance—largely because her husband tackled his own neurosis and stopped blaming her for being disturbed. Hard work on the husband's part, therefore, led to a considerable reduction in his own disturbance and in the disturbed marital interaction while some, though limited, work on the wife's part led to a better marriage in spite of the maintenance of many of her own negative premises about herself.

Similarly, I find that whenever I can induce any of my psychotherapy patients or marriage-counseling clients to *work* at changing their underlying neurosis-creating assumptions, significant personality changes ensue, and their interactions with their mates, families, or other intimate associates almost always improve. More specifically, this work usually consists of: (a) fully facing the fact that they themselves are doing something wrong, however mistaken their intimates may *also* be; (b) seeing clearly that behind their neurotic mistakes and inefficiencies there are invariably important irrational, unrealistic philosophic assumptions; (c) vigorously and continually challenging and questioning these assumptions by critically examining them and by actively doing deeds that prove that they are unfounded; (d) making due allowances for the intrinsic difficulties and frustrations of certain human relationships such as monogamous marriage; (e) learning to keep their big mouths shut when one of their close associates is clearly behaving badly, or else objectively and unblamefully pointing out the other's mistakes while constructively trying to show him or her how to correct them in the future; and (f) above all, continually keeping in mind the fact that a relationship *is* a relationship, that it rarely can spontaneously progress in a supersmooth manner, and that it must often be actively worked at to recreate and maintain the honest affection with which it often starts.

To sum up: Disturbed marital interaction arises when a marital partner is neurotic or psychotic in his own right and when he consequently has unrealistic expectations of what his mate's behavior *should* be. Whatever the original source of these irrational premises may be, the important thing is that the individual usually does not clearly understand what they are, and, even when he does, he stubbornly refuses to work against them and give them up. Basically, therefore, he is a drifter or goofer, and his disturbed marriage will usually continue until he realizes that cognitive goofing simply does not pay, and that there *is* no way out of individual and human relationship dilemmas other than work, work, work.

References

1. Beck, A. T. Thinking and depression. *Arch. Gen. Psychiat., 9:*324, 1963.
2. Ellis, A. *How to Live With a Neurotic.* New York: Crown, 1957.
3. Ellis, A. *Reason and Emotion in Psychotherapy.* New York: Lyle Stuart, 1962.
4. Ellis, A. *The Origins and the Development of the Incest Taboo.* New York: Lyle Stuart, 1963.
5. Ellis, A., and Harper, R. A. *A Guide to Rational Living.* Englewood Cliffs: Prentice-Hall, 1961a.
6. Ellis, A., and Harper, R. A. *Creative Marriage.* New York: Lyle Stuart, 1961b.
7. Ellis, A., and Sagarin, E. *Nymphomania: A Study of the Over-Sexed Woman.* New York: Gilbert Press, 1964.
8. Freud, S. *Collected Papers.* London: Imago, 1924–1950.
9. Fromm, E. *The Art of Loving.* New York: Harper, 1962.
10. Gordon, R., Gordon, K., and Gunther, M. *The Split-Level Trap.* New York: Bernard Geis, 1961.
11. Human Development Institute, Inc. *Improving Communication in Marriage.* Atlanta: Human Development Institute, 1964.
12. Rogers, C. *On Becoming a Person.* Boston: Houghton, 1961.
13. Selye, H. *The Stress of Life.* New York: McGraw, 1956.

10

Characteristics of Psychotic and Borderline Psychotic Individuals

Albert Ellis

Chapter 10 reminds the reader of the key part that biological factors play in emotional disturbance. "The human animal is biologically predisposed to think crookedly on many occasions . . . and to become both anxious and hostile with very little or no objective provocation and to continue to reinforce himself with anxiety and hostility no matter what kind of up-bringing he has or what kind of society he has been reared in," Ellis notes. In basically psychotic individuals, the biological push toward crooked thinking is greater. Ellis describes the basic characteristics of psychotic and borderline psychotic individuals. These people have severe cognitive focusing difficulties and a good many of the traits that neurotics have, including habits of self-downing; low frustration tolerance; a rigid, devout thinking style that resists change; a belief that they "need" complete love and approval; and a tendency toward emotional overreactivity. Borderline psychotics and outright psychotic individuals hold these traits to an extreme degree, however.

SOME OF YOU MAY RECALL that several years ago an article appeared in the *American Journal of Psychiatry* which pointed out that Freud had misdiagnosed most of his early patients, since he referred to them as hysterics or neurotics when actually, in the light of our modern diagnostic methods, they would be labeled schizophrenic. I think that this Freudian type of misdiagnosis is still prevalent. Particularly if a psychotherapist is in private practice, he will soon find that because he charges forty dollars or more per session and because his patients (partly because of their severe sickness) tend to be unwealthy individuals, he is largely seeing people who are literally driven to seek help, rather than those who would merely benefit if they did receive it. These patients, who need steady and often prolonged support from a therapist, are most likely to be overt or borderline psychotics.

A part of Chapter 10 was delivered at the Symposium on Therapeutic Methods with Schizophrenics, V.A. Hospital, Battle Creek, Michigan, May 16–17, 1963.

When I first started to do psychotherapy, I was convinced that almost all highly disturbed individuals, including those who are basically psychotic, are made the way they are by their early environment—especially by traumatic occurrences during their first few years of life. After close observation of literally thousands of seriously aberrated people, I no longer believe this. I believe, instead, as I have noted in my book, *Reason and Emotion in Psychotherapy* (Ellis, 1962), that probably all human beings are born with a pretty distinct "hole in their heads" and that psychotics are born with a much bigger hole than the rest of us inherit.

By this I mean that the human animal is biologically predisposed to think crookedly on many occasions, to defeat his own ends, to be over-suggestible and overgeneralizing, and to become both anxious and hostile with very little or no objective provocation and to continue to reinfect himself with anxiety and hostility no matter what kind of upbringing he has had or in what kind of society he has been reared. As I noted above, I did not start out with this hypothesis, because I am by no means biologically trained and have not, in fact, had any courses in biology since I last took one in junior high school. But the belief that men and women are *first* genetically predisposed to emotional disturbance, and that they then later are the victims of environmental traumata which help actualize these predispositions and which induce them to become perhaps four or five times as disturbed as they might biologically tend to be has been forced on me by clinical observation during my last twenty years of practicing intensive psychotherapy.

My conversion to a strongly biologically oriented point of view has been appreciably aided by my giving up psychoanalytic therapy, which I used to practice years ago, and by my taking a much more direct and rational approach to psychotherapy. For, in addition to its many other disadvantages, psychoanalysis is such a highly disorganized, diffusive, and highly religious form of therapy that it obscures what is really going on in the patient's mind and prevents the ardent researcher from seeing what truly makes and keeps the patient sick. Thus, when my psychoanalytically treated patients often did not get better, in spite of their accepting the mystically "deep" interpretations of their behavior that I kept feeding them, I could always easily convince myself and them that they were employing negative transference, or didn't really want to get better, or desired to punish themselves, or were blocked, or some other clever explanation of that sort. I thereby could nicely avoid facing the fact that maybe I wasn't really showing them why they were disturbed or what, precisely, they had to do to overcome their disturbances. I also could easily interpret their resistance in terms of psychoanalytic theory, instead of in terms of what might actually be occurring in the patients' heads.

Once I developed an exceptionally clear and precise method of showing patients exactly what they were telling themselves to make themselves upset and what they could do to challenge their irrational thinking and thereby immediately restore their own emotional equilibrium, I no longer had the psychoanalytic obscurantism to serve as an excuse for my patients' resistance to treatment. For I soon saw that many patients did *not* resist in the usual way; some, in fact, started getting better after a session or two of rational-emotive psychotherapy and kept steadily improving; what is more, they maintained this improvement long after the therapy, which sometimes consisted of relatively few sessions, had ended.

Other patients, however, did continue seriously to resist getting better. In some of these cases, it soon became clear that they resisted because they were telling themselves that they *couldn't* help themselves; or because they resented having to *work* at therapy; or because they wanted to spite me; or for some other ideological reason. In many other instances, however, it eventually became evident that the patients very much *did* want to improve and *were* working hard at doing so. They just had great *difficulty* helping themselves; it was highly probable that this difficulty was inborn, had plagued them all their lives, and was an essential component of their disturbance. In other words, whereas many neurotic individuals, for various perverse reasons, simply *will not* think straight about themselves, it appeared that the patients who resisted getting better on nonideological grounds were usually psychotic or borderline psychotic individuals who could not think straight, or who could not do so except with great difficulty.

Further observation of these patients convinced me that they seemed to have severe focusing difficulties. Either they did not focus very adequately on solving their life difficulties and instead were unusually diffuse, discursive, and disorganized in their thinking, or else, in many instances, they overfocused, in a highly rigid manner, on some specific aspect of their life, usually some negativistic or catastrophic aspect, and therefore were unable to focus adequately on other aspects of any problem-solving situation. The more of this behavior I began to observe, the more I started to realize that these patients were not in the neurotic range, even though their behavior was often typical of that of so-called neurotics, but that they were basically psychotic. They had, I realized, a true thinking disorder—as Bleuler (1950) insisted is fundamentally true of schizophrenics.

David Shakow (1963) has summed up his thirty years of studying schizophrenics with this observation: "If we were to try to epitomize the schizophrenic person's system in the most simple language, we might say that he has two major difficulties: first, he reacts to old situations as if they were new ones (he fails to habituate), and to new situations as if they were recently past ones (he perseverates); and second, he overresponds when the stimulus is relatively small, and he does not respond enough when the stimulus is great." In both major difficulties that Shakow notes, it is obvious that the schizophrenic is at one time or another underfocusing and over-focusing.

Recent studies by Dr. Aaron T. Beck (1963) also confirm my clinical observations that seriously disturbed people have a fundamental, and probably innate, focusing or thinking disorder. Beck notes: "The present study indicates that, even in mild phases of depression, systematic deviations from realistic and logical thinking occur. . . . The thinking-disorder typology outlined in this paper is similar to that described in students of schizophrenia. . . . These findings suggest that a thinking disorder may be common to all types of psychopathology."

Beck (1963) also notes: "Magnification and minimization refer to errors in evaluation which are so gross as to constitute distortions. As described in the section on thematic content, these processes were manifested by underestimation of the individual's performance, achievement or ability, and inflation of the magnitude of his problems and tasks. Other examples were the exaggeration of the intensity or significance of a traumatic event. It was frequently observed that the patients' initial reaction to an unpleasant event was to regard it as a catastrophe. It was generally found on further inquiry that the perceived disaster was often a relatively minor problem."

Beck's statement has two important implications. It implies, first, that the Freudian theory of the great importance of childhood trauma is nonsense since individuals who are thus "traumatized" may very well invent their "traumas" by exaggerating the significance of the usual life difficulties that occur to them. And it also implies that these patients have a basic thinking disorder with probably innate as well as socially determined roots that causes them to be qualitatively different from so-called neurotics, who are unduly upset about life's problems but who can fairly easily be taught to cope with such problems.

In addition to and perhaps in part because of these focusing difficulties, what I refer to as psychotic and as borderline or basically psychotic individuals usually have a good many other highly disturbed or self-defeating traits; very frequently they have virtually all these traits to some considerable degree. Not always, however! Sometimes, as is the case with a woman I have seen recently and who has benefitted so much from RET that she now behaves quite "neurotically," and hardly at all "psychotically," the patient has one outstanding disruptive trait, but has this to such a degree that it practically rules her life. This woman gets along very well socially; does wonderfully well at her job as an editor of a magazine;

and in many ways leads a joyous, effective existence. But for all of her adolescent and adult life she has had an overweening demand that males with whom she has a close relationship indubitably and completely love her and she has felt constant and acute panic whenever it seemed likely, as of course it often did, that her current lover might criticize her or leave her.

Why do I think of her as "borderline psychotic"? Mainly because of the exceptionally serious degree of her one-faceted disturbance and the fact that, through ten years of therapy with effective practitioners, she *rigidly* held on to this disturbance and carried it into the therapeutic process itself. When I first saw her two years ago she described herself as an "emotional basket case"—and very correctly! Only after very persistent and almost brow-beating efforts on my part could I get through to her and get her to see—and I mean *really* see—that she could live happily whether or not a current man in her life truly cared for her. She now still very much *wants* a good primary relationship, but has truly given up the *dire need* for it; consequently, she has lost virtually all her panic and lives much more happily than ever before. Moreover, although she still may possibly fall back, some day hence, to her previous state of love slobbism, I doubt whether she ever will. So she acts clearly in the "neurotic" range today and has to all appearances achieved a therapeutic "cure."

But even this has occurred only after immense effort on her part and after many returns, over the last two years, to her previous state of overwhelming "need" and panic. Significantly, she still has to fight vigorously against her "natural" tendencies to put herself down when her current lover acts irritably or nastily to her—and she at times only barely wins this fight. She still *tends* to need security, support, approval, and love from a man, although she lives successfully, these days, with this underlying tendency.

Much more typically, however, I have seen Walter, a seriously borderline psychotic male for five years now. Although he has made enormous progress and comes in for therapy only about once every two months, he still has virtually all the tendencies that basically psychotic individuals have and he still suffers immensely, from time to time, from these tendencies. He is now 40 years of age, with a record of intermittent psychological treatment with several good therapists since the age of 18 (when he felt suicidal and had to quit college for awhile). He has never entered a mental institution (though he came close a couple of times!) and has always worked steadily at his medical practice. No one has ever diagnosed him as "schizophrenic" or "psychotic," and most people who know him think of him as a charming, though somewhat bizarre and peculiar, individual. Despite his success in his profession, however, he has virtually all the common borderline psychotic traits. So I shall use him as an example as I list these traits below.

Pandemic love slobbism. Psychotics and borderline psychotics tend to "need" the complete love and acceptance of every person they define as significant in their lives and, perhaps more importantly, to feel horrified about the disapproval or criticism of scores of people who even have little relevance to them. My client Walter not only thinks he needs the approval of his wife and shrivels up when she mildly points out the error of his ways, but also feels "destroyed" or "annihilated" when near-strangers look at him cross-eyed or indicate they disapprove of him. He inherited a two-family house from his parents and lives on the ground floor with his wife and two children. He has almost literally kissed the backside of every tenant of the upstairs apartment; he has felt afraid to ask for the rent when it was due, and has let virtually all his tenants take unfair advantage of him, lest they think him a "bastard."

Arrant self-downing. Psychotics and borderline psychotics commonly put themselves down, and I mean *severely* condemn themselves, for relatively minor imperfections and peccadillos. Although bright, charming, and physically attractive, Walter excoriates himself constantly for his skin blemishes, for little errors he makes with his friends or patients, for things he has done years ago, for lacking great artistic talents, for talking too much or too little, for having emotional problems, etc., etc.

Rigidity. Borderline psychotics (and, of course, outright psychotics) cling rigidly to their dysfunctional thoughts, affects, and behaviors. As Lauretta Bender indicated years ago, they resist many years of psychotherapy; when they improve, they still cling to many of their outlandish and self-destructive ideologies; and they frequently remain convinced that they cannot possibly make basic changes in themselves. Walter has certainly improved over his many years of therapy, and particularly through his two years of rational-emotive treatment. But he frequently thinks that he absolutely *has to* perform a new project well. He overreacts enormously to unfortunate situations over which he has little or no control. And he withdraws for weeks at a time when something goes wrong between himself and his family members. He previously had little insight into why he behaved in this manner, but now sees that he does so as a result of his own inordinate demands on himself, on others, and on the universe. This insight hardly stops him from overreacting similarly again and again!

Gross logical errors. Although virtually all humans fairly frequently tend to make gross logical errors—and conclude, for example, that because they once got very upset about something, they have to keep upsetting themselves about it forever—psychotics and borderline psychotics seem to make these errors more frequently and to have more difficulty than "neurotics" in giving them up. Although he has realized on many occasions that his relations with his father do *not* make him react antagonistically to strong men today, Walter still tends to fall back to this false position and to claim a specious connection when he currently sees a colleague as doing him in. He wrongly and easily concludes, in this connection: (1) the colleague has deliberately treated him unfairly (when nothing of the kind seems to have happened); (2) the colleague acts just the way Walter's father did (when the colleague clearly has not); (3) Walter's past hatred of his father *makes him* suspicious of the colleague (when Walter would probably feel suspicious even had his father died before Walter's birth); and (4) he has no choice but to try to get back at the colleague (when, of course, he has many other ways of behaving). His overgeneralizations lead him to see the facts of the case falsely; then he wrongly concludes that the "facts" *cause* him to think the way he does. Like a typical borderline psychotic, Walter *invents* specious conclusions from dubious data; he seems to have a natural talent for doing this. Nor does his native high intelligence and his knowledge of medicine stop him in these respects!

Emotional overreactivity. When normal "neurotics" overreact to unfortunate stimuli, they tend to do so relatively briefly and then calm down. Psychotics and borderline psychotics tend to overreact much more mightily and to continue their self-defeating reactions almost indefinitely. Walter can easily hate a patient, a nurse, or another physician for the slightest wrong that this person has perpetrated. He would practically like to "kill them" when he notices their wrongdoings. And he can easily remain utterly incensed about them for days, weeks, or even years. He feels positively aghast at their behavior and doesn't permit himself to forget it for a long time to come. He similarly overreacts to his own errors and to poor environmental conditions.

Abysmally low frustration tolerance. Borderline psychotics, as well as psychotics, tend to have abysmally low frustration tolerance—and consequently to do little or nothing about conquering their basic problems. If my theory of their behavior bears truth, it is because they *easily* tend to react self-defeatingly that they normally have to work much harder than other disturbed individuals to overcome their deficiencies. They rarely do! They define changing themselves as "too" hard; complain inwardly that it shouldn't remain that hard; and work only inconsistently, and often cavalierly, at self-change. Walter, even though he knows all about whining (from his RET experiences) and loathes this behavior in others, almost automatically whines and screams when something really goes wrong in his life and preoccupies himself with ranting to himself and to others about it. This low frustration tolerance not only directly prevents him from working to overcome his other problems but also consumes time and energy and indirectly interferes with his reaching better solutions.

Trigger-happy hostility. Not all psychotic individuals continually make themselves very hostile at others and seem to "automatically" react with overweening hostility at the drop of a hat. But many do! When they do, they trigger themselves off at both consequential and inconsequential things, do so in a split-second fashion, and often insist that they cannot prevent themselves from reacting in this manner. Walter incessantly hates, though often for a short period of time, people who act stupidly, who block him from doing what he really wants to do, who act in any way unfairly, and who do not love him as he thinks they indubitably *should*. He consumes much more time in feeling anxious and depressed than in feeling angry. But his anger often disrupts his life, consumes him entirely for a period of time, and represents a highly bigoted form of reaction from this otherwise enlightened and sensitive person.

Resistance to understanding and to new teachings. Although they frequently do well in school and at complicated jobs, borderline psychotics in many important ways resist understanding—particularly, they resist understanding of themselves and others. And although they agree with various therapeutic tenets, including the main ones in RET, they do not follow these views and frequently don't seem to comprehend them. Walter, for example, doesn't really listen to a great deal that goes on during therapy sessions—unless I break in very strongly and persistently and hammer away at practically forcing him to hear some of the things I say. He listens very well, during group therapy, to other people's problems, and can act very helpfully to them. But when they talk to him about his, he frequently gets so upset about some of the things they say that he really doesn't hear, misunderstands their points, and rushes on to something else on his mind rather than hear them out and feed back to them what they keep saying. He acts very politely to most people most of the time; but under these therapeutic conditions, he almost rudely edits others out, not because he feels angry at them but because he autistically sees things *only* from his own defensive frame of reference and therefore closes them out.

Negative conclusions about therapy. As pointed out above, psychotics and borderline psychotics often resist therapy because they have low frustration tolerance and because they listen poorly. But they also jump magically from the thought, "This therapeutic method hasn't worked yet," to "It will never work for me," or "It doesn't work at all!" They have a short-term perspective and will not patiently work at many things, including therapy, until the new ways catch on and turn into "second nature." Walter, in spite of enormous progress in therapy (which his friends and relatives keep pointing out to him), will try a suggestion half-heartedly (e.g., trying to stand up for himself in some business deal) and then, when it doesn't work quickly or perfectly well, he will conclude: "I tried very hard, but it won't work." Hell, he tried very hard! Or else he tried hard for a very short period of time. Only with constant therapeutic monitoring do I get him to go back to the drawing board and try, really try, until the new behavior starts working.

Easy and continual retrogression. When psychotics and borderline psychotics improve at therapy, either by their own efforts or with the help of a professional therapist, they easily and often fall back, and fall back to near-zero. Sometimes physical illness, such as a serious cold or the onset of influenza, seems to set them back. More often, they take some external setback too seriously, or they fall back for no good reason. Walter can make progress for several weeks at a time; then, when one big thing in his life goes wrong, he assumes that he can't do anything, will always remain "sick," and has made no real progress.

Devoutness. Borderline psychotics (and, of course, psychotics) de-voutly—and I mean devoutly!—believe in the basic irrational ideas which afflict other disturbed individuals and which RET emphasizes in therapy. Thus, Walter fairly consistently believes that he absolutely *has to* do well and avoid disapproval of significant others; that people who promise him something *must* keep their promises; that his parents and others have *got to* take care of him emotionally; that he completely *can't* have sex without love; that he *in no wa*y can act nicely toward those who have treated him badly; etc. Although not religious in the usual sense of the word, Walter compulsively follows many orthodox Jewish rituals which his family members do not follow and which he superstitiously hangs on to.

Autism. Psychotics and borderline psychotics tend to act in a highly autistic manner. They seem almost completely absorbed in themselves, not necessarily in enjoying but in "proving" themselves: in showing others how much greatness they have. In such pursuits, they frequently *appear* highly interested in others but they are not, really! As noted above, they do not particularly listen; they talk largely to themselves; and they sometimes feel so hurt about the deprivations and lack of appreciation that they gain in life that they withdraw into themselves, refuse to take various normal risks, and sometimes almost turn into hermits. Walter on the surface appears quite outgoing and often acts as the life of the party. But he obsesses about how well he does at the affairs he goes to; he often speaks *at* rather than *with* the people he meets; and after the party has ended he withdraws to his own quite empty state. He also egocentrically thinks that others *should* do whatever he wants them to do and he returns to his condition of inner hurt, and sometimes outer whining, when they do not.

Other traits. Some other traits which psychotics and borderline psychotics, including Walter, frequently exhibit include: (1) They tend to think in a loose or slippery way, or to have what Meehl (1962) calls cognitive slippage; consequently they tend to have great difficulty in making some of the finer discriminations that help people have adequate social relations. (2) They often have little insight into their disturbances, blame others for their problems, and act defensively when shown some of their major errors. (3) They frequently have low energies, or erratically work on all cylinders one day and feel blah the next day. (4) They may display major inefficiencies and disorganization, even though they do well in certain specific areas. (5) They tend to exhibit serious lack of discipline in such realms as overeating, oversmoking, overdrinking, and procrastination. (6) They sometimes note that they have serious disturbances. But then they tend to awfulize about their instability and make themselves phrenophobic, bringing on an acute and intense fear of going crazy.

Let me again emphasize that many neurotic individuals have traits similar to the ones just listed. But the borderline psychotic and outrightly psychotic individual has such traits to an extreme degree; rigidly holds on to them; falls back to dysfunctional behavior quite easily when he or she temporarily overcomes it; functions with great inefficiency during his or her entire lifetime; and generally has several serious inadequacies rather than one or two. From an RET framework, these borderline people *must*urbate with a real vengeance; helping them truly dissipate or largely eradicate their abysmal demandingness and whining constitutes an exceptionally difficult and often a thankless job. Cognitive-behavior therapy in general and RET in particular can help such individuals enormously and uniquely, but let's honestly admit that even then it helps to a somewhat limited degree.

References

Beck, Aaron T. Think and Depression. *Arch. Gen. Psychiatry,* 1963, *9,* 324–333.
Bleuler, Eugene. *Dementia Praecox or the Group of Schizophrenias.* New York: International Universities Press, 1950.
Ellis, Albert. *Reason and Emotion in Psychotherapy.* New York: Lyle Stuart, 1962.
Meehl, P. E. Schizotaxia, Schizotypy, Schizophrenia. *American Psychologist,* 1962, *17,* 827–838.
Shakow, David. Psychological Deficit in Schizophrenia, *Behav. Sci.,* 1963, *8,* 275–305.

Part Three

Rational-Emotive Therapy: Primary Techniques and Basic Processes

11

The Rational-Emotive Facilitation of Psychotherapeutic Goals

Albert Ellis

Chapter 11 shows the direct relationship between the rational-emotive theory of emotional disturbance and the derived goals and basic techniques of RET. Given the position that people create their own anxieties, guilts, depressions, and angers by the irrational beliefs they hold, the goal of therapy is to induce the client to give up these beliefs, as well as the self-defeating behaviors that often accompany them, and to maximize their rational thinking and believing. Chapter 11 discusses RET's basic methodology. Within the context of a direct, verbally active, and didactic stance, the rational-emotive therapist makes full use of the Socratic method of disputing the client's irrational beliefs in order to get him or her first to recognize them, then think them through, and finally relinquish them. The therapist repeatedly and vigorously insists that clients think about their beliefs and insists that they offer evidence to prove the things they have for years simply accepted. A psychotherapeutic excerpt illustrates this process.

THE MAIN GOALS in treating any psychotherapy clients are simple and concrete: to leave clients, at the end of the psychotherapeutic process, with a minimum of anxiety, guilt, depression (or self-blame), anger, and low frustration tolerance (or blame of others and the world around them); just as importantly, to give them a method of self-observation and self-assessment that will ensure that, for the rest of their lives, they will continue to make themselves minimally anxious and hostile.

I and others have explained the psychodynamics of various emotional problems in Part II, including problems of self-esteem, chronic anxiety, guilt, depression, and low frustration tolerance. Suffice it to say at this point that these negative states are by definition symptomatic of irrational thinking and, unlike apprehension, regret, irritation, and the like, practi-

Chapter 11 is adapted from "Goals of Psychotherapy," in *The Goals of Psychotherapy*, ed. Alvin R. Maurer (New York: Appleton-Century-Crofts, 1967), pp. 206–220.

cally always lead to unfortunate results: defensiveness, prolonged and/or intense suffering, ineptness in dealing with problem situations, and self-condemnation, among other things.

It does not seem possible for human beings to become totally un-anxious, undepressed, unguilty, or unhostile. They appear to have distinct inborn, biological tendencies to think unclearly about their own and others' behavior and hence to confuse anxiety with fear and hostility with annoyance, for example. However, they can laboriously learn, or train themselves over a considerable period of time, to be anxious or hostile only intermittently and moderately, instead of (as they normally do in our society) to be persistently and intensely angry at themselves and others.

Core Methodology

How does rational-emotive psychotherapy go about its therapeutic task? Unlike many other therapies today, RET is not primarily interested in getting clients to *express* or *abreact* or *act out* their anxiety, guilt, depression, and anger. RET tries to get them to admit that they are self-blaming or angry and then, as quickly as they are able to do so, to work *against, change,* and *eradicate* their anxious and angry feelings. If, in the process, they express previously suppressed or repressed negative attitudes toward themselves or others, fine. The rational-emotive therapist uses the material they express and works with it—or gets them to work with it. But the expression of their feelings per se is of little interest and, in fact, therapists who encourage such expression frequently help their clients adjust to their anxiety and hostility (that is to feel more comfortable with it), or enhance it—both of which results may be undesirable. Virtually all anger, anxiety, depression, and guilt can be and would better be purged from human affairs—not reality-based annoyance and fear, but needless hostility and self-damning that invariably exist over and above, and are unwittingly or consciously added to, normal irritation and vigilance.

In RET, clients are clearly and concretely taught three kinds of insights, rather than the limited "insight" that is usually given them in psycho-analytic therapies. Insight Number 1 occurs when the clients see that their present neurotic behavior has antecedent causes. Insight Number 2 is more important: this takes place when the clients come to understand that the reason why the original causes of their disturbance still upset and disorganize them is because they still believe in, and endlessly keep repeating to themselves, the irrational beliefs that they previously acquired. More precisely, the therapist can take, let us say, a male client who presently hates his parents, and first show him that this hatred originally arose from, let us assume, jealousy over his mother's paying too much attention to his father and too little attention to him when he was a child. This would also be helping him acquire Insight Number 1.

At the same time, however, the therapist would show this client that the real cause of his disturbance, even during his childhood, was not his mother's relative neglect of him for his father, but his early belief that it was horrible for her to neglect him in this way and that she and his father shouldn't have been the kind of people they were. Without this value system or philosophy of life, the client never would have become upset in the first place, no matter how much his parents tended to neglect him; it is therefore not their neglect but his beliefs about it that originally led him to hate.

More important, if he still hates his parents and is upset about them, this proves that he is still endlessly repeating to himself the original philosophy that he had about their behavior toward him: he still continually tells himself that it is horrible for parents to be neglectful and that they shouldn't be the way they are. If the therapist enables this client to see, very clearly and precisely, that he still upsets himself by continuing, most actively and vociferously, to subscribe to his childish philosophies about the horror of being neglected, and that his own internalized sentences about parental neglect, rather than that neglect itself, are now bothering him, the therapist has thereby helped him to acquire Insight Number 2.

Still more to the therapeutic point, the therapist then tries to help the client attain Insight Number 3. This is the full acknowledgment by the client that there is probably no other way for him to overcome his emotional disturbance but by his continually observing, questioning, and challenging his own belief systems, and his working and practicing to change his own irrational philosophic assumptions by verbal and motor counterpropagandizing activity. Thus, the therapist would show the client who hates his parents that if he is to overcome this irrational hatred (and a host of psychosomatic and other symptoms that may well accompany it), he'd better keep looking at his own idiotic assumptions about the horror of being neglected by them when he was a child and work tirelessly against these superstitions until he rids himself of them. Unless he acquires Insight Number 3, all possible degrees of Insights Number 1 and 2 are not likely to help him overcome his emotional disturbances.

Exactly how does the rational-emotive therapist induce clients to look their own irrational assumptions straight in the eye and to question and challenge these self-defeating philosophic premises? In the main, the therapist, believing that most people are generally allergic to thinking (that is, that most people tend to blindly accept the assumptions they hold and to unthinkingly repeat them to themselves as gospel truth), teaches clients to look at the exclamatory sentences they are telling themselves to create their emotions. Whenever a client says, for example, "My husband accused me of having an affair and that got me terribly angry, because it was so untrue and unfair of him to accuse me," the therapist stops her immediately and asks: "What do you mean *that* got you angry? You mean, don't you, that your husband accused you unjustly and then you got yourself angry by idiotically telling yourself: (1) 'I don't like his false accusations,' and (2) 'Because I don't like it, he shouldn't make them.' Isn't that what got you upset—your own irrational conclusion, rather than his accusation?"

Once the therapist has helped clients uncover and clarify their philosophic, disturbance-creating assumptions, he tries in a hard-nosed and persistent manner to annihilate them. By encouraging clients to think rigorously about these assumptions, perhaps for the first time in their lives, the therapist helps them to see their falseness and to acknowledge that, as long as these beliefs are maintained, the clients *will* get the neurotic emotional and behavioral results that they are now getting. Most of the time, the therapist takes a Socratic questioning stance rather than making declarative sentences. Getting back to the wife mentioned above, the therapist would repeatedly and vigorously ask: "Why shouldn't your husband act the way he does? Where's the evidence that he or anyone else for that matter, *must* treat you fairly? Why are you so special that you deserve to always get what you want from him or anyone else?"

The following excerpt from a rational-emotive therapy session will more fully illustrate the technique. The client, George, came to therapy ridden with guilt and anxiety. The core of his neurotic problem was that he unrealistically and stupidly demanded perfection from himself and, when he failed to always perform perfectly, as was inevitable, he thoroughly condemned himself. In this excerpt Russell Grieger, the therapist, challenges the client to think about the validity of his assumptions and pushes him to think for himself instead of merely parroting rational phrases:

GEORGE   It is true. There is still some part of me that says it shouldn't be true. It is true. People *should* be able to attain perfection. We ought to be more than just human.

THERAPIST   Why should that be true? Why must a person be more than human? Ask yourself: "Why must I, George, be more than human?"

GEORGE   Oh, because I'd like to be more than human.

THERAPIST   You've read the books now, so you know the slogans. But stop and think. OK, "I would like to be so effective that it would dazzle you." Right? "Because I would like to and because you would like to." But why *must* you and how *can* you be more than human?

GEORGE   Well, the only reason I must is because I tell myself that I must.

THERAPIST   I know you do. But let's think it through! *Why* must you? Think about that notion that you have.

GEORGE   Well, it is not so much that I must, it's that I would really like to. Well, because it would really be neat to be very competent.

THERAPIST   OK. I am with you. But the reason you go through so much grief is because you go over that border from, "My, that would be nice," to "therefore I must." Once you step over that border, it starts getting uncomfortable. Now why *must* you—you, one human being in the universe—why *must* you always, or put to it a little differently in our terms, why *must* you in the next instant have to absolutely be on top of the situation? Not, "why it would be nicer." I know that, and we can both agree that it would be nicer, but why *must* you?

GEORGE   Logically thinking, there is no reason.

THERAPIST   What is the logic?

GEORGE   Well, logically thinking it through, there are a number of things. The first thing: my being is intrinsically separate from what I do so that just because I do well or do shitty in the next instance that doesn't make me well or shitty intrinsically.

THERAPIST   That's true, it doesn't. But why doesn't it though?

GEORGE   Why doesn't it?

THERAPIST   Yeah. Why does your performance in this next conference, say, not mean you are a good or evil person?

GEORGE   Logically, it doesn't. Because that would be assuming that you can have perfection. So that being good in the next instance, for that to make *you* good would mean that in *all* those next instances you would be good. You'd have to be perfect to say, "If I'm good in this next instance that makes me perfect." You'd have to be perfect in the next instance and in the next one . . . and in the next one . . . and in the next one.

THERAPIST   And is that possible?

GEORGE   No. It is not possible.

THERAPIST   That's true. What does that mean?

GEORGE   OK. That means that you can't perform as well as you would want to perform. Nor would I want to perform perfectly in every instance. You can break it down; even in a field, even in a part of your field, you can break it down as small as you want to, but the chances are of your performing perfectly every time are . . . it is not possible to do so. There is too much going against it.

THERAPIST   There is too much going against it, including your humanness.

GEORGE   OK.

THERAPIST   If you were more than human you'd be godlike; you would either be dead or godlike. Right?

GEORGE   Right.

THERAPIST   Everybody is human except those who are dead or those who are gods. I know no gods, I have never sat down and talked to a god. I never have! Have you ever met another human being, have you ever sat with another human being in this world whom you could in all honesty say has not made a mistake? I am talking about a living human being.

GEORGE   No. (*Laughs*)

THERAPIST   Seriously?

GEORGE   (*Emphatically*) NO! Sometimes I felt that I had. Well, until I knew them long enough.

THERAPIST   Right. They were able to hide their humanness.

GEORGE   Right.

THERAPIST   And probably the longer it took you to see their humanness, it probably was an indication that they were scared to death about being, you know, just a human. So they had to hide it. Probably the longer it takes to find a flaw in somebody, the more they were hiding it and therefore the more scared they are.

GEORGE   I'll have to think about that sometime.

THERAPIST   OK. But anyhow, getting back to the point, you have never met another human being who is totally perfect. In other words, other than humanlike. Now why should you be different than everybody else? Just to say it crassly, what is so special about you? I mean I know that you are unique in that there is no other person like you in the universe, but being unique and being special are different.

GEORGE   Ah. Well, there is not something special about me.

THERAPIST   Right. There is not.

Derived Therapeutic Postures

Given the basic although not exclusive tool of the rational-emotive therapist of questioning and disputing (See Chapter 12), what else can be said about the therapist's style? In several main ways, the following are typical styles of the rational-emotive therapist.

1. The rational-emotive therapist is active-directive with most clients. Clients not only think the nutty and disturbing things they think, but they think them in the worst possible style: on the one hand, they actively and daily continue to propagandize themselves with their own nonsense; on the other hand, they lazily refuse to think about their thoughts and beliefs, much less the fact that they are always thinking. The system of RET states that clients often require a vigorous, direct therapeutic approach to first get their brains working and to then help them depropagandize themselves.

In RET, moreover, actual homework assignments are frequently given to individual and group therapy clients: assignments such as dating a girl whom the client is afraid to ask for a date; looking for a new job; or experimentally returning to live with a spouse with whom one has previously continually quarreled. The therapist quite actively tries to persuade, cajole, and at times even command the client to undertake such assignments as an integral part of the therapeutic process.

On one occasion, I very firmly gave a 30-year-old male, who had never really dated any girls, an assignment to the effect that he make at least two dates a week, whether he wished to do so or not, and come back and report to me on what happened. He immediately started dating, within two weeks lost his virginity, and quickly began to overcome some of his most deep-seated feelings of inadequacy. With classical psychoanalytic and psychoanalytically oriented psychotherapy, it would have taken many months, and perhaps years, to help this man to the degree that he was helped by a few weeks of highly active-directive rational therapy.

2. Rational-emotive therapists are exceptionally active verbally with their clients, especially during the first few sessions of therapy. They do a great deal of talking rather than passively listening to what clients have to say. They do not hesitate, even during the first session, to directly confront people with evidences of their irrational thinking and behaving. They actively interpret many of the things clients say and do without being too concerned about possible resistances and defensiveness. They consistently try to persuade and argue the client out of firmly held irrational and inconsistent beliefs; they unhesitatingly attack the client's neurosis-creating ideas and attitudes after first demonstrating how and why they exist. As noted in *Reason and Emotion in Psychotherapy* (Ellis, 1962): "To the usual psychotherapeutic techniques of exploration, ventilation, excavation, and interpretation, the rational therapist adds the more direct techniques of confrontation, indoctrination, and reeducation. He or she thereby frankly faces and resolutely tackles the most deep-seated and recalcitrant patterns of emotional disturbance."

3. The rational-emotive approach is unusually didactic. The therapist continually explains to his clients what the general mechanisms of emotional disturbance are, how these usually arise, how they become ingrained, and what can be done to combat them. He freely assigns reading material and discusses any questions the client may have about the material he reads. He firmly believes that people with emotional disturbances do not understand how and why they got disturbed, any more than physics students at first understand how and why the universe got the way it is. He therefore enlightens his clients as soon as possible and teaches them many things a good psychology professor would teach them except that the teaching is usually of an individual nature and is specifically designed to utilize the facts of the client's current life.

4. Rational-emotive therapists make little use of the transference and countertransference relationship in their work with clients. They may purposely not act very warmly with some clients, especially those who crave and ask for much warmth, since their main problem is often that they absolutely think they need to be loved, when they actually do not. RET therapists can teach such clients that they can get along very well in this world *without* necessarily being approved or loved by others. They therefore refuse to cater to inordinate love demands.

Transference phenomena are also minimized in rational-emotive psychotherapy because therapists usually see their clients once a week or less; speak directly to them in a face-to-face situation; directly answer any personal questions that they may ask; and do not go out of their way to interpret transference manifestations that do arise unless they are pertinent and helpful. Moreover, clients are encouraged to work out their problems with the significant people in their own lives, rather than with the therapist.

At the same time, one highly important aspect of relationship does enter into RET, since rational therapists serve as a much different kind of model for clients than do the other significant figures in their lives. Thus, if clients become angry during therapy sessions, rational therapists do *not* return their feelings with anger of their own. And if clients indicate that they do not love or approve of them, RET therapists do not feel that that is awful and that they cannot live successfully without their approval. In the course of RET sessions, therapists tend to show clients that it is possible for a human being to act sanely and appropriately, with a minimum of anxiety and hostility; they do this by serving as a more rational model than clients normally encounter in the rest of their lives. In this way, they help the clients to see that it is possible to behave in a less self-defeating manner. RET therapists distinctly endorse Albert Bandura's concept of modeling as an effective procedure and use it in theoery and practice.

5. The rational-emotive approach to therapy is often more philosophic than psychological. Rather than simply showing clients the psychodynamics of their disordered behavior, RET therapists demonstrate to them what might be called the philosophical dynamics of this behavior. That is to say, they show the clients that the real reasons they act in certain self-defeating ways do not lie in their early experiences or their past history, but in the philosophic attitudes and assumptions they have been making, and still are making, about these experiences and history.

Quite didactically, moreover, rational therapists present to clients what is usually a quite new, existentialist-oriented philosophy of life. They teach that it is possible for people to accept themselves as being worthy of life and enjoyment just because they exist; because they are alive. They vigorously attack the notion that people's intrinsic value depends on the usual socially promulgated criteria of success, achievement, popularity, service to others, devotion to God, and the like. Instead, they show clients that they had better, if they really are to get over their deep-seated emotional disturbances, accept themselves whether or not they are competent or achieving, whether or not others value them highly.

Final Points

The above are some of the main methods used in rational-emotive psychotherapy. In addition, some of the more conventional methods of psychotherapy, such as dream analysis, reflection of feeling, reassurance, and abreaction are also at times employed, but to a much lesser extent than they are used in most other forms of treatment. The main emphasis is ordinarily active-directive, confrontational, didactic, and philosophic. It is interesting to note that the unusual effectiveness of rational-emotive psychotherapy is duplicated by several other modes of therapy (particularly those reported by the late Eric Berne, E. Lakin Phillips, John Nathaniel Rosen, Frederick C. Thorne, and Joseph Wolpe), all of which seem to have in common the element of an active-directive approach to the client's problems.

Although the main emphasis in RET is on analyzing and challenging the negative thinking of the client, rather than on accentuating the positive aspects of his philosophy of life—as advocated by Emile Coué, E. S. Cowles, Viktor Frankl, Hornell Hart, Maxwell Maltz, Norman Vincent Peale, and others—there are very specific positive implications of what is done in the therapeutic relationship. Rational therapists distinctly teach clients that they can fully accept and enjoy themselves just because they are alive, and that they can choose or create special meanings for their existence. Several other positive goals of mental health are implicit or explicit in the teachings of rational-emotive psychotherapy: self-interest; self-direction; tolerance; acceptance of uncertainty; flexibility; scientific thinking; commitment; risk taking; and self-acceptance.

These constructive goals of psychotherapy interrelate with the other primary goals: the minimization of clients' anxiety, guilt, depression, and hostility. For as long as humans are needlessly anxious or hostile, they block their achievement of self-interest, self-direction, tolerance, acceptance of uncertainty, flexibility, scientific thinking, commitment, risk taking, self-acceptance, and virtually any other road to positive mental health —largely because they ceaselessly consume their time and energy in anxious and hostile behavior and sidetrack themselves from doing almost anything else but being self-blaming and angry at others.

It is unfortunately all too easy for people to cover up their underlying negative views of themselves and others with some kind of "positive thinking" that will temporarily divert them from their negative evaluations and make them "happy" despite their still holding such views. But sooner or later, if they mainly use this technique of diversion, their negative thinking will out and will rise to smite them. A permanent solution to basic neurosis, therefore, is for clients constantly to observe, challenge, question, and counterattack their self-defeating philosophies of life until they really evaporate and the clients no longer are basically influenced by them.

12

The Rational-Emotive Approach to Sex Therapy

Albert Ellis

Rational-emotive psychotherapy is often thought to be solely a highly verbal, intellectualized, and exclusively cognitive form of psychological intervention. To people who may have the above impression of RET, the value of Chapter 12 lies mainly in its description of the breadth and diversity of techniques generally employed by rational therapists, and only secondarily in its descripton of sex therapy. While recognizing the primacy of the Socratic method of helping clients challenge their own irrational philosophies (see Chapter 11), Albert Ellis outlines RET's comprehensive therapeutic approach, including the regular use of a combination of cognitive, emotive, and behavioral methods. This methodological eclecticism is well-grounded in theory, for RET believes: (1) that humans simultaneously and transactionally think, emote, and behave; and (2) that when people disturb themselves, they usually do so in all three spheres so that a "multimodal" therapeutic endeavor is desirable.

I FIND IT ALMOST impossible to present the rational-emotive approach to sex counseling and therapy within a chapter as brief as this. This approach has a comprehensiveness that purports to go far beyond the techniques usually employed by sex therapists attached to other schools, such as those used by psychoanalysts, behavior therapists, Reichian and bionergetics practitioners, or Masters-and-Johnson-schooled therapists. It not only includes many of the main methods utilized by these other schools, but it does so on theoretical rather than mere practical grounds, as part and parcel of an integrated theory of psychotherapy. It abjures

Chapter 12 originally appeared in *The Counseling Psychologist*, 1975, 5, 14–21, and is reprinted here by permission of that journal.

I have written Chapter 12 in E-prime, a form of writing invented by D. David Bourland, in accordance with the principles of Alfred Korzybski, the originator of general semantics. E-prime avoids all forms of the verb *to be:* such as *is, was, am, has been, being,* etc. My usage also preferably avoids forms of the word *become,* which one can employ as substitutes for *to be.* The purpose of this form of writing remains the getting rid of the "is" of identity: a form of overgeneralization that most writing and speaking employs and that somewhat falsifies and distorts the meaning of the writer or speaker (or makes it false to reality).

some of the highly popular methods of sex counseling, such as psycho-analytic and Reichian procedures, because it considers them distinctly nontherapeutic or harmful.

I shall not, therefore, try to state in this chapter everything that goes on—and that does *not* go on—in the rational-emotive treatment of sex problems. I have devoted two popular books to this subject (Ellis, 1972a, 1976) and I shall someday probably do a thoroughgoing professional text on it as well. Meanwhile, in the present chapter I shall try to mention briefly various aspects of rational-emotive therapy (RET) that significantly overlap with various other kinds of sex therapies; I shall emphasize those aspects that seem rather unique to RET and to allied cognitive-behavior practices.

I originated rational-emotive therapy early in 1955 as a kind of pro-test against the rather narrow and constricted cognitive-emotive thera-pies, particularly psychoanalysis and client-centered therapy, that then prevailed in the field. I believed, from my own practice of psychoanalysis, that the main psychotherapies of the day had three major defects: (1) on the cognitive side, they failed to include sufficient incisiveness, clarity, directness, and activity; (2) on the emotive side, they lacked solid con-frontation, risk-taking, shame-attacking, and here-and-nowness; (3) on the behavioral side, they almost totally avoided homework activities, training procedures, systematic desensitization, assertion training, and the use of operant conditioning. RET tried to make up for most of these important deficiences by consciously and deliberately using a wide variety of cog-nitive, emotive, and behavioral methods, and by using them within a sys-tematic theoretical framework, rather than outside of or even against such a therapeutic theory.

From the start, partly because I had recognition as a sex and marriage counselor even before I practiced as a full-fledged psychotherapist, RET was vigorously applied to human sex problems, particularly those of im-potence and frigidity. Indeed, had I not done a great deal of sex therapy first, I might never have developed rational-emotive methods, since, al-most more than any other human psychological problem, sexual mal-functioning practically *requires* (as Masters and Johnson [1970] later found) the effective use of direct teaching, training, homework-assigning methods by an effective therapist. And by experimenting in these respects, especially after I discovered that the "depth-centered" techniques of psy-choanalysis frequently harmed rather than helped sexually dysfunctioning people, I probably led myself to give up traditional psychotherapy and develop the rational-emotive approach long before I otherwise would have done.

Anyway, the rational-emotive treatment of sex difficulties uses a comprehensive, interlocking cognitive-emotive-behavioral approach. Let me outline some of its main elements.

Cognitive Sex Therapy

Information Giving

Like Masters and Johnson (1966, 1970), Hartman and Fithian (1972), Kaplan (1974), and other therapists, the RET practitioner sees that most clients with sex anxiety, hostility, or compulsiveness get a good amount of corrective information which, at the start, they usually seem to lack. In accordance with RET theory, this information serves largely to disabuse them of several irrational ideas: e.g., that they must have conventional coitus to have successful and enjoyable sex; that all normal men and women desire sex incessantly and can easily get aroused and satisfied; that spontaneous arousal by both partners must occur if they have good sex; that loving partners automatically and often feel aroused by their mates; that varietism proves unimportant in sex relations; that adulterous desires exist illegitimately and immorally; that foreplay, to seem proper, must wind up in penile-vaginal copulation; that any knowledgeable individual can easily turn on and give many orgasms to his or her partner (Ard, 1974; Ellis, 1972a, 1976).

Rational-emotive therapists give as much or more down-to-earth information as any other sex therapists. But they do it not only to provide more knowledge and training procedures to sexually maladjusted individuals, but to try to help them achieve a generally open, experimenting, individualistic, rational attitude toward sex, love, and marriage and to help them surrender self-defeating and couple-sabotaging myths, superstitions, and dogmas. In regard to such problems as fast ejaculation, I also tend to go beyond the somewhat obsessive use of the squeeze technique by many sex therapists and often recommend a whole variety of alternative procedures: such as the rapid ejaculator's getting more orgasms with his mate or himself, using diverting thoughts, employing one or two condoms, using nupercainal solution, having regular intercourse and interrupting it by intermittent halts as he sees he may come, using breathing exercises, and making use of anal sphincter contractions (Ellis, 1960). Because RET also employs its well-known anti-awfulizing techniques (described below), I and other rational-emotive practitioners can afford to recommend various methods (such as the use of diverting thoughts), which I think Masters and Johnson (1970) wrongly abjure.

Imaging Methods

In line with its emphasis on cognition, again, RET employs a good amount of imaging methods in sex therapy. In particular, males and females who have difficulty in feeling aroused or reaching orgasm get taught how to fantasize intensely and how to use any kind of a fantasy that will work in their individual cases—and to do so without any shame or guilt, if their fantasy seems "bizarre" or socially disapproved. The therapist may help them use regular sex fantasies, various kinds of "pornographic" images, romantic fantasies, focusing on their own or their partner's sensations and responses, or fantasies mutually verbalized with their partners. When advisable, written or pictorial materials may get recommended as fantasy aids.

A special kind of imaging that has powerful cognitive, emotive, and behavioral elements included in it remains in the special province of RET: rational-emotive imagery (REI), originally developed by Maxie C. Maultsby, Jr. (1975) and incorporated as one of the main techniques of RET (Maultsby and Ellis, 1974). I employed REI effectively with Sally, whose case I present in an article, "The Treatment of Sex and Love Problems in Women" (Ellis, 1974a) [see Chapter 8 of this handbook]. Sally came to see me because she only occasionally achieved a climax even when her lovers massaged her clitoral region for fifteen or twenty minutes and, at the time she came for therapy, started to feel completely turned off to sex, so that virtually nothing aroused her. As I explained the REI procedure to her, in the course of her second session:

"Close your eyes, right now, and fantasize, just as vividly as you can, having sex relations with your lover. Can you do that?"

"Yes."

"All right. Continue in your imagination, having sex with him. But picture, quite vividly, that little or nothing happens. You do not get in the least aroused; the whole thing proves a complete bust; and he starts feeling quite irritable and disappointed in you, because you keep failing. In fact, he wonders and makes overt remarks about your continually failing and he indicates that he begins to suspect you are just a dud, sexually, and that you will not likely ever satisfy any man in that respect. Picture these scenes just as dramatically as you can. See it as really happening!"

"I can see it. I can clearly see it now."

"Fine. How do you feel? How do you honestly feel, right in your gut, as you envision this kind of sexual failure?"

"Awful! Depressed!"

"Right. You normally feel that way when you think of this kind of thing happening. Now, change the feeling in your gut to a feeling of ONLY disappointment and frustration. Keep the same fantasy in your head, exactly the same picture, but ONLY feel sorry, disappointed, and frustrated. *Not* awful, *not* depressed. ONLY disappointed. Can you do that?"

"I see I have great trouble feeling that way. I find it hard!"

"I know. But I know that you can do it. You do have the power to change your feelings—if only for a short time. So try some more. Feel ONLY disappointed and frustrated. See if you can do that."

(*After a pause*): "All right. I guess I can do it."

"Do what?"

"Feel *just* disappointed. It keeps running back into depression. But I can feel it, at least for a while."

"Good. I knew you could. Now, what did you think about to make yourself feel that way?"

"Let me see. I guess I keep thinking. 'It doesn't equal the end of the world. I really would *like* to feel much more aroused and to please Henry. But I don't *have to.*'"

"Yes. Anything else?"

"Yes, I guess: 'I won't turn into a rotten person, even if I *never* get very sexy again. It only represents *one* of my traits, sexiness, and doesn't constitute *me*. If I lose that, I still very much have the *rest* of me.'"

"Fine. You could continue to think exactly that, if you want to feel disappointed but *not* depressed. For you *don't* turn into a rotten person if you lose your sexiness. There *does* exist much more to you than that. And you *can* enjoy yourself, and even have a good love relationship going, if you never get very sexy again."

"Yes. I see now that I can."

"Right! Now, if you will practice this rational-emotive imagery technique every day, for a minimum of ten minutes a day, for the next few weeks, if you really keep practicing it, it will emerge as more and more a part of you. You'll see, more clearly than you ever did, that you have a *choice* of what you think when you envision sex failure, that you can *choose* to feel sorry and disappointed—or awful and depressed. And you will get *used* to feeling the former and not the latter, until it develops into almost an automatic part of your thinking and feeling. Up to now, you have really vigorously practiced the opposite—*making yourself* feel depressed whenever you think, as you often do, of not becoming aroused or orgasmic. Now you can *make yourself* feel differently, until you 'naturally' keep feeling that way. So every day, for the next few weeks, practice this kind of rational-emotive imagery that we have just done, until it becomes 'second nature.' Will you do that?"

"Yes, I will," said Sally. And she did practice it steadily for the next few weeks, and reported that when she had sex with her lover, and she began to feel depressed at the thought of failing, she quickly and almost automatically started making herself feel sorry and disappointed instead. After a few weeks, she even had trouble feeling depressed! And she then, much easier and better than before, proved capable of practicing intense sexual imaging of an exciting nature and of arousing herself considerably and coming to orgasm.

Anti-awfulizing and anti-absolutizing. Rational-emotive imagery, as just demonstrated, usually constitutes an anti-awfulizing and anti-absolutizing technique, since it helps sexually malfunctioning individuals, imaginatively, emotively, and behaviorally, to *practice* thinking and acting differently and, notably, to change their awfulizing, anti-empirical philosophies of life. The main premise of RET holds that humans mainly feel disturbed and act dysfunctionally, in sex-love and other areas, when they escalate almost any desire, preference or wish into an absolutistic, perfectionistic *should, ought, must, command,* or *demandingness* (Ellis, 1962, 1972a, 1972b, 1973, 1975a, 1975b; Ellis and Harper, 1961, 1975; Harper, 1975; Hauck, 1974, 1975; Knaus, 1974; Kranzler, 1974; Lembo, 1974; Maultsby, 1975; Meichenbaum, 1974, 1977; Morris and Kanitz, 1975; Theisen, 1973; Tosi, 1974.) RET especially sees *mast*urbation as good and harmless but *must*erbation as pernicious and disturbance-creating. It consequently teaches people to look for their irrational *musts* and vigorously and persistently to dispute them and change them back to *it would be betters*.

In RET, we teach most people with sexual problems the A-B-C's of emotional disturbance and we help them acquire cognitive (as well as emotive and behavioral) tools to change these A-B-C's significantly. We deal, as does Helen Kaplan (1974), not only with the client's specific sex problems but usually, as well, with his or her general tendencies to create emotional disturbance in nonsexual areas of life.

I will now illustrate RET procedures in this connection with a summary of my treating a 29-year-old male with a fairly typical case of impotence. Although he had succeeded sexually with his ex-wife, to whom he remained married for four years, he had not regularly achieved a good degree of erection with other females, both before and after his marriage—except with prostitutes or "low-level," "whorish" women who look to him like hookers. He had explored his presumed Oedipal feelings toward his mother (who kept criticizing him sexually since his early childhood) and its supposed connection with his impotence in the course of a five-year period of psychoanalysis. But he had only got more impotent during this time.

I quickly showed this client that although his inability to get aroused may have at first partly stemmed from his fear of sex and his horror of having it with a "nice woman," who may have symbolized a mother figure to him, its continuing and main cause probably had little to do with the irrational idea that he would prove a sinner if he succeeded sexually with any mother-surrogate, but had other philosophic sources. At point C, his emotional Consequence (or neurotic symptom), he failed with "nice women." And, as an additional Consequence, he felt exceptionally ashamed of his failing. At point A, his Activating experience or Activating event, he got permission from a "good woman" to have sex with her and he got into bed and attempted to have it. Since, in RET terms, C follows A but does not really create or *cause* it (as assumed in psychoanalysis and several other therapeutic systems), the thing to look for and change consists of B—this individual's Belief system. What, in other words, does he irrationally keep believing or telling himself, at B?

As in many cases like this, I first start with the client's *second* C: his shame *about* his impotence. In this RET model, A (his Activating experience) represents his sexual failure, and C (his emotional Consequence) represents his feelings of shame, depression, and self-downing *about* A. B (his Belief System) has two parts: a rational Belief (rB) and an irrational Belief (iB). His rational Beliefs (as he soon agreed) seem obvious: "I would very much like to succeed sexually with all types of females, including 'nice women,' and since I have just failed with this present one, I find that unpleasant and inconvenient. How sad that I failed! I wish I had succeeded, instead. Now let me see what I can do, the next time I go to bed with her, so that I can get aroused and enjoy myself, and please her sexually."

This set of rational Beliefs, if he ONLY stayed with them, would tend to produce in the client (at C) *appropriate* feelings of sorrow, regret, frustration, and annoyance about his impotence at A. Thus, he would feel *appropriately* sad, sorry, and frustrated about his impotence. But since we (he and I) know that he feels *in*appropriately ashamed and self-downing about it (at C), we strongly suspect that he has *ir*rational Beliefs, at B, in addition to his rational Beliefs. And, looking for these irrational Beliefs (iB's), we soon find that he keeps telling himself: "How *awful* that I proved impotent! I *can't stand* having such symptoms! I *must* not act that way; and what *a worm*, what a *complete slob* I turn into if I behave as impotently as that!" He then, after having these profound beliefs, feels ashamed and self-downing at C.

If this client wishes, as we hope he does wish, to minimize or eliminate these *in*appropriate feelings, at C, I help him to go on to D—Disputing his irrational Beliefs. To do this, he asks himself four main questions: (1) "What makes it *awful* (or *terrible* or *horrible*) if I prove impotent?" (2) "Why can't I *stand* having such symptoms?" (3) "Show me the evidence that I *must* not have them." (4) "If I do behave impotently, how do I turn into *a worm* or *a complete slob* for behaving that way?"

He can then answer himself, at point E (the *Effect* or new philosophy of Disputing his irrational Beliefs): (1) "Nothing makes it *awful* (or *terrible* or *horrible*) if I prove impotent. It remains *inconvenient* and *frustrating*. But that doesn't amount to *awful* or *horrible! Awfulness* means 101% inconvenience. And that hardly exists. *Horror* stems from my believing that things *shouldn't* work out inconveniently. But if they do, they do! Tough! No matter how inconvenient or disadvantageous it proves for me to have impotence, it never will prove *more than* that." (2) "I can, again, *stand* impotence, though I of course need never *like* it. I can also *stand* having *any* symptoms that I do have. And I'd better not make myself *ashamed* of my impotence, only *distressed* about having it." (3) "I can find *no* evidence supporting the proposition that I *must* not act impotently. I would find it highly *desirable* to act potently, but that hardly means that I *must*. I will hardly die if I remain impotent. More importantly, I can have sex pleasure, distinctly satisfy my partner, and have many kinds of nonsexual joy in life, even if I stayed sexually impotent forever." (4) "My impotence definitely doesn't make me *a worm* or a *complete slob* but, at worst, a *person with a handicap*. Having a *poor trait* never makes me a *bad person*. I can fully accept myself and keep determined to lead as happy a life as I can lead, even though I have important deficiencies, such as sexual impotence."

By helping this client to go through his A-B-C-D-E's in this fashion, I first helped him to accept himself *with* his impotence and to feel unashamed of having it. Once he began to feel better in this respect, he could work more adequately on the impotence itself. In this respect, as I quite commonly find, his A-B-C's went as follows: Activating experience (A): "This 'nice woman' permits me to have sex with her." Rational Belief (rB) "Wouldn't it prove unfortunate if I failed with her, especially in view of the fact that I have failed in these circumstances before." Irrational Beliefs (iB): "I would find it *terrible* if I failed! I *have* to succeed, else I prove myself a thorough weakling, instead of a man!" Emotional Consequence (C): Lack of adequate erection. Disputing of irrational Beliefs (D); "How does everything turn *terrible* if I fail? What evidence exists that I *have* to succeed? How does it prove, if I fail, that I exist as a thorough weakling instead of a man?" Effect of Disputing (E): "Nothing really turns *terrible* if I fail. Things still remain unfortunate, handicapping, and inconvenient. But nothing more! No evidence exists that I *have* to succeed, though it obviously would prove highly desirable if I did. I don't *have* to succeed, though it obviously would prove quite fortunate if I did. I don't *have* to do anything! If I fail, I clearly don't exist as a Failure, a Weakling, or a Non-man. I still remain a human, a man, who presently fails—and who may well succeed in the future. Even if I never get fully sexually potent. *I* don't develop into a *bad* person. Only my behavior, not my essence, get thereby proven bad or weak."

As he kept going through these A-B-C's, my client grew more and more potent. After the third session, he had intercourse with a "nice woman" and succeeded reasonably well. Immediately thereafter, he assertively picked up another "good woman" on a bus and spent a "wonderful week-end" in bed with her. Thereafter, he had virtually no sex problems, no matter what kind of a partner he selected. He also, at first spontaneously and then with my help, began to tackle his feelings of inadequacy at his job, accountancy, and after several more months made great strides in that respect. As I find common, his sex problems got conquered much more quickly and thoroughly than his general feelings of worthlessness. But the mastering of the former helped him go on to the latter.

I used several of the other techniques mentioned in this chapter with this client—particularly that of helping him imagine "nice women" as "sexy" and that of getting him to question and challenge all his guilt feelings about sex. However, doing his A-B-C's about his shame about impotence and about his impotence itself proved most useful to him.

Removing sex guilt. As just noted, my impotent client found it quite helpful to rid himself of his feelings of guilt. In treating people with sex problems, the technique of shame- and guilt-reduction often proves valuable. As I have shown in several of my books (Ellis, 1958, 1960, 1965a, 1965b), even in today's relatively enlightened age, millions of people still make themselves needlessly ashamed or guilty about some of their sex acts. Although other therapies such as gestalt therapy (Perls, 1969), client-centered therapy (Rogers, 1961), and Reichian therapy (Reich, 1942, 1945) tackle this problem in their own ways, RET specializes in the minimization of shame and guilt.

When, for example, people feel guilty (at point C) about what they have done sexually (at point A), the rational-emotive therapist immediately looks for their Beliefs (at point B). In the sexual area, they have usually convinced themselves of two major Beliefs: (1) this sex act that I have done definitely seems wrong; and (2) because of its wrongness, I should not have done it and must consider myself a lousy person for having committed it. Normally, Belief No. 1 here might possibly emerge as rational, since people obviously can and do commit many wrong, mistaken, foolish, or unethical sex acts (such as compulsive peeping or rape). However, this Belief may have little or no wrongness about it. Such acts, for example, as masturbation, noncoital sex play leading to orgasm, and frequent sex fantasizing have often got labeled as "wrong" or "wicked" when no evidence exists for their foolishness or immorality. Consequently, people frequently make themselves ashamed of or guilty about perfectly harmless, even beneficial sex acts. And in RET we help them question the "erroneousness" of such acts, just as we would get them to ask themselves whether various nonsexual acts (such as primarily devoting oneself to one's own life rather than following the kind of existence one's parents want one to lead) truly prove wrong.

Secondly, and more importantly, RET teaches people that even when they commit an indubitably wrong, self-defeating, or antisocial act, they'd better not go on to Belief No. 2: "Therefore, I must consider myself a lousy person!" According to the RET theories, *no* lousy people exist—only those who do rotten things (Ellis, 1972b, 1973). Guilt (as well as feelings of shame or self-downing) cannot, therefore, get legitimized. We'd better feel highly *responsible* for but not *guilty* about our poor behaviors. RET therapists, ever since the inception of this system of therapy, have specialized in guilt removal. Consequently, they frequently do a bang-up job of helping sexually troubled clients attain freedom from guilt and maximum satisfaction (Ellis, 1962, 1972a, 1973).

Supplementary psychoeducative procedures. As an integral part of its program of cognitive restructuring, RET employs a great deal of bibliotherapy and recorded therapy. Following as it does the educational model, it uses all kinds of audiovisual modalities, including pamphlets, books, recordings, films, talks, and workshops. Thus, clients at the clinic of the Institute for Advanced Study in Rational Psychotherapy in New York City frequently use various kinds of supplementary psychoeducative procedures. They get encouraged to read scientific and disinhibiting sex books, such as *Sex Without Guilt* (Ellis, 1958), *The Art and Science of Love* (Ellis, 1960), *The Sensuous Woman* (Anonymous, 1970) *The Sensuous Person* (Ellis, 1972a), and the *Joy of Sex* (Comfort, 1974), and also to read nonsexual self-help articles and books, such as *Humanistic Psychotherapy: The Rational-Emotive Approach* (Ellis, 1973), *A Guide to Rational Living* (Ellis and Harper, 1975), *How to Live with a "Neurotic"* (Ellis, 1975), *Help Yourself* (Lembo, 1974), *Help Yourself to Happiness* (Maultsby, 1975), and *Overcoming Frustration and Anger* (Hauck, 1975).

They listen to recorded tapes and films, such as those distributed by the Institute. They frequently record their own sex therapy sessions on a cassette recorder and listen to the recordings several times in between sessions. They fill out Homework Reports about their therapeutic progress and use the report forms to help them with their A-B-C's of RET. They participate in live workshops, lectures, and seminars at the Institute. They have motto cards and games available to help them acquire rational-emotive teachings. In these and similar ways, sex therapy at the Institute for Advanced Study in Rational Psychotherapy consists not only of regular therapy sessions but of large and small group educative procedures and various supplementary psychoeducational methods.

Emotive Sex Therapy

Although RET's most unique and best-known procedures tend to lie in the cognitive area, it also includes a considerable amount of emotive-dramatic-evocative methods. Let me exposit a few of these in connection with RET sex therapy:

Unconditional acceptance by the therapist. RET only gets rivaled by Rogerian therapy (Bone, 1968; Rogers, 1961) in its unconditional acceptance of the client by the therapist. True to RET principles, the therapist accepts people with sex problems no matter how foolishly or anti-socially they behave (Ellis, 1974). RET group therapy (where a good deal of sex therapy often gets done) also specializes in teaching all the members of the group to accept (though not necessarily love) the other members and to help show these others, in theory as well as action, that they have a perfect right to accept themselves in spite of their sometimes execrable conduct.

Shame-attacking exercises. According to RET notions, shame or self-downing constitutes perhaps the most important part of many human disturbances. Clients, therefore, frequently get given shame-attacking exercises of a nonsexual nature, so that they thereby can prove to themselves that if they actually perform so-called shameful, foolish, or ridiculous acts, and even do so publicly, their world will not come to an end, and, in fact, good results often will ensue. When given such "shameful" acts to perform, either in the course of individual or group RET sessions, they do not do anything that would lead to real trouble or self-defeatism, such as behaviors that would encourage them to get fired or jailed. But they do get encouraged to perform nonharmful "shameful" behaviors: such as wearing sexy or ridiculous clothing, acting highly assertively and forwardly with members of the other sex, wearing conspicuous buttons, including those that may have antipuritanical views emblazoned in large letters, starting discussions of controversial topics in the kind of a group in which they might normally feel ashamed to bring up such topics, talking intimately to strangers about some of the details of their love and sex lives, and pushing themselves to perform supposedly "far-out" sex acts with some of their regular partners.

I and my RET associates find that these kinds of shame-attacking exercises frequently bring inhibited, unassertive, uptight individuals good results, sometimes in a short period of time. This especially proves true because, in the course of RET individual or group therapy, we not only assign such exercises as emotive or behavioral procedures to get acted upon rather than merely talked about but we *then* follow them up with anti-awfulizing discussions that show how and why there really exists nothing shameful about them. Just as we give our cognitive procedures an emotive vector, we give these emotive procedures a cognitive vector; the two vectors nicely tend to interact with and reinforce each other.

Risk-taking exercises. Along with shame-attacking, rational-emotive therapists specialize in the use of risk-taking exercises. Humans, in sex-love as well as in other areas of their lives, stubbornly refuse to take risks because they largely *define* them as horribly or awfully dangerous when they really involve little danger. The most frequent risk they seem horribly afraid of involves that of acting foolishly in the eyes of others, and they appear utterly determined to down themselves and consider themselves almost utterly worthless if they take such a risk and actually do get severely criticized by significant (or even nonsignificant) others. This naturally bollixes them up sexually, since they frequently define various sex acts as "risky" or "dangerous" and avoid them like the plague. In RET, we often persuade, encourage, and urge our clients to do emotive risk-taking things.

In both our individual and group therapy sessions, we may give our sexually troubled clients risk-taking exercises. For example: (1) "Do something that you consider risky or dangerous, right now in this room." (2) "Pick a partner in this group with whom you would like to have a ten-minute personal encounter and ask this partner if he or she will have such an encounter with you." (3) "Go to a dance, singles bar, or other social gathering and talk to at least five members of the other sex and try to make a date with at least one of them." (4) "Take the risk of asking your regular partner to engage in a sex act that you feel afraid that he or she would not like to perform or would criticize you for asking him or her to perform." (5) "Pick a person for whom you have a special liking and with whom you feel you would therefore feel a risk of getting rejected and ask that person to go on a date with you, to have sex with you, or to do something else that you would normally feel afraid to ask this person to do." (6) "Get together with a member of this (marathon or therapy) group and try to touch various parts of this person's body that you would like to touch. The other person can immediately signal you when he or she does not want you to touch that body part."

Rational-emotive imagery. As noted above in the section on cognition, we frequently employ rational-emotive imagery (REI) with our sex therapy clients because it not only involves cognitive elements but important emotive factors as well. We therefore use it with RET clients who have either sexual or nonsexual problems.

Nonverbal exercises. Since many RET clients have difficulty doing nonverbal activities (far more, sometimes, than they have difficulty with verbal activities) we frequently give them nonverbal exercises. We have them express their feelings to each other, as they mill around the room slowly, or get one of them to stand in a circle while the other members of a group show nonverbally how they feel toward him or her, or do various kinds of hand-holding, face massaging, or back rubbing exercises, or behave foolishly in a nonverbal manner, or act like an animal, or do other kinds of nonverbal activities with group members, with the therapist, or as outside homework assignments with their regular friends and associates.

We see most of these nonverbal procedures as nonsexual and use them for general loosening up processes but some of them have clearcut sexual meanings or implications. Thus, we sometimes have two males and two females respond to each other physically, to see if they bring out any hangups about homosexual feelings when doing so. Or we have males and females caress each other, to see what problems they reveal in the course of this kind of exercise. Or we have a person, as a homework assignment outside of group, try nonverbal contacts with a sex partner: a male, for example, may make a physical overture to one of his dates without his necessarily asking her verbally whether he can do so or if she would like it.

Emotive verbalizations. According to the theory of RET, people create their own emotional upsets largely by *strong* beliefs and *vigorously* held philosophies. Thus men or women who have trouble achieving an orgasm may very *powerfully* feel convinced that they *must* achieve it, *can't* obtain it easily, and prove *worthless* if orgasm remains unachieved. If these individuals merely *mildly* contradict such beliefs, they may still mainly hold them and remain emotionally upset by them. Consequently, in RET we not only attempt to get people to see their disturbance-creating ideas but to contradict and dispute these in a highly emotive manner.

Thus, when I ask an impotent male why it would prove *awful* or *horrible* if he remained unarousable with his favorite partner, and he finally answers, in a rather namby-pamby way, "Well, I guess it wouldn't," I frequently say, almost mockingly, *"But it really would!"* Or I say: "You don't convince me one bit, by that tone of voice, that you think it wouldn't prove awful. Now let me hear you say, much more vigorously, 'No matter how many times I fail sexually with my partner, I can still find it highly inconvenient but *not* awful!' " And I insist that he repeat this strongly to me (and later, to himself), until he starts to truly believe it.

In other instances, RET therapists help clients to powerfully convince themselves that they *can* succeed sexually, that they *have* a right to enjoy themselves in bed, that their parents and other early teachers held very *wrong* views about sex, that masturbation and various other kinds of "shameful" acts really test out as thoroughly unshameful and *good*. We not only, in RET, encourage clients to actively work and practice against their pernicious sex views and in favor of saner, health-creating views, but to keep doing so with as much strength and forcefulness as they can muster.

Emotive feedback. In RET individual and group sessions, we frequently give emotive feedback to clients. If, for example, we talk with a woman with a desperate need for love who keeps messing up her sex-love relations with males because she exudes this need, the therapist or one of the group members may say to her: "Look: if I went on a date with you and I saw how you keep acting—thoroughly obsessed with how much I care for you and not really, because of your obsession, giving a shit about me, I'd say to myself: 'Who needs this? She may have lots of brains and good looks but she obviously won't prove a good partner when she obsesses with, 'Do you *really* love me?' Screw it! I think I'll look for someone who shows much more interest in *me*." Or to a male, the therapist or a group member might say: "If I went with you and you asked me to have sex with you in the manner you just indicated you used with your woman-friend, I'd feel very turned off. I'd feel that you *only* cared for my tits and ass, and hardly a fig for me as a human with many other traits. So even though I might feel attracted to you, I'd run!"

This kind of emotive feedback, when used in RET, doesn't merely show the person with a sex problem the reactor's feelings, but also shows him or her how *others* will likely react and how he or she may change to bring about more favorable reactions. The therapist and group members employ it educatively and correctively, not just expressively.

Behavioral Sex Therapy

As indicated above, RET utilizes a great deal of behavior therapy and does so as an integral part of the rational-emotive method. Its theory states that humans rarely change and keep believing a profound self-defeating belief until they *act* often against it. Consequently, RET therapists have pioneered in giving activity, in vivo homework assignments to their clients, and notably use such assignments with sexually malfunctioning individuals. Since RET behavioral therapy overlaps significantly with the techniques of behavior therapists in general and of Masters and Johnson in particular, I will only briefly mention some of its main methods here.

Activity homework assignments. RET favors gradual in vivo desensitization in many instances. Thus, sexually malfunctioning clients get assigned to have more sex activities, instead of their common avoidance of such acts: to have sex with a partner without at first attempting any kind of penile-vaginal intercourse (Masters and Johnson call this technique the sensate focus); to experiment sexually with new partners if something interferes with satisfactory relations with their present ones; to deliberately work on their hostility or avoidance while remaining with an unsatisfactory partner instead of copping out and running away from sex with that individual; to practice certain activities over and over until they acquire adeptness at them; to practice sexually arousing imaging; and to steadily work at rational-emotive imagery (REI) or other cognitive-emotive methods of changing themselves, until they achieve good results almost automatically.

Operant conditioning. RET often employs operant conditioning or self-management techniques. Thus, clients get taught to reinforce their having sex with their mates and to penalize (but *not* to *damn*) themselves when they avoid sex, or they get shown how to reinforce so-called "shameful" but harmless activities and how to use self-management principles to minimize or stop their dysfunctional sex compulsions. Following the procedures of Stuart (1969), LoPiccollo, Stewart, and Watkins (1972), and other behavior therapists, RET practitioners frequently supervise clients in making sex-love contacts with their mates and monitor their carrying out of these contacts.

RET also specializes in the use of operant conditioning techniques to reinforce cognitive and emotive changes. If, for example, clients get assigned to anti-awfulizing or to disputing some of their irrational ideas about how horrible things would turn out if they failed sexually, and if they don't persistently carry out these cognitive homework assignments, we show them how to reward and penalize themselves so as to increase the probability of their performing their assignments. We find that operant conditioning techniques, when voluntarily accepted by clients, serve as one of the best methods of backing up the kind of homework assignments originally invented by Herzberg (1945), Salter (1949), and other active-directive therapists a good many years ago, and now incorporated as routine RET procedures.

Assertion training. Assertion-training procedures, used especially with shy and unassertive individuals, now constitute one of the most common behavior therapy procedures (Alberti and Emmons, 1970; Jakubowski-Spector, 1973; Lazarus, 1971; Salter, 1949; Wolpe and Lazarus, 1966). Though not called by this name, such procedures have existed as an integral part of RET since its beginnings. In my book, for example, *The Intelligent Woman's Guide to Manhunting* (1963), I showed how women can train themselves to overcome their "natural" passivity and can get themselves to act just as assertively as males in sex-love affairs.

More specifically, RET practitioners often help female clients, through a series of graduated homework assignments, to pick up attractive males in public places (such as dances, singles gatherings, or bars), to phone their men friends instead of passively waiting for the men to call, to make sexual overtures when they wish to do so, to ask their partners to engage in sex-love practices that they particularly enjoy, to stop taking too much responsibility for their children, and to do many other "unfeminine" things they truly would like to do (Wolfe, 1973, 1974). As Patricia Jakubowski-Spector (1973) has shown in an incisive article, "Facilitating the Growth of Women Through Assertive Training," rational-emotive techniques, along with the usual kind of behavioral assertive training, can immensely help females in our society. At the same time, of course, this same combination gets used by RET therapists to enable a large number of overly passive, unassertive males to succeed much better in their sex-love relations.

Summary

In this brief presentation of the rational-emotive approach to sex therapy, I have necessarily skimmed over some of the main details of this complicated, comprehensive, cognitive-emotive-behavioral system. The main thing I would like to note, in summary, is: RET *consciously* and on *theoretical grounds* employs many of the methods used by other well-known therapies. It strongly holds that humans simultaneously and transactionally think, emote, and behave, and that when what we call their emotions or behavior get disordered, we'd better also seriously take into account their thinking, imagining, and evaluating. It especially stresses the desirability of profound cognitive or philosophic change if people want to elegantly and permanently modify their sexual and nonsexual malfunctioning. But it never neglects changing beliefs through altering emotions and actions (Ellis, 1973, 1975). As a general system of psychotherapy, RET envisions most serious sex problems within a framework of prevailing emotional upsetness and it strives for reduced *general* disturbability along with minimizing of specific *sexual* malfunctioning. It recognizes, however, that *some* sex problems require concrete informational and training procedures, without the individual's having to receive extensive or intensive psychotherapy, and it tries to remain practical, hardheaded, and efficient as well as philosophically depth-centered. It now has gotten recognized as an important and, I hope, still pioneering aspect of the broad field of cognitive-behavior therapy. So may it remain!

References

Alberti, R. E., & Emmons, M. L. *Your perfect right: A guide to assertive behavior.* San Luis Obispo, California: Impact, 1970.

Anonymous ("J." pseudonym for Garrity, Terry). *The sensuous woman.* New York: Lyle Stuart, and Dell Books, 1970.

Ard, B. N. *Treating psychosexual dysfunction.* New York: Jason Aronson, 1974.

Bone, H. Two proposed alternatives to psychoanalytic interpreting. In Hammer, E. (Ed.) *Use of interpretation in treatment.* New York: Grune and Stratton, 1968, 169–196.

Comfort, A. *Joy of sex.* New York: Crown Publishers, and Simon and Schuster Paperbacks, 1974.

Ellis, A. *Sex without guilt.* New York: Lyle Stuart, 1958. Rev. ed. Hollywood: Wilshire Books, 1970.

Ellis, A. *The art and science of love.* New York: Lyle Stuart, 1960. Rev. ed. New York: Lyle Stuart, and Bantam Books, 1969.

Ellis, A. *Reason and emotion in psychotherapy.* New York: Lyle Stuart, 1962.

Ellis, A. *The intelligent woman's guide to man-hunting.* New York: Lyle Stuart, and Dell Books, 1963.

Ellis, A. *Sex and the single man.* New York: Lyle Stuart, and Dell Books, 1965a.

Ellis, A. *The case for sexual liberty.* Phoenix: Seymour Press, 1965b.

Ellis, A. *The sensuous person.* New York: Lyle Stuart, 1972a. New York: New American Library, 1974.

Ellis, A. Psychotherapy and the value of a human being. In Davis, J. W. (Ed.) *Value and valuation: Essays in honor of Robert S. Hartman.* Knoxville: University of Tennessee Press, 1972b, 117–139. Reprinted: New York: Institute for Rational Living, 1972b.

Ellis, A. *Humanistic psychotherapy: The rational-emotive approach.* New York: Julian Press, 1973; McGraw-Hill Paperbacks, 1974.

Ellis, A. The treatment of sex and love problems in women. In Franks, V. and Burtle, V. (Eds.). *Women in therapy.* New York: Brunner/Mazel, 1974a, 284–306.

Ellis, A. *Disputing irrational beliefs (DIBS).* New York: Institute for Rational Living, 1974b.

Ellis, A. *How to live with a neurotic.* Rev. ed. New York: Crown Publishers, 1975.

Ellis, A. *Sex and the liberated man.* New York: Lyle Stuart, 1976.

Ellis, A., & Harper, R. A. *Creative marriage.* New York: Lyle Stuart, 1961. Republished as *A guide to successful marriage.* Hollywood: Wilshire Books, 1971.

Ellis, A., & Harper, R. A. *A guide to rational living.* Rev. ed. Englewood Cliffs, N.J.: Prentice-Hall and Hollywood: Wilshire Books, 1975.

Harper, R. A. *The new therapies.* Englewood Cliffs, N.J.: Prentice-Hall, 1975.

Hartman, W. E., & Fithian, M. *The treatment of the sexual dysfunctions.* Long Beach, California: Center for Marital and Sexual Studies, 1972.

Herzberg, A. *Active psychotherapy.* New York: Grune and Stratton, 1945.

Hauck, P. A. *Overcoming depression.* Philadelphia: Westminster Press, 1974.

Hauck, P. A. *Overcoming worry and fear.* Philadelphia: Westminster Press, 1975.

Jakubowski-Spector, P. Facilitating the growth of women through assertive training. *The Counseling Psychologist.* 1973, *4*(1), 75–86.

Kaplan, H. S. *The new sex therapy.* New York: Brunner/Mazel, 1974.

Knaus, W. H. *Rational-emotive education.* New York: Institute for Rational Living, 1974.

Kranzler, G. *You can change how you feel.* Eugene, Oregon: Author, 1974.

Lazarus, A. A. *Behavior therapy and beyond.* New York: McGraw-Hill, 1971.

Lembo, J. M. *Help yourself.* Niles, Illinois: Argus Communications, 1974.

LoPiccolo, J., Stewart, R., & Watkins, B. Treatment of erectile failure and ejaculatory incompetence with homosexual etiology. *Behavior Therapy.* 1972, *3*, 1–4.

Masters, W. H., & Johnson, V. E. *Human sexual response.* Boston: Little, Brown and Company, 1966.

Masters, W. H., & Johnson, V. E. *Human sexual inadequacy.* Boston: Little, Brown and Company, 1970.

Maultsby, M. C., Jr. Systematic written homework in psychotherapy. *Rational Living.* 1971, *6* (1), 16–23.

Maultsby, M. C., Jr. *Help yourself to happiness.* New York: Institute for Rational Living, 1975.

Maultsby, M. C., Jr., & Ellis, A. *Techniques for using rational-emotive imagery (REI).* New York: Institute for Rational Living, 1974.

Meichenbaum, D. H. The clinical potential of modifying what clients say to themselves. *Psychotherapy: Theory, Research and Practice.* 1974, *11*, 103–117.

Meichenbaum, D. H. *Cognitive behavior modification.* New York: Plenum, 1977.

Morris, K. T., & Kanitz, H. M. *Rational-emotive therapy.* Boston: Houghton-Mifflin, 1975.

Perls, F. C. *Gestalt therapy verbatim.* Lafayette, California: Real People Press, 1969.

Reich, W. *The function of the orgasm.* New York: Orgone Institute, 1942.

Reich, W. *The sexual revolution.* New York: Orgone Institute, 1945.

Rogers, C. R. *On becoming a person.* Boston: Houghton-Mifflin, 1961.

Salter, A. *Conditioned reflex therapy.* New York: Creative Age, 1949.

Stuart, R. Operant-interpersonal treatment for marital discord. *Journal of Consulting and Clinical Psychology.* 1969, *33*, 675–682.

Theisen, J. C. *A study of a psychotherapist: Albert Ellis.* M.A. Thesis. San Diego: United States International University, 1973.

Tosi, D. J. *Youth: Toward personal growth, a rational-emotive approach.* Columbus, Ohio: Merrill Publishing Company, 1974.

Wolfe, J. L. What to do until the revolution comes: an argument for women's rational therapy groups. Talk presented at the University of Wisconsin, November 1973.

Wolfe, J. L. *Rational-emotive therapy and women's assertive training.* Tape recording. New York: Institute for Rational Living, 1974.

Wolpe, J., & Lazarus, A. A. *Behavior therapy techniques.* New York: Pergamon, 1966.

13

A Rational Approach to Interpretation

Albert Ellis

Interpretation is an important aspect of all schools of psychotherapy. In Chapter 13, Albert Ellis compares and contrasts the RET use of interpretation with those of other therapies. In contrast to analytic and neo-analytic therapists, whose interpretation focuses on the distant history of the client and its relation to present disturbances, the client's unconscious processes, and the so-called transference relationship between the therapist and client, rational-emotive therapists interpret to the client what his or her basic irrational beliefs and philosophies are and the self-defeating consequences of holding them. They furthermore show the client that, since he or she "chooses" to believe in and reinforce these irrational beliefs, he or she has the ability to give them up and adopt new ones. To do all this, RET therapists are highly direct and vigorous. They waste no time waiting for the client to come up with the irrational beliefs and quickly make interpretation. RET therapists selectively use only those aspects of the therapist-client relationship that may be employed to teach the client how to relate better to others. They report their interpretations to the client as often as necessary.

PRACTICALLY ALL SCHOOLS of psychotherapy take a distinct approach to interpretation, even if they mainly caution against it. In the practice of rational-emotive psychotherapy, the therapist takes a definite stand on many problems of interpreting the client's verbalizations and behavior so that the latter comes to understand much more fully what he is thinking and doing and uses his insight into his own (and others') behavior to change fundamentally some of the aspects of his functioning and malfunctioning. Interpretations made in RET are in some respects similar to, or overlap significantly with, the approaches of other schools, but many of them are also radically different.

Chapter 13 is an adaptation of "Rational Therapy: A Rational Approach to Interpretation," in *Use of Interpretation in Treatment,* ed. Emmanuel Hammer (New York: Grune and Stratton, 1968), and of a paper delivered at the Symposium on Interpretation as a Tool in Psychotherapy of the American Psychological Association in New York on September 5, 1966.

Several kinds of interpretation, however, are usually *not* emphasized in rational-emotive psychotherapy, although they are highly important in psychoanalytic and neopsychoanalytic therapies.

1. The rational therapist for the most part ignores connections between the client's early history and his present disturbances. He does not believe that the client was made neurotic by his past experiences, but by his own unrealistic and overdemanding *interpretations* of these experiences. He therefore spends little time in digging up and interpreting past occurrences and events; rather, he *interprets the interpretations* of these events. Thus, instead of showing the client that he feels angry at dominating women today because his mother dominated him when he was a child, he shows him his irrational thinking processes that made him, when he was young, *demand* that his mother not be dominating, and that in the present are still leading him childishly to demand that women be passive or warm rather than ruling and cold. The rational therapist consistently keeps interpreting the client's *responses* to his history, rather than that history itself and its hypothesized intrinsic connections with his current behavior.

2. Most analytic schools of therapy spend considerable time interpreting deeply unconscious or repressed material to the clients. The rational-emotive school holds that there is no such entity as *the* unconscious or *the* id; that although thoughts, feelings, and actions of which the individual is partly unaware frequently underlie his disturbed behavior, practically all the important attitudes that exist in this respect are not deeply hidden or deliberately kept out of consciousness because the client is too ashamed to acknowledge them, but are just below the level of consciousness, or (in Freud's original formulations) in his preconscious mind, and are relatively easy for the client to see and accept if the therapist will forcefully, persuasively, and persistently keep confronting him with them. The rational therapist, therefore, probably does more interpreting of unconscious or unaware material to the client than do most other therapists; but he does so quickly and directly, with no mysticism or mumbo jumbo, and no pretense that this material is terribly hard to discover and face.

3. Most contemporary psychotherapists appear to aggrandize the significance of the transference relationships between themselves and their clients and expend much energy interpreting to the latter their deep-seated feelings for themselves. The rational therapist believes that the client's relations with other human beings are normally far more important than his relations with the therapist, and that how he likes or hates the therapist has little to do with his basic problems, though it may well be an illustration of its difficulties. He therefore ignores most of the feelings which the client has about him and selectively uses only those aspects of these feelings that truly seem important and that may be employed to teach him

how to relate better to others and to people in the outside world. Instead of interminably analyzing the client's attitudes toward him (and his own attitudes toward the client), he interprets and attacks the general philosophy that the client employs to *create* his transference reactions: namely, his irrational belief that he *needs* the therapist's approval and that he cannot accept himself without it.

4. A great many therapists concentrate on interpreting to their clients their resistances and defenses: showing them how they rationalize, project, repress, compensate, and resist getting better. The rational-emotive psychotherapists probably overlap with analytic therapists more in this than in any other respect, since they particularly show clients the rationalizing, inconsistent, and illogical modes of thinking. Going much further than most other therapists in this regard, however, the RET therapist directly and vigorously *attacks* the clients' illogical thought processes and evasions and forces them, by giving them activity homework assignments, into positions where they no longer employ self-defeating mechanisms or irrational thinking.

5. Many schools of therapy today, such as the Freudian and the Jungian, emphasize the interpretation of dreams. The rational therapist does not believe that the dream is the royal road to the unconscious, nor that it usually gives important aspects of the patient's thoughts and wishes that are not easily available from an examination of waking life and fantasies. He consequently spends little time on dream analysis and prefers, instead, to examine the client's current nondreaming thought and behavior, to see how it reveals—as it almost invariably does—the underlying irrational philosophies and self-defeating attitudes toward himself and others. By the same token, the rational-emotive therapist rarely interprets the client's obscure symbolisms, whether these occur in sleeping or waking life, because he believes that there are too many allowable interpretations to many symbolic processes, and that it is often impossible to define exactly what a given symbol means. He would rather focus on specific events in the client's life and his concrete responses to these events; from these (and especially from the responses) he can determine exactly what the client's basic postulates about himself and the world are, how irrational are these postulates, and what can be done about changing them or eliminating their irrationality.

6. Some schools of psychotherapy, particularly the experiential and the Gestalt schools, emphasize the desirability of interpreting to the client the meanings behind his physical gestures and postures. The rational therapist does some of this kind of interpretation, but in a minimal way in most instances, because he is more interested in attacking the ideas behind the client's gestures rather than in demonstrating their mere existence. Thus, if he sees that the client is holding himself back physically or is speaking

in a stilted manner, he will not only point this out, but will try to get him to see that this posture or gesture is a direct result of his believing that he dare not let himself go because then people would find out what he really was like and would hate him. The rational therapist questions and challenges this hypothesis that the client holds about himself, rather than emphasizing its symptomatic results, such as postural inhibitions.

7. The psychoanalytic, experiential, and expressive schools of therapy tend to interpret almost *all* the client's expressions, fantasies, and behaviors as significant and to show him the unconscious meanings behind these manifestations. Thus, they will make an issue of his being late to the therapy session, or his slips of the tongue, or his writings or drawings, and will find notable underlying meanings in all these kinds of productions. The rational therapist will ignore much of this activity and expression and will, in a most selective manner, interpret what he considers to be the most meaningful aspects of the client's life: such as, his procrastination at work or at school, his problems relating to others, and his evaluation of himself. It is not that he thinks various of the client's behaviors unmeaningful, but that he selects some of them as being much *more* significant than others and prefers to concentrate the therapeutic work, in the interests of efficiency, on these more important areas.

So much for what the rational-emotive therapist tends to deemphasize or not do in the realm of interpretation. What, now, does he tend to emphasize and do?

His main interpretations are invariably philosophic rather than expository or even explanatory. If the client, for example, is unaware that he is overly dependent on others, the rational therapist not only shows him that he is, but also shows him that dependency is the result of an idea, a belief, or a value system; namely, the belief that he *must* have other people's help or approval in order to like himself. The therapist then forces him to question and challenge this hypothesis, to prove to himself how invalid it is, and to replace it with another hypothesis—e.g., that it is fine to have other people's approval but that he is a perfectly valuable person in his own right *whether or not* he does have it.

The main philosophic ideologies which the rational-emotive therapist keeps showing the client are the underpinnings of his disturbed behavior, the irrational ideas that: (a) he must totally condemn himself and others for wrong or inefficient conduct; (b) he must attain a high degree of perfectionism in his and others' eyes; (c) he must be absolutely sure that certain desirable events will occur and other undesirable events will not; (d) he (and others) are utter heroes when they follow a proper line of conduct and complete villains when they do not. The rational therapist, in other words, continually shows the client that he is an absolutist, a bigot, a moralist, a perfectionist, and a religious dogmatist and that only by accepting reality, uncertainty, and tolerance is he likely to surrender his emotional disturbances.

The therapist who takes a rational approach to interpretation keeps showing his client that there are highly probable consequences to his irrational premises; that if he believes that others must approve him, he probably *will* become anxious and depressed; that if he intolerantly condemns people for their mistakes and failings, he very likely will become incessantly hostile and suffer pains in his own gut. He continually proves, by the laws of logic, that certain unrealistic philosophies of life *do* result in self-defeating symptoms, such as phobias, obsessions, and psychosomatic disorders and that only if the client changes these philosophies is he likely to get significantly and permanently better.

Instead of interpreting to the client the historical causation of his present aberrations, the rational therapist shows him that *he* is in the saddle seat ideologically, that *he* brought on that original inappropriate responses to failure and frustration, and that *he* is continuing to respond destructively in the same basic manner in which *he* chose to respond years ago. The therapist fully acknowledges that the client's biological inheritance as well as his sociological conditioning make it very easy for him to get into certain dysfunctional habit patterns and to continue to behave in self-sabotaging ways. But he shows the client that *difficult* does not mean *impossible,* that he *can* change, with sufficient work and practice on his part, and that he'd *better* force himself to do so if he wants to live with minimal anxiety and hostility.

The rational therapist, in other words, interprets to the client the essential *two*-sidedness which underlies his past, present, and future behavior. He demonstrates how, on the one side, the client is biosocially predisposed to allow himself to sink into neurotic pathways, and how, on the other side, he has a special faculty called reason and a unique ability, self-propelled effort and practice, which he can employ to overcome largely his oversuggestibility, short-range hedonism, and rigid thinking. He interprets to the client not only how he got the way he is, but exactly what kinds of irrational beliefs he keeps reindoctrinating himself with to keep himself that way and how he can logically parse, reflectively challenge, and ruthlessly uproot these beliefs. His interpretations, therefore, go much deeper and make wider inroads against disturbed ideas, emotions, and actions than do the interpretations of many other therapists.

The rational-emotive therapist also interprets and teaches the general principles of scientific method and logic to his clients. He shows them that false conclusions about either objective reality or oneself stem from: (a) setting up false premises and then making reasonably logical deductions from these premises; or (b) setting up valid premises and then making illogical deductions from them. He shows his clients exactly what are their false premises and illogical deductions from valid premises. He teaches them to accept hypotheses as hypotheses, and not as facts, and to demand observable data as substantiating evidence for these facts. He also shows them how to experiment, as much as is feasible, with their own desires and activities, to discover what they truly would like to have out of life. He is in many such ways a scientific interpreter who teaches his clients—who in many ways resemble the students of other science teachers—how to follow the hypothetico-deductive method and to specifically apply it to their own value systems and emotional problems.

The rational therapist interprets to clients how their ideas and motivations are unconsciously influenced by their actions and how they can consciously change the former by forcefully changing the latter. He urges them not only to question and challenge their irrational philosophies of life on theoretical or logical grounds, but he gives them practical homework assignments, so that they can *work* against reimbibing these false and inimical values. In the course of so doing, he interprets to them what happens in their heads when they overinhibit their activities—for example, when they withdraw from social relations because of their inordinate fears of rejection—and what likewise happens in these same heads when they force themselves to do things that they have been afraid to perform. Instead of endlessly interpretively connecting the client's past with his present, he more often focuses on connecting his present with his present: that is, his current inactivity with his contemporary uncritical acceptance of unvalidated hypotheses. And he tries for reciprocal change in the client, by inducing him to modify two-sidedly both his thinking and his motor behavior.

In several important respects, then, rational-emotive psychotherapy encourages interpretation which is rather different from the kinds that occur in most other forms of therapy. The RET practitioner tends to interpret in the following ways:

1. Interpretation is usually made in a highly direct, not particularly cautious, circumlocutious, or tortuous manner. The rational therapist feels that he knows right at the start that the client is upsetting himself by believing strongly in one or more irrational ideas; he usually can quickly surmise which of these ideas a particular client believes. As soon as he does see this, he tends to confront the client with his irrational notion, to prove to him that he actually holds it, and to try forcefully to induce him to give it up. Where the majority of other therapists tend to be passive and nondirective in their interpretations, the rational-emotive therapist is almost at the opposite extreme, since he believes that only a direct, concerted, sustained attack on a client's long-held and deep-seated irrationalities is likely to uproot them.

2. Most analytic therapists follow Lewis Wolberg's rule that "it is im-

portant to interpret to the patient only material of which he has at least pre-conscious awareness," but the rational therapist has no hesitancy in trying to show him, from the first session onward, material of which he may be totally unaware and that even may be (on occasion) deeply repressed. He frequently directly confronts the client with two conflicting behaviors or values, to show him that the position that he says he consciously believes in or follows obviously is coexistent with an opposing, and presumably an unconsciously held, position which he also follows. The rational therapist is not intimidated by the client's possibly becoming temporarily more upset when he is confronted with some of his own covert thoughts and feelings, since he then immediately goes to work on showing the client how he is *creating* his own upsettedness and precisely what he can do to calm himself down again by changing the ideas with which he is creating this state of disorder.

3. Most psychotherapists only dare to make deep interpretations when, as Wolberg again states, "the therapist has a very good relationship with the patient." The rational-emotive therapist, however, usually starts making direct, depth-centered interpretations from the very first session, long before any warm or intense relationship between him and the client may be established. He is frequently highly didactic and explicatory and relies much more on the client's potential reasoning powers than on his emotional attachment to the therapist to induce him to accept his teachings and explanations.

4. While rarely being warm, fatherly, or loving to the client, the rational therapist consistently has what Carl Rogers calls "unconditional positive regard" for him, in that he is quite nonjudgmental. The core of rational-emotive therapy consists of teaching the client that no one is to be blamed, condemned, or moralistically punished for any of his deeds, even when he is indubitably wrong and immoral—because he is a fallible human and can be accepted as such even when he makes serious blunders and commits crimes. The therapist, following this philosophy that an individual does not have to be evaluated *as a person* though his *performances* may be measured and rated, fully accepts all his clients, even when he has to point out to them that their deeds are irresponsible and reprehensible. Giving them unconditional positive regard, he can afford to actively-directively confront them with all kinds of undesirable aspects of their behavior, since his interpretations in this connection are quite consonant with his own tolerance for *them,* as individuals, in spite of their deplorable *ways.*

5. Because, again, the rational-emotive therapist keeps forthrightly and ceaselessly attacking, not the client but his feelings of guilt and shame, he does not have to watch the timing of his interpretations too carefully.

He does not wait for the client to be ready for major interpretations; usually instead, he *makes* him ready by presenting the realities of the client's presumably shameful ideas and feelings and concomitantly fighting against the belief that they need be shameful. Occasionally, with an especially anxious client, the rational-emotive practitioner may have to wait to make certain revelatory interpretations; but most of the time he quickly jumps in with them and not only gets them, but also the irrational ideas that induce the client to keep himself from facing them, out of the way.

6. Much of the time, the rational therapist puts his interpretations in the forms of questioning rather than of declarative statements—not because he is afraid to upset the client by being more direct, but because one of his prime goals is to teach the client to question himself and his own thinking. Thus, instead of telling the client what he is saying to himself to make himself anxious, the therapist will say to him: "What could you be telling yourself? Why would you think this event, if it occurred, would be terrible? What evidence is there that it would be catastrophic if you failed at this task?" By these leading questions, the client is led to make his own interpretations of his behavior—and, more importantly, to *keep* making these interpretations when the therapist is no longer present.

7. Like many other therapists, the rational-emotive practitioner frequently makes the same interpretation repetitively. He deliberately does this, knowing that the client has been repeatedly overlooking this interpretation, or pushing it out of his mind, or making some false interpretation instead. He therefore wants to give the client an opportunity to go over the same ground, again and again in some instances, until he begins to see that the interpretation is really true and workable, and not merely to overlook it or give it lip service.

8. The rational-emotive therapist is unhesitatingly vigorous about many of the interpretations he makes. He believes that the client clings relentlessly to his self-defeating irrationalities partly because he has very strongly continued to reindoctrinate himself with them over the years, and that he is not going to give them up unless he strongly and courageously gives himself some alternative ideas. The therapist therefore vigorously shows him that he *cannot* be happy with some of his absurd values, that he'd better give them up if he wants to become minimally anxious, and that *there is no other way* than steady work and practice on his part if he is truly to surrender his superstitions and become less disturbed.

The rational therapist, therefore, quickly and persistently interprets to most of his clients the philosophic sources of their disturbances, namely, the specific irrational ideas that they keep telling themselves to create and maintain their psychological aberrations. He explains exactly what these ideas are and how they are biologically rooted as well as sociologically instilled. Thus, he shows the client that he is born with a tendency to desire approval from others and to believe mistakenly that he absolutely *must have* that approval and is a worthless individual without it and that, in an other-directed society such as our own, he is raised to accentuate rather than to minimize this belief and is conditioned to feel that prestige and popularity are all-important. Thus, again, the therapist shows the client that he is physiologically predisposed to be a short-term hedonist (or to adhere to what Freud called the pleasure principle and to strive for immediate satisfaction rather than future gain), and that in our culture, and with his particular set of parents, he is usually also socially conditioned to believe that he *must* have what he wants and that it is catastrophic when his desires are not fulfilled.

The rational therapist indicates to the client what these biosocial irrational beliefs inevitably *do* to the person who believes them, how illogical and self-defeating these ideas are, and how they can be attacked and uprooted by the client's challenging and questioning them, in theory as well as in practice, and working against them to the best of his ability in ideomotor ways. Because of his theory of human disturbance and its philosophic causation, his content and manner of interpretation is in many respects quite different from that of most other psychotherapists.

His interpretations do not ignore the unconscious, but are largely concerned with material that is conscious and not always deeply repressed. He is not overly involved with transference phenomena; directly attacking in regard to resistances and defenses; little concerned with dreams and obscure symbolic processes; highly selective in regard to what is significant in the client's life; very concerned with the fundamental irrational ideas which underlie the client's disturbed emotions; emphasizing of the inevitable consequences of his false premises and illogical deductions from sensible assumptions; strongly favoring general principles of scientific method; and distinctly involved with impelling the client into action that will help him change his value system. Because of their strong philosophic flavor, rational-emotive interpretations are usually made in a manner that is exceptionally direct, independent of the therapist's warm relationship with his client; indicative of a nonjudgmental attitude on the part of the therapist; not particularly dependent on any kind of special timing; largely given in the form of forthright questioning; quite repetitive in many cases; and unhesitatingly vigorous. Both the content and the form of rational-emotive interpretation unquestionably have dangers and drawbacks and may be pragmatically and experimentally modified as time goes by.

14

Rational-Emotive Imagery

Maxie C. Maultsby, Jr.

*What makes the emotionally disturbed person's behavior so confounding
is its continuation in the face of obviously self-defeating consequences.
Within rational-emotive theory, this is partially explained in terms of
habit strength. While many rational-emotive therapy techniques are designed to help clients give up their neurotic thinking habits, rational-
emotive imagery (REI) is designed to help clients learn rational, facilitative
habits of thinking and believing that are usually mirror opposites of the
old irrational thinking habits. In this chapter, Maxie Maultsby describes
how he uses REI. He discusses how to appropriately prepare the client
for REI, describes the methodology of REI itself, and elucidates several
problems which may occur with the use of REI.*

*Maultsby's version of REI is slightly different from the one described
by Ellis in Chapter 12, "The Rational-Emotive Approach to Sex Therapy."
It might be helpful for the reader to refer back to Ellis' chapter for comparison purposes. I (R.G.) have found it most facilitative to use the type of
REI described by Ellis in the earlier stages of therapy because it is
particularly useful in facilitating insights. I then typically switch to
Maultsby's version in later stages to help clients practice and ingrain their
rational thinking insights.*

REGARDLESS OF HOW sincerely clients may want to eliminate undesirable habits of emotional response that are long-standing and
well learned, they have a strong tendency to automatically continue having the same responses. The reason for this phenomenon is that,
like all other habits, habits of emotional response practiced over a long
period of time become in large part conditioned reflexes; that is, they are
almost completely under the cue control of external situations. It is that
reflex character of well-learned emotional habits which makes them appear to be almost completely beyond the conscious control of clients and
thus impossible to eliminate or change. However, clients learn in rational-
behavioral or rational-emotive therapy that this appearance is untrue.

Regardless of how long-standing undesirable habits of emotional re-

A version of Chapter 14 appeared in *Rational Living*, 1971, *6*, 24–26, and in Maxie
C. Maultsby, Jr., *Help Yourself to Happiness* (New York: Institute for Rational
Living, 1975), ch. 7, pp. 87–103.

sponse may be, clients can almost always learn either to eliminate or to significantly change them. In order to accomplish this, clients must first extinguish their irrational emotional responses to the external situations in which they usually occur. At the same time, they can condition (learn) personally desirable rational emotional responses to the same situations. The most efficient therapeutic technique for accomplishing that end is rational-emotive imagery (REI).

Rational-emotive imagery is based on the neurophysiologic hypothesis that both real experience and the use of the imagination serve to pattern nerve impulses (Eccles, 1958). Thus, mental practice can serve to habituate rational thinking and facilitative feelings that are consistent with rational thinking.

In the remainder of this chapter I explain how to do rational-emotive imagery. I discuss necessary preliminary steps before instructing clients to do REI's and various problems with the use of REI's; finally, I mention what the clients get from all this.

How To Do Rational-Emotive Imagery

Before attempting REI, clients are first instructed to write a complete A-B-C analysis of the event which was the stimulus for their specific undesirable emotional response and then to Dispute (D) their thinking in the "B" section of their analysis. They are cautioned to be as certain as they can that each statement in their "D" section is a rational statement based on the five criteria for the definition of rationality (Maultsby, 1970). To the extent that their "D" section statements do not meet the criteria cited for rational thinking, the REI is likely to be relatively ineffective. Clients are, therefore, instructed to check their attempts at A-B-C-D analysis with their therapist prior to attempting REI.

Immediately after writing an A-B-C-D analysis of irrational emotional responses in a specific situation, clients are to decide which specific responses they probably will have in that situation after they have learned to think rationally according to their "D" section. They then write those responses down in the following manner: "When I have really learned to think rationally, I will have the rational emotional and other behavioral responses of. . . ." When clients have a clear concept of the emotional responses which would be logical if they thought rationally in similar circumstances in the future, they are ready for REI.

Then, clients are given the following instructions to facilitate relaxation:

1. In one slow but continuous motion, take in a deep breath and force it out. As you are breathing out, think just one word: "Relax."

2. At the end of breathing out, hold your breath for approximately ten seconds. To estimate the seconds, count "One-thousand one, one-thousand two, one-thousand three," etc. (It takes about a second to say "one-thousand one.")

3. Keep repeating steps (1) and (2) for two to three minutes or as long as it takes for you to feel calm.

When the client experiences calmness, he recreates in his mind the events of the original situation exactly as they happen, but with two important exceptions: (1) Instead of picturing himself irrationally feeling and behaving as he did, he pictures himself thinking only the rational thoughts from the "D" section of the A-B-C-D analysis; (2) At the same time that he sees himself thinking rationally, he is to try to make himself feel emotionally appropriate to his rational thoughts.

REI is to be continued in this manner for at least ten minutes; a half-hour's duration is ideal. All the while, the client is to involve himself in REI as completely as he can, both intellectually and emotionally.

Sometimes clients tend to become more rather than less upset when they first start an REI session. If so, they are to immediately stop the session, reread the "D" section of their A-B-C-D analysis, and carefully compare each sentence to the criteria for rational thinking or beliefs (Maultsby, 1970). If they decide that their "D" section statements are rational, they are to try REI again immediately. By concentrating more strongly on their "D" section rational thoughts, such clients usually begin to feel less and less upset after about ten minutes of REI. If they do not, they are to discontinue REI on that situation until they check the homework with their therapist.

Very rarely, clients attempting to do REI on therapist-checked, well-done homework analysis will continue to get progressively upset during REI. Careful questioning usually reveals that such clients are not doing REI; instead they are having antitherapeutic associations and images. Such clients can usually be taught to do REI correctly within a few short REI sessions under the therapist's direction. If that fails, it probably means that the client is not suited for the REI technique.

Necessary Client Insights

REI progresses best when the client understands certain aspects of its nature and purpose. Hence, it is advisable for the therapist to arm the client with certain preliminary insights before undertaking REI proper.

REI is not a game. First of all, it is essential that the client take REI seriously. Rather than being a game, REI is an effective training and retraining exercise for the brain. Because REI is "as-if" practice or mental rehearsal of the rational habit that the client is trying to learn, it has almost all of the advantages of real-life practice with virtually none of the hazards. In addition, by doing daily REI, the client can gain three important advantages: (1) he gets practice in dealing with problematic real-life situations with much more rational skill, which would tend to eliminate past mistakes in the future; (2) his emotional re-education progresses significantly faster than it would otherwise; (3) he begins to feel self-confident in his ability to cope with life experiences.

Practice versus pretending. It is secondly important to explore with the client any notions he might have that REI is simply pretending. REI is practicing rather than pretending and I take pains to help clients see the distinction. REI is simply one of the most effective ways to use the brain to learn new habits. "But," many people ask, "can't people just use REI to pretend to be working on their problems, while, in fact, they are avoiding working on them?" My answer is yes and no. Yes, people can avoid working on their problems. But no, those people will *not* be using REI. They will merely be practicing their old habit of trying to trick themselves into feeling better without having first begun to think better. Since they will be thinking and reacting in their usual ways, they will get their usual results.

Pretending to become more rational is like pretending to learn to play the guitar. When an individual is pretending to learn to play, he doesn't follow instructions, he changes the suggested fingering techniques, and he doesn't make music. He just makes musical noise. Even if he often pretends to be learning, his ability to play the guitar doesn't increase.

When practicing the guitar, he follows instructions and he uses the suggested fingering technique. He still makes a lot of musical noise, but he also begins to make some music. And, most important, his ability to play the guitar gradually increases. But he would not stop practicing the guitar after one or two weeks and expect to maintain or increase his skill in playing. Instead, he would logically expect to lose rapidly whatever skill he has gained. The same logic applies to practicing rational thinking in general and REI in particular.

Rational-emotive imagery versus irrational emotive imagery. It is thirdly important to help the client distinguish between rational-emotive imagery and irrational-emotive imagery. Rational-emotive imagery is practicing the habit you want to learn. Irrational emotive imagery is practicing the habit that you want to get rid of.

Most people unfortunately practice thinking and feeling irrationally most of the time. Take the case of Lynn. Lynn was a very angry young woman who incidentally had difficulty getting along with her mother-in-law. She reported in therapy that she was very "uptight" about her mother-in-law's impending visit. An examination of her thinking revealed that she regularly practiced thinking upsetting thoughts about this woman's visit that could only lead to anger. She reported that she pictured her emerging from the airplane with a frown on her face and immediately complaining about something. She then thought almost all the themes that lead to anger: "She *shouldn't* be griping so much! Who the hell does she think she is! I don't know if *I can stand this*! The *bitch*!" It was when she understood the self-defeating nature of this practice that she calmed herself and began to practice thinking rationally about the visit. With her prior practice it was inevitable that she would arrive at the airport angry, and highly probable that little or no provocation would be needed for an aggressive encounter to ensue.

Problems with REI and Their Solution

My extensive research and clinical use of REI have revealed only two problems in correctly using it: (1) having vague, unclear images and (2) having distracting thoughts. I'll discuss each in that order.

People vary greatly in their ability to evoke vivid mental images. Some people do it effortlessly; I call them image thinkers. Other people (like myself) do it poorly, in spite of intense concentration; I call them concept, idea, or word thinkers.

The ability (or lack of ability) to evoke images is probably an inherited trait. If so, nothing much can be done to change it. Fortunately, however, the ability to evoke vivid images at will is merely helpful; it's NOT essential for efficient emotional re-education.

The brains of concept thinkers process concepts with the same ultimate thorough learning that results when the brains of image thinkers process images. It just takes concept thinkers a bit longer on the average to achieve the same level of immediate desirable results.

That fact does *not* mean that image thinkers are necessarily more fortunate than concept thinkers. As a rule, concept thinkers tend to be much less irrational, sensitive, changeable, moody, and phobic than image thinkers. Consequently, concept thinkers usually have fewer intense emotional hang-ups that need REI. So the extra effort concept thinkers must put forth tends to be balanced by their having fewer problems to solve in the first place. On the average, therefore, concept thinkers and image thinkers end up requiring about the same total time to achieve relatively comprehensive emotional re-education. In the beginning, I advise telling clients not to worry about their inability to evolve clearcut, vivid images when they try to do REI's. They should just rethink their "D" sections with as intense mental and emotional concentration as possible for at least ten minutes, four times per day.

Usually just ignoring distracting thoughts during REI is the best way to handle them. Sometimes though, people have the same persistent thoughts so often that REI is temporarily impossible. Whether they realize it or not, such people usually are having those thoughts as a subtle form of civilized voodoo, to magically prevent some feared event from happening. In short, these people are usually afraid not to have their distracting thoughts.

In my experience, all the other complaints clients have had about REI have disappeared rapidly when they diligently do it strictly as directed. That means excluding all, I repeat, ALL, personal short-cuts or interesting but untested personal variations on REI as it is described here.

Results of REI

When REI is done as described, clients accomplish three psychotherapeutic results: (a) they efficiently decondition themselves to the most important external stimuli which are usually eliciting the major parts of their undesirable emotional responses; (b) they create mental frames of reference for behaving rationally, thereby increasing the probability of actually behaving in that rational manner in the future; and (c) they learn to "self-talk" (think) rationally as easily and as reflexively or "naturally" as they were irrationally doing prior to rational psychotherapy. When clients begin to achieve those goals, they will have begun to benefit maximally from knowing their A-B-Cs of emotions and doing REI. Progressive rational self-mastery is the invariable result.

References

Eccles, J. The physiology of imagination. *Scientific American.* 1958, *199*(3), 135.

Ellis, A. *Reason and emotion in psychotherapy.* New York: Lyle Stuart, 1963.

Maultsby, M. C. Routine tape recorder use in RET. *Rational Living.* 1970, *5*(1), 8–23.

Maultsby, M. C. Systematic written homework in psychotherapy: a clinical study of 87 unselected OPD patients. *Rational Living,* 1971, *6*(1), 16–23.

Wolpe, J., and Lazarus, A. A. *Behavior therapy techniques.* New York: Pergamon, 1966.

15

Emotional Reeducation

Maxie C. Maultsby, Jr.

As the reader has already seen, rational-emotive therapy is an active, directive form of psychological intervention that usually bypasses the typical diagnostic and relationship-building processes of most other types of psychotherapy. The therapist quickly assesses the client's problems and almost immediately attempts to show the client what is causing him or her to have the disturbance and what can be done immediately to alleviate it. This process tends to be opportunistic.

One of Maxie Maultsby's major contributions to the theory and practice of rational therapy is his conceptualization of its process. Being more structured in his approach to RET than most rational therapists, he conceptualizes the process as a cognitive-emotional reeducation experience and purposely programs each client to pass through five discrete stages: (1) intellectual insight, or learning what thoughts lead to the particular emotional disturbance and learning the rational thoughts that lead to healthy consequences; (2) converting practice, or practicing the intellectual insights through rational-emotive imagery and various real-life activities; (3) cognitive-emotive dissonance, or helping clients deal with the discouragement that results from still feeling bad despite beginning to think more rationally; (4) emotional insight, or reacting emotionally in a way compatible with rational thinking; (5) personality trait formation, or developing rational thinking to the point that it is habitual. Chapter 15 explains each stage and illustrates them with dialogue from an actual case study.

A noteworthy aspect of Chapter 15 is Maultsby's description of rational self-analysis (RSA), one of the major tools he uses to help clients think rationally. This is a written homework format which he recommends using with all clients to aid them in identifying, disputing, and giving up their irrational thinking. He encourages his clients to do an RSA between each session and uses the generated data as material for each therapeutic session. Maultsby discusses how the use of RSA fits into the process of emotional reeducation.

Chapter 15 is a modified version of a chapter in Maxie C. Maultsby, Jr., *Help Yourself to Happiness* (New York: Institute for Rational Living, 1975).

RATIONAL PSYCHOTHERAPY IS a reeducational process. To say it simply, the goal of therapy is to help the person correct his misconceptions, to unlearn old habits of thinking irrationally, and to learn new rational thinking habits to replace the old ones.

The key concept is HABIT or HABITUAL REACTION. Habitual perceptions and thoughts cause habitual emotions; irrational thought habits cause most emotional problems. For example, most people react with jealousy and other negative feelings every time they learn their sweethearts are romantically interested in other people. Many of those people never learn to stop their negative feelings. So, they logically conclude that they just can't get over such an event in any other way. They don't forget the event, actively remember it, and make themselves chronically miserable, which often leads to the dissolution of the relationship. Since all habits work the same way (i.e., tend to repeat themselves over and over), it follows that this person, like all clients, must engage in repeated, conscious, and purposeful action to replace his habits with more helpful ones. This requires learning through practice and downright hard work.

Since the process of affective education and reeducation is the same for any type of learning, I usually use the example of an American trying to learn Spanish. When children are born, they have no language. All they have is the ability to learn language. So, when American-born children learn to speak English, they get a language education. When they later decide to learn another language, they get a language reeducation. That is, they learn a new speaking habit to replace their old speaking habit. But, they must learn to counteract their tendencies to think and speak in the old ways until the new ways of thinking and speaking become just as strong or stronger. At that point Spanish will flow easily and naturally.

Emotional reeducation is no different. To help himself to happiness, all the client has to do is to work at improving his emotional habits as hard as he would to learn to speak Spanish. The stages and problems are exactly the same. In my experience, there are five stages to reeducation in general, and to emotional reeducation in particular. They are: (1) intellectual insight; (2) converting practice; (3) cognitive-emotive dissonance; (4) emotional insight; and (5) personality trait formation. I thoroughly expect my clients to go through each stage and have devised and elaborated techniques to facilitate this process, which I will now discuss.

Intellectual Insight

Intellectual insight merely means learning *what* you must practice to get the reeducation you desire. In Spanish-language reeducation, intellectual insight means learning the Spanish alphabet, the grammar, pronunciation, and so on. In emotional reeducation, it means learning the objective perceptions and rational thoughts that lead to the feelings you desire.

One of the first necessary insights is the dynamics of how emotions are caused. Through the use of analogies, I help the client understand that thoughts cause feelings and that disturbed thoughts cause disturbing feelings. Once he or she has learned these basic insights, I teach him or her how to use rational self-analysis (RSA). Rational self-analysis, I think, is the best way to get intellectual insight into one's irrational thinking. It has six parts: A is the facts and events section. B is the self-talk section. C is the habitual feeling section, under which the person writes these five questions for rational thinking: (1) Is this thinking factual? (2) Will this thinking help me protect myself? (3) Will this thinking help me achieve my goals today and tomorrow? (4) Will this thinking help keep me out of significant trouble with others? (5) Will this thinking help me feel the emotions I want to feel? Then there's Da, the camera check of A section (here the person corrects his A section to what a camera with sound would have recorded of the event described at A). Db is the rational debate of the B section, and E is the way I want to feel and act.

Normally, when a client brings a written RSA to a session, he reads the A, B, C and E sections first. These sections indicate to the therapist what the problem is, how the client feels about it, and how the client wants to learn to feel and react about similar future events. Then, the therapist usually asks for the Da, or camera check of A. After helping the client critique the Da, the therapist helps the client challenge the B statements in the Db section.

The following case example shows what happens when a client uses RSA to gain the intellectual insights needed to solve his emotional problem. Remember as you are reading it that my aim is to help the client gain insight into his disturbed thinking, to help him dispute all this, and assist him in deriving rational alternatives. At various points you will find a *Dialogue*. These are summaries of the rational discussions Dan (my client) and I had during the actual session.

Case History

Dan consulted me because of severe depression. A month previously, Mary (his regular date) had casually admitted to dating another man. She had no intention of breaking up with Dan, as she much preferred him to the new fellow, but Dan had told her several times that marriage was out of the question for him. In addition, he more than once told her that he expected her to meet and have relationships with other men. So, when an interesting new fellow began asking her out, she accepted, never dreaming

Dan would care. Just the opposite was true. Dan immediately went into a deep depression.

When Mary saw Dan's reaction, she immediately terminated her new relationship. In addition, she sincerely reassured Dan that, had she ever imagined that he'd object, she never would have dated the new guy in the first place. From Mary's point of view, therefore, the event was nothing more than a surprising bit of miscommunication which was regrettable but not significant. Still, Dan felt crushed and trapped. He didn't want to break off with Mary and resolved not to do it "even if it kills me!" As the first rational step in getting over those miserable feelings, Dan did an RSA (Rational Self-Analysis) of the event.

Dan's RSA

A	Da
FACTS AND EVENTS	CAMERA CHECK OF A
I found out Mary had been dating another guy and it almost killed me. Even though she voluntarily stopped seeing the guy and promised not to do it again, I just can't forget it. It's always there to hurt me.	A camera would show Mary telling me she had been dating this guy; that she did not think I would care about her doing it; that she's not that interested in him; that she really loves me; that nothing has changed between us; and that she'll never see him or any other guy again without discussing it with me first. Those are objective facts about what happened. Nothing almost killed me; I am irrationally upsetting myself about what Mary told me. It's probably not true that I can't forget it; it's just that I haven't done it because I probably haven't tried hard enough.

DR. M   I agree with everything you said in your Da section except your idea that you haven't forgotten about the event because you might not have tried hard enough. In reality, that's probably your problem or a big part of your problem—namely, trying to forget it. Trying to forget an event is the best way to guarantee that you will go on remembering it. To actively do anything, you have to pay attention to what you are doing. Therefore, to actively forget something, you have to remind yourself of it in order to remember to forget it. It's sort of like saying: "Remember to forget the word 'elephant'." If you remember, then you're not forgetting it. I would say that you have been trying diligently to forget the event, using an ineffective method of forgetting. More specifically, you haven't forgotten the event because you have no conscious knowledge of the process of forgetting.

DAN   But how can you say I don't know the process of forgetting? That's one of my biggest problems at work; I'm too good at forgetting; I'm forever forgetting things.

DR. M   That's true. You have also been making yourself depressed when you have been depressed. You have not had any conscious knowledge of how you did that either, and that's why you are in this bind, with reference to not being able to get over your depression. You have no useful knowledge about how you have been doing it in the past or about how you have stopped doing it in the past. That's why you are having the problem now. The same thing holds for forgetting. Granted, most people forget things all of their lives. But rarely does a person bother to become thoroughly acquainted with the essentials for forgetting. That's why it's so important to do a thorough rational self-analysis of this event. Once you fill your mind continuously with the rational view of the situation and begin to do rational emotive imagery on it, you will desensitize yourself to the situation. Then you will forget it due to lack of interest in it. At the present time you are irrationally fascinated with it and that's why you have not been able to forget it, but we'll get to that later. For now, I just want you to realize that the reason you haven't forgotten is not because you have not been trying; it's because you have been trying too hard using an ineffective method.

B	Db
SELF-TALK	RATIONAL DEBATE OF B
B-1 How could she do this to me?	Db-1 I couldn't think of any rational challenge for that; I really can't see how she could do that to me.

DR. M   As I see it, there are at least three parts to a rational debate of your "B-1" idea. First, you need to realize that your question is inappropriate. She did not do anything to you; what she did, she did with the other fellow. So, a more accurate or relevant question would be: "How could she do that with him?" Now, you maintain you could not think of a rational challenge to that idea. However, if you merely look at the first rule for rational thinking, namely, it is based on objective reality, you would realize that the objective answer to the question is, "Easily." It didn't require any significant effort on her part to do what she did. All she had to do was accept an invitation. She probably didn't give it a second thought. Now, the fact that you didn't see that obvious answer to the question indicates to me that you were not asking a real question in the first place. Instead, I think you were asking a common rhetorical question. Rhetorical questions are not real questions. They are statements of arbitrary beliefs, in the form of questions. People put their beliefs in the form of questions in an attempt to create the illusion that they are being objective about the situation with which they are concerned. In reality, all they are doing is stating an arbitrary opinion about the situation; it's that opinion stated in the form of a question that triggers their emotional response. Now, if you were to restate your question in the form of a statement that you believe sincerely, what would that statement be?

DAN   Why, "She shouldn't have done that."

DR. M   Precisely. Your strong belief that she shouldn't have done it makes you feel miserable because she did it. Then, your miserable feeling makes it appear to you to be an objective reality that she shouldn't have done it. That incorrect perception of objective reality made it appear to you that there was no rational challenge to your belief. But, when you think about it rationally, what is the evidence that she should not have done what she did?

DAN   Why, she just shouldn't do that. You just don't do those things.

DR. M   Well, people obviously *DO* do those things and she obviously *DID* do it. So, your statement that people don't do those things is nonsensical. It just isn't true. Now, if you were to be truthful and honest about the situation, what statement would you make?

DAN   Why, I guess if I were really going to be honest about it, "I didn't want her to do that; I wish she hadn't done it."

DR. M   Precisely! That's what most people mean when they say "shouldn't"; they really mean "I don't want, I wish it hadn't." If they really get upset about the situation, their upsetness indicates that they really *demand* that the situation not be the way it is. But, then, how much sense does it make to demand that a situation not be the way that it objectively is? None at all. It's nonsense to waste time demanding that something that obviously is should not be, just because you don't like it.

DAN   What should people do when the situation exists that they really hate?

DR. M   It would be well for people who are faced with situations that they hate to rationally analyze the situation and see if there is anything they can do to quickly change the situation. If they discover something they can do that will effectively change the situation, then the most rational thing would be to do it as efficiently as possible. And that usually means as calmly as possible. In any event, whether there is anything they can do to change the situation or not, being upset serves no useful purpose. So, it seems to me that a rational challenge to your B-1 idea would go like this: "That's an irrational, rhetorical question hiding my belief that she should not have done what she did. Now, I have something I can check against the five questions for rational thinking. Is this thinking factual? No. Will this thinking help me protect myself? No. Will this thinking help me achieve my goals today and tomorrow? No. (My goal is to stop being miserable and go on enjoying my relationship with Mary. If I keep thinking this way, I will go on being miserable and ultimately break off with her as I have always done in situations like this in the past.) Will this thinking help me avoid significant trouble with others? No. (It will either lead to my continuing to have these long, emotionally charged arguments with Mary, which neither of us like, or it will lead me to break off with her which, in my mind, would be even more painful and self-defeating than what I'm doing now.) Will this thinking help me feel the emotions that I want to feel? No. To the contrary, thinking that she has done something that she shouldn't have done and, more specifically, that she has done it to me, leads to my feeling painfully angry and desiring revenge. My desire for revenge leads to an equally painful fear that I will lose her, which in my mind would be the worst situation of all. That's why I feel so trapped. So, my thinking here disobeys all five of the rules of rational thinking. A more rational way of thinking would be: everything is always exactly as it should be. Mary did what she did because of the beliefs she had about the situation at the time. And, although I didn't realize it at the time, I see now that I actively contributed to her having the beliefs that led to her dating another fellow. But, the main thing for me to focus on now is the objective reality that everything is exactly as it should be and therefore I have no rational reason to feel hurt or otherwise unfairly treated."

DAN Wow! That's a mind-blowing way to think, man!

DR. M But, does it make sense? And, more specifically, does it make more sense than what you're thinking in terms of your goals of feeling better and remaining in the relationship?

DAN Yes, I have to admit, in that sense, it makes a whole lot of sense.

DR. M And it's for those reasons alone that I recommend it to you as a replacement for your irrational *shoulds*. Let's hear your B-2.

DAN I see now that you're really going to dislike this one because I can see now that it was just as irrational as B-1.

DR. M No, I'm not surprised. If you knew how to do Rational Self-Analysis perfectly well, you wouldn't have the problem you're having now. So, let's hear it.

B-2 If she really loved me, she never would have done it.

Db-2 (1) Is this thinking factual? No. People can love people and still have romantic interests in other people, especially if they believe and have been told in no uncertain terms that the other person doesn't care. (2) Will this thinking help me protect myself? No. By continuously thinking this way and making myself depressed, I may become suicidal. (3) Will this thinking help me achieve my goals today and tomorrow? No. It is likely to make me abandon my goal of being happy and continuing my relationship with Mary. (4) Will this thinking help me avoid significant trouble with others? No. (5) Will this thinking help me feel the way I want to feel? Definitely, no, no, no. More rational thinking is: The fact that she did what she did only proves that she did it. It has no necessary relationship to her love for me. However, the fact that she says she loves me and does not love him and she voluntarily broke off with him when she saw that I really did care about her dating other guys is evidence in favor of her telling the truth when she says she loves me. I see now that I had the common irrational attitude that if a woman really loved me her love would make her blind and otherwise incapacitated to have any feelings whatsoever or any interests whatsoever in another man. It only takes a minute of objective thought to see that that is utter horseshit. Still, that's been the attitude that I have had all these years and why I have always ended up breaking off with girls when I believed that they were interested in someone else.

DR. M   I would agree wholeheartedly with your challenge there. I can't think of anything more rational to add to it. Let's hear your B-3.

B-3   How can I think of my-   Db-3   I don't see how to challenge that.
self as a man when I wasn't
man enough to keep her from
doing that?

DAN   I see now that is also a stupid rhetorical question, hiding the belief that I can't think of myself as a man now because if I had been a real man she would not have done what she did.

DR. M   Precisely. Now you have something you can apply the five questions for rational thinking to and see how rational the beliefs hidden in those rhetorical questions really are.

DAN   Yeah. I see what you mean and it's obvious that it's all irrational. The objective reality is that I am a real man now and I'm just as much a man now as I ever have been. And she went out with that guy because she thought I didn't care and because she wanted to. It had nothing to do with how much of a man I am or am not.

DR. M   Is it possible for you to be anything less than a whole, 100% male?

DAN   When I think about it objectively, the answer is obviously I can't be anything other than an objectively whole male.

DR. M   Exactly. Even if you have a transsexual operation, you will still be a genetically whole male without your external genitalia. And even when you're not alive, you'll be a real dead man.

DAN   Man!

DR. M   Precisely.

DAN   Yeah. It's just another one of those stupid rhetorical questions that I don't see how I could challenge rationally.

B-4 What if it happens Db-4 I don't know how to challenge that.
again?

DAN   Now, if I were doing it I would say: "I am afraid it might." I would answer the question by saying: If it happens again, it happens again. It will happen. And I will react whichever way I react. But if I get what I hope to get out of this rational behavior therapy, I will certainly react more rationally than I do now. However, I was not really asking the question, "What if it might happen?" I was really stating my belief that it is going to happen again.

DR. M   Beautiful. Now we have something we can apply the five questions for rational thinking to, again. Okay, what is the objective evidence that it is going to happen again?

DAN   None.

DR. M   Will thinking that way help you protect yourself?

DAN   Well, yeah, I'll be prepared for it.

DR. M   You'd be prepared for it? How will you be prepared for it?

DAN   Well, if you are expecting something, then you won't be surprised if it happens.

DR. M   That's true, but if you don't give yourself an emotional reeducation, will you be any less miserably depressed if it happens and, until it happens, will you be any less painfully afraid and upset than you are now?

DAN   Yeah, I see what you mean.

DR. M   The reality is that you cannot prepare yourself emotionally in the way that you do physically, like stockpiling guns or something. All you can do is replace your present irrational thinking with the type of rational beliefs which would not trigger the type of painful depression you are experiencing now. Then you would not have anything to be afraid of because if she does it again you will not feel as miserable as you do now and you won't have anything to be afraid of. What you are afraid of now is not her doing it again, but of experiencing the miserable feelings that you have now. Right?

DAN   Right.

DR. M   Well, if you adopt the rational thinking that she hasn't done anything to you and everything she did she should have done, therefore, you have no rational reason to feel miserably upset. Now, this doesn't mean you're supposed to like what she did, but you don't have to make yourself miserable to prove to yourself that you don't like something. Do you?

DAN   No. I don't have to be depressed to prove that I don't like something.

DR. M   Right, so all you're doing here with your so-called "being prepared" is making yourself miserably afraid and not allowing yourself to enjoy the reality that you have what you hope to have from Mary, namely, her unshared romantic attention. Is that not a fact? Isn't it true that so far as you can tell, you now have her unshared romantic attention?

DAN   Yes, so far as I can tell.

DR. M   So, therefore, all you have to do is change your thinking so that you will stop upsetting yourself and that rational change will also prevent you from being as upset in the future, regardless of what she does. Now, are you really, sincerely committed to adopting this new rational way of thinking that we've just described as your permanent replacement for the irrational thinking that lead to your being so depressed for the last four or five weeks?

DAN   Yeah. It sure makes more sense than what I'm doing now.

DR. M   Okay, let's hear your C section.

C	E
MY HABITUAL FEELINGS	THE WAY I WANT TO FEEL AND ACT
Angry, depressed, afraid.	Rationally accepting of the objective reality without significantly upsetting myself. Calmly behaving in my best interest.

This lengthy example shows how I help Dan begin the process of emotional reeducation. He now has insights into the causes of his depression and also insight into what he needs to do to become undepressed. But more is required and I will now turn my attention to the next stage of emotional reeducation.

Converting Practice

Converting practice means acting on one's new intellectual insights. This is done by ignoring old habits and regularly practicing the intellectual insights. The two ways to act out intellectual insight are: by doing rational emotive imagery (REI), explained more fully in the preceding chapter, and by real-life practice. When these techniques are combined, irrational thinking habits are most quickly brought under voluntary control and then given up. Daily *PRACTICE* is all that is needed.

To return to our language analogy, converting practice means practicing Spanish until you can speak it without English first popping into your mind. Then you'll have converted your involuntary English-speaking habits back to their voluntary stage. That lets you keep English out of your mind at will and you can then speak Spanish as much as you desire. An important point is that learning Spanish *does not* rob a person of his or her ability to speak English. And *neither* does learning to feel less miserable rob clients of their ability to feel. I want to emphasize that point. Many people naively believe that learning to feel less miserable may rob them of their ability to feel any emotion. That CANNOT happen. As long as one has a normal nervous system, he or she will be able to feel all normal human emotions, even if some of them are irrational. *All* rational emotional control does is help one feel *more* of the emotions one likes and less of those one doesn't like.

Since rational-emotive imagery is thoroughly discussed in the previous chapter, I will not go into detail at this point about its mechanics. Suffice it to say that it involves practicing the Da, Db and E sections of the RSA and ignoring the A, B, and C sections. Gradually clients will stop automatically having the old perceptions, thoughts, and gut feelings; instead, they will start replacing them with the more rational ones of the E section of RSA.

In Dan's case, converting practice meant picturing himself reacting to Mary in a personally enjoyable fashion despite her past action. He could do that only by practicing replacing the irrational thoughts he had had about her action for the past six weeks with the rational ideas in his RSA. Let's pick up where we left off in Dan's therapy session.

DR. M   Good, now you're ready for the second step in your emotional reeducational process—practice.

DAN   (*With a surprised expression*) How can you practice a feeling?

DR. M   Easily, if you use your brain rationally and do systematic rational-emotive imagery. You've read about rational-emotive imagery in your *Cartoon Booklet,* right?

DAN   Yeah, oh yeah. You must mean imagining yourself doing something the way you want to do it.

DR. M   Right. I suggest you reread that section and start doing rational-emotive imagery at least four times per day. Okay. I see our time is up now, so I'll see you next week.

The following are excerpts from Dan's sixth rational behavior session.

DAN   Doc, your RBT just isn't working.

DR. M   Oh? Why do you say that?

DAN   I still feel so bad about this Mary thing, I don't think I'll ever get over it.

DR. M   Have you been doing REI?

DAN   No, I don't do it any more because it's too painful.

Dan wanted to learn to rationally accept this personally undesirable event and go on enjoying his relationship with Mary. To practice that behavior would not be painful; it would be pleasant. I therefore suspected that Dan was doing irrational emotive imagery rather than rational-emotive imagery.

Experience has taught me that it is never rational for the therapist to accept at face value the patient's description of the failure of a rational self-help technique. In my experience, such instances have always been the failure of the patient to correctly utilize the technique. Consequently, I asked Dan to tell me exactly what he had been picturing in his mind when he tried to do his rational-emotive imagery. He reported that every time he tried to picture Mary in bed with this other fellow, he would get so upset that he would have to stop the imagery. I immediately pointed out to him that rational-emotive imagery is done using the correctly done rational self-analysis of the event that you want to handle more rationally. The goal in his "E" section was for him to learn to calmly accept the knowledge that Mary had had an affair with this fellow and that it did not mean that she did not love him (Dan) or that anything had changed between them. Instead, it was the result of an unfortunate bit of miscommunication. What he was doing was ignoring the rational self-analysis and trying to calmly picture himself seeing Mary and this other fellow engaged in love-making. There would be no more reason for him to want to enjoy seeing that than there would be for him to want to enjoy seeing any couple in the act of love-making. Such activity would be voyeuristic and therefore irrational, if not abnormal, behavior. So, when I pointed all this out to him, he readily agreed that he was not doing rational-emotive imagery the way it was described in the book.

Cognitive-Emotive Dissonance

Engaging in converting practice typically puts the client into cognitive-emotive dissonance. This means having mental behavior that's NOT logical for your habitual GUT feelings. In learning Spanish, you are in cognitive-emotive dissonance when you speak it correctly but feel uncomfortably strange, as if you are pretending to be what you aren't—namely, Spanish. Most people call that strange feeling feeling phony. Regardless of what you call it, you usually experience it as a strong urge to switch back from Spanish to English. But, you can't learn to speak Spanish while speaking only English. That urge to act contrary to what you know is correct is caused by cognitive-emotive dissonance. People who don't understand it give in to it; they then end up going back to their old habits.

In emotional reeducation, cognitive-emotive dissonance occurs when the client begins to think rational thoughts but still has the old miserable feelings. Those miserable feelings seem so natural, normal, and right to some clients that they are sometimes afraid to work against them. In addition to feeling "right," those old feelings somehow seem to protect them from further hurt. That's because almost everyone believes a little in the magical idea: "If I had just worried more before I felt so badly, it might not have happened." That subtle but effective magical thinking is the main reason people in emotional distress are often afraid at first to become undistressed.

Dan demonstrated cognitive-emotive dissonance in his sixth RBT session. He'd catch himself thinking rationally and feeling like his old satisfied self with Mary; then he would think irrationally about her affair and frighten himself into a depression again. He knew his depression was irrational, but it felt so natural, normal, right, and protective that he was afraid to work against it. It seemed that working against it might open him up to an even deeper emotional pain. So he logically but irrationally settled for what he incorrectly believed was a lesser pain and ironically achieved only useless suffering.

Let's return to Dan's sixth session. When I asked him why he was not following the REI directions, he responded:

DAN   Because when I picture myself thinking and acting as if it's no big thing that Mary stepped out on me, that it was really just stupid miscommunication which I caused, my gut tells me that's just horseshit. It just doesn't feel right, and I can't believe it.

DR. M   I wouldn't say that you can't believe it; I'd just say that you are refusing to believe it.

DAN   Right! I just damn well refuse to believe that her screwing another guy doesn't say something about me as a person. I really feel it does say I'm not a real man; otherwise, why would she have done that to me?

To benefit from rational thinking, the person not only has to think the rational ideas, he has to communicate them to himself as well. It is only by communicating an idea to himself that he demonstrates that he believes it. It's essential that he believe the rational ideas which he describes in his RSA because they will be the basis of rational emotional reeducation. It's obvious from Dan's remarks that he was merely entertaining the rational ideas we went over together in his RSA, not communicating them to himself. The only thing I needed to do was to get Dan to start focusing on the rational ideas that he described in his rational self-analysis. That is why I calmly went back to the content of his rational self-analysis in my response.

DR. M   Well, objectively speaking, she didn't do anything to you. What she did, she did to and with the other guy. Also, she did what she did, in part because you told her more than once you wouldn't care and that you even expected her to date other fellows. Of course, we have to believe that she wanted to do it. There is no reason to believe that he raped her, is there?

DAN   No! But damn it, I'd feel a hell of a lot better if he had.

DR. M You mean you would have preferred her to experience the objective dangers of being raped, as opposed to having a harmless affair?

DAN I know it sounds crazy; but it's true. At least she would have been trying not to hurt me. I don't care what you say, I really feel that she hurt me, made me feel inferior, worthless, less than a man. I really feel she did that to me. Sometimes I catch myself feeling halfway undepressed and get the weirdest feeling. In fact, I actually get scared and seem to bring the depression back. I know you're going to say that's crazy: but, damn it, it just doesn't feel right not to be depressed when you know the woman you love has been screwing another guy. It's phony, and I feel phony when I think that way, and I can't stand being phony; I hate it. I feel I have a right to be depressed.

DR. M Oh, I agree completely; you have a perfect right to be depressed. But that doesn't mean it's rational to exercise that right, does it?

DAN I don't see why not.

DR. M Look at it like this; when you walk, you have the right to take five steps forward and two steps backwards; so, why don't you exercise that right?

DAN That'd be stupid; I'd never get where I'm going.

DR. M Nope, you're only half right. It would be a stupid thing to do; but you would get where you were going; it would take about 50% more time to get there, but you'd get there. So, it's not a question of having the right to do what you do; it's a question of how much rational sense does it make to exercise your right? Do you see what I mean?

DAN (*After a pause*) Yeah, I see, but it still feels phony; not like the real me.

DR. M (*Smiling*) Are you saying you'd rather be real, even if it means being real miserable?

DAN (*With a sheepish grin*) Well, yeah, sort of. I mean, I don't want to be a damn phony. I hate phonies. If being rational means being phony; well, I just don't know.

DR. M So, you really would rather be real miserable, huh?

DAN It sounds stupid doesn't it? Actually, it's really crazy. I mean, I can see the sense in what you're saying; actually, if I stop and think about it, I mean *really* think about it.

DR. M (*Smiling*) Rationally, I hope.

DAN (*Pause*) Yeah, when I think about it rationally, I see that she really didn't do anything to me and I'm just as much a man as I ever was. But, I just don't know. You know it's like I'm afraid not to be depressed. It seems like a big mistake to stop feeling hurt. It seems so unnatural, so abnormal, even obscene. I mean, it really feels strange, weird; more like a nightmare than reality.

DR. M I think you are hanging yourself by your GUT. I mean, you are trying to use your gut rather than your brain to tell you what's best for you to do. That habit is rational *ONLY* if your beliefs and attitudes that produced your habitual gut feelings are really rational for you now. The fact that you are in therapy means that they are not. If so, that means

your gut feelings are now being triggered by irrational beliefs and attitudes. If you are really committed to rational emotional control, you
will replace those irrational beliefs, attitudes, and gut feelings with more
rational ones. But, you won't do it until you get the courage to feel ab-
normally and unnaturally *less* miserable and then are willing to keep on
feeling that way until feeling *less miserable* becomes natural and normal
for you and feeling *more miserable* is *unnatural* and *abnormal*.

DAN   (*Incredulously*) But how do you do that?

DR. M   First, you must learn about the five stages of emotional reeducation,
especially the third stage, cognitive-emotive dissonance. That will clear
up your present confusion. Then it will be simply a matter of you letting
your brain rather than your gut do your thinking for you. I see our
time is up, so I'm going to have you listen to a recorded lecture on the
process of emotional reeducation before you leave today. I think the
tape will help you see that you have made much more rational progress
than you think you have. In fact, you have your problem half solved.
But the halfway point is where most people get discouraged, frustrated,
and want to give up. The fact that your reaction is so common, but easy
to handle once you understand it, is the reason I made a tape recording
to tell patients about it, rather than wasting a therapy session on it. I
want you to listen to the tape once a day for the next five days. After
listening to it and thinking about it three or four times, I think you will
solve the other half of this problem in short order, Okay?

DAN   If you say so; I'm at the point where I'll try anything.

Cognitive-emotive dissonance is relatively easy to eliminate once you
understand it. Mainly, you convince the client to ignore it and continue his
or her rational thinking and actions using REI and real-life practice. Then
miserable feelings become less and less intense and the rational feelings
that are logical for rational thoughts will become habitualized.

The Last Two Stages

The fourth stage of emotional reeducation is called emotional insight. In
learning Spanish, emotional insight means feeling natural about speaking
Spanish. In emotional reeducation, emotional insight means the client
feels the way he or she wants to feel when thinking rationally about old
events. It only requires diligent practice.

Merely by continuing to have emotional insight, emotional insight
quickly turns into *a new personality trait*. This is the fifth stage of reeducation in which one makes the new habits of thinking become as natural,
normal, and involuntary as the old irrational habits used to be.

After Dan had listened to the tape and practiced REI's three times per day for one week, he had an important insight: His fear of not being depressed was not protecting him from further hurt; instead, it merely kept him feeling miserable. That insight freed Dan to stop being afraid of ceasing to be depressed. Then when he caught himself feeling fearful, he'd correctly label the emotion a "magical worry." Next, he'd do two to five minutes of REI, seeing himself rationally continuing his romance with Mary as if nothing had happened. Within another six weeks, Dan had completely resolved his cognitive-emotive dissonance in favor of new emotional insight.

That doesn't mean Dan felt good then or even completely neutral about Mary's past affair. To the contrary, he still didn't like the thought of it. That let him know for sure that he was neither ready for nor did he want to have an open relationship. Equally important, Dan realized for the first time that he could dislike a past event without feeling miserable to prove it. Even several months later, Dan still had negative thoughts about Mary's affair, but he no longer felt miserable about it. And it no longer felt phony to refuse to feel miserable about it. By consistently feeling rationally calm about the affair, Dan was able to forget it more or less completely within seven to ten months. That's not a long time in which to overcome an emotional habit of fifteen years' duration. Dan only needed three months of RBT to be able to continue progressing by himself.

Summary

Replacing an old habit with a new one is a process. It's *NOT* a one-trial act. Old habits just don't roll over and die. During the first few weeks of emotional reeducation, the client probably will experience the old emotions much more than the new ones. He or she has to work out each of the old habits; it's quite logical, therefore, to have to work out of and into any new ones.

Converting practice will be most effective if the client takes these five steps: (a) He should read the Da, Db, and E sections of a well-done RSA every night at bedtime. When doing REI, the client should imagine as vividly as possible acting out in real life his rational Da, Db, and E script, repeating the scenes over and over, seeing himself feeling emotionally and physically appropriate while acting out the more rational role in real life; (b) When waking up in the morning, the client should immediately repeat the bedtime REI for ten minutes; in that way, the day starts with the pleasant feeling of rational success and self-confidence; (c) Instead of making meaningless small talk during cigarette breaks or coffee breaks, the client should use the first two or three minutes of each for a quick REI;

(d) The client should repeat his REI ten minutes before going to lunch and dinner, for what the client thinks about most is what he or she will most likely do at any given time; (e) Finally, the client must put the REI into diligent real-life practice, otherwise it will be a waste of time. In terms of emotional reeducation, it means reexperiencing over and over without emotional pain the real-life events habitually associated with emotional pain. The client will be able to do that because he or she will be making only Da perceptions, thinking only Db thoughts, thereby creating E feelings. In Dan's case, that meant learning to think about Mary's past affair without feeling depressed. Both with language and emotional reeducation, converting practice puts the client in the third or halfway state of reeducation—cognitive-emotive dissonance.

The phony feeling of cognitive-emotive dissonance is the unavoidable result of practicing new beliefs and attitudes. The fastest way to resolve cognitive-emotive dissonance in favor of new emotional insight is daily REI and real-life practice. In Dan's case, that meant daily REI's seeing himself feeling neutral about thoughts of Mary's affair; then he would see himself calmly dismiss those thoughts as being irrelevant to his life in the present. Next, he'd see himself continuing to enjoy his romance with Mary. Finally, and most important, Dan acted out his REI's daily, to both his and Mary's enjoyment. In the face of that kind of daily practice the phony feelings of cognitive-emotive dissonance can't persist.

16

Psychotherapeutic Responses to Some Critical Incidents in RET

Russell Grieger and John Boyd

Rational-emotive psychotherapy is a special kind of psychological inter-
vention that often places unusual demands on clients. For some clients,
these demands precipitate irrational thoughts and cognitive distortions that
can lead to premature termination or to a superficial process of psycho-
therapy. In Chapter 16, Russell Grieger and John Boyd discuss four types
of cognitive distortions and offer concrete suggestions as to how the
therapist can respond to each.

RATIONAL-EMOTIVE PSYCHOTHERAPY (RET) is a relatively direct, time-saving form of psychological intervention. Because it is so conceptually and parsimoniously grounded in the now-famous A-B-C theory, it is easy for the well-trained rational therapist quickly to discern the client's irrational beliefs, to get the client to articulate these in short order, and swiftly and directly to challenge their irrationality. Ellis (1971), talking about one of his clients, described the RET therapist's approach best:

> Although I, as the therapist, know very little about the client, I size him up quickly and decide to take a chance, on the basis of RET theory, and to try to get to one of the main cores of his problem quickly: his terrible feelings of inadequacy, of shithood . . . and I make an attempt to show the client, almost immediately, what he is doing to cause his central upsetness and what he presumably can do about understanding and changing him-self. . . . I know fully that I may be barking up the wrong tree, and am prepared to back down later if I turn out to be mistaken. But I know, on the basis of considerable prior evidence, that there is an excellent chance that I may be right; and I want, by taking that chance, to try to save the client a great deal of time and pain. . . . I also try to show how human beings in general easily think the way he does and how so many of them, no matter what their abilities and talents, wind up by hating themselves because of this type of crooked thinking. I am thus exceptionally educa-tional in the first minutes of this first session—just as, presumably, any good teacher would be. (p. 106)

While all this is well and good, RET tends to place unusual demands on clients. For one, it puts the responsibility for change directly on the client's shoulders—a burden often difficult to carry in the initial phases of treatment. The burden is complicated by the fact that the client is shown a straightforward method for solving his problems before he acquires the capacity to apply it. This is often frustrating. Furthermore, RET requires the client to exert a great deal of effort, both in and out of therapy, without necessarily receiving support from the therapist. Finally, RET forcefully encourages the client to immediately reflect upon strongly held beliefs about himself that are often painful to face.

What happens when clients are faced with these demands? Some respond in a constructive manner. They conclude that it would be better for them to change and they tolerate the distress that often accompanies therapy as a necessary requisite for improved psychological functioning. Some others present simple resistances, such as a reluctance to self-disclose or a mistaken expectation that the therapist's role is to make them better. For others, however, the burdens mentioned above precipitate thoughts and beliefs that quite often present the therapist with critical incidents for which he is unprepared. These incidents usually develop in the intermediate or later stages of therapy and reflect rather significant cognitive distortions which are part and parcel of the client's existing problems. It is imperative that these incidents be dealt with directly and effectively, for a less than adequate therapist response can lead to premature termination or at best a benign treatment of the client's problem.

This paper discusses several critical incidents and their cognitive distortions: cognitive-emotive dissonance; the "I-Won't-Be-Me" syndrome, self-hatred, and the fear of mediocrity. For each we describe the dynamics and then suggest how the therapist might strategically respond.

Cognitive-Emotive Dissonance

Some clients make significant changes in only one or two sessions; however, most people's habits of thinking irrationally are so well ingrained by the time they come to therapy that they tend to persist in this mode until new thinking habits become, through practice, stronger and more general than the original irrational ones. Because of this, most clients are prone to cognitive-emotive dissonance. This occurs at the point in therapy when the client recognizes his irrational beliefs, understands their rational alternatives and begins to think rationally, but still feels the same negative ways (Maultsby, 1971). These clients see a better way, but cannot immediately actualize it, so they conclude that they cannot possibly overcome their self-made mess and/or that the A-B-C principles make no sense.

It is sufficient, with many clients, simply to advise them to ignore the dissonance and continue RET. Sometimes, however, clients develop one of three cognitive distortions that present a crisis to the therapist:

1. *"My mountain is too high."* The client often believes that his irrational philosophies are too well-ingrained to overcome. It is ironic that clients who believe this usually understand that it is their habitual beliefs that are indeed the bases for their emotional disturbances. One of my [Grieger's] clients expressed it this way: "I know that my problems are simply that I've developed a momentous habit of thinking nonsense, but my mountain is just too high to climb."

Two types of clients are particularly prone to this. One is the perfectionist. In the arena of psychotherapy no less than other arenas, he will demand that he perform exceptionally well by achieving immediate and total rationality. Once he perceives himself as being unable to attain perfection, he becomes discouraged and/or depressed. As a result, he often concludes that the attainment of therapeutic goals is too difficult. A second type of client who is prone to this type of cognitive-emotive dissonance is the one who generally sees the world as overwhelming and himself as inadequate. He has high values for achievement but low expectations for effecting change. A feeling of helplessness results from this discrepancy and he then becomes discouraged.

2. *"It's too hard."* A similar cognitive-emotive dissonance occurs when the client believes that maximizing his happiness is not worth the effort. Instead of setting realistic goals of minimizing his negative emotional reactions, this client becomes discouraged that he will have to work with himself throughout his life. Clients give messages to this effect in a variety of ways, but some of the more common are: "I can do it OK at a particular time, but I have to be vigilant all the time"; "I'll need to make a maximum effort every day of my life or I'm doomed"; "I'll be contending with this sort of thing the rest of my life." It is interesting that clients often arrive at such conclusions after they comprehend the validity of the A-B-C theory and have had some success in reducing their misery by using rational-emotive principles. When they again become upset, which is inevitable, they become quite discouraged.

The dynamics of this critical incident are prototypic of most neurotic problems. The client is a magical believer in his own "specialness." He sees himself as more than a unique individual; he sees himself as somehow separate and different than the rest of the human race so that *he should not* have to contend with the same problems and miseries that the rest of us do. Thinking of himself as special, he literally demands that he not have to make such efforts in life and he upsets himself because things are not as pleasant and easy as *they should be* for him.

In part because of the above belief, this client is also one who does not tolerate frustration well. In addition to believing in his own specialness, he believes that unpleasant experiences are *awful* and that he *cannot stand* them. The reality is, of course, that he can always stand these things although not necessarily comfortably. Believing all this, he finds it difficult to accept the fact that he will periodically experience discomfort and often gives up trying in therapy.

3. *"RET is nonsense."* Two types of clients tend to conclude that RET makes no sense. One is the client whose pathology centers around the belief that he is worthless. Believing this, and not achieving magical success in therapy, he finds himself at a point where he can either blame himself for this alleged failure or find something or someone else to blame. Many defensively choose the second alternative and conclude that the system and/or the therapist is useless. The second type of client prone to disparage RET is the one whose problems involve hostility. Hostility, as Ellis (1973) has noted, involves the person's first believing: "Because I want this to be, it *should* be exactly that way." After convincing himself of this, he usually concludes: "Because it isn't just the way it should be right now, I *can't stand it* and it *deserves* every ounce of my anger." The result of this process is blame. Specifically applied to the topic of this paper, the hostile client is prone severely to blame the therapeutic system and the therapist when they do not magically provide him with the positive outcome he immediately demands.

The rational-emotive therapist can do several things to respond to clients in cognitive-emotive dissonance. First, he may help the client accurately conceptualize the dynamics of his discouragement. Most people tend to mystify their emotional experiences and become catastrophized by them. By explaining to the client how he makes himself discouraged, the therapist helps the client demystify and make sense of the phenomenon and, in the process, gives him support. All this tends to make the client perceive his dissonance as manageable.

At this point the therapist may also help the client deal with any magical notions that he might have about psychotherapy itself. Many clients expect (or demand) magical cures from therapy. "When is this going to make me better?" they ask. We advise the therapist to deal directly with this issue. He should first admit to the client that neither he nor RET has a magic answer; then, he should forcefully tell the client that only he can effect his own cure by willingly engaging in a period of determined work. We then advise challenging the client as to whether or not he is willing to make this start. Assuming that he chooses to continue, we then

educate him about what he can reasonably expect with regard to therapeutic progress. We find it helpful to show him the typical stages a client
travels in therapy, including: (1) being able to identify his beliefs and to
understand and challenge the irrationality of them; (2) being able to catch
himself thinking these irrational things when they occur; (3) being able
to regularly and effectively challenge these beliefs when they occur; and
(4) being able to habitually think more rationally in real-life situations. In
addition to encouraging realistic expectations about psychotherapy, this
tactic also lends support to the client by further helping him perceive a
workable road to recovery.

In a similar vein, it is extremely useful to help the client set appropriate
therapeutic goals. Many clients, particularly perfectionists, irrationally
conclude that they must never again feel upset. They mistakenly think
that they are not healthy if they ever feel blue. The reality is that all people become upset at times; the trick is to minimize these in terms of
frequency, intensity, and duration. In this light it is often helpful to teach
the client the difference between mastery and coping. Meichenbaum
(1976) defines mastery as the perfect attainment of a skill, while coping
is the ability to deal effectively, but not necessarily perfectly, with a problem when it arises. The goal of the therapist in this instance is to help
the client set coping goals rather than mastery ones. From a coping stance,
the client can attempt to maximize his rational thinking by using his negative feelings to cue him to begin a rational problem-solving process, rather
than panicking and resorting to habits of irrational thought.

Another strategic therapist response is to directly confront the irrational
notions behind the various forms of cognitive-emotive dissonance and to
tie them back to the client's general problems. With the perfectionist who
thinks his "mountain is too high," the therapist would persistently ask him
why he has to, and how he can, be perfectly rational. With the client with
low frustration tolerance, the therapist can take the client through the irrational notions that make frustration tolerance difficult: "Why should you
have it so easy?" "Why are you so special that you should not have to
work through problems?" "What do you mean you can't stand it? You
look unhappy, but you look like you're standing it." Such challenges are, of
course, designed to force the client to think about his own thinking; they
represent the heart of RET.

The "I-Won't-Be-Me" Syndrome

Our society is quite effective in brainwashing people to believe that they
have no alternative but to be terrifically upset in the face of adversity
(Ellis, 1962). Most believe that they cannot help being disturbed when

certain unwanted frustrations occur; some even believe that not reacting strongly and negatively to such circumstances is unnatural and inappropriate. These notions, of course, are irrational. Existing evidence
strongly suggests that people upset themselves by the learned philosophies
and beliefs they hold. Furthermore, people can unlearn maladaptive beliefs and develop new ones in order to reduce unnecessary emotional stress.
In essence, the individual *always* directs his own emotional reactions and
can therefore choose to be upset or not.

Three aspects of the mistaken notion that people must become emotionally upset often prompt a critical incident in rational-emotive psychotherapy:

1. *"I'll lose my identity."* After successfully working through the basic
philosophies that led to their emotional disturbance, some clients find it
strange to react calmly or only mildly negatively in situations in which they
previously reacted catastrophically. They marvel at the unusualness of
their reactions and even find it fascinating.

Some clients unfortunately go further; they disturb themselves about
their new way of responding and tend to resist further psychotherapeutic
work. The client usually gets caught up in some metaphysical nonsense
about a loss of integrity regarding his "inner essence." He worries: "Who
am I now?" and "What will be my purpose in life?" Not surprisingly,
clients who have previously been exposed to nondirective therapy and
"humanistic" theory are most prone to perceived loss of identity.

An example of how this critical incident unfolds in psychotherapy is
illustrated by the following therapeutic interchange:

STAN It's really strange. I don't get upset the way I used to, and it's
scary.

THERAPIST How so? What's scary about that?

STAN Well, I don't know. I've lost something and there's nothing to replace it.

THERAPIST I'm not sure that makes sense. What have you lost?

STAN The pain. The depression and anxiety.

THERAPIST So what? What's the bad thing in that? That sounds like a good
thing to me.

STAN I know it doesn't make sense. Being depressed is being me. I've
identified that with me. If I don't get depressed, I won't know
myself.

THERAPIST How so? How will you not know yourself? Will you look in the
mirror and not recognize your face?

STAN I just won't know myself anymore.

The most important thing for the therapist to do is to directly dispel
these silly notions by challenging their validity. As per the above inter-

change, the therapist might ask: "What do you mean you won't know yourself?" "How can part of you be lost?" "What does it mean to not be you?" "How can you possibly be anyone else but you?" After insisting that the client think rigorously about these nutty assertions, the therapist is in a good position to educate the client about a more valid notion concerning what he has or has not lost. Basically, the client has only lost or, more accurately, given up his troublesome *habits* of thinking and in their place substituted a new and better way of responding.

A useful way of doing the above is to explain or re-explain the A-B-C theory to the client. We find the use of analogies, examples, and visual aids often helpful. The therapist can explain that thought habits (at point B) are no different from any other habits; what one is therefore losing is only a neurotic, self-defeating habit which is being replaced with a rational, more facilitative one. An analogy that we particularly like concerns handedness: We ask the client whether he would lose his identity if he were required to change from being right-handed to left-handed. Then we show him that, although he would find it awkward for a period of time to switch handedness, he would with persistent effort ues his left hand more often, more comfortably, and perhaps with more facility until it became "natural" for him.

2. *"I'll be a phony."* It is not uncommon for a client to conclude that he will become a phony if he tries to think and believe differently than he normally does. Rational therapists often hear such comments as: "It's unnatural not to go with my true feelings"; "I can't pretend to feel something I don't"; or even directly, "I'll be a phony if I don't feel as I naturally do." Clients who maintain such thoughts are prone to active resistance: they will not challenge the philosophies behind their feelings and, instead, insist on thinking in self-defeating ways.

The dynamics of this pretense are twofold. First, it is a self-evaluation that, like all self-evaluations, is invalid. As Ellis (1973) has noted on numerous occasions, it is scientifically invalid and practically impossible to judge, rate, or evaluate a person as totally anything. A person may on occasion act phony, but it could never be proven that he, indeed, is a phony.

The distinction between brain thinkers and gut thinkers (Maultsby, 1974) is also helpful in understanding the dynamics of this issue. The brain thinker accurately realizes that it is his thoughts that cause feelings; the gut thinker mistakenly places inappropriate emphasis on feelings. The gut thinker believes that feelings are entities that just happen and that, because he feels something so strongly, the thing he holds feelings about must be consistent with the feelings. For example, the client who hates someone concludes that his hatred validates that the other person is, indeed, despicable. A diametrically opposite explanation is, in fact, accurate. The client thinks of another as despicable and then feels angry at him. All in all, the gut thinker reverses the natural order of events (i.e., thoughts cause feelings) so that feelings are seen as: (1) caused by events; (2) the most important entities in the universe; and (3) the criteria for the definition of objective reality. Thinking thus, it is understandable that this client often works only half-heartedly in rational therapy or simply quits.

In addition to challenging the self-evaluation component of this cognitive assertion, it is important for the therapist to directly attend to the phoniness issue in two other ways. The first is to reiterate the A-B-C theory in terms of this irrational idea. We find it helpful at these times to diagram the theory and to visually show how the "phony" belief is just another B. Following the diagram, the client is helped to think through his reversed notions with the fact emphasized that the brain, not the gut, is, indeed, the most important human organ.

In addition to the diagram strategy, the therapist can help the client see the difference between *pretending* and *practicing* (Maultsby, 1974). A person is pretending (i.e., acting in a phony fashion) when he does not have a sincere desire to bring about permanent change and only goes through the motions. A person is *practicing* (i.e., behaving genuinely) when he diligently tries to learn something new with a sincere desire to change. Thus, sincerely and diligently practicing something is not phony.

3. *"I'll become a machine."* Some clients want to terminate rational therapy because they conclude that they will become mechanized or cold and unemotional. We often hear such things as, "I won't have feelings anymore," or "I'll become a robot." One guilt-ridden client said: "I'm not sure I really want to think differently; I'm more alive when I feel strongly about things even though my feelings are so painful." Other clients worry about becoming "contented cows" who will simply accept life as it is and passively bear the insults of others. "People will walk all over me" is a common complaint in this realm.

Similar to the client who thinks he will be a phony, this client is gut thinking. He mistakenly thinks that events directly cause his feelings and/or that feelings are independent entities that somehow magically represent truth in the universe. In addition, this client commonly does not distinguish between the negative feelings of sorrow, regret, frustration, and irritation that result from rational thinking, and the negative feelings of depression, guilt, anxiety, and anger that result from irrational thinking. He then mistakenly fears he will give up all negative feelings and perhaps even the positive ones as well.

Regardless of how it is expressed, these conceptions call for an immediate response on the therapist's part. Our main advice is to attack this notion along the same lines as that of the client who dredges up the phoniness issue. That is, the therapist should first reintroduce the A-B-C theory and teach the client the difference between brain and gut thinkers.

Another important strategy is to directly dispel the mistaken notion that once his neurotic feelings are minimized the client will be rendered feelingless. The therapist can help the client understand that all sorts of negative feelings, such as irritation and regret, result from thinking rationally. For example, a client can rationally conclude that a particular setback in his love life is unfortunate and appropriately feel sad; or he can feel depressed by irrationally concluding that it is an *awful* thing that *should not* have happened. Furthermore, it is often useful for the therapist to point out that the minimization of neurotic feelings literally frees a great deal more time to devote to experiencing pleasure. Rather than becoming mechanized, therefore, the client who maximizes his rational thinking really has a chance to experience more frequent and more intense positive feelings, as well as a whole host of mildly negative ones, rather than no feelings at all.

Self-Hatred

One of the more common bases for emotional disturbance is the general philosophy that a person's self-worth is dependent on his performance. Habitual self-condemnation is inevitable for those who take this superstition seriously, because every human being at times performs poorly and inappropriately. The end product is literally self-hatred. The irrationality of this notion has been so thoroughly discussed elsewhere in this book that no further discussion need be made here.

In addition to causing a person to become disturbed, the habit of self-evaluation often leads to resistance in psychotherapy. Sometimes a client will resist working on his irrational beliefs about his worthlessness for fear that he might find evidence of its truth—this client is so traumatized by his belief in his apparent worthlessness that he goes to extreme lengths to avoid facing them. When his neurotic belief is pointed out to him, he often refuses to admit it, engages in long-winded philosophical discussions of the matter, or only superficially thinks through the philosophy.

In contrast to the above, some clients are so thoroughly convinced of their worthlessness that they conclude that they deserve to suffer. They consider the issue of their worthlessness closed and, in fact, *insist* that they continue to suffer. What follows is an illustration of this from a therapy session with a self-hating, overweight, middle-aged woman.

SUSAN   Yesterday, I thought it was sort of a breakthrough, you know. I felt very good about the work I did here. And, uh, this has happened before. I felt really great and thought it was a breakthrough. I felt high, you know, and I couldn't sleep.

THERAPIST You mean you felt so good you couldn't sleep?

SUSAN   Yeah. But, I'm now thinking that wasn't a breakthrough at all.

THERAPIST You've changed your mind on that?

SUSAN   Yes. You see, now I'm doubting all the thinking I did yesterday. I'm doubting it because, you know, maybe it's really right. In other words, maybe I'm right and I am really worthless. And maybe I'm trying to keep the irrational ways of acting. I didn't have self-control so therefore I was punished or deserved the bad things that happened. So this means that the world is sort of, well . . . sort of made sense. The bad things that happened to me made some sense, because maybe I deserved them for not having self-control.

THERAPIST So you believe that something or someone is punishing you for not being—

SUSAN   I sort of deserved to suffer, yeah. . . .

The therapeutic strategy for this critical incident is rather straightforward. We think it best to help the client to conceptualize the reasons for his resistance and lack of progress. With Susan, for example, we want her to understand that she is acting in therapy on the belief that she deserves grief. A useful way to get this across is to compare her behavior toward herself with her behavior toward someone else she hates. We point out to her that she very probably would not go out of her way to do a favor for this hated other; likewise, she does not go out of her way to do a favor for herself, whom she also hates. This explanation tends to decathect the issue and makes it appear manageable.

At this point the therapist can begin to encourage the client to think empirically about his beliefs about himself. Where is the evidence that he or anyone else can legitimately be judged worthless? How can someone be a louse because he makes mistakes in any one area? Why does anyone deserve to suffer? In typical RET fashion, the therapist continues in this way to assist the client to first question and then give up these erroneous, self-defeating notions.

An interesting way to help the client see the illogicalness of his self-evaluation has been developed by Maxie Maultsby and his colleagues at the University of Kentucky. It involves drawing a circle and placing within the circle a great many dots. The therapist communicates to the client that a person's "selfhood" is comprised of literally hundreds of thousands of experiences, actions, and characteristics, each represented by a dot. The therapist then asks the client how many "dots" a person can reasonably remember. With the answer obviously being only a small percentage, the therapist then asks the client to prove how reasonable it is to conclude that *all* his known "dots," much less all the dots in his circle and much less his total circle, are worthless because of one or several inadequate ones. The point is, of course, that total self-evaluation is a gross overgeneralization that is conceptually and pragmatically invalid.

The Fear of Mediocrity

A final impediment to persistence in rational-emotive psychotherapy has to do with the fear of mediocrity. The basis of this resistance is the client's conclusion that if he gives up his irrational idea that far-reaching competence is necessary and appropriate for him to be worthwhile, he will condemn himself to the "god-awful, inhuman state of averageness." Success for him is an all or none thing that can only be achieved with all-consuming effort. He worries that he will lose his motivation to succeed at anything and often fears he will doom himself to total nonachievement.

Some clients resist rational therapy from the beginning because this irrational idea is the heart of their neurosis. Other clients develop this notion in the process of therapy and begin resisting at that point. The dynamics of this critical incident for the latter group can best be conceptualized as a mourning process. After comprehending the irrationality of the demand for perfection and the goals and modus operandi of RET, the client sees himself at a choice-point in his life where he can either give up his perfectionistic demands once and for all or retreat safely into his neuroticism. It is the fear of the *supposed* consequences of making the former choice, along with some lingering fascination with godlike conquests, that make him pause. Essentially, this critical incident represents the last vestiges of the client holding onto his neuroticism.

An excerpt from a session with one of our clients illustrates how this often arises in rational-emotive psychotherapy:

MIKE   You know I'm really doing well. But you know I had no dreams last week of conquering worlds. I found that sad.

THERAPIST   Thinking of imperfection led you to conclude that maybe your limits are not so far out there?

MIKE   Yeah.

THERAPIST   What's so sad about that? Let's assume that your limits are short of being outstanding. OK? So what? What's bad about that? There is a possibility you won't be super. Now, what's awful about that?

MIKE   It shouldn't be that way. My impact is going to be limited.

THERAPIST   What does that mean?

MIKE   The impact of my creativity or skills on whatever.

THERAPIST   That's true. If you don't have the skills of a Van Gogh, you won't paint the pictures of a Van Gogh. But, why is that so awful?

MIKE   It's disappointing. (*Long pause*) It's just very sad.

THERAPIST   Why?

MIKE   Um, OK, um, well, it's a loss. I'm not going to be able to do those things. I may never become dedicated or organized to, say, spend three or four years of my life to make an impact on the field, for instance.

THERAPIST   But, let's say that you don't make an impact like you want. Now, that would be unfortunate for the field because they won't get the goodies of your efforts. But, why would that be sad for you personally? It seems to me that you find it sad for you, not for the rest of the world. Now, why is that sad for you?

MIKE   It's really a matter of finally letting go. To be wonderful is still very attractive.

THERAPIST   I know. In a sense, this is one of the last vestiges, one of the last hurdles in a therapy process, with people who have habitually demanded perfection of themselves. You have gotten to a point where you say: "Hey, I can give this up; I'm on the verge." But, when push comes to shove, you are saying, "Hey, wait a minute, I'll be mediocre if I give it up, and, Jesus, that'll be horrible and terrible."

MIKE   Yeah, I can see that. I can see the process.

THERAPIST   It's almost that if you can get over this last hurdle, you've got it made. You're to a point now where you can stay where you are and even go backward, or you can jump over this last hurdle. Because once you get over this notion that being mediocre is horrible and being not-mediocre is wonderful, you're past your nuttiness.

MIKE   I've not felt nutty, just sad. And resistant.

THERAPIST   It's just from this mourning process. The fear leads to resistance. Because you're telling yourself, "This is my last chance to hold onto what I've always believed."

MIKE   Right. Yeah, I see. That's right.

THERAPIST   So, you're at a crossroads.

MIKE   Yeah, the image I have is that I'm taking the last boat to Australia and, if I go, I'll live in Australia forever and I'm not sure I want to go there. Australia looks pretty bleak.

THERAPIST   Be careful not to get discouraged.

MIKE   No, I'm not. Just resistant. It's going to take some work to get over this. But, it's giving up a magical notion.

Because we see this as a very critical incident in rational-emotive psychotherapy, we recommend that the therapist make a forceful and detailed response. What follows is a recommended sequence of action.

1. First, explain to the client the dynamics of this mourning process and relate it to his basic pathology. We have found it helpful to point out to the client how his irrational ideas lead directly to the mediocrity crisis and

how in turn this makes resistance probable. This explanation places his anxiety into perspective and helps undercut his tendency to become discouraged. It is also helpful at this point to encourage the client to view this issue as just another hurdle, perhaps the last, on the way to adjustment.

2. A second strategy we recommend is to distinguish between concern and worry. Many clients believe that being rational means not feeling at all. The opposite, of course, is true. The person who thinks rationally will often become discouraged, frustrated, and concerned. The person who thinks irrationally feels all the above, but also anxious, depressed, and guilt-ridden. We strongly recommend that the therapist help the client accurately conceptualize the dynamic difference between these separate processes and point out that motivation that facilitates achievement often arises from concern but rarely from anxiety.

3. After the above has thoroughly been discussed, we recommend that the therapist again take the typical RET role of the logical-empirical scientist. Through this process, the therapist challenges the client's irrational belief system: "Why is it so awful not to achieve perfection?" "Why are you so special and different from the rest of us?" "How can anyone, including you, achieve perfection?" "How is your self-worth diminished by a mediocre performance, or even by doing poorly?" This process, of course, is the core of RET. It is important that the therapist again help the client see his perfectionistic demands (i.e., musting), help him think through the unreasonableness of achieving such total competence, and analyze how it is impossible for a person's self-worth to be affected one way or the other.

4. Finally, we find it helpful to add a few extra tidbits. We like to point out to the client that he is ironically getting very little from his efforts; he never enjoys his achievements, much less the efforts. Furthermore, we find it helpful to point out to him that he has completely lost sight of the viable goals of happiness and enjoyment. Then, after showing him how the goal of perfectionistic achievement blocks enjoyment, we challenge his mistaken notion that he cannot find life rewarding unless he achieves at an exceptionally high level in all endeavors.

Lastly, we simply point out to the client that he can always readopt his neurotic notions at some later date if his fears of mediocrity are realized. He really is not, in other words, on the last boat to Australia; he can choose to be unhappy again if he wants.

Conclusion

The four critical incidents described in this paper are not exhaustive; there are many others which can lead to the demise of the rational therapy process. Indeed, any situation in which the client uses a cognitive distortion to successfully thwart the therapist is a "critical incident." But the authors suggest that the four incidents presented herein deserve special attention, not only because of their difficulty, but particularly due to their reliability: they occur with enough regularity to be termed "characteristic" of the rational therapy process. If a rational therapist engages in an ongoing practice, we believe he will encounter all of these incidents sooner or later. As mentioned earlier, how the therapist responds to the incident will probably determine whether or not therapy successfully progresses. The strategic responses which we have suggested were developed through trial and error, success and failure, and much analysis of our therapeutic efforts. Hopefully this paper will shortcut the learning process for other therapists.

As rational-emotive therapy continues to gain in repute and empirical support, we except to see many more treatises on the RET therapeutic "process." We believe that the practice of RET belies the simplicity of the A-B-C theory and that, just as in any other therapeutic approach, there are high-level skills which separate the common-place practitioner from the expert. Successful resolution of the four critical incidents described in this paper represent the manifestation of truly high-level RET skills.

References

Ellis, A. *Reason and Emotion in Psychotherapy*. New York: Lyle Stuart, 1962.

Ellis, A. *Growth Through Reason*. Palo Alto, California: Science and Behavior Books, 1971.

Ellis, A. *Humanistic Psychotherapy: The Rational-Emotive Approach*. New York: The Julian Press, 1973.

Maultsby, M. C. *More Personal Happiness Through Rational Self-Counseling*. Lexington, Ky.: M. C. Maultsby, 1971.

Meichenbaum, D. Toward a cognitive theory of self-control. In G. Schwartz and D. Shapiro (Eds.), *Consciousness and Self-Regulation: Advances in Research*, Vol. 1. New York: Plenum, 1976.

17

Fun as Psychotherapy

Albert Ellis

In whatever form it takes, psychopathology consists of taking life and ourselves too seriously: demanding that we get exactly what we want, or else; concluding that it is tragic when our wants are thwarted or delayed; judging that we and others are either devils or gods depending on how we or they act. It follows that a major purpose of psychotherapy is to undermine people's over-seriousness.

Chapter 17 serves to review in a humorous vein some of the over-serious beliefs that constitute psychopathology and to reorient the reader to more rational ways of thinking. More germane to this unit, it describes how the rational-emotive therapist uses various types of humor to get clients to quit taking things so seriously and to accept life gracefully in all its fallible forms. Finally, it lists the advantages of the use of humor in psychotherapy, including helping clients accept themselves and their fallibilities and showing people the absurdity of their actions.

E MOTIONAL DISTURBANCE largely consists of taking life too seriously; of exaggerating the significance of things; of what I have called, with humor aforethought, catastrophizing, awfulizing, or horribilizing—like the reading of papers at scientific meetings, for example, an obvious disturbance in its own right. For at such meetings, presumably intelligent men and women, with hell knows how many academic degrees behind them (which we may unhumorously refer to as degrees of restriction rather than degrees of freedom), consistently take themselves too seriously; enormously exaggerate the significance of the papers they present; and catastrophize, awfulize, and horribilize about the size of their audience and the amount of mention they may or may not receive in the public press.

I shall not, at least for the nonce, expand on the overseriousness, otherwise known as the emotional disturbability, of the participants in scientific and professional meetings. That would, I fear, take a presentation of encyclopedic proportions and the APA and my dear fellow panelists have gracelessly allowed me a total of a mere twenty minutes. So back

Chapter 17 was originally presented at the Symposium on Humor, Play, and Absurdity in Psychotherapy, American Psychological Association Annual Meeting, Washington, D.C., September 3, 1976.

to the more specific fray—and on to a consideration of humor in psychotherapy!

I assume again, and have elsewhere expanded on this thesis ad nauseam, that we disturb ourselves emotionally largely by taking things too damned seriously—or by defensively going to the other asinine extreme and not taking them seriously enough. Instead of mainly wanting, preferring, and desiring various things and relationships, we frequently demand or command that we get them, insist that we absolutely *must* have them; with this kind of *musturbation,* a form of behavior infinitely more pernicious than masturbation, we render ourselves disturbed and seriously defeat ourselves. So says the noble theory of rational-emotive therapy (Ellis, 1962, 1971, 1973, 1975; Ellis and Harper, 1975; Maultsby, 1975; Morris and Kanitz, 1975).

If I judge correctly in this respect—and we may ignore the infinitely small probability of my proving wrong—psychotherapy includes showing people their erroneous demanding or absolutizing and of seriously combatting their over-seriousness. My brilliant views in this connection have fortunately been endorsed, sometimes before I doffed knee pants, by several other latter-day psychotherapeutic saints, such as Alfred Adler (1973), Eric Berne (1964), George Kelly (1955), and Victor Raimy (1975). Even the redoubtable Sigmund Freud occasionally saw fit to note, before he became anally fixated on the notion of having to bugger his mother, that emotional disturbance arises from what he called *ideogenic* sources—meaning, from nutty and highly exaggerated ideas (Breuer and Freud, 1953). Unfortunately, when he failed to figure out a good mind-blowing method (such as RET) of helping people dynamite themselves away from their *meshugge* thinking, Freud retreated into a loony transference-*schmansference* routine from which most of his followers, not to mention Carl Rogers (1961) and *his* followers, have not yet recovered. Which tends to validate one of my main personality theories: namely, that even the brightest of humans seem biologically prone to take good ideas to idiotic extremes and gratuitously to invent incredible balderdash which they then call "science." This biological proneness of humans to conduct their lives in accordance with stupendous irrationalities calls for still another sagacious and profound scientific paper—which, fortunately, I have already written and presented elsewhere (Ellis and Harper, 1975).

Back to the boring board! If human disturbance largely consists of over-seriousness; and if, as in rational-emotive therapy, therapists had better make a hardheaded attack on some of their clients' fatuous thinking, what better vehicle for doing some of this ideological uprooting than humor and fun? If neurotics take themselves, others, and world conditions too solemnly, why not poke the blokes with jolly jokes? Or split their shit with wit?

We try—or at least I try—to do exactly that in RET. I use humor in many different ways, with the aim of directly and forcefully attacking my clients' crazy ideas. Not, mind you, my clients! For one of the main tenets of rational-emotive therapy consists of unconditionally accepting people with their mistakes and idiocies: of fully acknowledging their human fallibility and pigheadedly refusing to condemn or damn them no matter what they do or don't do. So I consider it *verboten,* in the course of therapy, to poke fun at people, even though I frequently ridicule their fatuous and self-sabotaging ideas. How can I, or anyone, accurately distinguish between these two modes of humorous attack? Not with any degree of perfection, I admit. But we can at least try!

In writing this paper, I at first considered describing some of the different humorous techniques which I employ in the course of my regular RET therapy. But I decided that though that would amount to an interesting linguistic analysis, it would have little to do with the process of psychotherapy. So let me briefly mention here that my therapeutic brand of humor consists of practically every kind of drollery ever invented—such as taking things to extreme, reducing ideas to absurdity, paradoxical intention, puns, witticisms, irony, whimsy, evocative language, slang, deliberate use of sprightly obscenity, and various other kinds of jocularity. Someday I may do a systematic study of the frequency count of these different kinds of humorous sallies; I suspect that when I do so, my use of exaggerated language and the taking of things to deliberate extremes will probably lead all the rest of the things I do. For, again, human disturbance largely consists of exaggerating the significance or the seriousness of things and the ripping up of such exaggerations by humorous counter-exaggerating may well prove one of the main methods of therapeutic attack.

Rather than consider this matter right now, let me instead outline some of the main messages that I try to get over to my clients as I engage in individual and group therapy. RET, remember, bases itself on the theory that humans largely, though not completely, get disturbed—or, more to the point, disturb themselves—with various kinds of irrational ideas or philosophies. It therefore directly and didactically makes a distinct effort to puncture these asinine ideas and to help the clients replace them with saner, more effective views. And it does so in the course of individual and group therapy sessions, as well as in large-scale presentations such as lectures, workshops, and films.

In observing some of my attempts at humor in the course of my recent sessions I note the following kinds of RET-sponsored ideas, which I often seriously promulgate but which I also, I hope, effectively present with some degree of humor.

Responsibility for your own disturbances. RET teaches that you mainly have the responsibility for your own disturbances; that external events, at point A, do *not* make you disturbed, at point C. Rather, you disturb yourself by telling yourself, and for the most part creatively inventing, irrational beliefs at point B. I therefore continuously interrupt people, in an exaggerated and humorous manner, when they say things like, "She hurts me with her criticism," with, "You mean, '*I* hurt me. She, for her own nutty reasons, tries to stick me with verbal arrows. But I foolishly sharpen them up, and stick them in my own breast, and viciously twist. I vastly enjoy that sort of thing—for then I can blame her for my hurt and convince St. Peter that I have sufficient nobility to get into heaven. Of course, he may doubt my nobility and foolishly think that I hurt myself. But that merely would show his bigotry and make me more noble than ever!' "

When my clients insist, as they often do, that they automatically or unconsciously overeat or start smoking against their own will, and deny that they tell themselves anything, at point B, their Belief system, to make themselves act that way, I say something like: "What do you keep telling yourself immediately before you cram that stuff down your gullet and into your craw? 'I hate food? I just eat to keep up my strength? I'll fix my dead mother by showing her that I can eat all I want without getting fat?' Or do you mean to tell me that the food automatically jumps out of the refrigerator, onto your plate, into your mouth, and forces you to swallow it?"

Unconditional self-acceptance. Like Rogerian therapy (Rogers, 1961), RET espouses unconditional self-acceptance and directly and actively teaches clients that they have almost unlimited human fallibility and that they'd therefore better accept themselves with their errors and never down or damn themselves for anything, even though they'd better note and change their immoral or self-defeating behavior. To this end, I often humorously point out to members of my group, when they confess some stupid act for which they obviously keep condemning themselves, "Of course, no one else in this group ever makes that kind of mistake! Maybe we all had better boycott you for life!" Or, conversely, "You mean you only repeated that idiotic act five times this week? I don't see how we can let you remain in a crummy group like this one. Now don't you think you'd better go out next week and do it at least ten times more, so that you can remain a worthy member of this group of complete fuckups?"

When one of my clients complains of the horror of his getting rejected, I use clever word play to underscore his negative self-rating. "Don't you see," I ask, "that you make her rejection not merely the absence of *her* but the absence of *you*? Instead of merely losing her, which seems the only real result of this rejection, you insist on losing *yourself*. Quite a magical power you have there!"

To emphasize how people try to deify themselves, and consequently end up by devil-ifying themselves, I steadily use exaggerated terms to describe what they do—terms like *love slob, nobility nut,* and R.P. (for rotten person). I have found, over the years, that if people refer to themselves as worthless or a bad person, it often helps to reindoctrinate them, over-seriously, with negative self-concepts. But if I keep referring to their slob-hood, their wormhood, or their shithood, they not only realize how they keep rating themselves but also laugh at their own self-downing and tend to help themselves give it up.

Anti-perfectionism. Practically all humans not only try to act well but insist on doing perfectly well and winning complete, total approval from others for doing so. RET continually attacks this kind of perfectionism in both serious and humorous ways. Thus, when my clients show inordinate fear of dancing, playing tennis, speaking, or doing something else imper-fectly, I often say something like, "And of course, if you do dance poorly, everyone on the dance floor will stop and guffaw, do nothing else but think about you all night, and keep remembering your crummy dancing for-ever. Right?" Or, when I get them to admit that they must make no mis-takes in their encountering of other people and must perfectly impress these others with everything they say, I exclaim, "Lots of luck! I think you really should keep working at perfect encountering. I, in your place, wouldn't permit myself any lapse whatever. That way, I'd have a nice, challenging goal to work at."

Again, when one of my clients told me that he could not defecate in a public toilet because someone in the next stall might hear him make im-proper sounds and might think badly of him, I asked, "What do you expect when you sit on the john and make the right noises—that the guy in the next stall will play 'The Star-Spangled Banner'?"

I often use emotive, humorous language to get over to my clients that they haven't a devil-damned chance of performing perfectly; instead of my old term, FHB, fallible human being, I now often refer to people as FFH's, fallible fucked-up humans. When they stop laughing about such deliber-ately exaggerated terms, they frequently go to work on accepting them-selves with their fucked-upness.

In my use of humor, incidentally, I hardly confine myself to my own invention, but frequently use the appropriate humor of others. Thus, in regard to perfectionism I often quote Oscar Wilde's clever statement: "Anything that's worth doing is worth doing badly." I find that this kind of clever statement really hits home and helps clients give up, by heartily getting themselves to laugh at, their own perfectionistic tendencies.

Acceptance of reality. Disturbed people take reality so seriously that they often refuse to accept it at all; and in RET we try to help them accept, or gracefully lump, many aspects of reality that they don't like. Thus, I humorously—and seriously!—tell my clients and my public audiences: "If you think that you absolutely need others' love, you invariably cook yourself. For in your entire lifetime, perhaps ten or twelve people—such as your mother, father, wife or husband, and children—really love you. And they do so with nauseating intermittency. They mainly focus, of course, on how much you love them!" And I tell people, on many occasions, "Life, whether you like it or not, generally gets spelled H A S S L E. You rarely get gain without pain. Tough!"

Along similar lines, RET specializes, probably more than any other popular form of psychotherapy, in helping people raise their low frustration tolerance. To this end, when clients keep telling me, "I find it hard to diet, to give up smoking, or to study for my exams," I quickly agree: "Yes, it certainly appears hard. But don't you find it harder *not* to?" In regard to his procrastination about his schoolwork, one of my clients recently remarked, "I always wait and do the hard things last." "Yes," I said, "and that way they finally do it themselves. Your term papers write themselves the last day of the semester. Right?" To another client, who noted that she had great difficulty working at getting along with people, I observed, "And so you nicely goof—and instead of getting *along* with people, you make yourself get *a short* with people. Great!"

In regard to low frustration tolerance, I find that people often refuse to recognize it and admit its disadvantages. Instead, they try to cover it up or perfume it by calling it "righteous indignation," "healthy anger," or a "genuine feeling" of despair. Abetted somewhat by some very nutty psychotherapists who have no intention of giving up their own feelings of LFT and of growing up, these clients resist facing reality and accepting responsibility for their own disordered feelings. I consequently find it highly effective to use strong, semi-humorous words to describe their behavior, to underscore the desirability of giving it up. I tell them, for example, "What you call anger and depression indeed often have a common cause—whining. Almost all human disturbance, in fact, consists of whining—of demanding and commanding, like a 2-year-old, that you must get exactly what you want immediately when you want it. Do you intend, now, to continue this kind of whining and of making yourself needlessly miserable for the rest of your life—or have you any intention of stopping your whining and winning what you want, instead?" And I sometimes sing for them,

in my broken baritone, the song that I have written to the tune composed
by a Harvard man and used in the famous Yale "Whiffenpoof Song":

> I cannot have all of my wishes filled—
>   Whine, whine, whine!
> I cannot have every frustration stilled—
>   Whine, whine, whine!
> Life really owes me the things I miss,
> Fate has to grant me eternal bliss;
> And if I must settle for less than this—
>   Whine, whine, whine!
>   (Ellis, 1977)

Anti-absolutizing. RET theorizes that human disturbance largely stems
from absolutizing, from necessitizing, or from demanding utter certainty
when the world seems to provide only certain degrees of probability. I
humorously keep after my clients, on many occasions, to give up this self-
destructive idea. When one of my group members clearly keeps asking for
a guarantee that he win someone's love or that she succeed at school, I
interrupt with, "Well, you really have luck today! We just happen to have
printed a beautifully engraved certificate which guarantees that you will
get exactly what you want. Just ask for it downstairs in the office and we'll
gladly give it to you, absolutely free."

Similarly, I show my public workshop audiences that no absolute musts
seem to exist in the universe and I tell them, "If you even take a good
thing, like rationality, and tell yourself, 'I *must* act rational, I *must* act
rational, I *must* act rational!' what will happen?" And they quickly get the
point and respond, "I'll drive myself crazy!" I also, as noted above, have
coined several humorous terms, like awfulizing, terribilizing, and musturbation—to highlight to my clients that unconditional *musts* simply do not
exist and that if they think they do, they almost certainly will—no, not
must!—defeat themselves.

I teach various other sensible, efficient, happiness-producing philosophies in the course of my RET presentations, such as the point that nothing proves awful in life, though lots of things seem damned inconvenient;
that people don't have to rate themselves, their totalities, even though
they'd better rate many of their traits and performances; and that damning
others for their deficiencies usually does immense harm and little good.
My advocacy of these ideas includes a heavy and heady dose of humor.
For my clients, I assume, mainly desire to get more fun and less misery
out of life; and humor constitutes fun in its own right, as well as a fine
vehicle to help dissipate a hell of a lot of needless gloom.

A number of professionals have advocated the use of humor in psychotherapy—including Farrelly and Brandsma (1974), Frankl (1966), Greenwald (1975, 1976), Haley (1963), Klein (1974), and Whitaker (1975). If I add some of the main points they have made to some of my own clinical findings, I come up with these advantages: (1) Humor can help clients laugh at themselves and thereby accept themselves with their vulnerabilities and fallibilities. (2) It clarifies many of the client's self-defeating behaviors in a nonthreatening, acceptable manner. (3) It provides new data and potentially better solutions, often in a dramatic, forceful way. (4) It relieves the monotony and overseriousness of many repetitive and didactic points which often seem essential to effective therapy. (5) It helps clients to develop a kind of objective distancing by participating in the therapist's humorous distancing. (6) It dramatically and rudely interrupts some of the client's old, dysfunctional patterns of thought and sets the stage for using new, more effective patterns of thinking, emoting, and behaving. (7) It helps many clients paradoxically think and act oppositely to their usual ways and thereby enables them to do many things, such as behave unanxiously, that they think themselves unable to do. (8) It serves as a distracting element that will at least temporarily interrupt self-downing and hostility-creating ideas. (9) It shows people the absurdity, realism, hilarity, and enjoyability of life. (10) It effectively punctures human grandiosity—quite a disturbance in its own right!

As I have noted elsewhere (Ellis, 1971, 1973, 1975; Ellis and Harper, 1975), humans disturb themselves cognitively, emotively, and behaviorally; by the same token, good psychotherapy includes cognitive, emotive, and behavioral methods of helping them change some of their basic personality difficulties. Humor, quite naturally and because of its very nature, works in all three of these basic ways. Cognitively, it presents new ideas to the absolutistic, rigid client in an insightful, hard-hitting way. Emotively, it brings enjoyment and mirth, makes life seem more worthwhile, and dramatically intrudes on gloom and inertia. Behaviorally, it encourages radically different actions; it constitutes an anti-anxiety activity in its own right; and it serves as a diverting relaxant.

Humor, then, has a powerful, multifaceted therapeutic effect. Psychotherapy can indeed prove fun; and fun can lead to good psychotherapy. A sense of humor, in itself, will not cure all emotional problems. But the refusal to take any of the grim facts of life *too* seriously largely will.

Since the members of this audience seem to have nicely survived one rational humorous song, let me risk my scientific reputation and your mental health by trying another. Putting words to Luigi Denza's "Finiculi, Finicula," I come up with:

Some think the world must have a right direction—
And so do I, and so do I!
Some think that with the slightest imperfection
They can't get by—and so do I!
For I, I have to prove I'm superhuman,
And better far than people are;
To show I have miraculous acumen—
And always rate among the Great!

Perfect, perfect rationality
Is, of course, the only thing for me!
How can I even think of being
If I must live fallibly?
Rationality must be a perfect thing for me!

(Ellis, 1977)

References

Adler, A. *Understanding human nature.* Greenwich, Conn.: Fawcett, 1973.

Berne, E. *Games people play.* New York: Grove Press, 1964.

Breuer, J., & Freud, S. Studies on hysteria. In J. Strachey's *The standard edition of the complete psychological works of Sigmund Freud.* London: The Hogarth Press and the Institute of Psychoanalysis, 1953.

Ellis, A. *Reason and emotion in psychotherapy.* New York: Lyle Stuart, 1962.

Ellis, A. *Growth through reason.* Palo Alto: Science and Behavior Books, 1971. Hollywood: Wilshire Books, 1973.

Ellis, A. *Humanistic psychotherapy: The rational-emotive approach.* New York: Julian Press, 1973 and McGraw-Hill Paperbacks, 1974.

Ellis, A. *How to live with a "neurotic."* New York: Crown Publishers, 1975.

Ellis, A. *A garland of rational songs.* Songbook. New York: Institute for Rational Living, 1977.

Ellis, A., & Harper, R. A. *A new guide to rational living.* Englewood Cliffs, N.J., and Hollywood: Wilshire Books, 1975.

Farrelly, F., & Brandsma, J. *Provocative therapy.* Millbrae, Calif.: Celestial Arts, 1974.

Frankl, V. *Man's search for meaning.* New York: Washington Square Press, 1966.

Greenwald, H. Humor in psychotherapy. *Journal of Contemporary Psychotherapy,* 1975, *7,* 113–116.

Greenwald, H. *Direct Decision Therapy.* New York: Aronson, 1976.

Haley, J. *Strategies of psychotherapy.* New York: Grune & Stratton, 1963.

Kelly, G. *The psychology of personal constructs.* New York: Norton, 1955.

Klein, J. P. On the use of humour in counseling. *Canadian Counsellor,* 1974, *8,* 233–237.

Maultsby, M. C., Jr. *Help yourself to happiness.* New York: Institute for Rational Living, 1975.

Morris, K. T., & Kanitz, H. M. *Rational-emotive therapy.* Boston: Houghton Mifflin, 1975.

Raimy, V. *Misunderstandings of self.* San Francisco: Jossey-Bass, 1975.

Rogers, C. R. *On becoming a person.* Boston: Houghton Mifflin, 1961.

Whitaker, C. Psychotherapy of the absurd: With a special emphasis on the psychotherapy of aggression. *Family Process,* 1975, *14,* 1–16.

Part Four

Rational-Emotive Therapy: Additional Techniques and Related Approaches

18

Rational-Emotive Therapy in Groups

Albert Ellis

Although RET began as an individual method of psychotherapy, rational-emotive psychotherapists make considerable use of groups. Unlike most other psychotherapy groups, however, rational-emotive groups do not stress the relationship between the members as an avenue for bringing about change, although strong interpersonal bonds often develop. RET groups do not stress various forms of emotive experience to cathect feelings, nor do they stress interpersonal support to provide troubled members with "ego strength." Rather, they are designed to bring together individuals who can help each other think and behave more rationally. Like individual RET, these groups are multimodal, yet highly cognitive-philosophic. Chapter 18 describes how rational-emotive psychotherapy groups help clients and the therapist's role in the process.

RATIONAL-EMOTIVE THERAPY MAKES considerable use of group work to facilitate a change to rational and goal-producing thinking and appropriate emoting. Assuming that my hypotheses about emotional disturbance and psychotherapy are correct (as a good deal of evidence suggests; see Chapter 2), how do the group processes specifically abet the aims just mentioned? They abet them in many ways. In RET, I and my associates at the Institute for Advanced Study in Rational Psychotherapy in New York City, and at various of our branches in other parts of the country, find group work exceptionally advantageous.

At the moment, we employ five main kinds of group processes.

1. Family groups meet with the therapist for regular sessions. These may consist of a husband and wife, a couple and its children, a single parent and one or more children, or two or more children without their parents.

2. Regular group therapy sessions are held with a therapist and an assistant or co-therapist leading. Usually they meet on a once-a-week basis for about 2¼ hours and have 10–13 group members.

3. Marathon sessions of rational encounter with a therapist (and often a co-therapist) spend 14 hours straight with 10–16 participants who are

A slightly different version of Chapter 18 appeared in *Rational Living*, 1974, *9*, 15–22.

led in specially devised encountering exercises, including a good many hours of showing the members of the group specifically how to solve some of their major life problems in a rational-emotive manner.

4. Workshops are held in rational living, with a therapist demonstrating the rational-emotive method with a volunteering individual who talks about his specific problem, but does so before an audience of 20 to a few hundred people. After the therapist speaks with the volunteer for about 20 or 30 minutes, the members of the audience who wish to do so are actively encouraged to speak to the therapist and to the volunteer; thus, the volunteer encounters the feelings and hears the suggestions of as many as 25 people in addition to the therapist.

5. Lectures, seminars, films, tape recordings, and other kinds of educational presentations on the principles of rational living are given at the Institute's adult education program during the year and at the Living School, a private school for normal children which the Institute operates in New York City.

All these methods of group therapy have proven to be highly effective, each in its different way, for individuals having minor or major emotional problems, as well as for individuals (such as those at the Living School or those who participate in the Institute's Friday-night workshops) who may not be afflicted with any emotional upsets at the moment, but who can prophylactically learn what to do if and when they make themselves disturbed about anything. After conducting and observing these various kinds of groups for the past twenty years, I find that they help the individuals who participate sporadically or regularly in them in a number of important ways.

1. Since the essence of RET is to teach the person how to accept reality and to try to change it by concerted work instead of by whining demands, several members of a group usually are more effective in bringing the client's dictatorialness to his attention than is a single therapist. Because some of the members of a group process are themselves, as different circumstances arise, often rigidly enmeshed in 2-year-old thinking and emoting, they can fairly easily recognize its manifestations in others and dramatically can bring these manifestations to a complainer's attention.

2. RET, perhaps more than any other of the major therapy systems, emphasizes not only showing individuals what they are thinking and how muddled thoughts are causing self-destructive feelings, but also demonstrating the logical parsing, the vigorous attacking, and the empirical contradicting of this disordered thinking. In a group situation, querying, contradicting, and attacking the individual's crooked cognitions can be forcefully done by several group members, who are likely to have a greater impact, all told, than a single therapist has.

3. In RET, therapists are exceptionally active, probing, challenging people. In group therapy, they may well be aided in all these functions by suggestions, comments, and hypotheses from other group members, which may deflect them from neglecting some important factor, give them hypotheses which they can check on and add to, reinforce some of their main points, and allow them at times to stand on the emotive and intellectual shoulders of other group members and thereby add to their therapeutic effectiveness.

4. RET notably includes specific activity-oriented homework assignments. Thus, a client may be assigned the outside task of looking for a new job, dating a woman he is afraid to date, or deliberately visiting his mother-in-law whom he detests. Such homework assignments are often more effectively given and followed up when given by a group than when given by an individual therapist.

5. RET includes a number of role-playing and behavior modification methods—such as assertion training, in vivo risk-taking, and behavior rehearsal—which can partly be done in individual sessions but which sometimes require a group process. Thus, if an individual is afraid to talk before a group of people, she/he may be induced to talk regularly in the group itself.

6. The group provides a laboratory where emotional, gestural, and motorial behavior can be directly observed rather than learned through the client's secondhand reports. Clients who keep telling their individual therapist that they no longer become enraged at others may get away with this report for quite awhile. But the same people engaged in a group process may unwittingly give away their enraged feelings by the way they act in the group; such defined feelings may then be spotted by the therapist or other group members. When this occurs, RET procedures can then be effectively employed to show them exactly what irrational Beliefs they are holding to create their rage and what they can do about changing them and it.

7. In RET, clients frequently fill out homework report forms and give them to the therapist at the beginning of each session to go over and correct. These forms teach them how to go through the A-B-C's of their most upsetting experiences and, when they are corrected, enable them to use the RET theory and practice more effectively the next time. In group sessions, a few homework assignment forms are often read and corrected during the session, so that all the members of the group, and not merely the individual handing in the form, may be helped by seeing specifically what disordered emotional Consequence was experienced (at point C); what Activating Events occurred to spark it (at point A); what rational and irrational Beliefs the individual told himself (at point B) to create his

dysfunctional Consequences; and what kind of effective Disputing he could do (at point D) to minimize or eradicate his irrational Beliefs and his subsequent disordered Consequences. By hearing about other group members' main problems and how they dealt with them on the Homework Report, most clients are helped to use these Reports properly themselves.

8. In the group process, people are helped to see that they are hardly alone in being troubled and that they have the same foolish, disturbance-creating ideas as many others have. They are thereby shown that they are not unique in this respect and that they need not condemn themselves for having disturbances. They gain the help of others who are in much the same boat, and learn how to try to talk these others out of their irrational Beliefs and thereby to unconsciously and consciously attack their own similar Beliefs. In the group, they learn the RET theory and application by actually *practicing* it; or, as John Dewey (1930) stated many years ago, they learn by doing.

9. People get valuable feedback from the group. They begin to see themselves more and more as *others* see them, to realize some of the poor or wrong impressions they make on these others, and to learn how to change some of their behaviors which encourage these impressions. They frequently gain social skills during the group process and in socializing with group members after or in between sessions. Some of these gains are only palliative, since they largely learn better skills rather than accepting themselves *whether or not* they are notably skillful. But they also can be philosophically jogged by other group members, especially in their social relations with them or in the course of telephone conversations, so that they acquire a distinctly new view of themselves and the world.

10. When the individual tries to deal with other people's problems in the group and questions them wrongly, makes inappropriate conclusions about them, advises them foolishly, or keeps offering them only palliative solutions to their basic problems, the therapist and other group members are able to observe his errors, immediately bring them to his/her attention, and get him to think through what more appropriate responses would be. She/he thereby receives a corrective emotional and didactic experience as the session is proceeding.

11. The individual is able to observe the progress, and especially the philosophic and behavioral progress, of other group members, and thereby to see that: (1) treatment can be effective; (2) she/he can similarly change; (3) there are specific things to do to help; and (4) therapy is hardly magic but almost always consists of persistent hard work.

12. Group members are frequently offered a wider range of possible solutions to their problems than they would normally be offered in individual

therapy. Out of ten or twelve people present at a given group session, one person may finally zero in on a central problem (after several others have failed) and another person may offer an elegant solution to it (after many ineffectual or lower-level solutions have hitherto been offered). Where a single individual, including a single therapist, may well give up on a difficult issue (or person), a few group members may persist and may finally prove to be quite helpful.

13. Revealing intimate problems to a group of people may be in itself quite therapeutic for the individual. In a regular RET group, clients disclose many ordinarily hidden events and feelings to a dozen or so peers; by being encouraged and occasionally almost forced to do so, they frequently see that nothing is really so shameful as they previously thought it was. In RET workshops they may reveal themselves to a hundred or more people; especially when they are normally shy and inhibited, they often find that this is one of the most useful risk-taking experiences. Such disturbance-dispelling experiences occur in almost all kinds of therapeutic groups. But in RET groups, in particular, the therapist (or another group member) specifically tries to show the previously held-in people that they have taken a risk of others' disapproval; that they have come through it with little of the criticism and attack they falsely predicted; and that even if they were roundly excoriated and laughed at, that would not in the least be ego-downing or catastrophic—it would merely be unfortunate.

14. RET, like most cognitively oriented systems of therapy, is highly educational and didactic. It frequently includes explanations, information-giving, and the discussion of problem-solving techniques. It is usually more economical for the therapist to do this kind of teaching in a group rather than an individual setting, and is of course more time- and money-saving for the client. Teaching, moreover, is more meaningful in a group than in an individual setting, and encourages certain kinds of questioning of the therapist and discussion of the points she/he is raising that would be less effective in one-to-one teacher-pupil relationships. Education, moreover, as John Dewey (1930) and Jean Piaget (1970) have shown, is much more effective when individuals actively enter the teaching-discussing-doing process than when they are mainly passive recipients. And group therapy tends to provide a more stimulating and more activating kind of involvement than individual treatment often does.

15. The group session tends to be a highly effective interrupting device for many clients, partly because of its length. Whereas individual sessions tend to run for a half-hour or three-quarters of an hour, group sessions at our Institute run for a total of 2¼ hours and are frequently followed by the group members spending another hour or so with each other without a formal leader. This somewhat massive time intrusion during which they

think and act against their strongly held self-defeating philosophies can be therapeutically cogent and potent.

16. Group procedures can be especially helpful for rigidly bound individuals who have a most difficult time jolting themselves out of old, dysfunctional behavior patterns into newer, healthier ones. Individual therapists, for example, frequently have considerable trouble inducing fixed deviants, alcoholics, or food addicts to experiment for a sufficient length of time with radically different modes of living. If, however, one or two such individuals are placed in a group where most of the other members unblamefully accept them with their problems but keep showing them that they *can* change and that they intend to keep after them until they do, then such severely phobic or addicted individuals are frequently helped to try to continue new behaviors until they become accustomed to them and even learn to enjoy them.

For many reasons, of which the foregoing list is hardly exhaustive, group processes are not only exceptionally useful in attacking troubled individuals irrational premises and illogical deductions and helping them reconsider and reconstruct their basic self-destructive philosophies, but are frequently more effectual in this respect than are the same therapies used individually. That is why many of the leading cognitive-oriented therapists —such as Berne (1964); Corsini (1966); Dreikurs (Dreikurs and Grey, 1968); Ellis (1962, 1971, 1972; Ellis and Harper, 1970a, 1970b); Lazarus (1971); Low (1952); and Phillips and Wiener (1966)— have made such extensive use of various kinds of group procedures.

This is not to say that group methods do not have intrinsic disadvantages when compared to other therapy modes, for they definitely do. In my own work, I have often found that group members can easily, out of over-zealousness and ignorance, mislead other members. They give poor or low-level solutions and they can waste so much time that there is little opportunity for the client with a problem to be shown a higher-level solution. They can bombard the individual with so many and so powerful suggestions that she/he is overwhelmed and partly paralyzed. They can allow a member, if the therapist does not intervene, to get away with minimal participation and hence minimal change. They can irrationally condemn the person for poor behavior or for refusing to do anything about it.

In onesidedly-oriented encounter-type groups, the group process is much more likely to be inelegant or even antitherapeutic and to discourage rational thinking and appropriate emoting. For the basic attitude—or may I say religion?—of such groups is that the group members should mainly "get in touch with their feelings" or let their emotions unreflectively hang out; that intense emotionality of *any* kind is marvelous in itself; that if individuals stop to think about feelings they are being overintellectual, defensive, and mechanical; that they have several powerful and unchangeable needs, such as the need to be approved by others and the need to get terribly angry at them when they reject; and that if they do not fulfill these needs directly and immediately they can only remain in terrible anguish or can be bottled-up zombies. Because of the highly indulgent, irrational, emotion-deifying philosophy of many encounter groups, they tend to coerce their members into conforming behavior, aggravate their dire love needs, and give them various kinds of physical diversions (such as body massage, screaming, wailing, and muscular relaxation) which enable them to feel better rather than to get better and to avoid the basic issue of ever interrupting and changing their childish demandingness (Ellis, 1969). A considerable amount of experimental and clinical evidence exists to show that emotional catharsis usually does little good and some harm (Berkowitz, 1971), but since the encounter movement is now often led by actors, dancers, architects, masseurs, housewives, gym teachers, and other nonprofessionals who are not too eager to read or to heed the psychological literature, this evidence is not likely to help stop the present questionable group therapy trends.

Let me say in conclusion that humans are exceptionally prone to self-defeating thinking and inappropriate emoting and behaving and perhaps, unless they radically change their entire biosocial makeup, they will always be. They can significantly change cognitions, emotions, and behavior, however, in a number of ways—most of them accidental and some of them designed. Considering the enormous amount of needless emotional suffering which they now tend to experience—including long periods of intense anxiety, depression, guilt, and hostility—they would be wiser if they clearly understood exactly what they think and do to create their so-called emotional upsets, and if they exerted the choice which they uniquely have as humans to think and to act differently and thereby quickly undo their upsets and arrange for their infrequent subsequent occurrence.

People can most elegantly do this if they avoid preoccupying themselves with A, Activating events, and fully acknowledge but resist endlessly re-experiencing C, the inappropriate emotional Consequences which frequently follow after and falsely seem to stem from A. They have the choice, instead, of keenly discerning, parsing, examining, modifying, and uprooting B, the irrational Beliefs which they so easily tend to believe about some of the Activating Events at A. They can decide to persistently and vigorously work at changing irrational Beliefs on their own, or can get help in doing so from straighter-thinking friends, books, lectures, demonstrations, tape recordings, and other sources. They can also work with an individual therapist or group leader. If they choose the group process and pick a cognitively-oriented group that also employs a comprehensive method of attacking stubbornly held irrationalities and illogicalities and includes selected evocative-emotive and activating-behavioristic techniques, they will thereby avail themselves of a multifaceted and powerful therapeutic procedure. I stoutly hypothesize that this kind of group intervention is more likely to lead to a quicker, deeper, and more elegant solution to the ubiquitous human condition of childish demandingness and perennial disturbability than any other contemporary form of psychotherapy.

References

Berkowitz, L. Experimental investigations of hostility catharsis. *Journal of Consulting and Clinical Psychology,* 1971, *35,* 1–7.

Berne, E. *Games people play.* New York: Grove Press, 1964.

Burton, A. (Ed.), *Encounter.* San Francisco: Jossey-Bass, 1969.

Corsini, R. J., with Cardono, S. *Role-playing in psychotherapy: a manual.* Chicago: Aldine, 1966.

Dewey, J. *Human nature and conduct.* New York: Modern Library, 1930.

Dreikurs, R., and Grey, L. *Logical consequences: a handbook of discipline.* New York: Meredith, 1968.

Ellis, A. *Reason and emotion in psychotherapy.* New York: Lyle Stuart, 1962.

Ellis, A. A weekend of rational encounter. In Burton, A. (Ed.), *Encounter.* San Francisco: Jossey-Bass, 1969.

Ellis, A. *Grow through reason.* Palo Alto, California: Science and Behavior Books, 1971.

Ellis, A. *Humanistic psychotherapy.* New York: Julian Press, 1973.

Ellis, A., and Harper, R. A. *A guide to rational living.* Englewood Cliffs, N.J.: Prentice-Hall and Hollywood: Wilshire Books, 1970a.

Ellis, A., and Harper, R. A. *A guide to successful marriage.* (Original title: *Creative marriage).* New York: Lyle Stuart, and Hollywood: Wilshire Books, 1970b.

Kelly, G. A. *The psychology of personal constructs.* New York: Norton, 1955.

Lazarus, A. A. *Behavior therapy and beyond.* New York: McGraw-Hill, 1971.

Low, A. A. *Mental health through will-training.* Boston: Christopher Publishing, 1952.

Phillips, E. L., and Wiener, D. N. *Short-term psychotherapy and structured behavior change.* New York: McGraw-Hill, 1966.

Piaget, J. *Science of education and the psychology of the child.* New York: Orion Press, 1970.

19

A Structured Approach to Group Marriage Counseling

Thomas A. McClellan and Donald R. Stieper

One of the advantages of rational-emotive psychotherapy is its adaptability to diverse client populations. Another is its didactic nature. In Chapter 19, Thomas McClellan and Donald Stieper report on an innovative and exciting method of group marriage counseling that makes rational-emotive psychotherapy a key component. They describe a 9-month group process that begins with a presentation of rational-emotive concepts and follows with several months of psychodrama and between-sessions homework to facilitate the clients' use of rational thinking. The evaluation of the study indicated that the procedure used was an effective tool for group marital therapy.

OVER THE PAST SEVERAL YEARS, a number of new approaches have been developed to enhance effectiveness in changing maladaptive behavior. One such approach has been increased use of brief psychotherapy based on educational, social, and cognitive models. Another has emphasized increased involvement of family members other than the patient: the spouse, parents, and children.

This paper describes a pilot study in group marriage counseling which combines four approaches: programmed instruction, rational-emotive therapy (RET), role-playing, and systems theory.

Location

The study was conducted in a Veterans Administration outpatient psychiatric clinic located in St. Paul, Minnesota. As with most well-established outpatient psychiatric clinics, the patient population is composed to a large degree of chronically ill psychotic and neurotic patients. Over the years, marriage counseling has been offered on a limited basis, generally as an adjunct to traditional psychotherapeutic practices. Interviews were either

Portions of Chapter 19 originally appeared in "A Structured Approach to Group Marriage Counseling," *Mental Hygiene,* 1971, *55,* 77–84, and are reprinted by permission of that journal.

281

with the patient alone, with the focus on marital problems, or jointly with the spouse. Marriage counseling in groups was rare and was built on the traditional, dynamically oriented discussion model.

Method

Basic to the new approach was the assumption that psychotherapy is primarily a teaching process—regardless of how it is packaged or delivered to the patient. Among the many things that it teaches, psychotherapy presumably teaches patients to problem-solve in new, hopefully more effective, ways. Group psychotherapy is then analogous to a classroom situation with one or more teachers and several students. However, one problem has been the reluctance of group therapists to make maximum use of known effective educational techniques (Bandura, 1961). Other writers have also pointed out the failure of group therapists to apply available knowledge about small-group dynamics (Hunt, 1964; Rosenbaum, 1963).

The group was scheduled to run for nine months. This limited the number of sessions and also limited the group experience to the academic year, avoiding the summer months with its intrusions of summer vacations and children home from school. Sessions were scheduled weekly and were an hour and a half long each.

Couples were selected from the active case loads of clinic therapists. By and large, they were couples where the husband had been treated for some time for chronic psychiatric conditions and where, in addition, there appeared to be crystallized marriage problems. During the first group session, the members, five couples in all (one couple later dropped out), were introduced to each other and to the therapists. The structural plan (along with the time allotments) of the group therapy meetings was described to them. After they were given a battery of psychological tests for research purposes, the members were introduced to programmed instruction and received the first lesson. Approximately 17 weeks were required to complete the presentation of this formal educational material. The material involved basic principles and concepts of Albert Ellis's rational-emotive therapy (RET) (1962), which have been developed into a programmed instruction format by one of the authors and two co-workers (Ells, Stieper, & Ellis, 1968).

The formal educational material was presented in didactic, classroom fashion—with one of the therapists reading the item aloud and the members responding first by writing their answers, then by saying them aloud. For example, an item might be: "Anxiety is another type of emotion for which we have a lot of other words. On Line Four put down another word that means the same thing as FEELING ANXIOUS." Another item: "Suppose, for example, a man who believes he must have everyone's love and approval has just been called in by his boss and criticized for an error in his work. How is this man likely to feel? Write your answer on Line Five." Since there was a high probability (a 90% chance) of members' giving the "correct" response, they got a great deal of social reinforcement from this procedure. Also, where there was great variation in "correct" responses, discussions following each item's presentation were often long and fruitful. At the end of each session, total correct responses were calculated, and each member of the group was kept aware of his or her own accuracy scores on the material.

The first seven lessons instructed members in basic RET theory, with illustrations of how it might apply in their own lives. Basic psychological terms and concepts necessary to understanding the psychology of emotion were also covered. The second phase of the programmed material went into some of the more common "irrational" beliefs held by individuals with psychological problems. The material dealt directly with four basic "superstitions" (demanding love and approval, demanding perfection in themselves, demanding things be their own way, and insisting on fixing blame). It also dealt indirectly with a number of other misconceptions: the beliefs that sources of problems lie outside oneself, that one has no power to control one's own emotions, and that events (rather than interpretations of events) lead to unpleasant feelings; the importance of fretting and worrying over other people's problems; and the preoccupation with unhappy events. Discussions of these "beliefs" were also often long and fruitful. Workshop-type materials were employed, and each group member was encouraged to see how the misconceptions applied to his or her own behavior both in and out of marriage.

The third and final phase of the programmed instruction series was one lesson dealing specifically with marital functioning. The content of this program covered the frequently-too-high expectations married partners had of one another and the complementary tendency to condemn or blame the married partner when expectations were not met. The program focused on two key ideas: EXPECT and RESPECT, showing how both unreasonable expectations and too little respect (both for oneself and the spouse) can lead to disastrous marital consequences. Also, in coping with the common marital complaint of "too little communication," the program provided exercises in the art of listening. Members were taught the simple task of paraphrasing, in which they were asked to repeat, in their own words, what they thought their partner meant—to their partner's satisfaction. This exercise gave many opportunities to introduce role-playing, which became a major tool later in the group experience. Each couple went through the exercise of paraphrasing each other's comments and complaints. Misinterpretations were commonplace, and all members were impressed with how little they really "listened" to or understood what their partners had to say.

During the first 17 weeks of the group, discussion was limited to clarification of the material being presented and to a review of previously discussed material. In the last weeks, members took self-rating scales and also predicted how their spouses would rate themselves. They rated their own tendencies to behave in accordance with four major irrational beliefs: (1) demanding love, appreciation, affection, and approval from practically everyone; (2) expecting everything to go the way they wanted; (3) expecting perfection or near-perfection in practically everything they did; and (4) blaming others (and themselves) when things went wrong.

The last 19 weeks of the group experience moved into an "application" phase where, through role-playing and homework assignments, members were asked to apply the principles they had learned to their own marital and family situations. Sessions were structured according to the following format: During the first 20 minutes of each session, a report was given by group members on a chapter from Albert Ellis and Robert A. Harper's *Creative Marriage* (1961). Couples were assigned chapters, and each spouse participated in the oral report to the group. In this way, the content of the book was covered and group members were given an additional opportunity to "appear before the group," desensitizing them to public performance and breaking down their resistance to the role-playing tasks that lay before them. The remainder of each session was given over to role-playing, discussion, and homework assignment.

The content for the role-playing skits was selected from the previously administered questionnaire on marital functioning. Specifically, group members were asked to complete the following two sentences, by writing in those areas about which they were most concerned: (Question 3), "I find it hard to talk with my spouse about _____." (Question 14), "We disagree mostly in the areas of _____." Three problem areas, selected on the basis of frequency, were drawn from these questions. In descending order of importance, they were: difficulties with money and budgeting; sexual problems; and problems related to the discipline and adjustment of children. A series of three separate group therapy sessions, each an hour and a half long, was spent on *each* of these problem areas. The focus of these sessions was the role-playing of various aspects of these problems, with special emphasis on the part irrational beliefs and expectations had on creating difficulties. Solutions were commonly handled in RET terms.

For example, in the area of money and budgeting, a skit was prepared and performed by the therapists, depicting a neurotic, self-defeating form of communication between a couple attempting to discuss their budget problems. (Because both therapists were men, feminine guests were often brought into the group at this point to play specific roles.) This particular skit highlighted hostile interaction between the pair, general unreasonableness, and an inability to bring the discussion to a fruitful, decision-making conclusion. Following this explosive introduction, group members commented upon and discussed the salient features: unreasonable expectations, blaming tendencies, refusal to listen, insistence on having their own way, and general crappiness. The irrational approaches to interaction were dealt with via the medium of the programmed instruction materials—members were taught to challenge and dispute irrational beliefs and to substitute more reasonable statements for them. The "listening" problem was handled through a repeat of the paraphrasing exercise, demonstrating that neither spouse was really listening to or understanding his partner. Subsequent role-playing skits worked toward practicing more mature, problem-solving discussions about budgeting by all of the members. The final skit in the "budgeting" series involved a couple from the group working out their own "real-life" difficulties with money, using their newly learned approaches and problem-solving techniques.

Dealing with the second area of concern—sex—began with a role-reversal playlet wherein male group members acted out the way they believed females talked about sex, and female group members repeated the procedure in an attempt to show how they thought men talked about sex. This little series helped destroy the myth that men are more comfortable talking about sex than women—despite the locker room lore. The larger and more basic problem uncovered, however, was the traditional sex-role discrepancies, which neither men nor women understood very well. They disagreed on the frequency of sex; men required it more often than women. They also disagreed (as a group) on the appropriateness of using sex for recreational purposes. The men were largely on the side of recreation, while women felt the primary function of sex was procreation. And they disagreed on the place of sex in marriage. The men felt it was their right and privilege and the women felt it was something to be earned—and then only infrequently. A great deal of time was spent in desensitizing members to the point where they would talk more openly about sex and in getting the men and women to understand and appreciate the culturally determined expectations of their partners. Finally, once the heat had been drawn from the first two areas, attention was turned to the problem of improving communication about sex between the partners. Subsequent role-playing skits centered around improved communication about: (1) sexual frequency; (2) rights and privileges in sexual behavior; (3) signaling systems; and (4) the use of sex for recreational as well as procreative purposes. Basic cultural differences between female and male sexual attitudes—a constant intrusion—were dealt with openly throughout this series of sessions.

The third area of concern was relationships with children; however, as therapy progressed, it became evident that this was only a symptom of a larger and more basic problem: disagreement over rule-making and lines of authority in the family, specifically, Who's in control? This, of course, went to the core of the marriage relationship and constituted a fundamental misalignment in the whole marital structure.

This problem was approached through an avenue somewhat new to RET application: systems theory. First it was explained to group members that any marriage and any family was constituted of more than just the sum of its members and really represented an organic unit to which each of the family members made his own unique contribution. Alter one family member and the system was altered. It was explained that if an imbalance in power occurred, this imbalance was the creation of all members. There were no victims and persecutors as such, no controllers or controllees. Approached from this point of view, each partner was asked to assess his own contributions to the imbalance of power and what he was likely to receive from being either "victimized" or being the "controller." It was repeatedly illustrated through the use of role-playing exercises that often the passive, unresponsive partner was the one exercising the most power in the relationship. For example, one wife complained that she had to make all the decisions and do the major chores around the house. She felt she had become dictatorial and shrewish, to which her rather passive husband agreed. He complained that she was always ordering him around and demanding that he behave in ways that she wanted. It became quickly apparent, through role-playing a typical household situation, that the more passive husband was indeed in the most favorable "power" position, forcing his wife through his passivity to assume most of the responsibilities and the decision-making risks. He had in fact put her almost totally in his service, even though to the casual observer she was an unmitigated shrew and dictator. (This ensemble—the "bossy" wife and the passive husband—was common in this group; the wives having had to take over family leadership responsibilities while their husbands were busy being "psychiatric.")

Approaches to altering the system involved getting each partner to share responsibilities on the one hand and avoid taking responsibility for his or her partner's behavior on the other hand. Previous RET training was extremely valuable in demonstrating to the members that, in assuming the roles they had, they were testifying to several irrational beliefs; e.g., events in and of themselves are terrible; they had to be perfect in everything they did; they felt compelled to fret and stew about other people's problems; and someone should always be blamed and labeled the villain when something goes wrong.

Specific role-playing skits went into the need for communication to be simple, direct, and congruent (Satir, 1964) and for the channels of communication to be kept open; and explored the need for a rational approach to the issues of who is in charge and in what area, what rules need to be made and how they are made, and what procedures are helpful when there is disagreement. Finally, much time was spent on getting input (and shared responsibility) from both members of the marriage in decision-making behavior. Vigorous counters to the cop-out plea of the husbands (in this case) when they said, "I'll let my wife take care of things!" were frequently necessary. This turned out to be one of the most difficult and energy-consuming portions of the group experience.

Following completion of the above nine sessions, each couple was assigned responsibility, in rotation, for one week's role-playing skit. Each couple was instructed to bring in a problem about which it was concerned and with which it was willing to accept help from the group. The couple was to structure the role-playing presentation, decide how the problem would be illustrated (or reenacted), and cast the psychodrama, using other members of the group if necessary. Following each such presentation, a series of recommendations by the therapists and group members were made in the form of specific "homework assignments," about which the couple had to report the following week.

One couple brought in the problem of how to get other relatives to cooperate in the care of an aging parent. While this was not specifically a marital interaction situation, it was a matter of concern to the family. It was particularly urgent since the parent had many health-care needs and the capabilities of the family were somewhat limited. Other group members suggested throwing a party for the relatives, during which the family "laid their cards on the table," asking cooperation from the relatives. The husband and wife thought this was a good idea, but neither thought he could do an adequate job of presenting the situation to the relatives. So it was role-played in the group. With group members playing the roles of relatives, the target couple enacted its presentation. The "relative" members threw up as many obstacles and objections as they could think of, and the husband-wife team tried to field them. They were continually plagued by their irrational belief that they had to "please" the relatives and not incur their disapproval—a belief that was vigorously attacked by the therapists. Ultimately, after several role-playing run-throughs, the husband-wife team felt that they were sufficiently fore-armed so that they could face the real-life confrontation with confidence and with somewhat decreased irrational expectations. Their homework: throw the party, invite the relatives, and get on with the confrontation. A week later they reported a successful solution to their problem: most of the relatives had more than willingly flocked to their aid.

A second problem, brought in by another couple, revolved around the passive husband who loaded his wife with responsibilities in decision-making and work. He was assigned a number of household tasks by the group, including making lunch for himself and his wife, for which he was given a number of easily prepared recipes. He was to have full responsi-bility as well as full authority for these tasks. His report the following week reflected somewhat less success than the family confronting their relatives. He had come to like his life of leisure and no responsibility, and was reluctant to give it up. This position was vigorously attacked by the group and by the therapists—as well as his wife's position that she "needed" to take care of him. While some headway was made after repeated role-playings of "role-reversals" and shared responsibility, less progress was made with this couple than with any other in the group.

A third family brought up the problem of a deteriorating father-son relationship. A number of reality problems intruded, such as the father's unpredictable working hours, the son's many outside activities, and the wife's siding with the son in family squabbles. After a great deal of dis-cussion and a number of role-playing skits, the following were accom-plished: the mother was to stay out of father-son conflicts; father was to make appointments for "dates" with his son so that they could attend ball-games, etc.; and communication among all three was increased through scheduled "family meetings." The family carried out the homework assign-ments in dogged but ultimately successful fashion, and the father-son relationship was improved.

The final husband and wife disagreed about where they should live. The husband liked the overcrowded mobile home in which they currently re-sided; the wife wanted a house with more rooms for their expanding fam-ily. Neither was listening to the other; each wanted his own way; and each blamed the other for the dilemma. After vigorously attacking the irra-tional beliefs which underlay their problem, the therapists recommended role-playing the paraphrasing exercises again, making both of them more active listeners. After several run-throughs, the husband and wife were able to move to a reasonable compromise, based on what they had learned from each other. They ultimately bought a house, but only after having settled some financial problems about which the husband was concerned. They were both content—if not outrageously happy—with this solution.

The final contact with group members consisted of individual sessions with each couple, during which the therapists summarized and described their pretest and posttest results. The therapists also solicited feedback from the couples about their experiences in the group, all of which were generally favorable.

Discussion

All of the husbands had been treated on an individual basis in the Mental Health Clinic prior to this group experience. Treatment had been extensive—and had occurred over several years—with, for the most part, only marginal results. They suffered from relatively serious mental disorders—paranoid schizophrenia, manic-depressive psychosis, chronic anxiety reaction, and psychotic depression. In fact, during the course of therapy, one couple dropped out due to job problems and the husband was subsequently hospitalized. Three of the couples had been involved in marriage counseling in the clinic previously, one on a group basis. Again, it was not believed that this had been particularly successful.

MMPIs on the wives indicated greater variation than that found in the men. Two of the wives had no profile elevations above standard score 70; one had elevations above 70 on K and 4; and the fourth had a pre-psychotic profile. Clinical survey of all the nonclinic spouses revealed a certain amount of disturbance, corroborative of the MMPI findings. The age-spread was quite wide. The women were age 25, 40, 41, and 48; the men were age 31, 44, 47, and 50. The couples had been married from 10 to 22 years, notable achievements in the face of their many problems. All had one or more children still living at home.

At the completion of therapy, the group was tested on a number of variables to ascertain what, if any, change had occurred. The group made significant improvement, reporting less psychic distress, lessened discomfort over specific problems existing in the home, and greater capacity for positive communication about those continuing problems. While there was continued concern about the three major problem areas—money, sex, and child discipline—intensity of feeling over these problems was lessened and the participants now had available to them some new techniques for dealing with these problems.

It is worthwhile mentioning that the couples were generally in high agreement that they had similar value systems (largely traditional in orientation) and similar marriage goals; this opinion did not change after therapy. This common cultural bond may well have been one of the factors holding the marriages together in spite of some rather devastating problems, although the "systems" they had developed between them must be seen as the major contributing factor.

The results obtained with this experimental group are encouraging inasmuch as the members had serious, chronic psychiatric difficulties and long-standing marital discord. It is believed that this approach may have general applicability to adult psychiatric outpatient clinics with large numbers of chronically ill married patients. Some of the advantages of this approach, at least with our patient population, are as follows:

1. The whole style of approach was radically different from anything they had experienced in the clinic before. Chronic patients seem to accommodate themselves to any mode of therapy which is easily accessible and offered indefinitely, with resultant problems in dependency and secondary gain. It would therefore seem advisable to expose chronic patients to an occasional radically different therapeutic experience.

2. It is obviously more expeditious to provide therapy—including marriage counseling—on a group basis in large psychiatric clinics with great numbers of patients. As with any form of psychological treatment, we would anticipate that results would be better with less chronic patients.

3. Many of our patients, even those that have been treated psychotherapeutically over several years, show minimal psychological orientation or sophistication. (Often we assume that sophistication is correlated with length of time in treatment, which turns out to be the case in this instance.) The emphasis of the programmed instruction on clarifying and reducing psychological concepts to simple, basic terms seems advantageous for this group inasmuch as it effectively teaches them a conceptual base roughly congruent with that of the therapists. As a prelude to therapy proper, the use of programmed instruction seemed to facilitate a more profitable use of subsequent therapeutic time.

4. The fact that this treatment program begins in a highly structured manner, with a focus on specified learning tasks, may be an advantage with patients who are highly defensive and have low motivation toward improvement. Also, the paper-and-pencil work and the regular assessment of performance throughout the period of programmed instruction may be less threatening to this group of patients than the early "self-exposure" found in traditional discussion-type group therapy.

5. Throughout the 9-month program, both group members and therapists reported that they enjoyed the experience. High attendance rates and timely arrivals on the part of the members attest to their high interest level. There were obvious signs of social growth on the part of group members, marked by improved appearances, increased volubility, and

improved mood levels. The fact that the therapists enjoyed the experience may be an important side effect of this approach inasmuch as it allows therapists a new kind of encounter which is inherently more rewarding than previous contacts with this same group of chronic patients.

References

Bandura, A. Psychotherapy as a learning process. *Psychological Bulletin,* 1961, *58*(2), 143–159.

Ellis, A. *Reason and emotion in psychotherapy.* New York: Lyle Stuart, 1962.

Ellis, A., & Harper, R. A. *Creative marriage.* New York: Lyle Stuart, 1961.

Ells, E., Stieper, D., & Ellis, A. Programmed instruction in rational living. Unpublished manuscript, 1968.

Hunt, J. McV. Concerning the impact of group psychotherapy on psychology. *International Journal of Group Psychotherapy,* 1964, *14*(1), 3–31.

Rosenbaum, M., & Berger, M. (Eds.). *Group psychotherapy and group function,* New York: Basic Books, 1963.

Satir, V. *Conjoint family therapy.* Palo Alto, California: Science and Behavior Books, 1964.

20

Cognitive-Behavioral Assertion Training

Arthur J. Lange

A number of people in recent years have successfully used rational-emotive techniques together with other therapeutic approaches. Arthur Lange's chapter on cognitive-behavioral assertion training describes another such successful attempt. After discussing the nature of assertion, Lange goes on to describe a 4-stage model of assertion training designed (1) to assess the cognitive and behavioral aspects of nonassertiveness in specific situations and (2) to utilize those cognitive and behavior procedures appropriate for the client. The 4-stages in the assertion-training process are: (1) the development of a belief system which maintains a high regard for one's own personal rights and the rights of others; (2) discrimination between unassertive, assertive, and aggressive responses; (3) cognitive restructuring in specific situations; and (4) behavioral rehearsal of assertive responses in specific situations.

ASSERTIVENESS AS A personal quality has become increasingly desirable, due partly to the several liberation movements supporting greater personal freedom and partly to a more pervasive and emerging conviction that people can improve the quality of their daily personal lives by establishing relationships which are more functional, direct, and genuine. Assertion training is a process which helps people communicate what they choose to express in more effective ways.

Expressing caring, warmth, and support are certainly examples of assertiveness. Unlike the encounter movement of the 1960s, however, assertion training is not solely directed toward greater intimacy, sensitivity, or self-disclosure. Moreover, there is not an exclusive emphasis on the "here and now" or on developing closer relationships by the group members' sharing of positive and negative perceptions of each other within the group, although a supportive atmosphere usually does develop as the participants work closely together to increase their assertiveness. Group members might give each other information regarding the assertive or nonassertive qualities of interactions right within the group. However, the focus is primarily on handling situations which occur outside the group.

Assertion training focuses on specific situations or types of interactions that group members believe they are not handling as well as they would like. People in assertion groups work on varied concerns: refusing invitations from friends, giving compliments, confronting fellow workers with something they are doing that negatively influences one's work, responding to an obstreperous supervisor, telling one's lover what one does and does not enjoy sexually, confronting a roommate with sharing financial or housekeeping responsibilities, carrying on social conversations, being interviewed for a job, talking with a professor outside class, asking for a date, requesting service in a store when ignored, seeking information from just about any agency administrator, supervising employees, dealing with one's ex-spouse, planning a vacation, and asking for a raise. The situations range from relatively simple day-to-day events to more significant or intimate interactions. The goal is to handle them in an effective manner.

Assertiveness can be defined as communicating one's opinions, beliefs, feelings, and wants in a direct, honest, and appropriate manner (Lange and Jakubowski, 1976). Moreover, assertive behavior maintains a high regard for one's own personal rights *and* the rights of others. Assertiveness is often associated with conflict situations, refusing requests, or taking care of one's own wants; however, positive expressions like giving and receiving compliments, initiating and carrying on conversations, and making positive statements about oneself all involve assertive behavior.

Assertive behaviors can be classified into at least three types: empathic, simple, and confrontative assertions (Lange and Jakubowski, 1976). When refusing a request for a date from a friend, a person might wish to express some understanding and caring while also refusing ("It's really nice of you to ask, but I'd rather not have a dating relationship with you"), particularly if the entire statement is an honest one. When a person on the street asks you for your "spare change" as you are leaving the store, you may respond with a simple "no." Or if a person persists in asking you to change your plans for the weekend, you might become less empathic and simply say, "No, I've decided I really want to go sailing." If, however, the person persists even further, you might confront the person by saying, "Lynn, when you persist in trying to convince me to change my plans even after I've said no several times, it seems that you won't take no for an answer and I'm really frustrated with that." All these types of responses are within an assertive range of behavior. Assertiveness is not a cold, singularly abrupt standing up for one's rights and the hell with others or with the consequences.

A Model for Assertion Training

Assertion training, unlike other treatment modes which have emerged from a primarily behavioral orientation, does not consist of a generally agreed upon set of procedures. A variety of cognitive and behavioral interventions (in differing combinations) have been employed under the rubric assertion training (Salter, 1949; Wolpe and Lazarus, 1966; Lazarus, 1972; Wolpe, 1973a; Alberti and Emmons, 1974; Rimm and Masters, 1974; Bloom, Coburn, and Pearlman, 1975; Lange and Jakubowski, 1976; Cotler and Guerra, 1976; Liberman, King, DeRisi, & McCann, 1976).

The model of assertion training presented in this chapter (Lange and Jakubowski, 1976) combines behavioral components with cognitive ones. It thus in large part attests to the importance of cognitive procedures, as suggested by Rimm (1973); Meichenbaum (1974, 1975); Ellis and Harper (1975); Goldfried and Sobocinski (1975); Kazdin (1975); Thorpe (1975); Wolfe (1975); Beck (1976); Goldfried and Davison (1976); Glass, Gottman, and Schmurak (1976). The behavioral interventions, however, have been more widely researched (Wolpe and Lazarus, 1966); Wagner (1968); McFall and Marston (1970); McFall and Lillesand (1971); Friedman (1971a, 1971b); Eisler, Hersen, and Miller (1973); McFall and Twentyman (1973); Rathus (1973); Young, Rimm, and Kennedy (1973); Rimm and Masters (1974); Galassi and Galassi (1976).

The cognitive-behavioral assertion trainer believes that: (a) people's thinking influences the way they feel and behave and therefore intervention at the cognitive level is appropriate, and (b) people think about and evaluate their feelings and behaviors and therefore changing one's behavior will also lead to changes in attitudes and other cognitions. Thus, the cognitive-behavioral assertion trainer teaches clients the basic principles of RET and several other cognitive orientations which have emerged from RET principles. Trainees then move on to practice and carry out in vivo behavior changes based upon the new, more rational cognitions. In addition, some treatment interventions utilize behavior therapy principles to alter or cope with cognitions as well as behaviors. Basic to the cognitive-behavioral approach is client understanding of the RET principles regarding the relationships between thinking, feelings, and behaviors *and* the procedures for altering and coping with irrational thinking. These procedures are described below and elsewhere in this text.

More specifically, the model of assertion training presented in this chapter (Lange and Jakubowski, 1976) is a 4-stage process designed to: (1) assess cognitive and behavioral aspects of nonassertiveness in specific situations and (2) utilize those cognitive and behavioral procedures which seem most appropriate for that client. Thus, it is conceivable that with one client greater attention would be given to the identification and challenging of irrational thinking in a specific situation, while a second client may recognize the faulty thinking and require considerable behavior rehearsal since specific assertive responses are missing.

The four stages of the assertion model are: (1) development of a belief system which maintains a high regard for one's own personal rights *and* the rights of others; (2) discrimination between unassertive, assertive, and aggressive responses and behaviors; (3) cognitive restructuring of one's thinking in specific situations; and (4) behavior rehearsal of assertive responses in specific situations. The stages are not necessarily sequential; they often overlap in time, and, in fact, may be rearranged or modified in a variety of ways to be more appropriate to the participant. These stages might also be stated as outcome goals for clients along with reduction of excessive anxiety, intense anger, or depression.

Group assertion training is the setting described in this chapter; however, any of the exercises or procedures might be used with an individual client. The author uses two formats for group assertion training. For the first several sessions, the format consists of a series of structured exercises. The remaining sessions focus on situations on which individual participants choose to work, utilizing the 4-stage process mentioned above. The exercises accomplish several purposes: (1) they enable the participants to interact with each other and to do so successfully, which can be especially important for the more pervasively unassertive or aggressive person; (2) they introduce information which focuses on some aspect of assertiveness, for example, nonverbal behavior, irrational thinking, self-assessment methods, and specific assertive responses; and (3) they train participants in the 4-stage process mentioned above so that the second format for the group can run more smoothly. The author has attempted to begin assertion groups by working on specific situations that group members believed they weren't handling as well as they would like to. Unfortunately, this process proved painfully slow and required continual interruption to explain such concepts as personal rights and to teach skills that members were not skilled in, such as role-playing or giving behavioral feedback. The author now uses a series of exercises, each one of which focuses on a different content or process aspect of the four stages of training.[1] After doing

[1] Space limitations prohibit extensive elaboration of many of these exercises. For a detailed, step-by-step description of these and other exercises, see Chapter 4 of *Responsible Assertive Behavior: Cognitive-Behavioral Procedures for Trainers* by A. Lange and P. Jakubowski, published by Research Press of Champaign, Illinois, in 1976.

structured exercises first, the group members can go on to work more efficiently on their own specific situational concerns.

Session One: Positive Assertions and Nonverbal Behaviors

After providing a brief overview of assertion training, the initial exercises of the first session focus on: (1) briefly introducing oneself to another member of the group; (2) identifying nonverbal behaviors which members are employing as they carry on brief conversations, and identifying those behaviors which the participant would like to change; (3) giving and receiving compliments; (4) making positive statements about oneself; and (5) practicing such conversational skills as asking open-ended questions, responding to free information from others, and paraphrasing.

Even when performing these brief initial exercises, group members usually mention having thoughts or beliefs that have kept them from behaving assertively; for example, "I can't say such good things about myself, people will think I'm bragging!" or "What if I do start talking with someone and run out of things to talk about?" At this stage in the group, trainers might mention that thinking has a very important role in assertive behavior and that the group will focus on the relationships between what we think and how we feel and behave very soon.

Session Two: Personal Rights and Discrimination Training

The second session focuses on the first two stages of assertion training: developing personal rights and discriminating between unassertive, assertive, and aggressive responses. Most people in assertion groups have not given extensive consideration to what personal rights they believe they have, particularly in specific situations.

The reader might be wondering what the relationship is between such an abstraction as "personal rights" and assertive behavior. Ample evidence has been presented in earlier chapters which demonstrates how one's cognitions affect one's feelings and behavior. The beliefs persons hold regarding their personal rights are likely to have a significant bearing on whether or not they act on those personal rights. The first step is to identify the personal rights that group members believe they can act on if they choose to do so.

One way to help participants identify their personal rights is to ask them to list all the personal rights they believe a person has: (1) when accused of a crime; (2) as a child; (3) when on a date; or (4) when being interviewed for a job. They could literally list hundreds if they were very specific (the right to a phone call; the right to express legitimate feelings;

the right to refuse the date; the right to decide what to do; the right to refuse sex; the right to get information about salaries, time requirements, work load). These rights can be generalized into the following groupings:

—the right to express your beliefs, ideas, opinions, wants, desires, and feelings
—the right to decide how to spend your time
—the right to decide what you do with your body
—the right to decide what you do with your property.

The group members might discuss how others violate their personal rights *and* how they themselves violate their own personal rights by not acting on them or by responding ineffectually when others violate their rights. For some group members, the process of identifying personal rights and seeing how they manifest themselves in specific situations (particularly where others are denying those rights) can provide substantial insight and lead to more assertive behaviors in those situations. Many assertion trainers use a series of stimulus films (Jakubowski-Spector, Pearlman, and Coburn, 1973) in which a person comes on the screen and talks to the group members in a manner that violates their personal rights. In the vignettes either the issue (content) or the manner in which the person behaves somehow violates the viewers' personal rights. After watching a vignette, participants are asked to identify the personal rights at issue and specify how the other person is violating them.

After one or two vignettes, the trainer might review the definitions of unassertive, assertive, and aggressive behavior and ask each participant to think of one example of each type of response.

Trainers can make up their own stimulus statements which might be more appropriate for their group and put them on audio or video tape for this discrimination exercise. The group members can also be specific about what they thought made their statement unassertive, assertive, or aggressive. As with developing a conceptual system for personal rights, group members here are creating a cognitive model for assessing any response.

In the process of discriminating between unassertive, assertive, and aggressive responses, the question of taking responsibility for the impact of one's behavior on others often comes into play. Three issues seem to be at play: (1) taking responsibility for one's own actions and their intent (to express one's own rights and preferences vs. to hurt or put someone down); (2) not taking responsibility for the way others choose to respond; and (3) in some cases being concerned about how the other person reacted.

It is possible to take responsibility for one's actions without also taking responsibility for the emotional reactions of others. This follows from the rational-emotive premise that people do *not* have the power to make others feel angry, depressed, or anxious. Thus, if a person behaves in an aggressive manner when refusing a date ("For crying out loud, can't you take obvious hints? Why don't you just leave me alone? Get lost!"), or in an unassertive manner ("Gee, uh, I think I'm probably going to be doing something else that night," when that is clearly not true), or in an assertive manner ("It's nice of you to ask but I'd rather not have a dating relationship with you"), the refuser can take responsibility for that behavior, apart from its effect on the requestor.

Taking responsibility for the reactions of others becomes an important issue when the refuser begins to define his or her own behavior as unassertive or aggressive *because of the way the other person responded*. Thus, if the refuser made an assertive refusal and the other person expressed hurt or anger, the refuser might then label his or her own response as aggressive. Many times, the reactions of others to us can be a valuable source of information. However, those reactions can sometimes be inappropriate, exaggerated, distorted, or manipulative. Therefore, participants are encouraged to first assess their own manner of refusal and then evaluate the appropriateness of the reactions of others. Many nonassertive persons short-circuit this process by presuming that they did something to "cause" the other's response and then work toward changing what might have been a quite reasonable, appropriately assertive response. Thus the belief that one's feelings are externally caused can have a significant effect on defining one's own behaviors as nonassertive.

Lastly, not taking responsibility for the reactions of others does *not* preclude one from being *concerned* about another's reactions. For example, if a person assertively refuses a date and the requestor appears quite down in the dumps, the refuser might choose to express concern and a willingness to talk about the requestor's reaction ("You seem pretty down because I said 'no' "). This is not to suggest that the refuser imply a change of decision; nor is it a suggestion that refusers "rescue" people by soothing their hurt feelings. Rather, in some cases, a person refusing a date might be willing to discuss what is prompting the requestor's reactions and to be concerned.

Session Three: Cognitive Restructuring

The third session is most heavily directed toward teaching cognitive restructuring, primarily in a RET and stress-innoculation fashion. The cognitive-behavioral assertion trainer believes that the images, values, expectations, perceptions, attributions, meanings, and evaluative self-statements in which persons engage have considerable influence on the assertive quality of their behavior. In some instances, clients tend to not think at all, as opposed to engaging in faulty thinking. The cognitive-behavioral trainer considers one's thinking (or lack of it) to be as appropriate a focus for change as are the resultant overt behaviors. Moreover, assertion training is a most likely context to combine techniques which might be applied to both client's *thinking* and *behaving*.

Ellis' rational-emotive approach (Ellis, 1974; Ellis & Harper, 1975) is designed to substitute rational for irrational thinking, particularly with regard to the basic underlying assumptions upon which a person might be operating. Meichenbaum (1975) offers what he calls a coping model designed to control and delimit the influence of faulty thinking. I work toward helping clients learn effective coping self-statements (c.f. Meichenbaum) *and* identify and challenge their underlying irrational beliefs (c.f. Ellis).

The first information the trainer provides is Ellis' A-B-C's (see Chapter 1 of this book). On a blackboard, the trainer defines point A: a situation, for example, of being upbraided unfairly by one's boss in front of everyone else in the office. Then the trainer explains that point C represents feelings and behaviors: for example, intense upsetness, excessive anger, and terrible embarrassment. The trainer then asks the participants to think of all the behaviors people might engage in at point C when they feel these ways. In my experience, participants become quite actively involved in thinking of all the dysfunctional behaviors in which they or others might engage. With the unfair boss, they might cite the following behaviors: shouting back indignantly, crying, running away to the rest room, verbally putting the boss down, hitting the boss, getting revenge by sabotaging the work project (some people are unusually creative in how they would accomplish the breakdowns), tattling on the boss to superiors, getting the other staff members to dislike the boss, and cowering and looking sheepish and guilty.

The trainer then gives a mini-lecture and explains how such situations and the feelings and behaviors described are quite visible but what is often overlooked is that something is happening at point B. That something is thinking, and without that particular thinking a person would not feel and behave as was described on the board; rather, he would feel and behave some other way. The trainer explains that this thinking often takes the form of an internal dialogue (Meichenbaum, 1975), or a conversation one has with oneself. The trainer then asks the participants to think of some of the thoughts that might lead to *excessive* anger, upsetness, or embarrassment. The following are examples of internal thoughts: "You can't speak to me this way! How dare you, you creep!" "Oh, why does he always

pick on me? What am I doing wrong all the time? I can't stand it!" "Oh
no, what must everybody be thinking of me!" "Everybody's looking. Oh
no!" "I'll get you for this, you rat!"

Trainers can teach participants at least two important principles of
irrational thinking during such a session. They can teach the participants
the irrational beliefs articulated by Ellis (Ellis and Harper, 1975). Trainers might particularly note the catastrophic ("What if"; "Oh my gosh")
and the absolutistic ("I must"; "I need"; "I've got to") qualities of most
irrational thinking. Trainers also can provide specific techniques for
changing both the content of one's internal dialogues and the basic irrational thinking.

Trainers actually begin the cognitive restructuring process when introducing the Ellis and Meichenbaum models (A-B-C's, irrational ideas, inner
thoughts) for conceptualizing the relationships between thinking, feeling,
and behavior. The trainer might then teach participants how to challenge
and change irrational ideas (point D in the Ellis model) and how to substitute one's thoughts (Meichenbaum's stress innoculation). During this
third group session, the trainer might ask participants first to challenge
the validity of one of the irrational ideas: "What if I don't get the job?
It would be awful and I must be a real turkey." Participants might ask:
"How awful is it? Is it the end of the world? Am I really a shit because I
didn't get the job? Where is the evidence that I am a shit? What *does* it
mean not to get the job?" The trainer then has the participants identify
more rational, realistic thoughts as alternatives to the faulty thinking.
These alternatives can be specified either at the inner-dialogue level ("I
didn't get the job and I can handle that") or at the irrational idea level
("I am disappointed that I was rejected and I am not a 'bad' person nor
am I a failure or a shit"; "I'd like to be competent at everything I undertake and I will try to do so. If I'm not, I can handle it.").

The example below contrasts some irrational thinking and faulty inner
dialogue with more rational alternatives in a specific situation.

SITUATION	FAULTY INNER DIALOGUE AND IRRATIONAL THINKING	POSSIBLE RATIONAL ALTERNATIVES
On a date	"What if he gets angry if I say I don't want to go to bed with him; maybe he'll really be turned off and not want to see me anymore; then I'll wind up alone, maybe forever! I'll probably never get married; that would be awful! What am I gonna do! What can I	"If he does get angry that would be unfortunate, but I can handle it; if he never comes back I'll probably miss sharing all the good things we've had, but I'm not will-ing to do something I don't want to do to avoid his anger and rejection; if I am alone

say! Damn him anyway! All they want is sex!" for some time I can handle that too, even if I might not prefer it; I can be happy and I don't *need* a romantic relationship, although I would like to have one; even if I never have a sexual or romantic relationship the rest of my life, it's not the end of the world; I may not like it or prefer it, but I *can* handle it. It's likely I will have another relationship."

The reader can see that the irrational dialogue is likely to lead to feelings of distress, anxiety, and possibly anger toward the other person and oneself so that the potential for unassertive or aggressive behavior is great. The woman might avoid contact with the man, offer a variety of excuses when directly asked, become indignant and abusive if asked, or unassertively go ahead and be sexual when not wanting to do so.

Meichenbaum (1975) offers another direction. In addition to disputing the truth of one's earlier thinking, the women might also focus on what is actually happening in the moment and internally "talk herself through," handling the situation assertively. For example, she might go through several stages. In anticipation of his suggestion to be sexual, she might think: "Don't worry, I can think this through without getting upset. I won't say anything negative about myself. What do I want to do?" When he actually makes the suggestion, she might say to herself: "I can handle this anxiety. One step at a time. Relax. I'm in control. Take a deep breath. This anxiety is just what I expected. I can use it as a reminder to start saying coping statements to myself. Just think about what I want to do. Good." If she starts to feel increasingly anxious, she might say to herself: "I expected this might happen. Just pause and relax a moment. Just let the fear go down a little. I don't have to eliminate it." After the interaction is completed, she might also think: "I did it and it wasn't nearly as bad as I thought it might be. It works; when I control my thinking I control my fear." She might also employ a somewhat similar set of coping statements if she was feeling *excessively* angry and believed that that was getting in the way of her handling the refusal in an effective manner. It is important to remember that cognitive principles are *not* designed to suppress or eliminate all feelings. Irritation, annoyance, some degree of anger, sadness, disappointment, and anxiety can lead to appropriate, functional behaviors. Moreover, the cognitive procedures are designed to enable people to prevent and control maladaptive and excessive affective and behavioral responses *when they choose to do so.*

To summarize, a session on cognitive restructuring includes introducing the A-B-C's and such concepts as inner dialogue and irrational thinking in a manner which demonstrates the relationship between nonassertive or assertive behavior and one's cognitions. Participants then learn to challenge the irrational or faulty components of their cognitions and to substitute more rational, realistic thoughts.

During this third session trainers can also introduce a series of questions which participants can run through either just before or during a particular interaction. The goal of asking oneself these questions is to maintain cognitive control of one's thinking, feelings, and behaviors. The following questions exemplify such self-assessment efforts:

What am I doing?	(sweating, rapid heart beat, stammering)
What am I feeling?	(anxious, worried, afraid)
What am I thinking?	(What if she laughs at me when I ask her for a date? I'll probably mess this up terribly.)
What do I want to be thinking?	(That I can ask directly and if I get turned down I'll be disappointed but I won't get embarrassed or feel terribly rejected.)
How do I want to feel?	(calm, a little excited)
What do I want to do?	(I want to tell her I like her and that I would like to invite her over for dinner.)
What's keeping me from doing what I want to do?	(only my irrational, catastrophic thinking which I *can* change)

Not all the questions need to be asked and answered in every situation. They can, however, be asked in a very few seconds, particularly if the person has given some thought to similar situations in the past. Group members report that their self-assessments become more precise and occur more rapidly as they continue to use the procedure.

Trainers might also employ the specific procedures developed by Ellis and Maultsby, Rational Self-Analysis (RSA), Rational Emotive Imagery (REI), and Disputing Irrational Beliefs (DIBS), to help group members assess and alter their cognitions.

Session Four: Behavior Rehearsal Exercises

The fourth session is usually directed toward behavior rehearsal. Since this handbook is primarily oriented toward rational-emotive and other cognitive principles and practices, only a brief description of the behavioral procedures will be presented. It is important to note, however, that the behavioral procedures are fully as important as the cognitive interventions. Moreover, actual time spent in the group using behavioral procedures is usually about equal to the cognitive restructuring time.

During the fourth session, exercises focus on responses for specific types of assertion situations, for example: (1) conflict resolution when someone is doing something that has negative consequences for you (Gordon's conflict-resolution procedures and I-message responses are taught); (2) making and refusing requests without feeling guilty; and (3) responding to persons who are overly persistent toward you (training in learning empathic, simple, and confrontative assertions occurs at this point).

Trainers might in some cases model several assertive responses, particularly if the person working is having difficulty responding at all assertively. Very often, clients can observe such modeling and integrate such response modes into their own repertory. One caution with modeling is that some participants seem to become more adaptive and imitative than integrative. That is, they treat the modeled behavior as something external which they *should* try to become rather than a type of response which they decide is an effective one and which they choose to integrate into their own style. The difference appears to be in the locus of control and evaluation of the appropriateness of one's responses: the former is more externally based.

Meichenbaum (1975) has suggested that therapists or other group members might model more functional (assertive) cognitions in addition to the actual assertive behaviors. The modeler would verbalize inner thoughts that would be counter to the maladaptive thoughts that led to excessive anger, anxiety, guilt, or depression.

When conducting the behavior rehearsals, trainers can also make substantial use of videotaping. After a rehearsal, trainers can play back the interaction, enabling the person to assess his own behavior. Trainers might also use this playback process to have the participant recall the thinking and feelings he experienced at various moments during the role-play. I have found that a good deal of cognitive, affective, and behavioral activity is going on during a role-play that is outside the person's immediate awareness. The recall process helps group members to recognize and become more aware of those thoughts, feelings, and behaviors and their interrelationships. When done in a supportive, analytical and not critical, and improvement-oriented manner, this self-assessment can be a valuable experience. The technique of Interpersonal Process Recall, or IPR (Kagan and Krathwohl, 1967), has been adapted by Resnikoff (1976) to assess cognitions, affects, and behaviors in assertion training behavior rehearsals.

In addition to learning several response modes in specific situations, clients also learn the basic procedures to help them participate in the more complex behavior rehearsals occurring in the remaining sessions. Two exercise formats are employed: the coached client triad and the 5-person line exercise.

In the coached client triad, the whole group is divided into threes. One participant takes a role of making a request, a second person (the asserter) practices refusing the request assertively, and the third person coaches the asserter. The coach has several functions: to help the asserter clarify his goals; to keep the practiced interactions brief; to provide positive behavioral feedback to the asserter and to elicit same from the requester; to help the asserter identify specific improvements she would like to make; to make *suggestions* for change which the asserter decides whether or not to try (the coach can also elicit such suggestions from the requester); and to keep the number of specific changes being worked on at one time to a maximum of three or four. The asserter might practice the interaction several times, with assessments between each practice. The coach might then suggest that the requester become more persistent or nasty, or try to induce guilt or act helplessly. The asserter thereby has an opportunity to practice more difficult situations requiring not only her own assertiveness in response to the request, but also assertiveness in dealing with the other person's nonassertive or manipulative behavior.

The line exercise developed by Patricia Jakubowski (Lange and Jakubowski, 1976) is used with a stated type of situation as, for example, confronting someone about something he is doing that has negative consequences for you. Briefly, the first person in line faces the second person and practices bringing up the concern (keeping the exercise to three or four interactions). The four line members give positive feedback, and the asserter and line members develop suggestions for improvement. Then the asserter faces the next person in the line and practices, particularly working on the changes that the asserter decided upon. When working with the last two line members, the asserter can either continue to practice improving the initial interaction, continue the conversation longer, or ask the line member to become obstreperous in some way.

The remaining sessions can be used primarily for working on situations that the participants themselves identify as ones which they have not handled as well as they would like to or which they have been avoiding. All four stages of the assertion training model are utilized. Time and attention are given to each area (personal rights; discrimination between unassertive, assertive, and aggressive responses; cognitive restructuring; and behavior rehearsal), as needed. Usually, however, the group will not work with one person for more than a half-hour at one time.

Out-of-Group Activity

Primary attention in this chapter has been given to procedures conducted within the group. A significant component of assertion training, however, involves clients going out and trying their new approaches in particular situations. The cognitive-behavioral assertion trainer also encourages group members to develop "out-of-group" plans for changing their cognitions. These plans might include any of the cognitive procedures described or referred to in this chapter (DIBS, REI, RSA, stress innoculation, self-assessment questioning, identification of personal rights, or challenging one's inner dialogue). Group members are not only encouraged to use cognitive interventions to accomplish desired changes, but also to assess and evaluate continuously what is happening with them before, during, and after the particular interaction. Often trainers begin sessions with participants briefly discussing what happened when they worked on a particular type of assertive behavior or when they respond in a specific situation outside the group. Some trainers make planning of group activity a systematic part of each session. Clients make verbal agreements to do a specific cognitive or behavioral task outside the group. Behavioral or contingency contracting (Malott, 1972) can often be employed at this stage.

Self-Evaluation and Control

A major goal of the cognitive aspects of this model is to develop an internal locus of control (which may be quite new for some). Training provides several conceptual frameworks to help people think more clearly about their own thinking, feelings, and behavior: the personal rights system, the internal dialogue process, irrational ideas, the A-B-C's, the self-assessment questions, the disputation of irrational beliefs, the stress innoculation coping procedures, rational-emotive imagery, and even the systematic behavior rehearsal procedures. The goal is to help people make sense of their actions and to utilize their cognitive capabilities to effect desired changes. As Meichenbaum (1975) notes, clients are having a dialogue about the treatment process itself. If the process is believable, relatively safe, and logical, clients will more likely enter into it and profit from the experience. A cognitive-behavioral assertion training group itself should be a process which encourages client thinking, client self-control, and client self-assessment.

Several concerns regarding assertion training warrant attention. Some people can take on assertiveness as their "always to be strived for" cause.

Every opportunity to assert oneself is sought diligently; the assertion antennae are always up and on the prowl. As Arnold Lazarus notes: "Some of these compulsively 'assertive' individuals go through life chalking up interpersonal 'victories' while remaining puzzled by the consequent lack of emotional intimacy. I have heard people actually boast about pushing little old ladies to the back of lines!" (Lange and Jakubowski, 1976). Trainers can be careful to present assertiveness in its realistic light. First, while it is not a cure-all, many persons can improve the quality of their relationships through such training. Second, people can misuse assertiveness by making it another set of "shoulds" by which to measure their o.k.-ness. Third, assertiveness is not a cold set of responses. Assertiveness can lead to warm, caring, honest relationships when used appropriately.

It is also worth noting that some persons have a great psychological investment in maintaining their nonassertive behaviors and that a brief assertion group will not likely be of great benefit in itself. Careful screening of participants by trained counselors and psychologists can prevent inappropriate placements. Some persons would likely profit more from an intensive form of psychotherapy in conjunction with assertion training.

Assertion training can be a powerfully impactful experience for participants through the utilization of cognitive and behavioral procedures. Although many of the techniques might involve extensive practice with supervision, they can eventually become self-help procedures which can be applied to any situation. The union of cognitive and behavioral interventions for modifying thinking, feelings, and behaviors is one of the most exciting and potentially valuable directions emerging in psychology today. Assertion training is an excellent context for such an integrative approach to change.

References

Alberti, R. E., & Emmons, M. L. *Your Perfect Right: A Guide to Assertive Behavior* (2nd ed.). San Luis Obispo, Calif.: Impact Press, 1974.
Beck, Aaron. *Cognitive Therapy and the Emotional Disorders.* New York: International Universities Press, 1976.
Bloom, L. Z., Coburn, K., & Pearlman, J. *The New Assertive Woman.* New York: Delacorte Press, 1975.
Cotler, S., & Guerra, J. *Assertion Training: Humanistic-Behavioral Guide to Self-Dignity.* Champaign, Ill.: Research Press, 1976.
Eisler, R. M., Hersen, M., Miller, P. M., & Blanchard, E. F. Situational Determinants of Assertive Behavior. *Journal of Behavior Therapy and Experimental Psychiatry.* 1973, *4,* 1–6.

Eisler, R. M.; Hersen, M.; Miller, P. M.; & Blanchard, E. F. Situational Determinants of Assertive Behaviors. *Journal of Consulting and Clinical Psychology,* 1975, *43,* 330–340.

Ellis, A. *Humanistic Psychotherapy: The Rational-Emotive Approach.* New York: Julian Press, 1973. (New York: McGraw-Hill Paperbacks, 1974).

Ellis, A. *Growth through reason.* Palo Alto, Calif.: Science and Behavior Books, 1971. Hollywood: Wilshire Books, 1974.

Ellis, A., & Harper, R. A. *A New Guide to Rational Living.* Englewood Cliffs, N.J.: Prentice-Hall, 1975.

Flowers, J., & Guerra, J. The use of client-coaching in assertion training with large groups. *Community Mental Health Journal,* 1974, *10*(4), 414–417.

Friedman, P. H. The effects of modeling and role-playing on assertive behavior. In R. D. Rubin, H. Fensterheim, A. A. Lazarus, & C. M. Franks (Eds.), *Advances in Behavior Therapy.* New York: Academic Press, 1971(a).

Friedman, P. H. The effects of modeling, role-playing and participation on behavior change. In B. Maher (Ed.), *Progress in Experimental Personality Research* (Vol. VI). New York: McGraw-Hill, 1971(b).

Galassi, M. D., & Galassi, J. P. The effects of role playing variations on the assessment of assertive behavior. *Behavior Therapy,* 1976, *7*(3), 343–347.

Glass, C., Gottman, J., & Schmurak, S. Response acquisition and cognitive self-statement modification approaches to dating skills training. *Journal of Counseling Psychology,* 1976, *23*(5), 520–526.

Goldfried, M., & Davison, G. *Clinical Behavior Therapy.* New York: Holt, Rinehart, and Winston, 1976.

Goldfried, M., & Sobocinski, D. Effect of irrational beliefs on emotional arousal. *Journal of Consulting and Clinical Psychology,* 1975, *43,* 504–510.

Jakubowski-Spector, P. Facilitating the growth of women through assertive training. *The Counseling Psychologist,* 1973, *4,* 75–86(b).

Jakubowski-Spector, P., Pearlman, J., & Coburn, K. *Assertive Training for Women: Stimulus Films.* Washington, D.C.: American Personnel and Guidance Association, 1973.

Kagan, N., & Krathwohl, D. *Studies in Human Interaction* (Research Report 20). East Lansing: Michigan State University, Educational Publications Services, 1967.

Kazdin, A. E. Covert modeling, imagery assessment, and assertive behavior. *Journal of Consulting and Clinical Psychology,* 1975, *43,* 716–724.

Lange, A., & Jakubowski, P. *Responsible Assertive Behavior: Cognitive-Behavioral Procedures for Trainers.* Champaign, Ill.: Research Press, 1976.

Lange, A., Rimm, D. C., & Loxley, J. C. Cognitive and behavioral procedures for group assertion training. *The Counseling Psychologist,* in press.

Lazarus, A. A. *Clinical Behavior Therapy.* New York: Brunner/Mazel, 1972.

Liberman, R., King, L., DeRisi, W., & McCann, M. *Personal Effectiveness.* Champaign, Ill.: Research Press, 1976.

Malott, R. *Contingency Management.* Kalamazoo, Mich.: Behaviordelia, Inc., 1972.

McFall, R. M., & Lillesand, D. B. Behavior rehearsal with modeling and coaching in assertive training. *Journal of Abnormal Psychology,* 1971, *77,* 313–323.

McFall, R. M., & Marston, A. R. An experimental investigation of behavior rehearsal in assertive training. *Journal of Abnormal Psychology,* 1970, *76,* 295–303.

McFall, R. M., & Twentyman, C. T. Four experiments on the relative contributions of rehearsal, modeling, and coaching to assertion training. *Journal of Abnormal Psychology,* 1973, *81,* 199–218.

Meichenbaum, D. H. *Cognitive Behavior Modification.* Morristown, N.J.: General Learning Press, 1974.

Meichenbaum, D. H. Self-instructional methods (How to do it). In A. Goldstein & F. Kanfer (Eds.), *Helping People Change: Methods and Materials.* New York: Pergamon, 1975.

Meichenbaum, D. H., & Cameron, R. The clinical potential of modifying what clients say to themselves. In C. Thoresen and M. Mahoney (Eds.), *Self-Control: Power to the Person.* New York: Brooks/Cole, 1974.

Rathus, S. A. A 30-item schedule for assessing assertive behavior. *Behavior Therapy,* 1973, *4,* 398–406(a).

Rathus, S. A. Instigation of assertive behavior through video-tape mediated assertive models and directed practice. *Behavior Research and Therapy,* 1973, *11,* 57–65(b).

Resnikoff, A. *Facilitation of Individual Assertive Issues Through the Use of Video Feedback.* Unpublished manuscript, Washington University, St. Louis, Mo., 1976.

Rimm, D. C. Thought stopping and covert assertion. *Journal of Consulting and Clinical Psychology,* 1973, *41,* 466–467.

Rimm, D. C., & Masters, J. C. *Behavior Therapy: Techniques and Empirical Findings.* New York: Academic Press, 1974.

Salter, A. *Conditioned Reflex Therapy.* New York: Farrar, Straus, & Giroux, 1949.

Schwartz, R., & Gottman, J. *A Task Analysis Approach to Clinical Problems: A Study of Assertive Behavior.* Unpublished manuscript, Indiana University, 1974.

Thorpe, G. Desensitization, behavior rehearsal, self-instructional training and placebo effects on assertive-refusal behavior. *European Journal of Behavioural Analysis and Modification,* 1975, *1,* 30–44.

Wagner, M. K. Comparative effectiveness of behavioral rehearsal and verbal reinforcement for effecting anger expressiveness. *Psychological Reports,* 1968, *22* (3, Pt. 2), 1079–1080(a).

Wagner, M. K. Reinforcement of the expression of anger through role playing. *Behavior Research and Therapy,* 1968, *6,* 91–95(b).

Wolfe, J. Short-term effects of modeling/behavior rehearsal, modeling/behavior rehearsal-plus-rational therapy, placebo, and no treatment on assertive behavior. Doctoral dissertation, New York University, 1975.

Wolpe, J. *The Practice of Behavior Therapy* (2nd ed.). New York: Pergamon, 1973(a).

Wolpe, J. Supervision transcript: V—Mainly about assertive training. *Journal of Behavior Therapy and Experimental Psychiatry,* 1973, *2,* 141–148(b).

Wolpe, J., & Lazarus, A. A. *Behavior Therapy Techniques.* New York: Pergamon, 1966.

Young, E. R., Rimm, D. C., & Kennedy, T. D. An experimental investigation of modeling and verbal reinforcement in the modification of assertive behavior. *Behaviour Research and Therapy,* 1973, *11,* 317–319.

21

The Treatment of Depression with Cognitive Therapy

Brian F. Shaw and Aaron T. Beck

Chapter 21 is a companion to Beck's and Shaw's chapter on the psychodynamics of depression (Chapter 6, "Cognitive Approaches to Depression"). Here the reader will notice the general agreement between cognitive therapy and rational-emotive therapy. In both, the therapist is an involved, active participant in the therapeutic process; in both the major targets of therapy are the automatic thoughts, basic beliefs, and general philosophies that underlie the client's emotional disturbance; in both the therapist tries to get the client to recognize and accept a valid, empirically based view of self and the world.

Chapter 21 describes some distinct features of cognitive therapy that provide additional resources from which the rational therapist can draw. One is the close relation between the "cognitive triad" of depression and the strategies of the cognitive therapist. A second feature is cognitive therapy's rather organized, step-by-step treatment approach. It progresses from a focus on the client's symptoms and behaviors, to a focus on the client's more situationally specific thoughts, to a focus on the client's more central beliefs and philosophies. Cognitive therapy's techniques to challenge and dispute the depressed person's tendencies to self-criticize and to apply inflexibly absolute standards for performance to himself are also described.

AN INCREASING BODY of literature indicates the efficacy of cognitive therapy in the treatment of depression (for example, Taylor, 1974; Shaw, 1975; Morris, 1975; Schmickley, 1976). These findings are highly significant since previous controlled psychotherapy-drug outcome studies have found minimal effects in reducing depressive symptomatology with "social casework therapy" (Klerman, DiMascio, Weissman, Prusoff, and Paykel, 1974); "group psychotherapy" (Covi, Lipman, Derogatis, Smith, and Pattison, 1974); and "marital therapy" (Friedman, 1975). For the first time, a form of psychotherapy (cognitive therapy) has been shown to effect changes in the symptoms of depression. The purpose of this chapter is to outline the therapeutic techniques employed by cognitive therapists in the treatment of depressed and suicidal patients.

The cognitive view of the development and maintenance of depression has been described in Chapter 6. Essentially, the cognitive view holds that "The affective response is determined by the way an individual structures his experience." Because of the dominance of certain cognitive schema, the patient tends to regard himself, his experiences, and his future in a negative way. This has been heuristically labeled the "cognitive triad of depression" (Beck, 1967).

The negative concepts of the cognitive triad are apparent in the way the depressed individual *systematically* misconstrues his experiences and in the content of his ideation. Specifically, the depressed person regards himself as a "loser." His thinking is distorted and thus errors such as arbitrary inference, overgeneralization, and magnification lead him to totally down himself. The depressed individual believes he has lost something of substantial value, such as a personal relationship, or that he has failed to achieve what he considers an important objective, and he blames himself for the loss. Moreover, he expects the outcome of any specific activity that he undertakes to be negative and therefore he is not motivated to set goals and in fact will avoid engaging in "constructive" activities. In addition, he expects his future life to be deficient in satisfaction and even filled with despair.

Rationale and Data Base

The Rationale

The rationale of cognitive therapy is derived from the cognitive theory of depression. If the source of disturbance in depression is a hypervalent set of negative concepts, then the correction of these prepotent beliefs may be expected to alleviate the symptomatology of depression. By identifying the distorted cognitions derived from the dysfunctional beliefs and subjecting them to logical analysis and empirical testing, the therapist and patient work together to realign the patient's thinking with reality. Cognitive therapy thus consists of techniques that enable the patient to see himself realistically rather than as inadequate, undesirable, and unworthy; and as capable of mastery rather than as helpless. The therapy also aims at providing an objective view of the future rather than indiscriminate pessimism and hopelessness.

Thus, the immediate goals of cognitive therapy center on the systematic modification of the depressed patient's arbitrary, distorted interpretations of reality. The techniques of cognitive therapy are oriented toward: (1) the specific target symptoms of depression, that is, the overt symptomatology which can be incapacitating and may increase the likelihood of suicide; and (2) the "silent assumptions" or beliefs from which the patient operates.

The collaborative aspect of the therapeutic relationship requires special emphasis. A scientific collaboration implies that the therapist and the patient concentrate together on problematic areas using an empirical methodology. It is evident that in order to collaborate both the therapist and the patient should work within the same overall frame of reference. It is critical that the therapist thoroughly understand the patient's conceptualizations and be able to see the world "through the patient's eyes." The patient also needs to have a clear understanding of what thought or belief (hypothesis) is being tested and, importantly, what purpose various homework assignments serve. When the patient's conceptualizations deviate from the therapist's view of reality, the "collaborators" attempt to reconcile the differences through a logical-empirical approach.

The major content areas discussed in the therapy sessions are targeted by the patient *and* the therapist. Therapeutic interchanges are structured as collaborative discussions and thus the patient and therapist prepare an agenda at the beginning of each session. It is essential that the therapist actively direct the discussion to the problematic areas targeted for intervention. This directive behavior is in marked contrast to therapeutic approaches in which the patient selects his own agenda (content areas) or rambles aimlessly while the therapist listens passively.

Cognitive therapy is planned as a short-term intervention and time limits are frequently employed (for example, a maximum of 20 sessions in a period of 12 weeks). Some clinicians (for example, Lewinsohn, Shaffer, and Libet, 1971) indicate that the time-limited approach has a facilitative effect on the behaviors of the depressed patient and therapist. The strategy of a defined therapy period requires that the therapist and patient use the limited therapy time judiciously. This means that every question or statement posed by the therapist should have a definite rationale or purpose. Thus, questions should be conceptually relevant to cognitive therapy and should be phrased to elicit concrete information. (Requests such as "Please give me a specific example," are frequently used.) Questioning is a major tool not only to elicit reliable information regarding specific cognitions, definitions, and meanings, but also to expose inner contradictions, inconsistencies, and logical flaws in the patient's conclusions. A well-timed, properly phrased question may serve to open a closed belief system.

The Data Base for Cognitive Therapy

We have likened the technical approach of cognitive therapy to a scientific investigation: (a) collecting data that are as reliable and valid as possible, (b) formulating hypotheses based on the data, and (c) testing (and possibly revising) hypotheses based on new data.

The primary data base of cognitive therapy consists of the patient's "automatic thoughts" (Beck, 1963), images, feelings, and wishes. The automatic thoughts and images are referred to as the patient's cognitions. These data are collected in a systematic manner from three sources: (1) oral reports by the patient of the cognitions and emotions he experiences between therapy sessions that are relevant to the defined goals of therapy; (2) thoughts, images, and feelings experienced during therapy; and (3) introspective material *written* by the patient as part of homework assignments. The patient's reported cognitions, feelings, desires, and actions are taken as "hard data" (unless there is reason to suspect false reporting) and constitute, along with a description of the external circumstances, basic information from which the therapist develops hypotheses and makes inferences.

The therapist of course does not accept the introspective data as accurate representations of reality but rather as the patient's peculiar construction (or misconstruction) of reality. Since the basic premise of the cognitive theory of depression is that the patient systematically misinterprets his experiences, it is essential for the therapist to obtain information that will provide the context of the patient's specific constructions. Thus, through skillful questioning regarding the total circumstances of a particular event, the therapist will be able to obtain evidence of the patient's distorted or dysfunctional thinking.

Once these automatic data are collected, the patient and therapist can conceptualize them on three levels of abstraction. The patient's "general idea," or the extracted meaning of his interpretation of past events, represent a first level of abstraction. These data are elicited by questions such as: "How did you interpret the situation in which you felt bad?" "What did it mean to you when you were late for the appointment?"

The second level of abstraction consists of generalizations usually made by the therapist about the patient's cognitions. One kind of generalization concerns the content of the patient's ideations. For example, the patient and therapist may see certain themes which are apparent in the patient's cognitions; for example, "expecting to fail" or "reading rejection into personal situations." A second kind of generalization involves the stylistic errors in thinking (for example, "all-or-none" thinking, arbitrary inference, overgeneralization). A third kind of generalization involves classifying the automatic cognition as realistic or unrealistic, adaptive or maladaptive.

The third level of abstraction concerns the beliefs, attitudes, and assumptions which, according to cognitive theory, often shape the automatic thoughts and images. An attitude may be so dominant and pervasive that despite changes in the environmental input or the assigned meaning (significance) of an event, the conclusion never varies (e.g., "I make a fool of myself in novel situations"; "I can't be happy unless I'm loved"). The articulation of these attitudes may be useful for the future recognition of cognitions as well as empirical validation.

Specific Application of Techniques

The techniques of cognitive therapy are employed to facilitate changes in both the target symptoms of depression (for example, inactivity, self-criticisms, lack of gratification, suicidal wishes) and their underlying cognitive causes. Generally, the therapy interviews proceed from a discussion of previously assigned homework, to a focus on the patient's thinking in the interview itself (i.e., response to therapist, treatment goals), to a review of his recent past behavior and thinking, and then to the homework for the next session.

In the initial sessions, the therapist first attempts to elicit the hopeless thoughts which are commonly observed in depressed patients. One example is a 27-year-old patient who was asked what "was going through her mind" while she was sitting in the waiting room. With some hesitation, she stated that she was convinced that she "couldn't be helped." The therapist asked for the evidence which led to her belief and the patient indicated a psychiatric history of 5 years, 3 previous psychotherapists, and her "need to suffer." In addition, after meeting her therapist she was certain that he wouldn't understand her problems as he wasn't an American. Pursuing this line of thinking, the patient said that she could "deceive" people and the therapist would probably be fooled into viewing her as a "cool, calm, and collected" individual when really she was a "blob who had nothing going" for her. The correction of these misconceptions by the process of examining the validity of the patient's conclusion was important. Otherwise, any positive achievements may have been viewed as examples of her ability to deceive others while negative experiences would confirm her basic belief. The example also serves to illustrate the therapeutic approach which focuses on the "hard data" (i.e. "automatic thoughts") in the session, an approach which is central to cognitive therapy.

Once this has been accomplished, systematic goals are identified. Initially, the therapist chooses techniques that emphasize behavioral changes, particularly with the more acutely and severely depressed person who is often less able to engage in many of the cognitive tasks; then, as the intensity of the affect begins to diminish and concentration improves, he proceeds to the collection, examination, and finally the testing of the cognitive assumptions which lead to depression. The cognitive techniques progress toward greater abstraction, thereby requiring greater logic and mental activity. However, if the patient is moderately depressed and has no major behavioral symptoms, the therapist may choose to employ the cognitive techniques from the beginning.

Focus on Behavior Change

The behavioral techniques used in cognitive therapy have a dual purpose: first, to produce change in the patient's passivity, avoidance, and lack of gratification; second, to stimulate empirical evaluation of his overgeneralized beliefs of inadequacy and incompetence. For instance, the *graded task assignment* is based on the assumption that it is difficult for the depressed individual to complete tasks which had been relatively simple prior to the depressive episode. As they grow increasingly inactive, severely depressed patients often think, "I can't do anything," or "It's useless to try." This cognitive reaction may be seen as a logical result of the overgeneralized belief that because an activity is no longer simple, it is therefore impossible. The cognitive therapist does not counter this belief by taking the opposing stance (e.g., "Yes, you can do it, if you try"), for this strategy may serve to alienate the patient. Rather, he approaches the problem from an empirical viewpoint ("Would you be willing to test your belief?") and the goal-directed activity in question is divided into mini-tasks which are within the patient's capability.

Other techniques aimed at behavioral change include: *cognitive rehearsal* (the patient imagines each step in the sequence leading to completion of the assignment); *activity scheduling* (the patient and therapist collaborate to schedule hourly activities); and, the *mastery and pleasure technique* (rating the scheduled activities according to the amount of mastery or pleasure obtained).

In applying behavioral change techniques, the therapist needs to emphasize that the immediate goal is to diminish the patient's self-debasement and low mood, *not* to achieve complete and significant therapeutic cure. Also, frequent reminders of the accomplishment of therapeutic targets, which had been established collaboratively by the patient and therapist, are necessary because the depressed patient tends to overlook or even actively devalue his successful experiences. Thus, conclusions, such as "Any 10-year-old would be able to do this activity," warrant a challenge by the therapist that performance has to be judged relative to the depressed state and that the empirical evidence shows that the initial target (i.e., increased activity and mood) was achieved. A reevaluation of the patient's initial negative belief may be pursued with the goal of making the appropriate cognitive change (e.g., "I *thought* that I couldn't do anything but the evidence is that tasks are harder to do but not impossible").

Collection and Examination of Cognitions

The cognitions (automatic thoughts and images) of depression have been described in detail in Chapter 6. In cognitive therapy, the patient is trained to observe the cognitions which are associated with unpleasant affect. The technique of *collecting automatic thoughts* makes the patient aware of the critical function of thinking in the experience of affect. Cognitions are collected by the therapist in the interview itself and by the patient at other designated periods between sessions (for example, at times of intense dysphoria or during specific environmental interactions). The therapist teaches the patient to view his cognitions as psychological responses rather than accurate reflections of reality, and to examine reasonableness and evidence supporting specific cognitions, such as "I'm a complete failure" or "Everyone is disgusted with me." This training period varies from patient to patient, but, given sufficient attention, particularly through homework assignments, the patient learns to identify his automatic thoughts.

At this point in therapy, the *triple-column technique* is often employed. On the left-hand side the patient records the situation or event associated with unpleasant affect and this serves to describe the context in which the cognition occurred. The middle section of the page is reserved for the actual cognitions and serves as the primary data base. The right-hand column is reserved for the patient's active attempt to answer the cognitions using concrete evidence ("facts"), thereby testing the validity and reasonableness of the cognitions. The therapist may help the patient categorize his cognitions under relevant themes such as self-blame, inferiority, or deprivation. It is important to emphasize that, of the innumerable ways to interpret life experiences, the patient tends to perseverate in a few stereotyped, self-defeating patterns. Cognitive distortions such as overgeneralization, arbitrary inference, and self-attribution may be evident and can be identified and categorized.

The depressive's closed system of logic and reasoning opens as he distances himself from his cognitions, analyzes his cognitions with concrete evidence, and identifies the pattern they follow in his thinking. Problems which previously were perceived as insoluble may then be reconceptualized and the therapist may utilize the *alternative technique*. In this approach, the patient actively searches for alternative solutions or interpretations of problematic events. This technique will be later detailed in the example which illustrates the cognitive approach to suicidal patients.

The aforementioned strategies are designed to involve the patient in a systematic testing of his cognitions in order that external problems may be approached realistically. There is no attempt to deny or invalidate realistic difficulties which evolve from external problems. Nevertheless, it is assumed that the patient who can recognize and correct his distortions of reality is better able to attack the problems which, in fact, exist in his domain.

Identification and Evaluation of Maladaptive Assumptions

The final stages of cognitive therapy involve the identification of the chronic beliefs and assumptions by which the patient constructs and orders his world. The content of such attitudes may be inferred from an examination of the recurrent themes in the patient's cognitive responses to specific situations. Recall that the therapist develops hypotheses about these attitudes from the beginning of therapy. Further information about the patient's basic premises may be obtained by ascertaining the evidence for a particular conclusion or the reasoning behind a particular judgment. Some of the attitudes which predispose individuals to excessive sadness and depression include the following: "I must be successful in whatever I undertake"; "I must be in control of my life at all times"; "My value as a person depends on what others think of me"; "If I make a mistake, it means that I'm inept"; and, "I can't live without love." The attitudes of the patient can be examined and assessed for their reasonableness and evidence, just as individual cognitions are evaluated for their validity.

Once the patient recognizes these attitudes, it is often profitable to review their cognitive, behavioral, and affective implications by referring to specific data previously discussed with the patient.

Specific Targets and Problems

In this section, two clinical examples are presented which allow us to detail other specific therapeutic techniques used to effect changes in target symptoms of depression. It should be noted that the techniques are designed to increase the patient's awareness of specific cognitions and, with practice, to change the cognitive pattern. The examples of target symptoms and techniques is not exhaustive, but only offered to provide a variety of potential interventions.

Target 1: Self-Criticism

The tendency for excessive self-blame is frequently found in depressives. One cognitive function associated with self-criticism or self-blame is the tendency to assume total responsibility for failures and to selectively discount responsibility for success. This tendency is excessive as the depressed patient may attribute the causality of negative events to himself when he has a minimal influence on the event in reality.

With the goal of changing the patient's self-criticism and predisposition to hold himself responsible for any adverse occurrence, the therapist may elect to: (a) counter this cognitive set by showing that the patient has a functional role in a success experience; or (b) demonstrate that the patient applies a different criteria of judgment to his own behavior than he does with others' behavior; or (c) challenge the assumption that he is "100 percent" responsible for a negative event. This class of techniques are referred to as *"reattribution"* techniques.

Clinical example. A 38-year-old married male owns a small manufacturing firm which has prospered over the past six years. Six months previously, he made a series of decisions which led to a significant personal financial loss and in the period following became severely depressed. Despite the company's moderate recovery, the patient continued to experience depression and ruminated almost continuously about his management errors and current indecisiveness.

Increase awareness of success experiences. The patient was asked to keep an activity log and to record mastery and pleasure experiences (mastery and pleasure technique). Initially, the patient's self-critical belief that he was "totally inadequate" was tested by an "experiment" in which the patient attempted to wash and dry his clothes. Despite a constant stream of negative predictions, the patient was able to see the results of his effort. This experience was the first of a number of tasks which were used to challenge his belief of "total" inadequacy.

Reverse role playing. The patient reported an incident during which he acted "like a fool." According to the patient, he added his charge card bill incorrectly at a restaurant and was distressed because "the other members of the group must have thought I was a basket case." The therapist initially pursued the patient's evidence for this belief but despite the patient's inability to present concrete data which would support his conclusion, he maintained his self-debasing stance. The therapist then used a reversal in roles in which the patient was to be a member of the group while one of the other men paid the bill and made the same error as the patient. In contrast to the verbal self-abuse he gave himself, the patient was sympathetic to the other person and readily conceded that "mistakes will happen." When confronted with the discrepancy in his application of criticism, the patient was able to provide alternative notions to the possibility that he was a "fool" for making the mistake. The result of this technique was to "defuse" the patient's continual self-criticism. Later in the session the therapist and patient attempted to define a "fool" and concluded that the term was undefinable.

Identification of excessive responsibility. Depressed patients are often unable to assess where their responsibility realistically ends in a situation and assume they control negative events. In this particular case, the patient spent considerable time ruminating about issues over which he had little control. Importantly, these issues were not abstract in the sense of his relationship with many of the world's problems (i.e., overpopulation, pollution), but rather involved specific interactions in which he had some minimal involvement.

One such incident which led to intense dysphoria involved a stock market purchase of a business associate. The patient had previously enjoyed his reputation as a conservative yet shrewd analyst of certain types of stocks. During his depression, he was approached by an associate at a dinner party and asked his advice. The patient wanted to decline, given the context in which the request was made, but instead simply responded that the investment "sounded okay." Later, after discovering that the stock prices had suffered a decline, the patient became convinced that he caused the financial ruin of his associate. He concluded: "I'm like the plague; I'm to blame for this disaster."

In order to counter these cognitions, the therapist clearly identified the patient's silent assumption. This identification facilitated the patient's awareness of his tendency to that excessive responsibility. It was accomplished by direct inquiry ("Do you believe that you are 100 percent responsible for your associate's loss?"). Once the assumption was identified, the therapist and patient proceeded to outline in a stepwise fashion the other factors involved in the process of buying a stock (i.e. other sources of advice, the associate's own decision-making process, the general status of stocks in a period of inflation, chance factors). The patient was then asked to assess the relative contributions of each factor and his personal control over these factors. He was asked to provide evidence as to why he assumed his advice was of critical importance.

When the patient recognized that the probability that he was *totally* responsible was almost zero, the therapist inquired as to whether he would have been elated and taken all of the credit if the stock had risen in price. Thus, the patient was confronted with the "double standard" of his own thinking; namely, that if there was a loss, he was 100 percent responsible but if there was a success, his responsibility was minimal.

Once the validity of his assumption was questioned, the patient was asked to investigate to what degree he was realistically responsible for his associate's loss. He contacted his associate and eventually obtained some "data" to test his new hypothesis and found that while his response had increased his associate's confidence in the decision, the decision had been made, for the most part, before the party. Finally, as a result of the party interaction, the patient concluded that he would take steps in the future to guard against "party advice," a realistic solution and response to his initial actions.

Target 2: Modifying the "shoulds"

A common cognitive schema seen in depressives is an extensive belief in the "shoulds" of living (Horney, 1950), or, as Ellis (1974) refers to them, "musturbation." Basically, the "shoulds" and "musts" are rules which the patient believes to be absolutely certain in all situations and represent part of the cognitive structure used to order his experiences.

Depressed patients frequently compare what they believe they *should* do with what they are doing in the present. After perceiving the discrepancy between how they behave and the ideal way, they usually conclude that they are worthless, inadequate, or in a process of deterioration. While nondepressed individuals commonly compare their behavior with a standard as a constructive means of self-control, the depressed person applies rules in an inflexible manner. The standard becomes a rigid goal instead of a guide, as evidenced by the intensity with which depressed patients maintain that they *should* do something and by the variety of situations in which the patient feels compelled to attain a certain standard. The depressed patient rarely recognizes the important fact that when depressed, expectations need to be reduced because of the effects of the depressive symptoms (i.e., fatiguability, loss of concentration). In other words, the guidelines, much less the rules, no longer apply since the condition of the patient is different.

An analogy such as the following may be helpful to illustrate this problem. An adult *should* be able to walk up a flight of stairs. This statement is probably true for most adults (notice that even this rule is not absolute). But if the adult is suffering from a paralysis of his legs, the rule no longer applies. This fact, of course, does not rule out the possibility of ultimately getting up the stairs, but doing so by a different procedure than his standard way of climbing the stairs is required.

Often the patient's "should" and "must" rules are supported by significant others. Rules are commonly outlines to direct socially appropriate behavior ("You should not cross the street on a red light"), but may also be overapplied in the communication of expectations ("You should go to college"). The rules may develop after specific unpleasant personal experiences and, from the patient's viewpoint, may function to prevent something undesirable from happening (for example, "I should always listen to those in authority or they won't like me"; "I must keep up with my work or I will lose my job"). The cognitive therapist may choose to target these rules in the sessions with the patient.

Clinical example. The patient was a 32-year-old female with intense dysphoria who had difficulty asserting herself. With regard to her inability to give negative feedback to her supervisor, the therapist asked her to consider the consequences of telling her supervisor her dissatisfactions about her duties as a salesperson. The patient indicated that the supervisor would be angry and think less of her. In addition, she thought her peers would be upset if she received special treatment and wouldn't like her for it. To prove her point, she noted, "If you want someone to like you, you shouldn't complain or put demands on them" and that if you do complain, others won't like you. She strongly adhered to these rules and applied them in the majority of her social and occupational relationships.

Some techniques for modifying the "Shoulds" are:

Examination of when "shoulds" apply. The patient is asked to consider various situations in his life. In a situation-by-situation analysis, he can be helped to apply differentially one or another of his "shoulds." In the present example, the patient developed a hierarchical list of situations in which the rule, "You shouldn't say how you're dissatisfied or they won't like you," applied. This prohibitive list included complaining about the service in a restaurant, stating to friends that she disliked politics, telling her boyfriend how he angered her, and telling her mother to mind her own business. The patient recognized the frequency and intensity with which she applied these prohibitions to herself. She then started to apply the rule flexibly on the basis of particular circumstances of a situation and the *probable* consequences, rather than rigidly in all situations.

Comparison of the "shoulds" with what the patient wants. When the patient's life is dominated by "shoulds," little attention and energy is left for obtaining what the patient himself wants. By asking the patient to state what he *wants* in contrast to the demands he places on himself, the therapist can demonstrate how much the patient has neglected his own desires. The patient and therapist can then establish the therapeutic goal of "catching the should" and then listing the advantages and disadvantages of following the dictates of these self-imposed prescriptions or restrictions.

Counting automatic self-commands. One way to highlight the overuse of "shoulds" is to have the patient count on a wrist golf counter or a similar device the number of times he tells himself what he must do. He may record the content on a homework form.

Exploring the consequences of giving up the "should" rule. In the present example, the patient was first asked to consider how she would state her "gripes" and then how others would act toward her. How long would they feel angry or sad? Would that permanently or transiently affect the relationship? In this way, she was helped to more realistically predict the consequences of her desired actions, rather than automatically presume the direct consequences.

Role reversal. In this technique, the patient may be asked to think of herself as the supervisor (or peer) while the therapist describes the patient's behavior in the supervisory contact. The patient (in the role of the other) is asked to draw conclusions about her own behavior.

In the above case, the patient concluded that she was seen as a timid person who denied others her opinions, originality, and talent. She believed that she was seen as insipid, uninteresting, and dull, *not* kind, gentle, and considerate, as she wanted to be seen. The therapist then proceeded to focus on her assertive behavior. In this particular case, the patient possessed the behavioral skills, but if a patient's skills are deficient a specific assertive training program may be indicated.

Supportive Data

A number of the reports in the literature which support the use of cognitive or behavioral techniques in treating depression involve case reports and analog studies. For example, Rush, Khatami, and Beck (1975) reported the successful treatment of three patients with chronic relapsing depression using a combination of cognitive and behavioral techniques. The main behavioral modality consisted of the use of activity schedules. The cognitive approach was directed at exposing and correcting the patient's negative distortions of the activities undertaken. These patients, although not substantially helped by drug therapy, showed prompt and sustained improvement with therapy, as reflected by their scores on clinical and self-report measures.

Recently, a number of studies with controlled research designs have evaluated the relative efficacy of cognitive and behavioral procedures, alone and in combination. The studies must be viewed as preliminary due to research issues such as the sample size and the severity of symptomatology in the population studied; however, it is notable that treatments which focus on cognitive and behavioral targets are effective in alleviating depression. Furthermore, they appear to be more efficacious than nondirective and supportive approaches.

Shipley and Fazio (1973) demonstrated that an individual treatment approach which provided functional problem-solving alternatives resulted in significantly greater improvement in depressed student volunteers than did a supportive control group. In their experiment, 24 treatment subjects and 25 controls were seen for three 1-hour sessions in a period of three weeks by one therapist. In addition to the significant treatment effects, the authors found that the effects were not contingent on the initial expectancies of the subjects.

Taylor (1974) conducted a controlled treatment comparison among groups which received cognitive modification, behavior modification, cognitive *and* behavior modification, as well as a waiting-list group. One therapist treated 7 depressed college student subjects in each group using a group therapy format. Taylor (1974) concluded that subjects in the treatment groups showed significant improvement in depression, compared to the waiting-list control subjects. Furthermore, the combination treatment was superior to the cognitive or the behavioral groups alone.

Increased confidence in the efficacy of cognitive procedures resulted from a study by Shaw (1975). He treated depressed students who were referred from a University Health Service and were assessed by psychometric ratings and independent clinical evaluations by two psychologists. A group therapy format was employed with one therapist treating 8 subjects in each group. Cognitive therapy was found to be more efficacious than behavior therapy (interpersonal skills training), nondirective therapy, and a waiting list control. The behavioral and nondirective procedures were significantly better than no treatment.

In a study of depressed female outpatients, Morris (1975) compared a "didactic cognitive-behavioral program," an "insight-oriented therapy" (an experiential and unstructured program which focused on self-understanding), and a waiting-list control group. Four therapists were used to treat two discrete subgroups within the treatment conditions. There were 22 subjects in the cognitive-behavioral group, 17 in the insight group, and 12 served as controls. Morris (1975) found that the cognitive-behavioral program was superior. He also found the cognitive-behavioral treatment to be as effective in a 3-week period as in a 6-week period when the number of sessions (6) remained constant. This finding is important as one of the notable features of the cognitive approach is that significant change can occur during a time-limited intervention period.

Using a single-subject design, Schmickley (1976) reported significant improvement in a sample of 11 clinical outpatients as a direct result of a cognitive-behavioral treatment intervention. The subjects were seen individually by one therapist for four 1-hour sessions. Changes in the direction of improvement were found on 11 or 12 psychometric and behavioral measures following treatment and these changes were maintained at a 2-week follow-up.

Hodgson and Urban (1975) demonstrated that both a behavioral interpersonal-skills procedure and a treatment program which altered the interpersonal perceptions of depressed college students were significantly more effective than no treatment. In addition, they found the behavioral procedures to be more effective than the interpersonal perception techniques.

Results from *two* outcome studies conducted by Rehm and his colleagues (Fuchs and Rehm, 1975; Rehm, Fuchs, Roth, Kornblith, and Romano, 1975) indicated the efficacy of a behavioral self-control therapy program with depressed female volunteers. In the first study, the self-control group and a nondirective placebo group produced changes in depression which were significantly different from a waiting-list control. These changes were maintained at a 6-week follow-up. In the second study, the self-control group was compared with a social skills training group. Two pairs of therapists treated one therapy group in each condition during six weekly sessions. While subjects in both conditions improved with therapy, the self-control group showed greater improvement on the symptoms of depression.

Gioe (1975) compared a modified cognitive modification treatment in combination with a "positive group experience," a cognitive modification treatment, a treatment consisting of a "positive group experience" alone, and a waiting-list control. Using a group therapy modality with 10 depressed students in each group, Gioe (1975) found that the combination treatment package was clearly superior in alleviating depressive symptomatology.

An intensive pilot study at the University of Pennsylvania (Rush, Beck, Kovacs, Khatami, Fitzgibbons, and Wolman, 1975; Kovacs and Rush, 1976) was undertaken to assess the relative efficacy of cognitive therapy and an antidepressant drug (imipramine hydrochloride) in the treatment of depression. The patients were adult outpatients, most of whom had been experiencing moderate or severe depression for over six months prior to coming for treatment. Treatment was initiated with a total of 19 cognitive therapy subjects and 22 chemotherapy subjects. Cognitive therapy subjects were individually treated twice a week for a maximum of 20 1-hour sessions. Chemotherapy subjects were seen once a week in a 15-minute session for a maximum of 12 visits, the last two of which involved tapering off and stopping the medication.

The findings of the ongoing study as of August 1976 indicate a significant advantage of cognitive therapy in reducing acute depressive symptomatology. Using appropriate analyses of variance and covariance, the groups were compared on the Beck Depression Inventory (Beck and Beamesderfer, 1974) and the Hamilton Rating Scale for Depression (Hamilton, 1969). There was a significant improvement as a result of treatment with each therapeutic modality. The cognitive therapy group, however, showed significantly greater improvement at termination than did the chemotherapy group. These findings were consistent on the self-administered measure of depression (the Beck Depression Inventory) and the clinical rating scale (the Hamilton Rating Scale for Depression).

One notable difference between the groups was the frequency of dropouts from treatment. Eight patients prematurely terminated treatment in the chemotherapy group; six terminated against the therapist's advice and two were withdrawn due to severe side effects. In the cognitive therapy group, only one patient prematurely terminated against the therapist's advice. Obviously, this differential dropout finding is preliminary, given the size of the sample. It is possible that psychopharmacological treatment in itself may be related to higher dropout rates (Kovacs and Rush, 1976). Nevertheless, based on these data, further investigation is warranted.

It should be clear from this brief review of the relevant research on the cognitive-behavior therapy of depression that more thorough work must be done. Specifically, the outcome studies which used only one therapist require replication. Also, the reported studies employed a variety of cognitive and behavioral interventions which need further investigation. Nevertheless, these studies reflect an optimistic outlook, one which is certainly encouraging to the clinician and researcher interested in cognitive approaches to depression.

Summary

The central assumption of cognitive therapy is that the affective response is determined by the individual's interpretation of events rather than the events themselves. Technically, cognitive therapy follows a scientific model in which the therapist and patients collaborate with the goal of modifying the distorted aspects of the patient's thinking. Cognitive therapy focuses on the manifest symptoms of depression and the assumptive or belief systems which predispose the patient to experience clinical depression. Based on clinical experience and controlled research studies, cognitive therapy appears to be an efficacious modality for the treatment of depressed and suicidal patients.

References

Beck, A. T. Thinking and depression: I. Idiosyncratic content and cognitive distortions. *Archives of General Psychiatry,* 1963, *9,* 324–333.

Beck, A. T. *Depression: clinical, experimental and theoretical aspects.* New York: Harper & Row, 1967.

Beck, A. T., and Beamesderfer, A. Assessment of depression: the depression inventory. In P. Pichot (Ed.), *Psychological Measurement in Psychopharmacology, Mod. Prob. Pharmacopsychiat.* (Vol. 7). Basel, Switzerland: Karger, 1974.

Beck, A. T., Kovacs, M., and Weissman, A. Hopelessness and suicidal behavior: An overview. *Journal of the American Medical Association,* 1975, *234,* 1146–1149.

Covi, L., Lipman, R. S., Derogatis, L. R., Smith, J. E., and Pattison, J. H. Drugs and psychotherapy in neurotic depression. *American Journal of Psychiatry,* 1974, *131,* 191–198.

Ellis, A. Rational-emotive therapy. Workshop presented at the Eighth Annual Meeting of the Association for the Advancement of Behavior Therapy, Chicago, 1974.

Friedman, A. S. Interaction of drug therapy with marital therapy in depressive patients. *Archives of General Psychiatry,* 1975, *32,* 619–637.

Fuchs, C. Z., and Rehm, L. P. A self-control behavior therapy program for depression. Unpublished manuscript, University of Pittsburgh, 1975.

Gioe, V. J. Cognitive modification and positive group experience as a treatment for depression. Unpublished doctoral dissertation, Temple University, 1975.

Hamilton, M. Standardized assessment and recording of depressive symptoms. *Psychiatria, Neurologia, Neurochirurgia,* 1969, *72,* 201–205.

Hodgson, J. W., and Urban, H. B. A comparison of interpersonal training programs in the treatment of depressive states. Unpublished manuscript, State College, Pa., 1975.

Horney, K. Neurosis and human growth: The struggle toward self-realization. New York: Norton, 1950.

Kovacs, M., Beck, A. T., and Weissman, A. The use of suicidal motives in the psychotherapy of attempted suicides. *American Journal of Psychotherapy,* 1975, *29,* 363–368.

Kovacs, M., and Rush, A. J. Cognitive-behavioral psychotherapy versus antidepressant medication in the treatment of depression. Paper presented at the Forty-Seventh Annual Meeting of the Eastern Psychological Association, New York City, 1976.

Klerman, G. L., DiMascio, A., Weissman, M., Prusoff, B., and Paykel, E. S. Treatment of depression by drugs and psychotherapy. *American Journal of Psychiatry,* 1974, *131,* 186–191.

Lewinsohn, P. M., Shaffer, M., and Libet, J. A behavioral approach to depression. Unpublished manuscript, University of Oregon, 1971.

Morris, N. E. A group self-instruction method for the treatment of depressed outpatients. Unpublished doctoral dissertation, University of Toronto, 1975.

Rehm, L. P., Fuchs, C. Z., Roth, D., Kornblith, S., and Romano, J. Self-control and social skills training in the modification of depression. Unpublished manuscript, University of Pittsburgh, 1975.

Rush, A. J., Beck, A. T., Kovacs, M., Khatami, M., Fitzgibbons, R., and Wolman, T. Comparison of cognitive and pharmacotherapy in depressed outpatients: A preliminary report. Paper presented at the Society for Psychotherapy Research, Boston, June 12, 1975.

Rush, A. J., Khatami, M., and Beck, A. T. Cognitive and behavioral therapy in chronic depression. *Behavior Therapy,* 1975, *6,* 398–404.

Schmickley, V. G. The effects of cognitive-behavior modification upon depressed outpatients. Unpublished doctoral dissertation, Michigan State University, 1976.

Shaw, B. F. A systematic investigation of two treatments of depression. Unpublished doctoral dissertation, University of Western Ontario, Canada, 1975.

Shipley, C. R., and Fazio, A. F. Pilot study of a treatment for psychological depression. *Journal of Abnormal Psychology,* 1973, *83,* 372–376.

Taylor, F. G. Cognitive and behavioral approaches to the modification of depression. Unpublished doctoral dissertation, Queens University, Ontario, Canada, 1974.

22

The Clinical Potential of Modifying What Clients Say to Themselves

Donald H. Meichenbaum and Roy Cameron

Since Chapter 22 is more a summary of research findings than a description of cognitive therapy techniques, it is useful to point out two basic concepts that underlie the discussion.

First, Meichenbaum and his colleagues, among others, distinguish various ways to conceptualize the client's internal dialogues or cognitions, for example: (1) as automatic and perhaps faulty styles of thinking; (2) as a mediational process between stimulus and response which serves to direct, guide, or inhibit behavior; (3) as a reflection of poor problem-solving skills; (4) as illogical and irrational ideas; and (5) as inadequate coping responses to stressful situations. (The interested reader can find a more complete discussion of alternative conceptualizations in Meichenbaum's chapter in Schwartz and Shapiro's text, Consciousness and Self-Regulation: Advances in Research, *1975.)*

Second, the cognitive-behavioral techniques that Meichenbaum and Cameron discuss take a coping-response perspective on cognition. It may be, argues Meichenbaum, that it is not the incidence of irrational beliefs per se that is the distinguishing characteristic between normal and abnormal populations. Nonclinical populations may also emit many of the irrational premises that characterize clinical populations. Instead, it may be what the nonclinical subjects say to themselves about the irrational beliefs, the coping mechanisms they employ, that forms the distinguishing variable. It may not be the absence of irrational thoughts per se, but rather the set of management techniques employed to cope with such thoughts and feelings that characterizes the nonpatient population.

This coping-skill approach to conceptualizing cognitions leads to the therapeutic procedures which have come to be called stress inoculation training. As the name of the procedure implies, stress inoculation tries to inoculate the client to future stresses by teaching him sets of cognitive and behavioral skills and then exposing him to real and imaginal stressors

Chapter 22 originally appeared in *Psychotherapy: Theory, Research and Practice,* 1974, *11,* 103–117, and is reprinted here by permission of that journal.

whereby he can practice his learned skills. The first treatment phase is educational and provides the client with an explanation of how he becomes emotionally aroused and what he must do to change this reaction. The therapist might, for example, use the A-B-C formula to illustrate that his fear or anger reaction is a result of how he labels and evaluates a situation, rather than a massive and direct reaction to the situation itself.

The second phase of stress inoculation is a rehearsal in which the client and therapist develop and rehearse a series of internal dialogues that help the client: (1) prepare for a stressor ("Here it comes. Now, what can I expect and what is it I have to do?"); (2) handle a stressor ("OK. Stay calm. One step at a time."); (3) cope with possible feelings of being overwhelmed ("When I become afraid, just pause, rate it from 0 to 10. It won't be the worst thing to happen, but probably will be manageable although uncomfortable"); and (4) reinforce himself for coping ("There. You did it! Good job.").

The final stage of stress inoculation has the client test and practice his new coping skills by employing them in stressful situations other than the one in question.

The technique of stress inoculation represents a compatible cognitive technique to add to the typical ones of the rational-emotive therapist. While recognizing the power of the more usual therapeutic tools described throughout this book, one can readily appreciate the value of stress inoculation, particularly with clinical populations such as the retarded, the brain-injured, and the psychotic that are unsuited to more abstract, Socratic techniques.

OUR RESEARCH EFFORTS BEGAN in an attempt to systematically assess the validity of behavior therapy procedures which have been described in a number of comparative studies and clinical case reports. The general research strategy has been to assess the efficacy of "standard" behavior therapy procedures (such as operant and aversive conditioning, modeling, and desensitization) relative to behavior therapy procedures which included a self-instructional component. In general, the results have indicated that when the standard behavior therapy procedures were augmented with a self-instructional package, greater treatment efficacy, more generalization, and greater persistence of treatment effects were obtained. Moreover, when the standard behavior therapy procedures were put under the scrutiny of experimentation, their limitations were highlighted and, in some instances, the basis of their conceptualizations challenged. The byproduct has been the development of new, and possibly more therapeutic, procedures.

One common theme has run through our research findings. It is that behavior therapies in their present form have overemphasized the importance of environmental consequences, thus underemphasizing (and often overlooking) how *S* perceives and evaluates those consequences. Our research on cognitive factors in behavior modification has highlighted the fact that it is not the environmental consequences per se which are of primary importance, but what *S* says to himself about those consequences. However, what *S* says to himself, that is, how he evaluates and interprets these events, is explicitly modifiable by many of the behavior therapy techniques which have been used to modify maladaptive behaviors. The following quasi-chronological summary of our research indicates how we have come to these conclusions.

Origins of Research Program

The research program began with a rather serendipitious finding which was observed in the senior author's Ph.D. dissertation (Meichenbaum, 1969). The study involved a laboratory operant training program in which a group of hospitalized schizophrenic patients were trained to emit "healthy talk" in an interview setting. The effects of operant training generalized over time to a followup interview administered by the experimenter, to a posttest interview administered by a patient confederate, and to other verbal tasks (e.g., proverbs test, word association test) administered under neutral conditions. Interestingly, a number of the schizophrenic patients who had been trained to emit "healthy talk" repeated aloud and spontaneously the experimental instruction "give healthy talk, be coherent and relevant" while being tested on the generalization measures.

This self-instruction seemed to mediate generalization by aiding the subject in attending to the demands of the task, thus preventing any internally generated distracting stimuli from interfering with his language behavior. An intriguing question thus arose: can schizophrenics (and perhaps other clinical populations) be explicitly trained to talk to themselves in such a self-guiding fashion and to spontaneously produce such internally generated discriminative stimuli? A paradigm for training schizophrenics to self-instruct emerged from a series of studies with impulsive children.

Application to Impulsive Children

A series of observational and experimental studies on impulsive children (Meichenbaum, 1971a; Meichenbaum & Goodman, 1969a) indicated that they exercise less verbal control over their motor behaviors and use private speech in a less instrumental fashion than reflective children. Hence it appeared that the impulsive children, like the schizophrenic patients, might benefit from a training procedure to learn how to talk to themselves in a directive, self-regulatory fashion. Developmental literature from the Soviet psychologists Vygotsky (1962) and Luria (1961) inspired the training paradigm. On the basis of his work with children, Luria (1961) has proposed three stages by which the initiation and the inhibition of voluntary motor behaviors come under verbal control. During the first stage, the speech of others, usually adults, controls and directs a child's behavior. The second stage is characterized by the child's own overt speech becoming an effective regulator of his behavior. Finally, the child's covert or inner speech comes to assume a self-governing role.

Our cognitive self-guidance training technique proceeded as follows: first, E performed a task while S observed (E acted as model); then S performed the same task while E instructed S aloud; then S was asked to perform the task again while instructing himself aloud; then S performed the task while whispering; and finally S performed the task while self-instructing covertly. The verbalizations which E modeled and S subsequently used included: (a) questions about the nature of the task; (b) answers to these questions in the form of cognitive rehearsal and planning; (c) self-instruction in the form of self-guidance; and (d) self-reinforcement.

The following is an example of E's modeled verbalizations which S subsequently used (initially overtly, then covertly):

> "Okay, what is it I have to do? You want me to copy the picture with the different lines. I have to go slowly and carefully. Okay, draw the line down, down, good; then to the right; that's it; now down some more and to the left. Good, I'm doing fine so far. Remember, go slowly. Now back up again. No, I was supposed to go down. That's okay. Just erase the line carefully . . . Good. Even if I make an error I can go on slowly and carefully. Okay, I have to go down now. Finished. I did it!"

Note that in this example an error in performance was included and E appropriately accommodated. This feature was included because prior research with "impulsive" children (Meichenbaum & Goodman, 1969a) indicated a marked deterioration in their performance following errors. E's verbalizations varied with the demands of each task, but the general treatment format remained the same throughout. The treatment sequence was also individually adapted to the capabilities of the S and the difficulties of the task.

A variety of tasks was employed to train the child to use self-instructions to control his nonverbal behavior. The tasks varied along a dimension from simple sensorimotor abilities to more complex problem-solving abilities. The difficulty level of the training tasks was increased over the training sessions, requiring more cognitively demanding activities.

One can imagine a similar training sequence in the learning of a new motor skill such as driving a car. Initially, the driver actively goes through a mental checklist, sometimes aloud, which includes verbal rehearsal, self-guidance, and sometimes appropriate self-reinforcement, especially when driving a stick-shift car. Only with repetition do the cognitions become short-circuited and the sequence becomes automatic. If this observation has any merit, then a training procedure which makes these steps explicit should facilitate the development of self-control.

The self-instructional training procedure, relative to placebo and assessment control groups, resulted in significantly improved performance on Porteus Maze, performance IQ on the WISC, and cognitive reflectivity on Kagan's (1966) Matching Familiar Figures test (MFF). The improved performance was evident in a one-month followup. A number of other investigators (Bem, 1967; Karnes et al., 1970; Palkes et al., 1972; Palkes et al., 1968) have also demonstrated the therapeutic value of similar self-instructionally based treatment programs.

In a second study (Meichenbaum & Goodman, 1971), it became evident that the experimenter's cognitive modeling was a necessary but not sufficient condition for engendering self-control in impulsive children. The results indicated that the impulsive child's behavioral rehearsal in self-instructing was an indispensible part of the training procedures. It was necessary that the impulsive child not only be exposed to a self-instructing model, but also "try out" the self-instructions himself. The treatment condition of cognitive modeling alone resulted in the impulsive child's slowing down his performance, but no concomitant reduction in errors on the MFF test. However, cognitive modeling plus self-instructional rehearsal resulted in both a slower and a more accurate performance.

Our recent clinical work with impulsive hyperactive children has raised a number of other treatment considerations. First, the self-instructional training regimen can be supplemented with imagery manipulations, especially in treating young children. One can train the impulsive child to image and to subsequently self-instruct, "I will not go faster than a slow turtle, slow turtle." Secondly, it is often more productive to begin self-instructional training on tasks at which the child is somewhat proficient. The therapist can model the use of self-instructions in the midst of ongoing play activities and in turn have the child incorporate these self-statements into his repertoire. Thus, the therapist can, in a "playful" manner, teach the impulsive child the concept of talking to himself. Thirdly, we have found that it is helpful to evolve toward the complete package of self-statements through a series of successive approximations. Initially, the therapist can model and have the child rehearse simple self-statements such as, "Stop! Think before I answer." Then, over the course of training sessions, the therapist can model (and have the child rehearse) a more complex set of self-statements. Another observation is that children readily seem to accept the demand to "think out loud" as they perform a task, whereas the instruction to "talk aloud to oneself" seems to elicit negative connotations (e.g., that is something crazy people do). The emphasis on playfulness needs to be underscored. In order to gain the impulsive child's attention, the therapist must actively participate in the child's play. For example, while playing with one impulsive boy, the therapist said, "I have to land my airplane, slowly, carefully, into the hanger." The therapist then encouraged the child to have the control tower tell the pilot to go slowly, etc. In this way the therapist was able to have the child build up a repertoire of self-statements to be used on a variety of tasks.

We have employed two additional treatment procedures to train impulsive children to develop better verbal control of their behavior. The first involves the impulsive child's verbally directing another person to perform a task such as Porteus Maze while the child sits on his hands. In this way, the child has to learn to use his language in an instrumental fashion in order to perform the task. Another technique designed to enhance self-control is to have an older impulsive child teach a younger child how to do a task. The impulsive child whose own behavior is actually the target of modification is employed as a "teaching assistant" to model self-instructions for the younger child. In both of these instances, the goal is to have the impulsive child come to appreciate the ways in which language can be used to effect change.

Impulsive children vary markedly in how much training they need. Some require many trials of modeling and many trials of overt self-instructional rehearsal, whereas others may go covert quickly. The speed with which the therapist fades the self-instructional rehearsal depends on the child's performance. The importance of individually tailoring the self-instructional treatment package was illustrated by a study on the development of verbal control by Meichenbaum & Goodman (1969a). They found that forcing first-grade children to talk to themselves aloud while performing a motor control task interferes with performance, whereas younger, kindergarten children benefited from such overt self-instructions.

Finally, it should be made clear that the treatment research results do not necessarily imply that reflective children actually talk to themselves in order to control their behavior. However, if one wishes to encourage an impulsive child to become reflective, then explicitly training him to talk to himself, initially overtly and eventually covertly, will enhance the change process.

Application to Schizophrenics

The next step was to try the self-instructional training paradigm with a group of schizophrenics. In an initial study, hospitalized schizophrenics were successfully trained to talk to themselves in order to improve their performance on attentional and cognitive tasks (Meichenbaum & Cameron, 1973). Using the same modeling and overt-to-covert cognitive rehearsal paradigm as the impulsive children received, schizophrenics were trained to use such self-instructions as "pay attention, listen and repeat instructions, disregard distraction." The cognitive self-guidance training resulted in a significantly improved performance on such tasks as a digit symbol task. On an individual case study basis, several schizophrenic patients were given more extensive self-instructional training (viz., six hours), during which they were trained to monitor their own behavior and thinking as well as interpersonal cues. In this way, the schizophrenic patients were trained to become sensitive to the interpersonal cues (viz., the facial and behavioral reactions of others) which indicated that they were emitting "schizophrenic behaviors" (e.g., bizarre, incoherent, or irrelevant behaviors and verbalizations). Both the interpersonal observations and the self-monitoring provided cues which were to be signals for the patient to emit a set of self-instructions which were "to be relevant and coherent, to make oneself understood." An attempt was made to modify how the schizophrenic perceived, labeled, and interpreted such interpersonal and intrapersonal cues.

The sequence of the self-instructional training regimen took into account Haley's (1963) hypothesis that schizophrenic symptoms function as covert messages aimed at grasping control of social interactions in a devious manner. This hypothesis was recently supported by Shimkunas (1972), who found that as the demand for intense interpersonal relationships increased, the incidence of schizophrenic symptomatology, such as bizarre verbalizations, also increased. Thus, the self-instructional training began with structured sensorimotor tasks where the demands for social interactions and self-disclosure were minimal. On these initial straightforward tasks (e.g., digit symbol, Porteus Maze), the schizophrenics were trained to develop a set of self-controlling self-statements. When the schizophrenics had developed some degree of proficiency in the use of such self-statements, the task demands were slowly increased, requiring more cognitive effort and interpersonal interaction (e.g., proverb interpretation and interviewing). In this way an effort was made to have the schizophrenic initially develop with high response strength a set of self-instructional responses which he could apply in more anxiety-inducing interpersonal situations. Moreover, an attempt was made to have the schizophrenic become aware of instances in which he was using symptomatology to control situations. This recognition was to be a cue to use the self-instructional controls which he had developed on the more simply structured sensorimotor and cognitive tasks.

The specific components of the self-instructional training included: provision of general "set" instructions, use of imagery; monitoring and evaluation of inappropriate responses; and administration of self-reinforcement. These components were presented to the subject via a variety of procedures; namely, administration of instructions (by the experimenter and the subject, overt and covert forms), modeling, provision of examples, behavioral rehearsal, operant chaining and shaping techniques, and discussion. The self-instructional training group, relative to a yoked practice control group, improved on a variety of measures. The consistent pattern of improvement was evident at a three-week followup assessment.

A word of caution is in order concerning the implementation of such self-instructional training with schizophrenics as well as other clinical populations. It is important to insure that the subject does not say the self-statements in a relatively mechanical, rote, or automatic fashion without the accompanying meaning and inflection. This would approximate the everyday experience of reading aloud or silently when one's mind is elsewhere. One may read the paragraph aloud without recalling the content. What is needed instead is modeling and practice in synthesizing and internalizing the meaning of one's self-statements.

With the impulsive children and schizophrenic patients, appropriate self-instructional statements appeared to be absent from the S's repertoires before training. Self-instructional training was used to develop what Luria (1961) calls the "interiorization of language" in these populations. However, a large population of clients, who generally fall under the rubric of "neurotic," seem to emit a variety of maladaptive, anxiety-engendering self-statements. Hence, the goal of intervention is not to remedy the absence of self-statements (as with the schizophrenics and impulsive children), but rather to make the "neurotic" patients aware of the self-statements which mediate maladaptive behaviors and to train them to produce incompatible self-statements and behaviors.

This approach is not basically new: there is a long history of educational and semantic therapies which emphasize cognitive factors and which focus on maladaptive self-verbalizations (e.g., Coue, 1922; Korzybski, 1933; Johnson, 1946; Kelly, 1955; Phillips, 1957; Ellis, 1963; and Blumenthal, 1969). Typical of this view is Shaffer (1947), who defined therapy as a "learning process through which a person acquires an ability to speak to himself in appropriate ways so as to control his own conduct (p. 463)."

The second phase of our research explored the variety of ways "neurotic" clients can be trained to talk to themselves differently. In a series of studies, using such varied populations as speech-anxious, test-anxious, and uncreative college students, phobics, and smokers, a variety of self-instructional training techniques was examined. These treatment procedures included "insight" therapy, desensitization, modeling, anxiety relief, and aversive conditioning, all modified to be consistent with a self-instructional approach.

Application to Neurotics

Interpersonal evaluation anxiety. The therapeutic approach which has most explicitly emphasized the importance of a client's internal verbalizations is the rational-emotive therapy of Ellis (1962). The Ellis approach attempts to make the client aware of his maladaptive self-statements and to change the client's behavior by means of persuasion, encouragement, and education in the form of rational analyses. The first experiment in treating speech-anxious clients (Meichenbaum et al., 1971) was designed to assess the relative merits of such a semantic "insight" therapy approach vs. systematic desensitization. In each case, treatment was conducted on a group basis. The procedure included progressive relaxation training, group hierarchy construction, imagery training, and group desensitization as described by Paul & Shannon (1966). The group "insight" treatment approach emphasized the rationale that speech anxiety is the result of self-verbalizations and internalized sentences which are emitted while thinking about the speech situation. The clients were informed that the goals of therapy were for each S to become aware of ("gain insight into") the self-verbalizations and self-instructions which he emitted in anxiety-evoking interpersonal situations. The group discussed the specific self-verbalizations they emitted in speech situations and interpersonal situations and the irrational, self-defeating and self-fulfilling aspects of such statements. In addition, they learned to produce both incompatible self-instructions and incompatible behaviors.

The major results indicated that the "insight" approach was equally as effective as desensitization in reducing the behavioral and affective indicants of speech anxiety. However, a most interesting post hoc finding was that different types of clients received differential benefit from insight and desensitization treatment. Clients with high social distress who suffered anxiety in many varied situations benefited most from the insight procedure, which attends to and modifies the client's self-verbalizations. More recently, other investigators (Lazarus, 1971; Karst & Trexler, 1970) have also reported successful treatment outcome with a similar rational-emotive-based treatment approach. Desensitization treatment appeared to be significantly more effective with Ss whose speech anxiety was confined to formal speech situations. This latter finding is consistent with an increasing literature (Clarke, 1963; Gelder et al., 1967; Lang & Lazovik, 1963; Lazarus, 1966; Marks & Gelder, 1965; Wolpe, 1961) which suggests that systematic desensitization works well with monosymptomatic phobias, and poorly with so-called free-floating anxiety states.

Test anxiety. Highly test-anxious clients represent another population whose self-statements or thinking processes evidently contribute to maladaptive behavior. Research by a variety of investigators (e.g., Liebert & Morris, 1967; Mandler & Watson, 1966; Wine, 1972) has indicated that high test-anxious persons, in situations in which their performance is being evaluated, spend more of their time (a) worrying about their performance and about how well others are doing; (b) ruminating over alternatives; (c) being preoccupied with such things as feelings of inadequacy, anticipation of punishment, loss of status or esteem, and heightened somatic and autonomic reactions. In other words, a worry component diverts attention away from the task and results in performance decrement. Thus, a treatment procedure aimed at controlling the worry component and the attentional style of the high test-anxious client should improve test performance.

Two studies have been conducted which use different training procedures to teach test anxious college students to talk to themselves differently in order to control their attention. The first sudy (Meichenbaum, 1972) compared the relative efficacy of a cognitive modification treatment procedure with that of desensitization and waiting-list control group. The cognitive modification treatment group combined the "insight"-oriented approach of the previous treatment study of speech anxiety with a modified desensitization procedure. The first aspect of cognitive modification therapy emphasized becoming aware of ("gaining insight into") the thoughts and self-verbalizations which are emitted both prior to and during test situations. The second phase of therapy was designed to train the test-anxious college students to emit task-relevant self-statements and to perform arousal-inhibiting behaviors such as relaxation. Whereas the self-instructional training procedures used thus far had involved explicit rehearsal and practice (e.g., with schizophrenics and impulsive children), the therapeutic strategy to be tried with the test-anxious client was to include self-instructional training as part of the imagery procedure of desensitization. In order to provide such self-instructional training, the desensitization component of the treatment was modified to include coping imagery. The *S*s were asked to visualize coping as well as mastery behaviors, viz., if they became anxious while imaging a scene, they were to visualize themselves coping with this anxiety by means of slow deep breaths and self-instructions to relax and to be task-relevant. The *S*s were encouraged to use any personally generated self-statements which would facilitate their attending to the task and inhibit task-irrelevant thoughts. Only if the coping imagery techniques did not reduce their anxiety were they to signal the therapist, terminate the image, and continue relaxing. Thus, the *S*s in the cognitive modification group rehearsed self-instructional ways of handling anxiety by means of imagery procedures. In this way they provided themselves with a model for their own behavior, one which dealt with the anxiety they were likely to experience in reality.

This self-instructional coping imagery stands in marked contrast to the mastery type imagery used in standard desensitization procedures. In the standard desensitization treatment procedure, the *S* is told to signal if the visualized image elicits anxiety and then to terminate that image and relax. This mastery image is consistent with the principle of counterconditioning which pairs the *S*'s state of relaxation with the visualization of anxiety-eliciting scenes. There is no suggestion within the standard desensitization procedure that, following the completion of therapy, *S* will in fact realize or experience anxiety in the real-life situation. In contrast, the coping imagery procedure required the *S* to visualize the experience of anxiety and ways in which to cope with and reduce such anxiety. The coping imagery technique was designed to have the test-anxious *S* view the anxiety he might experience following treatment as an "ally," a "signal" for employing the previously trained coping techniques of relaxation and self-instructions. The cognitive modification procedure required the client to explicitly rehearse by means of imagery the ways in which he would: (a) appraise, label, and attribute the arousal he would experience; (b) control his thoughts and cope with his anxiety; and, more specifically (c) what he would say to himself in evaluative situations.

The results of the study indicated that a cognitive modification treatment procedure, which attempts to make high test-anxious *S*s aware of the anxiety-engendering self-statements they *do* emit and of incompatible self-instructions and behaviors (viz., relaxation) they *should* emit, was significantly more effective than standard desensitization in reducing test anxiety. The superiority of the cognitive modification treatment group was evident in an analog test situation, on self-report measures, and on grade point average. This improvement was maintained at a one-month follow-up assessment. It is noteworthy that after treatment the Ss in the cognitive modification group did not significally differ from low test-anxious Ss on the performance and self-report measures.

Most significantly, only the Ss in the cognitive modification treatment group reported a posttreatment increase in facilitative anxiety as assessed by the Alpert-Haber anxiety scale (1960). Following treatment, the cognitive modification Ss labeled arousal as facilitative, as a cue to be task-relevant, as a signal to improve their performance. The self-report of reduced perceived anxiety *and* improved academic performance in the cognitive modification Ss is most impressive in light of other investigators' reports (Lang & Lazovik, 1963; Paul, 1966) that desensitization results in modified behavior but a minimal decrease in self-reports of fear and anxiety. Johnson & Sechrest (1968), who conducted a desensitization study of test anxious Ss, failed to obtain changes in self-report on the Alpert-Haber scale and they indicated that verbal behavior of reporting oneself as an anxious student is not dealt with directly by the desensitization procedures. The cognitive modification treatment demonstrated that the cognitions which accompany arousal are modifiable.

Further evidence for the effectiveness of training high test-anxious college students to self-instruct was provided by Wine (1971). Whereas Meichenbaum (1972) used a cognitive rehearsal self-instructional *imagery* procedure, Wine (1971) gave six hours of attentional training which involved the modeling and behavioral rehearsal of self-instructions (i.e., a training procedure similar to that used with the schizophrenics and impulsive children). Subjects in Wine's self-instructional attention training group improved significantly relative to Ss in an "insight" group, who concentrated on the explorations of self-relevant verbalizations, namely, the thoughts they had in evaluative situations. Wine's results suggest that an insight procedure which concentrates only on making Ss aware of their anxiety-engendering self-statements *without* exploring and practicing the use of incompatible self-instructions and behaviors is ineffective in reducing test anxiety and is likely to reinforce a deteriorative process.

One additional note should be made concerning the treatment of speech- and test-anxious adults. In both of the Meichenbaum studies, a comparison was made between the group versus individual administration of the "insight" treatment procedure. In both cases group administration of the "insight" treatment procedure was found to be as effective as individually administered "insight" treatment and thus represents a considerable saving in the therapist's time. In fact, the group administration of the "insight" treatment approach appears easier and somewhat more efficacious than individual administration. In the group administration, the *S*s can readily contribute and benefit by a shared exploration of the personalized cognitive events which they emit and the incompatible cognitions and behaviors they must emit to reduce anxiety and improve performance. In addition, group pressure can be therapeutically employed to encourage and reinforce behavior change.

Low-creativity college students. Interestingly, another population for whom a set of negative self-statements seems to interfere with functioning are college students who perform poorly on creativity tests. When such noncreative *S*s were asked to describe the thoughts and feelings they experienced while taking a battery of creativity tests, they reported task-irrelevant self-critical thoughts (e.g., "I'm not very original or creative. I'm better at organizing tasks than at being creative"), *or* thoughts which disparaged the value of the creativity tests (e.g., "Is this what psychologists mean by creativity, telling all the uses of a brick? What a waste"), *or,* if they did produce a creative response, they devalued their own performance by thinking that, "Anyone could have produced such an answer." Such cognitive activity is obviously counterproductive and likely interferes with the creative process.

Thus, the first aspect of self-instructional training of creativity was to make the *S* aware of the variety of self-statements he emitted which inhibited creative performance. These negative self-statements fall into two general classes: self-attributable statements whereby the *S* questions his own creative powers and those by which he externalizes by devaluating the task or situation.

The second aspect of training was to train *S*s to produce incompatible creativity-engendering self-statements. But what exactly do you train a *S* to say to himself in order to become more creative? Some suggestion for the content of the self-statements come from the burgeoning literature on creativity training (see Parnes & Brunelle, 1967). Three conceptualizations of creativity seem to underlie the range of techniques which have been used to train creativity. The conceptualizations include a mental abilities approach, which emphasizes deliberate training exercises (e.g., Guilford, 1967; Torrance, 1965); an ego analytic levels analysis of thinking, which focuses on the role of the regression of the ego and on associational techniques (e.g., Kris, 1953); and finally an approach which emphasizes the role of general attitudinal set, including factors which characterize creative individuals (e.g., Barron, 1969). Each of these conceptualizations was translated into a set of self-statements which could be modeled and then practiced by *S*s.

The following is an example of the type of self-statements that *E* modeled and *S*s subsequently practiced. In this case the task was product improvement, requiring a list of clever, interesting, and unusual ways of changing a toy monkey so children will have more fun playing with it.

"I want to think of something no one else will think of, something unique. Be freewheeling, no hangups. I don't care what anyone thinks; just suspend judgment. I'm not sure what I'll come up with; it will be a surprise. The ideas can just flow through me. Okay, what is it I have to do? Think of ways to improve a toy monkey. Toy monkey. Let me close my eyes and relax. Just picture a monkey. I see a monkey; now let my mind wander; let one idea flow into another . . . let my ego regress."

After inducing this general set, E then thought aloud as he tried to come up with answers. For example: "Now let me do the task as if I were Gordon" (i.e., William Gordon of Synectics training). "I have to use analogies. Let me picture myself inside the monkey" (i.e., a fantasy analogy).

On another occasion E would model:

"Let me do the task as if I were Osborn who did that brain-storming research. How many different ways can I change the monkey? Remember, the key word is SCRAM. It stands for substitute, combine, rearrange, reverse, adapt, modify, magnify, minify."

Using such procedures, E would continue to provide both obvious and original answers to the task. Throughout the modeling, E often used self-reinforcement by means of manifesting spontaneous affect of pleasure, surprise, eagerness, delight and by saying such things as "good," or "this is fun," etc. E tried to capture a mood of self-mobilization, of determination to do the task, and the desire to translate into answers the excitement of creative thoughts. The modeling also included E's coping with getting into a rut, feeling frustrated, and then talking himself out of it. An example of a set of such coping self-statements would be: "Stop giving the first answer that comes to mind. One doesn't have to press . . . let the ideas just play; let things happen. The ideas seem to have a life of their own. If they don't come now, that's okay. Who knows when they will visit? Remember, no negative self-statements."

Following such modeling, the group practiced talking to themselves while performing on a variety of tasks. Gradually, at the S's own pace, the explicit use of self-statements dropped out of the S's repertoire. Most importantly, Ss were not asked to merely parrot a set of self-statements but, rather, were encouraged to emit the accompanying affect and intention to comply with their self-statements. This involvement can be achieved by a variety of means including: (a) determining the S's conceptualization of creativity and expectations concerning training; (b) explaining the rationale for self-instructional training; (c) having Ss examine their personal experiences to find instances of when they emit similar negative and positive self-statements; (d) having *S*s rehearse or "try on" self-statements while performing personally selected meaningful activities (e.g., hobbies, homework, etc.).

In order to assess the beneficial effects of self-instructional training, two control groups were included in the study. The first group afforded an index of improvement on creativity tests due to factors of attention or placebo effects, exposure to creativity tests during training, and any demand characteristics inherent in our measures of improvement. An attempt was made to include a group which (a) received a type of training based on a conceptualization of creativity which did not emphasize cognitive or self-instructional factors and (b) whose face validity was sufficient to elicit high expectations from *S*s. These criteria were met by a procedure called "focusing" which Gendlin (1969) and his colleagues suggest can be used to enhance creativity. Focusing involves paying attention to one's present feelings and coming to a new formulation about them. In addition to the focusing group, a waiting-list control group was included in the study.

The self-instructional training group, relative to Gendlin's focusing training group and to the untreated waiting-list control group, manifested a significant increase in originality and flexibility on tests of divergent thinking, an increase in preference for complexity, a significant increase in human movement responses to an inkblot test, and concomitant changes in self-concept. In contrast, *S*s in the focusing training group showed no objective improvement on the creativity tests, although they indicated by self-report that they felt more creative.

Moreover, the self-instructional training engendered a generalized set to view one's life style in a more creative fashion. The *S*s reported that they had spontaneously applied the creativity training to a variety of personal and academic problems. This latter observation suggests that psychotherapy clients may benefit from such a self-instructional creativity or problem-solving regimen. Instead of the clinician's dealing with the details of the client's maladaptive behaviors, he could provide the client with self-instructional creativity training for solving personal problems. This suggestion is consistent with D' Zurilla & Goldfried's (1971) view of a problem-solving approach to psychotherapy.

The research with the college students indicated that behavior modification techniques such as desensitization and modeling could be improved by altering them in order to directly modify what clients say to themselves. For example, the addition of an "insight" procedure and coping imagery to the desensitization treatment resulted in greater improvement than standard desensitization. Would other behavior modification procedures similarly benefit from changes designed to directly alter the client's cognitive processes? In separate studies, the modification procedures of modeling, anxiety relief, and aversive conditioning were examined respectively in order to compare the standard "traditional" manner in which the therapy procedure has been used vs. a procedure which would explicitly attempt to modify the client's self-statements as well as his maladaptive behavior.

Phobics. The first study (Meichenbaum, 1971b) examined the use of modeling therapy to alter the self-statements of snake-phobic clients. The modeling study was designed to examine the differential efficacy of having models self-verbalize (i.e., the explicit modeling of self-statements the client could use) vs. the absence of any model verbalizations. A second factor included in the study was the modeling style: multiple models demonstrating coping behaviors (i.e., initially modeling fearful behaviors, then coping behavior, and finally mastery behavior) vs. mastery models, demonstrating only fearless behavior throughout. The results clearly indicated that a coping model who self-verbalizes throughout facilitates greatest behavioral change and most self-report affective change. The effectiveness of a model who verbalizes self-instructions along with self-reassuring and self-rewarding statements was indicated by the fact that five of the nine clients in the coping condition spontaneously overtly self-verbalized in the posttest assessment.

It may be instructive to illustrate the coping verbalizations which were modeled. Initially, the models commented on their anxiety and fear and the physiological accompaniments (sweaty palms, increased heart rate and breathing rate, tenseness, etc.). But at the same time, the models attempted to cope with their fear by such means as instructing themselves: (a) to remain relaxed and calm by means of slow deep breaths; (b) to take one step at a time; (c) to maintain a determination to forge ahead and handle the snake. The models were—to us a colloquial term— "psyching" themselves up to perform each task and, upon completion of that task, they emitted self-rewarding statements and positive affective expressions at having performed the task. One model stated to the snake: "I'm going to make a deal with you. If you don't scare or hurt me, I won't scare or hurt you," and after concluding the final step added, "Wait until I tell my mom I was able to handle a snake barehanded for a full minute; she won't believe it. I'm so happy with myself; I was able to overcome my fear." It is interesting to note that two subjects who observed this series of coping verbalizing statements, upon return to the posttreatment assessment room, stated aloud (in essence): "You (referring to the snake) made a deal with her (referring to the model); I will make a similar deal. If you don't hurt me, I won't hurt you. I'm going to pick you up."

Bandura (1965, 1969) has emphasized that the information which observers gain from models is converted to covert perceptual-cognitive images and covert mediating rehearsal responses which are retained by the client and later used by him as symbolic cues to overt behavior. The results of the modeling study suggest that the explicit modeling of self-verbalizations facilitates the learning process which Bandura has described. It is also interesting to note that treatments which provide clients with techniques that deal with coping styles via modeling films or imagery techniques (as in the previous study with test-anxious clients), facilitate greater behavioral change than do mastery, fearless models, or mastery images.

Another example of the efficacy of therapy designed to modify what clients say to themselves came from a series of studies (Meichenbaum & Cameron, 1972a) on Wolpe & Lazarus' (1966) anxiety relief procedure. The latter authors have described their paradigm and its rationale as follows: "If an unpleasant stimulus is endured for several seconds and is then made to cease almost immediately after a specified signal, that signal will become conditioned to the changes that follow cessation of the uncomfortable stimulus (p. 149)." Typically, the word "calm" is the signal which is paired with the offset of aversive stimulation (usually electric shock). Theoretically, the self-instruction "calm" takes on counterconditioning anxiety-relief qualities which generalize across situations. A number of investigators (Solyom & Miller, 1967; Solyom et al., 1969; Thorpe et al., 1964) have presented data which demonstrate the therapeutic value of such anxiety-relief techniques in alleviating phobic and obsessive behaviors.

The first study in the series further assessed the therapeutic value of Wolpe & Lazarus' (1966) anxiety relief procedure in reducing persistent avoidant fear behavior of harmless snakes. The anxiety relief group received five one-hour sessions of escape and avoidance training in which the self-instructions "relax" and "calm" terminated ongoing shock to the forefinger and eventually avoided the onset of shock. This shock-contingent group was compared to a self-instructional rehearsal group which did not receive shock, and to a waiting list control group. The anxiety relief group was found to facilitate most behavioral and affective change, being significantly improved relative to the rehearsal and control groups.

A second study on the anxiety relief procedure attempted to break new ground. First, we added a self-instructional component to the procedure. Phobic clients in an expanded anxiety relief group now terminated shock by generating and emitting coping self-statements (e.g., "Relax, I can touch the snake; just one step at a time"), rather than by verbalizing a single cue word such as "relax" or "calm." Our second revision of the paradigm involved employing the aversive stimulation as a punishing agent as well as to provide the basis for anxiety relief. The client was asked to verbalize the thoughts associated with his avoidant behavior (e.g.. it's ugly, it's slimy, I won't look at it, etc.). Shock onset was then made contingent upon these verbalizations. Throughout training all self-statements (both positive and negative) were to be said in a meaningful, personalized manner.

In addition to a waiting-list control group, two additional groups were included in study II in order to assess (a) the rehearsal effects of such self-instructional training, and (b) the importance of the contingency of shock onset and offset to the expanded anxiety relief treatment paradigm. The contingency variable was assessed by means of inverting the expanded anxiety paradigm so that now the expression of avoidant thoughts was paired with relief, whereas positive, coping self-instructions were punished.

The results proved most revealing. Consistent findings were found across all behavioral and self-report measures as indicated in the posttest and followup assessment. The two anxiety relief groups (regular and inverted) which employed shock were both equally effective in reducing fears. The cognitive rehearsal group led to less substantial and less consistent behavioral change. Moreover, the two anxiety relief shock groups in study II yielded significantly more change than the anxiety relief clients in study I. The results of studies I and II suggest that: (a) self-instructional training in the form of anxiety relief is an effective treatment procedure in reducing persistent avoidant behavior; (b) the efficacy of Wolpe's anxiety relief paradigm can be enhanced by having the client embellish his self-statements; (c) the addition of shock to the treatment paradigm has a therapeutic benefit in facilitating change; and (d) the importance of the contingency variable and the plausibility of a "conditioning" explanation for treatment efficacy is seriously called into question.

This last finding is especially noteworthy. Two other investigators (Carlin & Armstrong, 1968; McConaghy, 1971) have also recently reported similar instances of therapeutic benefit accruing from noncontingent and inverted aversive conditioning paradigms. These studies, as well as our own research on anxiety relief, render suspect the basic "learning theory" assumptions which have been offered to explain the treatment efficacy of aversive conditioning. A variety of alternative theories deriving from social psychology, such as dissonance theory, attribution theory, and self-perception theory, each provide likely alternative explanations to explain the effects of aversive conditioning. In each case, these theories implicate the importance of the client's cognitions or self-statements to explain treatment efficacy. More research is obviously required to assess the validity of each of these alternative interpretations.

Our research on the anxiety relief procedure suggested that clients were developing a set of self-instructional coping skills which they could employ to deal with the stressor of shock and that these skills were in turn employed by clients in overcoming their fear of snakes. This observation raised the possibility that one could further enhance the client's skills by making the training more explicit and by giving the client application training in a more anxiety-inducing situation. A number of investigators (D'Zurilla, 1969; Goldfried, 1971; Suinn & Richardson, 1971; Zeisset, 1968) have provided data to indicate that a skills training approach followed by an opportunity for application, practice, or rehearsal is effective in reducing anxiety.

Working within a skills training framework, Meichenbaum & Cameron (1972b) developed a stress inoculation training procedure to treat multiphobic clients. The stress inoculation training was designed to accomplish three goals. The first was to "educate" the client about the nature of stressful or fearful reactions; the second, to have the client rehearse various coping behaviors; and finally, to give the client an opportunity to practice his new coping skills in a stressful situation.

The educational phase conceptualized the client's anxiety in terms of a Schacterian model of emotion; that is, the therapist reflected that the client's fear reaction seemed to involve two major elements, namely: (a) his heightened arousal (e.g., increased heart rate, sweaty palms, bodily tension); and (b) his set of anxiety-engendering thoughts and self-statements. The therapist then suggested that treatment would be directed toward helping the client (a) control his psychological arousal by learning how to physically relax and (b) learning how to modify his self-statements along more productive lines. Once having mastered such coping skills, the phobic client was given an opportunity to practice the coping mechanisms in a stress-inducing situation of unpredictable electric shock. Numerous investigators (Elliott, 1966; Previn, 1963; Skaggs, 1926; Thorton & Jacobs, 1971) have demonstrated that unpredictable shock (in terms of intensity and timing) represents a very stressful, anxiety-inducing situation.

One can view this treatment approach as the client receiving an inoculation to stress, one which builds "psychological antibodies," "psychological strategems and skills," which could be employed in a variety of settings which induce anxiety and fear. The skills training treatment approach was designed to translate the phobic client's sense of "learned helplessness" into a feeling of "learned resourcefulness" that he could cope with any anxiety or fear-inducing situation.

An interesting comparison would be to examine the efficacy of treatment procedures which were based upon self-instructions, such as stress inoculation, with a treatment procedure which was based on imagery, such as desensitization. In order to assess the relative effectiveness of the two procedures, a group of multiphobic clients (i.e., phobic to both rats and snakes) were selected for treatment. One group received desensitization treatment (half being desensitized to rats and the other half to snakes). The other groups included two self-instructionally based treatments, namely, stress inoculation training and the expanded anxiety relief regular procedure of study II.

The results proved most interesting. The most effective treatment approach was stress inoculation. These clients showed the most significant improvement in both behavioral approach and self-report measures with respect to both the snake and the rat. The expanded anxiety relief groups did not differ behaviorally from the desensitization group for the feared objects to which the desensitized group had received treatment. However, the desensitization group showed minimal generalization at posttest and only slight improvement at followup to the nondesensitized phobic object. This latter result is consistent with the findings of Meyer & Gelder (1963) and Wolpe (1958, 1961), who indicate that desensitization seems to alleviate only those phobias that are being treated, without mitigating other coexisting phobias which remain at a high level, indicating a specific treatment effect. On the other hand, the clients who received the expanded anxiety relief procedure showed marked reduction in avoidance behavior to both phobic objects.

The stress inoculation training procedure is a complex, multifaceted treatment package and further research is required to assess the relative contribution of the different treatment components. However, one hypothesis which may explain the greater treatment generalization of the self-instructionally based treatment programs as compared to the imagery-based programs may be in the nature of the respective mediators. Visualizing an object or stimulus even is quite different from describing or talking about the same object. The visualization process or imagery which is involved in desensitization is a more concrete representation of specific stimuli and therefore should lead to minimal treatment generalization across multiple phobias. In contrast, the stress inoculation procedure emphasizes words and cognitive coping processes which are more abstract representations of stimulus events and should result in greater treatment generalization. Lang (1968 p. 94) has indicated that "the absence of programs for shaping cognitive sets and attitudes may contribute to the not infrequent failure of transfer of treatment effects." This set of studies, which directly modified what phobic patients said to themselves, demonstrated the importance of such cognitive mediators in behavior modification.

With the increasing demand for individuals to deal with stress, the possibility of providing stress inoculation training is most exciting. It was quite common for clients in the stress inoculation group to spontaneously report that they had successfully used the training procedure in other stress situations, such as final exams and visits to the dentist. One client even taught the procedure to his pregnant wife. One could think of a variety of additional stressors which could be employed for inoculation purposes (e.g., cold pressor test, stress films, fatigue, deprivation conditions, giving speeches, etc.). The more varied and extensive the training to deal with a variety of stressors, the greater likelihood the client will develop a general learning set, a general way to talk to himself in order to cope. The research on stress by Janis (1958) and Lazarus (1966) provides further evidence for the importance of cognitive rehearsal and stress inoculation in learning to cope.

Cigarette smokers. The last behavior modification procedure that was examined in order to determine how a client's self-statements and behavior can be modified was aversive conditioning. The aversive conditioning paradigm typically involves showing the client a taboo stimulus or its representation (e.g., a slide) and when the client responds (as indicated by GSR, penile erection, etc.), he is shocked. Shock is terminated by the reduction of the autonomic arousal or by an instrumental response such as choosing another slide. In some paradigms the onset and offset of shock is made contingent upon the initiation and termination of an instrumental act such as drinking alcohol or smoking. A study was conducted in which the aversive conditioning paradigm was elaborated in order to modify what clients say to themselves. Steffy et al. (1970) treated a group of smokers by making the shock contingent upon the self-statements, thoughts, and images which accompany the smoking act. Termination of the shock was contingent upon the expression of self-instructions to put out the cigarette or such self-statements as not wanting "a cancer weed." In this way an explicit attempt was made to influence the chain of covert behaviors that control the smoking behavior. The clients were very inventive and serious in generating self-persuasive and self-rewarding self-statements which they could use to combat their urges to smoke.

This treatment approach is consistent with Premack's (1970) analysis of the self-control mechanisms which contribute to the termination of smoking behavior. Premack proposed that the decision to stop smoking results in a self-instruction which interrupts the automatic quality of the smoking chain. An increase in self-monitoring of one's smoking behavior sets the stage for such self-instructions. Thus, a treatment procedure which focuses on the development of such self-instructions should prove efficacious.

Postassessment and six-month followup indicated substantial and significant improvement for the treatment group whose attention to covert verbalizations was accentuated as compared to a standard aversive conditioning group. The addition of having the clients verbalize an image while smoking and then making the onset and offset of shock contingent upon the verbalized covert processes was highly effective in modifying what clients say to themselves and in reducing smoking behavior.

Our self-instructional treatment approach might also be applied to aversive conditioning of other clinical populations. For example, if one were treating a pedophile by means of such an aversive conditioning procedure and the conditioned stimuli were slides of young children, the therapist could make the onset of shock contingent upon the meaningful expression of the set of self-statements and descriptive images, feelings, and fantasies the pedophile experiences when confronted by a real child. Shock offset could then be made contingent upon incompatible self-statements which may involve self-instructions that he is mislabeling his arousal as sexual, that he should remove himself from the playground, or that he is not that kind of person.

It should be apparent by now that, as Farber (1963) has indicated, "the one thing psychologists can count on is that their *S*s will talk, if only to themselves; and not infrequently whether relevant or irrelevant, the things people say to themselves determine the rest of the things they do (p. 336)." The present set of studies indicates that the recently developed armamentarium of behavior modification techniques can be successfully used to modify what the client says to himself.

Finally, evidence (Krasner, 1962; Truax, 1966) has convincingly indicated that the therapist can and does significantly influence what the client says to him. Now it is time for the therapist to directly influence what the client says to himself.

References

Alpert, R., & Haber, R. N. Anxiety in academic achievement situations. *Journal of Abnormal and Social Psychology*, 1960, *61*, 207–215.

Bandura, A. Vicarious processes; A case of no-trial learning. In L. Berkowitz (Ed.), *Advances in Experimental Social Psychology*, Vol. 2, New York: Academic Press, 1965.

Bandura, A. *Principles of behavior modification.* New York: Holt, Rinehart & Winston, 1969.

Barron, F. *Creative person and creative process.* New York: Holt, Rinehart & Winston, 1969.

Bates, H., & Katz, M. Development of the verbal regulation of behavior. Proceedings, 78th Annual Convention, APA, 1970, *5*(Part 1), 299–300.

Bem, S. Verbal self-control: The establishment of effective self-instruction. *Journal of Experimental Psychology*, 1967, *74*, 485–491.

Blumenthal, A. The base of objectivist psychotherapy. *The Objectivist*, 1969.

Carlin, A., & Armstrong, H. Aversive conditioning: Learning or dissonance reduction? *Journal of Consulting and Clinical Psychology*, 1968, *32*, 674–678.

Chapman, J., & McGhie, A. A. comparative study of disordered attention of schizopherenia. *Journal of Mental Science*, 1962, *108*, 187–200.

Clarke, D. The treatment of mono-symptomatic phobia by systematic desensitization. *Behaviour Research and Therapy*, 1963, *1*, 63–68.

Coue, E. *The practice of autosuggestion.* New York: Doubleday, 1922.

Davison, G. Systematic desensitization as a counter-conditioning process. *Journal of Abnormal Psychology,* 1968, *73,* 91–99.

D'Zurilla, T. Reducing heterosexual anxiety. In J. Krumboltz and C. Thoresen (Eds.), *Behavioral counseling: Cases and techniques.* New York: Holt, Rinehart and Winston, 1969.

D'Zurilla, T., & Goldfried, M. Problem solving and behavior modification. *Journal of Abnormal Psychology,* 1971, *78,* 107–126.

Elliott, R. Effects of uncertainty about the nature and advent of a noxious stimuli (shock) upon heart rate. *Journal of Personality and Social Psychology,* 1966, *3,* 353–356.

Ellis, A. *Reason and emotion in psychotherapy.* New York: Lyle Stuart, 1962.

Farber, I. The things people say to themselves. *American Psychologist,* 1963, *6,* 185–197.

Geer, J., & Turtletaub, A. Fear reduction following observation of a model. *Journal of Personality and Social Psychology,* 1967, *6,* 327–331.

Gelder, M., Marks, I., Wolff, H., & Clarke, M. Desensitization and psychotherapy in the treatment of phobic states: A controlled inquiry. *British Journal of Psychiatry,* 1967, *113,* 53–73.

Gendlin, E. Focusing. *Psychotherapy: Theory, Research and Practice,* 1969, *6*(1), 4–15.

Goldfried, M. Systematic desensitization as training in self-control. *Journal of Consulting and Clinical Psychology,* 1971, *37,* 228–235.

Guilford, J. Some theoretical views of creativity. In H. Helson & W. Bevan (Eds.), *Contemporary approaches to psychology.* New York: Van Nostrand, 1967.

Haley, J. *Strategies of psychotherapy.* New York: Grune & Stratton, 1963.

Janis, I. *Psychological stress: Psychoanalytic and behavioral studies of surgical patients.* New York: Wiley, 1958.

Johnson, W. *People in quandaries.* New York: Harper, 1946.

Johnson, S., & Sechrest, C. Comparison of desensitization and progressive relaxation in treating test anxiety. *Journal of Consulting and Clinical Psychology,* 1968, *32,* 280–286.

Kagan, J. Reflection-impulsivity: The generality and dynamics of conceptual tempo. *Journal of Abnormal Psychology,* 1966, *71,* 17–24.

Karnes, M., Teska, J., & Hodgins, A. The effects of four programs of classroom intervention on the intellectual and language development of 4-year-old disadvantaged children. *American Journal of Orthopsychiatry,* 1970, *40,* 58–76.

Karst, T., & Trexler, L. Initial study using fixed role and rational-emotive therapy in treating public-speaking anxiety. *Journal of Consulting and Clinical Psychology,* 1970, *34,* 360–366.

Kelly, G. *The psychology of personal constructs.* Vol. 2. New York: Norton, 1955.

Korzybski, A. *Science and sanity.* Lancaster, Pa.: Lancaster Press, 1933.

Krasner, L. The therapist as a social reinforcement machine. In H. Strupp & L. Lubrosky (Eds.), *Research in psychotherapy,* Vol. 3. Washington, D.C.: APA, 1962.

Kris, E. *Psychoanalytic explorations in art.* London: Allen & Unwin, 1953.

Lang, P. Fear reduction and fear behavior: Problems in treating a construct. In J. M. Shlien (Ed.), *Research in psychotherapy.* Vol. 3. Washington, D.C.: APA, 1968.

Lang, P. The mechanics of desensitization and the laboratory study of human fear. In C. Franks (Ed.), *Assessment and status of the behavior therapies.* New York: McGraw-Hill, 1969.

Lang, P., & Lazovik, A. Experimental desensitization of a phobia. *Journal of Abnormal and Social Psychology,* 1963, *66,* 519–525.

Lazarns, A. *Behavior therapy & beyond.* New York: McGraw-Hill, 1971.

Lazarus, A., & Rachman, S. The use of systematic desensitization in psychotherapy. In H. Eysenck (Ed.), *Behavior therapy and the neurosis.* London: Pergamon, 1960.

Lazarus, R. *Psychological stress and the coping process.* New York: McGraw-Hill, 1966.

Liebert, R., & Morris, L. Cognitive and emotional components of test anxiety: A distinction and some initial data. *Psychological Reports,* 1967, *20,* 975–978.

Luria, A. *The role of speech in the regulation of normal and abnormal behavior.* New York: Liveright, 1961.

Mandler, K., & Watson, D. Anxiety and the interruption of behavior. In C. Spielberger (Ed.), *Anxiety and behavior.* New York: Academic Press, 1966.

Marks, I., Boulougouris, J., & Marset, P. Flooding versus desensitization in the treatment of phobic patients. *British Journal of Psychiatry,* 1971, *119,* 353–375.

Marks, I., & Gelder, M. A controlled retrospective study of behavior therapy in phobic patients. *British Journal of Psychiatry,* 1965, *3,* 561–573.

McConaghy, N. Aversive therapy of homosexuality: Measures of efficacy. *American Journal of Psychiatry,* 1971, *127,* 1221–1223.

Meichenbaum, D. The effects of instructions and reinforcement on thinking and language behaviors of schizophrenics. *Behavior Research and Therapy,* 1969, *7,* 101–114.

Meichenbaum, D. The nature and modification of impulsive children. Paper presented at the Society for Research in Child Development, Minneapolis, 1971(a).

Meichenbaum, D. Examination of model characteristics in reducing avoidance behavior. *Journal of Personality and Social Psychology,* 1971, *17,* 298–307. (b)

Meichenbaum, D. Enhancing creativity by modifying what *S*'s say to themselves. Unpublished manuscript, University of Waterloo, 1972.

Meichenbaum, D. Cognitive modification of test anxious college students. *Journal of Consulting and Clinical Psychology,* 1972, *39,* 370–380. (b)

Meichenbaum, D. Therapist manual for cognitive behavior modification. Unpublished manuscript, University of Waterloo, 1974.

Meichenbaum, D., & Cameron, R. An examination of cognitive and contingency variables in anxiety relief procedures. Unpublished manuscript, University of Waterloo, 1972(a).

Meichenbaum, D., & Cameron, R. Reducing fears by modifying what clients say to themselves: A means of developing stress inoculation. Unpublished manuscript, University of Waterloo, 1972(b).

Meichenbaum, D., & Cameron, R. Training schizophrenics to talk to themselves: A means of developing attentional controls. *Behavior Therapy,* 1973, *4,* 515–534.

Meichenbaum, D., Gilmore, J., & Fedoravicius, A. Group insight vs. group desensitization in treating speech anxiety. *Journal of Consulting and Clinical Psychology,* 1971, *36,* 410–421.

Meichenbaum, D., & Goodman, J. Reflection-impulsivity and verbal control of motor behavior. *Child Development,* 1969, *40,* 785–797. (a)

Meichenbaum, D., & Goodman, J. The developmental control of operant motor responding by verbal operants. *Journal of Experimental Child Psychology,* 1969, *7,* 553–565. (b)

Meichenbaum, D., & Goodman, J. Training impulsive children to talk to themselves: A means of developing self-control. *Journal of Abnormal Psychology,* 1971, *77,* 115–126.

Meyer, V., & Gelder, M. Behavior therapy and phobic disorders. *British Journal of Psychiatry,* 1963, *109,* 19–28.

Paivio, A. Mental imagery in associative learning and memory. *Psychological Review,* 1969, *76,* 241–263.

Paivio, A. On the functional significance of imagery. *Psychological Bulletin,* 1970, *73,* 385–392.

Palkes, H., Stewart, M., & Freedman, J. Improvement in maze performance of hyperactive boys as a function of verbal-training procedures. *Journal of Special Education,* 1972, *5,* 337–342.

Palkes, H., Stewart, W., & Kahana, B. Porteus maze performance of hyperactive boys after training in self-directed verbal commands. *Child Development,* 1968, *39,* 817–826.

Parnes, S., & Brunelle, E. The literature of creativity. Part 1. *Journal of Creative Behavior,* 1967, *1,* 52–109.

Paul, G. *Insight vs. desensitization in psychotherapy: An experiment in anxiety reduction.* Stanford: Stanford University Press, 1966.

Paul, G., & Shannon, D. Treatment of anxiety through systematic desensitization in therapy groups. *Journal of Abnormal Psychology,* 1966, *71,* 124–135.

Phillips, F. *Psychotherapy: A modern theory and practice.* Englewood Cliffs, N.J.: Prentice-Hall, 1957.

Premack, D. Mechanisms of self-control. In W. Hunt (Ed.), *Learning and mechanisms of control in smoking.* Chicago: Aldine, 1970.

Previn, L., The need to predict and control under conditions of threat. *Journal of Personality,* 1963, *31,* 570–585.

Shaffer, L. The problem of psychotherapy. *American Psychologist,* 1947, *2,* 459–467.

Shimkunas, A. Demand for intimate self-disclosure and pathological verbalizations in schizophrenia. *Journal of Abnormal Psychology,* 1972, *80,* 197–205.

Skaggs, E. Changes in pulse, breathing and steadiness under conditions of startledness and excited expectancy. *Journal of Comparative and Physiological Psychology,* 1926, *6,* 303–318.

Solyom, L., Kenny, F., & Ledwidge, B. Evaluation of a new treatment paradigm for phobias. *Canadian Psychiatric Association Journal,* 1969, *14,* 3–9.

Solyom, L., & Miller, S. Reciprocal inhibition by aversion relief in the treatment of phobias. *Behavior Research and Therapy,* 1967, *5,* 313–324.

Steffy, R., Meichenbaum, D., & Best, A. Aversive and cognitive factors in the modification of smoking behavior. *Behavior Research and Therapy,* 1970, *8,* 115–125.

Suinn, R., & Richardson, R. Anxiety management training: A nonspecific behavior therapy program for anxiety control. *Behavior Therapy,* 1971, *2,* 498–510.

Thorpe, J., Schmidt, E., Brown, P., & Castell, D. Aversion-relief therapy: A new method for general application. *Behavior Research and Therapy,* 1964, *2,* 71–82.

Thornton, J., & Jacobs, P. Learned helplessness in human subjects. *Journal of Experimental Psychology,* 1971, *87,* 367–372.

Torrance, E. *Rewarding creative behavior.* Englewood Cliffs, N.J.: Prentice-Hall, 1965.

Truax, C. Reinforcement and nonreinforcement in Rogerian psychotherapy. *Journal of Abnormal Psychology,* 1966, *71,* 1–9.

Valins, S., & Ray, A. Effects of cognitive desensitization on avoidance behavior. *Journal of Personality and Social Psychology,* 1967, *7,* 345–350.

Vygotsky, L. *Thought and Language.* New York: Wiley, 1962.

Wine, J. Test anxiety and direction of attention. *Psychological Bulletin,* 1971, *76,* 92–104.

Wine, J. Investigations of attentional interpretation of test anxiety. Unpublished doctoral dissertation, University of Waterloo, Waterloo, Ontario, 1972.

Wolpe, J. *Psychotherapy by reciprocal inhibition.* Stanford: Stanford University Press, 1958.

Wolpe, J. The systematic desensitization treatment of neuroses. *Journal of Mental Disease,* 1961, *132,* 189–203.

Wolpe, J., & Lazarus, A. *Behavior therapy techniques.* New York: Pergamon Press, 1966.

Zeisset, R. Desensitization and relaxation in the modification of patients' interview behavior. *Journal of Abnormal Psychology,* 1968, *73,* 18–24.

23

Personal Science: A Cognitive Learning Therapy

Michael J. Mahoney

Chapter 23 describes a therapeutic approach removed from the mainstream of rational-emotive psychotherapy, yet within the cognitive-behavioral camp, as is RET, and sharing with RET many important things. Like RET, Michael Mahoney's "Personal Science" emphasizes the teaching of broad coping skills to the client so that he or she may function more independently and effectively. It attempts to teach the client to become a responsible agent of self-control or self-regulation via the development of a set of personally relevant problem-solving skills. It views the therapist as a coach or consultant who collaborates with the client in applying various techniques to problem-solving.

Personal Science represents a cognitive-learning approach to treatment that takes the client through seven steps in personal problem-solving. The client learns to: (1) specify general problem areas; (2) collect data; (3) identify patterns or sources, including cognitive sources of problems; (4) examine options, including cognitive change options; (5) narrow and experiment; (6) compare data of change; and (7) extend, revise, or replace. Mahoney discusses each stage and offers techniques for accomplishing the goals of each.

ONE OF THE MAIN GOALS of clinical science is to provide clients with experiences which will enhance their adaptation and growth. Judging from the track records of traditional therapies, that goal is not easy to achieve. To date most psychotherapies have failed in one or more of the following areas:

1. *effectiveness,* particularly as defined from the client's perspective;
2. *generalization* of positive effects to situations and experiences outside the therapy enterprise;
3. *maintenance* of positive effects for prolonged periods of time;
4. *cost-efficiency* as measured by both monetary and phenomenological standards; and
5. *ethics,* respect for the client's rights and responsibilities.

The therapeutic paradigm presented here does not purport to have resolved all of these issues, but it does claim improvement over traditional approaches. While its effectiveness needs further evaluation, the preliminary data suggest that it has made a promising start (cf. Mahoney, 1974; Arnkoff & Mahoney, 1977, in press; Meichenbaum, 1974, 1977; Beck, 1976; Goldfried & Goldfried, 1975).

Relative to the five aforementioned areas, this would seem to warrant a cautious optimism. First, personal science is specifically geared toward personal effectiveness. The client is encouraged to continue and expand only those techniques which have been constructive or successful in personally conducted experiments. Second, because it emphasizes broad coping skills, this approach specifically addresses the issues of generalization and maintenance. Likewise, in its emphasis on helping the client to become a responsible agent of self-change, it may offer substantial advantages in cost-efficiency and the protection of client's rights.

The model presented here might be called *personal science* in that it applies empirical skills of problem-solving to intimate personal problems. It is a cognitive-learning therapy in that it recognizes the simultaneous importance of cognitive *processes* and learning *procedures* (Bandura, 1975). It adopts a broad coping skills perspective in combination with a bias toward self-regulation and cybernetic problem-solving. Its roots can be traced back well over two decades (cf. Kelly, 1955) and probably even further; I shall not here attempt to delineate its history and development. Suffice it to say that it draws upon literatures ranging from personality theory and social psychology to information processing and psychophysiology (cf. Mahoney, 1974). In this approach, the therapist is viewed as a technical consultant or coach whose assistance will primarily take the form of instruction and training in the development of relevant coping skills. Therapy is used as an apprenticeship in these skills, and the role of the client is therefore one of active collaboration and participation.

A general outline of the personal scientist approach is presented in Table 1. The overall orientation which is presented to the client is one of problem-solving and growth, rather than rehabilitation or medical cure. Personal distress is viewed as an understandable consequence of unfortunate exigencies and/or inadequacies in the development or utilization of coping skills. The client is informed that counseling will involve a collaborative endeavor in which both he and the therapist cooperate in collecting information, assessing the problem(s), selecting and implementing therapeutic options, and so on. Critical emphasis is placed upon the importance of accurate information—particularly as this is provided by client self-report, structured recording systems, etc.

The personal science sequence is divided into seven steps, which are mnemonically represented by the letters in the word "science." These seven steps are as follows:

S   Specify general problem area;
C   Collect data;
I   Identify patterns or sources;
E   Examine options;
N   Narrow and experiment;
C   Compare data;
E   Extend, revise, or replace.

Table 1

General Schema of Personal Science

S   *Specify general problem area*
    1. *Labeler*—who says it is a problem?
    2. *Affect,* e.g., anxiety, depression, anger, frustration.
    3. *Sphere,* vocational, medical, financial, social relationship, self-concept, etc.
    4. *Urgency,* e.g., suicide, imminent events.
    5. *Goals*—short-term and long-term.

C   *Collect data*
    1. *Biomedical status,* as reflected in current health condition, medical examination, nutrition, sleep and activity patterns, etc.
    2. *Cognitive status,* personal perception of the problem and its cause, outcome expectancies, locus of control, attribution, perceived options, perception of the nature of therapy and personal role in therapy, etc.
    3. *Affective status,* especially in terms of extreme sympathetic arousal and/or apathy-helplessness; attention is given to ANS prerequisites for optimal learning.
    4. *Assessment of problem-relevant skills,* e.g., social communication (verbal and nonverbal), assertiveness, ability to control autonomic arousal—via direct (in vivo) or analog assessment; emphasis placed on assets as well as liabilities.
    5. *Current physical, social, and phenomenological correlates,* as suggested by self-monitoring, behavioral diary, reports from significant others, etc.
    6. *Retrospective assessment*—problem history and development.

I   *Identify patterns or sources*
    1. *Portion primarily attributable to physical environment,* e.g., physical living conditions, biomedical status, finances.
    2. *Portion primarily attributable to social environment,* e.g., family, intimate relationships, nonintimate relationships.
    3. *Portion primarily attributable to cognitive factors and/or skill deficiencies,* e.g., irrational beliefs, self-arousal patterns, maladaptive fantasies, unrealistic performance standards,

E   *Examine options*
   1. *Survey potential goals*
      a. *Physical environment options,* e.g., alteration of problem-relevant stimuli, prearrangement of response consequences.
      b. *Social environment options,* e.g., participation of significant others in counseling, expansion of social contacts.
      c. *Cognitive environment options,* e.g., belief alterations via cognitive restructuring, self-instruction, coping skills training, problem-solving training.
   2. *Survey potential means*
      a. *Stimulate,* e.g., via programmed cueing, response priming, stimulus control, self-instruction.
      b. *Motivate,* e.g., reward or punishment systems, symbolic self-evaluation, rationalization, engineering social support.
      c. *Graduate,* division of problem(s) into manageable and specific subunits; usually with hierarchialization according to temporal sequence, approximation of a stimulus, approximation of a response, approximation of a contingency, work or distress involved, urgent priority, etc.
      d. *Imitate,* e.g., select a *coping* model and attempt role-playing and reproduction of relevant patterns.
      e. *Practice,* emphasis on symbolic (cognitive), analog (e.g., role-playing), and actual rehearsal of relevant skills with attention focused on their execution, their consequences, and their attribution.

N   *Narrow and experiment*
   1. *Eliminate unfeasible options,* e.g., those which would be physically impossible or illegal.
   2. *Eliminate least-feasible options,* e.g., those which are deemed less likely to succeed or poor in cost-efficiency.
   3. *Select or consolidate most-feasible option(s).*
   4. *Rehearse the option and its consequences,* e.g., via mental imagery.
   5. *Revise (if necessary) and implement.*

C   *Compare data*
   After a reasonable period of personal experimentation, compare initial and present indices of the target phenomenon. Look for *any changes* (desirable or undesirable) in:
   1. *Frequency.*
   2. *Intensity or magnitude.*
   3. *Duration.*
   4. *Patterning.*

E   *Extend, revise, or replace*
   1. *Continue or expand,* if the data reflect a reasonable degree of progress.
   2. *Revise,* when so doing might make the strategy more effective, cost-efficient, comfortable, etc.

3. *Replace,* if the data suggest no change or deteriorization.
   Note: negative results are always informative. Before cycling back to alternate options, consider:
   a. *Validity:* Are you confident in the accuracy of the data upon which you are basing your evaluation?
   b. *Follow-through:* Are you confident that the option(s) selected were conscientiously implemented?
   c. *Tenure:* Was the experiment given sufficient time to adequately test the option(s)?
   d. *Undetected progress:* Are there signs of change or improvement which may not have been noticed?
   e. *Implications:* Do these experimental results reflect poor problem definition, inadequate identification of patterns or sources, deficient options or poor option selection, unanticipated obstacles to implementing options, etc.?
4. *Assess attribution:* Are the obtained results being attributed to personal causation?

The object of clinical apprenticeship, of course, is not simply to guide the client through a series of inflexible assignments. Rather, it is to set up learning experiences which will facilitate the development of coping skills which are relevant to the current problem as well as future or additional areas of personal crisis. The 7-stage sequence is intended to optimize opportunities to develop these skills. By providing the client with a mnemonic blueprint for personal problem-solving, generalization and maintenance are hopefully facilitated.

In stage one of the personal science paradigm, the client is assisted in defining the area or areas which are of current concern in his or her adjustment. This is primarily accomplished via direct questioning and reflective listening. Since therapists often impose some of their own diagnostic biases on their clients' complaints, particular attention is given to the importance of phenomenology (the client's perception of the problem). Likewise, every effort is made to encourage a receptive and supportive atmosphere which will be conducive to self-disclosure and candid information-gathering. To minimize categorical and labeling biases, questions directed to the client are intentionally open-ended (e.g., "How do you feel?) rather than restrictive (e.g., "Are you depressed?"). The client's short-term and long-term goals are solicited, along with his or her expec· tancies regarding therapy outcome. In cases of extreme arousal, panic, or fatigue, immediate attention is given to client support and reassurance and the therapist assumes a more directive role. This directiveness is gradually decreased at later stages in accordance with the client's development of independent coping skills.

In the second therapeutic stage, more specific information is collected on the parameters and correlates of the presenting problem. Biomedical status becomes a first concern, and the possible role of malnutrition, sleep disturbance, and other physiological factors is evaluated. Attention is given to the history of the problem, and particularly to aspects of the client's autobiography which may be relevant to his current situation, e.g., religious beliefs and parental patterns of problem resolution. Where appropriate, psychometric tests such as the Beck Depression Inventory are employed. Homework assignments are used to clarify aspects of the client's self-concept, attributions, and problem-relevant skills. The greatest assessment focus, however, is directed at three methods of information-gathering: (1) self-observation; (2) analog assessment, and (3) direct observation of in vivo performance. The self-observation may take many forms—ranging from a global daily self-rating scale to a structured checklist or an open-ended behavioral diary. Practical aspects of designing and implementing these systems have been discussed elsewhere (Mahoney, 1976a). The client's participation in data collection is emphasized as an important element in both the process and outcome of therapy. Since therapeutic techniques will be partly determined by assessment of data and ongoing evidence of change (or no change) in the client's distress, the accuracy and comprehensiveness of that personal data can hardly be over-emphasized. Self-observation may also lend reactive benefits to the situation and underscores the client's active role in his own apprenticeship. This may be an important factor in influencing attributions of improvement.

In addition to client-collected data, analog assessments are conducted. These may take the form of role-playing (e.g., to assess social skills or assertiveness), or they may involve covert (symbolic) performances. In the latter, a client might be asked to generate a "mental movie" of heterosexual interaction (e.g., approaching a person and asking her for a date). The clients's narrative during this exercise may reveal important aspects of his problem. When given this task, for example, a client might describe his imagery as follows:

> "I go up to this girl who is in my math class. She is not very pretty. She doesn't look up when I get near her. I say 'Excuse me,' and she looks at me very suspiciously. She looks like she is dreading something. I am sweating a lot and my hands are all wet. I say 'Would you be interested in going to a movie with me?' She looks shocked, stares down at her feet and I feel sick. I begin to stammer and she bursts out laughing."

This brief hypothetical episode may contain important clinical considerations. For example, the fact that the girl in the scene was unattractive may reflect that the client feels inadequate or unworthy of attractive partners. His description of her as seeming "suspicious" and "dreading something" suggests that he may be attributing many of his own negative self-evaluations to her—expecting her to be avoidant. Such an expectation might have serious self-fulfilling characteristics in social interactions. By acting the role of a to-be-avoided person, the client may be molding many of the social reactions he encounters. Finally, his imagining her laughter in response to his invitation may reflect unrealistically catastrophic beliefs about the consequences of being heterosexually assertive. This technique of covert assessment is obviously projective in some respects, but it may often reveal important and idiosyncratic aspects of a client's beliefs, coping skills, and general reality contact.

Direct naturalistic observation is sometimes unfeasible, but is often considered one of the preferred methods of information-gathering. Home visits in the case of marital or family counseling may offer valuable insights into coping skills and problem patterns. Reactivity is again a problem, however, and efforts are made to combine several different methods of assessment to increase the likelihood of accurate, relevant, and representative information-gathering.

The third stage of therapy involves identification of possible factors which may have been involved in either the development or maintenance of the problem. Three general categories are considered: aspects of the physical environment, aspects of the social environment, and cognitive or skill factors. For many clinical problems, of course, all three of these categories may be represented. The identification of patterns or sources must take into account not only the client's perceptions of causation, but also any spatiotemporal correlations between episodes of distress and various environmental parameters. For example, in the case of a client with anxiety attacks, what are the events and stimuli associated with the attacks? Are there temporal patterns (time of day, day of week, part of month, season)? Do they occur more frequently in some physical situations than in others (home, office, auto)? Are certain persons consistently present or absent? What thoughts or images preceded the attack? What were its immediate and long-term consequences? The accurate identification of problem sources is, of course, an important prerequisite to effective problem resolution.

In the fourth personal science stage, possible solutions are examined. These are divided into goals (changes to be effected) and *means* for implementing those goals. Identification of these options may be facilitated by (but should not be restricted to) a matrix such as the one in Table 2. Fundamental strategies of intervention are here crossed with the three basic environments (physical, social, cognitive). During this phase of therapy, emphasis is placed on developing creative skills in *generating*

Table 2

An Option Matrix

	Environment		
Strategy	Physical	Social	Cognitive
Stimulus control	Regulation of relevent physical cues (e.g., an alarm clock)	Regulation of relevant social cues (e.g., a discussion group)	Regulation of relevant thoughts, images, fantasies (e.g., self-instruction, self-relaxation)
Motivation	Regulation of automatic physical consequences (e.g., a seat belt buzzer)	Regulation of social feedback (e.g., by publicly announcing progress and/or requesting encouragement)	Regulation of self-evaluative patterns (e.g., self-reward, self-punishment)
Gradation	Regulation of successive physical demands (e.g., stimulus encountered, response required, etc.)	Regulation of successive social demands (e.g., hierarchy for heterosexual anxiety)	Regulation of successive self-demands (e.g., goals, performance standards)
Modeling	Observation of nonhuman models (e.g., a computer, an animal, etc.)	Observation of persons performing a targeted response (e.g., in films, lectures, etc.)	Imaginal observation of a model performing a targeted response (e.g., in covert modeling)
Practice	Rehearsal without other persons present (e.g., as in practicing a speech alone)	Rehearsal with other persons present (e.g., role playing, analog practice, etc.)	Rehearsal via such cognitive processes as imagery (e.g., "mental practice" by athletes)

options (regardless of their feasibility). Stimulus-control options include such procedures as self-instruction and self-relaxation. Since the client may be unaware of some of these strategies, it is the therapists's responsibility to increase client awareness of options and provide whatever skills training may be required. The gradation strategies may include (a) approximation of a response (e.g., in assertiveness training); (b) approximation of a stimulus (e.g., in a phobic hierarchy); (c) approximation of a contingency (e.g., in standard setting); or (d) any combination of the above. Likewise, practice of a targeted performance may be combined with gradation such that a client moves from imaginal (symbolic) rehearsal to live analog practice and, finally, actual in vivo performance.

The fifth stage requires a narrowing of the possible options to those which are most feasible and promising. This is usually accomplished via a process of successive elimination. Evaluation of feasibility and unanticipated complications can often be facilitated by having the client cognitively rehearse each contending option. For example, a person experiencing marital difficulties may perceive divorce as a simple and sure-fire solution until he or she is asked to act out this option in a mental movie. A step-by-step narrative on "what life would be like if . . ." may reveal overlooked difficulties which might be reduced or avoided by appropriate foresight. When the most feasible option has been selected, it is implemented in the form of a personal experiment.

Ongoing collection of data is necessary to evaluate the impact of this self-change enterprise. In the sixth stage, the effects of the personal experiment are assessed by comparing current problem parameters (e.g., frequency, intensity, duration) to those present prior to intervention. Depending on the outcome of that comparison, the experimental solution is either extended, revised, or replaced (stage seven). In personal science there are no "unsuccessful" experiments in the sense that all are informative, potentially constructive in their information content, and embody the critically important process of scientific hypothesis-testing. Before an option is declared unsuccessful, other possible interpretations are considered (e.g., inaccurate data, inconsistent application, or insufficient evaluation). Should it still appear to have been unsuccessful, the sources of this are constructively considered (e.g., poor problem analysis, inappropriate goal setting, or poor option selection).

The client's successful apprenticeship in coping skills training can also be facilitated by several aspects of the therapist's behavior. For example, he can model many of the problem-solving skills which are being recommended to the client. In fact, the modeling experiences provided by the therapist may constitute one of his most valuable contributions (Bandura, 1974). Recent studies have begun to suggest that the form which this modeling takes may be very important (e.g., Meichenbaum, 1971; Kazdin, 1974a, b, c). These investigations have addressed the distinction between a "coping" model and a "mastery" model. A coping model is one who shows signs of fallibility, initial distress, and apprehension, while a mastery model performs effortlessly and without error. In a sense, the mastery model is a movie-star version of the perfect client—self-confident, motivated, and competent in a variety of skills. The coping model, on the other hand, shows initial signs of self-doubt, his performance often reflects a sometimes crude trial-and-error perseverance rather than Hollywood perfection. In the experimental studies comparing these two model forms, the coping model eventually arrives at the same level of performance as that demonstrated by the mastery model. The major difference is in their route and the relative ease with which they have reached their destinations. Although the data here are still quite preliminary, the available studies have reported greater effectiveness on the part of coping models in reducing avoidance patterns.

I have incorporated the coping model strategy into my own clinical endeavors (as well as my conduct of clinical supervision), and the results have been subjectively encouraging. While there are undoubtedly clients who might better respond to a mastery (high placebo, high prestige) model, I believe that a large percentage of clients may be significantly aided by the use of a coping model in therapy. This does not require total and unrestrained self-disclosure on the part of the therapist, but it does necessitate what I think is a reasonable and therapeutic revelation: i.e., that life is basically a coping process in which a person attempts to react to and influence the complex and ever-changing array of factors which may be of personal relevance to him.

Therapists who criticize the iatrogenic effects of psychiatric diagnosis and classification but who are unwilling or unable to admit that their own lives include personal problems should evaluate the implicit message contained in this hypocrisy. If psychotherapy is indeed a learning process and if psychological problems are primarily a reflection of maladaptive histories and/or deficient coping skills, it should come as no surprise to either the therapist or the client that there are no paragons of adjustment. The therapist may be more skilled and experienced in coping, but this does not mean that he will always cope perfectly or that he is always well-prepared for any exigencies.

In my own endorsement of this strategy, I find it useful to view psychotherapy (and indeed, life itself) as a process rather than a product, a journey rather than a destination. Absolute lists and perfect adjustment are unattainable goals. The client who naively believes that one morning he will wake up to find himself "cured" (normal, healthy, etc.) may be in for some very rude clinical awakenings. If he is waiting for the moment when he will have his life "totally together" and will be able to face a future of self-confidence, happiness, and the *total* absence of future problems, he may find that his wait is an exceedingly long one. In fact, I often consider it one of the best signs of clinical progress when a client comes to recognize that his adjustment and coping skills can always be improved —but never perfected. In one sense, he has "arrived" in realizing that arrival is impossible. By sharing this realistic coping philosophy, the therapist may also help the client to set more reasonable goals for therapeutic improvement and long-range personal growth. Inequity, uncertainty, and change are inevitable aspects of human life. Coping does not, however, mean a simple passive acceptance of these realities. Rather, it entails a tolerance for personal variance, an acceptance of those aspects of one's life which are indeed immutable, and an active commitment to maximizing one's personal impact on the forces which shape one's life.

In addition to the use of a coping model strategy, the therapist can also employ those options which are recommended in the personal science approach (cf. Table 2). In my opinion, the five most powerful techniques utilized by helping professionals have been: (1) stimulus control, (2) motivational incentives, (3) task gradation, (4) observational learning, and (5) active practice. The therapist should give appropriate attention to each of these options, and particularly to the manners by which they could be incorporated into his clinical conduct. For example, I use a clinical session log which—in addition to requesting information on the content of a given therapeutic session—requires me to record my own behaviors which might be relevant to the client's motivation (e.g., my praise, criticism, encouragement, etc.). Likewise, the conduct of therapy can be graduated in a manner such that the therapist begins in a relatively authoritarian role and eventually fades into a less directive consultantship. I have found the use of Socratic dialogue helpful in facilitating this gradual transition (Mahoney, 1974).

In addition to providing valuable feedback and structured experiences, the therapist may also play a very important role in the client's perception and attribution of therapeutic change. It may matter little to the client that his therapist believes that he is making progress. Unless he, the client, sees that progress and considers it to be acceptable in both its direction and rate, he may be dissatisfied with his clinical experience. This problem of discrepant perceptions is especially important since the traditional therapist often sees only 50 minutes of client verbal behavior per week. That is, he seldom follows the client out the office door and into the real world of his personal distress. Simply noting adaptive changes in the client's verbalizations may not be sufficient. While it is often helpful, many clients will selectively attend to their failures rather than to their successes. There are several techniques which may be of use in this situation.

First, it is probably here that the action-oriented behavior therapist is best equipped in that graduated task performances seem to play a very important role in both perceptual and conceptual alterations. It was, in fact, this realization which led George Kelly (1955) to develop his "fixed role therapy" for changing personal constructs. Another writer whose works I have found useful in this regard is Thomas Kuhn (1962). Although Kuhn makes no pretense to presenting a model of therapeutic intervention, his analysis of belief systems and belief changes in science offers some stimulating suggestions for clinical practice (Mahoney, 1976b). In particular, I was intrigued by his observations that (a) individuals (in his analysis, scientists) seldom abandon an old belief system unless they have an alternative one to adopt, and (b) the shift to a new belief system is often preceded by a crisis or anomaly (i.e., an event or phenomenon which strongly challenges the validity of the prior belief system). If Kuhn's ideas do indeed have clinical implications, they would seem to include the importance of alternate "assumptive worlds" (cf. Frank, 1961) and the possible significance of anomalous experience in psychotherapy. These suggestions are congruent with the growing consensus that a therapeutic rationale may enhance clinical outcome. They may also reflect on the growing complementarity between cognitive and behavioral therapeutic approaches. Behavioral procedures may be powerful partly due to the fact that they force clients into anomalous experiences—i.e., they lead the client (through a graduated hierarchy) into behaving in a manner which is contradictory to his or her personal belief system (such as "I am afraid of snakes" or "I have no will power"). To the extent that this anomaly is perceived, and to the extent that the therapist has planted the seeds of an alternate personal belief system, the client may experience a rather dramatic shift in affect, in perception, and perhaps even behavioral repertoire.

The therapist should bear in mind that the degree of client improvement may be partially moderated by attribution processes. Clinical improvement per se may be short-lived and situation-specific if the client attributes this improvement to powers or forces which are temporary and external. This is another reason for the graduated shift in responsibility from therapist to client. As the client perceives himself progressively behaving in manners which are congruent with a new and more adaptive belief system, the probability of adopting that system may be facilitated by emphasizing the extent of his personal involvement and responsibility for these improvements. To the extent that the therapist has in fact assumed a progressively less directive role in solving the client's problems, this attribution is of course warranted. One recent client described it very vividly:

"When I began therapy, I felt handicapped and unable to run my own life. You assumed the role of a coach—telling me what I needed to do, encouraging me to give it a try, and so on. Now I feel like I am on my own, and even though I am "walking by myself," I feel good that I can look over my shoulder and see you in the distance nodding improvement. Thanks, Coach."

Another technique which I have used to facilitate attribution and the positive transfer of in-session improvements might be called "therapeutic paranoia." This strategy is particularly useful in situations where a client is capable of performing adequately in a clinical analog situation, but has had difficulties in generalizing these skills to actual real-life situations. The client is asked to voluntarily agree to a system of unobtrusive in vivo evaluations of his or her behavior. Thus, for example, a recent client reported difficulties in assertively declining propositions made to her by males at local bars. Although she was able to rehearse appropriate assertiveness skills in the therapy room, they were slow to transfer to the real-life situation. She was therefore asked to agree to a contract which stipulated that a male confederate would approach her in a bar and proposition her sometime during the forthcoming six weeks. She would not know who he was ahead of time, and it was agreed that he would later provide feedback on the manner in which she handled his sexual proposal. Congruent with this contract, the client was required to inform the therapist of her whereabouts each evening. Interestingly, while plans were being made to train a confederate, the client reported dramatic improvements in her in vivo assertiveness. She came into each session with glowing reports of self-commendation, and repeated certainty that she had detected the nonexistent confederate. There are, of course, both ethical and empirical limitations to the use of this technique, but its potential relevance should not be overlooked.

In keeping with the emphasis on a graduated apprenticeship in coping skills, the later stages of counseling are geared toward "graduation" rather than "termination." Therapy sessions are not abruptly terminated (with the implication that the client is now "healed" and on his own). Instead, the gradual shift to client self-direction is combined with some anticipatory discussions of graduation and long-term maintenance. Eventually, therapeutic sessions are distributed over longer time intervals and progressively moved into situations which are conducive to other forms of social interaction. That is, the demand characteristics of a therapy room are replaced by those of a restaurant or park bench. This is intended to facilitate the transition from an intimate and perhaps dependent helping relationship to one more conducive to responsible self-direction and maintenance.

Paul Meehl (1960) once described psychotherapy as "the art of applying a science which does not yet exist." I have no delusions about the personal science paradigm being free of problems and limitations, and I would not defend it as a monolithic blueprint for all psychotherapeutic endeavors. However, I believe that its liabilities are offset by certain strengths—some of which are unique in the sense that they are absent from more traditional ideologies. Despite the growing trend toward cognitive learning perspectives, I view them all (including the present) with a skeptical optimism which is, I believe, in their best interests (Mahoney, 1976b). And in this, I would concur with another statement offered by Meehl (1955): "We know so little about the process of helping that the only proper attitude is one of maximum experimentalism."

References

Arnkoff, D., & Mahoney, M. J. Cognitive and self-control therapies. In A. E. Bergin & S. L. Garfield (Eds.), *Handbook of psychotherapy and behavior change.* 2nd ed. New York: Wiley, 1977, in press.

Bandura, A. Behavior theory and the models of man. *American Psychologist,* 1974, *29,* 859–869.

Bandura, A. Divergent trends in behavior change: Some thoughts on a unifying theory. Paper presented to the Association for the Advancement of Behavior Therapy, San Francisco, December, 1975.

Beck, A. T. *Cognitive therapy and the emotional disorders.* New York: International Universities Press, 1976.

Frank, J. D. *Persuasion and healing.* Baltimore: Johns Hopkins Press, 1961.

Goldfried, M. R., & Goldfried, A. P. Cognitive change methods. In F. H. Kanfer & A. P. Goldstein (Eds.), *Helping people change.* New York: Pergamon, 1975.

Kazdin, A. E. Effects of covert modeling and model reinforcement on assertive behavior. *Journal of Abnormal Psychology,* 1974, *83,* 240–252. (a)

Kazdin, A. E. The effect of model identity and fear-relevant similarity on covert modeling. *Behavior Therapy,* 1974, *5,* 624–635. (b)

Kazdin, A. E. Covert modeling, model similarity, and reduction of avoidance behavior. *Behavior Therapy,* 1974, *5,* 325–340. (c)

Kelly, G. A. *The psychology of personal constructs.* New York: Norton, 1955.

Kuhn, T. S. *The structure of scientific revolutions.* Chicago: University of Chicago Press, 1962.

Mahoney, M. J. *Cognition and behavior modification.* Cambridge, Mass.: Ballinger, 1974.

Mahoney, M. J. Some applied issues in self-monitoring. In J. D. Cone & R. Hawkins (Eds.), *Behavioral assessment: New directions in clinical psychology.* New York: Brunner/Mazel, 1976 (a).

Mahoney, M. J. *Scientist as subject: A psychological imperative.* Cambridge, Mass.: Ballinger, 1976 (b).

Meehl, P. E. Psychotherapy. In C. Stone (Ed.), *Annual Review of Psychology,* 1955, *6,* 357–378.

Meehl, P. E. The cognitive activity of the clinician. *American Psychologist,* 1960, *15,* 19–27.

Meichenbaum, D. H. Examination of model characteristics in reducing avoidance behavior. *Journal of Personality and Social Psychology,* 1971, *17,* 298–307.

Meichenbaum, D. *Cognitive behavior modification.* Morristown, N.J.: General Learning Press, 1974.

Meichenbaum, D. *Cognitive behavior modification.* New York: Plenum, 1977.

Part Five
Rational-Emotive Therapy with Children

24

A Behavioral Approach to RET with Children

Catherine DeVoge

Most theorists and practitioners recognize that psychotherapy as it is usually practiced must be modified to be effective with children. This is particularly true of rational-emotive psychotherapy since its format is highly verbal and requires some degree of abstract conceptualization from its clients. Chapter 24 outlines a theoretical rationale and procedure for the use of operant conditioning procedures to teach rational thinking to children. Informally comparing one group of emotionally disturbed children who were systematically reinforced for rational thinking with a second group who were not so reinforced, Catherine DeVoge found that those who received the rational-emotive, operant treatment improved significantly whereas the others did not.

RET IS BASED ON the principle that people *feel* the way they think, and overt behavior is reasonably considered to be an expression of these feelings. RET therapists operate under the assumption that although an individual was once influenced to think in a certain way at a certain time in his life, he may later challenge and change *any* belief (Ellis, 1962).

The acquisition of a belief system is an integral part of speech (Luria, 1966). Much of our command of both word usage and belief system develop in the early years of childhood when we are in our most suggestible state. As infants we *know* nothing and so we repeat after others white is "white" and square is "square." A child learns a language by imitating. He hears someone say, "da da," and soon he says, "da da." As he grows he begins to incorporate a sub-language—the *meaning* of the *facts* in the environment. This knowledge may be termed his belief system. Just as the speaking nationality of his model determines what language the child will use, the belief system of the significant person or persons in his life will largely determine whether he thinks rationally or irrationally about the *facts* of his environment. This social aspect of attitude learning has been described by Luria (1966).

Children learn their attitudes through observing significant adults. For

Chapter 24 originally appeared in *Rational Living*, 1974, *9*, 23–26.

instance, the child who behaves imperfectly and is told by his parent that he should be beaten to "within an inch of his life," even if he is never touched, will have learned the attitude that "if I make a mistake I'm hardly worthy to live," and that it is horrendous not to perform perfectly well. The child who observes his father, while driving the automobile, yelling and cursing at the driver ahead because he is going too slowly will be learning that he is justified in expecting others to perform in exactly the manner he wishes.

Just as a child can continually acquire additional vocabulary, could not a child who has been taught a neurotic belief system be taught a *new* attitude language? Further, if he is influenced so as to *use* this new attitude language over a period of time, could it not then become the more dominant system? To discover whether children *could* be taught new thought and attitude patterns, the writer proposed and tested a method of teaching disturbed children a rational system of thinking. It was hypothesized that those children who were strongly and consistently rewarded for verbal expressions of rational thinking would gain more control of their behavior than those who were not so reinforced (Meichenbaum, 1971).

Method

All children on the Children's Unit at Larned State Hospital between the ages of eight and thirteen years who were not mentally retarded were included and randomly assigned to one of the two groups. Group A was designated to receive RET therapy. Each group met twice weekly for four weeks.

Group A was given the following instructions:

Good, 'sensible' ideas coming from members of this group will be written here on the blackboard.

You will receive one mark after your name on the blackboard for the following:
1. Arrival on time
2. Helping a member of the group with a problem
3. Giving good homework assignments
4. Appropriate behavior during the group meeting
   a. Staying in your place
   b. Not hurting yourself or anyone else
5. Leaving quietly with your place in order.

Every five marks may be traded at the end of each group meeting for one of the things in this bowl [various candies], or you may save up your marks and trade fifty of them for a model car.

Group B was given the following instructions:

> You will receive one mark after your name on the blackboard for the following:
> 1. Arrival on time
> 2. Participating in a discussion about a problem of someone in the group
> 3. Appropriate behavior during the group meeting
>   a. staying in your place
>   b. not hurting yourself or anyone else
> 4. Leaving quietly with your place in order.
>
> Every five marks may be traded at the end of each group meeting for one of the things in this bowl [various candies], or you may save up your marks and trade fifty of them for a model car.

Examples of statements which were reinforced in Group A:

> I don't like school, but I can stand it.
> I did something bad, but I'm not a bad person.
> I don't like to be called [insulting] names, but being insulted is not awful.
> Just because someone calls you a 'dumb-dumb' doesn't mean you are one.

Examples of statements which were not reinforced:

> I can't stand school.
> I'm bad.
> I can't do anything good.
> I'll never get out of here.
> If he calls me a ——————, I'm going to bust him!

Children in both groups were reinforced for verbal behavior, but those in Group A were reinforced for a particular kind of verbalization while those in Group B were rewarded regardless of how sensible or rational were their statements. All children in both groups continued to receive the same milieu treatment and to attend school regularly.

Results and Discussion

The following excerpts from the annecdotal record speak only of behavior problems seen on the Unit and not of the children's problems before admission.

Group *A Before Therapy*

I-A   Refused to work in school; feigned illness often to get out of going to school. Complained of all school work as being "too hard." Made snide remarks to aides and other children almost constantly. Was often involved in fights among the children. Would not cooperate well at anything.

II-A   Extremely uncooperative. If aide asked him to do something he wanted, or if he did not get something he wanted, or if another child called him a derogatory name, he would scream, cry, curse, destroy property, and appear very disturbed. Performance in school was nil. When the group itself began he would not stay in his place; he hit children who were sitting near him.

III-A   Severe withdrawal in general; nervous tic-like shrugging of his shoulders and blinking of his eyes are sporadic. Reacted with great anger when another child called him a bad name. Very cooperative with the aides.

IV-A   Very cooperative with the aides. Performed well in school. Would become very depressed whenever his mother would not call or come to visit him. When he made visits home he did not behave well for even one day. He said he was a bad boy because his father had told that he had come from the devil.

V-A   Speaks very rapidly and inappropriately. Cooperates with aides well. Works in school well.

VI-A   Physically attacked other children whenever they called him, or someone he liked, a bad name. Often uncooperative with aides. Worked fairly well in school.

VII-A   Physically attacked other children often and without provocation. Would tolerate no name-calling or any frustration of his wishes. When denied something he wanted he would scream, hit others, and destroy property.

Group *A After Therapy*

I-A   Following four weeks of RET, still considered school "too hard," but ceased feigning illness to get out of it. Improved noticeably in the amount of schoolwork he did. Became much more cooperative and was seldom involved in fights among the children anymore.

II-A   Very cooperative and helpful. Never acts out in any way when he is called a name by another child or has to deal with any other frustration, though he still cries over these incidents occasionally. Performs so much better in school that teachers wondered what had happened. Started to stay in his place in the group and to participate verbally. He often told the therapist with a smile that 'so-and-so' called him a bad name but he just walked on and other children would report the same about him. He told his father that he had "learned a secret" about how not to get mad.

III-A   Still has tic-like movements. Tolerates being called anything by another child. He usually retorts with a calm, "I'm not that," and walks on or goes about his business.

IV-A   Remained cooperative with aides and continued to perform well in school. Dropped his insistence that he was a bad boy and began to help the other children see that we're all "just human beings" (he came up with this terminology himself) and that they would always be making mistakes but that that would never cause them to be less than or worse than they were. Verbalized that he really did not like it that his mother did not visit him often but took a noncatastrophic view of it. *Dismissed.*

V-A   Speaks more slowly and appropriately. No change in other areas.

VI-A   By his own report, when another child called him a bad name he would remember what they had talked about in group therapy and, though he still did not like it at all, he did not feel the need to attack. He was reported involved in fights only occasionally. He became cooperative and helpful to the aides. *Dismissed.*

VII-A   Never hits other children without provocation. He very seldom hits another in anger. When he was denied something he wanted, he accepted it very well, especially if it were explained why. His father expressed how he now enjoyed visiting with him. He has been *dismissed* and is reported to be getting along very well in school.

Group *B Before Therapy*

I-B   Expressed suicidal and homicidal wishes very often. He hates his mother and himself. Threatened to kill her or himself because she is giving him up to a foster home while still keeping his three sisters. Cooperates fairly well with aides and in school.

II-B   Cooperative with aides. Works far under his potential in school. Extremely sensitive to ridicule or teasing of any kind and becomes withdrawn and sullen. Says he's treated unfairly at home because his mother blames him for things his brothers do.

III-B   Goes to school very infrequently. Hides out. Highly uncooperative. Has unexpected outbursts of temper in which he screams and threatens to kill others.

IV-B   Screams loudly at even the slightest frustration of his wishes. Attacks other children or staff members when he perceives rejection. If he is not served first or responded to immediately, he insists no one likes him because he is a "nigger." Mimics the behavior of the autistic child on the unit. Threatens suicide often.

V-B   Very cooperative. Worked well in school. Not liked by other children because he insists on being in power. Enjoyed making visits home.

VI-B   Does not get on well with his peers at all. Rejects them for not being completely knowledgeable in all things. Performs far below his capacity in school. Insists his father is a worthless piece of "junk" because he has behaved so badly.

VII-B   Very depressed and lacks energy. Doesn't work in school. Does nothing in crafts class but sit. Physically attacks other children without provocation and then laughs.

Group *B After Therapy*

I-B   Says that his mother has some sort of problem. Continued expression of suicidal wishes. Cessation of homicidal wish expressions. No change in other areas.

II-B   He reports he is glad that now that he is gone, his mother can see that it was not he who was doing all the bad things. No change noticed otherwise.

III-B Attends school regularly now. Decreased temper outbursts.

IV-B   His behavior has worsened in all these areas *except* that he has ceased threatening suicide.

V-B   Not cooperative. Makes snide remarks to aides and other children. Often tells people to "shut up" even when they are not talking to him. Verbalized suicidal wishes. Does not ever want to go home again because his stepmother expressed anger at him the last time he was home. Still not liked by other children.

VI-B   Improved slightly in his ability to socialize with other youngsters and did not appear so withdrawn. Still is very rejecting of others and still performs very poorly in school. His feeling toward his father is the same. However, he now expresses it openly to the father.

VII-B No change.

When each group began, there was much confronting and loud expressions of anger among the children. After three meetings of Group A, the children were observed to confront each other in a relatively calm manner. The children in Group B continued to confront in a loud, blaming manner.

The nursing staff reported that the children of Group A were consistently less upset by frustrations, personal rejections, and failures. The children of Group B often became upset, depressed, destructive, or withdrawn in reaction to unpleasant aspects of their environment.

By the end of the study, three Group A children were considered by the staff to be sufficiently in control of their behavior and reactions to frustrations to recommend their dismissal. None of the Group B children was judged to be able to control his reactions to his environment well enough to leave the Unit.

Conclusions

On the basis of this pilot work, it appears that consistent and exclusive reinforcement of rational statements results in change toward more self-controlled behavior. The use of behavior modification techniques affected children's verbal expressions of their belief systems and ultimately their emotions and behavior.

References

Ellis, A. *Reason and emotion in psychotherapy.* New York: Lyle Stuart, 1962.
Luria, Aleksandr Romanovich. *Higher cortical functions in man.* New York: Basic Books, Consultants' Bureau, 1966.
Meichenbaum, D. *Cognitive factors in behavior modification: Modifying what clients say to themselves. Research Report No. 25,* University of Waterloo, Waterloo, Canada, July 23, 1971.

The Use of Behavior Modification To Establish Rational Self-Statements in Children

Raymond A. DiGiuseppe

Chapter 25 is another report of an effort to modify the process of RET to accommodate child clients. Raymond DiGiuseppe describes a therapeutic program to alter the irrational thinking of emotionally disturbed children. This program combines rational-emotive psychotherapy, behavior modification, role playing, and social modeling. He provides several case examples to illustrate the procedures.

RATIONAL-EMOTIVE THERAPY (RET) is based on the theory that emotions and subsequent overt behaviors are caused by a person's antecedent thoughts or private speech. Behavior is changed by altering the covert cognitions which precede the behavior. Research to support this theory comes from the work of Luria (1966), Vygotsky (1962), and many others.

Recently several studies have focused on more effective means to establish rational self-statements in children with behavior-modification techniques. DeVoge (1974) used an operant procedure with children at a state hospital. She found that "reinforcement of rational self-statements resulted in a change towards more self-controlled behavior."

Meichenbaum and Goodman (1971) demonstrated that they could change the "impulsive" behavior of second graders by using behavioral principles to establish appropriate self-statements. This was done by first having a model speak aloud the self-statements while performing the target behavior. Then the child performed the behavior while saying aloud the model's statements. On succeeding trials the verbal stimulus was faded by having the child perform the target behavior while saying the statements in a whisper and eventually covertly. This procedure was successful in slowing down the children's behavior and in reducing their errors on several dependent measures. This study demonstrates that significant behavior change can result by using the behavioral principles of modeling, fading, and reinforcement of antecedent cognitions.

Chapter 25 originally appeared in *Rational Living*, 1975, *10*, 18–19.

RET already has been shown to be effective with children (Ellis, 1972; Knaus, 1974). It would appear that RET could become more effective with very young and nonverbal children. The behavioral principles of modeling, fading, and reinforcement utilized by Meichenbaum and Goodman can be systematically employed to establish rational self-statements in therapy. The first step would be to have the child describe the activating events and his emotional consequences. After the therapist explains that it is the child's thoughts that are upsetting him they can then role-play the activating event with the therapist playing the part of the child and the child playing the part of the significant other who is supposedly upsetting him. At this point in the scene, where the child usually gets upset, the therapist verbalizes aloud rational self-statements about the activating event and demonstrates an appropriate behavior. After this is done several times, the roles are reversed and the child role-plays himself. When the activating event occurs in play the child is instructed to say aloud the self-statements of the model. Reinforcement should follow the child's attempt at this. Social approval is preferable, but material reinforcement could be used if the child is very young or if the behavior is very difficult to elicit. If the child fails to repeat the rational self-statement correctly, a shaping procedure can be devised with successive approximations being rewarded. When the self-statement is firmly established, the role playing is continued with a gradual fading of the verbal response. The child is instructed to repeat the self-statement, on each trial lowering the volume of his voice a little. Finally the role playing is done with the child repeating the self-statement covertly.

This technique has been used many times by the author. The following are some examples.

John was a 12-year-old boy in a special class who was referred for his continual fighting with his brothers and his extreme anxiety in class. Each situation was dealt with separately. John reported that his brothers were always making him angry by calling him names. After several sessions, John seemed to understand the A-B-C theory and that his thinking was getting him angry, but his behavior just wasn't changing. We then role-played the situation with myself being John and he playing the role of his brothers. He called the therapist all the names his brothers called him. I would then say aloud, "Just because they call me a name doesn't make it true. It isn't nice to be called a name but it's not so terrible and I can stand it." Then roles were then reversed and I called John the same names. He repeated the statements aloud and they were faded over the next two sessions. At this time John's parents reported that he was no longer fighting with his brothers. John later reported that since he had stopped getting angry, his brothers had stopped the name calling. A similar exercise was worked out with John's nervousness in class and it was equally successful. John had limited conceptual abilities and did not seem to gain from the sessions where his irrational beliefs were disputed. But he made significant, rapid gains when the behavioral principles were employed to change his self-statements.

Keith was a 7-year-old black boy with a low average IQ. He was very aggressive and disruptive in class and his teacher wanted him placed in a special class. Keith usually acted out when he was called names by his peers. He was extremely nonverbal and a didactic approach to RET as well as an operant procedure that reinforced appropriate behavior failed. After several frustrating weeks, the role-playing exercise was tried. Keith threw many barbs at me, and I responded with rational self-statements. Then Keith received the barbs and responded with the self-statements. The statements were faded over six half-hour sessions in three weeks. During this time Keith still received reinforcement for periods of non-aggressive behavior. By the end of the third week his troublesome behavior had been eliminated.

This procedure is designed to modify the child's behavior in situational disorders. It is not as elegant a solution as might be desired with adults or older children. Certainly it does not reach Ellis' goal in therapy of developing rational thinking in all situations. It does not teach the child how to use RET in other situations so he can ward off future disturbance. Thus the generalization to be expected is less than is usually the case with RET. But Meichenbaum (1974) has pointed out the behavioral procedures which aim at changing rational self-statements produce more generalization than traditional behavior therapy techniques. The total effectiveness and generalization produced by this procedure can only be speculated upon until empirical studies are completed.

References

De Voge, C. A behavioral approach to RET with children. *Rational Living*, 1974, *9* (1), 23–26.

Ellis, A. *Reason and emotion in psychotherapy*. New York: Lyle Stuart, 1962.

Ellis, A. Teaching emotional education in the classroom. *School Health Review*, 1969, Nov., 10–13.

Ellis, A. Emotional education in the classroom. *Journal of Clinical Child Psychology*, 1972, *1*, 19–22.

Knaus, Wm. *Rational emotive education: A manual for elementary school teachers*. New York: Institute for Rational Living, 1974.

Luria, A. R. *Higher cortical functions in man*. New York: Basic Books, 1966.

Meichenbaum, D. The clinical potential of modifying what clients say to themselves. *Psychotherapy: Theory, Research and Practice*, 1974, *11*, 103–117.

Meichenbaum, D., & Goodman, J. Training impulsive children to talk to themselves. *Journal of Abnormal Psychology*, 1971, *77*, 115–126.

Vygotsky, L. *Thought and language*. New York: John Wiley, 1962.

26

Training Impulsive Children To Talk to Themselves: A Means of Developing Self-Control

Donald H. Meichenbaum and Joseph Goodman

Chapter 26 describes two studies that tested the effect of the development of cognitive self-guidance in impulsive children. The first study presents a systematic cognitive modification technique in which: (1) the therapist modeled appropriate verbal mediation while working on a task and the child observed; (2) the child did the task while the therapist continued to instruct the child aloud; (3) the child performed the task while instructing himself aloud; (4) the child performed the task while whispering to himself; and (5) the child performed the task while thinking (or talking silently) to himself. The results of the first study indicated that the cognitive self-guidance program was effective in modifying the children's impulsive behavior. The second study examined the different effects of self-instructional training and modeling procedures. It was found that cognitive modeling plus self-instruction was most effective in altering decision time and in reducing errors on several measures.

THE DEVELOPMENT OF THE functional interaction between self-verbalization and nonverbal behavior has received much attention (Luria, 1961; Piaget, 1947; Reese, 1962; and see especially a review by Kohlberg, Yaeger, & Hjertholm, 1968). Two general research strategies have been employed to assess the influence of self-verbalizations on behavior. The first strategy is characterized by S's performance on a task and E's subsequent inference as to the presence or absence of specific cognitive activities. In general, this approach has used the concept of "deficiency" to explain poor performance. Reese (1962) has suggested a mediation deficiency hypothesis; Flavell and his co-workers (Flavell, Beach, & Chinsky, 1966; Moely, Olson, Halwes, & Flavell, 1967) have offered a production deficiency hypothesis, and most recently Bem (1970)

Chapter 26 originally appeared in the *Journal of Abnormal Psychology*, 1971, 77 (2), 115–126, and is reprinted here by permission of that journal.

379

has suggested a comprehension deficiency hypothesis. The developing child is characterized as going through stages during which he (*a*) does not mediate or regulate his overt behavior verbally; (*b*) does not spontaneously produce relevant mediators; and (*c*) does not comprehend the nature of the problem in order to discover what mediators to produce. Thus, problem solving is viewed as a three-stage process of comprehension, production, and mediation, and poor performance can result from a "deficiency" at any one of these stages. The deficiency literature suggests that a training program designed to improve task performance and engender self-control should provide explicit training in the comprehension of the task, the spontaneous production of mediators, and the use of such mediators to control nonverbal behavior. The present cognitive self-guidance treatment program was designed to provide such training for a group of "impulsive" children.

The other strategy, which is designed to assess the functional role of private speech in task performance, directly manipulates the child's verbalizations and examines resulting changes in nonverbal behavior. Vygotsky (1962) has suggested that internalization of verbal commands is the critical step in the child's development of voluntary control of his behavior. Data from a wide range of studies (Bem, 1967; Klein, 1963; Kohlberg et al., 1968; Lovaas, 1964; Luria, 1959, 1961; Meichenbaum & Goodman, 1969a, 1969b) provide support for the age increase in cognitive self-guiding private speech, and the increase in internalization with age. These results suggest a progression from external to internal control. Early in development, the speech of others, usually adults, mainly controls and directs a child's behavior; somewhat later, the child's own overt speech becomes an effective regulator of his behavior; and still later, the child's covert or inner speech can assume a regulatory role. The present studies were designed to examine the efficacy of a cognitive self-guidance treatment program which followed the developmental sequence by which overt verbalizations of an adult or *E,* followed by the child's overt self-verbalizations, followed by covert self-verbalization would result in the child's own verbal control of his nonverbal behavior. By using this fading procedure, we hoped to (*a*) train impulsive *S*s to provide themselves with internally originated verbal commands or self-instructions and to respond to them appropriately; (*b*) strengthen the mediational properties of the children's inner speech in order to bring their behavior under their own verbal or discriminative control; (*c*) overcome any possible "comprehension, production, or mediational deficiencies"; and finally (*d*) encourage the children to appropriately self-reinforce their behavior. We hoped to have the child's private speech gain a new functional significance, to have the child develop a new cognitive style or "learning set" and thus to engender self-control.

Two studies are reported which apply the cognitive self-guidance treatment regimen to impulsive school children. The first study, using second-grade children who had been assigned to an "opportunity remedial class," provided four ½-hr. individual training sessions over a 2-wk. period. The effects of training on performance measures and classroom behavior is reported. The second study examines the modification value of a particular component of the treatment regimen, namely, modeling, which is designed to alter the child's impulsive cognitive style in one treatment session as assessed on Kagan's (1966) Matching Familiar Figures (MFF) Test. The impulsive Ss in the second study have been selected from kindergarten and first-grade classes as assessed by their failure to follow an instruction to "go slower" on a preassessment of the MFF test. Both studies indicate the general treatment regimen designed to train impulsive children to talk to themselves, a possible means of developing self-control.

Study I

Method

SUBJECTS

The Ss were 15 second-grade children (8 females, 7 males) whose ages ranged from 7 to 9 yrs. with a mean of 8 yr., 2 mo. and who had been placed in an "opportunity remedial class" in a public elementary school. The children were placed into the opportunity class because of behavioral problems such as hyperactivity and poor self-control, and/or they had low IQs on one of a variety of school-administered intelligence tests. The cutoff point on the IQ measures was 85, but for several Ss the last assessment was several years prior to the present research project. The children's behavior both in class and on performance measures was measured before and after treatment as well as in a 1-mo. follow-up assessment described below. Following the pretreatment assessment, Ss were assigned to one of three groups. One group comprised the cognitive self-guidance treatment group ($N = 5$). The remaining two groups included in the study were control groups. One control group met with E with the same regularity as did the cognitively trained Ss. This attention control group ($N = 5$) afforded an index of behavioral change due to factors of attention, exposure to training materials, and any demand characteristics inherent in our measures of improvement. In addition, an assessment control group of Ss who received no treatment was included. The assessment control group ($N = 5$) provided an index of the contribution of inter-current life experiences to any behavioral change (e.g., being a member of the opportunity remedial class). Assignment to these three groups was done randomly, subject to the two contraints of (*a*) equating the groups on sex composition and (*b*) matching the groups on their pro-rated WISC IQ performance scores taken prior to treatment.

TREATMENTS

Cognitive training group. The *S*s in this group were seen individually for four ½-hr. treatment sessions over a 2-wk. period. The cognitive train-ing technique proceeded as follows: First, *E* performed a task talking aloud while *S* observed (*E* acted as a model); then *S* performed the same task while *E* instructed *S* aloud; then *S* was asked to perform the task again while instructing himself aloud; then *S* performed the task while whispering to himself (lip movements); and finally *S* performed the task covertly (without lip movements). The verbalizations which *E* mod-eled and *S* subsequently used included: (*a*) questions about the nature and demands of the task so as to compensate for a possible comprehen-sion deficiency; (*b*) answers to these questions in the form of cognitive rehearsal and planning in order to overcome any possible production de-ficiency; (*c*) self-instructions in the form of self-guidance while perform-ing the task in order to overcome any possible mediation deficiency; and (*d*) self-reinforcement. The following is an example of *E*'s modeled ver-balizations which *S* subsequently used (initially overtly, then covertly):

"Okay, what is it I have to do? You want me to copy the picture with the different lines. I have to go slow and be careful. Okay, draw the line down, down, good; then to the right, that's it; now down some more and to the left. Good, I'm doing fine so far. Remember go slow. Now back up again. No, I was supposed to go down. That's okay. Just erase the line carefully. . . . Good. Even if I make an error I can go on slowly and care-fully. Okay, I have to go down now. Finished. I did it."

Note in this example an error in performance was included and *E* appropriately accommodated. In prior research with impulsive children, Meichenbaum and Goodman (1969b) observed a marked deterioration in their performance following errors. The *E*'s verbalizations varied with the demands of each task, but the general treatment format remained the same throughout. The treatment sequence was also individually adapted to the capabilities of the *S* and the difficulties of the task.

A variety of tasks was employed to train the child to use self-instruc-tions to control his nonverbal behavior. The tasks varied along a dimen-sion from simple sensorimotor abilities to more complex problem-solving abilities. The sensorimotor tasks, such as copying line patterns and color-ing figures within certain boundaries, provided *S* with an opportunity to produce a narrative description of his behavior, both preceding and accompanying his performance. Over the course of a training session, the child's overt self-statements on a particular task were faded to the covert level, what Luria (1961) has called "interiorization of language." The difficulty level of the training tasks was increased over the four training sessions requiring more cognitively demanding activities. Such tasks as reproducing designs and following sequential instructions taken from the Stanford-Binet intelligence test, completing pictorial series as on the Primary Mental Abilities test, and solving conceptual tasks as on the Ravens Matrices test, required *S* to verbalize the demands of the task and problem-solving strategies. The *E* modeled appropriate self-verbalizations for each of these tasks and then had the child follow the fading procedure. Although the present tasks assess many of the same cognitive abilities required by our dependent measures, there are significant differences between the training tasks and the performance and behavioral indexes used to assess improvement. It should be noted that the attentional control group received the same opportunities to perform on each of the training tasks, but without cognitive self-guidance training.

One can imagine a similar training sequence in the learning of a new motor skill such as driving a car. Initially the driver actively goes through a mental checklist, sometimes aloud, which includes verbal rehearsal, self-guidance, and sometimes appropriate self-reinforcement, especially when driving a stick-shift car. Only with repetition does the sequence become automatic and the cognitions become short-circuited. This sequence is also seen in the way children learn to tie shoelaces and in the development of many other skills. If this observation has any merit, then a training procedure which makes these steps explicit should facilitate the development of self-control.

In summary, the goals of the training procedure were to develop for the impulsive child a cognitive style or learning set in which the child could "size up" the demands of a task, cognitively rehearse, and then guide his performance by means of self-instructions, and when appropriate reinforce himself.

Attention control group. The children in this untutored group had the same number of sessions with *E* as did the cognitive training *S*s. During this time, the child was exposed to identical materials and engaged in the same general activities, but did not receive any self-instructional training. For example, these attentional control *S*s received the same number of trials on a task as did the cognitively trained *S*s, but they did not receive self-instructional training. An attempt was made to provide both the experimental and attention control groups with equal amounts of social reinforcement for behavioral performance on the tasks.

Assessment control group. This untreated control group received only the same pretreatment, posttreatment, and follow-up assessments as the cognitive treatment and attention control groups.

INSTRUMENTS

Two general classes of dependent measures were used to assess the efficacy of the cognitive self-guidance treatment regimen to improve performance and engender self-control. The first class of measures involved performance on a variety of psychometric instruments which have been previously used to differentiate impulsive from nonimpulsive children. The second class of measures assessed the generalizability of the treatment effects to the classroom situation. The female *E* who performed the pretreatment, posttreatment, and follow-up assessments on the performance measures and the two female *E*s who made classroom observations during pretreatment and posttreatment periods were completely unaware of which children received which treatment.

Performance measures. Three different psychometric tests were used to assess changes in behavioral and cognitive impulsivity during the pretreatment, posttreatment, and follow-up periods. Several investigators (Anthony, 1959; Eysenck, 1955; Foulds, 1951; Porteus, 1942) have demonstrated that the Porteus Maze test, especially the qualitative score which is based upon errors in style and quality of execution, distinguishes between individuals differing in impulsiveness. Most recently, Palkes, Stewart, and Kahana (1968) have reported that hyperactive boys significantly improved on Porteus Maze performance following training in self-directed verbal commands. Thus, the Porteus Maze performance provided one indicant of behavioral change. Because of the length of the assessment (some 45 min.), only years 8–11 of the Porteus Maze test were used. On the posttest the Vineland Revision form of the Porteus Maze test was used.

A second measure which has been used to assess cognitive impulsivity is Kagan's (1966) MFF test. The *S*'s task on the MFF test is to select from an array of variants one picture which is identical to a standard picture. The tendency toward fast or slow decision times and the number of errors are used to identify the degree of conceptual impulsivity. Further support for the use of the MFF test in the present study comes from research by Meichenbaum and Goodman (1969a), who have reported a positive relationship between a child's relative inability to verbally control his motor behavior by means of covert self-instructions and an impulsive conceptual tempo on the MFF test. Parallel forms of the MFF test were developed by using six alternate items in the pretreatment and posttreatment assessments, with the pretreatment MFF test being readministered on the follow-up assessment.

The final set of performance measures was derived from three performance subtests of the WISC. The three subtests selected were Picture Arrangement, Block Design, and Coding. Respectively, these subtests are designed to assess (*a*) the ability to comprehend and size up a total situation requiring anticipation and planning; (*b*) the ability to analyze and form abstract designs as illustrated by *S*'s performance and approach to the problems; and (*c*) the child's motor speed and activity level (Kitzinger & Blumberg, 1951; Lutey, 1966; Wechsler, 1949). The results from the WISC subtests are reported in scaled scores and as a prorated IQ performance estimate.

In summary, the performance measures were designed to assess the range of abilities from sensorimotor, as indicated by qualitative scores on Porteus Maze and Coding tasks on the WISC, to more cognitively demanding tasks such as the MFF test, Block Design, and Picture Arrangement subtests.

Classroom measures. Two measures were used to ascertain whether any of the expected changes would extend into the classroom. The first measure behaviorally assessed the 15 children on their appropriateness and attentiveness within the classroom setting. We used a time-sampling

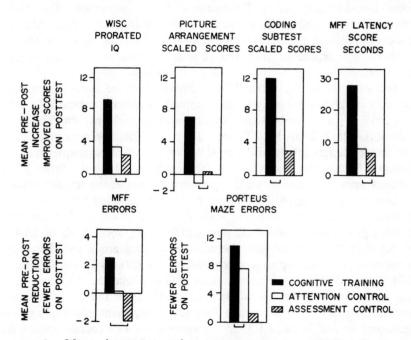

FIGURE 1. Mean change scores from pretreatment to posttreatment on performance measures. (Groups not connected by solid line are significantly different at .05 level.)

observational technique (10 sec. observe, 10 sec. record) which was developed by Meichenbaum, Bowers, and Ross (1968, 1969) to rate inappropriate classroom behavior. Inappropriate classroom behavior was defined as any behavior which was not consistent with the task set forth by the teacher, that is, behavior which was not task-specific. The children were observed for 2 school days, 1 wk. before and immediately after treatment. The second measure involved a teacher's questionnaire which was designed to assess each child's behavioral self-control, activity level, cooperativeness, likeability, etc. The questionnaire consisted of 10 incomplete statements, each of which was followed by three forced-choice alternative completions. The teacher filled out the scale immediately prior to treatment and 3 wks. later at the conclusion of the posttreatment assessment.

Results

The relative efficacy of the cognitive self-guidance treatment program was assessed by means of a Lindquist (1953) Type I analysis of variance which yields a treatment effect, trials effect (pretreatment and posttreatment assessments), and a Treatment × Trials interaction. The results from the 1-mo. follow-up measures were analyzed separately. Multiple t-test comparisons (one-tailed) were performed on the change scores for each of the dependent measures. Figure 1 presents the performance measures.

The analyses of the three WISC subtests revealed only a significant Group × Trials interaction on the Picture Arrangement subtest ($F = 4.56$, $df = 2/12$, $p = .033$) and a strong trend towards significance on the Coding subtest (Group × Trials $F = 2.87$, $df = 2/12$, $p = .10$). The performances on the Block Design subtest did not yield any significant groups, trials, or Group × Trials interactions. When the performances on the three WISC subtests were combined to yield a prorated IQ score, the relative efficacy of the cognitive training procedure is further revealed in a significant Group × Trials interaction ($F = 3.97$, $df = 2/12$, $p = .05$). The cognitive training group improved 8.3 IQ points ($SD = 3.8$), from an IQ of 88.4 to an IQ of 96.7. In comparison, the attention control group and the assessment control group improved, respectively, 3.4 ($SD = 4.1$) and 2.2 ($SD = 3.0$) IQ points. Multiple t comparisons indicated that the cognitive training group was significantly different ($p < .05$) from the attentional and assessment control groups on the Picture Arrangement and Coding subtests, and on the prorated IQ scores, whereas the two control groups did not significantly differ from each other on the WISC measures.

Further evidence for the efficacy of the cognitive training is derived from the measure of cognitive impulsivity, namely, the MFF test. A significant Group × Trials interaction ($F = 9.49$, $df = 2/12$, $p = .004$) was found on the initial decision time or latency score on the MFF test. The cognitive training group increased its mean total decision time for the six MFF items from pretest to posttest by 27.4 sec. ($SD = 10.3$), in comparison to the attention and assessment control groups who, respectively, increased their total posttest decision times by 7.4 sec. ($SD = 3.8$) and 6.8 sec. ($SD = 9.9$). The differential increase in response time indicates that the impulsive Ss in the cognitively trained group took significantly longer before responding on the posttest. The analyses of the error scores on the MFF test did not yield any significant differences, although the trend of the results did suggest differential effectiveness for the cognitively trained Ss. The cognitively trained Ss had a group total decrease on the posttest of 8 errors in comparison to the attentional control Ss, who had a group total decrease of only 2 errors on the posttest, and the assessment control Ss, who had a group total increase of 10 errors on the posttest. The absence of statistical significance on the error scores may be due to the relative ease of the MFF test for this age level and the use of a shortened version of the test in order to develop parallel forms (i.e., 6 items were used instead of the usual 12-item test). The potential usefulness of the cognitive training procedure in altering cognitive impulsivity was examined in the second study which is described below.

An analysis of the performance on the Porteus Maze test indicated a significant Group × Trials interaction ($F = 5.52$, $df = 2/12$, $p = .02$), with the cognitive training and the attentional control groups making significantly ($p < .05$) less errors on the posttest than the assessment control group. The mean change scores indicated that (*a*) Ss who received cognitive training improved most with 10.8 ($SD = 4.3$) less errors on the posttest; (*b*) Ss in the attentional control group made 7.8 ($SD = 6.8$) less errors on the posttest; and (*c*) the assessment control group made 1.2 ($SD = 4.7$) more errors on the posttest. Both the cognitive training group and the attentional control group decreased errors on the posttest by cutting fewer corners, crossing over fewer lines, lifting their pencils less frequently, and producing fewer irregular lines. Palkes et al. (1968) have reported a significant improvement on the Porteus Maze test for a self-directed verbal command group relative to an assessment or no-treatment control group, but they did not include an attentional control group. The present results indicated that an attentional control group which received only practice on a variety of sensorimotor and cognitive tasks also significantly improved their performance on the Porteus Maze test. The inclusion of such an attentional control group is thus necessary in order to exclude alternative hypotheses.

The analyses of the S's classroom behavior by means of time-sampling observations and by teachers' ratings did not yield any significant differences. The absence of a significant treatment effect in the classroom may be due to a lack of generalization because of the limited number of training sessions and/or the lack of sensitivity of the assessment measures. The analyses of the 4-wk. follow-up assessment revealed that the cognitive training group maintained their improved performance on the test battery, relative to the attentional and assessment control groups. The analyses of the follow-up test performances relative to the pretreatment performance indicated that on the Picture Arrangement subtest, the WISC prorated IQ score, and the decision time on the MFF, the cognitive training group was significantly different ($p < .05$) from the two control groups. The analysis of the qualitative performance on the Porteus Maze test indicated that both the cognitive training group and the attentional control group maintained their improved performance relative to the assessment control group.

The results of the first study proved most encouraging and suggested that a cognitive self-guidance training program can significantly alter behavior of impulsive children. The purpose of the second study was to examine the differential contribution of the various components of the treatment program in modifying impulsive behavior. The cognitive training procedure involved both modeling by E and subsequent self-instructional training by S. In this study a comparison is made between the relative efficacy of modeling alone versus modeling plus self-instructional training in modifying cognitive impulsivity as measured by the MFF test. Kagan (1965) has defined cognitive impulsivity as a conceptual tempo or decision-time variable representing the time S takes to consider alternate solutions before committing himself to one of them in a situation with high response uncertainty. Kagan and his associates (Kagan, 1965, 1966; Kagan, Rosman, Day, Albert, & Phillips, 1964) have shown that performance on the MFF test has high stability and intertest generality and is related to performance on visual discrimination tasks, inductive reasoning, serial recall, and reading skills. Most recently, investigators have been interested in the modification of cognitive impulsivity. Kagan, Person, and Welsh (1966) have attempted to train, in three individual sessions, inhibition of impulsive responding by requiring the child to defer his answer for a fixed period of 10 to 15 sec. During this period the child was encouraged to study the stimuli in the task and to think about his answer, but he did *not* receive training in more efficient procedures to emit during this interval. Significant changes in latency or decision time occurred, but no corresponding significant change in errors was evident. Debus (1970) examined the usefulness of filmed modeling of reflective behavior and found a decrease only in decision time, and, like Kagan, Pearson, and Welch (1966), no corresponding change in errors. The studies by Kagan et al. (1966) and Debus (1970) have concentrated on increasing latency times without paying sufficient attention to inducing improved cognitive and/or scanning strategies in the impulsive child. Siegelman (1969) and Drake (1970) have demonstrated that different attentional and cognitive strategies seem to underlie the performance of impulsive and reflective Ss. The data from Siegelman and Drake indicate that the impulsive child on the MFF test (*a*) displays a greater biasing of attention both in extent of scanning and in number of alternatives ignored; (*b*) is simply in search of some variant that globally resembles the standard and is not very discriminating or analytic in his viewing. In comparison, the reflective child seems to follow a strategy designed to find explicit differences among alternatives and then to check the standard for verification. The impulsive child's approach or strategy on the MFF task results in many errors and quick decision times. The purpose of the present study was to examine the usefulness of the cognitive self-guidance training procedure in altering the attentional strategy of the impulsive child on the MFF test. The efficacy of the self-instructional training procedure in modifying cognitive impulsivity is compared with a modeling-alone procedure. An attentional control group which received exposure to the practice materials but no explicit training was included for comparative purposes.

Study II

Method

SUBJECTS

The 15 impulsive children who received training were selected from a larger group of kindergarten (*N* = 30) and first-grade (*N* = 30) public school children on the basis of two behavioral criteria. All of the children were individually tested on parallel forms of six items each of the MFF test. Interspersed between the two MFF forms the instruction "You don't have to hurry. You should go slowly and carefully" was given to all Ss. The 15 impulsive Ss (4 male and 4 female kindergarteners and 4 male and 3 female first graders) were selected on the basis of the S's initial performance on Form I of the MFF test and the absence of any appreciable improvement in performance on Form II of the MFF test. Thus, the selected impulsive children were initially cognitively impulsive, and they did not significantly alter their style of responding even though they were instructed to do so. The use of an instructional manipulation to select Ss is consistent with Vygotsky's (1962) suggestion that a child's capabilities are best reflected by his response to instructions.

Following Session 1, the 15 selected impulsive Ss were randomly assigned to one of the treatment groups (viz., modeling alone or modeling plus self-instructional training) or to the attentional control group, subject to the constraint of comparable age and sex representation in each group. One week later in a second session, each of the impulsive Ss was individually seen by a different E (female), who conducted the treatment, after which Ss were tested on a third form of the six-item MFF test by the first E (male) who had conducted the testing in Session 1. The E who administered the three forms of the MFF test was thus unaware into which group S had been placed. The training materials consisted of the Picture Matching subtest from the Primary Mental Abilities (PMA) test and items from the Ravens' Matrices test. These materials elicit similar task abilities to the MFF test and provide a useful format for modeling reflective behaviors. The training procedure, which lasted some 20 min., consisted of E performing or modeling behavior on one item of the practice material and then S doing an item. There were in all eight practice trials.

TREATMENTS

Cognitive modeling group. The Ss in this group ($N = 5$) initially observed the E who modeled a set of verbalizations and behaviors which characterizes the reflective child's proposed strategy on the MFF test. The following is an example of E's modeled verbalizations on the PMA Picture Matching test:

"I have to remember to go slowly to get it right. Look carefully at this one (the standard), now look at these carefully (the variants). Is this one different? Yes, it has an extra leaf. Good, I can eliminate this one. Now, let's look at this one (another variant). I think it's this one, but let me first check the others. Good, I'm going slow and carefully. Okay, I think it's this one."

The impulsive child was exposed to a model which demonstrated the strategy to search for differences that would allow him successively to eliminate as incorrect all variants but one. The E modeled verbal statements or a strategy to make detailed comparisons across figures, looking at all variants before offering an answer. As in the first study, E also modeled errors and then how to cope with errors and improve upon them. For example, following an error E would model the following verbalizations:

"It's okay, just be careful. I should have looked more carefully. Follow the plan to check each one. Good, I'm going slowly."

After E modeled on an item, S was given an opportunity to perform on a similar practice item. The S was encouraged and socially reinforced for using the strategy E had just modeled, but did not receive explicit practice in self-instructing. This modeling-alone group was designed to indicate the degree of behavioral change from exposure to an adult model.

Cognitive modeling plus self-instructional training group. The *S*s in this group were exposed to the same modeling behavior by *E* as were *S*s in the modeling-alone group, but in addition they were explicitly trained to produce the self-instructions *E* emitted while performing the task. After *E* modeled on an item, *S* was instructed to perform the task while talking aloud to himself as *E* had done. Over the course of the eight practice trials, the child's self-verbalizations were faded from initially an overt level to a covert level, as in Study I.

Attentional control group. The *S*s in this group observed the *E* perform the task and were given an opportunity to perform on each of the practice items. The *E*'s verbalizations consisted only of general statements to "go slow, be careful, look carefully," but did not include the explicit modeling of verbalizations dealing with scanning strategies as did the two treatment groups. The *S*s were encouraged and socially reinforced to go slow and be careful, but were not trained to self-instruct. In many ways this group approximates the methods teachers and parents use to demonstrate a task in which they make general prohibitions, but do not explicate the strategies or details involved in solving the task. This group can be considered a minimal modeling condition or an attentional control group for exposure to *E* and practice on task materials.

An attempt was made to provide all three groups with equal amounts of social reinforcement for their performance. At the completion of the modeling session, all *S*s were told, "Can you remember to do just like I did whenever you play games like this? Remember to go slowly and carefully." The *E* who conducted the training departed, and the first *E* then administered Form III of the MFF test.

Results

SELECTION OF *S*s

Table 1 presents the performance of reflective and impulsive *S*s on the initial MFF test (Form I) and on the MFF test (Form II) which was administered immediately after the instructions to "go slower." Of the original 60 *S*s tested, 45 were classified into either the reflective or impulsive groups, based on the *S*'s response time and errors relative to the performance of the same age and sex peer group. The instructions to go slower resulted in a significant ($p < .05$) increase in the mean total response time on initial decisions for reflective *S*s (i.e., from 99.8 to 123.8 sec.), but no comparable change in errors. The latter finding may be due to a "ceiling effect" and/or a slight decrement in performance resulting from anxiety. Several reflective *S*s indicated that they interpreted

Table 1

**Impulsive and Reflective Ss' Performance on Initial
MFF Test (Form I) and on the MFF Test (Form II)
Administered after Instructions to "Go Slower"**

Ss	MFF performance			
	Form I		Form II	
	X̄	SD	X̄	SD
Reflectives (N = 20)				
Total errors	6.3	3.5	7.7	4.0
Total decision time	99.8	6.5	123.8	10.5
Impulsives (N = 25)				
Total errors	16.4	3.8	11.4	7.0
Total decision time	42.9	5.5	58.1	7.6

E's instruction to go slower as an indicant that they were not performing adequately. Ward (1968) has reported that anxiety over failure played a greater role in the performance of reflective children than it did in the performance of impulsive children. The impulsive *S*s demonstrated a marked variability in how their performance changed as a result of the instructional manipulation. This variability permitted selection of the 15 most impulsive *S*s whose performance changed minimally. In a second session, these impulsive *S*s were provided with treatment. Table 2 presents the performance scores for the impulsive *S*s who were selected for treatment and those impulsive *S*s who significantly improved their performance from the minimal instructional manipulation.

Table 2

**A Breakdown of Impulsive Ss' Performance on
Forms I and II of the MFF Test**

Ss	MFF performance			
	Form I		Form II	
	X̄	SD	X̄	SD
Impulsive *Ss* selected for treatment (N = 15)				
Total errors	15.2	3.5	12.2	4.6
Total decision time	42.8	5.3	51.2	5.9
Impulsive *Ss not* selected for treatment (N = 10)				
Total errors	17.6	4.2	10.5	5.4
Total decision time	43.0	6.0	65.0	8.3

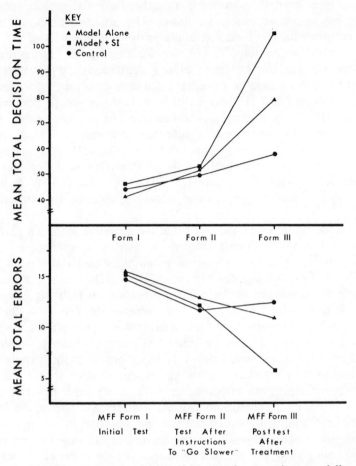

FIGURE 2. MFF performances of impulsive *S*s who were in a modeling-alone group, a modeling plus self-instructional training group, and an additional control group.

In summary, from a group of 60 kindergarten and first-grade children, 15 *S*s were selected who were most cognitively impulsive on initial testing and who minimally altered their response style when explicitly given the instruction to do so.

ANALYSIS OF TREATMENT EFFICACY

Figure 2 presents the performance of the modeling group, modeling plus self-instructional group, and the attentional control group for the three 6-item forms of the MFF test. The analyses of the decision times and error scores on Forms I and II of the MFF test yielded no significant group, trials, or Group × Trials interaction, indicating that prior to treatment the three groups performed comparably on initial performance and in response to instructions to go slower. The differential efficacy of the treatment procedures is indicated in the analysis of Form III of the MFF test which was administered immediately after treatment. On the decision time measure, the two treatment groups significantly ($p < .05$) slowed down their decision time on Form III relative to their own prior performances on Forms I and II and relative to the control groups performance on Form III. The modeling plus self-instructional training group which slowed down the most was significantly different ($t = 18.0$, $df = 8$, $p < .001$) from the modeling-alone group on Form III. The analyses of the error scores indicated that *only* Ss who received modeling plus self-instructional training significantly ($p < .05$) improved their performance relative to the other two groups and relative to their own prior performances.

In summary, the results indicated that the cognitive modeling plus self-instructional group was most effective in altering decision time and in reducing errors. The modeling-alone group significantly decreased decision time, but did not significantly reduce errors. The efficacy of the self-instructional component of the training procedure in fostering behavioral change is underscored by the fact that three of the five Ss in the self-instruction group spontaneously self-verbalized on Form III of the MFF test, whereas none did so in the other two groups. Similarly, in Study I several Ss in the self-instructional training group spontaneously self-verbalized in the posttest and follow-up sessions. It does appear that self-instructional training can bring an impulsive child's overt behavior under his own verbal discriminative control. At a macroscopic level, the impulsive children, after self-instructional training, do seem to be approaching psychometric tasks differently, taking their time, talking to themselves, and improving their performance. Research is now underway to explore the generality, persistence, and behavioral changes that result from self-instructional training.

Discussion

The results of the two studies indicate that a cognitive self-guidance program which trains impulsive children to talk to themselves is effective in modifying their behavior on a variety of psychometric tests which assess cognitive impulsivity, Performance IQ, and motor ability. The results of Study II indicate that the addition of explicit self-instructional training to modeling procedures significantly alters the attentional strategies of the impulsive children and facilitates behavioral change. The impulsive children were taught to use their private speech for orienting, organizing, regulating, and self-rewarding functions with the consequence of greater self-control. The present self-instructional procedure seems applicable to the culturally deprived child, who has been described by Bereiter and Engelmann (1966) and Blank and Solomon (1968, 1969) as having a "central language deficit," namely, the inability to relate what he says to what he does. The deprived child does not spontaneously use language to direct his problem-solving behavior, especially when specific demands to do so are removed, nor does he exhibit normal capacities for self-control. An examination of the usefulness of the present self-instructional training procedures over a prolonged period of time with such deprived children is now underway.

The present studies indicate that the therapist can now attempt to modify not only the patient's overt behavioral response, but also the antecedent and/or accompanying cognitions. For example, cognitive self-guidance training procedures may be used to influence the attentional and cognitive strategies patients emit in a variety of situations. The possibilities of using self-instructional training procedures to alter (*a*) the "attentional deficit" in schizophrenics (Lang & Buss, 1965); (*b*) psychophysiological reactions of psychiatric patients (Grings, 1965; Schachter, 1966); and (*c*) cognitive styles in general (Ellis, 1962) are most promising. The application of the self-instructional procedure to operant conditioning programs with human *S*s, especially children, also seems worthwhile. We suggest that having *S* self-verbalize, initially aloud and subsequently covertly, the contingencies of reinforcement will result in greater change and more generalization. Reinforcement can be made contingent upon not only the emission of the desired behavior, but also *S*'s self-verbalization of what he must do to secure reinforcement. The literature on awareness (see review by Bandura, 1969) provides further support for the possible efficacy of having *S* learn to self-verbalize the correct reinforcement rules which influence his subsequent responding.

With the cognitive training procedure, the response chain to be modified is broadened and may thus be subjected to such modification techniques as modeling, reinforcement, and aversive consequences. We have explored in a series of studies the use of behavior modification techniques to alter the self-verbalizations of such patients as phobics, schizophrenics, smokers, speech- and test-anxious *S*s, as well as impulsive children (Meichenbaum, 1970, 1971; Meichenbaum, Gilmore, & Fedoravicius, 1971; Steffy, Meichenbaum, & Best, 1970). In each case, therapeutically attending to the patient's self-verbalizations, as well as his overt maladaptive behavior, has led to greater behavioral change, greater generalization, and greater persistence of treatment effects. In each of these therapy studies the goal has been to bring *S*'s overt behavior under his own discriminative control, a means of developing the self-regulatory function of private speech.

In conclusion, a heuristic assumption underlying the present line of investigation has been that symbolic activities obey the same psychological laws as do overt behaviors and that private speech is teachable. Thus, behavior modification techniques which have been used to modify overt behaviors may be applied to cognitive processes. Only future research will indicate the validity of this assumption, but the by-products, in terms of the development of new treatment techniques, will be sizable.

References

Anthony, A. Normal and neurotic qualitative Porteus Maze performances under stress and non-stress. Unpublished PhD thesis, Columbia University, 1959.

Bandura, A. *Principles of behavior modification.* New York: Holt, Rinehart and Winston, 1969.

Bem, S. Verbal self-control: The establishment of effective self-instruction. *Journal of Experimental Psychology,* 1967, *74,* 485–491.

Bem, S. The role of comprehension in children's problem-solving. *Developmental Psychology,* 1970, *2,* 351–358.

Bereiter, C., & Engelmann, S. *Teaching disadvantaged children in the preschool.* Englewood-Cliffs, N.J.: Prentice-Hall, 1966.

Blank, M., & Solomon, F. A tutorial language program to develop abstract thinking in socially disadvantaged preschool children. *Child Development,* 1968, *39,* 379–389.

Blank, M., & Solomon, F. How should the disadvantaged child be taught? *Child Development,* 1969, *40,* 47–61.

Debus, R. L. Effects of brief observation of model behavior on conceptual tempo of impulsive children. *Developmental Psychology,* 1970, *2,* 22–32.

Drake, D. M. Perceptual correlates of impulsive and reflective behavior. *Developmental Psychology,* 1970, *2,* 202–214.

Ellis, A. *Reason and emotion in psychotherapy.* New York: Holt, Rinehart and Winston, 1962.

Eysenck, A. J. A dynamic theory of anxiety and hysteria. *Journal of Mental Science,* 1955, *101,* 128–151.

Flavell, J. H., Beach, D. R., & Chinsky, J. M. Spontaneous verbal rehearsal in a memory task as a function of age. *Child Development,* 1966, *37,* 283–299.

Foulds, G. A. Temperamental differences in maze performance. *British Journal of Psychology,* 1951, *42,* 209–217.

Grings, W. W. Verbal-perceptual factors in the conditioning of autonomic responses. In W. F. Prokasy (Ed.), *Classical conditioning: A symposium.* New York: Appleton-Century-Crofts, 1965.

Kagan, J. Impulsive and reflective children: Significance of conceptual tempo. In J. D. Krumboltz (Ed.), *Learning and the educational process.* Chicago: Rand McNally, 1965.

Kagan, J. Reflection-impulsivity: The generality and dynamics of conceptual tempo. *Journal of Abnormal Psychology,* 1966, *71,* 17–24.

Kagan, J., Pearson, L., & Welch, L. The modifiability of an impulsive tempo. *Journal of Educational Psychology,* 1966, *57,* 359–365.

Kagan, J., Rosman, B. L., Day, D., Albert, J., & Phillips, W. Information processing in the child: Significance of analytic and reflective attitudes. *Psychological Monographs,* 1964, *78* (1, Whole No. 578).

Kitzinger, H., & Blumberg, E. Supplementary guide for administering and scoring the Wechsler-Bellevue Intelligence Scale (Form I). *Psychological Monographs,* 1951, *65* (2, Whole No. 319).

Klein, W. L. An investigation of the spontaneous speech of children during problem solving. Unpublished doctoral dissertation, University of Rochester, 1963.

Kohlberg, L., Yaeger, J., & Hjertholm, E. Private speech: Four studies and a review of theories. *Child Development,* 1968, *39,* 691–736.

Lang, P. J., & Buss, A. H. Psychological deficit in schizophrenia: Interference activation. *Journal of Abnormal Psychology,* 1965, *70,* 77–106.

Lindquist, E. F. *Design and analysis of experiments in psychology and education.* Boston: Houghton Mifflin, 1953.

Lovaas, O. I. Cue properties of words: The control of operant responding by rate and content of verbal operants. *Child Development,* 1964, *35,* 245–256.

Luria, A. R. The directive function of speech in development. *Word,* 1959, *15,* 341–352.

Luria, A. R. *The role of speech in the regulation of normal and abnormal behavior.* New York: Liveright, 1961.

Lutey, C. *Individual intelligence testing: A manual.* Greeley, Colo.: Executary, 1966.

Meichenbaum, D. Cognitive factors in behavior modification: Modifying what people say to themselves. Unpublished manuscript. University of Waterloo, 1970.

Meichenbaum, D. Examination of model characteristics in reducing avoidance behavior. *Journal of Personality and Social Psychology,* 1971, *17,* 298–307.

Meichenbaum, D., Bowers, K., & Ross, R. Modification of classroom behavior of institutionalized female adolescent offenders. *Behavior Research and Therapy,* 1968, *6,* 343–353.

Meichenbaum, D., Bowers, K., & Ross, R. A behavioral analysis of teacher expectancy effect. *Journal of Personality and Social Psychology,* 1969, *13,* 306–316.

Meichenbaum, D., Gilmore, J. B., & Fedoravicius, A. Group insight versus group desensitization in treating speech anxiety. *Journal of Consulting and Clinical Psychology,* 1971, 36, 410–421.

Meichenbaum, D., & Goodman, J. The developmental control of operant motor responding by verbal operants. *Journal of Experimental Child Psychology,* 1969, *7,* 553–565. (a)

Meichenbaum, D., & Goodman, J. Reflection-impulsivity and verbal control of motor behavior. *Child Development,* 1969, *40,* 785–797. (b)

Moely, B., Olson, F., Halwes, T., & Flavell, J. Production deficiency in young children's recall. *Developmental Psychology,* 1969, *1,* 26–34.

Palkes, H., Stewart, W., & Kahana, B. Porteus Maze performance of hyperactive boys after training in self-directed verbal commands. *Child Development,* 1968, *39,* 817–826.

Piaget, J. *The psychology of intelligence.* London: Routledge & Kegan Paul, 1947.

Porteus, S. E. *Qualitative performance in the maze test.* Vineland, N.J.: Smith, 1942.

Reese, H. W. Verbal mediation as a function of age level. *Psychological Bulletin,* 1962, *59,* 502–509.

Schachter, S. The interaction of cognitive and physiological determinants of emotional state. In C. D. Speilberger (Ed.), *Anxiety and behavior.* New York: Academic Press, 1966.

Siegelman, E. Reflective and impulsive observing behavior. *Child Development,* 1969, *40,* 1213–1222.

Steffy, R., Meichenbaum, D., & Best, A. Aversive and cognitive factors in the modification of smoking behavior. *Behavior Research and Therapy,* 1970, *8,* 115–125.

Vygotsky, L. S. *Thought and language.* New York: John Wiley, 1962.

Ward, W. C. Reflection-impulsivity in kindergarten children. *Child Development,* 1968, *39,* 867–874.

Wechsler, D. *Manual: Wechsler Intelligence Scale for Children.* New York: Psychological Corporation, 1949.

27

Rational-Emotive Education

William J. Knaus

Rational-emotive therapy seeks to provide its clients with cognitive-emotive reeducation. The client is helped to unlearn old, irrational beliefs and to replace them with new, more rational ones. Rational-emotive education (REE) is a planned, systematic cognitive-emotive reeducational program for children. It is designed to teach children beliefs and problem-solving strategies that generally follow the tenets of rational-emotive therapy. More specifically, it aims to teach children such basic rational-emotive insights as how feelings develop, how to discriminate between valid and invalid assumptions, and how to think rationally in antiawful and antiperfectionistic terms. In Chapter 27, William Knaus, the person who has been primarily responsible for the development of REE, traces REE's historical roots, provides a description of its contents and uses, and reviews the literature on its efficacy.

WITH TODAY'S SEVERE manpower shortage in the mental health field, many educators and psychologists have advocated the development and use of programs to prevent emotional disturbance. Prominent among these programs have been various affective education programs whose aims are to facilitate psychological growth and adjustment and to teach the skills necessary to relate effectively to others.

Most psychological education programs represent adaptations of psychotherapeutic models. One therapeutic model currently contributing to affective education is rational-emotive therapy (RET). Rational-emotive education (REE) is an affective education program that I and my colleagues have developed that is consistent with RET.

The purpose of this chapter is to acquaint the reader with rational-emotive education. I first discuss the history of psychological education. Then I describe and discuss the content of REE. Finally, I review the research that I and others have accumulated on the effectiveness of REE.

Historical Overview of Emotional Education

Many views concerning what children are to be taught and how education is to be conducted have prevailed over the centuries. Plato, for example, viewed "training in the dialectic" as the "coping stone of the sciences." Capable persons were taught skills in asking and answering questions. This approach afforded the student the opportunity to develop true knowledge, i.e., ". . . the ability to distinguish between one and many, between ideas and the objects which partake" (Plato, p. 207). Implied in this passage is the desirability of teaching persons to distinguish between specific and general cases and between fact and fancy. Plato, in essence, wanted students to learn to think and thereby develop objectivity.

This Greek tradition, however, was abandoned by the colonial Americans who fostered an educational model based upon the inculation of Calvinist moral and religious principles. Such principles were dictated as guidelines and standards for behavior and *The New England Primer* (Ford, 1897) became the educator's bible for the instillation of these standards. The unfortunate outcome was that the primer served as a written vehicle for instilling fear and guilt in children.

During the latter half of the eighteenth century, the average American continued to reflect the religious doctrines and class prejudices of colonial days. In the nineteenth century, however, some important changes in educational thinking began to erupt. Leaders of the Enlightenment, specificaly John Locke, Jean Jacques Rousseau, and Johann Pestalozzi, stimulated a view of man as a product of his environment. The child was seen as a potentially good creature who could be developed and perfected through education (Butts and Crenin, 1953).

Pestalozzi in particular provided a concept of how young children learn best. He suggested that education should be an enjoyable process and emphasized that the teacher's role is to organize and correlate information rather than to drill, to use love rather than punishment as a disciplinary technique, and to aid children to learn through doing. This view was further emphasized by the associationist Herbart who believed that learning is best accomplished when related to something which is already known (Boring, 1957).

William James (1899) also emphasized the importance of a nonaversive learning environment. He rejected stern discipline, which he called "inhibition by negation," as a classroom management technique and, even more importantly, suggested that learning is most closely related to the emotions and feelings of the learner. He stated that the development of positive feelings of curiosity and interest ("inhibition by substitution") was most likely to ensure lasting desired results in the learner.

One of James' contemporaries, Dewey, advocated the position that values are not static entities, but rather grow from human experience. He viewed human intelligence as offering the best hope for man in solving his problems and living according to his values. The role of education, according to Dewey, was thus to enable students to develop their ability to actualize their values in their daily lives.

Following this leadership, a humanistic movement designed to aid the child in his intellectual-emotional development was already afoot at the turn of the twentieth century and continues to this day in American education. The core of ideas describing the emotional education wave of today are:

1. Each and every child has a right to develop his unique potentialities.

2. The role of education is to aid the child in understanding and adjusting to his world and in preparing himself for particpating in the process of change.

3. The child learns through active problem-solving.

4. Attitudes, feelings, and emotions play a vital role in teaching and learning.

In the last decade, an eruption of ideas and programs designed to foster emotional growth in the classroom has taken place. Many of these programs have been designed to prevent children from developing emotional-behavioral problems, to help children cope with problems when they do arise, and to generally promote the actualization of their potential. Indeed, the movement has been of such great importance as to prompt editors of the *Personnel and Guidance Journal* (May 1973, Vol. 51, No. 9) to commit an entire issue to the description and discussion of psychological educational programs in the schools.

Carl Rogers, a zealous advocate of humane learning environments, has continued to be a strong spokesman in advocating changes in the classroom which foster student self-determination and knowledge of how to learn. He strongly opposes pounding facts into children's heads through rote drill methods (Rogers, 1961, 1967). From a behavioristic vantage, Skinner's (1965) strong statement in "Why Teachers Fail" included specific ideas on the extinction of aversive teacher behaviors and the increase of facilitative behaviors in the teaching process. Bijou (1970) extends the behavioristic view by advocating that teachers employ principles derived from experimental analysis of behavior: "to look carefully to the relationships between observable environmental and behavioral events and their changes."

In applying Reality Therapy principles to the schools, Glasser (1968) posits teacher techniques, including a class meeting model, to promote development of student responsibilities and adaptive behavior and attitudes. He believes that the student's taking responsibility for himself is instrumental in learning and in fostering a sense of self-worth, and he therefore suggests that teacher facilitate self-direction in children. Furthermore, he emphasizes that guidance and teaching personnel would wisely make themselves more knowledgeable about group processes and use this knowledge in the creation of the learning environment.

Values clarification procedures have recently come into vogue. Simons, Howe, and Kirschenbaum (1972) have provided a program for teachers to employ with their classes in order to aid students to understand their personal values.

Major efforts have been made by other proponents of the psychological education movement, in particular Weinstein and Fantini (1970), Weinstein (1973), Alschuler (1969), and Ivey and Alschuler (1973). These educational specialists have directed their efforts to aid students in self-determination through the addition of self-help and psychological learning principles in the curriculum, and have evolved a variety of salient techniques to further this end.

Numerous other people from various psychological and educational schools of thought and traditions, in addition to the above mentioned psychological or emotional educational advocates, have made contributions (Lyon, 1971; Heath, 1971; Dinkmeyer, 1973; Besell and Palomares, 1970; Maslow, 1970; Roen, 1964; Stone, Hinds, & Schmidt, 1975; Mosher and Sprinthal, 1970; Brown, 1971). Specifically, these mental health advocates have tried to include the affective component of education in the academic phases of the curriculum (Keats, Leaman, Logan, Malecki, & McDuffy, 1975). Jerome Bruner, through *Man, A Course of Study* (1966), has introduced a curriculum in the schools which provides avenues for children to develop understanding of cultural differences and to develop tolerance for differences between peoples.

Among the prominent humanistic psychological-educational or affective educational programs currently available is rational-emotive education (REE). It provides the helping person with a comprehensive array of cognitive-emotive-behavioral strategies for helping students identify and accept their feelings, and cope with and change maladaptive thoughts and behavior.

An Overview of Rational-Emotive Education

Rational-emotive education (REE) provides a systematic approach for teaching problem-solving strategies that follows the tenets of rational-emotive psychotherapy (Ellis, 1962; Ellis and Harper, 1961; Goodman and Maultsby, 1974). While REE is philosophically identical to RET, it more strongly emphasizes experiential learning as advocated by Dewey (Bernstein, 1960) and Piaget and Inhelder (1970), and simulation strategies as described by Knaus and Wessler (1976). REE further assumes that children will learn rational coping strategies through the presentation of tasks and problems in a group atmosphere.

Rational-emotive education, unlike the psychotherapeutic process, is a planned sequence of emotional lessons that follows a thematic format (Knaus, 1974; Knaus and Eyman, 1974; Knaus and McKeever, 1977). REE provides an experiential avenue for both teachers and students to learn self-help skills and concepts by following a sequence of lessons that increasingly enables the participants to gain important emotional insights, to learn basic problem-solving skills, and to examine the outcome of their efforts. Thus, when a child encounters emotional-behavioral problems, he will have a firm foundation of knowledge and applicable practical skills.

The structured thematic format in REE includes units which aid children to learn about feelings and how they develop, to discriminate between assumptions and facts, to challenge ideas underlying inferiority feelings, to accept imperfection, to deal with painful emotional overreactions (depressions, anxiety), to develop perspective, to tolerate the discomfort of frustration, to get along better with others, to cope with bullies, and to deal with sex-role stereotyping.

Chapter 3 of *Rational Emotive Education* (Knaus, 1974) illustrates how REE is used. This unit is designed to help children define and identify common feelings and to demonstrate that feelings are influenced by thoughts. One lesson of this chapter emphasizes a pantomime game (The Expression Guessing Game), which helps students learn that persons do not uniformly express feelings in identical ways, and furthermore, that a person can only accurately determine the likelihood of what another person is feeling by asking. To demonstrate these individual differences, the classroom group leader selects several groups of volunteers to pantomime a particular feeling in their own individual styles. Each group takes turns pantomiming a different feeling while the rest of the class guesses the feeling being expressed through the pantomime.

The REE program provides for transfer of learning by encouraging the children to test in various situations in their lives the principles that they are learning. In The Expression Guessing Game described above, for example, the students may be assigned the task of asking the teacher how he/she may be feeling at various times of the day and thereby may check out their guesses. The principles may also be applied in spontaneously occurring problem situations. In one classroom, for instance, a child initially upset himself by concluding that his friend didn't like him when he perceived him angry. Rather than wallowing in depression or acting out, the child was able to use the concepts learned in The Expression Guessing Game to deal with the problem by checking his perceptions and discovering that his friend was indeed feeling angry, but that the anger was not directed towards him.

Rational-emotive educational concepts can be formally woven into the regular curriculum as a preventative mental health tool. In this instance the goal is to teach children to think objectively. This may be accomplished by assigning children the task of examining the impact that certain beliefs have on their own and others' behavior. Superstition, for example, can be examined in social studies units where children look at the basis for fearing black cats and fearing Friday the thirteenth as a day of bad luck. Once the child has learned to recognize his own personal irrational fear-inducing assumptions, these methods of challenging beliefs may then be later employed as personal problem-solving tactics.

Indeed, the classroom can be a fertile ground where children learn a multiplicity of rational coping strategies through the REE program. For example, children can be taught an emotive vocabulary to enable them more accurately to identify and express feelings. Many youngsters are handicapped in terms of this skill. They speak in generalities and fail to specify feelings accurately. Teaching students to use descriptive and concrete words and phrases thus aids them in their work and in their everyday life situations.

Behavioral strategies can be employed adjunctively with REE. Token economies as described by Kazden (1975) can be established with the intent of reinforcing youngsters for actively testing rational coping behaviors. Within problem circumstances, a child may be reinforced with tokens exchangeable for prizes when he strives to cope rationally with the difficulty. Tokens may further be employed to encourage positive experimental risk-taking behaviors, such as when a shy child volunteers to speak in front of the class.

The author has also developed an evocative technique combining REE with reinforcement to challenge resistive children to assert their power in appropriate ways. For example, in a first group meeting with eight hyperactive, emotionally disturbed 11-year-old and 12-year-old boys, the author suggested that the group probably wouldn't focus on what the leader was saying because he doubted if the group could sit still for even one-half hour. When one member challenged him, the author told the group that he would be willing to give each member a dime if the group could stay in focus for one-half hour, but that he doubted that he would have to pay off since the group ". . . was sure to goof up." The stipulation was that all members would have to stay focused on the "feeling lesson," actively ask and answer questions, and not get up from their seats. The group successfully rose to the challenge, and the author was short eighty cents at the end of the half-hour. Consistent with the REE focus, the author actively interacted with the youngsters to help them see how one's thinking influences his feelings and actions. Using examples supplied by the group members themselves, he began to show the group how to cope with frustrations and impulsivity. In the second group meeting, the dime reward was withdrawn; however, the group remained attentive through-out the one-half-hour session. A new motivational concept was intro-duced. In conference with the author, the group became enthusiastic about learning rational concepts to develop mental muscle. The approach was labeled "mental karate." It was pointed out that in karate one learns physical defense methods. In mental karate, one learns to cope by learn-ing how to ward off insults and other means by which people come to needlessly upset themselves. Different-colored wrist bands were created to represent varying levels of competency in this coping process. The group members chose to wear these wrist bands only during group meet-ings as they decided that mental karate would be their secret weapon for self-control and they did not want to advertise their competency.

Research in Rational-Emotive Education Methods

Evidence for the efficacy of rational-emotive techniques with children derives from two lines of evidence: case studies and controlled experi-mental studies.

Ellis (1966) has provoided numerous supporting case examples in which RET has been used therapeutically with children. His contention (1966) that rational-emotive therapy is effective with youngsters has gained widespread support from various practitioners (Lafferty, Den-nerll, and Rettich, 1964; Hauck, 1967; McGrory, 1967; Wolfe, 1970; Knaus, 1970; DiGiuseppe, 1975; DiNublie and Wessler, 1974; Daly, 1971; Wagner and Glicken, 1966).

RET's efficacy with children, however, goes far beyond testimonials and descriptive reports and finds firm support in the experimental litera-ture. In the forefront of this literature is burgeoning literature on REE. In two pilot studies designed to examine the effectiveness of rational-emotive education lessons, Albert (1971) compared a rational-emotive group with an attention-placebo group. The population for the first study consisted of fifth-grade inner-city school children with a multiplicity of overt signs of emotional disturbance. The subjects for the second study consisted of youngsters in the same grade and school who were rela-tively free of overt signs of emotional disturbance. Both studies were run during the same time period. Subjects were pretested and posttested using the Test Anxiety Scale (TAS) and rated according to eleven dimensions of classroom behavior on a behavioral rating scale (BRS). Subjects met in their respective groups one hour per day, four days per week, for five consecutive weeks. Results showed that children participating in the rational-emotive education groups demonstrated significantly less test anxiety and significantly more positive classroom behaviors than their attention-placebo group counterparts.

Knaus and Bokor (1975) completed a 6-month study comparing REE with a Self-Esteem Enhancement Group (SEEG) procedure and a no-treatment control condition. The groups were three intact, heterogeneous eighth-grade classrooms in a low-income school district. All groups were posttested one month after the completion of the program. Both the REE and SEEG conditions demonstrated significantly more positive results on the TAS and the Coopersmith Self-Esteem Inventory (SEI), but the REE group demonstrated significantly more positive results on the TAS and SEI compared to the SEEG condition.

Working with fifth-grade youngsters in a middle-income school district, Brody (1974) found that, in a comparison between a group taught using rational-emotive skills and an attention-placebo and no-treatment control condition, the rational-emotive education group demonstrated significantly higher self-esteem, less test anxiety, and greater tolerance for frustration. On a follow-up study the trend continued; however, the difference between conditions no longer remained statistically significant.

DiGiuseppe and Kassinove (1976) examined the effectiveness of a rational-emotive mental health program for children's emotional adjustment and found that rational-emotive procedures can be acquired by school children and that such acquisition corresponded with lowered trait anxiety and neuroticism scores.

In a program using rational-emotive education lessons with inner-city 17-year-old and 18-year-old students with high absenteeism and academic failure rates, Knaus and Block (1976) found that a 6-month REE program effectively reduced subject failure rate, increased school attendance, increased self-concept and socialization and ethical awareness as compared to a passive, nondirective condition and to a no-treatment control group.

Katz (1974) investigated rational-emotive education versus a mental health program founded on psychoanalytic principles. The rational-emotive education children had significantly higher posttest scores than the analytic mental health program children on the Coopersmith Self-Esteem Behavior Rating Form, but not on any of the other measures employed.

It is obvious that the research necessary to fully substantiate the efficacy of REE and to work out all its bugs is far from complete. Yet, across the various reported studies, results consistently favor rational-emotive education approaches as most effective. This has been found to be true utilizing different measures, using different rational-emotive procedures, and in comparison with attention-placebo, nondirective, psychoanalytic, and self-esteem enhancement comparison groups.

Although the application of rational-emotive education is still in its infancy and almost certainly will be modified as warranted by further research, it surely merits consideration as a viable preventive mental-health approach within the schools. Furthermore, REE appears to have excellent face and content validity, in addition to its rapidly growing empirical support regarding its effectiveness as a cognitive-behavioral approach to human problem-solving.

References

Albert, S. A study to determine the effectiveness of affective education with fifth-grade students. Unpublished master's thesis, Queens College, 1971.

Alschuler, A. Psychological education. *Humanistic Psychology,* 1969, *9,* 1–15.

Bernstein, R. J. *Dewey on experience, nature and freedom.* New York: Liberal Arts Press, 1960.

Besell, H., and Palomares, A. *Methods in human development: theory, manual and curriculum activity guide.* San Diego: Human Development Training Institute, 1970.

Bijou, S. What psychology has to offer education—now. *Journal of Applied Behavioral Analysis,* 1970, *3* (1), 65–71.

Boring, E. G. *A history of experimental psychology* (2nd ed.), New York: Appleton-Century-Crofts, 1957.

Borton, T. *Reach, touch and teach.* New York: McGraw-Hill, 1970.

Brody, M. The effect of the rational-emotive affective education approach on anxiety, frustration tolerance, and self-esteem with fifth-grade students. Unpublished doctoral dissertation, Temple University, 1974.

Brown, G. I. *Human teaching for human learning: An introduction to confluent education.* New York: Viking Press, 1971.

Bruner, J. S. Man: a course of study. *E.S.I. Quarterly Report,* 1966 (Spring/Summer), 2–13.

Butts, R. F., and Cremin, L. A. *A history of education in American culture.* New York: Henry Holt and Co., 1953.

Daly, S. Using reason with deprived pre-school children. *Rational Living,* 1971, *5* (2), 12–19.

DeVoge, C. A behavioral approach to RET with children. *Rational Living,* 1974, *9*(1), 23–26.

DiGiuseppe, R. The use of behavioral modification to establish rational self-statements in children. *Rational Living,* 1975, *10*(2), 18–20.

DiGiuseppe, R., and Kassinove, H. Effects of a rational-emotive school mental health program on childrens' emotional adjustment. *Journal of Community Psychology,* 1976, *4*(4), 382–387.

Dinkmeyer, D. *Developing understanding of self and others.* Circle Pines, Minn.: American Guidance Services, D-1 (1973); D-2 (1973).

DiNublie, L., and Wessler, R. Lessons from the Living School. *Rational Living,* 1974, *9*(1), 29–32.

Doress, I. The teacher as therapist. *Rational Living,* 1966, *2*(1), 27.

Ellis, A. *Reason and emotion in psychotherapy.* New York: Lyle Stuart, 1962.

Ellis, A., and Harper, R. *A guide to rational living.* New York: Prentice-Hall, 1961.

Ellis, A. *How to prevent your child from becoming a neurotic adult.* New York: Crown, 1966.

Ellis, A. Rational-emotive therapy and its application to emotional education. Paper delivered at the 17th International Congress of the International Association of Applied Psychology, Liege, Belgium, 1971.

Ellis, A. An experiment in emotional education. *Educational Technology,* 1971, *11*(7), 61–64.

Ellis, A. Emotional education at the living school. In M. M. Ohlsen (Ed.), *Counseling children in groups.* New York: Holt, Rinehart and Winston, 1973.

Ford, R. (Ed.) *The New England primer.* New York: Dodd Mead, 1897.

Glasser, W. *Schools without failure.* New York: Harper & Row, 1968.

Goodman, D. S., and Maultsby, M. C. *Emotional well-being through rational behavioral training.* Springfield, Ill.: Charles C Thomas, 1974.

Greenberg, H. M. *Teaching with feeling.* New York: Macmillan, 1969.

Hauck, P. *The rational management of children.* New York: Leber, 1967.

Heath, D. H. *Humanizing schools: New directions, new decisions.* New York: Hyden, 1971.

Ivey, A., and Alschuler, A. Psychological education: An introduction to the field. *Personnel and Guidance Journal,* 1973, *51*(9), 591–597.

James, W. *Talks to teachers on psychology: and to the students on some of life's ideas.* Boston: George H. Ellis, 1899.

Katz, S. The effect of emotional education on locus of control and self concept. Unpublished doctoral dissertation, Hofstra University, 1974.

Kazden, A. *Behavioral modification in applied settings.* Homewood, Ill.: Dorsey, 1975.

Keats, D. B., Leaman, L., Logan, W., Malecki, D., and McDuffy, I. Psychological education: The formulation of twenty-first century man. *Psychology in the Schools,* 1975, 12, 43–49.

Knaus, W. Innovative use of parents and teachers as behavior modifiers. Paper presented at combined Seventh Annual School Psychology Conference and Second Annual Special Education Conference. New York: Queens College Publications, January, 1970.

Knaus, W. *Rational-emotive education: A manual for elementary school teachers.* New York: Institute for Rational Living, 1974.

Knaus, W., and Block, J. Rational-emotive education with economically disadvantaged inner city high school students: A demonstration study. Unpublished manuscript, 1976.

Knaus, W., and Bokor, S. The effect of rational-emotive education lessons on anxiety and self-concept in sixth-grade students. *Rational Living,* 1975, *11*(2), 7–10.

Knaus, W. and Eyman, W. Progress in rational-emotive education. *Rational Living,* 1974, *9*(2), 27–29.

Knaus, W. and McKeever, C. Rational-emotive education with learning disabled children. *Journal of Learning Disabilities,* 1977, *10*(1), 10–14.

Knaus, W. and Wessler, R. Rational-emotive problem simulation. *Rational Living,* 1976, *11*(2), 8–11.

Lafferty, G., Dennerll, A. and Rettlich, G. A creative school mental health program. *National Elementary Principal,* 1964, *43*(5), 28–35.

Leonard, G. B. *Education and ecstasy.* New York: Delta, 1968.

Lyon, J. C. *Learning to feel—feeling to learn.* Columbus, Ohio: Charles E. Merrill, 1971.

Maslow, A. H. Peak experiences in education and art. *Humanist,* 1970, *30*(5), 29–31.
Maultsby, M., Knipping, P., and Carpenter, L. Teaching self-help in the classroom with rational self-counseling. *Journal of School Health,* 1974, *44*(8), 445–448.
McGrory, J. Teaching introspection in the classroom. *Rational Living,* 1967, *2*(2) 23–24.
Mental health and learning: A joint publication of the U.S. Office of Education and the National Institute of Mental Health. Rockville, Maryland, (HSM), 72–9146, 1972.
Mosher, R., and Sprinthal, N. Psychological education in secondary schools: A program to promote individual and human development. *American Psychologist.* 1970, *25,* 911–124.
Personnel and Guidance Journal, 1973, *51*(9) (whole number).
Piaget, J., and Inhelder, B. *The psychology of the child.* New York: Basic Books, 1970.
Plato. *The Republic.* New York: Random House, n.d.
Roen, S. The behavioral sciences in the primary grades. Paper presented at the American Psychological Association convention, Washington, D.C., September, 1964.
Rogers, C. R. *On becoming a person.* Boston: Houghton-Mifflin, 1961.
Rogers, C. R. The interpersonal relationship. In Robert Harper (Ed.), *The facilitation of learning humanizing education: The person in the process.* Washington, D.C.: Association for Supervision and Curriculum Development, 1967, 1–18.
Rogers, C. R. *Freedom to learn: A view of what education might become.* Columbus, Ohio: Charles E. Merrill, 1969.
Sanford, G., and Sanford, C. Affective approaches to literature. *English Journal,* 1973, *62*(1), 64–68.
Simons, S. G., Howe, L. W., Kirschenbaum, H. *Values clarification: A handbook of practical strategies for teachers and students.* New York: Hart, 1972.
Skinner, B. F. Why teachers fail. *Saturday Review,* October 16, 1965, 80–82 and 90–103.
Stone, G., Hinds, W., and Schmidt, G. Teaching mental health behaviors to elementary school children. *Professional Psychology,* 1975, *40,* 34–40.
Todd, K. *Promoting mental health in the classroom: A handbook for teachers.* Rockville, Maryland. National Institute for Mental Health (ADM) 74-25, 1973.
Wagner, E., and Glicken, M. Counseling children: Two accounts. *Rational Living,* 1966, *1*(2), 26–30.
Weinstein, G. Self-Science Education: The trumpet. *Personnel and Guidance Journal,* 1973, *51*(9), 600–606.
Weinstein, G., and Fantini, M. D. *Towards humanistic education: A curriculum of affect.* New York: Praeger, 1970.
Wolfe, J. Emotional education in the classroom. *Rational Living,* 1970, *4*(2), 23–25.

28

Irrational Parenting Styles

Paul A. Hauck

It is an interesting phenomenon in the field of child psychotherapy that the least effective modes of intervention are often the ones most frequently practiced. In particular, most child psychotherapists ignore the many outcome studies which show that the most productive focus of intervention is working with the parents of a referred child, while the least productive focus is on working with the child alone. Instead, most psychotherapists focus exclusively or at least predominantly on the child client. No doubt this misplaced emphasis has in large measure been caused by the prevalent notion that emotional disturbance represents a psychic disease.

Paul Hauck has for years been a leading RET figure associated with the treatment of disturbed children, parents, and families. In Chapter 28 he speaks to therapists as he focuses on common parental practices that lead to and help sustain emotional disturbances in children. He discusses three of the more common yet erroneous beliefs about child-rearing that are particularly destructive to children: children must *not disagree with their superiors; children* must *not be frustrated; and children should be calmed first, adults second. He then outlines three patterns of child-rearing grounded on combinations of these erroneous beliefs. Throughout Chapter 28 there is an emphasis on how to work with parents in helping them and their children overcome problems.*

IF THERE IS ONE THING parents want from a counselor, it's advice. They don't want a long spiel about feelings, a delving into their history, or a kindly, pipe-smoking therapist who nods his head gravely and murmurs, "I see," every so often. Parents want advice because they need it. Though they may have studied philosophy, religion, music, and even psychology, chances are they know next to nothing about being parents. Come to think of it, lots of therapists don't know a heck of a lot about parenting either. It's only been of late (the last ten years) that real strides have been made in the area of parent and child psychology. These gains have enabled us to do a solid job for parents and children for the first time since the mental health movement began. Much of this is due to contributions from RET and the work of Rudolf Dreikurs (Dreikurs,

Gould, & Corsini, 1974), an Adlerian. Any counselor with a good exposure to both of these schools of thought will be well-equipped to advise
parents on how to raise stable children.

Reactive versus Manipulatory Behavior

One of the first issues the clinician wants to settle on initially meeting a
child and his parents is whether the objectionable behavior is the result
of typical irrational thinking and shows itself as neurotic symptoms
(fear, anger, depression, poor self-discipline), or if it is the product of
manipulations by the child to attain one or more of four specific goals:
attention, power, revenge, or disability.

If you decide the behavior in question is of the reactive type, you
will listen to the events in the child's life which may have indirectly
precipitated his symptoms and, with your knowledge of cognitive-behavior
techniques, pick out the irrational ideas causing the symptoms and pre-
scribe homework assignments to the child or parent to decondition them
out of their poor habits. Should you conclude the behavior is manipulative, you will be focusing on the target that his behavior is gauged to elicit.
He may be depressed for attention; angry to prove he is more powerful
than his parents; fearful to revenge himself against worrying parents; or
poorly self-disciplined to prove he is weak and so afraid of growing up
that no adult demands will be made of him. All of these behavior
disorders stem from a series of parenting errors which are so frequent
they form patterns of conduct.

Common Errors of Parenting

I shall focus on only several of the ten erroneous beliefs of child management which I first wrote of in *The Rational Management of Children*
(Hauck, 1967). These are so common and so devastating they deserve
to be singled out. As long as a parent is guilty of one of these practices
he or she can someday expect trouble.

1. Children Must Not Question or Disagree with Their Superiors.

Some parents will not take kindly to a bit of advice contrary to this.
They want you to back them on all issues and when you intimate here or
there that the child might be right, watch out! That's how psychology
gets a bad name. We're accused of spoiling the next generation when, in
fact, we're giving it confidence and strength we don't get credit for.

Teaching children to think for themselves carries with it the essential ingredient of mental health. RET is based on that very skill: challenging one set of beliefs that are commonly thought to be sound until their incorrectness is detected. To get the parent to accept this piece of advice, the therapist emphasizes the need for the child to learn through hard experience. If he, the parent, is so right, why get so uptight over the youngster's rebellion? All he has to do is wait long enough and his child will bump his nose on some error and prove in a bloody demonstration how right his parents were. Doing the opposite, namely, shoving your wisdom down the boy's throat, can cause immediate psychological vomitus in the form of a power struggle.

This phenomena is becoming increasingly common in this period of greater freedoms for adolescents: i.e., voting and drinking. Instead of snapping his heels obediently at an order as he might have done a few generations ago, the modern boy becomes a "smart aleck" and does the opposite of what he's told. However, that's not all bad. Advise the father to give his advice once or twice and then hold his peace. What happens to the boy thereafter is the boy's responsibility. This can be serious, as for example if the parent's warning is not heeded. That's how some youngsters get killed riding motorcycles, or end up arrested for drugs. The parent is proven correct at great price. That's a chance you tell the parent to take.

Actually the parent has no option in the matter. Even if we would advise him not to let up on his warnings about bike accidents or drug busts, the kid in a power struggle is going to do the opposite of what he's told. So your best bet is to caution the parents against pushing an oppositional youngster too far. By reminding mother and father that they do not *need* to be upset over other people's problems and disturbances and that it is not *vitally* important to their existence what the boy does, you assure them of taking a sane course which has a chance eventually of making an impression on the boy and which puts the responsibilities for his behavior on his back.

The common age at which a child questions the wisdom of his parents is when he approaches teenhood. Overnight that sweet boy or girl becomes a mean and disobedient demon. That's the power struggle and the child is questioning everything he or she has ever been told. So be it. Back off, let them question and shape their lives according to what they find out the hard way. When they aren't injured by their foolishness, they also help change the world for the better with their fresh views on politics, religion, sex, and fashion. The society that does not encourage the challenging of tradition (the Indians or the Australian aborigines) can go on for centuries with practically no change.

2. Children Must Not Be Frustrated.

Something serious is happening to us as a people and especially to our children. We have developed a condition which can be called frustration-phobia. We seem hell bent on making life so easy and pleasant that frustration has become a dirty word. Parents who come to therapists over guilt for the frustrations they cannot remove from their children can have that burden relieved if we make it clear to them that protecting children from many of life's frustrations is actually harmful for children. The value of living through frustrations and growing strong in the process is currently not sufficiently appreciated. We so much want to spare our children pain that they often do not know how to tolerate it and work effectively at the same time.

It seems most people honestly believe they cannot be expected to continue with their responsibilities if they are frustrated. A young husband does not like taking orders from his boss. He finds it frustrating and feels completely justified in telling the employer to go soak his head. The idea that the young man is expected to do his work whether he's unhappy or not is foreign to him. Nonsense! Let him learn to put up with the unpleasantness in life. Who the dickens ever told him in the first place that this was supposed to be a fair world? And what about the high school senior who bugs his parents for a car because he wants one and all his friends already have one? We surely could let the young man earn the money for his car, or have him ride a bike, or, if that's too inconvenient on the parents, let him walk.

One father, well-meaning, wanted to spare his son the frustration of running out of money through foolishly spending his allowance. The father constantly advised his son about spending his money carefully until the son angrily defied his dad. Not knowing how to reach the boy, the man sought me out for help in sparing his son the frustrations he was sure to endure if he did not handle his funds more wisely.

There it was again—that dread of leaving someone frustrated, the need to do something, anything, about sparing someone a few moments displeasure. I had no such problem and therefore advised the father to stop advising his son what to do but to allow him to suffer with his errors.

"But," protested the man, "if I do that John will be broke in a couple of days and I'm not supposed to give him his allowance again for about two weeks. What's the boy going to do?"

"Suffer," I responded, calmly but very seriously.

"Yes, I know. But what can I do to spare him that?"

"You've already done all you can. You've warned and advised him against being reckless. If he doesn't follow your advice, let him go without money and let the unpleasantness of being penniless convince him where you couldn't."

This approach makes constructive use of frustration. It takes it as an unavoidable quality of life and welcomes the good that comes from it. And when you think of it, isn't the inability to bear frustration a major characteristic of the neurotic and the immature?

It's time we counselors saw the great benefits to be gained through suffering. Instead of always sparing people stress, let's help them endure some of it. Starting with the parents is one of the soundest approaches. Self-discipline and the demands it makes for delayed satisfaction is one of the great benefits to be gained through temporary distress. Learning to overcome fears requires the same tolerance of tension that self-discipline does, often more. If a person escapes from frustration each time he faces a stressful situation, such as dancing before a crowded ballroom for the first time, giving a public address, risking failure and humiliation, he will never master any of these skills. The best way to conquer fear is to face the fear repeatedly until familiarity breeds contempt. But during that period of adjustment and desensitization, the fear takes its toll. The subject is made nervous, tense, worried, depressed, and what not in anticipation of the worst. Too bad! Our advice had better be from henceforth: Stay with it. Do not run from the experience merely because it is painful. If you endure some pain now you will endure less pain eventually. Do not excuse yourself by insisting you cannot be expected to perform merely because you are upset. Rubbish. Actors on an opening night are often filled with stage fright. No one in the audience nor in the stage production would accept this as a valid excuse for not making the show go on.

Good work can be performed by people under great frustration, while they are frustrated, fearful, and tense. The effort will have to be greater, of course, but it can be done. That is why children had better be taught to live with some frustrations for limited periods of time. They don't stand a snowball's chance in hell of growing strong unless they do.

3. Children Should Be Calmed First, Adults Second.

This is a critical error. The family that defines the child as sick fails to realize its own significant contribution to the disturbance. Not only is it unfair to assume everything will be all right as soon as that kid shapes up, but expectations for the child to accomplish a degree of control the parent won't achieve is unrealistic. For example, if you as a parent get angry at the fresh backtalk of your children, stop and think how unreasonable you're being. You want your 10-year-old boy to control himself in a fully mature way, but you, the supposedly mature adult, can get as angry as you like. You insist he get hold of himself first, then you will get hold of yourself.

That's putting the cart before the horse. Get yourself in tow first, then deal with the child. In this way you avoid a great deal of unfairness. You will generally be more calm when you get back to the problem with the child and that automatically means more fairness. Parents who put the responsibility for their composure on their children attack the child, sometimes literally, and then regain themselves at the cost of the child's efforts. This is wrong. Children do not upset us, only frustrate us. They have a greater right to behave neurotically than we do because they're children. And they have less expectation to talk themselves back to stability, again because they are the children and we the adults. But this is precisely the opposite of what we expect. I've seen many parents scream at their offspring because they weren't doing what the parents themselves could not do.

Helping parents gain control is quite possible if you assure them that with much practice they can learn to first calm themselves and then deal fairly with the disturbances of their children. This would easily diminish child-abuse brought on by impulsive actions. It would also reduce those extreme penalties parents sentence their children to in the heat of a quarrel. In the fury of an altercation, some children have been grounded to their rooms after school for a month at a time. An hour later the extravagance of that penalty becomes clear, but only when Mom or Dad lets the dust settle.

A final benefit from getting the parents to focus upon themselves first is the lessened amount of blame to which the child is exposed. Blame is just about the most neurotic of all the neurotic acts. It stirs your blood to a mean point where you're often unreasonable and saying things only calculated to hurt. What this does to you physically can be serious. Blaming your child, however, can ruin him for years. The inferiority feelings he must deal with, the depressions, and the training he or she gets in the act of hating can cause all kinds of misery to all kinds of people.

In summary, as a therapist it is your task to explain to your parent-clients that they wrongly believe: (1) we upset children by frustrating them; (2) they upset us after they become disturbed; (3) to restore peace and harmony, the child's emotions must be calmed first; (4) this will cause the parent's disturbance to diminish.

You will want instead to get them to accept the following thinking: (1) We frustrate our children, who, because of their immaturity, upset themselves; (2) we do not use this problem as a reason for us to create a greater problem—self-disturbance; (3) having focused on our feelings and tried to limit our problems just to the children, we devote our attention to them and apply all our knowledge to helping them calm down and then teach them to remove, minimize, or avoid future frustrations.

Patterns of Kindness and Firmness

The errors mentioned above are several of almost a dozen which are often practiced in such a combination that they fall in common patterns. These patterns have predictable effects on the rearing of children.

Unkind and Firm

There's nothing wrong with being consistent in your discipline, following through with your promises or threats, and teaching a child self-discipline. Unfortunately, this aspect of child-rearing is often flavored in many families with a strong dose of unkindness. The combination is often demonstrated in instances where a child has failed to do a chore. The irate mother wisely says, "You'll not be able to come to the dinner table until you wash your hands," and then gets mean by saying, "Why do you always have to be so difficult? Do you always have to give me so much trouble?" Can you see the two separate messages? One is sound and leads to strength; the second leads to guilt, depression, and resentment.

Past generations have been raised largely by this pattern. Unquestioning obedience toward authority coupled with a kick in the ego has given the world some of its finest neurotics. Masochists throughout history have felt deserving of their suffering because someone was hard as nails with them and also convinced them that they deserved it. Your typical depressive and your obsessive-compulsive, even your anxiety neurotic, are all products of those daily put-downers and criticisms while still demanding total conformity.

Parents with this pattern are well-advised to continue expecting sensible behavior from their children but to leave off the blame, the dirty digs, and the slaps. And this is where the psychology of anger is so vital. It is practically impossible to convince a child you love him if you are angry much of the time. Even if you accept the new psychological thinking which suggests that you separate the child as a person from his actions and say to him, "I love you but I don't like what you did," you would not make much sense to the child because he wouldn't believe you. Just about the only way a boy or girl is going to believe that an irritating action does not turn mother or father against him or her is if the complaint is made in a relatively matter-of-fact way, not with great feeling.

If the child says, "George Washington was our second president," most parents would simply point to the error and let the matter rest. The child could accept that correction and not even question whether he was a worthwhile person for erring since no one has suggested with word or feeling that he was a nothing. But if the parent corrects the child with, "Washington was our first president, stupid," you have a situation where a self-rating will surely take place. The child will modify his belief about Washington (which is fine), but he will now also modify his belief about himself (and that is neurotic and painful).

Kind and Not Firm

The opposite of the above pattern is to be kind and not firm. Instead of raising scared, nervous, insecure, and inferior-feeling children, parents who practice this second combination develop personalities in their children which are very different. These kids, being seldom frustrated, set up their own rules, often get their way, and tend to be spoiled brats. They are the whiners of the world, the darlings of Mom and Dad who can't stand ice cream if it's older than a week, who get threatened and furious if you turn your back on them to talk to someone else, and who act like eternal babies. Even when they do turn out to be fairly pleasing people, they still live under great fear of having to live on their own someday.

Just this week I saw a middle-aged adult who still lived at home with Mommy and Daddy, who hadn't earned $25 in all of his life, and who was so protected by his folks that he couldn't stand up without looking around to see what the strong people in his life thought. He was quick to let it be known that he's fragile and always had been, that he was picked on by kids when he was in school and, therefore, couldn't we see why he couldn't continue in school.

Strength of character does not come from being too helpful. It especially does not come from hesitating to let a child suffer. When will some parents learn that suffering (up to a point) is very productive? Had Junior been allowed the privilege of working his own way out of his pain, he would have developed into a real man. But this was denied Mr. Marshmallow, whose life will forever be lonely, unfulfilled, and largely unhappy. And just imagine what he's going to go through when his parents die!

Mental health professions are seeing more and more such people who, when they burn their toast, get upset. If hubby comes home late a few times they go into a major depression. If he can't have a new motorcycle or she a new freezer, watch out! The backlash can be serious.

What these people had better learn is the ability to put up with frustration like an adult. They simply haven't grown up yet, and react to each disappointment as though they were five years old and were denied an ice cream cone. The stoic philosophy is foreign to them because they were reared with kindness but little firmness.

Unkind and Not Firm

This is a wicked combination. How can the child win if he's yelled at, scolded, told he's no good, but at the same time has no strong hand over him making him correct his irritating behavior? It's one thing to yell at an adolescent for not studying but then ground him or penalize him until he bring his grades up, and its entirely another thing for him to be screamed at for poor grades and then allowed to stay out every night after dark. The help he needs to control or change his behavior is lacking. He, in effect, is expected to be his own conscience and supervisor, his own parent, with the widom to do what is right even though he's only a child.

People who get in trouble with the law often suffer from this combination. The truant child is yelled at by his wishy-washy mother, but she doesn't sit on him hard enough to bring him in line. All she does is complain more and more and do less and less.

I see a lot of this today. Parents are afraid to face an angry child, or to face the rejection of a child they feel like disciplining. We are so unsure of ourselves that we can't even stand being disliked by our own children. These kids don't mind it all that much whether you love them or not (just as long as you give them their way), so why should you mind that much? What they don't learn at home they finally learn the hard way in jail. When Dad won't pick his boy up by the seat of the pants and make him leave the room when asked, the police will eventually act like the father he would have been better off having. Maybe Dad hasn't the stomach to smack the boy for a fresh remark, but when he talks that way to his boss, a neighbor, or the police, he'll soon learn the rules of the game have changed.

Kind But Firm

All of the above leads to one conclusion. It is important to be decent, understanding, patient, and so on with our children, *but* it is equally important to expect, unangrily and unblamingly, that our children face life and its frustrations squarely. Love is not enough, as the title of a book once suggested. In fact, love, as often conceived, can be ruinous to the character development of a child.

I hope counselors stop being bleeding hearts as they once were and begin to adopt the attitude of the stoic. It matters little that the thief being tried in court had a wicked stepmother and an alcoholic father. What matters is that he understands *he* has a problem and by golly he's going to spend a lot of time in the slammer unless he learns to leave his hands off other people's property. No excuses for him any more, please. We don't have to hate him because he stole. We don't blame him for being under the sway of antecedent conditionings. It's well understood that he is. However, all that is fairly *irrelevant*. What he will want to develop (if he wants to stay out of jail, or the state hospital, or mental health center) is to accept responsibility for his *current* behavior and work like a demon to change it. To do so we will have to be both kind and firm toward our disturbed clients: kind by controlling our angers and always seeing the subject as the victim of genetic deficiencies, ignorance, or emotional disturbances, and firm by not making apologies for his negative behavior. He is now talking himself into his irrational acts and he had better talk himself out of them, or suffer the consequences.

References

Dreikurs, R., Gould, S., & Corsini, R. J. *Family Council: The Dreikurs Technique for Putting an End to War between Parents and Children (and between Children and Children).* Chicago: Henry Regnery, 1974.

Hauck, Paul A. *The Rational Management of Children.* New York: Libra Publishers, 1967.

Addendum

29

The Present and the Future of RET

Albert Ellis and Russell Grieger

A S THIS BOOK goes to press, RET is entering its twenty-third year since I [A.E.] created it around the early part of 1955 and presented my first paper on it at the 1956 meetings of the American Psychological Association in Chicago (Ellis, 1958). Since that time RET has undergone many substantial developments and has been established as one of the major cores of the cognitive-behavior therapy movement. This is shown by acknowledgments and endorsements of rational-emotive therapy in a great many recent cognitive-behavior texts and self-help books —for example, those by Beck (1976), Blazier (1975), Church (1975), Davison and Neale (1974), Diekstra and Dassen (1976), Fensterheim and Baer (1975), Goldfried and Davison (1976), Goldfried and Merbaum (1973), Goodman and Maultsby (1974), Greenwald (1976), Harper (1959, 1975), Hauck (1972, 1973, 1974, 1975a, 1975b), Knaus (1974), Kranzler (1974), Lange and Jakubowski (1976), Lazarus (1971, 1976), Lazarus and Fay (1975), Lembo (1974, 1976), Lewis (1972), Mahoney (1974), Maultsby (1975), McMullen and Casey (1974), Meichenbaum (1974, 1977), Morris and Kanitz (1975), Raimy (1975), Rimm and Masters (1974), Thoresen (1975), Tosi (1974), and Young (1974).

Imitation, said Charles Calb Colton early in the nineteenth century, is the sincerest flattery. We note with satisfaction, therefore, that many popular writers and group leaders have effectively used some of the most important aspects of the RET approach without giving any credit to rational-emotive therapy or to its philosophic ancestors, Epictetus and Marcus Aurelius. Thus, we have what appear to be RET-inspired or RET-imitated works (often, alas, in a watered-down and sadly bowdlerized fashion) by Barksdale (1977), Dyer (1976), Werner Erhard (Marks, 1976), Ginott (1965), Glasser (1965), Keyes (1975), Maltz and Barker (1969), Masters (1973), and Smith (1975). So many articles and books now keep appearing that use rational-emotive principles in either an acknowledged or unacknowledged way that it is almost certain that the future of modern psychotherapy and self-help procedures will be strongly influenced by these principles, whether or not the term RET itself survives. The cognitive-behavior movement in therapy seems definitely here to stay; rational-emotive therapy is probably the main force in instigating and furthering this movement.

What are some of the recent developments in RET, as well as some of its predictable future trends? In the last chapter of *A New Guide to Rational Living* (Ellis and Harper, 1975), these developments are summarized. Let us, because of space limitations, give an even more condensed summary here before looking to the future.

Combating absolutistic thinking. RET has always seen absolutistic, magical, and illogical thinking as the source of practically all "emotional" disturbance, and it emphasizes the role of antiempirical assumptions as well. Thus, if you are afraid to take airplane flights, you often irrationally assume that there is a *good chance* that if you fly your plane will fall and you will be killed—when actually, of course, there is an almost infinitesimal chance of such an accident occurring, since commercial airplanes are one of the safest forms of transportation ever created (Ellis, 1972b). Most sane therapists, therefore, try to show you, if you come to them for help, that you are viewing flying in an antiempirical manner and they try to get you to view it more realistically.

RET recently emphasizes, more clearly than ever before, that behind antiempirical statements lie absolutistic or *musturbatory* ideas. Thus, your basic assumption, when you think about flying is, "I *must* not die before my time; and I especially *must* not get killed in a sudden, and perhaps gruesome, airplane accident." Once you devoutly believe in this *must,* you almost always derive other subideas, all equally irrational, from it: (1) "Because I *must* not die in a plane crash, it would be *awful, horrible,* and *terrible* if I did"; (2) "Because I have to avoid dying in an airplane, I *can't stand* flying, or even thinking about flying, in one"; (3) "Because I *must* not get killed in a crash, and it would be *awful* it I did, airplanes are horrible contrivances; and the world makes it *too hard* for me (what with possible airline crashes and what with my terrible anxiety *about* such crashes!), and I can hardly see life in such an unbearably grim world as being worth it."

Once you believe that you *must* not die in an air crash and that it *would be* awful to die, that you *can't stand* flying, and that it's too hard for you to live anxiously in such an uncertain world where you have no guarantee that you will not prematurely die, you then will almost always make up the antiempirical notions that there is a *good chance* that any plane you fly in will fall and that you will die a horrible death. If you gave up your musturbation, however, accepted the reality that nothing is awful in the universe, that you can stand whatever occurs, and that the world doesn't have to arrange itself to give you guaranteed satisfaction, you could then fairly easily accept empirical reality: that planes rarely crash and that even if one that you were on did go down, there still would be a possibility of your survival.

In using RET with all kinds of clients, we find that virtually all feelings of emotional disturbance stem from three fundamental *musts:* (1) "I must do well and be approved by significant people in my life, or else I become an R.P. (rotten person)"; (2) "You *must* treat me kindly, fairly, and considerately, else you are a louse!" and (3) "The universe *must* arrange things so that I easily and quickly get what I want; otherwise it stinks and life is awful!" If any disturbed individual, with the help of RET, zeroes in on these *musts* and really eliminates them his or her disturbance will quickly evaporate, and after awhile will tend to return rarely or only lightly.

Giving up self-rating. In the early RET writings, particularly *A Guide to Rational Living* (Ellis and Harper, 1961) and *Reason and Emotion in Psychotherapy* (Ellis, 1962), people were taught to stop rating themselves as "worthless," "no good," or "bad," and to give themselves a good or worthwhile rating only because of their aliveness, their existence. It was later seen that this pragmatic solution works satisfactorily but is philosophically unsound, since to say, "I am good because I'm alive" cannot be proven, any more than "I am bad because I perform badly" can be validated.

In RET, as shown in Chapters 4 and 5 of this handbook, we now teach people to refuse to rate their "selves," "essences," or totalities" at all —but only to rate their deeds, acts, and performances. We do this because we clearly see that any self-rating is an overgeneralization that cannot be proven. What can only be proven about a person is threefold. You can empirically observe: first, that you are alive; second, that you are capable of remaining alive for seventy years or so if you choose to do so, barring some unforeseen misfortune; third, that you have some degree of control over your happiness—can choose to remain alive fairly happily or miserably. You can logically stop right there, and make the choice of remaining alive and keeping yourself happy (and relatively free from pain) and in that sense "accept" yourself (that is, accept your aliveness and choose to enjoy yourself) rather than "rate" yourself (that is, label yourself as "good" or "bad"). You can also say *"This* is good or bad," because it contributes to or sabotages your aliveness and enjoyment, without adding, *"I* am good or bad." By not rating your "youness" or your "self," RET helps you achieve maximum satisfaction with minimum "ego." It abolishes the heaven of "self-esteem" and the concomitant hell of "self-downing," but leaves "self-acceptance," or the determination to accept life and enjoy yourself to the hilt, whether or not you perform outstandingly and whether or not others approve or love you (Ellis, 1972a, 1972c, 1973a, 1975, 1976, 1977a).

Doing homework assignments. RET has emphasized, right from its inception, that humans *practice* crooked thinking, inappropriate emoting, and self-defeating behavior and that, in order to change themselves and keep changed, they usually have to *practice* thinking, emoting, and behaving much differently. It consequently has always advocated active-directive homework assignments of a cognitive, emotive, and behavioral nature. It has particularly always been a form of behavior therapy since it encourages people to do in vivo homework assignments (such as taking the active risks of encountering members of the other sex or riding in automobiles if they have a phobia about these acts) that would help them change their irrational beliefs.

RET also emphasizes operant conditioning, self-management, and contracting procedures. Thus, if you refuse to write assigned papers and get them in on time, we recommend that you reward or reinforce yourself with something pleasant (e.g., music or sex) *after* you have finished a stipulated amount of writing each day and that you stiffly penalize yourself (e.g., by burning a twenty-dollar bill) every time you fail to do the agreed-upon amount of writing (Ellis, 1973a).

To help people do their homework consistently, we have developed regular homework reports which they fill out at least once a week, and sometimes every day, about the things that they feel most upset about. Maxie C. Maultsby, Jr. (1975) has created Rational Self-Analysis (RSA) forms. At the Institute for Advanced Study in Rational Psychotherapy in New York City we have been using a printed homework report ever since our clinic opened in 1968. The latest edition of this report, which graphically illustrates the basic theory of RET and also serves as a self-help form, is reproduced here as Figure 1.

Combating self-damnation. RET has always emphasized, more perhaps than any other form of psychotherapy, self-forgiveness. We try to get people to accept the responsibility for their errors—and in that sense accept "blame"—but to refrain from damning, berating, denigrating, or devil-ifying themselves for these errors. The essence of RET is that you are not only human but a very *fallible human person;* and that therefore you can only reasonably expect that you will always, for the rest of your days, commit light and serious errors. We rarely use the original RET language, in this respect, of not "blaming" yourself for your mistakes, since your acts may truly be blameworthy but, in the newer RET formulations, we teach you to stop "downing," "damning," or "condemning" yourself—

FIGURE 1. Rational self-help form. © 1976 by the Institute for Rational Living, Inc., 45 East 65th Street, New York, N.Y., 10021

INSTRUCTIONS: Please fill out the ueC section (undesirable emotional Consequences) and the ubC section (undesirable behavioral Consequences) first. Then fill out all the A-B-C-D-E's. PLEASE PRINT LEGIBLY. BE BRIEF!

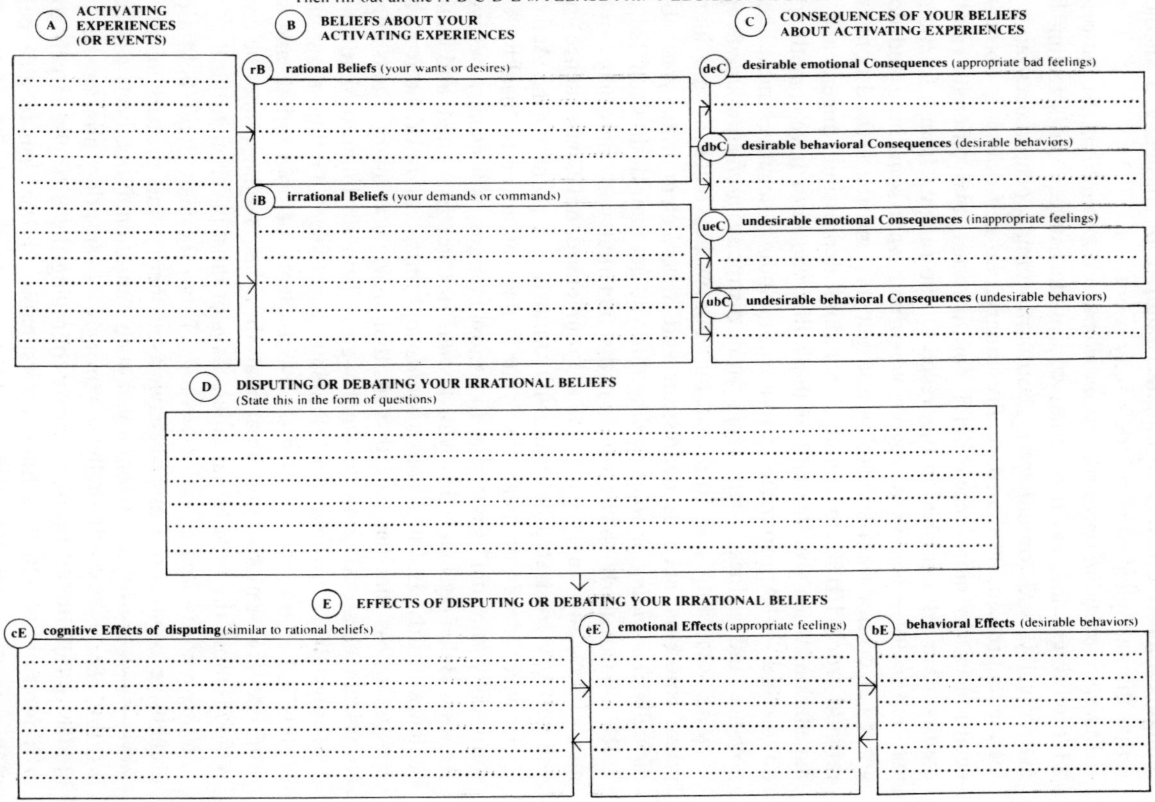

(A) ACTIVATING EXPERIENCES (OR EVENTS)

(B) BELIEFS ABOUT YOUR ACTIVATING EXPERIENCES

(rB) rational Beliefs (your wants or desires)

(iB) irrational Beliefs (your demands or commands)

(C) CONSEQUENCES OF YOUR BELIEFS ABOUT ACTIVATING EXPERIENCES

(deC) desirable emotional Consequences (appropriate bad feelings)

(dbC) desirable behavioral Consequences (desirable behaviors)

(ueC) undesirable emotional Consequences (inappropriate feelings)

(ubC) undesirable behavioral Consequences (undesirable behaviors)

(D) DISPUTING OR DEBATING YOUR IRRATIONAL BELIEFS
(State this in the form of questions)

(E) EFFECTS OF DISPUTING OR DEBATING YOUR IRRATIONAL BELIEFS

(cE) cognitive Effects of disputing (similar to rational belief(s)

(eE) emotional Effects (appropriate feelings)

(bE) behavioral Effects (desirable behaviors)

since damnation of one form of another (damning yourself, other humans, or the world) seems to be the main essence of human disturbance. Although criticism often is legitimate, damnation (basically a theological rather than a logical concept) definitely is not.

Discriminating inappropriate from appropriate emotions. In the original RET writings, no clear distinction was made between one's feeling legitimately sorry, sad, or unhappy about unfortunate occurrences and one's feeling depressed, ashamed, guilty, angry, or self-downing about such occurrences. In more recent RET formulations, two different emotional continua are distinguished in this respect: one ranging from a fraction of a per cent to 99% sorrow or regret, when you want something and do not get it (or do not want something and get it); and the second continuum, ranging from 101% to infinity, including depression, anger, and self-flagellation, when you demand or think that you *must* have something and do not get it. Appropriate emotions, including negative ones like annoyance and sadness, stem from your distinctly *preferring, desiring,* or *wanting* something and from getting your wishes blocked; and inappropriate emotions, such as depression and anger, stem from your absolutistically *demanding* or *commanding* that you get your desires fulfilled.

RET particularly shows you that the fact that you "naturally" or "humanly" feel, say, angry (at point C, your emotional Consequence) when you get very frustrated or dealt with unfairly (at point A, the Activating Experience) does not mean that your feeling of anger is "healthy." It is statistically "normal" since you, like most humans, will usually believe (at B, your Belief system) that you *should not* get frustrated and *must* be dealt with fairly. But it is your *shoulds* and *musts,* and not the frustration and unfairness that happens to you, that make you angry. Such anger is empirically "natural" and "normal"—and distinctly inappropriate or self-defeating. RET, to help you eliminate your anger (rather than merely express it better), gives you a clear-cut theory of appropriate and inappropriate and rational and irrational thoughts, feelings, and behaviors. Which is more than can be said these days of most psychotherapies!

Using emotive and affective methods. From the start, RET held a comprehensive cognitive-emotive-behavioristic theory and practice of psychotherapy and consequently employed such "emotional" methods as accepting the client unconditionally, vigorously confronting him or her with hidden or defensive behavior, and encouraging the therapist largely to act as himself or herself, as a human personality, rather than to hide behind silence or other therapeutic masks. In more recent years, RET has created or adapted a variety of other emotive methods, such as variations on psychodrama, encounter groups, and self-actualizing exercises. Some particularly RET-oriented emotive techniques have been invented and widely used, including Maultsby's rational-emotive imagery, or REI (Maultsby, 1975; Maultsby and Ellis, 1974); Knaus and Wessler's (1976) rational-emotive problem simulation; and Ellis' (1973b, 1977a) shame-attacking exercises. RET theory says that not only is it good for people to get in touch with disturbed feelings—such as those of anxiety, guilt, and hostility —but that it is also good for them to have at their disposal techniques of *strongly, vehemently,* and *powerfully* thinking, emoting, and acting against these feelings. RET therefore encourages the use of any emotive methods that will help this process. In this respect it departs from the "rationality" espoused by Epictetus, Marcus Aurelius, and other thinkers who over-emphasize feelings of calm and serenity and tend to forget that strong ap-propriate feelings—such as distinct annoyance, sorrow, and determina-tion—help humans to correct the unnecessary unpleasantries of their lives and to live much more joyous existences in the future.

New cognitive methods. As Mahoney (1974), Meichenbaum (1974, 1977), and other cognitive-behavior therapists have pointed out, cognitive therapy hardly consists only of arguing or disputing with clients about their irrational beliefs. RET is famous for this kind of disputing, because it often seems necessary, especially when clients have firmly entrenched and long-standing irrational ideas, to show them that they cannot support these by any empirical or logical arguments, and that, since they lead to such un-pleasant results, they'd better surrender them. But a myriad of other cognitive methods exist of showing people how to overcome their self-defeating philosophies, and RET keeps exploring these methods and us-ing them in many instances.

As shown in this book, particularly in Parts Three and Four, RET procedures now include (1) lecturing and instructing; (2) teaching logical thinking; (3) thought-stopping and focusing on nondisturbing ideas; (4) problem-solving methods; (5) attacking false attributions; (6) the use of general semantics, referenting, and other forms of semantitherapy; (7) cognitive modeling; (8) the use of imaging and fantasy; (9) biofeedback techniques; (10) bibliotherapy; (11) recordings and films; and (12) paradoxical intention. I [A.E.] have recently added a new cognitive-emotive method: that of using rational songs to help people see how foolish many of their ideas are and how they can change them to saner philoso-phies of living (Ellis, 1977b, 1977c).

Future Directions

Having outlined some of the major changes and refinements in rational-emotive psychotherapy during the last twenty years or so, we can now

briefly look to the future. In what directions would it be profitable for RET
and similar forms of cognitive-behavioral therapy to go? Well, in many directions, including the following.

Refining RET Theory and Practice via Further Research

When rational-emotive psychotherapy was originated, it was based on a
small amount of research that amounted to little more than a hill of beans.
Since that time, a massive amount of research has accumulated that bears
on rational-emotive theory. I [A.E.] have gathered most of these materials and put them together in Chapter 2 of this handbook. In that chapter, I reviewed the literature surrounding 32 core hypotheses of RET and
found over 90% of the studies supportive. It is particularly interesting,
as I noted in that chapter, that the great bulk of these studies did not
originate from researchers who specifically set out to test RET. Moreover,
DiGiuseppe and Miller reviewed the literature pertaining to the effectiveness of RET (see Chapter 3) and have likewise found that RET works
quite well when compared to other forms psychotherapy.

Despite the fact that RET is so convincingly established by all this, we
still think it important to continue to test it—to further tease out the
subtleties of its theory and practice, to add or subtract crucial dimensions, and to continue to break new ground. As an illustration, take Goldfried's and Sobocinski's (1975) study that compared the emotional reactions of subjects who scored high and low on the Demand for Approval
subscale of the Irrational Belief Test (Jones, 1968) when confronted with
a simulated social disapproval situation. The results confirmed the relationship between "need" for approval and emotional arousal, in that subjects high in this irrationality became more emotional than those low in
this irrationality. Going beyond this general and expected result, Goldfried and Sobocinski also found that the high irrational subjects not only
experienced significantly more anxiety and depression after being exposed
to the social rejection than before, but they also experienced significantly
more anger as well. This result raises some interesting questions, not the
least of which is why the high "need" for approval group reacted with
anger. Could it be that anger reactions are typical of most people high in
approval "needs" who experience social rejection? Could it be that the
emotional reactions of people who strongly believe that they must receive
love and approval are affected by the holding or not holding of other irrational beliefs, specifically the tendency to blame others as well as themselves for behaving poorly? Could it be that individual differences rest
more in the expression of the feeling of anger and not in the holding of
the anger? Could it be that the dimension of frustration tolerance typically
plays a part in negative emotional arousal and precipitated the anger? In-

teresting speculations, but we do not know for sure without further experimentation.

Desirable directions for research pertaining to the practice of RET are extensive and space does not permit us to expand at length on them in this chapter. Some interesting as well as profitable questions for research, however, are:

1. What are the differential effects of various components of RET? What are the major and minor ingredients of change—cognitive, behaviorial, emotive—and what combinations of ingredients are more powerful than others?

2. Similarly, what are the effects of such things as bibliotherapy, pretherapy training of clients regarding how to behave in therapy, and in vivo and written homework assignments?

3. What are the effects of combining RET with various other techniques —hypnosis, desensitization, sexual and sensual exercises, operant procedures, and so on?

4. How does RET compare with other forms of psychotherapy, particularly gestalt therapy, transactional analysis, psychodynamically oriented insight therapy, relationship therapy, and modeling?

5. With regard to outcome, how effective is RET with a variety of psychopathological populations (for instance, psychopaths); sociological populations (the aged, people on probation, and the like); and people with particular life problems (such as those suffering from loneliness, those lacking career or social goals, overeaters, the unassertive and so on)?

6. In RET, does the "hard sell" or "soft sell" approach work best? Is a dramatic therapeutic style better than a calm one?

7. What variables make clients more likely to benefit from RET?

Content Analysis of RET

A major motivation for putting this handbook together was to combine in one resource the main ideas and techniques that make up rational-emotive psychotherapy. In reviewing material to do this, we became aware that we still did not entirely capture to our satisfaction what RET therapists actually do. This may be partly because each individual therapist does RET somewhat differently depending on his or her personality and ingenuity. Another reason is that we in the RET field have been somewhat remiss in *precisely* articulating what specific things we regularly do in RET and for what exact purpose we do them. We talk about the rational therapist being direct, philosophic, socratic, and so on, but we do not tell precisely how to do that.

I [R.G.] in my role as trainer of psychotherapists have keenly felt a need for more concrete articulation of methods. Unlike teachers at the advanced training center at the Institute in New York City, where trainees are immersed full-time for a year or two in supervised RET experiences, I and other university-based trainers are forced to teach RET to students in a rather structured, typically time-limited format because of a high trainee-to-teacher ratio, the seminar and semester system, and limited resources. I often find at the end of a semester or two that students know RET theory and the general postures of the therapist, yet do not know specifically how to implement their knowledge.

While noting this current deficiency, we can also say that we are taking steps to rectify the situation. I [R.G.] and one of my colleagues at the University of Virginia, Dr. John Boyd, in consultation with many prominent rational-emotive therapists throughout the nation, are in the process of preparing a competency-based training manual [1] that attempts to concretely spell out in an organized fashion the more typical and prominent therapeutic activities in RET. We are also attempting to suggest ways to best teach students these skills in a systematic fashion. Space does not permit us to go into detail about all this. Briefly, however, Dr. Boyd and I believe that most of what the therapist does in RET can be classified into one of four skill areas: (1) Rational-Emotive Psychodiagnosis—skills in recognizing the client's irrational thinking patterns or his irrational thoughts, beliefs, and philosophies; (2) Rational-Emotive Insight—skills in helping clients recognize and acknowledge that they do hold irrational thinking patterns; (3) Rational-Emotive Working Through—skills in helping the clients challenge and dispute their irrational thinking patterns; and (4) Rational-Emotive Reeducation—skills in helping the client learn and act upon new, more rational thinking patterns. We conceptualize these four skill areas as following a logical sequence, but see them as being recyclable, even within a single session. When the skills book is finished, we intend to show the reader through description and example what various things can be done to facilitate each of these four rational-emotive goals. We also intend to delineate both therapist and client pitfalls that interfere with the realization of these goals. Hopefully, this text will be useful in many ways—as a RET training manual, as a jumping-off point for research on the power of various components of RET, and as a basis for continuing refinement of the practice of RET.

RET with Lay Persons and Paraprofessionals

We think it is fair to state that rational-emotive and other forms of cognitive-behaviorial therapy are gaining a rather wide acceptance in pro-

---

[1] This book is tentatively titled *A Skill-Based Model of RET and RET Training.* It is currently being written and will be published in 1978.

fessional circles. This acceptance parallels a trend toward viewing pycho-
therapy in large part as a teaching rather than a curative process (Lazarus, 1976). Maultsby (see .Chapter 15), for example, coined the phrase
"emotional reeducation" when referring to rational-emotive psychotherapy. Many other therapies outside the analytic fold (see Meichenbaum's and Cameron's Chapter 22 and Mahoney's Chapter 23 of this
book) envision the therapist as one who helps the client to cope with life
more effectively.

Since RET is very distinctly a teaching and learning process in which the
therapist openly and unabashedly sets out to educate and reeducate the
client, it makes sense to us to extend the theory and practice of RET via
structured or semistructured programs to various lay populations for self-
help and preventive mental health purposes. I [A.E.] and others have
written many texts, such as *A New Guide to Rational Living* (Ellis &
Harper, 1975), with just this in mind, as have others; Bill Knaus' *Rational-Emotive Education* (1974), a program designed for educators to
teach rational thinking and effective problem-solving to elementary school
children (see Chapter 7 of this book), is another example.

The field is wide open in this regard and limited only by the imagination
of the reader. Some potential populations, in addition to teachers, include:
(1) parents, particularly foster parents, single parents, and parents of
children with various physical handicaps; (2) professionals in other fields
who regularly work with people who experience emotional stress; for
example, lawyers, physicians, welfare department workers, law enforce-
ment officers, public health workers; (3) the aged; (4) the chronically ill
and those with various physical problems, such as diabetics, the obese,
arthritics; (5) people who work in bureaucratic settings and who steadily
contend with the pressures of both protocol and production.

In many ways, such as those briefly discussed above, RET has changed
over the years and added new cognitive, emotive, and behavioral methods
to its already effective armamentarium. It is predicted that these kinds of
changes will lead toward an increasingly more efficient system of procedures within the general RET framework and will continue indefinitely.

References

Barksdale, L. S. *Essays on self-esteem*. Los Angeles: Barksdale Foundation, 1977.
Beck, A. T. *Cognitive therapy and the emotional disorders*. New York: International
    Universities Press, 1976.
Blazier, D. *Poor me, poor marriage*. New York: Vantage Press, 1975.

Church, V. A. *Behavior, law and remedies.* Dubuque, Iowa: Kendall/Hunt Publishing, 1975.

Davison, G. C., & Neale, J. M. *Abnormal psychology: an experimental-clinical approach.* New York: John Wiley, 1974.

Diekstra, R. F. W., and Dassen, W. F. M. *Rationele therapie.* Amsterdam: Swets & Zeitlinger, 1976.

Dyer, W. D. *Your erroneous zones.* New York: Funk and Wagnalls, 1976.

Ellis, A. Rational psychotherapy. *Journal of General Psychology,* 1958, *59,* 35–49.

Ellis, A. *Reason and emotion in psychotherapy.* New York: Lyle Stuart, 1962.

Ellis, A. Psychotherapy and the value of a human being. In J. W. Davis (Ed.), *Value and valuation. Axiological studies in honor of Robert S. Hartman.* Knoxville: University of Tennessee Press, 1972. Reprinted, New York: Institute for Rational Living, 1972 (a).

Ellis, A. *How to master your fear of flying.* New York: Curtis Books, 1972 (b).

Ellis, A. *Executive leadership: a rational approach.* New York: Citadel Press, 1972 (c).

Ellis, A. *Humanistic psychotherapy: the rational-emotive approach.* New York: Julian Press and McGraw-Hill Paperbacks, 1973 (a).

Ellis, A. *How to stubbornly refuse to be ashamed of anything.* Cassette recording. New York: Institute for Rational Living, 1973 (b).

Ellis, A. Are cognitive behavior therapy and rational therapy synonymous? *Rational Living,* 1973, *8*(2), 8–11. (c)

Ellis, A. *How to live with a "neurotic."* Rev. ed. New York: Crown Publishers, 1975.

Ellis, A. *Sex and the liberated man.* New York: Lyle Stuart, 1976.

Ellis, A. *How to live with—and without—anger.* New York: Reader's Digest Press, 1977 (a).

Ellis, A. Fun as psychotherapy. Paper delivered at the American Psychological Association Convention, Washington, D.C., September 3, 1976. Cassette recording. New York: Institute for Rational Living, 1977 (b).

Ellis, A. *A garland of rational songs.* New York: Institute for Rational Living, 1977 (c).

Ellis, A., and Harper, R. A. *A guide to rational living.* Englewood Cliffs, N.J.: Prentice-Hall, and Hollywood: Wilshire Books, 1961.

Ellis, A., and Harper, R. A. *A new guide to rational living.* Englewood Cliffs, N.J.: Prentice-Hall, and Hollywood: Wilshire Books, 1975.

Fensterheim, H., and Baer, J. *Don't say yes when you want to say no.* New York: Dell, 1975.

Ginott, H. *Between parent and child.* New York: Macmillan, 1965.

Glasser, W. *Reality therapy.* New York: Harper, 1965.

Goldfried, M. R., and Davison, G. C. *Clinical behavior therapy.* New York: Holt, Rinehart and Winston, 1976.

Goldfried, M. R., and Merbaum, M. (Eds.). *Behavior change through self-control.* New York: Holt, Rinehart & Winston, 1973.

Goldfried, M. R., and Sobocinski, D. Effect of irrational beliefs on emotional arousal. *Journal of Consulting and Clinical Psychology,* 1975, *43,* 504–510.

Goodman, D., & Maultsby, M. C., Jr. *Emotional well-being through rational behavior training.* Springfield, Illinois: Charles C Thomas, 1974.

Greenwald, H. *Direct decision therapy.* San Diego: Edits, 1976.

Harper, R. A. *Psychoanalysis and psychotherapy: 36 systems.* Englewood Cliffs, N.J.: Prentice-Hall, 1959.

Harper, R. A. *The new psychotherapies.* Englewood Cliffs, N.J.: Prentice-Hall, 1975.

Hauck, P. A. *Reason in pastoral counseling.* Philadelphia: Westminster Press, 1972.

Hauck, P. A. *Overcoming depression.* Philadelphia: Westminster Press, 1973.

Hauck, P. A. *Overcoming frustration and anger.* Philadelphia: Westminster Press, 1974.

Hauck, P. A. *Overcoming worry and fear.* Philadelphia: Westminster Press, 1975 (a).

Hauck, P. A. *The rational ' ~agement of children.* New York: Libra, 1975 (b).

Jones, R. G. *A factored measure of Ellis' irrational belief system, with personality and maladjustment correlates.* Doctoral dissertation, Texas Technological College, 1968.

Keyes, K. *Handbook to higher consciousness.* Berkeley: Living Love Center, 1975.

Knaus, W. J. *Rational-emotive education: A manual for elementary school teachers.* New York: Institute for Rational Living, 1974.

Knaus, W., and Wessler, R. Rational-emotive problem simulation. *Rational Living,* 1976, *11*(2), 8–11.

Kranzler, G. *You can change how you feel.* Eugene, Ore.: Author, 1974.

Lange, A., and Jakubowski, P. *Responsible assertive behavior.* Champaign, Ill.: Research Press, 1976.

Lazarus, A. A. *Behavior therapy and beyond.* New York: McGraw-Hill, 1971.

Lazarus, A. A. *Multimodal behavior therapy.* New York: Springer Publishing, 1976.

Lazarus, A. A., and Fay, A. *I can if I want to.* New York: Morrow, 1975.

Lembo, J. *Help yourself.* Niles, Ill.: Argus Communications, 1974.

Lembo, J. *The counseling process: A cognitive-behavioral approach.* Roslyn Heights, N.Y.: Libra Publishing, 1976.

Lewis, W. C. *Why people change.* New York: Holt, Rinehart and Winston, 1972.

Mahoney, M. J. *Cognition and behavior modification.* Cambridge, Mass.: Ballinger, 1974.

Maltz, M., and Barker, R. C. *The conquest of frustration.* New York: Constellation International, 1969.

Marks, P. R. *EST: the movement and the man.* Chicago: Playboy Press, 1976.

Masters, R. *How your mind can keep you well.* Greenwich, Conn.: Fawcett, 1973.

Maultsby, M. C., Jr. *Help yourself to happiness.* New York: Institute for Rational Living, 1975.

Maultsby, M. C., Jr., and Ellis, A. *Technique for using rational-emotive imagery (REI).* New York: Institute for Rational Living, 1974.

McMullen, R., and Casey, B. *Talk sense to yourself.* Denver: Creative Social Designs, 1974.

Meichenbaum, D. H. *Cognitive-behavior modification.* Morristown, N.J.: General Learning Press, 1974.

Meichenbaum, D. H. *Cognitive behavior modification.* New York: Plenum, 1977.

Morris, K. T., and Kanitz, H. M. *Rational-emotive therapy.* Boston: Houghton Mifflin, 1975.

Raimy, V. *Misunderstandings of the self.* San Francisco: Jossey-Bass, 1975.

Rimm, D. C., and Masters, J. C. *Behavior therapy.* New York: Academic Press, 1974.

Smith, M. *When I say no, I feel guilty.* New York: Bantam, 1975.

Thoresen, E. *Learning to think: A rational approach.* Clearwater: Florida Branch of the Institute for Rational Living, 1975.

Tosi, D. J. *Youth: toward personal growth, a rational-emotive approach.* Columbus, Ohio: Merrill Publishing Company, 1974.

Young, H. *A rational counseling primer.* New York: Institute for Rational Living, 1974.